THE
BUSH
STILL
BURNS

THE PRESBYTERIAN AND REFORMED FAITH
IN AUSTRALIA
1788–1988

By the same author:

Spiritual Gifts in the Apostolic Church (1972)

Presbyterianism in Tasmania 1821-1977 (1977)

The Making of An Australian Church (1978)

Psalm-singing in Scripture and History (1979, revised edition 1985)

Learning the Christian Faith (1981, 3rd edition 1987)

The Free Presbyterian Church of South Australia (1984)

CORRECTIONS

Most of the gremlins which got through the proof-reading process are rather obvious. The following corrections could be noted:

p.95: McLeod was ordained June 25,1851 (5th last line).
p.148/504: Dr Mackay was inducted to St George's on May 12, 1856.
p.157: †72 should be James Henderson.
p.312; the name in the 5th last line should be Ronald not Robert.
p.360: The last word in the 1st line of the paragraph beginning (a) should read 'members' not 'ministers'.
p.396: the date in the 3rd line of the footnote should be 1963.
p.416: the Frankston RPC was wound up in June 1989.
p.454: the year in the 10th last line of text should be 1972.
p.484: Mr D.S.Harman (uncle of AMH) was an elder 1937-1977.
p.514: Geelong in 7th line should read Grafton. The Geelong property was sold in 1989; it is planned to relocate in Newcomb.
p.523: Knox Presbyterian Church was opened February 28,1987.
p.524: Premises at 183/185 Grange Rd, Glenhuntly were opened on April 28, 1990, and the North Caulfield work relocated there.
p.541: McSkimming was born 1823 and arrived near end of 1858.
p.545: Livingstone served the PCV at Scarsdale & Carisbrook c.1902/1908. In retirement he was an elder at St John's Hobart and then South Yarra (Melbourne
p.555: Ward was editor to 6/87 not 6/86. Cromarty married 1962 not 1963.

THE
BUSH
STILL
BURNS

THE PRESBYTERIAN AND REFORMED FAITH
IN AUSTRALIA
1788–1988

Rowland S Ward

THE BUSH STILL BURNS
Copyright (c) - Rowland S. Ward, 1989

First Edition - June 1989

ISBN 0 949670 05 7

This book is available from:
Rowland S. Ward,
358 Mountain Highway,
Wantirna, Victoria, 3152

Tel: (03) 720 4871

RRP A$25 plus postage

Typeset 10 on 11 Theme by the Author
Cover design by The Booksmith, Canterbury
Printed by Globe Press Pty Ltd, Brunswick

CONTENTS

NOTE RE MONEY CONVERSION

In 1966 Australia changed from the pound, made up of 240 pence, to the dollar with 100 cents. Generally in this book, pre 1966 amounts are converted into dollars.

Inflation renders old figures somewhat misleading. As an approximate guide to inflation of building construction costs, costs in 1888 must be multiplied by 70 to produce an approximate 1988 cost. An index of building prices as well as an inflation and wages index may be conveniently seen in *The Australians: Historical Statistics* (Sydney 1987).

FOREWORD

by the Reverend Doctor J.Campbell Andrews, MA, MB, ChB

It is a privilege to be asked to commend this book and its author.

Rev Rowland S. Ward is a minister of the Presbyterian Church of Eastern Australia. He is a graduate in Arts and Theology (BA, BTh Hons.) of the University of South Africa, and also holds the Diploma of the Free Church of Scotland College, Edinburgh, which he attended 1972-75. Licensed to preach the Gospel in 1975, he has held pastorates in Ulverstone, Tasmania, and in Melbourne where he now labours. A tireless worker he has both by voice and pen shown his devotion to Christ and His Church and his interest in her constitution, history, doctrine, procedure and practice.

Mr Ward has an alert, enquiring, receptive mind, as well as a retentive memory and a ready pen. He has carefully researched available resources and consulted a wide range of persons and documents as his numerous references and foot-notes show. He has shown both his considerable knowledge and balanced judgement in selecting relevant facts, taking account of trends and making observations on events and their outcome.

His adherence to the Reformed Faith in the Presbyterian tradition of doctrine and practice is obvious. He shows that tradition to be based on Scripture, to have been stimulated by Calvin, and defined further by Knox, Melville, Henderson, Chalmers and others against the background of Scotland's chequered history. It has become the birthright of Christians of Reformed and Presbyterian persuasion in the Australian Colonies and later Commonwealth.

This book revolves around the contendings of a small, conservative Presbyterian Church in the context of Presbyterianism generally, of the Christian Church generally, and of the even wider social and political background of the Australian Nation's striving for and achievement of independence and identity. It is a contribution to the Bicentenary of Australia within this particular field. It is a notable publication and should command the close attention of students of Australian Church History, and will be especially welcomed by the members of the denomination in which Mr Ward ministers, and by all interested in Australian Presbyterianism.

ACKNOWLEDGEMENTS

The Synod of the Presbyterian Church of Eastern Australia on May 22, 1986 resolved unanimously that I be asked to prepare a history of the PCEA for publication in 1988. I appreciate the confidence shown by my brethren, and I appreciate being given a completely free hand to write the history as I saw fit. I have set the history of the PCEA in the setting of the Presbyterian and Reformed Faith in Australia, since no one denomination, and certainly no one denomination in the Reformed tradition, can understand itself and its mission without regard to the wider context, and to the joys and trials of those who in whole or in part share that tradition.

I owe a considerable debt to those who have worked in the field before me or have been involved in the events described. My greatest debts would be to Barry Bridges, MA, MEd, MTh, PhD, DLitt et Phil., of Sydney, and to F.Maxwell Bradshaw, MA, LLM of Melbourne. Dr Bridges, who is not formally connected with any church, is a most diligent and exact researcher, and a specialist in pre-1865 New South Wales Presbyterianism as well as in the Boer War. Mr Bradshaw has been the Procurator of the Synod of the Presbyterian Church of Eastern Australia for about 40 years and of the General Assembly of the Presbyterian Church of Australia since 1959. He is an expert in the historical and constitutional aspects of Presbyterianism in the form derived from Scotland. Dr Bridges has read portion of the manuscript and Mr Bradshaw virtually the whole, and I record my thanks for their comments and suggestions.

I record my appreciation for access to the collections of the State Library of Victoria, the Joint Theological Library at Ormond College, Melbourne, the Presbyterian Theological College Library, Melbourne, the Mirchell Library in Sydney, State Archives in Adelaide and Hobart, and the Ferguson Library of the Presbyterian Church of Australia in the State of New South Wales, Sydney. F.M.Bradshaw loaned me rare copies of early magazines given to him by a former chronicler of things Presbyterian, J.Campbell Robinson. Presbytery and Session Clerks of the PCEA were generally very helpful, although records were often defective.

Mr W.M.Mackay of Melbourne kept me from a number of errors. Iain Mackay turned my rough maps into something presentable at short notice. Mr W.F.G. Gadsby, a member of my congregation, took the major burden of proof-reading, but he will agree that remaining errors and infelicities are mine!

Without the loving support of my wife Anna, and the patience (?) of the children, who were always wondering when Daddy's book would stop, as I was myself, this book would not have been finished. One knows what the comment at the close of many copies of the Greek New Testament means: 'Writing bows one's back, thrusts the ribs into one's stomach, and fosters a general debility of the body.' While the men feature most in this volume, it is, after all, the women of the church who play just as vital a part as heirs together with their men of the grace of God.

INTRODUCTION

To see a thorn bush burning in the desert is not so unusual, but to see such a bush burning but not being consumed is indeed extraordinary. When Moses saw such a sight in the wilderness of Horeb his scientific instincts drew him to investigate. But God spoke to him from the bush, the ground on which Moses stood was pronounced holy, and Moses worshipped, hiding his face, because he was afraid to look upon God (Exodus 3:6).

The burning bush has become the symbol of many Presbyterian Churches throughout the world. It was used by the French Reformed Church as early as 1583, and is found in Holland and Italy 50 years later. It became identified with the (reformed) Church of Scotland in 1690 when the printer of the Acts of the General Assembly of the church placed the symbol on the title page. Not being officially approved nor registered many variations of the logo appeared. From Scotland the symbol came into use in the British colonies together with the motto 'Nec tamen consumebatur' [Nevertheless it was not consumed] taken from the Latin Bible of Tremelius and Junius, Frankfurt 1579.

The use of the burning bush logo invites the question: 'What does it mean?' A not uncommon explanation is to see the fire as a symbol of the fiery trials of God's people whom Moses was to lead out of Egyptian bondage. In agreement with this idea one can find representation of the burning bush with an aura of light symbolizing the Divine presence behind the burning bush itself. So the meaning is; 'God is with his church in her trials.' And that is surely a great comfort.

ix

However, perhaps this explanation does not focus the text clearly. Is not the thornbush a reminder of the fruits of sin (Genesis 3:18), even as the crown of thorns our Saviour wore speaks of the sin's curse which he bore and so won for us a crown of glory? And is not the fire itself (and not some light behind the bush of which the text says nothing) the token of the presence of God himself, of that God who is 'a consuming fire' (Hebrews 12:29), destroying all that is sinful? Thus, the miracle on the physical level points to the spiritual miracle: God's people should be consumed by God's righteous judgement but in fact are preserved by his presence!

As the unfolding of the Gospel shows us, this paradox is explained by the coming of Immanuel (God with us!) to bear the Father's curse and so put away sin on behalf of his chosen ones. The burning bush thus declares that the existence of God's people is entirely a matter of divine grace: 'It is of the Lord's covenant kindness that we are not utterly consumed' (Lam 3:22).

When Moses set off for Egypt to liberate his people from oppression and slavery it was this marvellous and sustaining hope that he took with him. He was not merely to gain some earthly advantages for his countrymen but he was to proclaim in his mission the mercies of a covenant God whose presence does not consume, but preserves, blesses and brings peace between God and man. In the knowledge of that reconciliation Moses could speak to the tyrannical Pharaoh, even as John Knox, the Reformer of the Scottish Church, feared not the face of man because he had learned what it was to fear the Lord in truth. And it is in the knowledge of a reconciliation initiated, accomplished and applied in the sheer wonder of divine graciousness in Christ, that the people of God in every age persevere through all earthly trials.

The sign that speaks of the centrality of God's grace must assuredly be an appropriate one with which the entitle the story of the Presbyterian and Reformed faith in Australia. To be sure, the Presbyterian Church is but part of the Church Catholic. Still, she has always in her best moments majored on the marvellousness of God's grace and in fact in her doctrine seeks to preserve and formulate that truth in the full consistency which Scripture allows. And yet in her practice she has often been like the Israelites of old. God's covenant is not with an institution but with believers and their children. So we would not glory in institutions as such. Rather, we would glory in the Cross and record the Lord's doings despite the unfaithfulness and unbelief of men.

Part One

BACKGROUND

1: PRESBYTERIAN PRINCIPLES

The churches known as 'Presbyterian' in English-speaking countries are termed 'Reformed' in mainland Europe. At the time of the 16th century Reformation of the Western Church those influenced by John Calvin (1509-1564) aimed to reform the church according to the Bible as the supreme and final authority to the exclusion of human tradition. Their thorough-going work of restoring the church to its original order meant also that the government of the church had to be reformed. They held that the government of the church was given in Scripture to mature men called *elders* (in Greek: *presbuteroi*) whose function was that of oversight so that they are sometimes called *bishops* or *overseers* (Greek: *episcopoi*). This conviction contrasted very much with prevailing practice in Britain where the Church of England in her *Thirty-nine Articles* (1563) was 'reformed' in most points but retained much of the medieval system of government. 'Reformed' can be used to refer to the basic theological position of those who adhere to Calvinistic teaching even if this is not carried through in the area of church order, but in general 'Presbyterian' and 'Reformed' as denominational labels are synonymous and refer to the same kind of church even if there are some variations in practice arising from particular ethnic or historical factors. In theory, a Presbyterian or Reformed Church aims to be nothing other than a consistently Biblical Church.

The Swiss Reformer, Huldreich Zwingli (1484-1531) was a Roman Catholic priest at Zurich who preached reform at about the same time as Martin Luther (1483-1545) and in a measure independently of him. Zwingli was a humanist who sought reform on the basis of the Scriptures in a thorough-going way. However, his influence was limited chiefly to Switzerland. The true founder (or recoverer!) of the Reformed Church was John Calvin, a Frenchman trained for the law. He gave a coherent theology and programme to the reform movement through his classic work *The Institutes of the Christian Religion*, first published in 1536 when he was 26 years of age. Calvin too was a humanist who wished to live a scholar's life. However, his conversion to the Reformation and his sense of duty resulted in his work in the strategic city of Geneva. Here, save for a break of several years, he spent the rest of his life as preacher, scholar, churchman and theologian. He wrote catechisms, commentaries on most of the books of the Bible which laid the basis of scientific exegesis and are still in print, promoted the singing of the Psalter in metrical translation, and carried on a voluminous correspondence with leaders of reformation in other lands. An Academy (now the University) was formed in 1559 and enrolled over 800 students in the first year. At this time there were almost as many receiving lectures in Biblical subjects in order that they might take the Gospel to their own countries. Geneva, small in population (say 15,000), was a centre for the spread of the robust Biblical faith.

Calvin had a multitude of health problems which were not helped by his tremendous workload and the difficulties of the time. He did not always get his own way and often had difficulty securing the independence of the church in its exercise of discipline. He was not the dictator of popular legend. No Roman Catholic was executed in Geneva, but the death of an anti-trinitarian activist named Michael Servetus has been laid at his door. Servetus was burnt on the order of a secular court with a majority of members opposed to Calvin. Still, Calvin acted as plaintiff in the case. Servetus had been condemned to the same fate by the Inquisition at Vienne earlier in the year. He escaped and came to Geneva despite warnings. Reformed people of a later time have regarded this as a blot and an 'expiatory monument' was erected in 1903.

While there have been countless thousands of Calvinist martyrs (such as the 20,000 or more in France on and after St Bartholomew's Day in 1572), and there has been persecution of Calvinists by Lutherans, Calvinists themselves, for all the sturdiness of their faith, have rarely persecuted. The Calvinist faith put iron into men's souls so that they were able and willing to work in countries hostile to reformation. Its system of organisation proved adaptable to a variety of circumstances so that the Reformed and Presbyterian churches spread to many lands and developed their own life there. The Netherlands, Scotland, France, Germany and Hungary had very large numbers of Calvinists. The promising movement in Spain and Poland was crushed by persecutions as was also largely the case in France (the Huguenots). Today there are large numbers of Presbyterian and Reformed people in Scotland, the Netherlands, Hungary, Southern Africa, the United States of America and South Korea (where nominally a majority of the 10 million Christians are Presbyterian). There are smaller groupings in more than 100 other countries.

Some basic principles

Presbyterianism rejects the idea that each local church is independent and has no responsibility towards other parts of the church. It rejects the idea that church membership is of little importance and that the organised church has no power of spiritual discipline. It rejects the idea that it is perfectly proper for anyone to set himself up in an evangelistic ministry answerable only to himself with no accountability to the wider church. It also rejects the idea that church government is simply a matter of following practices which seem to work even though they are not based on Scripture.

The distinctive features of Presbyterian and Reformed churches which are true to original principles are:

1. *Acceptance of the Bible as the fully reliable written word of God*, the judge of all teaching and behaviour as well as of church government (2 Tim 3:16). In other words, the Bible is the Supreme Standard.

2. *The public setting forth of the church's understanding of the teaching of Scripture in a Confession of Faith* which is adhered to by all office-bearers (Titus 1:5,9; 2 Timothy 2:15; I John 4:1-3). The Belgic Confession of 1561 together with the Canons of the Synod of Dort in 1619 and the Heidelberg Catechism [the so-called *Three Forms of Unity*] form the doctrinal basis of most Reformed churches of Dutch origin. The *Westminster Confession* of 1647, sometimes with variations, is the principal Subordinate Standard of Presbyterian churches.

Confessions are intended to be a witness to the world, a rallying point for those agreed, a defence against error, and a safeguard for the people of God. Church members are not usually required to subscribe the Confession in detail as a pre-requisite for membership, but subscription is required of office-bearers. If subscription vows are not made intelligently and honestly, or if the church does not insist upon its Confession being maintained, the church is in peril.

3. *The allowance of only two orders of office-bearers - elders* or overseers, of whom the minister is one (1 Timothy 5:17), who are equal in ruling power and who oversee the spiritual needs; and *deacons*, who care for the poor and look after the finances as a kind of adjunct to the elders' meeting (Acts 14:23; Acts 6:1-6; Philippians 1:1; 1 Timothy 3:1-13). Sometimes the minister is sharply distinguished from the other elders as if there were three

5

orders of office-bearers, but it is largely a case of terminology and it seems more Scriptural to speak of distinction of function within the order of eldership rather than to speak of two quite different orders of elders.

The word 'presbyterian' comes from the Greek word for an elder. It is the Presbyterian conviction (backed by the more candid Anglicans!) that the bishop or overseer of the New Testament is just the elder described in terms of his work rather than in terms of his maturity (Titus 1:5-7); I Timothy 3; Acts 20:13,28). The events of history have demonstrated the dangers of a higher order of 'bishop' above the presbyter as found in Anglican and Roman communions. Such an order, through control of it by monarchs, was a ready means of controlling the church. Scottish Presbyterians had repeated experience of this. Control of the church by the civil government is also rejected on principle on the grounds that Christ has instituted a government in his church distinct from and not subordinate in its own province to civil government. There ought to be a good relationship between church and state but neither should intrude into the jurisdiction of the other.

The deacon's ministry is to bring the care and compassion of Christ to the needy. In many situations in developed societies this ministry almost seems to have been swallowed up by the property maintenance function. Yet the basic aim should not be forgotten.

4. *The unity of the church being expressed through a system of representative assemblies or courts of elders,* thus allowing for united action and for difficulties to be resolved in an orderly way (Acts 15). The basis of all action is the Bible, and the elders administer according to the rules God has given in the Bible.   Hence, while office-bearers are chosen by the members, the church is not a democracy but a Christocracy: Christ is the Head and accountability is to him. Of course this does not mean that the people have no say in important decisions affecting them as a congregation. Elders are not to lord it over God's people, and obviously harmony is to be furthered by keeping the members informed on significant matters. The members have a decisive voice in calling a minister from among those approved by the church, and property sales normally require majority approval. Many checks and balances are built into the system of government to prevent anarchy or tyranny that all might be done to God's glory.

The elders in a local congregation form the *Session*; representative elders from congregations in a region [usually the minister and one other elder of each congregation] form the *Presbytery*; a *Synod* or *Assembly* includes commissioners from the Presbyteries. In Reformed churches following the Dutch pattern, the assemblies are called the *Consistory*, the *Classis*, and the (Provincial or National) *Synod*.

6

In churches of the Scottish pattern the tendency is to emphasise the unity of the member congregations in one church, hence Presbyterian *Church* (singular) of Eastern Australia. In churches of Dutch pattern the emphasis is on the local church as having a certain completeness in itself, hence Reformed *Churches* (plural) of Australia. However, at root there is no difference of principle.

Doctrinal position

Presbyterian and Reformed churches accept the beliefs about God enshrined in the Apostles' Creed, the Nicene Creed and the Athanasian Creed of the early centuries, and in this sense are Catholic Christian. The doctrinal conclusions in these creeds are regarded as Scriptural and accordingly they are embodied in the Reformed Confessions. Presbyterian and Reformed churches are also Protestant, that is, they affirm the word of God written as authoritative and sufficient over against unwritten traditions.

The Calvinist wants to put God first. He believes that we are not to be religious merely to satisfy our desires or to obtain meaning for our lives, but because God has created us and it is our chief and highest good to glorify our Creator. So the glory and praise of God is a major theme. It is reflected in the polemic against idolatry and the emphasis on the highest loyalty being to God that is particularly evident in English Puritanism - an essentially Presbyterian movement.[1]

The Calvinist believes God is working out a holy purpose in human history with a view to the glorification of his name throughout creation. All should own his rule, hence Presbyterians have been concerned to see a godly society and a good working relationship between the Church and the State without either intruding on the province of the other. In the light of the grace of God in Christ which brings believers into the family of God as his dear children, Calvinism emphasises the ethics of gratitude. Its emphasis on the law of God is not to be seen as embracing legalism or self-righteousness, although, no doubt, some Calvinists have been guilty of such distortions. The disciplined and simple life of the genuine Calvinist has often been thought to account for the rise of capitalism. It is true that the 'Protestant work ethic' owes much to the Reformed Faith, but the sins of capitalism are the sins of capitalism and not of Calvinism.

The Calvinist believes God is to be loved with the mind as well as the heart. Education is prized and a well-trained ministry (commonly six years study at tertiary level) is characteristic. Its pattern of worship is simple, sometimes

1. Leland Ryker, **Worldly Saints: The Puritans As They Really Were** (Grand Rapids 1986) presents a balanced treatment of a much misunderstood people.

embracing a relatively plain but sober liturgy. The preaching of the Word of God is a major feature (indicated visually by the centrally located pulpit), since it is especially through this means that God speaks to men and brings them to himself. The church is regarded as very important since it is a major means, instituted by God, for bringing the knowledge of Christ to men and building them up in the faith. The sacraments of baptism (including infants of believers) and the Lord's Supper are observed. The former is commonly by pouring or sprinkling and is seen as the token of God's covenant and in succession to circumcision in the Old Testament. The latter is observed with a frequency according to the discretion of the Session. In Australia a quarterly celebration is common. The sacraments are not regarded as converting ordinances but as signs and seals of God's covenant of grace and of benefit where faith is present.

In Calvinism belief in the sovereignty of God is reflected in the understanding of the grace of God. God is not under obligation to any but has predestined the salvation of his elect. Predestination is not the same as fatalism since the means as well as the end are alike ordained by God. The atonement of Christ is admitted to be sufficient for all but the intention is the question at issue. The Calvinist holds that the intention was to make satisfaction for the sins of the elect - those given by the Father to the son in the eternal purpose. So Christ's redemption was particular and definite and the work of the Holy Spirit is in harmony with it. The Holy Spirit applies the work of Christ by working faith in the heart and so uniting the individual to Christ. Election is not because of holiness but in order to holiness. Calvinists affirm that the nature of man is flawed from his birth so that while each person acts freely he cannot act contrary to his nature. Thus, apart from the re-creating power of God, he cannot do anything spiritually pleasing to God. However, this spiritual bankruptcy is man's fault and he remains fully accountable to God. Those who are lost are not lost because God prevents their salvation but because they abide in their sin. Infants (and imbeciles) can be saved since it is ultimately grace which creates faith. Hence, those too young to believe personally are not beyond the gracious influences of God's Spirit.[2]

The number of the elect is known only to God. Earlier Lutheran and some Reformed theologians thought the number of the elect was relatively few. However, there has always been a more positive note among Reformed writers from early times, and the leading writers of the 19th century also articulated this hope.[3] The Calvinist has confidence in the future because

---

2. Suitable introductory literature includes L.Boettner, **The Reformed Doctrine of Predestination** (Philadelphia 1965); A.W.Pink, **The Sovereignty of God** (revised edition, London 1961); John Murray, **Redemption Accomplished and Applied** (London 1961).
3. A good introduction is I.H.Murray, **The Puritan Hope** (London 1971).

of his belief in God's control of all things and God's promise of Christ's kingdom as a world-transforming power although the danger of linking this expectation to advances in social and scientific progress in the 19th century was not always appreciated. As for the last things, Calvinism has thought of the Anti-Christ as a movement of error in history to be overcome by the triumphs of the Gospel[4] although the thought of a personal Anti-Christ and apostasy near the end of human history is rather common in the 20th century.[5] The return of Christ is regarded as closing human history and as being co-terminous with the resurrection of the dead, the last judgement and the ushering in of a new heavens and earth where righteousness has its home. The millennium of Revelation 20 is seen as the period between the advents (a-millennialism) or else as a time of gospel triumphs yet in the future after which Christ comes (post-millennialism). The view of pre-millennialism (ie. that Christ comes to reign on earth during the millennium and closes the period with the final resurrection, judgement and eternal state) has always been a minority opinion and not favoured among Reformed writers because of its pedantic literalism in interpretation of the Old Testament contrary to the principles of Scripture itself and because of its inconsistencies and incongruities.

Perhaps it will be appropriate to note at this point the Presbyterian view of Scripture. One is fully aware of the attempts made to show that Calvin did not believe in the inerrancy of the text of Scripture in the autographs. These attempts have often been based on taking Calvin's comments in reference to copyists' errors as if Calvin was reflecting on the integrity of the original text. It has also been common for critics of verbal inspiration (and some of its friends) to argue that verbal inspiration means meticulous precision in every detail disregarding accepted forms of speech and the canons of Biblical interpretation in the Bible itself. This leads either to the more extreme forms of harmonisation and pre-millennial interpretation common in American evangelicalism, or to the contention that verbal inspiration is nonsense and that the Bible is only reliable in the facts of salvation and not necessarily accurate in matters of history and science. Both extremes are avoided in orthodox Calvinism which affirms the inspiration of the Scriptures in the original autographs so that what men spoke was what God intended them to speak and does not partake of error (compare 2 Peter 1:20).[6]

4. I have expounded this view of 2 Thessalonians 2 in **Banner of Truth Magazine,** December 1977, pp.26-32.
5. Eg. William Hendriksen, **Commentary on Thessalonians** (London 1972)pp.173ff.
6. For Calvin's view see John Murray, **Works** Vol. 4 (Edinburgh 1982) pp.158-175. The classic presentation of the Church doctrine is B.B.Warfield, **Inspiration and Authority of the Bible** (Philadelphia 1970). On the transmission of Scripture see J.H.Skilton in **God's Infallible Word** (ed. Stonehouse & Woolley; 3rd edition, Philadelphia 1967) pp. 141-195, and as a general treatment J.M.Boice (ed), **The Foundations of Biblical Authority** (Grand Rapids 1978).

APPENDIX:

Some Historical Dates

Council of Jerusalem (Acts 15)	AD 49
Constantine's Toleration Edict	313
Council of Nicea (Arian dispute)	325
Augustine of Hippo, North Africa	354-430
Patrick, British missionary to Ireland	c389-461
Columba, Irish missionary to Scotland	c521-597
Pope Gregory the Great	590-604
Rise of Islam	from 622
Seventh Ecumenical Council (icons)	787
East and West drifting further apart	
Pope Innocent III - papal high point	1198-1216
The Age of Crusades	1095-1291
Thomas Aquinas, scholastic theologian	1225-1274
Papacy in Avignon, France	1305-1377
Rival popes	1378-1417
Jan Huss, Bohemian Reformer, burned	1415
Martin Luther's 95 Theses	1517
John Calvin, Geneva, Reformer & Theologian	1509-1564
John Knox, Scotland, Reformer	c1514-1572
Council of Trent (Roman)	1545-1563
Synod of Dort (Reformed)	1618-1619
Westminster Assembly (Reformed)	1643-1648

2: THE SCOTTISH EXPERIENCE

Australian Presbyterianism is largely the daughter of the Scottish Church, and a knowledge of the Scottish background is essential to our story.

Scotland is a country about the size of Tasmania but with a current population in excess of 5 million. The Reformation came to Scotland in 1560 under John Knox (c.1513-1572) and others when the Scots, with English help, defeated the French army of occupation. The Scottish reformation was a popular movement which swept away the gross doctrinal and moral corruption that had brought the church to a degraded condition.[1] The population was then about 850,000.

John Knox
John Knox was the man for the hour. A man under middle height he was possessed of great vigor, directness, faith and invincible courage. It was said that others lopped the branches but Knox struck at the root of 'Papistry.' He was a mighty preacher. Queen Elizabeth's envoy, Randolph, wrote: 'I assure you the voice of one man is able in one hour to put more life in us than 500 trumpets continually blustering in our ears.' Knox was uncompromising in his adherence to the word of God. Mary cried tears of frustration, for he was the obstacle to her ambitions to return Scotland to Rome. Near his life's end, when he had to be helped into the pulpit, James Melville records that 'ere he had done with his sermon, he was so active and vigorous that he was like

---

1. D.Hay Fleming, **The Reformation in Scotland** (London 1910) is a standard work which provides many details. Knox has found a recent biographer in W.Stanford Reid, **Trumpeter of God** (New York 1974).

to ding that pulpit into blads and flee out of it.' At his death in November 1572 the ruthless regent, the Earl of Morton, rightly said: 'Here lieth a man, who in his life, never feared the face of man, who hath often been threatened with dag and dagger, but yet hath ended his days in peace and honour.'

The First Reformation

Historically important is the *First Book of Discipline* prepared at short notice in May 1560 by six Johns including John Knox. All but one of them were travelled men and all were men of depth and breadth. The Book of Discipline was not, as modern usage might suggest, merely a book of rules for dealing with delinquent church members. Rather, it was a document setting out the order appropriate for reformation in the judgement of the six ministers. Prepared at the request of the Great Council of Scotland, it was not ratified by Parliament because too many of the nobility saw it would impair their own designs on the lands and property of the old Church.

The First Book states: 'seeing that Christ Jesus is he whom God the Father hath commanded only to be heard and followed of his sheep, we judge it necessary that his gospel be truly and openly preached in every church and assembly of this realm; and that all doctrine repugnant to the same be utterly repressed, as damnable to man's salvation.' It asserted that all things necessary for the instruction of the church and to make the man of God perfect are contained and expressed in holy Scripture, and that all which lacks command-ment or assurance from Scripture, as, for example, the keeping of holy days including Christmas, ought to be abolished. Idolatry is defined as including 'all honouring of God not contained in his holy Word.' The true preaching of God's word, the right administration of the sacraments and the due exercise of church discipline are regarded as essential marks of the true church. The rudiments of Presbyterian polity are present. One order of ministry together with elders and deacons appears. Possession of suitable gifts and graces is needful to office, so election and examination occur before admission.

Although there was a groundswell of popular support for the Reformation, there were very few persons suitably qualified for the ministry. There were only 12 ministers in 1560, and only six of them are noted among those present at the first General Assembly later that year. Rather than lower the standards they judged required of ministers, as a necessary expedient two temporary offices were allowed - superintendents and readers. The superintendents, ten or twelve of whom were suggested, were to organise congregations in areas where this had not already occurred, staying perhaps three weeks or a month in one place. While episcopacy is not expressly condemned in the Book of Discipline, there was no room for it by reason of the provisions made. The attempt by some to make the superintendent an hierarchical bishop falls flat on its face in the light of the evidence. As for the readers, these were not assistants to the ministers, but a temporary substitute to ensure some provision of the word of God to the people until sufficient ministers were available. There were 252 ministers and 621 exhorters and readers by 1567, and a total of some 900 parishes.

The final point worth noting is that the six Johns proposed that the vast revenues of the church (nearly half the revenue of Scotland) should be applied to ensure a school in every parish, reform of the universities and the relief of the poor and the provision needful for the church. The ideal was the creation of a thoroughly Christian nation. All were to be compelled to bring up their children with learning and virtue rather than in ignorance and vice. The educational programme was not carried into effect because of the avarice of the nobility, but it remained an ideal that was of major influence in succeeding generations.

Soon after the presentation of the First Book of Discipline, the same six Johns drew up the *Scots Confession*, which was ratified by Parliament on August 17, 1560, and the first General Assembly of the (reformed) Church of Scotland met in Edinburgh on December 20, 1560 with 42 members, only six of whom are noted as ministers. The Scots Confession was drawn up in only four days. It 'does not elaborate any of its doctrines with the precision and fullness we would like. At some points the arrangement is highly illogical and the movement of thought confusing. Yet it nowhere transgresses the norm of Reformed orthodoxy. Its formulations are emphatic enough to preclude subscription by anyone who is not both an Evangelical and a Calvinist. And it never allows us to forget that truth is in order to holiness. As a religious document and as a manifesto of Christian radicalism the Scots Confession is superb.[2] In February 1556, a service book including fifty metrical psalms and an English translation of Calvin's 1541 French Catechism was published in Geneva. This book already had currency in Scotland before 1560, and was subsequently approved by the General Assembly in 1562 and again in 1564 when the whole Psalter had been versified in a total of 30 metres.[3]

In 1567, seven years after its recognition, Parliament gave the church financial support. Knox died in 1572, the same year that the Regent obtained an Act of Parliament restoring the old hierarchical titles with a view to conferring them on persons who would, as a condition of receiving them, sign away most of the revenues to an avaricious patron. While not an actual restoration of full episcopacy it had potential to cause trouble.

2. Donald Macleod, 'The Scots Confession' in **Our Banner** (PCEA) September 1976,p.5.
3. For more details see Rowland Ward, **Psalm-singing in Scripture and History** (2nd edition Melbourne 1985) pp.41ff.

The forme of pray-

ERS AND MINISTRA-
tion of the Sacraments, &c. vſed in the
Engliſhe Congregation at Geneua: and
approued, by the famous and godly learned man, Iohn Caluyn.

and fewe finde it. Mat.7.

INTRATE:PER

ARCANVIAM

The way to life is ſtreiſte

They haue forſaken me. the well of the water of lyfe, and dygged
thcym ſelues pyttes. yea vyle and broken pyttes, that
can hold no water. Iere 2.

IMPRINTED AT GENEVA BY
IOHN CRESPIN M. D. LVI

Andrew Melville

Knox's successor in the leadership of the church was Andrew Melville (1545-1622). He returned from Geneva in 1574 to become Principal of Glasgow University. An accomplished scholar and a man of true courage, he was later (1607) confined to the Tower by King James, and ended his days in exile. He is one of Scotland's greatest sons. Melville championed the cause of presbytery over prelacy. The Church commissioned a *Second Book of Discipline* and it was adopted in April 1578 without a dissenting voice. It was the work of a Committee of ministers most of whom belonged to the era of the 1560s. This book developed the principles of church order in the right direction in the light of experience. No provision was now made for superintendents, the eldership was declared to be perpetual and annual election was replaced by life tenure. Episcopacy in all forms was expressly rejected, the liberty of the church to convene its Assemblies was asserted, and it was affirmed that patronage (the right to nominate to a benefice) ought not to have place any longer, and none should be intruded upon any congregation without lawful election and the assent of the people.

The Presbytery was not yet in general operation but in 1581, when the General Assembly ordered the Second Book to be engrossed in its records, it also ordered the erection of 50 presbyteries. King James was seeking to further his absolutist claims. Episcopacy was revived in 1581 and in 1584 the Black Acts were passed prohibiting meetings of the Assembly without the King's permission, prohibiting criticism of the Government in public or private, branding as guilty of treason any who declined the jurisdiction of the privy council in any matter (Melville had done so in reference to his preaching), and requiring all ministers to acknowledge the bishops as their ecclesiastical superiors.

However, the tide seemed to turn for a time and in June 1592 , Parliament consented to pass an Act ratifying the Assemblies, Synods, Presbyteries and Sessions of the Church of Scotland, declaring them, with their jurisdiction and discipline, as agreed to by the King, and embodied in the Act, to be in all time coming 'most just, good and godly.' This was the charter of Presbyterianism, and by implication gave the Second Book the force of law.

However, James was not to be relied upon to keep his word. Holding that 'Presbytery agreeth as well with a monarchy as God and the devil' he was told by Melville in 1596: 'Sir, as diverse times before I have told you, so now again I must tell you, - there are two Kings and two Kingdoms in Scotland; there is King James, the head of the commonwealth, and there is Christ Jesus, King of the Church, whose subject King James VI is, and of whose kingdom he is not a King, nor a Lord, not a Head but a member.'

The Second Reformation
The conflict with episcopacy still continued. Episcopacy had the authority of civil law from 1612 to 1640, and from 1662 to 1689. The first of these periods was brought to an end by the famous Glasgow Assembly of 1638 - the first free Assembly of the Church of Scotland for more than 40 years. Under the able Moderatorship of Alexander Henderson (1583-1646), and in spite of orders from King Charles to dissolve the Assembly, the prelates were either excommunicated or deposed and presbyterianism - government by Scriptural bishops - re-established. The episcopal Primate had reason to bewail: 'Our work of thirty years is overthrown at a single stroke.' Henderson was a tactful statesman, a great patriot and an able defender of the church's liberties under Christ. He was responsible for most of the important church documents from 1637 until his death, including the drafting of the Solemn League and Covenant of 1643.

In subsequent years the *Westminster Assembly* of ministers and theologians convened with a view to a thorough reformation of religion in the British Isles based on the model of Scotland and the example of the best Reformed churches elsewhere, Scripture always being supreme. Convened at first for a more limited purpose, this thorough reformation was part of the price required by the Scots in return for military assistance to the English in the time of Oliver Cromwell. Accordingly, the Scots had several influential commissioners representing them at the Westminster Assembly. These included such luminaries as Henderson, Samuel Rutherford (c.1600-1661) and George Gillespie (1613-1648), an extraordinarily able debater and the youngest member of the Assembly. [4]

As it turned out the fruit of the Assembly's labours from 1643 to 1648 was of chief benefit to Scotland. The restoration of the monarchy in England in 1660 also brought the re-establishment of Anglicanism in England, and the work of the Westminster Assembly was ignored there. In 1662 nearly 2,000 of some 12,000 ministers were 'ejected' from the Church of England for refusal to conform. From these 'non-conformists' at the Great Ejection sprang the Presbyterian and most of the Congregational and Baptist churches in England.

Back in Scotland the work of the Westminster Assembly was valued. Its *Directory for the Public Worship of God* was adopted by the church in 1645, not as a code but as a directory to indicate the lines upon which a non-liturgical Reformed service should be conducted. It superseded the old Genevan service book. A few days later the General Assembly adopted the *Form of Presbyterial Church Government*. This document was somewhat of a compromise in the place given to ruling elders because of the opinion in England which was not in general so clear in asserting the view that the ruling elder is a true presbyter in Scripture. The action of the Assembly shows that if the practical effect is secured some compromise on argumentation is tolerable for the sake of the unity of the church. In the Church of Scotland the Form was accepted in such a way as preserved the doctrine in the Second Book of Discipline. The Scots Confession was superseded by the *Westminster Confession of Faith* in 1647, the latter being regarded, with a couple of small provisos, as 'most agreeable to the word of God, and in nothing contrary to the received doctrine, worship, discipline and government of this Kirk.' The *Larger* and *Shorter Catechisms* were adopted in 1648, and soon replaced the other catechisms which had been used (principally Calvin's, Thomas Craig's (1581) and the Heidelberg of 1563 which had considerable use in Scotland at least as early as the 1590s). In 1650 the 1564 Psalter was replaced by a more accurate version with fewer metres. This was not the version based on the work of Francis Rous which the Westminster Assembly had revised but a Scottish production, nearly half the lines being the independent work of the Scottish Committee. All this retained the great principles of the First Reformation but applied these principles to the conditions then existing. A new English Bible was also planned but not executed due to the unsettled political situation.

4. The most recent study of the ecclesiastical and political setting of the Westminster Assembly is R.S.Paul, The Assembly of the Lord (Edinburgh 1985).

The absolutism of Charles II (1661-1685) and his brother James VII (1685-1688) corresponded with 'the killing times.' The covenant to maintain the Reformed religion was taken insincerely by Charles, and he soon imposed episcopacy and 'bent all his energies through willing satraps to stamp out the Covenants and Covenanters in a manner so merciless and revolting as showed him and his menials men devoid of humanity, self-respect and responsibility, and of any regard for the laws of civilised warfare.'[5] By 1663, about 350 of the near 900 parish ministers were ejected because they would not conform to episcopacy or acknowledge the king's claim of supremacy over the church. Some, like John Brown of Wamphray, were exiled to Holland. Those who remained were forbidden to preach and were prohibited from living within 20 miles of their former parish. Defoe, the 18th century historian, says 18,000 people were killed, or suffered exile, imprisonment or torture - nearly 2% of the population.

Calvinistic thought rejected the 'divine right' claimed by Charles by which absolute obedience to his decrees was enjoined. It rejected the concept of passive submission irrespective of the character of the ruler. While hesitant to oppose tyranny with force they did not exclude it altogether where rule developed an irreligious and iniquitous extreme. Revolt broke out against the monarch who had placed himself above the oath he had sworn, and whose own life was flagrantly immoral. Some of the more strict Covenanters found leadership under Richard Cameron who was killed in 1680. The last preacher who was martyred was James Renwick in 1688. Later that year the English and Scottish leaders offered the crown to William of Orange and so occurred the 'Glorious Revolution'. The overthrow of the Stuart dynasty was justified on the grounds that abuse of power of the kind that had occurred destroys the right to exercise it, essentially the very position of the Covenanters. Though some went to an extreme yet they were driven to it. We owe much of our modern freedoms to their brave struggle which, however, was not for freedom to do whatever one liked, but freedom to live under the authority of Christ according to his Word.

The Revolution Settlement

On April 11, 1689, William and Mary were proclaimed King and Queen in Scotland. Two weeks later it was ordered that the 60 ministers remaining of the some 350 who had been ejected since 1661 be reinstated . On June 7, 1690, episcopacy was formally abolished, the Confession sanctioned as 'the avowed Confession of this Church', and Presbyterian government restored in terms of the legislation of 1592 and placed in the hands of the 60 ministers.[6]

5. D.Maclean, **Aspects of Scottish Church History** (Edinburgh 1927) p.48. On the Covenanters see J.D.Douglas, **Light in the North** (Exeter 1974).
6. The Confession as approved by the church in 1647 and by Parliament in 1649 includes references to the text of Scripture but not the verses themselves. The

The settlement was very popular after the strife and trials of the previous years. However, a small number of the stricter Covenanters, known as Cameronians, from whose midst the *Reformed Presbyterian Church* was formed later, refused the settlement. Their chief objections were (1) the binding obligation of the National Covenant (1640) and the Solemn League and Covenant (1644) were passed over, since the Acts of Parliament in favour of these had been rescinded by Charles and were not revived under William and Mary; (2) the Church of Scotland, in accepting the settlement, had made a bargain with an Erastian state, so fettering its own liberties and dishonouring Christ. Here William's position as king in episcopal England was relevant as also his intimidation of the Assembly with a view to requiring it to accept some of the episcopalian clergy into vacant parishes. The spirit of 1689 was certainly a more secular one than in 1638, but the church stood up for her spiritual independence, and most of what the Covenanters had stood for was secured in practice in Scotland.

Subscription and other safeguards 1690-1711

On October 29, 1690, the Assembly urged Presbyteries to take up the matter of a subscription of approval of the Confession by ministers and elders. In 1693, Parliament required subscription of each minister and preacher, in which he declared the Confession to be the confession of his faith, that he owned the doctrine in it to be the true doctrine to which he would constantly adhere, and that he owned the Presbyterian government as settled by the Parliament in 1690 to be the only government of the church to which he would submit, and that he would never, directly or indirectly, endeavour its prejudice or subversion. The Parliament also ordained that 'uniformity of worship and of the administration of all public ordinances within this Church be observed by all the said ministers and preachers, as the same are at present performed and allowed therein or shall be hereafter declared by the authority of the same, and that no minister or preacher be admitted or continued for hereafter unless he subscribe to observe, and do actually observe the foresaid uniformity.' The concern here was to settle the peace and quiet of the church, especially given the number of preachers of prelatic outlook who still served parishes. There were about 300 of these in 1693. On April 13, 1694 the General Assembly enacted a Formula of subscription in terms of what Parliament required for a continuation of the relationship with the church. In 1700 the Assembly required elders to sign the Formula too.

Confession as ratified by Parliament in 1690 has no proof texts or references at all (vide D.Hay Fleming, **Critical Reviews** (London 1912) p.314), and this is the legally inviolate edition for churches, like the Free Church of Scotland, who still adhere to the old constitution. On the Revolution period see also A.I.Dunlop, **William Carstairs** (Edinburgh 1967).

While the General Assembly had very limited powers constitutionally, the need for safeguards against hostile majorities was recognised. The form of commission adopted in 1695 specifically affirms the limits of the commission: 'to consult, vote and determine in all matters that come before them to the glory of God and the good of his Church, according to the Word of God, the Confession of Faith, and agreeably to the constitution of this church, as they shall be answerable.' Further, in 1697, the General Assembly adopted a measure, commonly known as the *Barrier Act*, by which all new laws of general application to the church had first to go to the presbyteries and receive majority consent before becoming standing rules. The aim here was to place a check on abuse of power as well as to ensure that changes that were within the power of the church had general support. It was not a procedural method for bringing about significant constitutional change, although this was later unsuccessfully claimed in the Free Church Case of 1900.

In 1707, the Kingdoms of England and Scotland united in terms of a Treaty of Union. Under the 'Act of Security' passed at the time, it was provided as an essential and fundamental condition 'that the true Protestant religion contained in the above-mentioned Confession of Faith with the form and purity of worship presently in use within this Church and its Presbyterian Church government and discipline....all established by the foresaid Act of Parliament pursuant to the Claim of Right, shall remain and continue unalterable.'

There was still concern because of Anglican practices by those clergy at heart not faithful to the Church of Scotland; hence on April 21, 1707, the General Assembly passed an *Act Against Innovations*, and on May 22, 1711, enacted a rather more tight Formula of Subscription together with questions. One was required to 'own and believe' the 'whole' doctrine of the Confession. One also had to 'own' the worship whereas in 1694 one was required to make only a simple promise to observe uniformity, a promise one could make while seeking to overthrow the worship and make it of a different kind, although the principles of worship in the Confession, XXI would be a restriction. Essentially, the 1711 formula has been carried through to the present time by such as the Free Church of Scotland and the Presbyterian Church of Eastern Australia. As the nexus between the minister and the Confession, the wording of the Formula of Subscription is vital.[7]

7. The formula of 1711, if and in so far as it requires more than is expressed or implied in the formula of 1694, may well be regarded as in excess of power given the Treaty of Union. This also appears to have been the view of the Church of Scotland in 1889, and in legal opinion given the CS Assembly in 1900. The questions are a kind of elucidation of the formula, rest on the authority of the Assembly alone, and, unlike the formula, may be changed.

Patronage

One aspect of the Revolution Settlement which was to lead to untold trouble was less than final. This dealt with patronage, that is, the right of lay 'patrons' (usually land owners) to present and have admitted by the Presbytery such duly qualified minister as the patron nominated. This provision in the 1592 legislation was not revived in 1690, since all along the presbyterians had opposed it as interfering with the liberties of the church given by Christ, and William had had to give in. In its place a method for regulating the settlement of ministers was enacted which gave the right to nominate to the elders and the heritors (land owners) of the parish, provided they were Protestants. The congregation might approve or disapprove and the presbytery had the final say. If no one was nominated within six months the right of appointment lapsed into the hands of the Presbytery. This was not an ideal measure and was found hard to work because of the number of vacancies and the aversion of landholders, who were often episcopalian, to Presbyterian preachers. The Assembly was in process of drafting legislation to aid in the settlement of vacancies when, without consulting the church, the British parliament rushed through an Act, which became effective in 1712, by which the right of nomination was transferred from the elders and heritors to whoever had the right of patronage. In a majority of cases this was the Crown itself, and in others episcopalian land-owners, and the aim of the measure was to spite the Presbyterians and undermine the independence of the church. This Act was in violation of the Treaty of Union, contrary to the constitutional principles of the church, and accordingly was regularly protested against by the Assembly for many years.

Doctrinal trends

The sceptical spirit around 1700 was not helped by the scope given to reason by a godly English non-conformist, Richard Baxter (1615-1691). Baxter was self-taught in theology and his eccentric views moved away from evangelical Calvinism. He taught that repentance was to be distinguished from faith and was prior to faith, and that one could comply with God's new law, receive God's graciously provided righteousness and gain eternal life. Such 'neo-nomian' views spread in Scotland and along with the impact of Deism created many difficulties. Professor Simson of Glasgow was influenced by Baxterian and Arian views, but after two attempts by the orthodox to have him dealt with (1714-1717 & 1721-1729) it was only with reluctance that he was suspended in 1729 from his teaching position though retaining the status and stipend of office. At the same time, men like Thomas Boston (1677-1732) of Ettrick, who were striving in this difficult time to maintain the freeness of the Gospel for sinners, found that swift and unjust action was taken by the Assembly against a book *The Marrow of Modern Divinity*, which, for all its inaccurate and injudicious expressions, was not without value in aiding an evangelical presentation of Calvinistic teaching. [8]

Divisions and Moderatism

As the century progressed there was a growing cleavage between ministers and the common people. By and large, the latter wanted evangelical pastors but did not get them. The pursuit of privilege and the lifeless teaching that were common worked together so as to contribute to a secession from the Church of Scotland under men like Ebenezer Erskine (1680-1754) in 1733. The Seceders were zealous for the cause of truth and they regarded themselves as having withdrawn 'from the prevailing party in the church' but represented the true Church of Scotland still. They even renewed the covenants passed over in 1690. In 1743, the Cameronians were able to organise a Presbytery too, although they continued to practise political dissent as a form of protest at the inadequacies of the Revolution Settlement, and so they did not unite with the Seceders. As well as division among the Seceders in 1747 over the wording of an oath, there was a further separation from the Established Church when Thomas Gillespie (1708-1774) of Carnock was deposed in 1752 for refusing to take part in the settlement of a minister at Inverkeithing who was opposed by the congregation. In 1761 the *Relief Presbytery* was formed by Gillespie and two others. The influence of English non-conformity was present in the Relief from the beginning and it rejected the obligation of the covenants and the State connection.

By 1765 there were 120 congregations of Presbyterians outside the Established Church with 100,000 worshippers - nearly 10% of the population. The proportion grew over the next 70 years to be about 15% on the eve of the 1843 Disruption.

The Assembly of the Established Church was dominated by what from the 1760s were called Moderates, their great leader being Principal William Robertson (1721-1793). Robertson was a man of erudition and culture, as were many of his school, although the latter part of the 18th century was to

---

8. There is an extensive literature on this subject which continues to raise its head from time to time as in Tasmania in the 1960s. The decision of the Assembly had some similarities to the Roman Catholic condemnation of Jansenism in that certain propositions in the book were lifted from their context and condemned as heretical despite the protests of the Marrowmen that they rejected the heretical sense themselves.

The Assemblies of 1720 and 1722 condemned the Marrow teaching under the persuasion that it embraced, inter alia, universal pardon. In 1831, when dealing with Macleod Campbell, who did teach universal pardon, appeal was made to the earlier decisions. This prompted the great historian, Thomas McCrie (1772-1835), to publish several articles on the Marrow Controversy [Edinburgh Christian Instructor, August, October & December 1831 and February 1832] which provide important background. A short summary is A.M.Harman, The Marrow Controversy in Our Banner (PCEA) September 1964. David C.Lachman, The Marrow Controversy 1718-1723 (Edinburgh 1988) is the definitive work thus far.

see many of a crassly secular spirit. They were great for law and order in the church and they customarily carried technical points to a legalistic extreme in the interests of their party. They owed their position to influential patrons and they believed in giving full support to this system (despite hypocritically continuing the annual protest against it until 1784), and they did not regard the will of the people in the settlements of ministers. Theatre-going and card-playing by ministers was characteristic. Missionary outreach was opposed, particularly the effort by the evangelicals in the Assembly of 1796. As one of them said: 'To spread abroad the knowledge of the Gospel among barbarous and heathen nations seems to me highly preposterous, in so far as it anticipates, nay, reverses the order of nature.' It was not until 1829 that the rising strength of the evangelicals resulted in Alexander Duff being sent to India as the first missionary of the Church of Scotland.

Evangelicals

Over against the Moderates were the Evangelicals - the High-flyers, as the Moderates were accustomed to call them. John Willison (1680-1750) of Dundee was one of them, and along with Thomas Boston's *Human Nature in its Fourfold State*, Willison's writings were favourite reading among the common people. John Erskine (1721-1803) of Edinburgh was another prominent Evangelical leader. Interestingly, he ended up as a colleague in Principal Robertson's church. He was a fine preacher and scholar and first advocated the cause of foreign missions in the Assembly. Such men lamented the administration of things in the church but did not consider they should withdraw since the constitution was sound, while the Moderates, though cold and formal and worldly, did not commonly openly deny the Confession since they received their stipend on the profession of adherence to it. Indeed, Robertson's successor from 1781 as leader of the Moderates, was Principal George Hill of St Andrews. He produced a standard text of Calvinistic theology (1821), although he did not intend that his students should actually go and apply it seriously! Andrew Thomson (1779-1831), 'A Great Scottish Churchman',[9] led the Evangelicals soon after Erskine's death.

All the Scottish Presbyterian churches shared in the evangelical revival which gathered momentum in the early years of the 19th century and was aided by the vindication of the Scottish Reformation by the work of such scholars as Thomas McCrie (1772-1835), whose *Life of Knox* was published in 1812. Thomson's influence among the elite of Edinburgh society was also marked, and the influence of his magazine *The Christian Instructor*, founded in 1810, very considerable. The Evangelical leader after Thomson's early death in 1831 was Thomas Chalmers (1780-1847), at first a Moderate with more

9. Cf. the monograph by R.S.Miller, A Great Scottish Churchman (Dunedin 1961).

interest in mathematics than his parish duties, but from 1811 a convinced and active evangelical successively in Kilmany, Glasgow, St Andrews and Edinburgh. The scholarship, preaching and literary work of these men may be noted - they were not pietistic. Chalmers was very concerned about social needs and made a contribution to education second only to that of Melville in the 17th century.

The Ten Years' Conflict 1834-1843

By 1834 the Evangelicals had a majority in the Assembly and were determined to remove abuses, not only because they valued the Scriptural principles of the church, but also because the abuses only encouraged attacks on the very idea of an established church by many of those outside it. In the year mentioned, the Assembly, having taken excellent legal advice, passed what was called the *Veto Act*. This declared that it was a fundamental law of the church that no minister should be intruded on a congregation contrary to the will of the people. To give effect to this the disapproval of the majority of male communicants who were heads of families would require the Presbytery to refuse induction. Also at the 1834 Assembly, the 'chapels of ease' which had been established in the absence of endowment for new parishes from the State, were reckoned for ecclesiastical purposes as if they were parish churches. Thus their ministers were given full standing and the churches involved were able to have their own Sessions.

Over the next few years there were a few cases where men were either vetoed or intruded on congregations, and legal decisions in the Court of Session (the highest civil court in Scotland) established a new interpretation of the contract with the State which gave the State the right to interfere in the spiritual affairs of the church. Melville's 'two kingdoms' doctrine had succumbed to the influence of a doctrine of the monolithic state which was found among men of privilege and position and anti-democratic temperament at that time. Various appeals were made - to the House of Lords, the Prime Minister, Parliament and the Queen, but to no avail. At length, having exhausted all remedies, a large section of the Established Church was forced to withdraw so as to keep a good conscience. This event is called 'the Disruption'. It occurred on May 18, 1843 in Edinburgh. Nearly 40% of the ministers withdrew representing about two-thirds of the Evangelical party.

A CLAIM, DECLARATION AND PROTEST was sent to Parliament in 1842. The CLAIM values the relationship with the State as calculated to enable the Gospel to be brought to all of the people, it recognises the jurisdiction of the State in civil matters, but claims as of right that the church shall enjoy her privileges according to law and be protected from the illegal encroachments of the civil law. Its DECLARATION is that the church will refuse to intrude ministers on congregations, even at the risk of losing the State's financial support. And it goes on to PROTEST that all Acts in derogation of the rights and privileges of the church are null and void. This 'Claim of Right' [the short title] was carried in the Assembly by 241 to 111. Parliament did not take it very seriously and rejected it 211 to 76.

When the Assembly of 1843 met, a PROTEST was read by the retiring Moderator, Dr David Welsh, the Protest having been signed by many members of the Assembly. He then laid it on the table, bowed respectfully to the Lord High Commissioner - the Queen's representative, and moved to the door followed by 120 ministers and 73 elders. The first General Assembly of the CHURCH OF SCOTLAND FREE was then held in Tanfield Hall, Dr Thomas Chalmers being the first Moderator. The Protest was engrossed in the minutes as the ground of their action. Its general principles were held as binding, and the questions used at ordinations/inductions were amended accordingly to make this explicit. The Deed of Demission was adhered to in due course by 474 of the about 1,200 ministers.

In 1876, the majority of the Reformed Presbyterian Church, having abandoned enforcement of political dissent in 1863, joined the Free Church, a small remnant continuing from the events of 1863.

The Disruption : The Protesters leave St Andrew's Church

It is not necessary to determine here if the Disruption could have been avoided although the answer is probably 'no'. The division occurred, for better or for worse, and involved major sacrifice for many of the ministers. We cannot stop to tell the inspiring story of the remarkable progress of the Free Church of Scotland nor its subsequent decline. Suffice it to say that the Disruption stirred the soul of Scotland. One could not be neutral and there was plenty of partisanship too. In all lands where Scotsmen had gone the repercussions were felt. At the same time the Established Church did not wither away but was stimulated to more activity, especially from the revival of Calvinism among the younger men which showed up in the 1860s alongside a very liberal stream of teaching.

Different Church/State views in 1843

Differences among Scottish Presbyterians in 1843 were chiefly related to differences on the church/state questions, although these differences often reflected class differences and also Highlander/Lowlander distinctions. Thus, those continuing in the Established Church in the main were Tory in outlook, while the Free Church had many from the rising middle class who were Liberal in politics. The Free Church also was strongly represented in the Highlands partly because the landed proprietors asserted their rights and tended to disregard the needs of the Highland peasantry. Disregarding the emphases of the smaller Presbyterian groups, the three major positions were as follows:

1. *National recognition and spiritual independence*

About 30% of Scottish Presbyterians held this position in theory and by practical involvement with the Free Church of Scotland. Given that Scripture requires all men to own the claims of King Jesus, and also sets forth a distinct government for the church, the Free Church position was the Scriptural one, and it was also the constitutional position of the Scottish church. Hence, the Free Church of Scotland regarded herself as the true Church of Scotland, the body which had that name in law having fallen away from its principles.

It should be noted that to believe in the national recognition or establishment of the church does not of necessity require financial support be given by the State. The Church of Scotland was established by law in 1560 but was endowed only in 1567. Thus, the Free Church was not inconsistent in giving up State-funded stipends, and State-provided churches and manses. It gave these up because the conditions under which it could continue to enjoy them could not be endured with a good conscience.

2. *National recognition with civil interference*

The Established Church believed in national recognition but was prepared to accept interference by the State in the spiritual affairs of the church. Naturally, she denied that there was such interference as constituted what is technically called 'Erastianism' but such was the case. This was a modification of a fundamental point of the constitution of the Church of Scotland. About 50% of Scottish Presbyterians accepted it to a greater or lesser degree, or were prepared to tolerate it.

3. *No national recognition or support*

Many of those who had seceded from the Church of Scotland in the 18th century had come to believe that it was sinful to receive financial support from the State, and some took the line that Church and State should have nothing to do with each other. About 16% of Scottish Presbyterians went along with such views. They had come about through jealousy of the privileges of the Established Church as well as the influence of unbiblical philosophy. This 'voluntary' position is associated with the Relief and major Secession bodies which united in 1847 as the *United Presbyterian Church.*

It should be noted that the Free Church was 'voluntary' in practice, since it relied totally on the givings of the people, but it believed very definitely in the State connection on a proper basis. Some United Presbyterians would have been happy with this, especially once they were in a country where there was no Established Church. The great fear of those holding the Free Church position was that the voluntary position of the United Presbyterians in principle led straight to the atheistic State which answered only to popular will and disregarded the word of God. Today we see the relevance of this with Western society on the verge of collapse.

With these thoughts in mind we can turn to our Australian story. However, for the sake of completeness and clarity, the following outline of subsequent developments is appended.

Scottish church history 1843-1988 in outline

Judged from marriage statistics, 46% of the Scottish population in the 1850s identified with the Established Church (the active following being far less), 23% identified with the Free Church, 14% with the United Presbyterians, 2% with the Episcopal Church and 9% with the Roman Catholic Church (chiefly people of Irish extraction in the Glasgow region). The figures for the Established Church remained steady until 1910, whereas the Free Church and United Presbyterians show decline setting in in the 1870s even as less definite doctrinal views come to prevail. In 1900 these two bodies were supported by about 29% of the population, and a union was effected that year under the name *United Free Church.* The UFC closed over 200 parishes and opened some 25 new ones prior to 1929. In that year, all but a small following which objected to the Church/State relationship, entered the Church of Scotland.

The 1900 union was opposed by a handful of members of the Free Church Assembly since it involved leaving the Church/State issue an open question and involved a new Formula of subscription which changed the relationship of the church to her creed. The continuing Free Church won their legal claim at the House of Lords in the famous Free Church Case in 1904. It then had about 30 ministers and a following of 50,000. Today it has about 100 ministers although the following has halved. The Free Church is to be distinguished from the *Free Presbyterian Church* formed in 1893 by two ministers who withdrew from the Free Church because of serious modifications in the Formula in 1892. However, these modifications were regarded by the majority of the constitutional party at that time as in excess of power, and they did not withdraw but constituted the minority who succeeded against the United Free Church in 1904. In 1905, the offending legislation was repealed, but union overtures have been rejected. Both churches are Highland-based and similar in position although the Free Presbyterians in general are more rigorous and would have a greater proportion of men of somewhat austere and narrow vision than the Free Church. The Free Presbyterians have about 30 ministers and a community of 4,000. There are two centres in Australia (Grafton and Sydney).

In the aftermath of the Free Church Case, the United Free Church needed Parliamentary sanction to retain a share of the old Free Church property. In consideration of her support for the measure the Church of Scotland secured an amendment to her own contract with the State by which she was given the freedom to prescribe a Formula of subscription from time to time. In 1909, the Church of Scotland suitably modified her subscription in a similar way to the United Free Church. This paved the way for the eventual union in 1929 referred to above. However, it left the church able to vary its creed within broad limits so long as the church remained officially Protestant and Trinitarian. The endowments for the benefit of the church are now fully under church control. However, the liberty obtained is not the spiritual independence intended by the Reformers since the church's creed is a fluctuating one somewhat less definite than the corresponding provisions of the Presbyterian Church of Australia. Compared with more than 3,000 ministers at the time of union in 1929 there are now well under 2,000. There is evidence of a revival of evangelical life, but for most of the 20th century the proportion of definite evangelicals has been less than 10% of the ministers.

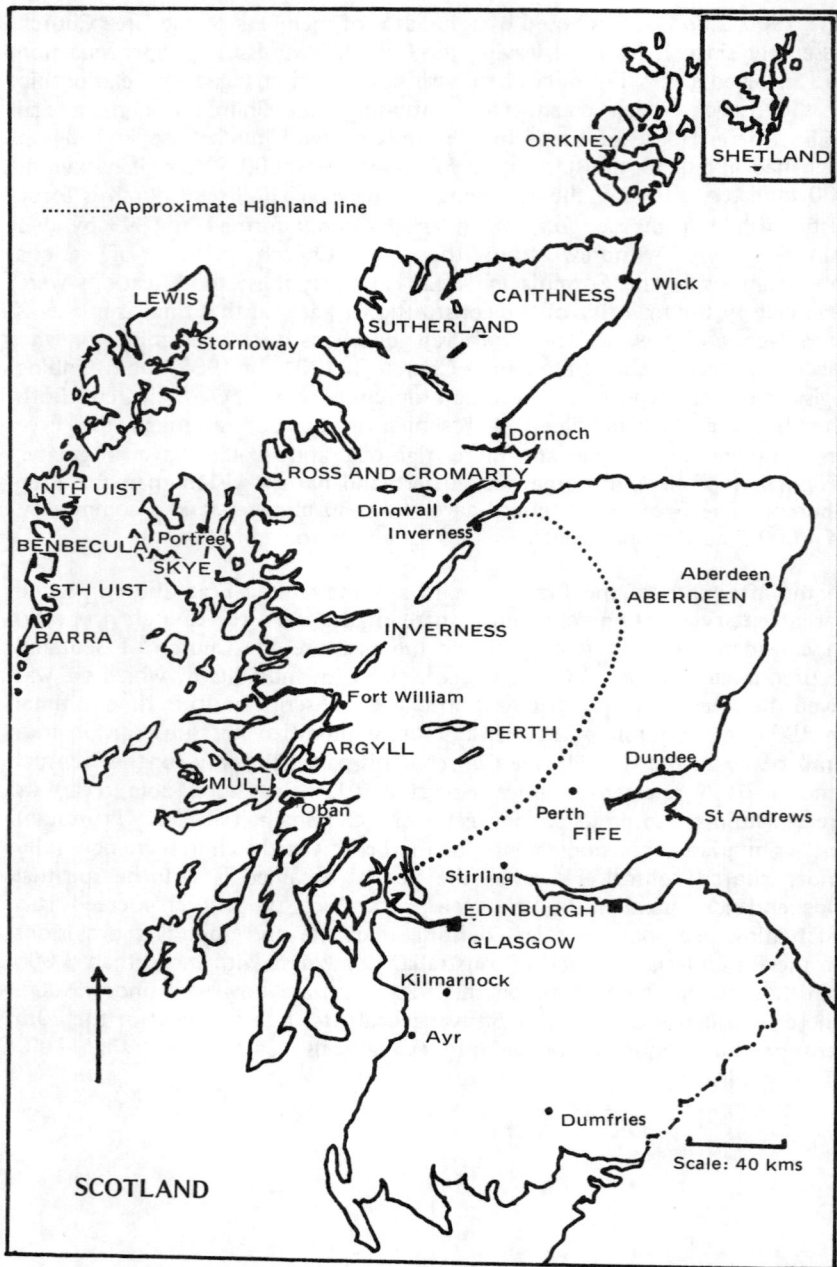

ORKNEY

SHETLAND

............Approximate Highland line

LEWIS

CAITHNESS   Wick

SUTHERLAND

Stornoway

Dornoch

ROSS AND CROMARTY

NTH UIST

Dingwall
Inverness

BENBECULA   Portree

Aberdeen
ABERDEEN

SKYE

STH UIST

INVERNESS

BARRA

Fort William

PERTH

ARGYLL

Dundee

MULL

Perth   St Andrews

Oban

FIFE

Stirling

EDINBURGH

GLASGOW

Kilmarnock

Ayr

Dumfries

Scale: 40 kms

SCOTLAND

Part Two

CONFLICT AND TROUBLE

1788-1846

3: AUSTRALIAN BEGINNINGS

The beginnings of Australian Presbyterianism

The first member of a Reformed Church to visit Australia was Abel Tasman, the Dutchman, who reached what is now called Tasmania in 1642 and named it Van Diemen's Land after the Governor of Batavia. The earliest Presbyterian settlers came in the First Fleet in 1788. They included the Assistant Surgeon, Dr Thomas Arndell. In due time others arrived and a Presbyterian settlement developed in the farming district of the Hawkesbury River near Windsor. Sydney, some 70 kilometres distant, was then very much a convict settlement. [1]

Few of those transported from Britain were Presbyterians - less than 3% - and then often for political offences. Thomas Muir of Dundee, who sought greater representation for Scotland, was one of these. He was a young advocate of great ability but was condemned and transported for 14 years. He reached Botany Bay about August 1794 and was given a measure of freedom because of his excellent conduct. He provided some spiritual services on the way out, and conducted services according to the Presbyterian form among his fellow convicts as an elder of the Church of Scotland. He escaped on a ship in February 1796, and later became a French citizen. [2]

1. The story of this settlement is told in R.M.Arndell, **Pioneers of Portland Head** (Brisbane 1976)
2. This paragraph is based on C.A.White, **The Challenge of the Years** (Sydney 1951) p. 1,2, whose source is Blackwood's Magazine, July 1950. See also Eris O'Brien, **The Foundation of Australia 1786-1800**, second edition, (Sydney 1950) p.242. I owe this reference to Professor A.M.Harman of the Presbyterian Theological College, Melbourne.

The early Presbyterian settlers were frugal, hard-working, intelligent and serious minded Scotsmen. They brought with them their religious principles, their desire for education and their love of good government. Early religious services were held in Dr Arndell's home, and in 1803 a temporary building with a thatched roof was erected. Here a godly Presbyterian by the name of James Mein (1761-1827) continued his practice on the voyage out in 1802: he would gather the families together for worship

'by singing the psalms of David in the Scottish metrical version, reading the Holy Scriptures with a sermon from some Puritan divine, and commending themselves to the Divine blessing in extempore prayer to God, agreeably to the hallowed customs of their native land.' [3]

There is no direct evidence that Mein was an elder, but he certainly had been a seat holder of the Presbyterian Church in Crown Street, Covent Garden prior to coming to New South Wales.

In 1809 a solid stone building with walls two feet thick was erected by this small band of settlers and called Ebenezer (see 1 Samuel 7:12). The original building with the addition of a porch (1929) stands to this day. It was the first church building erected in Australia entirely by voluntary subscription ($800), and is now the oldest church building in the country still used for public worship. In 1977 it ceased to be Presbyterian and came under the control of the Uniting Church formed that year.

3. J.D.Lang, **Reminiscences of My Life and Times** [edited by D.W.A.Baker] Melbourne 1972 p. 45

Originally the building (approximately 40 feet by 20 feet) served as both a church and a school. Dr G.R.S.Reid has written thus of the church in his *The History of Ebenezer*, 1964 edition:

In its plain austerity the building resembles many other older places of worship in Scotland, almost exactly the same in size, shape and style. 'Here in Ebenezer,' it has been said, 'we have a replica of the beginning of our faith in the land from which our faith was derived.' A lowly and lonely sanctuary it was, with no outward adornment, no interior decorations, nor organ or choir or hymns originally, only the singing of the Psalms, the reading of the Scripture, the preaching of the Word - the devout fellowship of praise and communion in the solemn sacrament of the Lord's Supper. 'The sacrifices of God are a broken spirit; a broken and a contrite heart, O God, thou wilt not despise' (Ps 51:17).

Such was the beginning of Presbyterianism in Australia.

It was not until December 1822 that Archibald McArthur arrived as the first Presbyterian minister. He was based in Hobart and commenced services in a building on the corner of Murray and Macquarie Streets on January 12, 1823. On the mainland the first minister, and one destined to play a leading role in future developments, was John Dunmore Lang. He arrived in Sydney on May 23, 1823, preached his first sermon on June 8, 1823 and founded the Scots Church in Jamison Street. Lang preached occasionally at Parramatta and to the small group of settlers at Ebenezer, Portland Head.

The Church of England had been represented in New South Wales from the beginning of European settlement, the first service being conducted by Rev Richard Johnson on February 3, 1788. Johnston was appointed chaplain through the influence of the evangelicals in the Church of England who adhered to the *Thirty-nine Articles of Religion*. Johnston's theological position was very close to that of the Presbyterians other than in matters of church government and order.[4] Rev Samuel Leigh, the Wesleyan Methodist, arrived in 1815, while John Joseph Therry arrived as the first official Roman Catholic priest in 1820. The population was principally Anglican (over 50%), with Roman Catholics in second place followed by Presbyterians. Methodists were a much smaller percentage at this stage.

4. The best biography of Johnson is N.K.Macintosh, **Richard Johnson** (Sydney 1978).

4: THE LANG ASCENDANCY 1823-1837

During the period between 1823, when the first minister arrived in New South Wales, and 1837, when there were many additions, there were five Presbyterian congregations: Ebenezer, Portland Head; Scots, Sydney; Scots, Maitland; Bathurst; and St Andrew's Scots, Sydney.   As we will see, James Forbes was right when he wrote in 1846:

'But unhappily, the persons placed in charge of them were either so injudiciously chosen, or the deteriorating influence of colonial society was such, that religion did not prosper under their ministrations. There were also continual jars and bickerings between the 'senior minister' and his juniors. For these, all parties seem much to be blamed; and it has ever appeared to us one of the most mysterious *permissions* of Divine Providence, that the founding of an infant Church in an infant colony should have fallen into such hands.' [1]

John Dunmore Lang - turbulent Scot [2]

John Dunmore Lang, the first Presbyterian minister on the Australian mainland was born at Greenock in 1799, the son of a small landowner and ship's joiner. His mother, Mary Dunmore, came from Largs where John received his education prior to entering on an eight year course in Arts and Divinity in the University of Glasgow (1813-20). Major influences were Thomas Chalmers (1780-1847), the leader of the Evangelical Party in the Church of Scotland and minister in Glasgow, and Dr Stevenson Macgill (1765-1840), the Professor of Divinity and a leading Evangelical.

1. **Port Phillip Christian Herald**, May 2, 1846, p.38 col.3
2. The best biography of Lang is D.W.A.Baker, **Days of Wrath** (Melbourne 1985) 562pp, although discussion of the ecclesiastical aspects is inadequate; cf. Barry Bridges' review ir **Church Heritage**, Sydney, September 1986, pp.271-280.

After preaching for some time in various congregations, Lang resolved to follow his brother George to New South Wales with a view to ministering in Sydney. He was therefore ordained for this work by the Presbytery of Irvine on September 30, 1822 and left for Australia two weeks later. He arrived in Sydney on May 23, 1823, and founded the Scots Church in Jamison Street (opened July 16, 1826). He occasionally preached at Parramatta and to the small group of settlers on the lower Hawkesbury. At his first communion at Ebenezer in August 1824, 20 communicants were present.

Lang was egotistical, vituperative, imprudent and even devious in financial matters, and yet an earnest evangelical with active interest in the benefit of his fellows. While his encouragement of immigration and his efforts in developing democratic institutions cannot be denied, yet as first and foremost a Presbyterian minister, it must be doubted whether the church was really advantaged by his activities. He was for ever speaking, writing and agitating, but his 25 years in the legislature and his frequent absences from his pulpit sat ill with his primary responsibilities. His gaol terms for libel or debt and his often scurrilous attacks on those who opposed him hardly enhanced his reputation. Though his theology was tolerably orthodox, his concern for ordinary people warm and genuine, and his vision often far ahead of his time, his serious weaknesses of character will always prevent him being recognised as one of the great Australian Christians, though highly influential in his day.

Lang's first voyage - 1824

In August 1824, Lang decided to return to Britain to secure a minister for Portland Head, and to obtain equal standing with the Church of England in the colony for the Church of Scotland. He returned in January 1826 with a DD conferred by the University of Glasgow, a matter in which his old Professor, Stevenson Macgill, had assisted. Presumably, the argument was that this would assist in negotiations with the colonial authorities. The minister Lang obtained was not the man he originally had in view but another who turned out to be just the opposite of Lang himself - John McGarvie.

John McGarvie - 'in moderation placing all my glory' [3]

John McGarvie was born in Glasgow in 1794, the son of a journeyman shoemaker who later had his own shop. He entered the University of Glasgow in 1808 and graduated in Arts in 1813. He completed a year of the Divinity course before taking up tutoring and engaging in travel and some journalism.

'It seems clear that, as with the majority of his contemporaries, the Church was for McGarvie a career rather than a vocation. He did not enjoy preaching and literature and art were at the centre of his interests, but he lusted after the social standing and security offered by the ministry of the Established

3. These words are part of one of the mottos of the Sydney Herald chosen by McGarvie in 1831, the full quote (from Pope) being 'In moderation placing all my glory, while Tories call me Whig - and Whigs a Tory.' They have a deeper meaning in McGarvie's case.

35

Church....McGarvie was by temperament, personality and principles a Moderate and it was natural that lacking a patron he should seek support within the Church from Moderate leaders.' [4]

In 1823 he wrote several anonymous letters to the press in support of Duncan Macfarlan, when the latter was seeking to hold a pastorate as well as his Principalship of the University, a situation opposed by evangelicals, and he thus gained the friendship of the older man. This stood him in good stead when Macfarlan became Convener of the Colonial Committee in 1836. So Lang unwittingly introduced a moderate into the colonial ministry.

Despairing of obtaining a settlement in Scotland - there were many more candidates than vacant parishes - McGarvie accepted the proposal to migrate to New South Wales, was ordained by the Presbytery of Glasgow, and reached Sydney in May 1826. True to form he preached only twice on the voyage out. When he went to Portland Head, he was very depressed at what he found. There was only a small number of people, there was no manse or stipend and he was isolated from social contacts. Lang secured a state stipend of $200 together with a manse and glebe, but McGarvie's four years at Portland Head were years he would rather have forgotten. He preached once each Lord's Day to a handful of people, and frequently spent the mid-week in Sydney. He did not visit and pray with his flock but he was always ready to help them in negotiations with the authorities over land grants and the like, so he was accepted though the people were disappointed in his ministry.[5]

Lang's second voyage - 1830

Lang had written in vain for further ministers. In August 1830 he went to Britain to see what he could do in person and also to promote the establishment of an educational institution (The Australian College). McGarvie was to look after Scots Church in Lang's absence. Lang's mission seemed crowned with success. He returned in October 1831 with his bride and with Rev Thomas Thomson, MA, and Rev John Cleland, MA, intended for the Hunter River district and Pitt Town respectively. Revs Henry Carmichael, William Pinkerton and John Anderson were also with him as Professors for the College, which was duly established on November 15, 1831. Lang also brought out 45 tradesmen and their families.

Early ministry on the Hunter

Maitland was the cradle of Presbyterianism in the Hunter Valley, and had an importance as a centre of population second only to Sydney at this time.

---

4. B.Bridges, 'The Reverend John McGarvie' in Church Heritage, op. cit., p.231
5. B.Bridges, ibid., is the most helpful recent published source on McGarvie.

It was convenient to the extensive estate of Andrew Lang, John's brother, at Largs ('Dunmore'), and had been surveyed as a town in 1829. Thomas Thomson had been ordained by the Presbytery of Glasgow for 'The Scotch Church in the district of Maitland', and after arriving with Lang at Sydney he conducted his first service at Castle Forbes Granary near Singleton on November 6, 1831. However, Thomson had to withdraw after a few weeks because of his serious intemperance. He was given another chance at Bathurst early in 1832. A licentiate, Rev William Pinkerton, was sent to supply the district. The first church, built of slab with a shingle roof, was opened on November 11, 1832 by Dr Lang with the name 'Scots Church.' This was the third Presbyterian church building erected in New South Wales. The probable location was St Andrews Street. Pinkerton left for Sydney in the middle of 1833 and died the following year. John Adair, a licentiate of the Church of Scotland, was appointed to supply on July 1, 1833 and continued until November 17, 1834. He was not ordained, and was acquitted of forgery on the grounds of insanity in 1836. John H.Garven replaced him in 1835.

St Andrew's Scots Church, Sydney

When Lang returned in 1831 he found that a portion of his congregation had become attached to McGarvie's ministrations.

'Lang's behaviour had already caused scandal in the Colony; a defamation suit had been brought against him, he had been rebuked by the Secretary of State, he had provoked several secessions from the congregation and he was frequently absent from his post.' [6]

On the other hand, Lang was shocked to find that McGarvie, who had become associated with his brother William McGarvie in the publishing of the *Sydney Herald*, sanctioned preparation of the paper's Monday issues on Sunday. Nevertheless, wanting McGarvie's services at the Australian College, and to prevent losses from the Presbyterian faith (and perhaps because the Portland Head people did not want McGarvie back), Lang endorsed the forming of a second congregation from those desiring McGarvie's less turbulent ministry. According to Lang the previously cordial relations broke up because McGarvie blamed Lang for Isabella Lang's refusal of his proposal of marriage, and resented Lang's nomination of John Anderson for the Launceston congregation, a position which, unknown to Lang, he desired. At any rate, from mid 1832 the breach between the two was obvious and would be lasting. McGarvie succeeded in opening his church in 1835, and called it St Andrew's Scots Church. In the early days 'Presbyterian' was not used as a denominational title. The site was in St Andrew's Lane between George and Kent Streets, behind where St Andrew's Anglican Cathedral was erected. Rev John Cleland went to Portland Head.

6. B.Bridges, op. cit., p.233

Presbytery of New South Wales formed - 1832

Despite the fact that both Cleland and Thomson were intemperate and McGarvie was unwilling to co-operate, Lang knew there must be a regular presbyterial structure. So, as he had foreshadowed in Edinburgh in 1831, he took steps to form a Presbytery. On December 14, 1832, the Presbytery of New South Wales was formed against the wishes of McGarvie in order to ordain John Anderson for the congregation at Launceston. New South Wales at this time included what is now Victoria and Queensland. Sydney's population was around 25,000, and Melbourne did not exist.

McGarvie's objections were essentially ecclesiastical. Dr Bridges summarizes: 'He would consent to nothing which could be interpreted as the forming of a new Church independent of the Church of Scotland, arguing that all their security in the form of State recognition and State aid derived from their being an extension of the Scottish Establishment. He persuaded his fellow-ministers to agree not to perform any other act as a Presbytery until the attitude of the Church of Scotland was ascertained.' [7]

McGarvie appealed through the Presbytery of Glasgow for a ruling on the position of the Presbytery, and this resulted in the General Assembly passing the following Act on May 24, 1833.

DECLARATORY ENACTMENT AND RECOMMENDATION AS TO COLONIAL CHURCHES

The General Assembly of the Church of Scotland did, and hereby do, enact and declare, That it is proper and expedient for ordained ministers of the Church of Scotland connected with fixed congregations in any of the British Colonies, to form themselves, where circumstances permit, into Presbyteries and Synods, adhering to the Standards of this Church, and maintaining her form of worship and government.

That no minister should be received as a member of any such Presbytery or Synod, when first formed, who has not been ordained by a Presbytery of this Church; that no minister of this Church should be afterwards received as a member who does not come specially recommended from the Presbytery by which he was ordained, or in which he has last resided; and that no probationer of this Church should receive ordination from any such Presbytery, except on his producing extract of licence, with a testimonial of his good character, from the Presbytery or Presbyteries within whose bounds he has resided, down to the time of his leaving Scotland.

That it is not expedient for such Presbyteries, in the present state of education in the Colonies, to exercise the power of licensing Probationers; but that licentiates of the Church of Scotland, who shall be ordained by any such Presbytery to particular charges in the manner above described, shall remain in full communion with the Church of Scotland, and retain all the rights and privileges which belong to licentiates or ministers of this Church; and that members of congregations, under the charge of ministers so ordained, shall, on coming to Scotland, be admitted to Church privileges, on the production of satisfactory certificates of their religious and moral character, from the minister and session of the congregation to which they have severally belonged.

And the Assembly earnestly recommend to all ministers and probationers of this Church, who remove to those Colonies in which such Presbyteries are constituted, to put themselves under the inspection of the Presbytery of the bounds within which they may reside; and, in the event of their returning to this country, to produce testimonials from such Presbytery or Presbyteries of their character and conduct during their absence.

7. B. Bridges, op. cit., p.235

The General Assembly further named a standing committee to correspond with such Churches in the Colonies, for the purpose of giving advice on any question with regard to which they may choose to consult the Church of Scotland, and affording them such aid as it may be in the power of the committee to give in all matters affecting their rights and interests.

Before the fact of this decision was known in New South Wales, Lang decided to visit Scotland in person to obtain any needed clarification which would satisfy local authorities and to obtain further ministers.

Lang's third voyage - 1833

Lang left for Britain in July 1833. When he heard of the Assembly decision he regarded it as vindicating his position (McGarvie thought the same of his stance). He returned in November 1834 with four ministers: Kirkpatrick Smythe, John Hill Garven, MA, David Mackenzie, MA, and Robert Wylde, MA. The last two were licentiates intended as masters for the Australian College. A further master, Rev Thomas Aitken, MA, was interviewed but did not come out until about 2 years later.

However, on his return Lang found that Rev William Pinkerton had died, while Rev Henry Carmichael resigned from the Australian College and commenced his own school at the close of 1834. If this was not enough, Rev Thomas Thomson at Bathurst was a notorious drunkard and his congregation insisted he should leave. He returned to Britain early in 1835 where he did useful work in the literary field. Smythe replaced him at Bathurst and did good work. Garven, after a period of probation because of a proneness for ardent spirits evident on the voyage out, became the first inducted minister at Maitland.

In January 1835, Lang commenced a weekly newspaper called *The Colonist* in which he sought to advance his own views, in particular rebutting attacks on his conduct and censuring immorality in the licentious colonial society. This included attacks on other ministers, particularly the delinquent men, and on McGarvie. Bridges rightly says that McGarvie was 'a skilful tactician and unprincipled in some of the ploys to which he resorted to help his friends escape conviction',[8] but as he also says, Lang showed contempt for due process, and the needless publicity injured the standing of the Church. Also, Lang conducted a campaign advocating voluntary support so that the people would have a greater influence over the ministry despite the fact that the country charges would not have been viable without state aid.

8. B. Bridges, op. cit., p. 237.

Presbytery of Van Diemen's Land - 1835

In October 1835, Lang took ship to Hobart with a view to constituting a Presbytery for the island - an area of similar size to his native Scotland. He was shocked to find that Archibald McArthur was justly accused of improper advances to female members of his congregation. McArthur, filled with remorse, acted on Lang's advice and resigned his charge since there was no church court in the colony which could try him. His wife died soon after, and McArthur returned to England.

Meanwhile, Lang, John Anderson of Launceston and John Mackersey of Macquarie River, constituted the Presbytery of Van Diemen's Land on November 6, 1835. Immediately thereafter, the Presbytery admitted James Garrett of Bothwell. He, like McArthur, had come from the United Secession Church. He arrived in 1828, while Mackersey came from the Church of Scotland in 1829. The new Presbytery for the island colony was in legal and moral connection with the Church of Scotland, just as was the Presbytery of New South Wales. It has its own distinct history.

Scots Church, Jamison Street, Sydney
opened July 16, 1826 - demolished 1926
replaced by Scots Church within the Assembly Hall
on essentially the same site

More problems but improved State aid

Back in New South Wales, Rev John Garven of Maitland had broken out in bouts of drunkenness, while Cleland was also addicted to the bottle. Lang's efforts to have the Presbytery discipline Garven were frustrated by Cleland and McGarvie, while Smythe in distant Bathurst was not of a robust constitution. The situation was quite unsatisfactory, and Lang decided he would have to make a fourth trip to Britain to obtain other and better ministers. He was encouraged in this course by Sir Richard Bourke's *Church Act*, 1836, which ended the privileged position of the Church of England. It provided in a regular way for support for the three major Christian groups - Church of England, Church of Rome, Presbyterian and, from 1839, Methodist. However, the assistance was on the basis of a certain number of persons attending on the ministry of the clergyman, and thus it appeared to Lang to safeguard the congregations against unworthy men, while at the same time giving vital help which would make it easier to obtain ministers from Britain. The formula was that a congregation of 100 adults was entitled to $200 as stipend for their minister, $300 if 200 adults, and $400 if 500. There was also assistance to a maximum of $2,000 on a $ for $ basis for buildings provided that at least $600 had been raised by the congregation. The fact that there was no discrimination between the four creeds was to cause trouble later: the endowment of Christianity was one thing, and the endowment of error was another. There would be strife over this matter, but the supplanting of ad hoc arrangements by the new measure was generally welcomed by the Presbyterians.

Lang's fourth voyage - 1836

Lang left in July 1836, and as a result of his exertions obtained about 20 ministers. They were obtained by more formal means than used before, and this time the quality was considerably better. Lang personally selected Rev William McIntyre, MA, and arranged for him to be chaplain on the good ship *Midlothian* which reached Sydney on December 12, 1837 with many Highland emigrants.

From the Colonial Committee of the Church of Scotland Lang obtained 11 men: James Allan, Irving Hetherington, John Tait, William Hamilton, MA, James Forbes, MA, John Gregor, MA, George MacFie, MA, George Anderson, MA, Matthew Adam (candidate), Malcolm Colquhoun (candidate) and Robert Stewart (licentiate). From the Synod of Ulster, which was deemed to have equivalent status to the Church of Scotland, Lang obtained four ministers who all accompanied him back to New South Wales. They were Hugh Gilchrist, Thomas Dugall, James Fullerton and Robert Blain (licentiate). Rev Cunninghame Atchison, ordained by the Synod of Original Seceders in 1833 but later a licentiate of the Church of Scotland, was also secured. Two

German missionaries who were to labour near Brisbane - Karl Schmidt and Christopher Eipper - were further recruits.

Scottish emigration

While in Britain Lang also played a significant role in arranging for some 4,000 destitute Highlanders to come to Australia as assisted migrants over the next few years. Many others came too, since poor crops in Britain in 1836 and 1837, together with the second phase of the Highland Clearances (1842-1854), demanded a location for the victims of destitution and displacement. While many were labourers, there was also an influx of Lowlanders who were mainly artisans and mechanics. Lang's congregation had more than 50% in this group. Overall, in the 1830's, farmers and settlers were nearly 50%, artisans and mechanics 21%, with labourers under 10%. [10]

SHIPS SAILING FROM SCOTLAND WITH BOUNTY EMIGRANTS UNDER THE BOUNTY SYSTEM, 1837-1840 [9]

Date	Ship	Port of departure	Number of emigrants
13 March 1837	John Barry	Dundee	323
6 July 1837	William Nicoll	Hebrides	321
7 August 1837	Midlothian	Hebrides	282
October 1837	Brilliant	Hebrides	298
11 January 1838	Duncan	Greenock	260
18 April 1838	Lady Kennaway	Leith	283
13 May 1838	William Roger	Greenock	296
4 July 1838	Saint George	Oban	326
31 August 1838	Boyne	Cromarty	285
18 September 1838	Asia	Cromarty	270
26 September 1838	Lady McNaghten	Cromarty	205
13 October 1838	James Moran	Loch Broom	210
October 1838	British King	Tobermory	326
7 May 1839	Hero	Leith	201
13 June 1839	David Clarke	Greenock	283
15 September 1839	George Fyfe	Tobermory	178
October 1839	Henry Porcher	Skye	211
December 1839	Glen Huntly	Oban	305
3 January 1840	Dauntless	Greenock	200 approx.
January 1840	Calder	Greenock	200 ,,
Totals	20 ships		approx. 5,263 persons

9. Table from David S. Macmillan, **Scotland and Australia 1788-1850** (Oxford 1967), p. 276. I think the figure for the Midlothian should be 262 cf. E.H.McSwan, **The McSwans in Australia, 150 Years:1837-1987** (Maclean 1987) p. 11
10. D. S. Macmillan, ibid., p. 298 based on Alan Dougan's research.

42

Calvinism, the Psalms of David and porridge

The Highland emigrants were not always thought of in a positive light. The *Newcastle Morning Herald* of November 20, 1837, characterised them as 'reared on Calvinism, the Psalms of David and porridge.' But the combination seemed not to be detrimental to their progress in the colony, and they were to make their mark in due time.

The case of those who came on the *Midlothian* was somewhat unusual. Many spoke only Gaelic, and they were not willing to be dispersed in the usual manner. They wanted to stay together and to have their own minister. The upshot was that they were allowed to settle on the Hunter, many of them on Andrew Lang's property. Here they worked small but productive farms of 15 to 20 acres each. Life was hardly easy: there was a drought in 1839 and a flood in 1840. But they persisted, and over the next few years gradually moved from the Dunmore estate, often to clearing leases.[11]

In 1856 some 16 families moved to the Barrington - the region now centred on Gloucester. The following year a large number moved north following the severe flooding of June/August 1857. They increased the numbers already on the Manning River, and soon moved up to the Clarence River, as land was opened for selection in the early 1860s. In these areas solid Presbyterian congregations developed, and in general stayed out of the unions of 1864/65. The genesis of all the coastal congregations in New South Wales today of the Presbyterian Church of Eastern Australia is in one way or another related to the early Highland migrations. The preponderance of Skye names in these areas goes back to them.

11. The special treatment of the Midlothian passaengers was the cause of some criticism at the time, and may not be unconnected with the Highlander/Lowlander tension in the PCEA from 1852.

5: SCHISM 1837-1842

Shortly before arriving in Sydney on December 3, 1837, Lang had gathered together the ministers with him on the *Portland*. He endeavoured to persuade them to join him in establishing a new church court to supplant the corrupt Presbytery of New South Wales. There were four pastors connected with the Presbytery when Lang had left New South Wales - McGarvie, Smythe, Cleland and Garven. Four men - Allan, Hetherington, Tait and Hamilton - had preceded him in leaving Britain, but Lang had asked the last two not to join the Presbytery until he arrived. Allowing for the men with him on the Portland or to arrive soon after, Lang calculated he had the numbers to destroy effectively the power of the original Presbytery. He baulked at joining it because 'he was revolted by the idea of transforming the Church's ecclesiastical court into a common sewer for the reception and examination of the whole mass of colonial filth and abomination of several years' accumulation,' [1] and the difficulty of enforcing discipline given the time delay and the capacity for shiftiness previously evidenced. To make his case plausible, Lang falsely represented that he had authority from the Church and Colonial authorities in the United Kingdom to reconstruct the church along the lines he proposed.

When Lang actually reached Sydney, he was dismayed to find that in response to a suggestion by the Colonial Government, an Act to regulate the temporal interests of the Presbytery had been passed by the Parliament. It was assented to on September 9, 1837. [2] Of itself, such a measure was not

1. D.W.A.Baker, **Days of Wrath** (Melbourne 1985)p.140
2. It was entitled: An Act to regulate the temporal affairs of Presbyterian Churches and Chapels connected with the Church of Scotland in the Colony of New South Wales [short title, Scotch Presbyterian Church Temporalities Act] 8 William IV, No.7

unusual. However, in regulating the aid for building purposes under the Church Act of 1836 to 'churches, chapels and ministers' dwellings of the Presbyterian Church connected with the Church of Scotland,' it tied the colonial church to the Church of Scotland. The legal basis given to the Presbytery of New South Wales by this Act meant it was regarded as the only colonial representative of the Church of Scotland. The certificate of the Presbytery Moderator was also required for the payment of ministers' stipends under the Church Act. Lang immediately saw the difficulties these arrangements created for him. He represented the passing of the Act as a plot by McGarvie 'monstrous and disgraceful in the highest degree to the persons concerned.'[3] In fact the initiative had come from the Governor. Even the connection to the Church of Scotland, though fully consistent with McGarvie's idea of the colonial church as an integral part of the Church of Scotland, was not of itself so objectionable to Presbyterians at that time. Many of them were from churches in Scotland which had broken from the Established Church, but they still tended to find value and security in the far away colony in asserting a connection with the Church of Scotland.[4] Moreover, such wording was consistent with the policy of the British authorities which was to give recognition only to the Church of Scotland.[5] Still, it was to be the cause of much future strife because it provided the means by which the Church of Scotland could interfere in the colonial church, and even coerce it or effectively exercise jurisdiction by having salaries withheld from those it might regard as delinquent. Legislative sanction would be required for any change in the Temporalities Act. Thus the church would in measure be in the hands of the Tory establishment. All in all, the Temporalities Act set the stage for conflict in the colonial church.

In fact, the conflict began at once. Lang's pre-arranged plan to form a separate church court was now promoted as necessitated by the Act. Writing for posterity, Lang even decribed himself and his supporters as being 'forced out of our Mother Church by the Government of the day, at the instance of a traitor to our cause; just as the Free Church-men of the period I refer to [1843] were forced out of their Mother Church in precisely the same way.'[6] Of course, this was complete nonsense. The four ministers who had arrived shortly before Lang had already applied to join the Presbytery, and three of the ministers with Lang were not convinced by Lang. These were

3. J.D.Lang, Reminiscences of My Life and Times (ed. Baker, Melbourne 1972) p.164
4. Thus in 1840 the Synod then formed was 'in connection with the Established Church of Scotland.' James Forbes states: 'the name of the Church of Scotland was then [1837] a tower of strength; and it was freely used by some who had no claim to it, not having belonged to it in the Mother country' - Port Phillip Christian Herald, May 2, 1846,p.39.
5. B.J.Bridges, Presbyterian Churches in New South Wales 1823-1865 (PhD Thesis) p.80.
6. J.D.Lang, Reminiscences... ibid., p.165

James Forbes (destined for Melbourne), George MacFie and John Gregor. If Lang is to be believed, MacFie and Gregor were concerned for secure stipends. Forbes was not so accused, and had a clear grasp of the issues. The three men refused to join Lang and 5 other ministers in constituting the *Synod of New South Wales* on December 11, 1837, and gave their reasons. [7] They argued that the worthlessness of several members of the Presbytery was no ground not to join it, since there would be sufficient men to deal with any discipline problems, while to set up a rival Synod, especially when only Lang himself was actually settled in a charge, would not only be a following of divisive courses, contrary to their vows, but improper from a scriptural and polity standpoint. Moreover, there was not the slightest evidence that Lang had a commission to reconstruct the colonial church, and everything pointed the other way. These three men therefore joined the Presbytery.

The Presbytery had passed some rules to entrench its power before the new-comers arrived. No minister could have a vote until he was duly settled in a congregation (the normal position but perhaps inappropriate in the embryonic colonial situation); the colony had been divided in such a way that the existing ministers had responsibility for the more populated areas, and further appointments were in the hands of Messrs McGarvie, Cleland and Garven. The intent of these arrangements seemed rather obvious, but could not endure for long once new ministers were settled. Lang took a very hostile view and aimed through his Synod to drive out the drunkards and McGarvie by putting his own men in the same localities to draw off the adherents of the existing congregations. So a full-blown schism was in operation until union was effected in 1840.

The Presbytery's work

The original Presbytery expelled Lang for schism on January 18, 1838, and settled its new ministers. Allan, a moderate, went to Parramatta, but was not particularly successful against the Synod man stationed there. Hetherington, Hamilton, Tait and Forbes were capable. They were settled at Singleton, Goulburn, Wollongong and Melbourne respectively. Smythe was still at Bathurst, Cleland at Portland Head and Garven at Maitland. However, the congregations of the last two had deserted their drunken pastors. Indeed, hardly had the new Synod begun when Garven was literally rolling drunk on a Sydney-Newcastle steamer on which Lang, Hetherington and Blain were passengers. Garven had no option but to submit his resignation. He was deposed without trial in February 1838, although the sentence was not pronounced by McGarvie, the 'moderate' Presbytery Moderator. John Gregor was sent to Maitland as a replacement but was no match for Blain, the Synod

7. **The Colonist,** December 21, 1837 prints the reasons with Lang's response.

minister. Three other pastors were stationed before the union of 1840. They included William Ross, MA, a Gaelic preacher settled at Paterson near the Lang estate late in 1838. In general the Highlanders did not approve of his position as a member of the disreputable Presbytery. In January 1839, Colin Stewart, MA, arrived and commenced an itinerant ministry in the Hartley district near Bathurst. His first service was in the Hartley Court House on February 17, 1839 with 21 or 22 present. Andrew Brown was a leading supporter. [8] Stewart was a good man but not a great preacher. Finally, Andrew Love arrived early in 1840 and was settled at Geelong. He was more of the moderate outlook.

The Synod's work

The new Synod held itself out as representing the Church of Scotland, but laid down as a fundamental article

that the said Synod shall, from the moment of its establishment, have an independent and supreme ecclesiastical jurisdiction over all and sundry its own members, whether clerical or laic, and shall by no means tolerate any appeal from that jurisdiction to any Church or Church Court beyond seas. [9]

All but one or two of the Presbytery ministers took the same view of their body, but it was not yet beyond dispute.

Stipends for 1838 were available in terms of a provision that any minister who came out with the sanction of the Secretary of State was entitled to a stipend of $300 for the first year. [10] The Synod entered energetically on its work. Lang, McIntyre and Dugall were stationed in Sydney, McIntyre as assistant to Lang and Dugall with a view to forming a new congregation in Pitt Street which would draw off McGarvie's adherents. Dugall was not successful and went to Sorell in Tasmania at the end of 1838. George Anderson was sent to Muswellbrook, and did some teaching. He was not very competent and left the colony in 1844. Robert Blain was ordained and sent to Maitland, where he was successful; Fullerton went to Windsor and Richmond but soon returned to Sydney where he served at Pitt Street in place of Dugall. He remained in this charge for the rest of his life, but in the early period does not seem to have had much of a following. His outlook was 'moderate' while his natural constituency of Ulster Presbyterians was not. Gilchrist went to Campbelltown and Liverpool, Atchison to Parramatta and Colquhoun to Brisbane Water now Gosford. Colquhoun was later removed

8. Cf. R.Ian Jack, **Andrew Brown, laird of Cooerwull** in JRAHS, Vol.73 †3 (December 1987)pp.173-186. In the **Australian Wtness**, March 22, 1873, Stewart stated he preached to 37 persons at Glen Alice, Capertee at his first service there in 1839, using Gaelic and English.
9. As quoted by Forbes in **PPCH**, op. cit., p.39 col.1
10. B.J.Bridges, op. cit., p.79.

from the ministry because of forged credentials. Robert Stewart was also ordained and was stationed on the Hawkesbury at Wiseman's Ferry for several years, and later was at Balmain then Newcastle. He was also of 'moderate' outlook, and possibly stayed with Lang because of the readier prospect of ordination. Schmidt and Eipper, the German missionaries, arrived in January 1838 to labour at the Aboriginal mission at Nundah, Moreton Bay. The former came to Sydney in 1845 and went to England the following year. Eipper left the mission in 1844 and went to Braidwood.

Moves to unite Synod and Presbytery

James Forbes of Melbourne indicates something of the contention and disrepute which fell on the Christian cause in general and the Presbyterian cause in particular through Lang's conduct:

It will readily be supposed that the rivalry to which this division of 1837 gave rise, was most injurious to religion, and painful to every right feeling mind. The leader of the Synod of New South Wales [Lang] was editor of a newspaper [The Colonist]; and week after week, he poured forth vollies of abuse against the Presbytery, unequalled for satanic bitterness and vulgar scurrility, by the worst of the London Sunday papers.[11]

Within the Presbytery there was deep division. Hamilton, Hetherington, Forbes and Tait found that McGarvie and his supporters were capable of every trick in the book, plus some that were not. Attempts at mediation and union were thwarted. A proposal from the Synod was sent to McGarvie, the Presbytery Moderator. He, knowing full well the contents, refused to open it so that he could deny having received it! Minutes were doctored, and novel rulings given to block reform. For example, McGarvie ruled that no elder could sit as representing a congregation unless there was a church building in his district. But it was then discovered that McGarvie had not submitted to the government applications by Hamilton and Hetherington for church buildings to be erected! Garven had been deposed, but Cleland was also notoriously drunk. Nevertheless, McGarvie was unprincipled in his handling of the case and Cleland was acquitted.[12]

In September 1838, the authorities made provision for stipends for the Synod ministers for a further year. This took some of the heat out of the strife, and terms of union were proposed and agreed in October, William Hamilton playing an important role. However, before the union was carried through, contention broke out again as a result of the Church of Scotland advising that the conduct of Lang was 'in all respects unjustifiable' and that only the Presbytery was recognised by the Church. The Synod of Ulster took

11. **Port Phillip Christian Herald**, op. cit., p.39.
12. B.J.Bridges, op. cit., p.82 refers to McGarvie's conduct as 'partial, even unprincipled.'

the same view. These conclusions were correct in law, but they were based on a partisan statement prepared by McGarvie in the name of the Presbytery, but without its knowledge or approval, and sent to Scotland early in 1838. McGarvie's object was to force the schismatics into the Presbytery on terms which would include recognition of the jurisdiction of the Church of Scotland. McGarvie and his henchmen, Gregor and Allan, continued their unprincipled course. Rev William Ross, who arrived in November 1838, was drawn into the rivalry by McGarvie, who stationed Ross at Paterson with a government stipend without the knowledge of the Presbytery and against its will when the matter was later raised.

However, the Colonial Committee of the Church of Scotland had by now a better understanding of the problems and urged the Presbytery to greater conciliation, and rebuked it for laxity in discipline. Lang now argued that the point of difference between the Presbytery and the Synod was that of the jurisdiction or otherwise of the Church of Scotland over colonial church courts. This was in some respects a bogey, since only McGarvie and Allan held that the Church of Scotland had jurisdiction, and there was every reason from parallel cases and the nature of Presbyterian church theory to reject the idea of jurisdiction by courts in which there was no representation. But Lang was determined to go to Britain to establish the point definitively, and the Governor let him go, shrewdly believing that matters could be resolved better in Lang's absence.

In Britain the Scottish Church rejected the argument that communion with the Church of Scotland implied jurisdiction over the colonial church. In declaring that the establishment of the Synod had not been authorised by the Church of Scotland, the Church was only declaring the facts, not exercising jurisdiction of any kind. It was urged that the Synod and Presbytery should unite on the basis agreed in October 1838 - a concession to Lang's influence which saved him the humiliation of having to dissolve his Synod to unite with the Presbytery. Nevertheless, Lang's prestige was further and seriously weakened in Scotland. He himself continued to take a very negative view of the Colonial Committee of the Church of Scotland. He resolved on going to America to see how the system of voluntary support for the ministry worked in practice, and to recruit ministers. He would not return to Australia until March 1841.

In October 1839, terms of union were agreed between the Presbytery and the Synod on the basis that (1) all past subjects of complaint would be buried; (2) jurisdiction of the Church of Scotland over colonial church courts was rejected; (3) Lang would be included on signing the terms of union even if the Church of Scotland took action against him; (4) three ordinations performed by the Synod were recognised. The inclusion of Lang was apparently at the insistence of William McIntyre, Lang's assistant at Scots.[13] Although McIntyre was the only ordained Church of Scotland minister, other than the unfortunate George Anderson, to join Lang's Synod, this was not because he had a sect mentality. McIntyre had not been chosen by the Colonial Committee but by Lang himself. Consequently, he felt an obligation to Lang, while it was also true that the moral ground in many respects was with the Synod not the Presbytery. McIntyre worked for union. He obviously hoped that with Garven deposed and Cleland dead (of *delirium tremens* in 1839), a new era would dawn as a united and numerically stronger Synod got down to work.

When the Bill to amend the Temporalities Act was being dealt with in the select committee of the Parliament, James Forbes and William Hamilton testified that it was the practice of the Church of Scotland to refuse to exercise jurisdiction over colonial courts connected to it by the fact of holding the same standards. Indeed, there had been a recent case on the very point, as James Forbes records:

In the negotiations of 1839, particular reference was had to the parallel case of the Presbyterian Synod in England. There had long existed in that country a number of churches claiming 'connexion with the Church of Scotland.' In 1836, a Synod was formed there under the designation of 'The Synod of the Presbyterian Church in England, in connection with the Established Church of Scotland,' and efforts were made to obtain representation in the Scottish Assembly, and to be brought under the jurisdiction and superintendence of that body. The Scottish Church declined any such intimate connexion with her sister in England. In May 1839, this matter was finally set at rest, representation and jurisdiction being refused, the Assembly 'expressing their heart-felt satisfaction at the formation of said Synod, as the supreme judicatory of the Presbyterians of England adhering to the Westminster Standards and Confession of Faith.' [14]

Against this view was McGarvie supported by Allan. McGarvie opposed the plan of union because he held the colonial courts to be an integral part of the Church of Scotland, and that the present absence of representation in the Assembly of the Church of Scotland would be overcome in the course of time as the church grew. His theory has similarities to the Church of England conception of the time. [15] In the event, McGarvie succeeded in having the passage of the Bill delayed until the opinion of the Church of Scotland was known. That opinion was only given at a meeting of a sub-

13. So McIntyre claimed: **PCEA Synod Minutes,** November 1863, p.11 (printed copy). Apparently at first McIntyre was virtually alone in advocating Lang's inclusion.

14. **Port Phillip Christian Herald,** May 2, 1846, p.39.

15. It was not until January 1, 1962 that the Church of England in Australia began functioning under its own constitution free of legal ties to England.

committee of the Colonial Churches Committee on August 11, 1840, and reached the colony about the close of the year. It was stated that

no doubt can now be entertained that the terms of the proposed Union, agreed to between the Presbytery of N.S.Wales and the separating ministers so far as constituting the basis of the intended Synod of Australia and the enactments of the 'Presbyterian Church Act Amendment Bill,' are in accordance with the Constitution of this Church, and the relations which she desires to subsist with her branches in the Colonies. [16]

But before this decision was known in the colony, Governor Gipps was satisfied that the union should be concluded without further delay, and accordingly the amendment to the Temporalities Act was approved and passed into law in October 1840. McGarvie still objected, but had to agree to sign in order to remain in the new Synod. He was silenced for the time being by the further decision of the Colonial Committee on October 6, 1841, that it had no objection to the confirming of the Act by the Queen.

The Colonial Committee in August 1840 did express concern about Lang's automatic inclusion, and stated a preference for writing in a requirement that the new Synod continue in connection with the Church of Scotland. This was not done as the union had already occurred. The Committee also felt there was sufficient safeguard in the fact that the Synod would forfeit its property if its connection with the Church of Scotland came to an end.

Synod of Australia formed - October 1840

The inaugural meeting of 'the Synod of Australia in connection with the Established Church of Scotland' was held on October 5, 1840, and a Bond of Union signed by all members of the court in the following terms:

We ministers and elders, whose names are undersigned, uniting ourselves together in the Synod of Australia, in connection with the Established Church of Scotland, do bind and oblige ourselves to pass over and bury in oblivion, all matters which, in times past, have been the subject of mutual complaint and accusation, and engage in every part of our future conduct towards each other to act in strict conformity to the laws of Christ and of the Scottish Church. We declare anew our adherence to the doctrines of the Confession of Faith, and to the other standards and formularies of the Established Church of Scotland, and promise that, in the exercise of discipline, we shall follow the laws of that Church so far as applicable in this colony; and whatever may be our individual opinions, will, so long as we remain members of the court, submit ourselves to the judgements and determinations of the majority of our number regularly met, and sitting in Presbyteries and Synod.

16. Text in Historical Records of Australia, Vol.XX, pp.820-822.

Some points about this Bond may be noted:

1) Consistent with the previous negotiations, the Bond provided no avenue of appeal to the Church of Scotland, and that body had no legislative or judicial jurisdiction - a fact the Scottish Church had fully conceded in 1840.

2) The standards and law of the Church of Scotland as at 1840 were the standards and law of the Australian Synod. This meant that it had the same powers as the Church of Scotland in so far as those powers could apply in Australia. Thus, within the framework of its basic doctrinal standards, it had capacity to develop its own legislation and practice. In the absence of such local legislation the practice of the Church of Scotland would be followed.

3) The concept seems to have been one of an independent church within a fellowship of churches based on the Scriptures and the time-honoured subordinate standards, and thus was quite different from McGarvie's dream of one church, with headquarters in Edinburgh and jurisdiction downwards over all its component parts throughout the world.

4) The failure to assert a distinct denominational name (eg. Presbyterian Church in Australia) must be counted a defect. The use of the name of a church court (The Synod of Australia) was hardly calculated to convey a clear idea of the independence of the church. [17]

5) Including a tie to another church in the Synod's name was also a mistake, since it virtually committed the testimony of the church to the care of another body over whom it had no control, and with hindsight was seen as calling in question the independence of the Synod.

6) The phrase 'so long as we remain members of the court' was to cause difficulty later since it left open the possibility that one could be removed from the ministry without thereby losing status as a minister of the Church of Scotland if such status was held prior to membership of the Synod. This is illustrated in the case of the deposition of Lang in 1842.

7) It should be remembered that the promise to submit to 'the judgements and determinations of the majority' is not an absolute promise but is qualified by the other terms in the Bond to which all Synod members were committed. [18]

17. The denominational use of the term 'Presbyterian' in the legal title of an Australian Presbyterian church began with the formation of the PCEA in 1846. Synod of Australia congregations commonly used the term 'Scots' or, especially later, 'St Andrews' as the prescriptive title of the congregation.
18. One may compare the customary form of commission given to commissioners to the General Assembly of the Church of Scotland which appointed them to 'deliberate and act in accordance with the Word of God, the Confession of Faith and the constitution of the Church.'

Resistance put down

The Governor insisted that only one stipend would be paid for each of Maitland and Parramatta, where there were ministers from each of the previous sections but insufficient Presbyterians to justify them. On February 11, 1841, it was decided to withdraw Allan and Atchison from Parramatta and that the congregations unite in calling another minister. John Tait of Wollongong was the choice, and Atchison replaced him at that centre. Similarly, Gregor and Blain were withdrawn from Maitland, and William McIntyre was settled. Blain confined his attentions to nearby Hinton and stations. Gregor and Allan resisted the authority of the church courts, as did McGarvie. But the upshot was that Gregor, who had been suspended by the Synod in June 1841, defected to the Church of England the following year, and was re-ordained as a deacon in September 1842. Allan, who had been suspended with Gregor, followed him into the Church of England in June 1843. Allan had sought to appeal to the General Assembly of the Church of Scotland, but the Scottish Church had declined to exercise jurisdiction as it had previously said it would. This was likewise a rebuff to McGarvie, who was now up against a brick wall and isolated. Although he would lie low for the moment, there was still fight in him as the future would show.

Ministerial moves

The Moderator of the Synod in 1840-41 was John Tait, and in 1841-42 William McIntyre. There were not many additions to the number of ministers. William Comrie arrived in the latter part of 1840. He was licensed by the Synod and supplied on the Williams River, principally at Dungog, until 1842. He went to New Zealand the following year. William Purves came to New South Wales in 1839. After a period as a squatter he was admitted to the Synod and settled at Port Macquarie late in 1840. In 1842, Messrs Mowbray, Laurie and Gunn arrived, and were settled in what is now Victoria. An additional Presbytery was formed for this area and held its first meeting on June 7, 1842.

Lang chafing at the bit

Upon his return to London from America, late in 1840 Lang published a substantial volume entitled *Religion and Education in America*. Among other things, this book spoke in admiring terms of the system of church support in America by voluntary givings, and went further to advocate no connection between church and state. Orthodox Presbyterians could hardly view some of these sentiments favourably, and some hostility arose against Lang.

When Lang returned to New South Wales in March 1841, he signed the Bond and joined the Synod. Although suspicions about his views had existed for a good while, Lang actually made application for an increase of his government stipend, and when it was refused agitated in a variety of ways. He declined Governor Gipps' dinner invitation in protest,[19]and tried to enlist the support of the Synod in October 1841.

In many ways the Synod showed extraordinary deference to Lang, appointing him Convener of 5 of the 6 Synod Committees. However, he operated these without much or any reference to other members, and he used his new paper, *The Colonial Observer*, to attack and even denigrate those with whom he disagreed. He was also caught up in a financial mess because of his incompetence and even deviousness in the affairs of Scots Church lands and the College.

The Australian College had declined to about 30 students during Lang's absence. He had not provided proper financing and the three masters (Revs Wylde, Mackenzie and Aitken) were engaged in pastoral operations and used the college as the city depot for their pursuits. Lang decided on a tour of Port Phillip and Van Diemen's Land to raise funds for the College. He came under some criticism for his absence from his pulpit on this mission. The Presbytery also directed him to have more regard for its rulings in future as a result of his allowing a person to preach in his absence who had recently been refused admission to the ministry by the Synod.

Lang leaves the 'synagogue of Satan' 1842

Lang let forth an extraordinary blast of invective against his ministerial colleagues from the pulpit of his church the following Lord's Day, February 6, 1842. He regarded the Presbyterian system of church government as ordained by God but its present administration in the colony had caused it to degenerate into 'an instrument of gross tyranny' with a series of unprovoked attacks on him. He considered that all he had done was regarded with rancorous hostility which could only have emanated from the Father of Evil. There was much more of the same. As well, Lang traced the strife, delinquency and inefficiency of the Church to the principle of government payment of stipends: she would not prosper until she renounced with indignant scorn the *Babylonish garment* of an infidel establishment of religion and abandoned the wedge of gold that corrupted all who touched it. Strangely, however, he told his congregation that his successor would likely receive the handsome stipend of $1,000 from the Government which would enable them to obtain a superior pastor from the home country. Lang himself would leave the colony and go to labour in New Zealand.

The congregation consisted of over 500 adults. The overwhelming proportion resolved to stand by Lang and agreed to his terms: that the congregation

19. B.J.Bridges, op. cit., p.129 (note 32)

renounce all state support and pay a stipend raised from voluntary subscriptions, and that the congregation renounce all connection with the Synod of Australia in connection with the Established Church of Scotland. Lang sent in his resignation and claimed the property for the congregation.

The upshot was that Lang was suspended and, after the usual confusion of procedure, on October 8, 1842, the Synod voted 8 - 4 to depose Lang from the ministry rather than the milder course of simply accepting his resignation which was advocated by McGarvie, Atchison, Adam and one elder. The Synod Moderator, Hamilton, indicated his approval of the deposition when pronouncing the sentence. Lang was not present as he had declined the Synod's jurisdiction.

The formal charges against Lang were slander - calling the Synod a synagogue of Satan was especially displeasing to the brethren - divisive courses and contumacy. Of these Lang was guilty. Some said the sentence was harsh in comparison to the mere declaration that Gregor was no longer a minister when he gave up Presbyterianism for the Church of England. But the Synod was right in recognising that right behaviour as well as right doctrine was required of a minister. Lang asserted the censure could have no force because it lacked the support of public opinion. It was true Lang had public sympathy, but not because of Lang's Christianity. It was rather his championship of popular causes and his ability as a speaker that gained him popular support.

The reason Lang gave for his resignation was patently untrue. Tait, Fullerton and McIntyre wrote a letter to the Presbyterians of New South Wales in February 1842 in which they asked

How is it that Dr Lang never discovered or avowed the guilt of 'eating the Queen's bread,' until he found out that the brethren of the Synod were not the pliant and submissive men he calculated upon finding them to be, or of making them? How was it that at the very first meeting of the court which took place after his arrival, when he had only recently left that land of liberty where voluntaryism was seen in such glory as to dispel all his Scottish prejudices, and convince him it was the best method of supporting the Church, he sought the interposition of the Synod's influence to have his government salary raised from three hundred to five hundred pounds... [20]

As William McIntyre said, 'Wounded pride had more to do in the matter than offended principle.'[21] The fact was that 'for almost two decades Lang had been able to make most of the important decisions himself, was given to rash decisions, tended to stick to a line once committing himself, and could not

20. Sydney Herald, February 15, 1842
21. Sydney Morning Herald, August 24, 1842 as cited by B.J.Bridges, op. cit., p.129

bear to be opposed.[22] Lang characterised Tait as the 'ecclesiastical Judge Jeffries', described Fullerton as 'a miserable Hibernian driveller, with neither ability nor respectability,' 'the ecclesiastical nightman of the Synod, doing all its dirty and disgraceful work'. He admitted respect for McIntyre but 'it was with a sinking spirit that he saw him banding against him with such contemptible creatures as Tait and Fullerton.' McIntyre, thought Lang, 'was too dogmatic, too fond of power, too apt to become the dupe of far inferior men who either flattered his vanity or wrought upon his fears.'[23]

The Synod sent advice of its action to the Church of Scotland, considering that the Presbytery which ordained him should ratify the sentence so that Lang would cease to be a minister of the Church of Scotland. In May 1843, the Presbytery was instructed to declare Lang no longer a minister if, after investigation, it found Lang had withdrawn from connection with the Church of Scotland. In the aftermath of the Disruption nothing was actually done, and it was only in 1850, when the Presbytery of Sydney resolved to apply for an extract of the Presbytery of Irvine minutes, that the matter was again taken up. Without giving Lang an opportunity to defend himself or even telling him what was afoot, the Presbytery of Irvine declared Lang no longer a minister of the Church of Scotland on September 9, 1851.

Lang's efforts to establish a voluntary church

One of the immediate results of Lang's resignation in February 1842 was that the German missionaries at Moreton Bay withdrew from the jurisdiction of the Synod. But they were too far away to help Lang in Sydney. In March 1842, Lang purchased land at Balmain and Pyrmont, and compact timber buildings were opened for worship on July 24, 1842 and April 28, 1843 respectively.[24] Lang was not against obtaining sites from the government, and applied without success for one at Paddington. He had formed a Presbyterian Church Society to organise funds and support. In October 1842 he appealed to the Relief and Secession churches in Scotland for no less than 25 ministers and for funds to assist their support. This and further efforts failed, except for the arrival of William Ritchie early in 1847. He supplied Scots Church during much of Lang's absence on his sixth trip to Britain (July 1846 to March 1850). When Lang returned he would set up a new Synod of New South Wales.

One other matter concerning Lang must be noted at this point. In June 1843 he was elected as one of the members of the newly-formed

22. B.J.Bridges, op. cit., p.129
23. D.W.A.Baker, Days of Wrath, op. cit. p.183
24. B.J.Bridges, op. cit., p.135

Legislative Council, representing the District of Port Phillip. This provided a platform for his views on state-aid and other questions. Indeed, in the next five months he served as chairman or member of nine select committees and made 184 speeches and statements! [25] Whatever happened over the next few years would have to take account of the redoubtable Doctor.

Still water before the storm

Leaving aside Lang, the Synod of Australia in connection with the Established Church of Scotland was now on a more even keel - at least one hoped so. The turmoil of the preceding years had not given the church a good name. One should not ignore the fact that in many instances the local parish picture was more serene than the public brawling might have suggested. Also we must remember that the church was in a frontier situation in a raw colony with many convicts. The moral weakness of many of the early ministers was symptomatic of the low regard for the colony's worth and potential, and was parallelled in other denominations.

The quality of the ministers was now somewhat better. Laurie was removed from office in 1848, but the rest were generally of respectable life and none professed unorthodox doctrine. They varied much in their individual qualities. McIntyre, Ross and Gunn were bi-lingual (Gaelic/English), and the latter was well known for the severity of his outlook on matters of worship. Ross was a leading Mason, and the Masonic fraternity erected a memorial pillar to him after his death at Goulburn in 1869. McGarvie was the archetype of moderatism, and Fullerton, Robert Stewart, Gilchrist and Purves were to take a generally similar position in the coming crisis. Forbes in Melbourne was a young man but a tireless worker in the cause of Christ with clear vision and wide interests. Some men showed a good eye for business, Purves in particular being involved in a number of ventures. Many seemed to be well off financially or became so as the colony developed. McGarvie accumulated a goodly fortune through careful use of his glebe and other investments. Purves had many business interests,, while McIntyre was well connected, his cousin Peter McIntyre (1783-1842), after whom the McIntyre River was named, having extensive pastoral interests. Many of these were inherited by William when he married Peter's sister and heir, Mary, in 1844.

But the calm, if it was that, was the calm before the storm. With the Scottish Disruption, the repercussions in Australia would be significant in shattering the appearance of unity, and dividing the infant church again.

25. 'J.D.Lang' by D.W.A.Baker in **Australian Dictionary of Biography 1788-1850**, p.79

6: DISRUPTION CRISIS 1843-1846

At the time of the Disruption of the Established Church of Scotland in May 1843 as described in an earlier chapter, Presbyterianism in the Australian colonies was organized as follows:

Eastern Australia [ie. the colony of New South Wales]
The Synod of Australia in connection with the Established Church of Scotland [Formed 1840 - 22 ministerial members.]

Scots Church, Jamison Street, Sydney [Dr Lang's independent congregation]

Tasmania [ie. the colony of Van Diemen's Land]
The Presbytery of Van Diemen's Land [Formed 1835 in connection with the Church of Scotland - 12 ministers.]

South Australia
No presbyery or synod formed but two ministers in colony:
 Ralph Drummond of the Associate Synod of Scotland arrived 1839
 Robert Haining of the Church of Scotland arrived 1841

Repercussions of the Scottish Disruption in outline
When news of the Disruption reached Australia late in 1843, several years' debate occurred before the dust settled. In South Australia there was no formal division since there was no presbytery or synod. About 25% of the census Presbyterians adhered to the views of the church question taken by the Free Church of Scotland, and *The Presbytery of the Free Presbyterian Church of South Australia* was constituted by 3 ministers and 2 elders (one of whom was James Benny) on May 9, 1854. On May 10, 1865, all but

the section of the Free Presbyterian Church led by James Benny, by then the minister at Morphett Vale, joined in a general union of Presbyterians which formed the *Presbyterian Church of South Australia.*

In Van Diemen's Land, the Presbytery professed to hold Free Church of Scotland principles but refused to break its moral and legal connection with the Established Church of Scotland. It desired the reputation of the Free Church but also the stipends granted because of its connection with the Established Church. Three of the twelve ministers resigned and left the colony as the available spheres of labour were already occupied and the population was not growing rapidly. A Free Church minister arrived in 1850, and on March 18, 1853, *The Free Church Presbytery of Tasmania* was constituted by three ministers. The most notable of these was Dr William Nicolson, MA, DD, of Hobart. Union with the original body to form the *Presbyterian Church of Tasmania* took place on March 18, 1896.

In the colony of New South Wales (covering the present states of New South Wales, Victoria and Queensland) the Synod professed the principles of the church question maintained by the Free Church of Scotland but declined to break the connection with the Established Church of Scotland. They, too, were concerned for their stipends and status. The legal name of the Synod became the point of debate. The majority refused to change the name expressive of connection with the Established Church and, as a result, six of the 22 regularly serving ministers withdrew. Messrs Mowbray and Hamilton were for neutrality and the one went to Queensland and the other to Victoria where later they participated in general Presbyterian unions. Three ministers protested and withdrew on October 10, 1846 to continue the church on true Presbyterian principles. They erected a new ecclesiastical court called the Synod of Eastern Australia, the church being called the *Presbyterian Church of Eastern Australia.* This was the first use of the word 'Presbyterian' in the legal title of an Australian church body.

The new Synod did not claim jurisdiction south of the Murray River because a further minister not present at the Synod, James Forbes of Melbourne, likewise protested and withdrew on similar grounds. Because of the vast distance from Sydney and anticipating that 'Australia Felix', as Victoria was then called, would become a separate colony, Forbes formed a separate ecclesiastical body on the same principles as those who formed the Synod of Eastern Australia. He called it the *Free Presbyterian Church of Australia Felix* and its Synod was formally constituted with three ministers (including one who had come from Van Diemen's Land) on June 9, 1847. Fraternal relations were established with the Synod of Eastern Australia.

We now come to look more particularly at the reasons for the division in the colony of New South Wales, and the position adopted by the protesting bodies.

THE SYNOD OF AUSTRALIA IN CONNECTION WITH THE ESTABLISHED CHURCH OF SCOTLAND
Constituted October 5, 1840

[Ministers in the year 1846 showing year of arrival in Australia]

Presbytery of Sydney

1826	John McGarvie, DD	St Andrew's Scots, Sydney
1837	James Fullerton	Pitt Street South, Sydney
1837	Robert Stewart	Newcastle
1837	**John Tait**	Parramatta
1840	William Purves, MA	Port Macquarie
1842	Thomas Mowbray, MA	Macquarie Street, Sydney

Presbytery of Windsor

1834	Kirkpatrick D.Smythe	St Stephen's, Bathurst
1837	Matthew Adam	Windsor
1837	George MacFie, MA	Ebenezer, Portland Head
1839	**Colin Stewart, MA**	Hartley/Bowenfels

Presbytery of Maitland

1837	**William McIntyre, MA**	Scots, Maitland
1837	Irving Hetherington	Singleton
1837	Robert Blain	Hinton
1838	William Ross, MA	Scots, Paterson

Presbytery of Campbelltown

1837	William Hamilton, MA	Scots, Goulburn
1837	Cunninghame Atchison	Wollongong
1837	Christopher Eipper	Braidwood
1837	High Gilchrist	Campbelltown

Presbytery of Melbourne

1837	**James Forbes, MA**	Scots, Melbourne (Collins Street)
1840	Andrew Love	Scots, Geelong (Yarra Street)
1842	Alexander Laurie	Scots, Portland (Percy Street)
1842	Peter Gunn	Scots, Campbellfield

The four men whose names are in bold print protested and withdrew to form new Synods. Mowbray and Hamilton also withdrew, the former going to Queensland and the latter to Victoria.

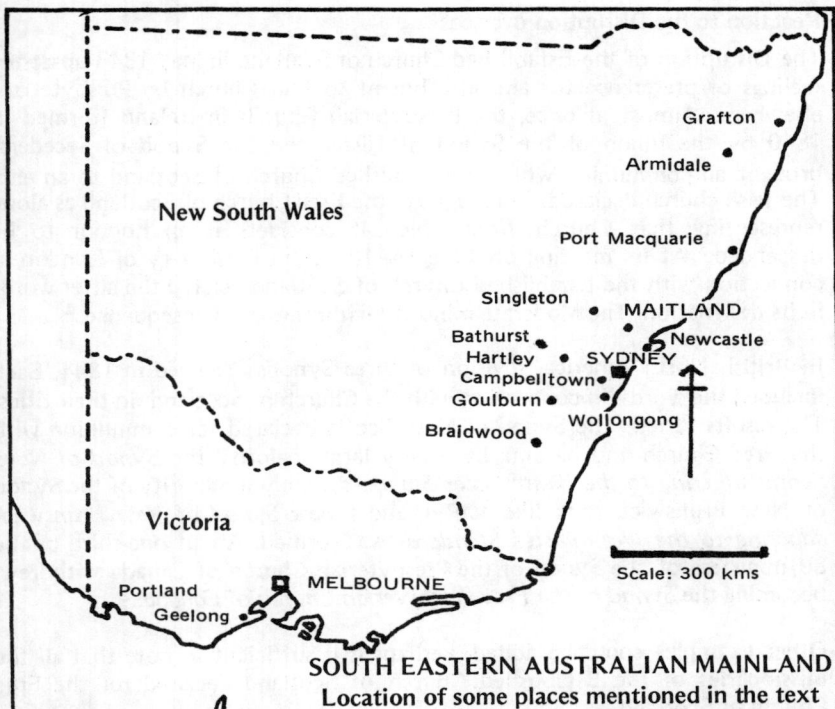

New South Wales

Grafton

Armidale

Port Macquarie

Singleton

MAITLAND

Newcastle

Bathurst

Hartley · SYDNEY

Campbelltown

Goulburn

Wollongong

Braidwood

Victoria

Scale: 300 kms

Portland

Geelong · MELBOURNE

SOUTH EASTERN AUSTRALIAN MAINLAND
Location of some places mentioned in the text

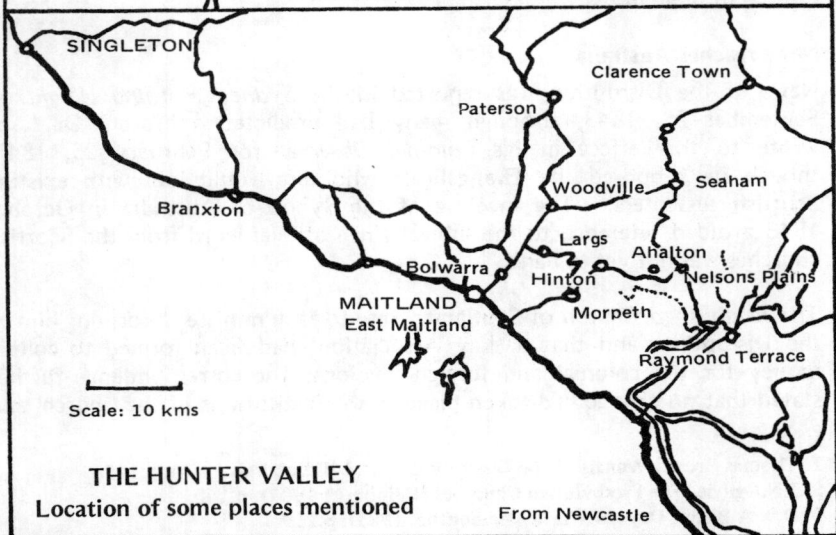

SINGLETON

Clarence Town

Paterson

Branxton

Woodville

Seaham

Largs

Bolwarra

Ahalton

Hinton

Nelsons Plains

MAITLAND
East Maitland

Morpeth

Raymond Terrace

Scale: 10 kms

THE HUNTER VALLEY
Location of some places mentioned

From Newcastle

61

Reaction to the Disruption overseas

The Disruption of the Established Church of Scotland in May 1843 upset the feelings of preference for and attachment to that Church by Presbyterians elsewhere. Almost at once, the Presbyterian Church in Ireland (formed in 1840 by the union of the Synod of Ulster and the Synod of Seceders) brought all communion with the Established Church of Scotland to an end. The Irish church declared: 'it recognizes the Free Church of Scotland as alone representing that Church from which it considers it an honour to be descended.' At its meeting on June 14, 1843, the Presbytery of London in connection with the Established Church of Scotland deleted the latter words in its designation. The Moderate minority withdrew as a consequence. [1]

In British North America, division of three Synods occurred in 1844. Each included the words 'in connection with the Church of Scotland' in their titles. The results varied. The Synod of Nova Scotia declared for communion with the Free Church and became by a very large majority the *Synod of Nova Scotia adhering to the Westminster Standards*. Only a minority of the Synod of New Brunswick took like action, and a new *Synod of New Brunswick adhering to the Westminster Standards* was formed. About one-third of the 80 ministers of the Synod of the Presbyterian Church of Canada withdrew, becoming the *Synod of the Free Presbyterian Church of Canada*. [2]

Other examples could be added. Perhaps it is sufficient to note that all the missionaries of the Established Church of Scotland declared for the Free Church of Scotland.

News reaches Australia

News of the Disruption was reported in the *Sydney Morning Herald* on September 25, 1843, although many had predicted a breach. Dr Lang wrote to this effect in his *Colonial Observer* for February 25, 1843, though he supposed the Evangelicals who left would join with existing Scottish dissenters.[3] The meeting of the Synod of Australia in October 1843 avoided reference to the subject since official word from the Scottish churches was not yet to hand.

The *Established* Church of Scotland wrote to each minister informing him of the Disruption, and that a 'Lay Association' had been formed to collect money for the colonial and foreign missions. The correspondence further stated that no change had taken place in the institutions of the Church, and

1. Thomas Brown, **Annals of the Disruption,** Part 3 (Edinburgh 1881), p.115
2. J.N.Ogilvie, **The Presbyterian Churches** (Edinburgh 1907), p.160
3. D.W.A.Baker, **Days of Wrath** (Melbourne, 1985), p.219

expressed the hope that the recipient was steadfastly adhering to the Church of his fathers.

The *Free* Church of Scotland wrote to the Synod Moderator as to an independent church, and said:

'...having all confidence in the wisdom and Christian principle of the Court over which you preside, we think it better to place the subject in your own hands, leaving it for the Synod to consider what, in all the circumstances, the course is, which it is their duty to pursue as a Church, and as individuals, and in what manner they should bring the question under the view of their people.

'In what measure the resolution to which you may come is likely to affect your temporal interests, we are unable to judge. We are satisfied, however, that you will follow what appears to you the path of duty, wherever it may lead. And we beg to assure you, that if in any instance the claims of conscience cannot be yielded to without suffering loss, our sympathies and active exertions, as well as those of our people, will be called forth to meet the evil in so far as we are able...'[4]

Agreement on principles, 1844

At the Synod of Australia meeting in October 1844, an overture from the Presbytery of Melbourne, moved by James Forbes and seconded by James Fullerton, affirmed unaltered attachment to two principles which embraced the distinctive views of the Free Church of Scotland, and also affirmed the independence of the Synod. Summarizing the overture, the three points were:[5]

1. The Lord Jesus Christ is the only King and Head of the church. He has provided its government in the hands of persons distinct from the civil power. While the civil power ought to further the interests of the church, if it lays down conditions for receiving support which infringe the spiritual liberties of the church under Christ, the church should decline such support rather than submit to the unlawful conditions. [This point embraces the 'separation of powers/co-ordinate jurisdiction' principle.]

2. No pastor should be settled over a congregation without lawful election and the formal or tacit consent of the majority of communicants first given. In the Colony of New South Wales the existing legal provisions provided an effective safeguard against intrusion, for the title to the state stipend supplement required the adherence of the congregation. [This point covered the rights of the Christian people.]

3. The Synod is the supreme legislative and judicial court for the Presbyterian

4. **Port Phillip Christian Herald** (hereafter PPCH), June 6, 1846.
5. Text in J.C.Robinson, **The Free Presbyterian Church of Australia** (Melbourne 1947) Appendix 5, and R.Sutherland, **The History of the Presbyterian Church of Victoria** (London 1877) pp. 49-53.

Church in the Colony. As an independent body its members are not morally responsible for the conduct of any body professing to hold the same standards over whose proceedings they can exert no influence.

The overture was adopted, Dr McGarvie alone dissenting. The Australian Synod had now reaffirmed its principles to be those espoused by the *Free* Church of Scotland. All that remained was to carry through the implications.

Disagreement in practice

The Synod next proceeded to take up the official correspondence from both Scottish churches, William Ross of Paterson being in the chair. In essence there were three possible positions, and each found support.

1. Neutrality
Cunningham Atchison, who in Scotland had at first belonged to the strict Original Secession Church, moved a proposal to do nothing, which was seconded by Hugh Gilchrist (originally from the Synod of Ulster), but this was later withdrawn. Neutrality was represented by William Hamilton's motion [6] which declined to 'adhere' to either church, but resolved, if the Scottish churches consented, to maintain communion with both and to accept assistance on that basis. The motion also allowed Synod ministers to divest themselves by a private act of the rights and privileges they possessed as ministers of the Established Church of Scotland (eg. the right to be nominated to an ECS parish). Finally, the motion proposed a change of name not, so the motion stated, because the name implied any degree of Erastianism, but rather to avoid the impression the Synod held exclusive communion with the Church of Scotland as now established, or more intimate communion with it rather than the Free Church of Scotland.

2. Solidarity with the Established Church of Scotland
McGarvie, supported by Robert Stewart and George Anderson (elder at McGarvie's church) held it was not necessary to change the Synod's name or to abandon the connection with the Established Church.

3. Solidarity with the Free Church of Scotland
A third lengthy motion, proposed by John Tait and seconded by William McIntyre, expressed deep regret and sorrow that the old principles of the Church of Scotland had been virtually surrendered by the portion of the church who remained in the establishment and deep thankfulness for the faithfulness of those who had sacrificed temporal benefits for the honour of Christ. The motion sought a name change on the ground of principle, and expressed thanks to the Free Church of Scotland and willingness to receive assistance from it. The key section of Tait's motion read:

6. Text in Sutherland, op.cit., pp.60-62

'...the relation in which the Synod stands to the Established Church...implies such a special preference for, and approval of her on our part as is inconsistent with the declaration we have now made of what those Standards teach and require...and that therefore while this Synod is deeply grateful for the valuable assistance and counsel they have received from the Established Church in times past, and have marked their sense of the honour and advantage of standing in such a relation by adopting as their official name, the Synod of Australia in connection with the Established Church of Scotland - they do not feel warranted in longer continuing the peculiar and close connection in which they have hitherto stood to her, or in retaining a name which is calculated to misrepresent them, give offence to many of their ministers and people, and lead to new dissensions and divisions in our Colonial Church; and that, therefore, immediate steps be taken for obtaining the sanction of the Colonial Government to the change of name now resolved on.'[7]

Vote for neutrality 1844

In the voting, McGarvie's amendment received only two votes. Accordingly, Tait's amendment carried, but when put against Hamilton's motion was defeated 6 to 9 with 4 abstentions (McGarvie, Anderson, Purves and MacFie) and with McGarvie and Anderson recording their dissent.

Neutrality	Established Church	Free Church
Fullerton	McGarvie	Tait
Mowbray	Anderson (elder)	Colin Stewart
Adam		McIntyre
Hetherington		Blain
Hamilton		Forbes
Atchison		Bowman (elder)
Eipper		
Gilchrist		
John Stewart (elder)		

Ministers absent: R.Stewart, K.D.Smythe,
Love, Laurie, Gunn.

Moderator: William Ross

A Committee was appointed to seek amendment of the Temporalities Act to incorporate a change of name to 'The General Synod of New South Wales'. Before being submitted to the legislature the draft amendment was sent to the five Presbyteries for approval in terms of the Barrier Act 1697, a procedural device inherited from the Church of Scotland by which due consideration is aimed at before changes affecting the church at large are implemented.

It was necessary to seek civil sanction for the change of name since, in the

7. Text in Sutherland, op.cit., pp.62-65. At the meeting of the Sydney Presbytery March 5, 1844, Tait and two elders were for calling a special Synod to discuss the Disruption, but were defeated. See M.D.Prentis, The Scots in Australia (Sydney 1983), p.242 where he cites McGarvie's Diary. McIntyre was in another Presbytery.

absence of such sanction, a dissenting minority resisting the authority of the Synod under a new name could destroy its authority and cause endless trouble. This could be the case even though none of the principles of the Synod had changed.

Thirteen of the 22 ministerial members had voted for a name change. The two who had declared themselves opposed and the absent members were supposed likely to acquiesce with the probable exception of McGarvie.[8] The declaration of principles plus the agreement to change the name reconciled the Free Church party to continuing in the Synod,[9] though they did not agree that the original name of the Synod was not objectionable in principle. However, they drew a distinction between the church's testimony and the administration of that testimony. Further, 'if they seceded, except in circumstances in which secession was the only means left to them of preserving purity of testimony and liberty of conscience, they would be guilty of schism.'[10]

Men with two faces

As a consequence of Fullerton, Atchison, Eipper and Gilchrist opposing at Presbytery level what they had voted for at Synod, two Presbyteries (Sydney and Campbelltown) rejected the proposed Bill to change the name, and one did not meet (presumably Melbourne). Thus, in the absence of a majority the process fell to the ground.

James Forbes' comment was: 'We will not trust ourselves to characterize such conduct. Since it took place we have in great degree lost all confidence in the majority of the Synod, and regarded a disruption as inevitable.' As a result of the temporizing policy of the majority he came to 'the painful conclusion that the declaration of principles was not worth the paper on which it was written.' [11]

Name change on principle 1845

When the Synod met in October 1845 the matter of the change of name was taken up afresh. Hamilton, seconded by Mowbray, proposed a Committee be appointed to draft a Bill to obtain civil sanction to a change of name which would be considered by a special Synod to be called in June 1846 after suggestions from Presbyteries had been obtained. McGarvie, seconded by Robert Stewart, proposed that a name change was inexpedient. McIntyre,

8. PPCH July 4, 1846 p.54 col. 2
9. PPCH July 4, 1846 p.58 col. 3
10. W.McIntyre, Narrative of the Disruption of the Presbyterian Church in New South Wales (West Maitland, 1859), p.30
11. PPCH July 4, 1846 p.53 col. 3 & July 29, 1846 p.59 col. 1

seconded by Tait, proposed a name change on the ground of the present name implying 'a decided though indirect testimony' in favour of the recent proceedings of the Established Church.[12]

It should be noted that McIntyre's motion did not expressly commit the Synod to communion with the Free Church of Scotland.[13] Certainly the logic was in that direction since the disapproval of the Established Church which *was* expressed certainly implied an end to communion with that church. Even so, it would not necessarily have ended communion with *good men* who remained in the Established Church.[14] Hamilton's proposal did not bear on relations with the Scottish Churches in an explicit way. As yet the reaction of Scotland to the decisions of the 1844 Synod had not been received.

When put to the vote, McIntyre's motion carried against McGarvie's and was then put against Hamilton's motion where it again carried with the following result:

Motion	Amendment	Abstained
Mowbray	Tait	McGarvie
Adam	Colin Stewart	Fullerton
Ross	McIntyre	Robert Stewart
Hamilton	Blain	MacFie
Kellman (Singleton elder)	Peter Stewart (elder-	Eipper
McMaster (Paterson elder)	Macquarie Street)	Gilchrist
	H.McDonald (elder-Hinton)	2 elders
	Ferguson (elder - Maitland)	
	Dr Hill (elder Parramatta)	

Absent: Smythe, Purves, Atchison, Forbes, Love, Laurie & Gunn.
Moderator: Irving Hetherington

This result was no real victory since 5 of the 7 absent ministers (ie. all but Smythe and Forbes) were opposed. Further, when the official reply of the Established Church came to hand shortly after the 1845 Synod, the 6 ministers who declined to vote and 5 who were absent, together with two elders (McMaster and Charles Gill of McGarvie's church) requisitioned a

12. Text in PPCH February 7, 1846 p.16 col. 1; also Sutherland, op.cit., pp.66-67
13. It is often said otherwise. Thus Sutherland, op.cit., p.73: 'In 1845 they voted in favour of connection with the Free Church, and to accept supplies of ministers from it.' Also R.Hamilton, A Jubilee History of the Presbyterian Church of Victoria (Melbourne 1888) p. 31, and A.Macdonald, One Hundred Years of Presbyterianism in Victoria (Melbourne 1937) p.27: 'It was decided to receive ministers from the Free Church alone.' Such statements are not correct.
14. PPCH June 6, 1846 p.47 col. 1 where Forbes states that the Synod might have declared the Free Church as truly constituting the Church of their Fathers. They might have done this, he writes, 'without shutting themselves out from communion with good men in the establishment, and in other churches, and in our opinion nothing less than this was their duty.'

special meeting of Synod with a view to rescinding the resolutions of 1845 and maintaining the connection with the Established Church. The Moderator declined to call the meeting, but the signs were ominous. At the beginning of 1846 two periodicals were commenced in the interests of the Free Church party, if for convenience we may call them that. James Forbes commenced the monthly *Port Phillip Christian Herald*, and William McIntyre began the fortnightly *Voice in the Wilderness*.

Views of the Established Church

The finding of the General Assembly of the Church of Scotland on June 2, 1845 was that the 1844 resolutions:

'...of necessity imply on the part of the Synod of Australia a total repudiation of its statutory connection with the Established Church of Scotland, and a virtual denial of the authority of the government and discipline of that church as determined by law - and farther, that such Ministers and Elders of the Synod of Australia as adhere to these resolutions are no longer to be regarded as Ministers and Elders in connection with the Church of Scotland, or as pastors have any just title to the privileges secured by law to such Ministers and Elders in the aforesaid colony. The General Assembly therefore direct copies of this minute to be transmitted to the Moderator and Clerk of the Synod of Australia, and also to Her Majesty's Principal Secretary of State for the Colonies, and they instruct their Colonial Committee, should the resolutions to which reference has been made above, continue to be adhered to by any Minister belonging to the Australian Synod, to take all competent steps in their name, in vindication of the rights and privileges of the Presbyterian population of Australia still maintaining their connection with the Established Church of Scotland.' [15]

This resolution went far beyond what was legitimate on the part of the Established Church towards an independent church. ' She assumes the attitude of a hostile invader; we are the feeble objects of her attack', wrote James Forbes. [16]

It does not appear certain that the Established Church was furnished a copy of the declaration of principles passed in 1844, although no doubt she had knowledge of it. The 'resolutions' referred to in the above minute are the propositions moved by William Hamilton and taking a neutral position. Of course, one can understand why the Established Church would not feel very friendly towards a Synod that held out hands of fellowship with those who had left her and formed the Free Church of Scotland. The Australian decision was stigmatized as 'milk and water' in the Established Church Assembly, and indeed it was pretty weak and inconsistent.

15. Text in **The Voice in the Wilderness** (hereafter **Voice**) June 15, 1846 p.96. While it is evident the disclaimer of jurisdiction made in 1840 is all but forgotten in this decision, the position was complicated by the statutory connection which did exist.
16. **PPCH** July 29, 1846, p.62 col. 2.

Views of the Free Church

The Free Church Assembly did not officially respond to the 1844 policy, since what with time delays in the post and the timing of the annual meetings in each country, it was felt better to wait until the Synod of October 1845![17] The Free Church anticipated a revision of what they regarded as an impractical policy. Indeed, one of the leaders of the Free Church, Dr Candlish, stated at the 1845 Assembly the attitude of the Established Church Assembly and declared: 'this resolution will not do us either; they will have to reconsider their position when I have no doubt another disruption may be expected.' This reaction was known in Australia by the beginning of 1846.[18]

Attempt to go backwards

As already mentioned, the response of the Established Church led to a request for a special Synod meeting which the Moderator did not accede to. Behind the request was the fear of losing the stipends paid by the Government; in other words, many took the threats of the Established Church seriously. When they saw that practical consequences would flow from what had been decided and affect their pockets, they saw the opportunity to force a reversal of policy, perhaps shrewdly reckoning that there would be waverers among the 'neutral' party.

Now it was quite true that stipends were not paid to Presbyterian ministers because they were ministers of the Established Church. Aid on the same basis was given to the major Christian groups including the Church of Rome. But the Temporalities Act tied the property and the Synod's designation together, so the property would be lost by that section of the church which went out because a name change was not secured. While that section could apply as an independent Christian body for stipend grants and site and building grants, there might well be a question as to obtaining such in practice. And even if there were a majority in favour of a name change, there was little reason to hope that the Legislative Council would grant it since its social makeup would tend to favour the Established Church. And then there was Dr Lang to reckon with. On the other hand, a good majority for a name change might be able to obtain the name change and keep the endowments. As it turned out, most did not want to take the risk.

17. This is stated in a letter dated May 19, 1846 to William McIntyre from Dr James Buchanan, the Convener of the Free Church of Scotland Colonial Committee; text in *Voice*, November 2, 1846 p.169
18. A number of writers give the impression the 'milk and water' expression originated with Candlish whereas he only took it up from the press reports of the Established Church Assembly. Sutherland, op. cit., p.73 suggests Candlish's handling of the issue by jest and sarcasm and without regard to the 1844 statement of principles resulted in loss of lay support in New South Wales for the Free Church.

Special Synod - May 1846

The Committee named in October 1845 proceeded to draft a Bill as instructed. The Moderator, Rev I. Hetherington, convened a special meeting for May 28, 1846 at noon 'to receive the Report of the said Committee, and to make such amendments on the Draft of a Bill prepared by them, as may be deemed necessary before submitting it to the Legislative Council.'[19]

In Presbyterian law such special *(pro re nata)* meetings must confine themselves to the objects for which they are called. This consideration did not stop the party who were fearful of the loss of state stipends. Atchison, seconded by McGarvie, moved that the Synod proceed no further and discharge the Committee. This motion should have been ruled out of order. McIntyre, seconded by Colin Stewart, moved that the Report be received and the Bill examined and amended as might be found necessary. This proposal carried on the casting vote of the Moderator:

Atchison's motion	McIntyre's amendment
McGarvie	Mowbray
Fullerton	Tait
R.Stewart	Purves
Ross	Adam
Eipper	MacFie
Gilchrist	C.Stewart
C.Gill (elder St Andrew's)	McIntyre
G.Whitelaw (Pitt Street elder)	Hetherington
- Innes (elder)	Blain
	Peter Stewart (elder)

Atchison himself did not vote (probably absent at the time), but he was present when the Synod resumed at 6pm. The pro-Establishment party found they had a majority and proceeded to 'break its backbone' (as one of them put it) by deleting whole clauses of the draft Bill. At length, further consideration was deferred until the annual meeting in October. The object of frustrating the decision to change the name was evident: McIntyre, Tait, Mowbray, MacFie, Hetherington, Blain and Peter Stewart dissented from the deferment. McIntyre warned that if the decision to change the name was retreated from at the annual meeting, he and those standing with him would be under the necessity of immediately withdrawing from the Synod.

Separation - when and how

The vacillating policy in the Synod had already led to resignations of elders - Messrs John Dumble and H.L.Black withdrew from Fullerton's Pitt Street congregation in March 1845.[20] Now, as a consequence of the special Synod,

---

19. See Voice, June 1, 1846 p.85 for full text of the draft.
20. Voice, April 16, 1846 p.64

Messrs Peter Stewart, John Little and William Buyers resigned in June from the Session of Mowbray's congregation in Macquarie Street.[21] However, in William McIntyre's view, the objectionable proceedings in May 1846

'...may have furnished data from which it may be calculated with a high degree of probability, if not with certainty, what course the Synod will take at its annual meeting. But, then, it is that course as actually taken, and not as foreseen, that would warrant separation from it. It is what a body *has* become, and not what we foresee or calculate it *will* become, that renders separation from it necessary...'[22]

McIntyre went on to stress the importance of separation by those with similar views being a collective act.

James Forbes in far-off Melbourne was sick at heart by this time but writes in similar vein:

'The last question we shall attempt to answer is, - why not go out at once? - why wait till October? To this our reply is, because we are Presbyterians, not independents. The decision of such matters is, in our system, vested in the *assembled pastors and elders*. Until these have departed from the resolutions of last year, and succumbed to the yoke attempted to be imposed on them by the Scottish Establishment, it would be a violation of our principles to separate. The ultimate issue may not be materially different; but it will be something to be able to say, amidst worldly loss, and the alienation of friends, and the forfeiture of temporal position, that not one principle of Presbytery has been lost sight of, and that we have been conducted to where we are, not by obstinacy or pride, nor the desire of being thought better than our neighbours, but by a determination to maintain the olden testimony of the Kirk of Scotland, - for Christ's Kingdom and Christ's Crown.'[23]

The importance of the name change

At the formation of the Synod of Australia in 1840 as an independent body, it was desired to express by the name the identity of principle with and preference for the Established Church of Scotland above all other churches. But following the new interpretation of the church-state relationship laid down by the civil courts and acquiesced in by those who continued in the Establishment, the Synod's name now indicated in the minds of many members and the community at large an identity of principle with those very points which had caused so many separations from the Established Church.

If the preference for the Established Church of Scotland had ceased to exist, the name ought to be changed if only to indicate the fact. 'To retain it on any consideration whatsoever would be to say the preference still continues; and

21. Voice, July 15, 1846 p.115/116
22. Voice, July 15, 1846 p.115/116
23. PPCH, July 4, 1846 p.54 col. 3

should in this way a preference for the Established Church of Scotland be declared, however tacitly, no one who, like us, considers the Free Church as truly the Church of Scotland, can remain in the body, be the consequences what they may.' [24]

The importance of an independent name
The existing Synod professed to be independent and a name that indicated this was appropriate. Given the division into two of the Established Church, the old name was forcing the division on to the Australian Synod.

'...a neutral name, a name that applies specially to neither should be adopted. We simply wish in consequence of the altered meaning that the words 'Established Church of Scotland' have come to bear, that they be left out of our title. We do not desire to substitute for these words, the other words, 'Free Church of Scotland'. [25] This would also be objectionable, though it would be less so than the other; for it so happens that we as a church take the same view of the great principles in dispute between the two divisions of the Parent Church, as that portion now constituting the Free Church does. But there is no desire nor intention on the part of any to put the Synod into special or exclusive connection with the Free or any other church, and the only effect of the change proposed would have been to leave us disconnected with any transmarine body whatsoever. And unless this is immediately done it is impossible that the unity of the Colonial Church can be maintained...[26]

What about those not wanting a name change?
McIntyre and others thus required a name change to prevent their separation. But if they obtained the name change, would there be others who would have to withdraw? McIntyre argued there would not be the same necessity since, as already stated, the opposite name (...in connection with the Free Church of Scotland) was not proposed. We

'propose that the Colonial Church should stand on independent Presbyterian ground, and be in connection with no transmarine Church at all. And is it not reasonable that this neutral ground be occupied by both parties?' [27]

What about the middle party?
Once communion with both sides was shown as impossible, the middle party of Mowbray and Hamilton should have supported McIntyre and

24. PPCH, July 4, 1846 p.54 col. 2

25. Voice, July 15, 1846 pp.109/110; similarly PPCH, August 15, 1846 p.129 col.2. This point is constantly missed. Thus, A.A.Dougan in the article 'Presbyterian Church' in The Australian Encyclopaedia 3rd edition (Sydney 1977) does not give the full title of the Synod of Australia once, and in one paragraph refers to 'The Synod of Australia,with Established Church sympathies...and The Synod of Eastern Australia, in connection with the Free Church of Scotland'. Thus the true position is reversed.

26. Voice, July 15, 1846 p.109

27. Voice, July 15, 1846 p.110 col. 1

Forbes in changing the name. Once this was done, the question of ministerial supplies could have been covered, and the numbers would have favoured the Free Church of Scotland and the Irish church. On this plan, the unity of the Synod would have been maintained. The doubtful aspect would have been the position of McGarvie's group and whether the Legislative Council would have amended the Temporalities Act.

In any case, the basis of opposition by Mowbray and Hamilton was pragmatic: they did not think the name was objectionable in principle. Thus, McIntyre considered their position one which would not require them to separate.

Narrow-minded or far-sighted?
As well as the need for a name change on the grounds of principle, there were other practical considerations too. The position of the Established Church was generally condemned by Presbyterians world-wide and thus many new settlers could not join her congregations if there was any alternative.

'What a short sighted policy is it for the sake of a present temporal advantage to occupy such narrow ground as actually to compel another rival Presbyterian Church to spring up alongside of the present; and that not on a narrow basis but on a broad basis that will include all the sections and no doubt be ultimately the chief governing body of the Presbyterian community.'[28]

For McIntyre, the choice was to place the Australian Church on the broad and secure foundation of Scripture as set out in the Westminster Standards, or to leave the Synod a small and dishonoured appendage of that half of the old Scottish Church that had so markedly lost the spirit and departed from the principles of her founders.

In addition, the Established Church was the church least likely to be able to send ministers to Australia   because of the shortage in Scotland caused by the exit of some 470 men at the Disruption.

Synod - October 1846
The annual Synod meeting convened in St Andrew's Scots Church, Sydney on Wednesday October 7 at noon. The matter of the change of name was taken up on Thursday evening. The resolution of the Established Church Assembly, as recorded above, was read. There was no official communication from the Free Church but her attitude was known. There was now no room for playing about. With a view to bringing matters to a head, it was moved by William McIntyre and seconded by Colin Stewart:
'That the Synod disapprove of the proceedings of the *pro re nata* meeting,

---

28. Voice, July 15, 1846 p.110 col. 2

held on the twenty-eighth of May last, in so far as they went to obstruct the carrying into effect of the resolution passed at the last meeting, with respect to the change of designation - and again solemnly determine that it will abide by and follow out those resolutions at all hazards; that with the view of carrying them into effect without further delay, the Synod now resolve itself into a committee to review the draft of the Bill proposed by the committee appointed for the purpose proposed at the last annual meeting, that it may be immediately laid before the Legislative Council; and that the Moderator shall be instructed to notify in the *Government Gazette*, so soon as the said Bill shall be passed or rejected by the Council, that the Synod shall hence-forth bear the new designation.'

Dr McGarvie with Robert Stewart as his seconder, proposed:
It is not necessary to proceed farther in the consideration of the change of designation, and the committee appointed thereanent, are hereby relieved of their duties in that matter.

Thomas Mowbray moved, seconded by Thomas Barker:
'1. That the Synod renew their adherence to the declaration of principles set forth by them on the 3rd October, 1844, respecting the sole headship of the Lord Jesus Christ over his Church - and respecting the supreme and independent jurisdiction of this Court in spiritual things; and they again declare their unaltered attachment to these principles, and their firm determination as a Church of Christ to maintain them, and in all circumstances to act in strict accordance with them.

2. That in the important charge with which they have been entrusted, of administering the ordinances of Christ, and preaching his Gospel in the land, it is their earnest desire to secure the support and co-operation of every faithful and evangelical church throughout the world that adheres to the same standards, and maintains the same form of worship and discipline.

3. That they rejoice that inasmuch as they are exempt from the evils of patronage and other causes of secession in the mother country, they are in such a position as enables them to invite, and warrants them to expect such support and co-operation.

4. That inasmuch as the present designation of this Synod is known to be offensive on various grounds to a considerable portion of its ministers and people, and is apt to convey to others an erroneous view of its position, and is thereby calculated to hinder that union and co-operation which it is the earnest desire of the Synod to secure and maintain, they resolve that instead of the clause, 'in connection with the Established Church of Scotland,' the words 'adhering to the Westminster Standards' be substituted.

5. That the Synod, during the present session, resolve itself into a committee of the whole Court to prepare the draft of a Bill embodying the change

resolved on and other amendments of the Temporalities Act, in accordance with former resolutions, and also to determine what steps shall be taken in order to render the application to the Legislature successful.'

The debate continued throughout Friday, K.D.Smythe being Moderator, and the vote was taken late in the evening. Mowbray's amendment was put against that of McGarvie and was defeated. Those who had supported a middle position did not now cast their votes for McIntyre's motion since most were not prepared to hazard the loss of their state stipends. Accordingly, McGarvie's amendment carried against the motion and became the finding of the Synod. The voting summarises as follows, and shows Robert Blain had retreated from his former support for McIntyre.

McIntyre's motion	McGarvie's amendment	Mowbray's amendment
Tait	McGarvie	Mowbray
Colin Stewart	Fullerton	Adam
McIntyre	Robert Stewart	MacFie
S.Martin (Hinton elder)	Purves	Hetherington
Dr Hill (Parramatta elder)	Ross	Blain
	Eipper	Hamilton
	Whitelaw (Pitt Street elder)	Barker (Macquarie Street)
	Ferrier (St Andrew's elder)	Kellman (Singleton elder)
	McMaster (Paterson elder)	

St Andrew's Scots Church, Sydney
Opened September 1835 - Closed November 1911

The name and certain fittings were transferred to the new church at Rose Bay, opened 1913

Atchison and Gilchrist declined to vote. The four ministers in what is now Victoria were absent, but only Forbes would have supported McIntyre's motion, and the rest were in favour of the status quo.

Repercussions

Mowbray, Hetherington, MacFie and Blain dissented from the finding for reasons to be given in. Dissent frees one from the sin conceived to be involved in a decision, but not from the obligation of submission to the judicatories of the church. Hamilton read reasons for his dissent and intimated his intention to resign his charge at Goulburn. On Saturday morning Hamilton and Mowbray submitted a written Protest against the decision and withdrew from the Synod.

In Presbyterian practice, a protest is rather stronger than dissent with reasons. Persons who are not members of the Synod or Assembly may adhere to it subsequently. Of itself, a protest does not imply a refusal to submit to the judicatories of the church nor a renunciation of the jurisdiction of the court,[29] since obedience under protest is still possible. But a protest may be accompanied by statements which indicate withdrawal or separation (as in Mowbray and Hamilton's case), or the protesters may conduct themselves in such a way as to incur the censures of the church.

About 12 noon on Saturday October 10, Messrs McIntyre, Tait, Colin Stewart and Samuel Martin entered the Synod meeting in St Andrew's Church. McIntyre read a Protest signed by them. Having laid it on the table, they withdrew to the home of William Buyers to constitute a new church court on the old principles - the Synod of Eastern Australia.

On October 25, soon after the report of the division reached Melbourne, James Forbes addressed his congregation and renounced connection with the Synod. His Protest dated October 29 was lodged with the Presbytery of Melbourne and he was declared no longer minister of Scots Church on November 17. Meanwhile, organisation of the Free Presbyterian Church of Australia Felix was under way. The first services were held in the Mechanics' Hall on November 22, and a Synod was formed the following year when Forbes was joined by two other ministers newly arrived in the colony.

29. The best source on the history of protest in the Scottish Church is **A Review of Events in the Free Presbyterian Church of Scotland 1925-1945** (Glasgow, 1948) 56 pp.

Part Three

EXPANSION 1846-1865

7: ACTIVITY IN NEW SOUTH WALES

THE SYNOD OF EASTERN AUSTRALIA 1846-1864

The three ministers and one elder who formed the Presbyterian Church of Eastern Australia, began a denomination which was to become, after a slow start, the most vigorous and evangelical branch of Presbyterianism in New South Wales. It had 22 active ministers (several not inducted) at the time in 1864 when the majority joined a union based on compromise of the position adopted in 1846. The Synod of Australia, with some exceptions, was a pretty lifeless church during most of its history. Disregarding ministers in what was to become Victoria and Queensland, its strength rose from 13 inducted ministers in 1846 to 23 in 1865, when it joined the general union. Lang's group was to have a fitful existence but its standards were lax and the quality of its ministers poor.

Constitution of the Synod of Eastern Australia

McIntyre, Tait, Stewart and Martin convened in an upper room in the house of William Buyers at 4 Hunter Street, and there constituted the Presbyterian Church of Eastern Australia. Buyers was a prominent businessman who acted as Sydney agent for McIntyre's pastoral interests. He had withdrawn with Peter Stewart from Mowbray's Sydney congregation in June 1846, and was to be Treasurer of the Synod until his death in 1875. The minutes of the inaugural meeting read as follows:

> At Sydney & within an upper room in
> Hunter Street. the 10th day of Oct. 1846

The ministers & elders of the Synod of Australia in connexion with the Established Church of Scotland being assembled in Synod this day in St Andrew's Church, the ministers and elders members of that Synod whose names are appended to the Protest then and there made and hereinafter inserted, having withdrawn from that place, and having convened in an upper room in Hunter St and having duly Constituted themselves in the name of the Head of the Church, the Revd William McIntyre was chosen to be their Moderator, and the Protest above mentioned, being produced, was read and thereafter ordered to be recorded as follows: (see text on next page)

Mr Tait was appointed Clerk. It was then resolved that this court should be called the Synod of Eastern Australia and that the ministers and elders constituting the court should renew and they do hereby renew their adherence to the Westminster Confession of Faith, the Directory for Public Worship, and the Form of Church Government, together with the Second Book of Discipline as the standards of this Church.

The Synod then adjourned till Monday at 10 o clk A.M. [1]

The report of the first meeting in McIntyre's paper shows certain differences when compared to Tait's hand-written record.

The Rev Mr Tait was appointed to be clerk of the court. It was then resolved that the body should be designated - The Presbyterian Church of Eastern Australia, and the Supreme Ecclesiastical Court - The Synod of Eastern Australia. The members present then declared anew their adherence to the confession of Faith, the Directory for Public Worship, and the Second Book of Discipline, as the Standards of the Church.[2]

The press report thus spells out the denominational title, not just the name of the supreme court, and it omits reference to the Form of Church Government. These are small variations which do not amount to anything, since the men who formed the PCEA were not forming a church with new standards but renewing their adherence to the old standards 'in their true and original import' - to quote their Protest. The Form of Church Government is one of these standards, but was accepted by the Church of Scotland in 1645 by an Act which purports to maintain the position set out in the Second Book of Discipline, adopted in 1578. Thus, it was really enough to mention the earlier Book, more especially as that Book contains very explicit teaching against patronage and the like evils which had led to the Disruption of the Established Church.

As would be expected from the earlier history, the name of the church was and is significant. McIntyre was opposed to the use of a name which would not bring out the reason for the distinctive position of the church. In reference to the opening of a church in Sydney he wrote:

it will be opened on Sabbath, the 29th instant, as the *Presbyterian Church, Pitt Street*; or, if the reader wishes a more distinctive name, he may call it

1. Minutes of SEA (Ferguson Memorial Library, Sydney), p.1
2. Voice in the Wilderness (hereafter Voice) October 15, 1846, p.160 col.3

We, the undersigned ministers and elders, members of the Synod of Australia in connection with the Established Church of Scotland—

Considering that the Synod, having resolved to remain in its present connection with the Established Church of Scotland, and to retain its present designation unchanged, does thereby declare its approval of the submission of the said Church to the encroachments of the Civil power on her spiritual independence and the liberties of her constitution, and thus concurs in the renunciation of the doctrine of Christ's sole' and sovereign Headship, which that submission involves.

And further, considering that, in virtue of the connection with the Established Church of Scotland, which the Synod has resolved to maintain,— asserted as that connection is, not only in the designation of the Synod, but also by the Bond of Union entered into by the ministers and elders who united in forming the said Synod, wherein it is set forth, that they engaged, in every part of their future conduct towards each other to act in strict conformity to the laws of Christ, and of the Scottish Church, declared anew their adherence to the doctrines of the Confession of Faith, and promised that in the exercise of discipline they should follow the laws of that Church, as far as applicable in this colony,—the unscriptural principles on which the government of the Established Church of Scotland is now administered, according to which the civil courts are invested with power to coerce the judicatories and individual members of that Church in the exercise of their spiritual functions and duties, and otherwise to interfere authoritatively in spiritual matters, and Presbyteries are authorised and empowered to disregard and overbear the voice of the people in the formation of the pastoral relation, are virtually adopted by the Synod: and the government and discipline of the Colonial Presbyterian Church under its superintendence are liable to be subjected to the operation of these principles.

We, therefore, the ministers and elders aforesaid, do protest, that the Synod, by its concurrence in the renunciation of the doctrine of Christ's Headship as aforesaid, has placed itself in a position at variance with the word of God, and with the standards of the Church of Scotland in their true and original import, and incompatible with the discharge of its great duty as a witness to Christ.

And we protest further, that, by the adoption of the principles aforesaid, the constitution of the Synod has been so changed, that the government of the church cannot be conducted in accordance with it, without violating the laws of God, dishonouring the Great King and Head of the Church, and invading the rights of the Christian people.

And finally, while we reserve any right, we, or any of us, or of such as may adhere to us, possess to the whole, or any portion of the property, held in behalf of the Synod of Australia in connexion with the Established Church of Scotland, we protest that, the Synod occupying such a position, and having adopted such principles, it is and shall be lawful for us, and such other ministers and elders as may concur with us, to withdraw from the Synod, and take such steps as may be competent to us and necessary for dispensing the ordinances of the Gospel, and administering the affairs of the Church in this land, agreeable to the mind of Christ and to the standards and constitution of our Church; and we do now withdraw accordingly.

81

the *Free Presbyterian Church, Pitt Street,* provided always that he bear distinctly in mind, that the Presbyterian Church of Eastern Australia, while it holds the principles of the Free Church of Scotland and desires to maintain relations of the closest friendship with it, is itself an independent Church, occupying in this Colony the same position which the Free Church occupies in Scotland.[3]

McIntyre had found some lay opinion in favour of the church being part of the Free Church of Scotland, and this he opposed. The clarity of McIntyre's vision was not always appreciated later. As well, the idea gained currency that the PCEA was formed as an imitation of the Free Church of Scotland, as if the local situation had not forced the division. Although subsequent history has rendered the PCEA name less distinctive than it was originally, and although the common way of referring to the church as the 'Free Church' or the 'Free Presbyterian Church' became prevalent and remains so, McIntyre's reasoning is still relevant. The PCEA was never in a position of being established by law so that it could become 'free'. Rather, it had to maintain the true Presbyterian testimony by freeing itself from a compromising name and association. It had to be seen as clearly independent and Australian, rather than as dependent and colonial. It would be good if the legal name was the only name commonly used, although there is no reason why a prescriptive name could not be used as well if it was really appropriate eg. if the PCEA operated in Western Australia in the future.[4]

Response to the Protest

The Synod of Australia issued a reply to the Protest lodged by McIntyre and those with him. It asserted that the Established Church was not Erastian and had not submitted to any encroachments on her spiritual independence; that the Veto Act of 1834, which prevented the intrusion of ministers, was an illegal Act on the part of the Church and the cause of all the subsequent troubles: the party which left to form the Free Church had not been prepared to abide by the contract with the state but sought to change it unilaterally. That ministers could be intruded in Church of Scotland parishes in the face of specific objections was denied; and the independence of the Synod of Australia was allowed by the Church of Scotland in 1839, so that the Synod was not in a state of vassalage as Mowbray claimed.

McIntyre's response was to point out that the assertion by the Established Church that she was not Erastian was a mere assertion. Many a guilty person

---

3. **Voice**, November 15, 1846, p.175 , col.2 (the opening was actually postponed to December 13, 1846 - **Voice**, December 1, 1846, p.186 col.1).
4. Change of the legal name would require (1) good unanimity throughout the church; (2) amendment of the Acts of Parliament by which the PCEA is incorporated for the purpose of holding property.

pleads not guilty when he is, and the evidence convicted the Established Church and was adequate in the eyes of virtually the whole Presbyterian world. In reference to the Veto Act, McIntyre held it was lawful, but if it was not, then it only proved the Established Church was Erastian before 1843, not that she was free from Erastianism at all. He noted: 'When the facts of the case are unpropitious, a special pleader will always resort to points of law.' Ministers could be intruded if the people were unwilling to have a man but did not give specific objection - the example of John Stewart of Plockton in May 1846 was adduced. Finally, the independence affirmed in 1839 was now, at any rate, a sham, since the 1845 Assembly had threatened punishment in the loss of salaries, if the Synod of Australia did not accept her position. To threaten punishment implies jurisdiction, on the best construction, or tyranny on the worst. The fact was the Synod of Australia gloried in her identification with the Established Church and

Constituting the Presbyterian Church of Eastern Australia
Sydney, October 10, 1846

Centre: William McIntyre; Left: Colin Stewart, Samuel Martin;
Right: John Tait, Peter Stewart, William Buyers

sought to justify her. This showed she was in the same position as the Established Church, and was also unwilling to be truly independent.[5]

The mission of the PCEA

McIntyre shared with Lang a vision for an evangelical church on Biblical lines. His stance was more theologically precise in the strict Puritan tradition to which he belonged. He was also concerned, as a Presbyterian, for the corporate life of the church. Thus he wrote before the division:

It is not necessary to conceal the conviction, which we entertain in common, we believe, with every true Christian in the colony, that the Presbyterian Church is in a deplorably dead condition. Where shall we find (making allowance for individual exceptions) any signs of *collective* vitality; of the life and energy of the Church *as such?* What is done for the missionary cause, what to overtake the heathenism of many parts of the colony; how many meetings for prayer are there among our ministers and congregations? and amidst all our unprofitableness, what proofs do we give that we bewail our condition, and earnestly seek our Master's presence and blessing?[6]

The coming division was not viewed with dread, for McIntyre considered that there were three distinct means by which a church may be revived and purified: the preaching of the everlasting gospel, the exercise of discipline, and divisions or disruptions. A church could become so corrupt as to be beyond the reach of reformation by the first two means, and even true servants of Christ remaining in such a church would be affected by the stupor and indifference so that their love grew cold and their spiritual sensibilities were blunted. While a church in such a condition might be revived, yet history did not furnish obvious examples. Rather, it seemed that God in his providence would bring his faithful people under a test so as to detach the pure from the impure and to accomplish what more ordinary measures could not.

Our Church is in a state of deplorable spiritual inefficiency. How shall it be revived and invigorated? In the providence of God, a question arising out of the circumstances of the Church of Scotland, has been proposed for our consideration, which bids fare, we venture to hope, to make such a separation in our Church, as a faithful discipline, were its exercise possible, would effect. It is no doubt extremely painful to contemplate the consequence of a new division in our small and already sadly shattered body, but, besides that adherence to duty leaves no alternative, we can discern no means so likely to restore to the presbyterians of this Colony a pure, spiritual and efficient Church. The consequences of the disruption will

5. The response is in the **Sydney Herald** November 21, 1846 also **Voice** December 12, 1846 pp.184-5. McIntyre's comments are in Voice December 1, 1846 pp.181-183 and December 15, 1846 pp.189-190.

6. **Voice,** October 1, 1846, p.151, col. 1

however depend greatly on the spirit of those who take part in it. If those who feel constrained by a sense of their duty to Christ to separate from those whom they must regard as unfaithful to their divine master, take the painful step with humility and brokenness of heart, yet with right hearted decision and hopefulness; if with lowly prostration before God, and unflinching firmness in the maintenance of principle, they combine a resolute determination to prosecute the work of the Lord with an energy that no difficulties can abate and a boldness that no opposition can quell, and a hope that no trials can extinguish, we shall see at no distant day a Presbyterian Church in this land, emulating the spirituality and zeal, and vigor and success of the Free Church of Scotland. Our disruption will prove to the Presbyterian Church in Australia, as real and lasting a blessing as the disruption of 1843 did to the true Presbyterian Church of Scotland. [7]

With such views as these, it should not be thought that the PCEA looked to be a 'holy huddle' in the midst of a needy community. The sectarian ideal was very far from the minds of those who formed the PCEA. Thus, in the *Voice* for November 15, 1846, there. is an article entitled, *The Presbyterian Church of Eastern Australia the True Representative of the Church of Scotland in the Colony*. It asserted that it was the duty of the PCEA to organise and extend a true and living Presbyterian Church in the colony since the original Synod had denied its Presbyterianism by involvement in the sin of the Established Church, and was also characterised by a secular spirit, a concern for outward forms, and a neglect of church discipline and missionary exertion. In Melbourne, Forbes said he had felt for a long time 'like one surrounded by icebergs.'[8] The clear vision is evident-

The Presbyterian Church of Eastern Australia deemed it its duty, from the very outset, to address itself to the entire work of the Presbyterian Church in this Colony - not only to continue to occupy the localities already occupied by its ministers, but to supply its ministrations, throughout the land, to every Presbyterian and to all others who would receive them. A more limited aim would be a departure from its principles. It maintains that it is the duty of the State to make adequate provision for the pure and scriptural dispensation of religious ordinances within its territory, and when the State failed to do this it was itself bound to do it to the utmost of its power.[9]

Support of the ministry
Under the *Church Act* of 1836, stipends and building grants were available to the different major churches, but in 1842, a ceiling of $60,000 had been imposed. As a consequence of this, government aid was going to decline in importance as the number of ministers grew. Ultimately, all such aid would

7. Voice, October 1, 1846, p.151, col. 1
8. Address to Scots Church Congregation, October 25, 1846
9. Voice, October 1, 1847, p.340, col. 1

be abolished, but if the Synod of Australia had held firm to principle it is probable that state-aid, even if withdrawn for a while, would have been restored. However, given the breach, it was the view of McIntyre in New South Wales and Forbes in Melbourne, that aid should be renounced, even for sites. While opposition to state-aid had not been voiced by these men before the division, they were not enthusiasts for it since the government endowed both truth and error, and thus breached its duty to God, while the practical effects in attracting careerists looking for a comfortable living had been detrimental. Forbes expressed his concern in an article in the *Port Phillip Christian Herald* for January 1, 1847. He thought indiscriminate aid had a superficial appearance of fairness, but proceeded on the ground that all religions were equally useful, did not promote truth because it was truth but supported truth and error alike, and did not recognise Christ's kingly claims over the rulers of the earth. He considered that the colony was of such a composition that truth could not be endowed, even if the state recognised it, without practical injustice to those who believed differently and, as in Ireland, the encouragement of prejudice against the gospel. Therefore it was better to let the truth prevail by its own intrinsic energy.

The PCEA Synod early had a request from Tait's congregation at Parramatta that steps be taken to secure a continuation of the government stipend previously enjoyed. The Synod resolved:

That it holds firmly to the doctrine, always held by the Church of Scotland and set forth in its standards, that it is the duty of the civil magistrate to provide for the people under his rule the pure and scriptural dispensation of divine ordinances; and that, when the civil magistrate rightly discharges this duty, the Church not only may but ought to avail itself of the support and assistance which he affords it.

That it regards the scheme of endowment which obtains in the colony, founded as it is on the principle of extending indiscriminate and equal support to truth and error, as involving a grievous violation of the civil magistrate's duty in this matter, and conceives that it was incumbent on the Church particularly when it availed itself of the operation of this scheme to have entered its solemn protest against it.

That entertaining these views, this Synod could not apply to the colonial Government to extend to it the benefit of this scheme, without at the same time protesting against it; and that as in the circumstances in which this Church is now placed such protest would be of little avail if the Synod applied for and continued to receive aid from the Colonial Treasury, this application shall not be made.[10]

Refusing state-aid also had the advantage of making it possible for Presbyterians of moderate voluntary views to find a home in the PCEA.

10. **PCEA Synod Minutes**, November 17, 1846

Central Sustentation Fund

In the *Voice* for May 1, 1846, McIntyre noted a calculation made at the time of the last census (1841) when there were 13,153 Presbyterians, 5,000 being adult males. Of these, 400 were landed proprietors, merchants, bankers etc., 150 were retailers, 950 mechanics and artificers, 2,650 agricultural and farming workers and 850 domestic servants. Allowing for contributions of $6-$10 a year from the property owners/professional people, $2-$4 from the retailers, $2 from the mechanics, $1 from the farming workers and 50c from the servants, a revenue of some $8,600 would be raised, about 50% more than was paid in 1846 in government stipends. In presenting this argument, designed to encourage adherence to principle in the coming conflict, McIntyre noted the amount consumed on alcohol and tobacco. There were 24 public houses in Maitland (East and West)while many a poor man spent more than $2 a year on tobacco; could he not afford but $1 for religious puposes? This is an argument that has a certain familiarity about it even today.

After the PCEA was formed, the Synod resolved to provide ministerial support by a Central Fund. The contributions of all the congregations were gathered into the fund and each half year distributed equally among all the ministers. This method was chosen because it had proved successful in the Free Church of Scotland, and was appropriate for the infant PCEA. The following reasons were adduced:

1. It brings the more wealthy and populous localities to the aid of the poorer and less populous in maintaining and extending the dispensation of Divine ordinances.

2. It is in accordance with the spirit and character of the Presbyterian system as securing the union and co-operation of all the congregations of the Church in prosecuting this common object.

3. While it affords full scope for the exercise of liberality on the part of the Christian people, it guards against the obvious disadvantages attending the dependence of each minister on the contributions of his own congregation.[11]

There are disadvantages in a Central Fund too. It is well known that people in a small congregation give better proportionately than many larger congregations, and this sense of Christian liberality can be lessened by a Central Fund, or only a minimum amount contributed sufficient to obtain an equal dividend but no more. Still, it was appropriate in the early stages of the PCEA, and continued for about 40 years. The first half-yearly distribution (October 1847) was less than $100, but it rose steadily to be $400-$440 per year by the early 1860s, and was higher than the general level of stipend in the Synod of Australia.

11. **PCEA Synod Minutes**, December 15, 1846

The Free Presbyterian Church of Victoria did not adopt a Central Sustentation Fund, but each congregation supported its own minister. The higher percentage of Presbyterians, the greater wealth in the community, and the receipt by some of state aid for stipends, following a controversial Synod decision in November 1854, were relevant.

In taking a position which made the church dependent upon the voluntary givings of the people, the PCEA did not adopt the 'voluntary' theory of church-state relations, nor did it impose any burden that the congregations were not already under.

Under any circumstances, it would be their unquestionable duty to contribute towards Christ's cause as the Lord prospered them; and they are not expected now to do more. [12]

Early PCEA activity

The formation of the PCEA was hardly the grand and popular event that the formation of the Free Church of Scotland had been. While McIntyre supposed that half the Presbyterians of New South Wales were in sympathy, that sympathy was not translated into active support in the absence of additional ministers. At a public meeting in the old Congregational Chapel in Pitt Street on October 22, 1846 at which the position adopted by the PCEA was explained, there was a numerous and respectable attendance,[13] which is a rather vague description, though about 100 people if Lang is to be believed, not all Presbyterians. Of the three ministers who constituted the PCEA, only McIntyre at Maitland had a solid congregation (some 200 people), and he apparently preached 5 times each Lord's Day.[14] Tait had division at Parramatta. While sympathetic, the people there, perhaps 60 communicants, did not enjoy losing the government stipend. Dr Hill, the Parramatta elder, voted with McIntyre's group in 1846, but did not subscribe the Protest with them, though perhaps he did so later. At any rate, Tait's position was not a happy one. The Presbytery of the Synod of Australia resolved in January 1847 to maintain supply as best it could until the building of St Andrew's Church could be completed. Rev James Coutts was duly inducted on April 22, 1849, and the first service in the new church was on November 14, 1849. What with several prominent Tait supporters moving to Sydney about this time, Tait's position was difficult. Colin Stewart's parish at Hartley/ Bowenfels (Vale of Clwyd) was really an itinerating one, as the population was sparse. 'Parson' Stewart's visits were appreciated, and he was bi-lingual. Nevertheless, not being a very effective preacher, he was unable to help the cause all that much.

12. Voice, April 1, 1847, p.246, col. 1
13. Voice, November 2, 1846, p.169ff.
14. B.J.Bridges, Presbyterian Churches in NSW 1823-1865 (PhD Thesis 1985), p.175

The fourth charge was at Jamberoo, south of Wollongong. In 1843 a request was made direct to the Ladies' Colonial Committee of the Free Church of Scotland for a suitable missionary. In 1845, Robert Taylor, an elder and student for the ministry, arrived at Jamberoo. He stayed apart from the Synod of Australia, but he and the congregation were received into the PCEA on October 12, 1846.

PCEA origins in Sydney

Four PCEA charges have been referred to but there was no organised work in Sydney which then had a population of 50,000, including about 6,000 'census' Presbyterians served by four congregations: Lang's Scots Church - large and well-to-do but usually in some ferment; McGarvie's and Fullerton's congregations - neither of which had appeal to evangelical Presbyterians; and the congregation which was ministered to by Thomas Mowbray, who took a neutral stand in the church crisis.

Mowbray's congregation had originated in April 1842. Lang had been suspended on the 7th of that month, and the Synod Moderator (William McIntyre) had been directed to go to Scots Church the following Lord's Day and conduct the service. As expected, McIntyre was denied entry, but the service was conducted in a room in the Sydney Exchange in Macquarie Place whither McIntyre and some of the congregation repaired. Services were continued under the sanction of the Presbytery and moved to the College High School the following year. At the first communion service in mid 1842 conducted by John Tait, it was found that 22 members of Lang's congregation plus their children and some adherents were present. Additions were gained from some who withdrew from McGarvie's and Fullerton's congregations.[15]

Back in 1837 Lang had planned for Tait to supplant McGarvie but, as we have seen, the schism was healed. However, Tait remained interested in a city parish - Parramatta being a small place then with local difficulties as already indicated. However, it was decided to call Thomas Mowbray from Campbellfield (north of Melbourne). Mowbray arrived in January 1845,[16] and was inducted on the 23rd of that month. The old Wesleyan Chapel opposite the Royal Mint was secured and a flourishing congregation was soon gathered. The idea of some that Mowbray supplant either Lang or McGarvie did not work out since Lang retained possession of Scots Church and McGarvie won the disruption struggle.

15. Many details in this paragraph are from E.A.Rennie, **An Outline of the History of St George's Church** (Sydney 1881)p.6
16. Not December 1844 as stated in R.Bardon's **Centenary History of the Presbyterian Church of Queensland**, p.27; Mowbray left Campbellfield on December 26, 1844, L.R. Moore, **A Time to Build Up...A History of Scots Church Campbellfield since 1842** (Melbourne 1982) p.6

Several months before the division of October 1846, two of Mowbray's elders with Free Church convictions withdrew. They were William Buyers and Peter Stewart, the latter a building contractor. [17] When Mowbray took a middle course, these men were joined by others. The opportunity to purchase the old Congregational Chapel in Pitt Street (built 1833) nearly opposite the new building (now Uniting Church) was seized. It was secured for $2,500, with William McIntyre, Dr Menzies of Kiama and William Buyers giving bills for the price and W.E.McIntosh, merchant, providing collateral security. After repairs were completed, it was opened as the Pitt Street Presbyterian Church on December 13, 1846. From January 1847 to February 1848, Colin Stewart gave supply, but was not effective in rallying a good congregation. He returned to Vale of Clwyd at the close of this period and the elders kept up the services, but they were normally attended by less than 50 people. Meanwhile, Mowbray's congregation was in difficulty as the loss of the Free Church element rendered it hardly viable, and Mowbray, who had not had good health in Campbellfield, fell seriously ill. The upshot was that the congregation broke up about the middle of 1847. Some families were lost to the Presbyterian Church at this time. Mowbray went to Brisbane but did not hold a charge. The Pitt Street PCEA became virtually a continuation of Mowbray's original congregation, and thus included a 'neutral' or 'comprehension' element.

Neutral party

The neutral element in the Pitt Street Free Church was satisfied that the PCEA was an independent church without a compromising name. However, they wanted to be muted in their attitude to the Scottish Churches, and desired no special fellowship with any of them. McIntyre resisted this outlook, for if it prevailed the church would become doctrinally unstable and would bear no clear testimony in practice to what it professed in principle. The need to ensure supplies of ministers was also relevant.

In April 1849, George Mackie, newly arrived from Scotland and intended as the minister of Jamberoo-Kiama, was appointed to supply Pitt Street PCEA. The attendance increased and on May 23 it was resolved to proceed to elect

17. Peter Stewart (1792-1882) arrived in Australia in January 1838, having previously been an elder in Hope Street Church, Glasgow. He left Lang's congregation in 1842, joined Mowbray's congregation then transferred to Pitt Street and ultimately to St George's. His daughter, Margaret, was married to William Buyers; another, Caroline, married Duncan McInnes, later PCEA minister at Maclean. - See **Australian Free Presbyterian**, June 1952.

elders and deacons, the following 35 men being recognised as communicants entitled to vote.

Billerwell, John	Maxwell, Alex. C.	McIntyre, Donald
Black, Henry L.	Melville, Andrew	Ogg, William A.
Buyers, William	Mein, John S.	Reynolds, James
Cargo, William	McDonald, John	Ronald, Rowan
Dumble, John	McDonald, Roderick	Rennie, Edward A.
Farnham, Henry	McDonald, Lachlan	Stewart, Peter
Gordon, Samuel D.	McLaren, Peter	Stenhouse, Nichol D.
Hughes, David B.	McGuffin, Richard	Simpson, Robert
Hutchinson, Charles	McKenzie, John	Tulloch, John
Learmouth, Alex.	McPherson, Dugald	Watson, James
Little, John	McIlrick, John	Wilson, James G.
Mitchell, Hugh	McKellar, Duncan	

Previous to this time, Peter Stewart, William Buyers, Henry L.Black and John Little had been the nominal elders who had kept up services. Each of them represented a different section of the church in the United Kingdom. The result of the election was that Peter Stewart, William Buyers, John Little and John McDonald were inducted as elders, and Alex Learmonth, E.A. Rennie, James G.Wilson, Henry L.Black, Peter McLaren and James Reynolds were chosen deacons. This was the first Presbyterian Deacons' Court formed as such in Australia.

Upon the arrival of Rev Alexander Salmon in September 1849, an experienced minister formerly of Barrhead, Scotland, Mackie went to Kiama and Salmon was inducted (October 10, 1849) to Pitt Street. Salmon was an able preacher and the congregation grew rapidly, and extension of the building was necessary. A predominantly 'neutral' element in the congregation proposed the calling of Tait to establish a new congregation. A call was got up and 29 signatures appended. Seven persons were appointed to see Salmon with a view to gaining his concurrence. They were Gilbert Eliot, formerly the Police Magistrate at Parramatta, Duncan Mackellar, Thomas Barker, John Mackay, John Brown and Messrs Hunter and Reynolds. However, the Synod decided one strong congregation should be fostered and rejected the proposal at its meeting in October 1850. Duncan McKellar complained to the Free Church Colonial Committee which, ignoring Salmon, responded by recommending Tait's translation to Sydney. But Tait had long since left for Victoria where he joined the Free Presbyterian Church and was settled at Geelong. The Colonial Committee, as well as James Forbes, fell into the mistake of making judgements based on only one side of the story. Mackellar, though willing to appeal to the Colonial Committee, objected to prayer for the Free Church of Scotland from the pulpit, and was content to sit under the ministries of McGarvie and Fullerton. While there is no reason to believe that McIntyre and Salmon were against receiving into membership Presbyterians of a variety of backgrounds, and indeed, the PCEA acted as if it was the custodian of Presbyterianism in the colony, it is easy to see that there were limits in practice to what could be tolerated if the testimony of the church was to be maintained. The less than pleasant incident outlined ended the power of the comprehension party for the next few years. [18]

Highlander/Lowlander strife - origin of St George's Congregation

The second division in the Pitt Street PCEA arose as a result of differences between Highlander and Lowlander sections. In 1852, there was interest in establishing a High School as there was then not one in the colony. This interest was among the well connected Highland element in the Pitt Street church and was shared by William McIntyre in Maitland. Salmon was not brought into the early proposals, though he was well qualified to establish educational institutions. Some in the congregation had other priorities, and in August 1853 it was resolved to import an iron church with seating for 800 persons. This was duly erected in Macquarie Street in 1855, and the old building was sold earlier that year. The mainly Highland section wanted to buy it as they had become a distinct congregation on February 22, 1854, but were not successful. After several attempts they obtained Macintosh Mackay as minister (inducted May 12, 1856) hoping his prestige would ensure a good congregation. His gifts were unsuited to colonial life and he repeated what had happened in St Andrew's, Carlton (Melbourne). A hugely expensive building (St George's, Castlereagh Street) was opened in 1860, and Mackay resigned in the middle of 1861 leaving a small congregation and a crushing debt. It might be noted that Mackay avoided the use of Gaelic because the congregation was mixed and some Gaels were ashamed to attend Gaelic preaching.

Further congregational development

Aside from St George's, five centres have been mentioned. In 1850 it was possible to provide help to William McIntyre on the Hunter. Late in 1849, Arthur Sherriff arrived with Alex Salmon. Sherriff was a catechist and student for the ministry. He completed his studies for the ministry under McIntyre and was ordained at Sydney for Clarence Town and district on April 3, 1851. Ahalton to the south was included in his charge until the arrival of Alexander McIntyre late in 1853, and Dungog in the north was also served.

In 1845, George Bowman, MLA, erected a church in Westmarket Street, Richmond, and gave his support to the PCEA after it was formed the

18. Sources for the preceding two paragraphs include, E.A.Rennie, op. cit., pp.7-9; **Voice,** October 15, 1850, pp.156-159; **Port Phillip Christian Herald,** December 6, 1850, pp.92-93; B.J.Bridges, op. cit., pp.177-179. From Tait's evident willingness to pastor the proposed second congregation we can see his concern was more for the independence of the church in Australia than for a clear practical testimony against the errors of the Established Church. The pressures at Parramatta must be allowed for, but Tait's attitude to church union in Victoria is consistent with his 1850 position.

following year. It seems that Bowman arranged for various Protestant preachers to take services, although the Synod of Australia man at Windsor either was not invited or refused to preach - the latter is the usual account,[19] but the former may have been true too as Adam does not appear to have had wide support anyway. By 1851, a PCEA man was available and on Wednesday November 12, 1851, after a period of supply, William Lumsdaine was ordained and inducted following a call signed by 51 members and 98 adherents. He did useful work for about 3 years, the charge including Castlereagh, some 15kms to the south. A 1-acre site was given on the corner of Church Lane and Castlereagh Road and a timber church/schoolroom existed. There being no Anglican parish, the Church of England people joined in the services. Some years later the building was destroyed in a flood. It was not rebuilt as the Church of England established a parish, and the Presbyterian element decreased. [20] On April 10, 1855, Mr Bowman, for ten shillings 'of lawful British money', transferred the property at Richmond to four trustees 'for the Congregation or Body of Christians at Richmond aforesaid belonging to the Synod of Eastern Australia.' On February 28, 1856, James Cameron (1826-1905) was inducted as the second minister. He married Mr Bowman's daughter the following year. Both he and the congregation entered the union of 1864.

Additional ministers - 1853

From 1846 to 1851, the number of PCEA ministers had increased from 3 to 8, including one in Brisbane (W.R.McLeod settled August 28, 1851). Tait had gone to Victoria but Mackie, Salmon, Sherriff and Lumsdaine were additions in New South Wales. There was a licentiate, D.M.Sinclair, a godly man and bi-lingual, who had been a pastoralist in New England for some years.[21] However, he went to Melbourne early in 1852. A special effort was made in that year. In May 1852, the Synod began a fund to aid in securing ministers. Salmon was initially appointed Convener, which upset McIntyre. Both seem to have been at fault. Salmon had rather exaggerated views of his abilities and importance as the minister in Sydney, and had sought to lay down the law to others. Appointing him as Convener was no doubt a

19. So James Cameron, **Centenary History of the Presbyterian Church in New South Wales** (Sydney 1905) p.251.
20. The title deed was held by the PCNSW and in 1885 steps were taken to transfer it to that church in terms of the provisions of the **Presbyterian Church Property Management Act, 1881.** However the purported transfer was not properly completed in accordance with the provisions of that Act. In the mid 1960s, the deed was given to the PCEA by the PCNSW. Rates continued to be paid, and in February 1986 a sale was effected to the Penrith Lakes Authority for $20,000, the proceeds being applied towards the new PCEA property at Mt Druitt.
21. In December 1845 Robert Blain stayed at Sinclair's property 'Newstead', describing it as a 'well ordered and happy home' and his experience 'one of the Sabbaths of my life never to be forgotten' - **Voice**, March 15, 1846 p.48

well-meant attempt to satisfy a difficulty. McIntyre saw it differently. He had local experience and good connections, and was probably right in thinking he would be able to carry the cause through successfully. A man of very superior ability, he too had difficulty playing second fiddle to others. The Synod bowed to McIntyre's pressure, and made him Convener instead. McIntyre arranged the scheme with great success and over $2,800 had been promised and $2,000 paid by the end of October 1852. McIntyre was appointed a delegate to assist in choosing the 8 ministers considered necessary, though in each case he was to have the sanction of the Free Church Colonial Committee.

The question of Highlander/Lowlander relations came into these matters. Highlanders regarded Lowlanders as 'city slickers' and Lowlanders thought of Highlanders as 'country bumpkins'. It is true many of the Highland migrants had lived in most depressed conditions in Scotland so that their lack of social graces combined with inability to speak English made them an easy target. As to Highland ministers, one Sydney merchant quoted by Salmon said, 'our money...will just be expended in sending out a lot of grunting and grainning highlandmen who however good they may be will drag us down in the Colony.'[22] The desire for high social status was strong.

Two Gaelic preachers came in 1853 - William Grant and Alexander McIntyre. William Grant (1806-1897), an Aberdeen man, was highly respected by all. After a short period of supply in the Vale of Clwyd district he was settled in 1854 on the south coast based at Terrara on the Shoalhaven River. He had a successful ministry. After initial disgust at the way the Free Church of Scotland abandoned its principles in the union matter, he joined the union of 1864. Alexander McIntyre (1807-1878) was born in Strontian, Argyllshire. He was well and favourably known among the Highland community in Scotland and Canada before he came to Australia. His great interest was evangelism, and his influence among the Highlanders in this country was very considerable. Despite the name, there is no evidence that he was related to William McIntyre. He was appointed to Ahalton where he had a valuable ministry. He went to Victoria in 1858, but often spent the winter in New South Wales, particularly on the Clarence River.

Six further ministers arrived in 1853 and thus it was possible to open up new work.

New England

John Morison of the Synod of Australia was at Armidale for about two years

22. B.J.Bridges, op. cit., p.188 (Source is letter November 8, 1852 by Salmon to Bonar.)

from 1851, and then removed to Walcha to the south. He did not receive a government stipend, had very few attending and was not successful.[23] Perhaps as a related development, Andrew Maxwell of the PCEA came to Armidale shortly after his arrival from Scotland in July 1853. He itinerated in a wide area including Wellingrove, then the centre of a district including the later parishes of Glen Innes and Inverell. Maxwell left for Victoria in May 1856. Archibald Cameron (1815-1905), who had also arrived as a rather raw recruit in November 1853, was settled at Wellingrove-Glen Innes in 1854 with Inverell as one of his stations. He entered the 1864 union, though there were some continuers at Inverell where the McIntyre family had pastoral interests.[24] At Armidale the people obtained Thomas Johnstone from the Synod of Australia and he was inducted April 17, 1857. Both Cameron and Johnstone were to chalk up over 45 years in their respective parishes.

South Coast

Hugh McKail arrived late in 1853 and went to Wollongong for a time where Cunningham Atchison was working under the Synod of Australia. Illawarra/Shoalhaven had been one PCEA charge to begin with, and George Mackie worked it energetically from his base at Kiama. Two additional charges were formed from the original district. George Mackie retained Kiama-Jamberoo, and had help from Charles Ogg in 1855-56 at Gerringong (church 1855), while William Grant, earlier referred to, took the Shoalhaven based at Nowra, some 45kms south of Kiama. McKail was settled at Shellharbour/Terry's Meadows (now Albion Park), between Wollongong and Kiama. Mackie left in 1857 and went to Victoria as did McKail in 1859. John Kinross, a man who would make his mark, was inducted to Kiama-Jamberoo on December 29, 1858. Shellharbour/Albion Park remained vacant for some years until joined to Wollongong upon union in 1865.

Queensland

Queensland originated as part of the colony of New South Wales containing the Moreton Bay penal settlement (1825-42) but did not become a separate colony until 1859. William R. McLeod was ordained at Sydney for Brisbane on August 28, 1851. He pastored the first Presbyterian congregation in Brisbane, which covered north and south of the river. Rev Thomas Mowbray was a member of this congregation and of the first session formed over it in 1856. McLeod's health failed and he left towards the end of 1852. A.W. Sinclair, who had arrived in November 1853, was McLeod's successor. He

---

23. B.J.Bridges, op. cit., p. 162.

24. Byron Plains was a McIntyre property. The PCEA church site at Inverell (allotment 6 section 1) on which a timber church was erected about 1857, was secured by the Inverell PCNSW congregation by the Inverell Free Church of Eastern Australia Land Sale Bill 1878, so that its sale would aid the financing of the impressive brick church built in 1878 on a site granted by the government.

began his ministry early in 1854, and a manse was erected in Ann Street, on the north side of the river, that year. Sinclair demitted in 1856 and for some time supplied Richmond in the absence of James Cameron overseas. In 1858 he went to Victoria. Charles Ogg (c1817-1895) succeeded him at Brisbane. He came in May 1856, was inducted November 7, 1856 and the following year continued with the part of the congregation which began Ann Street Church. The south Brisbane section was recognised as a distinct parish and retained the building in Grey Street which had been opened by Thomas Mowbray on May 25, 1851. An amount of $300 was given to the Ann Street congregation. For some years Grey Street had no settled minister and lost any distinctive character it had upon union in 1863. Ann Street built their church in 1858 and rebuilt it when it was destroyed by fire in 1870. It remains a significant centre of Presbyterian work in Queensland. The Ann Street congregation had applied to the government for a church site and duly received it. Later rises in property values enabled a good income to be derived from the use of the land.

Sydney

The origin of St George's, Castlereagh Street from the division in 1854 in the Pitt Street congregation has been outlined earlier. This was essentially a move by Highlanders. However, there were other moves too. Arthur Paul (1826-1910) was received by the PCEA Synod on November 2, 1853, and appointed to work in Sydney with a view to establishing another congregation. Paul was a native of Greenock and had excellent intellectual gifts. However, he was not a popular preacher and he did not get on very well with people. That was the assessment of educated Scots in Sydney and the assessment was accurate judging by his subsequent career in Victoria. His efforts to establish a second congregation were not successful, and after a year he went to Melbourne where he played a key part in the opposition to union. William Lumsdaine, formerly of Richmond, came to Sydney in 1854 and did missionary work in the southern suburbs in connection with Alex Salmon's congregation. In May 1855 a congregation was instituted which met in a hall called 'Providence Chapel' on the Parramatta Road near the present St Barnabas' Anglican Church. A site on Castlereagh Street South, Redfern was obtained for $1,000 and a large church erected which had a significant debt that was a burden for many years. It was known as Chalmers' Church. Lumsdaine was inducted in September 1856, the same year the church was built, but the pastoral tie was dissolved in 1858 when Lumsdaine intimated his desire to resign with a view to returning to the Church of England, which he duly did. John L.McSkimming arrived near the close of 1859 and was appointed to supply Chalmers' Church and was inducted in 1860. However, though his ministry was appreciated, he resigned the charge on February 3, 1864 on account of a drinking problem. The vacancy was not filled until after the 1864 union.

Bathurst and Hartley/Bowenfels were the earliest parishes west of the Blue Mountains. In 1848, some Presbyterian residents of Carcoar, some 65kms south-west from Bathurst, made enquiries of K.D.Smythe of the Synod of Australia in Bathurst as to the availability of a minister and a teacher. However, most of the people were in favour of the PCEA and resolved in March 1850 to seek assistance accordingly, and rejected McGarvie's proposal to continue to seek the help of the Synod of Australia. However, the state-aided Synod of Australia had funds and, more importantly, had a minister available in the person of James B.Laughton, who had been licensed on February 20, 1850. 'For the sake of peace and the benefit of immediate religious instruction' some or most of those adhering to the PCEA acquiesced in Laughton's settlement and he was ordained on September 20, 1850. Laughton was keenly evangelical, but he did not remain long, and was transferred to Paterson in 1851.

The PCEA supporters included J.T.Waddell, Thomas Kirkpatrick, William Bell and John McCrear of Carcoar; A. and R. McDiarmid and John Loudon of King Plains and Thomas McKell and William L. Jamieson. At a meeting on May 5, 1851 addressed by Colin Stewart, these supporters expressed their appreciation for the bi-monthly visits provided until a PCEA minister could be settled. They disclaimed party spirit or personal animosity to those of other views, recognised the fundamental principle 'to love one another,' but also expressed their determination to maintain what they confessed. No doubt they rejoiced when James Cameron (1826-1905) was inducted on February 22, 1854. He remained just two years before moving to Richmond, and the charge was vacant until James Adam (1830-1911) from the Synod of Australia arrived in March 1859. Known as 'the apostle of the saddle' he proved an excellent organiser. No less than 10 churches and 2 manses are credited to his efforts during his ministry from 1859-1877.[25]

In the early history of Carcoar parish one sees the practical situation in sparsely-settled rural areas with different views on the Scottish question. If the minister was a good preacher and could get on with people, which Synod he came from was of relatively small importance in practice.

25. For early details see **Voice**, April 15, 1850 p.63; June 1, 1850, p.86; June 1, 1851, p.88; and see C.A.White, **Challenge of the Years** (Sydney 1951) p.253 for Adam.

MINISTERS OF THE PRESBYTERIAN CHURCH
OF EASTERN AUSTRALIA, 1863

1 REV. JAMES S. LAING
2 „   WILLIAM BAIN
3 „   WILLIAM RIDLEY, B.A.
4 „   ADAM GORDON
5 „   DR. ROBERT STEEL
6 „   A. CONSTABLE GEIKIE
7 „   S. F. MCKENZIE, M.A.
8 „   JOHN KINROSS. B.A.
9 „   JOHN L. MCSKIMMING

18 REV. ALLAN MCINTYRE,
MODERATOR.

10 REV. COLIN R. GREIG
11 „   JAMES CAMERON, M.A.
12 „   ARCHIBALD CAMERON
13 „   JAMES MCCULLOCH
14 „   COLIN STEWART
15 „   ARTHUR M. SHERRIFF,
                    SYNOD CLERK
16 „   WILLIAM MCINTYRE M.A.
17 „   WILLIAM GRANT. M.A.

McIntyre returns from Scotland - 1854

The extra work made possible by the ministers who arrived in 1853 has now been covered. When McIntyre came back from his trip to Scotland as delegate (he left early in 1853 and returned in November 1854), he brought two further ministers. They were his older brother Allan McIntyre (1798-1870) who had been minister of the Gaelic Free Church at Paisley, and James McCulloch (1823-1873), a probationer who married McIntyre's niece, a Miss McKinnon, who came out with her sisters Mrs W.M.McLardy and Mrs M.M. Campbell, and their families at the same time. These two ministers laboured on the Manning and the Hunter, as described in a later chapter. 26

A church with two wings

Reference has already been made to the tension between Highlander and Lowlander which had come to a head in 1852. While the impression given by Dr Bridges is that McIntyre was the one ruthlessly pursuing power even by carnal means, his thesis labours under the serious disadvantage of not taking account of of such a prime source as *The Voice in the Wilderness*. Rather, he has relied on the correspondence that survives from those opposed to McIntyre. Unfortunately, other than the *Voice*, we have little or nothing of McIntyre's correspondence, so we do not know his private thoughts, and in any case, considerable care is needed in assessing the accuracy of allegations that are made by those in religious conflict.

Bridges rightly recognises that Salmon had wanted people to defer to him, and rather took his position in Sydney as giving him a superior status to others. It is also admitted that he was not of superior gifts though able and successful enough in a pastoral sense. It may also be allowed that McIntyre was a man of vision and ideas who did not like taking second place in matters affecting the development of the church. Perhaps if we say that McIntyre was strictly Reformed while Salmon, also Reformed, was influenced rather more by the wider views of the Evangelical Alliance, we will not be far out. The clash between McIntyre and Salmon was not over the basic principles of the church - Salmon was an ally of McIntyre against union later on, but it was a clash related to different personalities and styles, reflecting also the difference between Highland and Lowland culture and temperament, with a dash of human pride and jealousy mixed in.

Thus, while the Synod of November 1852 arranged for Salmon to take over the *Voice*, McIntyre, whose money supported it, closed it down at the end of 1852, shortly before he left for Britain. Salmon arranged to begin a new publication, *The Australian Witness*. Its first issue came out on April 2,

26. The family details are derived from a letter dated May 14, 1937 from D.A.McIntyre of Inverell (son of Allan) to Gordon Dennes, made available to me by Mr G.A.Neil, Session Clerk of the PCEA Congregation at Mt Druitt.

1853,[27] but it does not seem to have lasted long. It hardly seems likely that Bridges is right to say it was 'more friendly and less consciously superior' in its image than the *Voice*. A good amount of the original material in the *Voice* in 1852 was from Salmon himself on the controversy with the Church of Rome, while in general the *Voice* was not abrasive to other evangelical Christians anyway. On the other hand, Salmon gave his side of the conflicts to the Colonial Committee, and advised them against sending men selected by McIntyre on the ground that the prejudice against McIntyre would rub off on them to their detriment. Consequently, McIntyre received a polite but cool reception in Scotland. However, both Salmon and McIntyre were agreed that the standard of most men sent in 1853 was inadequate. Both wanted men of ability, but found the inexperienced and the second rate were all too commonly sent. Locally-trained men would be preferable in McIntyre's view.

While McIntyre at this time had the support of younger men like Sherriff and Mackie, and remained the leader of the PCEA for some years, the legacy was not helpful in handling the union controversy later.

The fading of a dream

In the early years McIntyre had had great hopes that the PCEA would become *the* Presbyterian Church in the colony, and exercise a powerful influence for good. For a variety of reasons, not least the lack of ministers and the lack of ability in some who were sent, this was not to be. The Synod of Australia had financial advantages through state-aid, but an even more severe problem in the matter of ministers. The PCEA was better organised and far more spiritually virile than the Synod of Australia or Lang's Synod, but it did not achieve the dominance that the Free Church section did in Victoria.

In a later chapter the subject of union debates which began in 1854 will be discussed. A proposal to co-operate with the Synod of Australia in the establishment of a Presbyterian College within the University was an issue in 1857. It was defeated, but in any event, such a College was an idea whose time was not yet if we may judge from the fact that St Andrew's College was not incorporated until 1873 - though it was agreed upon by the united church in 1866.

Extension work 1860-64

Most ministers from 1857 onwards were Lowlanders and were generally in

27. B.J.Bridges, op. cit., p.190. Copies of the magazine do not appear to have survived.

favour of union. Only from 1860 were the net additions sufficient to enable significant efforts in further areas. Work at Newcastle began in 1860, as described in the separate chapter devoted to congregations on the Hunter and to the north.

South Coast

South of Sydney near the Victorian border provided some openings. Colin Greig went to Twofold Bay (Eden-Bega-Pambula). He had been received by the Synod on November 8, 1860. He visited over a wide area until transferred to Bombala in May 1864. Alex Boddie replaced him at Eden and Bega in September 1864, and a brick church was opened at Eden in September 1866, the first built after the union. The congregation joined the union in 1864. Boddie demitted in 1867 on account of intemperance. Bega's first church was not opened until 1870.

Archibald Geike came to Bombala about November 1861, but transferred to Bowenfels in 1863. Colin Greig commenced his ministry at Bombala in May 1864. The usual 2 acre site was obtained from the government in 1865 (allotments 6-9, section 11), and St Andrew's Church was opened on February 6, 1870 by Greig. [28]

At Braidwood, services had been maintained by the Synod of Australia from an early date. Christopher Eipper was in the district in 1845-46, but details are sketchy. A.S.Pennycook came in the early part of 1854 as chaplain to the southern goldfields with 20,000 people in his parish. At Braidwood he preached in the Court House. He was a chronic drunkard, and was sometimes intoxicated when conducting weddings, yet the Synod of Australia did nothing. A modest church was erected in 1861 by all Presbyterians on an allotment granted for that purpose under the impression that the people would be able to have the minister of their choice. No sooner was the building completed than the Synod of Australia claimed it and asserted its exclusive right to deal with it. If this was not enough, a pastor was not provided. Pennycook was suspended in 1862, but the people seem to have had enough. They sought recognition by the PCEA and appear as a congregation for the first time in the Synod minutes of November 1863. The congregation joined the union and obtained John Johnstone in December 1865 but he remained only 18 months.[29]

28. As reported in **The Testimony**, 1870. The church was removed to the other (and more Protestant) side of the river in 1911 - vide Rev J.A.Davies, Bombala, June 20,1978.
29. D.W.A.Baker, **Days of Wrath** (Melbourne 1985) p.450 refers to the early period.

Sydney

In Sydney, the Pitt Street Free Church moved to their new iron building in Macquarie Street on a site next to Parliament House (now the Parliamentary Bowling Green) in 1855. Later, about 1871, it was called St Stephen's, as the Westminster Parliament had met in St Stephen's Chapel from 1543-1834.[30] Salmon was opposed to the inclusive union that had taken place in Victoria in 1859 but his congregation was generally in favour. He left in February 1860 and went to England where he died in 1864. Dr Robert Steel was the next minister. A man of capacity and leadership, he arrived in June 1862. He played a leading role in bringing about the inclusive Presbyterian union of 1864/65. He died still on active service in 1893.

The Presbyterian cause in Newtown originated in 1862 with W.S.Donald giving supply 1864-65. The minister of Fraserborough Free Church, Donald had taken extended leave to attend to some family matters in New South Wales. He was not inducted, was in sympathy with the 'continuers' and supplied at Clarence Town after the union for the PCEA. A brick church was opened at Newtown in August 1865. It was demolished and rebuilt in 1885.

Finally, one could mention Penrith, not that it was reckoned part of Sydney in 1860 though it is today a prominent municipality. As early as April 1850, the Penrith Presbyterians had resolved to identify with the PCEA as the most scriptural of the churches and the one most likely to edify their souls. The minister at Richmond gave services until 1860 when a new charge based on Penrith was established. A licentiate, J.S.Laing, gave supply from 1860. He was ordained in 1862. His charge included St Mary's. He left in the early part of 1863 and did extension work on the Lower Hunter in the Minmi and Wallsend district. Penrith was vacant at the time of union.

---

30. In 1873 St Stephen's Macquarie Street was resumed for the proposed new Parliament House and the last service was held in it early in 1875. It was then used as the lending branch of the Public Library. It was dismantled in 1899 and the 199 tonnes of components were re-erected as a dining hall at the Rosewood Asylum, Lidcombe. This was demolished in 1958. I am indebted to notes by Dr Miles Lewis of the Department of Architecture at the University of Melbourne for some of these details.

The congregation merged with the former United Presbyterian congregation in Phillip St (on the east side between Hunter and King), added galleries and a steeple and continued the St Stephen's name. In 1926 this site was also resumed so as to extend Martin Place through to Macquarie Street. The last service was held September 9, 1931. The current St Stephen's (now a Uniting Church) was opened in 1935 opposite Parliament House.

THE SYNOD OF AUSTRALIA (NSW) 1846-1865

The Synod of Australia's ministerial strength rose from 13 inducted ministers in New South Wales (excluding what later became Victoria) following the Disruption in 1846 to 23 in 1865 when union took place. Only 6 of the 13 ministers had been ordained in Scotland by the Established Church, and there was a certain tension among them about relations with that Church. The May 1847 Established Church Assembly resolved:

That the Assembly are much gratified to learn that the Synod of Australia have, by a large majority, resolved to maintain their connection with the Established Church, and the Assembly hereby cordially renew their relation with that Synod, and instruct the Colonial Committee to enter into a friendly correspondence with the Synod of Australia, and to offer such friendly advice as is in their power; and the Assembly recommend to probationers of the Church to take advantage of the important field of labour in Australia.

The majority was not 'large' but, as has already been recorded, the members had three choices and the final decision was carried by only one vote. The majority of members had actually voted for other choices. This unusual method of taking the vote was a matter of politics, as most of the neutral party did not want to support the exclusive connection with the Established Church but were not prepared to break if it meant the hazard of stipends. Of course one can always argue that in this they were acting responsibly: why deprive a people of a ministry by a withdrawal which forfeited state support in sparsely settled areas where self-support seemed impossible? While it would be folly to suppose all wisdom and goodness was on the PCEA side, it must be said that the Synod of Australia was rather lifeless and was looked upon by many as a body more interested in security than spreading the Gospel.

At McGarvie's request the Colonial Committee gave assurance that jurisdiction was not claimed by the Established Church. However, as the Synod remained in legal and moral connection with the Established Church, the Synod did not have true independence. Financial assistance from Scotland for buildings required the title deeds to attach the property inalienably to the Church of Scotland,[31] and when union came the consent of that Church was required and obtained.

The Established Church was not of great help with manpower. She had many vacancies as a result of the Disruption of 1843, and New South Wales was low on the list of priorities. Some financial help was given in 1848 to enable completion of the Parramatta building and Rev James Coutts arrived in

31. B.J.Bridges, op. cit., p.151 citing **Home & Foreign Missionary Record**, August 1857, p.215.

April 1849 as its pastor. Only with the dramatic increase of population on account of the discovery of gold in 1851 was there real assistance - this response being similar to that by the Free Church to the PCEA. Late in 1852 Rev William Purves was sent as a deputy to Scotland and was successful in obtaining a number of recruits so enabling a chaplain to be placed on each of the southern and western goldfields as well as a settlement at Paddington, a locality pioneered by McGarvie about 1847. [32]

The role of McGarvie

John McGarvie regained the leadership of the Synod following the Disruption of 1846. He had by this time greater confidence in the pulpit. His congregation numbered some 117 adults and 89 children in November 1846. In 1842 he had published a volume of sermons from which it appears that he was broadly Protestant rather than strictly Calvinistic. His sermons are pleasant compositions but are shallow rather than solid, and show the author lacked theological capacity. Exactness of theological expression is lacking, while his doctrine of faith is defective. While admitting man cannot originate saving faith he can, says McGarvie, do something to prepare himself for grace and 'God will assist man's humble efforts to prepare himself for grace.'[33]To the same effect is a statement noted by Dr Barrett: 'Whether faith is first, and grace succeeds, or whether grace prepares the heart for faith, the same consequence follows.'[34] His statements emphasising the free offer of salvation to whosoever will probably were not meant in the sense Calvinists accept, but do not of themselves reflect inconsistency with the doctrine of predestination as accepted by Calvinists.

There were many reasons accounting for McGarvie's influence on the Synod until his death in 1853.

McGarvie was deferred to because he was the longest serving minister,

---

32. In mid 1855 Alex Salmon asserted minimal attendances at Windsor, Richmond, Singleton, Muswellbrook, Pitt Town and Armidale - sometimes only the minister and his family. Salmon's claims appear to be correct. Cf. B.J.Bridges, op. cit., p. 162.

33. John McGarvie, **Sermons Preached in St Andrew's Church** (Sydney 1842) p.311. My copy of this book is inscribed by McGarvie and at one time was owned by James McCulloch. William McIntyre reviewed McGarvie's book in **Voice in the Wilderness**, August 1846 pp. 125-127, and concluded: 'Surely the author of these sermons should not occupy - he should not consent, and, though he consented, he should not be permitted to occupy, one of the pulpits of a body holding the standards of the Church of Scotland.'

34. ibid., p.271 cited also by John Barrett, **That Better Country - The Religious Aspect of Life in Eastern Australia 1835-1850** (Melbourne 1966) p.195. Concerning 'preparationism' see Paul Helm's article on Westminster Confession of Faith IX:3 'Or to Prepare Himself thereto' in **Banner of Truth Magazine**, April 1978, pp. 20-22. On the free offer, Barrett is inadequate: the free offer of the Gospel is an essential aspect of Calvinism though it may be held by those who are not Calvinists.

occupied the denomination's most important pulpit, had long dealt with the government on behalf of the Presbyterian body and represented it on public committees, provided the major link with the church at home through his friendship with Principal Macfarlan, and his role as Sydney agent for country ministers and the denominational schools. [35]

McGarvie was an organiser who continued to work behind the scenes even when he did not hold official positions. A bachelor, he was somewhat retiring but did engage in social work visiting the sick in his capacity as secretary of the Sydney Dispensary from 1836 to 1853. There was much truth in the observation made in 1862:

There is this difference between Dr Lang and Dr McGarvie; the former preaches more of the Gospel than he practises, and the latter practised more of the Gospel than he preached. [36]

McGarvie was adept at survival skills. He would always do what he could to smooth over the problems of any minister who got into difficulties so creating those bonds of affection and debts of gratitude which were a source of strength for himself in Church courts. [37]

This can be seen in the case of William Purves who was in strife in his parish prior to the Disruption. McGarvie exerted himself on Purves' behalf, received Purves' support in the crucial Synod of October 1846, and duly facilitated Purves' transfer from Port Macquarie to Maitland in 1849.

Extension work

Extension work of the Synod of Australia was patchy and generally due to financial or property considerations. Thus, in 1849 Purves was settled at East Maitland, a field already occupied by the PCEA, due to the availability of property income and not because of a significant following. Alexander Berry, the 'laird' of Shoalhaven and a close personal friend of McGarvie, facilitated the stationing of a Synod of Australia minister on his estate in the early 1850s despite the poor past record of the man in question (Garven) and the bulk of the people being supporters of the PCEA. At Paterson, a knot of Gaelic speakers stayed with the Synod of Australia, probably because of their connections with Andrew Lang's estate, but their minister (Ross) was unacceptable, and they never did succeed in obtaining a bilingual preacher thereafter. Additional centres at Braidwood and Paddington were established and state support was no hindrance in this.

---

35. B.J.Bridges, 'The Reverend John McGarvie' in Church Heritage Vol. 5:1 (1987)p.10.
36. The Presbyterian Magazine, June 1862p.33.
37. B.J.Bridges, Rev John McGarvie: A Scottish Moderate in the Presbyterian Church in New South Wales 1826-1853 (MTh Thesis, Sydney 1987) pp. 271-272.

State aid reduction

In 1842 a ceiling of $60,000 per year had been placed on the amount allocated for public worship, and the amount to each of the four denominations was on the basis of their census numbers in 1841 - in the case of Presbyterians this was 10.3%. As the churches expanded there would be less aid per capita. The Synod of Australia decided to continue state stipends to parishes existing before 1842, but provided assistance from its own extension fund for new parishes. This meant that by the early 1860s one in three of the Synod's ministers was voluntarily supported. This position came about after considerable effort to ensure that settlements of ministers did not proceed without very explicit commitment by the parish first. In 1860 the aimed at stipend was $400 a year of which half had to be available at the time of settlement. While the Government provided some extra amounts in the mid 1850s to meet special circumstances following the population influx on account of the gold discoveries, by the end of the decade it was clear that state aid would soon be withdrawn. This event occurred in 1862, though the rights of existing recipients were preserved.[38]

Ministers

Ten years after the 1846 Disruption the number of serving ministers had increased from 13 to 22, and when union took place in 1865 there were still only 23. The tables provided as an appendix to this chapter show that until 1858 virtually all recruits were from the Church of Scotland. This church lacked the missionary zeal and the man power to provide adequate numbers of men, while the number ordained after the Disruption in Scotland is generally indicative of the kind of men they were. There was something of a revival of orthodoxy in the Established Church after the events of 1843, but too many were attracted simply by the prospects of a good career. When union took place in 1865, something like 40% of the corps of ministers in the PCNSW at that time were Scots who had committed themselves to the Established Church after 1843 and there were few Irishmen. When union took place in Victoria in 1859 the corresponding percentage was about 10% and there were many Irishmen (24%) with their generally warmer evangelicalism. These differences continued to influence the churches into the 20th century.

---

38. William McIntyre wrote in 1851: 'It is extremely probable, I think -indeed, certain - that the State support now given to religious bodies in the colony will soon be wholly withdrawn; and I am satisfied that the Erastian Synod would not survive the withdrawal of it many years.' - Home & Foreign Record of the Free Church of Scotland, Jan 1852, p.202. Excluding what is now Victoria, the Presbyterian proportion of the population of New South Wales fluctuated slightly around the 10% level 1841-1861.

We have earlier noted Lang's efforts to organise a purely voluntary church which rejected a Church-State connection.[39] Upon his return from Britain in March 1850 he formally constituted what the minutes term 'The Australian Presbyterian Church' but what is commonly known from the name of its deliberative assembly as the 'Synod of New South Wales' - the second of this name. This Synod was extremely loose in its approach: it was enough if an applicant for ministerial status was evangelical in sentiment. By some it has been characterised as an attempt to establish a comprehensive Protestant body on the principles of the Evangelical Alliance which had been organised in the United Kingdom in 1846. While there may be some truth in this description one can also see it as an attempt by Lang to maintain a useful power base and to further his own ego. With him on his return in 1850 were about

twenty young men who were to be educated for the ministry in the Australian College, which he intended to re-open. Some of these forsook him soon after they landed; and for the benefit of the rest the Australian College was resuscitated, and professors at once appointed. Funds, however, were not forthcoming for the support of the undertaking; and it soon became evident that, however desirable it was that the young men should devote some years to preparatory studies, they and their teachers must immediately be placed in circumstances to procure bread for themselves. This was done, so far as it could be done, by the rapid succession of ordinations and settlements to which I have adverted. Such a procedure is deplorable in every point of view. In several localities it has thrown considerable obstacles in the way of our prospective operations...Its history I expect will be, that most of its ministers, deserted by the people on whom they are dependent for support, will betake themselves to secular occupations, and that the very few who are in any degree qualified for the duties of the ministry will seek admission into other bodies.[40]

A glance at the list in the appendix to this chapter will indicate the accuracy of McIntyre's analysis, and will also suggest that Lang's Synod was a most unusual one. Certainly its formal basis included the Westminster Confession and Catechisms 'with the exception of whatever in the said Confession and Catechisms warrants, or appear to warrant, the interference of the Civil Magistrate in the affairs of the Church of Christ,' and naturally it 'solemnly repudiated' support of the ordinances of religion from the public purse. But in fact the Synod was not Presbyterian in any real degree.

---

39. See page 56.
40. Letter of William McIntyre dated June 16, 1851 in **Home & Foreign Record of the Free Church of Scotland**, January 1852, p. 202. A list of those who came out with Lang is in James Cameron, **Centenary History of the Presbyterian Church in New South Wales**, (Sydney 1905) p. 415.

Lang himself was a deposed minister and his recruits were as mixed a bag as one could imagine. In practice standards were lax. A man who rejected the baptism of the infant children of believers was acceptable;[41] a man who rejected the authority of church courts and viewed them in the Congregational sense as places of fellowship only, could be a member;[42] persons planning to serve Lutheran congregations could be ordained by the Synod using Lutheran Confessions,[43] and still be regarded as members of the Synod while so serving; despite the rejection of state support, grants of land were accepted from the Government and at least one minister received a state stipend.[44] Such laxity and disorder, coupled with inadequate training in most cases, made relations with the Synod of Australia and the PCEA virtually impossible. Both the other churches ignored Lang's Synod. McGarvie of the Synod of Australia tried to poach the respectable men in Lang's Synod while Lang was overseas in 1852, and did secure two recruits (Carter and McGibbon). The PCEA men, especially the McIntyre group, had no time for Lang's Synod. While Lang had a policy of keeping out of areas the other Synods had occupied this was more a matter of practical politics than altruism. The success or otherwise of his Synod depended on being able to

41. **Minutes of the Synod of NSW** (Mitchell Library) pp.66-68 (April 2, 1851). Lang personally proposed the admission of Mr Stewart of the United Evangelical Church in Brisbane and received general support. For unrelated reasons Stewart did not in fact become a member.
42. ibid., p. 196 (March 25, 1857). Alexander Black was the man in question but his views were not unique. Gottfried Wagner was out of fellowship from 1852-55 because he had expressed positive objections to the Presbyterian view of church government and (and this seems the point really objected to) had moved from his charge at Tumut without consulting the Synod (p.117). Note also that a number of congregations did not accept the authority of the Synod of which their minister was a member, nor did most congregations have representation by elders.
43. ibid., p. 181 (November 4, 1856) recording the ordination of J.P.Nicquet and J.W.Gehricke at Scots Church, Sydney. Lang considered the Lutheran questions and Confession to be 'the same in substance with those of the British Presbyterians' p.180. A good few Lutherans came to scruple the lawfulness of these ordinations. Note also the minutes for February 3, 1860 (pp. 251-252) where the Synod is regarded as the Mother Church of the German Lutheran Church of Victoria. J.G.Hausmann was present and is described (p. 245) as 'corresponding member from the German Lutheran Church.' For history see, **The United Evangelical Lutheran Church in Australia** (Adelaide 1985 reprint) p.80ff and photographs of Goethe, Hausmann and Nicquet p.342. 'Old Lutherans' were critical of Goethe while Lang considered such little better than Puseyite (ie. sacramentarian).
44. ibid., p. 116 (April 8, 1852. Goethe asked whether it was necessary to renounce state support altogether. The founding declaration was read but upon Goethe indicating he did not think the voluntary system was the only just plan he was assured that the Synod would not object to his consistency. Perhaps unknown to the Synod, Goethe took a state stipend in Victoria. The acceptance of sites seems also to have been practised by the PCEA as early as 1856. What became St George's PCEA applied for a site and received one in Harrington Street which was later sold as the congregation purchased the site in Castlereagh Street.

supply a product in short supply, but if there was a choice his ministers were generally rejected in favour of more able men without connection with the disreputable Doctor. Distracted by Lang's political ventures, fights to have his deposition recalled, and family misfortunes, the Synod of New South Wales had a tenuous existence and would have collapsed very soon if union had not occurred in 1864. Even then, it was only the political influence of Lang which reconciled the other Synods to including him in the union, such was the legacy of hostility to him.

ORDAINED PRESBYTERIAN MINISTERS IN AUSTRALIA 1788-1846 EXCLUDING THOSE WHOSE SERVICE EXTENDED BEYOND 1846

†	Name	Ordination	Details of service
1	Archibald McArthur	US-1822	Scots Hobart 1823-35; to UK 1836.
2	T.N.Thomson, MA	CS-1831	Hunter Nov 1831 - Jan 1832; Bathurst 1832 - Dec 1834; forced resignation; to UK 1835; died 1869 aged 70.
3	John Cleland, MA	CS-1831	Ebenezer 1831-39 & died of alcoholism.
4	J.H.Garven, MA	OS-1831	Sydney (probation) 1834-35; Maitland mid 1835 & deposed Jan 1838 (drink). (Readmitted & reordained by S of A '53.)
5	James Allan	CS-1837	Parramatta Aug 1837-1842; joined C of E.
6	John Gregor, MA	CS-1837	Supply 1837-38; Maitland 1838-41; joined C of E.
7	Geo Anderson, MA	CS-1828	SNSW; applied to C of E 1838 & rejected; adhered to Presbytery Dec 1838; Upper Hunter (Scone) teaching & supply 1837-42; left colony 1843.
8	M.Colquhoun	SNSW	SNSW; Brisbane Water (Gosford) 1837-40; deposed due forged credentials; some teaching and supply. Died in 1861.
9	K.W.E.Schmidt	Lutheran	Aboriginal Mission Moreton Bay (Nundah) 1838-45; in Sydney 1846; to UK 1846.
10	William Comrie	SA-1840	Dungog 11/1840-1842/43; to NZ; d.1884.
11	Alex McKenzie	CS	West Tamar (Tas) 11/1842-12/1845; to Scotland 1846 & joined Free Church.

ORDAINED MINISTERS CONNECTED WITH THE SYNOD OF AUSTRALIA IN CONNECTION WITH THE ESTABLISHED CHURCH OF SCOTLAND

From Disruption, October 10, 1846 to Union, September 8, 1865

[Excluding Queensland, for which see page 162.]

†	Name	Ordination	Details of service
1	J.McGarvie, MA DD	CS- 1826	St Andrew's Scots, Sydney 1832-53.
2	K.D.Smythe	CS- 1834	Bathurst 1834-54; to Scotland, died 1864
3	I. Hetherington	CS- 1837	Singleton 1837-47; Scots,Melbourne
4	G.MacFie, MA	CS- 1828	Ebenezer 1842-67; died 1869
5	C.Atchison	OS- 1833*	Parramatta 1838-41; Wollongong 1841-64 St Peter's, Nth Sydney 1864-69.
6	R.Blain	SNSW- 1837*	Maitland 1837-41; Hinton 1841-60.

7	J. Fullerton	Ire- 1836*	Windsor 1837-38; Pitt Street 1838-86.
8	H.R.Gilchrist	Ire- 1837*	Campbelltown 1837-52; died 1852.
9	Robert Stewart	SNSW- 1838	Wiseman's Ferry 1838-41; Balmain 1841-42; Newcastle 1843-47 & retd. supply at Paddington & Alexandria 1847-66. Gaol chaplain 1847-72. Died 1872 aged 86.
10	Matthew Adam	SNSW- 1839	Windsor 1839-63; died 1863.
11	C. Eipper	UK-1837	Moreton Bay 1838-43; Braidwood 1845-46; Paterson 1848-50; became teacher.
12	William Ross MA	CS- 1838 G	Paterson 1838-47; Goulburn 1847-69.
13	William Purves	SA- 1840	Port Macquarie 1840-49; Maitland 1849-1869; left for Scotland 1870.
14	J.S.White	SA- 1847	Singleton 1847-1902.
15	William McKee	SA- 1849*	Port Macquarie 1849-53; Campbelltown 1853-67 suspended; died 1869.
16	James Coutts MA	CS- 1848	Parramatta 1849-1861; St Andrew's, Newcastle 1861-84.
17	J.B.Laughton BA	SA- 1850	Carcoar 1850-51; Paterson 1851-54; Bathurst 1854-65; Parramatta 1865-75; Tutor 1875-77; Orange 1877-82.
18	John Morison	SA- 1852	Armidale/Walcha district 1851-62
19	J.H.Garven	SA- 1853	Shoalhaven 1853-61; removed; died 1882.
20	J.T.Carter	SNSW-1850	Manning 1850-58 (to SA 1853)
21	Edward Holland	Cong-1841	Port Macquarie 1854-69; Campbelltown 1869-75; Grenfell 1875-77; Dubbo '77-86.
22	Robt Boag BA	CS- 1851	Sydney 1853-54 to Synod of NSW
23	Peter Gordon	USA- 1829	Braidwood district 1853-54; to USA.
24	William Nicol	SA- 1854	Western goldfields 1853-54;suspended '54.
25	John Dougall	CS- 1853	St Andrew's Scots, Sydney 1854-69; East Maitland 1869-71; died 1871.
26	John McGibbon	SA- 1854	Woolloomooloo 1854-82; died 1882.
27	James Nimmo	CS- 1853	St Andrew's Newcastle 1854-61; to Canada.
28	Alex S. Pennycook	SA- 1854	Braidwood 1854-62 & suspended (intemp)
29	James Milne MA	CS- 1832	Paddington 1854-74; died 1885 aged 86.
30	Alex McEwen	CS- 1853	Western Goldfields 1854-58; Mudgee 1858-60; Hinton 1860-64; Mudgee 1864-83.
31	Thomas Stirton	CS- 1854	Petersham supply 1854-55; Paterson 1855-73; Inverell/Moree 1873-98. Died 1906.
32	Duncan Ross MA	CS- 1856	Muswellbrook 1857-73; Nth Sydney 1873-78; Walcha 1878-81. Died 1901.
33	Thomas Johnstone MA	CS- 1856	Armidale 1857-1903; died 1909 aged 80.
34	James Adam MA	CS- 1858	Carcoar 1859-77; Penrith 1877-81; Tutor 1881-84; Carcoar 1884-91; Blayney 1895-1899; died 1911 aged 81.
35	Robert Hogg MA	PCV- 1858*	ex PCV; supply Bathurst 1861.
36	Thomas Craig	Ire- 1840*	ex PCV; Parramatta 1861-65; Tamworth 1865-67; Wagga Wagga 1867-70; Penrith/Springwood 1870-71; to Qld (Ipswich).
37	William Baker	Cong-1858	Yass 1862-65; Cooma 1865-72; Twofold Bay 1872-84; died 1905 aged 70.
38	David Moore BA	Ire-c1847*	ex PCV; Windsor 1863-69; Ebenezer 1869-77; Tutor 1877-81; Campbelltown 1881-97.
39	William Mitchell MA	CS- 1843	Shoalhaven 1863-64; Wollongong 1864-66
40	John Reid	US- 1829	ex Synod of NSW 1863; Mariners' Church

Note: The 23 serving ministers as at union are shown in bold type.
An asterisk indicates a minister with an Irish Presbyterian background.
The letter 'G' refers to a preacher able to minister in Gaelic.

ORDAINED MINISTERS CONNECTED WITH THE PRESBYTERIAN CHURCH OF EASTERN AUSTRALIA

From October 10, 1846 to the exit of the majority, November 15, 1864

†	Name	Ordination	Details of service
1 +	William McIntyre MA	CS- 1837 G	Assistant at Scots, Sydney 1837-40; Maitland 1840-62; St George's, Sydney 1862-70; died 1870.
2	John Tait	CS- 1837	Wollongong 1837-41; Parramatta 1841-51; to FPCV Geelong 1851. Died 1860.
3	Colin Stewart MA	CS- 1838 G	Bowenfels 1839-57; school at Bowenfels 1857-60 and preaching 1860-70 without charge; retired to Sydney 1872,died '86.
4	George Mackie	FC- 1848	Kiama 1849-57; to Victoria 1857.
5	Alex Salmon	CS- 1836	Pitt Street, Sydney 1849-60; to UK.
6	A.M.Sherriff	SEA- 1851	Clarence Town/Dungog 1851-64 & died.
7	W.R.McLeod	SEA- 1851	Sth Brisbane 1851-52; died in Scotland about 1855.
8	William Lumsdaine	SEA- 1851	Richmond/Castlereagh 1851-54; Sydney 1854-58;to C of E 1858; died 1902.
9	William Grant, MA	CS- 1836 G	Vale of Clwyd 1853-54; Shoalhaven 1854-91; died 1897 aged 93.
10	Andrew Maxwell	FC- 1852	Armidale 1853-56; to FPCV St George's Kilmore 1856-65 and died.
11	Alex McIntyre	Can- 1847 G	Ahalton 1853-58; to FPCV Geelong Gaelic (Myers St) oversight 1858-61 & various including Grafton 1865-66 until death at Geelong 1878.
12	Arthur Paul	FC- 1853	Supply at Sydney 1853-54; to FPCV 1854; Richmond (Bridge Road) 1854-55; St Kilda 1855-1910; died in 1910.
13	Hugh McKail	FC- 1853	Wollongong 1854-55; Shellharbour/ Terry's Meadows 1855-60; to PCV and died 1900.
14	Archibald Cameron	FC- 1853	Wellingrove/Glen Innes 1853-1905.
15	James Cameron MA	FC- 1853	Carcoar 1854-56; Richmond 1856-1905.
16	A.W.Sinclair	FC- 1853	Sth Brisbane 1854-56; supply Richmond 1856-58; to FPCV Bellarine 1858-64; to NZ then NSW Oct 1866; Windsor (supply) 1866-67; Bowenfels 1867-72; to PCV Golden Square, Bendigo 1874-76; d.1889.
17 +	Allan McIntyre	FC- 1846 G	Manning River 1854-1862; Clarence River 1862-65; Manning River 1865-70 & died.
18 +	James McCulloch	SEA- 1855	Singleton 1855-61; Ahalton/Raymond Tce 1861-1873 & died.
19	Charles Ogg	SEA- 1855	Gerringong 1855-56; Sth Brisbane 1856-57 then Ann Street 1857-95 (to PCQ 1863) and died.
20	M. Mackay MA,DD	CS- 1826 G	Ex FPCV (St Andrew's, Carlton); St George's, Sydney 1856-61; to Scotland; Tarbert FC 1862-68; d. 1873 aged 79.
21 +	S.F.Mackenzie MA	SEA- 1857 G	Bowenfels 1857-63; West Maitland 1863-66; (to PCNSW 1865) Ashfield 1867-69; Goulburn 1869-75; Braidwood 1875-94.
22	John Kinross	SEA- 1858	Kiama/Jamberoo 1858-75; Principal of St Andrew's College 1875-1901; Professor 1901-08 and died aged 75.

112

23 +J.L.McSkimming	SEA- 1859	Chalmers' Redfern 1859-64 & resd; Singleton 5/1866-8/67 & resd; deposed 11/67; teacher on Macleay 1873-83. Died in 1886 aged 60.
24 William Bain	SEA- 1861	Newcastle (Hunter Street)1861-95.
25 +Colin R.Greig	SEA- 1861	Twofold Bay 1861-64; Bombala 1864-72; to PCNSW Dubbo 1872-75; Hill End 1876-81; Walcha 1881-86. Died 1913.
26 J.S.Laing	SEA- 1862	Penrith/St Mary's 1860-63; Wallsend/Minmi 1863-64; Aberdeen/Scone 1865-66; Manning River 1866-74; Muswellbrook 1874-1905; died 1905.
27 Adam Gordon	FC- 1856 G	Arrived late 1860; without charge on Hunter River; inducted Singleton 1864; to Taralga 1866-71, and died 1871.
28 A.C.Geikie	Cong-1845	Ex Canada; Bombala 1861-63; Bowenfels 1863-66; Bathurst 1866-95. Died 1898.
29 W. Ridley, BA	SNSW- 1850	Ex SNSW; journalism & supply in Sydney area 1861-78; tutor 1875-78. Died in 1878 aged 59.
30 Robert Steel MA,PhD	FC- 1852	Macquarie Street, Sydney 1862-93.
31 William Dron	FC- 1851	Ex PCV; missionary Illawarra 1864; Manning River 12/64- 8/65; Tumut 1866; To Ireland; joined C of E.
32 +W.S.Donald MA	FC- 1844	Supply at Dubbo 1863; Newtown 1864-1865; Clarence Town 1868-90;died 1890.
33 H.S.Seaborn	Cong-1834	Ex PCV; supply at Forbes,Liverpool, Braidwood; resigned from General Synod PCNSW 1865; to C of E; died in 1889.
34 A.C.Smith	FC-	Gladstone Q 1863; to PCQ 1863.
35 A.C.Boddie	SEA-1864	Supply Chalmers' Redfern 1864; Twofold Bay 1864-67; deposed for intemperance.
36 John Thom MA	FC- 1856	Ex NZ; admitted SEA Nov 2, 1864; at Dubbo & Wellington to 1865; Coroki (Richmond/Brunswick/Tweed rivers) 1865-9/1869 and died (drowned).

NB: The 22 serving ministers as at union are shown in bold type. Not all were inducted. The seven men marked + did not join the 1864 union.

ORDAINED MINISTERS CONNECTED WITH LANG'S SYNOD OF NEW SOUTH WALES

Constituted April 3, 1850 & dissolved on union November 15, 1864

† Name	Ordination	Details of service
1 J.D.Lang, MA DD	CS- 1822	Scots, Sydney 1823-78 and died.
2 Barzillai Quaiffe	Cong- 1834	Upper Pitt Street 1847-50;resd 1854; joined General Synod PCNSW 1865.
3 William Ritchie	US- 1832	Yass from 6/50-10/54 and died.
SYNOD FORMED		
4 John Gibson	Cong- 1844	Grafton from 5/1850; to Sydney 1853. Died 1854.

5	Matthias Goethe*	9.10.1850	College 1850-52; East Melbourne 1853-1867 (Lutheran); to USA, died 1876.
6	Lorenzo Lodge*	10.4.1850	Newcastle 1850-52; to Tasmania 1853.
7	William Ridley BA*	10.4.1850	College 1850; Dungog 4/51 then various inc. Aboriginal mission; Brisbane; Portland (UP) 1857-58; supply in NSW. Resd 1860 to PCEA 11.61.
8	David Blair*	9.10.1850	Upper Pitt Street 1850-12/51; row with Lang, no longer minister 1.1.52; to Victoria; journalist and MP; died 1899.
9	James T. Carter*	25.12.1850	Manning 1/51-12/58 & died (to Syn of Aust 1853.
10	John McGibbon*	(by SA-1854)	Licensed 20.12.1850; supply at Scots; to Synod of Aust 1854.
11	Walter Robb*	9.10.1850	Gippsland to 11/51 & left charge.
12	Gottfried Wagner	9.10.1850	Tumut then Moreton Bay (not recognised 8.4.52 - 5.4.55); to Qld (Lutheran).
13	Alex Black	17.2.1851	Congregational; Murrurundi 1851-60 then Lands Commissioner at Wellington.
14	**Patrick Fitzgerald ***	17.2.1851	**Wagga 1851-52; Tumut 1853-62; Moruya 1863-71; Windsor 1875-96. Died 1902.**
15	J.G.Hausmann	25.12.1851	Qld; to Victoria 1854 (Lutheran).
16	John C.S.Handt	Baden- 1827	Recd 12/50 (was at Berrima 1847-52); To Victoria; Hospital and Prison Chaplain (C of E) at Geelong 1853-63 & died.
17	Thomas J. Kingsford	UP	Recd 11/52 at Warwick, Qld 1851-66;(to PCQ 1864) Allora 1873-78.
18	**William Chaucer**	**12.12.1853**	**Lower Hunter (previously lic. of Syn of A) 1853-66; Wollongong 1867-68;suspended.**
19	Robert Boag BA	CS- 1851	Ex Syn of A; assist to Lang 1854-59; to PCV 1859; without charge; teaching in Sydney 1863; joined General Synod PCNSW 1864; Hinton 1866-8%; died '91.
20	John McIlrea	UP- ?	Pyrmont 1854; Canterbury 1855; to Tas.
21	Robert Miller	28.6.1854	Grafton, died 1855.
22	James Collins	6.4.1855	Balmain; mid 1857 to Grafton where he died 7/1864 aged 66.
23	Thomas Bell	15.10.1856	United Evangelical Church, Brisbane 1856-57; Creek Street UP Church 1857-59 and died.
24	Peter Nicquet	4.11.1856	Victoria (Lutheran)
25	J.W.Gehricke	4.11.1856	Victoria (Lutheran)
26	John Reid	US- 1829	Ex UPC of Vic 4/58; assistant to Lang then Mariners Church 1862-67 (to Synod of Aust 11/63). Died 1867.
27	John Roberts	Cong ?	Recd 12/59 & suspended 4/60.
28	V.G.Williams	?.?.1860	Manning 12/59-60; Murrurundi 1860-64 & died 1.1.1864.
29	James Paterson	7.9.1862	Itinerant, Namoi, Yass, Hunter; to Uk '64.
30	**James Martin**	**27.8.1863**	**Upper Manning 1863-64; Queanbeyan 1864-67; resigned.**
31	George Graham MA	UPCS- 1861	Recd 8/63; assistant to Lang; to PCQ 11/64; Maryborough 1864-66; to PCV; Maryborough (Vic) 1866-69; Beechworth 1869-73; Bacchus Marsh 1874-78; St Arnaud 1878-83; died 1894.

NB †1, 14, 18 & 30 were connected with the Synod at the time of union.
The 8 men marked * were among the 20 or so brought out by Lang in 1850.

GENERAL SYNOD OF THE PRESBYTERIAN CHURCH IN NEW SOUTH WALES
Constituted November 15, 1864 & dissolved on union September 8, 1865

This was a union between 15 serving PCEA ministers and 4 SNSW ministers (see previous lists) together with two UP ministers:

1	Adam Thomson MA	US- 1833	Phillip Street, Sydney 1861-73; Principal St Andrew's College 1873-74 & died.
2	R.S.Paterson	UP- 1859	Pyrmont 1864-1900; died 1914 age 87.

The following ministers joined the General Synod after its formation:

1	Robert Boag BA	CS- 1851	admitted Nov 15, 1864 (previously Syn of Aust & SNSW & PCV); Hinton 1866-87.
2	T.A.Gordon	Cong- 1852	admitted Feb 1, 1865. Independent at Balmain 1853-57; Presbyterian at Balmain 1857-69; Inverell 1869-73; St Andrew's Newcastle 1874-96; died 1907 aged 85.
3	Barzillai Quaiffe	Cong- 1834	admitted May 3, 1865 (previously SNSW); without charge and died 1873 aged 74.
4	Wazir Beg	PCV- 1864	admitted June 15, 1865; Chalmers' Sydney 1865-1885 and died.

H.S.Seaborn (†33 in PCEA list) resigned from the General Synod, so at the time of union with the Synod of Australia, there were 24 ordained ministers, not all inducted.

GENERAL ASSEMBLY OF THE PRESBYTERIAN CHURCH OF NEW SOUTH WALES
Constituted September 8, 1865 by union of the General Synod and the Synod of Australia

Began with 47 serving ministers (Blain & R.Stewart were retired) plus S.F.Mackenzie of West Maitland (†21 in PCEA list) admitted immediately thereafter. Rev W.S.Donald (†32 in PCEA list) was without charge and has been classified as continuing PCEA. Rev William Ross MA,PhD (not to be confused with †12 in the SofA list) was at Wentworth near Mildura from 1861 but due to distance was not effectively connected with either the PCV or the PCNSW, and has been disregarded. Of the 48 serving men in 1865, 15 or 31.2% were ex PCEA, 10 or 20.8% could be classed as UP/Lang and 23 or 48% as S of A.

NB: In 1904 the legal name was inadvertently changed to The Presbyterian Church of Australia in the State of New South Wales.

SYNOD OF THE PRESBYTERIAN CHURCH OF EASTERN AUSTRALIA
Constituted October 10, 1846 & continuing outside the unions of 1864/65.

On the same day that the first stage of Presbyterian Union was accomplished (November 15, 1864), five ministers and an elder constituted a meeting of the Synod of Eastern Australia pursuant to Protests they had lodged. The final position after the union of September 1865 was that 5 of the 22 former PCEA ministers continued in a formal way with W.S.Donald (formally associated later) bringing the number to 6 or some 27% of the 1864 PCEA ministerial strength.

8: HUNTER VALLEY & NORTHERN RIVERS CONGREGATIONS

In this chapter attention will be given to the congregations in the Hunter Valley and the spread of work northwards to the Barrington, Manning, Hastings and Clarence Rivers which were opened up for settlement by 1865. The Hunter was a flourishing centre of Presbyterianism and the genesis of the congregations which continued the Presbyterian Church of Eastern Australia in 1864/65 will be found here. An additional reason for fairly detailed attention to this area is the inadequacy of existing printed accounts. Accordingly, an attempt has been made to relate the activities of the three sections of the Presbyterian Church which operated in the area prior to union in 1865.

Maitland (West & East)

The history of Presbyterian work on the Hunter from 1831 has been given on page 37. Rev John Hill Garven, who was settled in 1835, also proved grossly intemperate and was deposed in January 1838. Lang's Synod sent Rev Robert Blain to establish a congregation from those Presbyterians alienated by Garven's conduct and disillusioned by their experience with the Presbytery of New South Wales. The Presbytery was also anxious to retain the field and had already sent Rev John Gregor. Gregor was a 'moderate' in outlook and gained little support. He took services at Paterson and Morpeth, but apparently spent most of his time conducting a school. Blain was an accomplished preacher and zealous worker for the cause of Christ. It would appear that a building on the East Maitland road belonging to Andrew Lang [1] was opened for Blain's

---

1. B.J.Bridges, **The Presbyterian Churches in New South Wales 1823-1865** (PhD Thesis, University of St Andrews, 1985), p.136 citing **Colonial Observer**, 22 October 1842.

congregation in 1838. Blain also preached at Bowthorne, Morpeth - then the leading Port on the Hunter - and Dunmore (in the brick schoolhouse-church on the property), and had a total attendance of 175. Services at Harper's Hill (Stockade) drew 60, including convicts.[2]

Gregor and Blain were withdrawn from Maitland in 1841 following on the union of the Presbytery and Synod in October 1840, and William McIntyre was settled in their stead. He had a good mind and strong family connections with the Hunter through his cousins. He was also bi-lingual (Gaelic/English) which was very significant given the recent influx of Highland Scots, many of whom were only familiar with Gaelic. The first elders were installed on February 12, 1842 - Ross Coulter, Fergus Fergusson, Finlay Nicholson and Dr Andrew Liddell. In 1844 McIntyre married his cousin Mary, the sister and heir of her brother Peter McIntyre (1783-1842). In consequence, the considerable fortune Peter McIntyre had amassed passed to William, who resided at Pitnacree House, East Maitland. This was a 22 roomed mansion Peter had built from which to supervise his extensive property interests.

At the division of October 1846, in which McIntyre played a leading role, the large majority of Maitland Presbyterians adhered to the Synod of Eastern Australia led by McIntyre. Soon a new brick church was erected in what is now Free Church Street. It was seated for 400, cost about $2,000, and was opened on March 18, 1849. A large two-storey brick building costing about $9,000 was erected in 1855/56 to house the 'High School of Maitland' which began in the church in January 1855. It was co-educational, and the fore-runner of High Schools established by the Government in Maitland in 1884. McIntyre took a number of classes including Classics, acted as Headmaster without charge from 1857-59, and made the school one of the largest and best in New South Wales. It was separated from direct church control in1859, and declined soon after when the new Headmaster opened his own school. A modest brick building in East Maitland, which could hold about 100 when used as a church, was purchased by the PCEA in September 1847.[3] About the beginning of 1848 it was ready for use as a schoolhouse during the week and a place of worship on the Lord's Day. [4] David Dickson of Bolwarra was elected an elder in 1850 along with Michael Scobie. William Zuill and John Boggs were installed in 1852 and James Hamilton in 1857.

Meanwhile, Dr McGarvie of the Synod of Australia interested himself in the district. Although the vast majority of Maitland Presbyterians adhered to the Synod of Eastern Australia, there was a valuable property belonging to the

2. Catherine Boer, The Maitland Riot 1860, Presbyterian Church Union 1865: An Analysis of Religious Conflict (Sociology IV Honours, University of Newcastle 1981) p.62. Also of value is C.Boer, 'An Early Clergyman of the Hunter' William McIntyre 1806-1870' in Journal of the Royal Australian Historical Society, Oct. 1986, p.130/148.
3. Voice in the Wilderness (hereafter Voice), October 1, 1847, p.348.
4. Voice, February 1, 1848, p.22.

Church of Scotland Synod which was let out on building leases and returned a sum sufficient for a minister's stipend. Towards the close of 1848 moves were afoot to place William Purves of Port Macquarie in Maitland,[5] and this was carried into effect in the following year. Purves had a few followers but he confined his attention principally to East Maitland and to Largs, some 3kms to the north. He did not take a very major part in the disruption of 1846, although he wrote against the Free Church position some years later (1864). The first St Stephen's Presbyterian Church was opened on May 13, 1860. Purves resigned in 1869, and died the following year on a voyage to Britain.

When William McIntyre was translated to St George's Church, Sydney at the close of 1861, there were some 120 Gaelic speakers in the congregation, 30 of whom could not understand English. Failing to obtain Dr Grant of Shoalhaven, an able non-Highlander with Gaelic, Aberdeen-born Rev S.F. Mackenzie was called and inducted in 1863, though he was not proficient in Gaelic. At the PCEA Synod in November 1863, a Basis of Union was agreed with only James McCulloch of Ahalton and the elders from Ahalton, St George's, and the Clarence River dissenting.[6] However, immediately after the Synod meeting, the Free Church Highlanders at Bolwarra and Largs withdrew from the West Maitland congregation because they believed (rightly) that the resolutions accompanying the Basis placed the Free and Established Churches in Scotland on the same level.[7] In March 1864 they resolved to return, though protesting against the contemplated union, and to remain as long as they could without compromising their principles. This group included Finlay Nicholson, elder, who had come out on the *Midlothian* with William McIntyre and died in 1866, and Duncan McInnes, who was farming at Bolwarra, and who was later (1868) PCEA minister at Maclean on the Clarence River.

When the initial union was consummated in November 1864, the main Highland element of the West Maitland congregation continued with the PCEA and maintained services at the Presbyterian Schoolhouse at East Maitland, which they held by possession, and at Morpeth. James McCulloch of Ahalton/Raymond Terrace had oversight, and Duncan McInnes gave supply while completing studies for the ministry.

5. **Voice**, November 1, 1848, p.167. In the East Maitland parish history Purves is said to have come in 1846. This date is also given in the Biographical Register of Presbyterian ministers in **Church Heritage**, March 1984. However, 1849 is unquestionably the correct date and also agrees with the period of 20 years mentioned on the memorial tablet in the church.
6. Allan McIntyre of the Clarence was not present at the Synod but was also opposed.
7. **Presbyterian Magazine**, April 1864, inside rear cover.

The West Maitland Free Church, or Scots Presbyterian Church as it became known in 1865, did not manage well at this time. As Catherine Boer states, 'It lost the members that stimulated its growth. In 1865, the congregation could not pay the minister his full stipend.' [8] Mackenzie left in 1866, and there was only one elder in 1867. The Highland element, mainly farmers, had left, and the commercial interests in the area were in decline. In 1870 an Act of Parliament was obtained in order to divide the revenue from the original glebe between West and East Maitland PCNSW congregations, and so both parishes were able to survive. The original Free Church buildings in Free Church Street still stand, and the church, the oldest in Maitland, is still in regular use though affected by floods on many occasions.

Hinton

Rev Robert Blain (1796-1871), from the Synod of Ulster, ministered at Hinton and outstations from 1841 to 1861, after his withdrawal from Maitland. A quaint brick church with a metal spire was erected in 1841, as was a manse. Blain was a lucid and orthodox preacher who provided services at every little centre of population as often as he could. His stations in early times included Largs (at 'Dunmore', whose 2,560 acres were let in farms of 20 to 50 acres and supported 300 people), Morpeth (Mr Close's School), Ahalton, Seaham, and Clarence Town. Towards the end of 1845 he undertook a 1,500 mile preaching tour on horseback, visiting the Liverpool Plains and the New England district north of Armidale. [9] His inability to preach in Gaelic was a hindrance, but the fact he drew back in the church crisis of 1846 was probably a greater difficulty. In 1845 he married Sarah Keys, whose brother was married to a sister of Rev Irving Hetherington of Singleton. One assumes he took the view that the ministry could not or would not be supported by voluntary contributions, and so chose to remain in the Synod of Australia and thus to receive a government stipend. However, he was no mere time server as witness the fact that in 1860 he assigned his state stipend to Rev Alex McEwen, his successor, when he might have retained it. McEwen continued until the early part of 1864 and then removed to Mudgee retaining the state stipend. Hinton was vacant and not strong at the time of union. Rev Robert Boag, an unassuming man, was inducted by the PCNSW on September 26, 1866 and retired in 1888.[10]

8. Catherine Boer, op cit. p.91.
9. **Voice**, March 15, 1846, pp.48,49. Blain's report has been reprinted in Iain H. Murray's **Australian Christian Life From 1788** (Edinburgh 1988) pp. 186-192. Blain was away 9 weeks in all. In April/May 1844, William Purves of Port Macquarie had made a 3½ week tour of New England (see Allan M. Grocott's article in **Church Heritage**, September 1979, pp.101-113).
10. The PCNSW subsequently worked Hinton with various outstations. By 1931, Hinton and Morpeth could no longer sustain a pastor. In 1962, the Hinton church was in a state of disrepair. It was sold and demolished.

Paterson

A newly-ordained Gaelic preacher, William Ross (1803-1869), arrived in Sydney from Scotland in November 1838. He took up work on the Paterson, visiting also on the Williams River. In the small village of Paterson steps were initiated in 1840 to provide a plain brick church. This was opened by Mr Ross on Sunday August 27, 1842.[11] Ross did not favour making an issue of the Disruption and lost some support as a consequence. In 1847 he accepted a call to Goulburn. The following year he was suceeded at Paterson by Rev Christopher Eipper, a German minister of Lutheran background. From this time what had been 'Scots Church' became known as St Ann's, undoubtedly through Eipper's influence. He demitted in February 1850 and took up teaching at Muswellbrook. 'About this time an exodus of settlers took place owing to the Government opening up land on the Manning River, and the Paterson congregations suffered considerably.'[12] J.B.Laughton, an evangelical preacher, was minister from 1851 to 1854, although a Gaelic speaking minister would have been preferred. He was succeeded in 1855 by Rev Thomas Stirton who remained until 1873. Dungog was included in his parish though later separated leaving Paterson less than viable. For most of the 20th century it has been linked to Scots' Church in Maitland.

Ahalton/Raymond Terrace

After the 1846 division, a ½acre site was obtained by the PCEA from J.A. McClymont, the local proprietor, and a slab church with glazed windows and shingle roof was erected at a cost of $70 and opened on November 14, 1847 by William McIntyre. It was situated in the now forgotten locality of Ahalton, 'about 2 miles below Hinton, in the centre of a numerous population, chiefly Presbyterian.'[13] The site was immediately to the north of Kanwary Hill, about 1 mile north of the Hunter and 1½ miles west from the Raymond Terrace-Seaham Road, and probably adjoined the present Chichester Water Pipe Line.[14] The building was intended to serve folk on both sides of the Hunter, ie. those at Millers Forest as well as those in the Nelson Plains district. In fact, it appears that people came much further, even walking from Salt Ash, about 25 miles to the east. The building was 40' x 20' with seats sufficient for 192 - rather crowded by current standards.

---

11. The year 1840 has been claimed since one of the gable stones has that year cut into it. Compare **Australian Presbyterian Life**, September 1978, pp.10,11. However, the report of the opening appears in **The Australian**, September 2, 1842, p.3. On this basis St Ann's is the third oldest Presbyterian building now in use for such purposes after Kirklands, Tasmania (October 2, 1836), and Campbelltown (opened July 10, 1842 by Rev John Tait, according to C.A.White's history). The ecclesiastical use of the name St Ann(e) is virtually unknown in Scotland but is particularly common in Germany.
12. James Cameron, **Centenary History of the Presbyterian Church in New South Wales**, (Sydney 1905) p.277.
13. Voice, September 15, 1847, p.340.
14. The exact site has not been ascertained, but if one goes down Ralston Road to the pipeline, one is near the spot.

As early records have been lost there is some uncertainty about early events. However, it appears that Hugh MacDonald (1805-1889), formerly an elder at Hinton, was prominent in organising the Ahalton congregation. [15] He was active in conducting Gaelic prayer meetings, and was an able Bible expositor. About 1870 he removed to the Clarence. Another elder was Samuel Martin (1809-1889), also of Hinton at first after his arrival from Northern Ireland in 1839. Two years later he was working a property at Nelsons Plains. He shared in the constituting of the Synod of Eastern Australia in 1846. About November 1853, Rev Alexander McIntyre, a well known and loved Highland evangelist, came to the district. He soon had a strong group of people attending his ministry, though he was not inducted to the charge. Some two thirds of the 200 adults in the congregation were Gaelic speaking, and there is little doubt that very beneficial results flowed from McIntyre's ministry. He was a bachelor and resided with one of his flock.

By the mid 1850s people were increasingly moving north, and this accelerated following the severe flood of August 1857. Samuel Martin moved to the Manning about this time, but Hugh MacDonald remained until about 1870. In 1861, Rev James McCulloch of Singleton accepted a call, and began a much valued ministry as the first inducted minister. He lived in the manse built by the congregation, but it and its contents were destroyed by fire. However, McCulloch decided to take up residence in the more convenient centre of Raymond Terrace, and a timber church seated for 200 and costing $640 was opened on the present site on October 8, 1865. Mrs McCulloch's uncle, Rev William McIntyre, was the preacher at the opening. McCulloch himself did not have Gaelic, but was a soundly orthodox and earnest minister of amiable disposition, whose ministry was much appreciated by the people. He was not robust in health and died in May 1873 aged 50 years. He was buried in the (old) Raymond Terrace Cemetery. Elders 'holy' William McQueen and Malcolm Gillies of Millers Forest were installed by McCulloch. The first trustees of the Raymond Terrace site were John Thompson, Robert Phelan, Hugh Campbell, James Cameron, William Martin jr. and Donald Gillies. The pastor and congregation stayed out of the union of 1864/65. The PCEA Synod of 1867 gave permission for the sale of the Ahalton building.

McCulloch supplied East Maitland as well as Raymond Terrace, though the two congregations were reckoned as distinct and each sent a representative elder to the Presbytery and Synod. For a period in the 1860s McCulloch supplied a service at Morpeth, but his health was such that it was agreed to

15. Hugh McDonald was the great-grandfather of C.P.King, a prominent elder of the Hunter since his induction in 1958.
16. Two of Martin's great grandsons, John A.Anderson and Kenneth G. Anderson, are current elders of the PCEA Brisbane.

concentrate efforts on East Maitland and Raymond Terrace. Doubtless there were outstations which were regularly visited. Over at Port Stephens it appears the Cromarty family were connected with the church. Captain William Cromarty, RN (Retired), had come to Australia as early as 1822, and in 1824 he became the first European settler at Port Stephens, basing himself at Salamander Bay. He hailed from the Orkneys. A son, Magnus (died 1906), took up land at Bobs Farm. He had 12 children by his wife Christina McIntosh, including Magnus jr., who became a Member of Parliament.

Clarence Town

In the latter part of 1849, Arthur M.Sherriff, a student for the ministry of the Free Church of Scotland, arrived in the colony. He had been appointed by the Colonial Committee to work under the supervision of the Synod of Eastern Australia. He completed his studies while engaging in pastoral work. He was licensed on October 4, 1850, and ordained at Sydney for Clarence Town on April 3, 1851. At first he lived in West Maitland until a house was provided at Clarence Town. Services for up to 200 people were held on the wide verandah which was screened from the weather by a curtain. For a time he served Ahalton as well as the Williams River, both sides of which were dotted with farms. Later Sherriff lived at Dungog. He died November 1864.

Details of activity are sketchy. Clarence Town was a place of 100 people and some 20 houses in 1848, but by 1866 was a postal township with a population of 300, with two flour mills, three churches, two tobacco factories and a tannery. In 1853, two ½ acre allotments were purchased in Rifle Street (allotments 2 & 20 of section 20), with William Lowe, Donald McPhee, David Farquhar, Allan McCormack, William Johnston, Donald McDiarmid and Lachlan McDonald as trustees. In September 1855 the erection of a brick church - the first in the district - was commenced. It was named Chalmers' Church and cost $826. Following the union there was sufficient support to allow the area to be worked by the PCEA as a missionary district by Rev William S. Donald from 1868 until his death in 1890. The river trade was destroyed by the opening up of the North Coast Railway.[17]

Dungog

Dungog, 25kms up the Williams from Clarence Town, attracted the first settlers in 1824 because of the red cedar and fertile grazing land. William Comrie of the Synod of Australia gave supply 1840-42. Later it had visits from representatives of each of the Synods. Lang sent William Ridley into the

17. The materials of the church building were sold for $10 in 1904 but an offer of $100 for the sites was refused. They were sold for $1,000 in 1976 and the proceeds applied to the Hunter PCEA charge. The PCNSW made Clarence Town a station, probably in the 1890s, and erected a neat timber building next to the Public School.

area in April 1851 with a view to serving Dungog and Stroud.[18]At the Synod meeting in January 1852 he reported divisions existed, and he is soon after found in Sydney. From the scanty evidence, it seems that Dungog was mainly PCEA and Stroud Synod of Australia. Sherriff lived at Dungog during the latter period of his ministry. Thomas Stirton of the Synod of Australia at Paterson from 1855, seems to have visited too. In 1875 a PCNSW minister was stationed at Dungog, and at that time or earlier a building was erected, reputedly near the present Community Centre in Brown Street. [19] The PCNSW church building in Stroud dates from 1887.

The bulk of support coming from PCEA sympathisers, Thomas Abbott, the chief constable, gave a ½-acre site (allotment 12 section 2) in Dowling Street, and a brick church named after John Knox and costing $900 was opened on April 15, 1856. The chief supporters were the Mackay family who held extensive pastoral interests in the district. George Mackay,JP, and Alexander Mackay were early trustees. Services were conducted for some years. With the shortage of PCEA ministers and the distractions in the Synod in the 1880s, the property was sold to the PCNSW about 1892 for $200. Presumably it had already been used for some time as the place of worship for all Dungog Presbyterians.

Singleton

Singleton, some 50kms up the Hunter from Maitland was originally called St Patricks Plains because it was first visited by Europeans on St Patricks Day in 1820. Rev Thomas Thomson conducted his first service at Castle Forbes Granary near Singleton on November 6, 1831, and no doubt there were occasional visits from the ministers at Maitland until the first permanent minister was settled in September 1837. This was Irving Hetherington. His parish was 50 miles long by 30 miles broad, and his stations included Jerry's Plains and Muswellbrook. There were but eight families in the Singleton part of the parish in 1838, but they were influential and wealthy people. The work was arduous and Hetherington considered the people in general were unwilling to voluntarily support the work of the Gospel but were content to have a minister if the Government paid the stipend. Hetherington received the lowest stipend of $200 during his first year, but a church building and manse were erected in 1838. He was not a particularly good preacher although warmly orthodox, but he was an able administrator. He sought to take a neutral position in the Disruption crisis but stayed in the Synod of Australia. He thus retained his stipend and the opportunity to continue his ministry. However, he alienated many Presbyterians in the district by this

18. **Synod of New South Wales Minutes,** p.69 (April 2, 1851).
19. Vide letter May 15, 1987 from Rev R.C.Daley, PCNSW minister at Dungog.

stance. He left Singleton in April 1847 and was settled as minister of Scots Church, Melbourne, the pulpit vacated by James Forbes on grounds of principle. His successor at Singleton was the first Australian trained minister, James S. White. His pastorate covered 1847 to 1903, and in Bridges' opinion appears to have been in the 'moderate' tradition.

Those who adhered to the Synod of Eastern Australia maintained services among themselves. In the expectation of additional ministers arriving, George Bowman,MLA, offered the PCEA a ¼acre site at Singleton (allotment 270 in High Street near the present hospital).It was conveyed to G.P.Bowman, Alex Munro and William Waddell as trustees, and presumably Mr Bowman donated the purchase price of $80. James McCulloch was the first PCEA minister. He arrived from Scotland in November 1854, and was ordained and inducted on September 6, 1855 to the Upper Hunter with his base at Singleton. Early services were in the Court House. The first elders were Alexander Munro (Mayor of Singleton in 1866) and William Fraser. The Fraser family was very prominent and William Waddell (died 1895) was also a liberal supporter. While McCulloch did not have Gaelic, his ministry was a very helpful and appreciated one.

A brick church complete with gallery and costing $2,400 was erected and opened on April 30, 1860. Not all the funds were in hand and even in 1875 there was $600 owing - probably an interest free loan from one of the backers of the project. It was an over ambitious building reflecting the social position of some of the leading people. White's congregation was not very large - perhaps only a dozen attenders at Singleton,[20] and the Free Church had more than this - at a guess an average of 60.

In 1861, McCulloch accepted a call down river to Ahalton. He was succeeded by a Gaelic preacher, Rev Adam Gordon, of whom little is known. Aberdeen and Muswellbrook were included in his visits. Relatives of Rev William McIntyre had property interests in the Aberdeen/Scone area. His brothers Archibald and Donald lived at Blairmore near Scone (both died in 1860), while Donald McIntyre, a cousin, lived at Kayuga (between Muswellbrook and Aberdeen). Gordon and some of the people were in favour of the 1864 union, but others opposed it. The upshot was the the congregation continued under the PCEA, although depleted in numbers. Gordon transferred to Taralga in 1866 and was followed by John L. McSkimming, inducted May 23, 1866. He did not remain long, being a man of brotherly spirit but weak character, and he resigned effective August 21, 1867. He was later deposed. This left James McCulloch responsible for Raymond Terrace, East Maitland and the Upper Hunter, on behalf of the PCEA.

20. B.J.Bridges, op. cit., citing Rev Alex Salmon's speech in The Empire, July 17, 1855.

Newcastle and district

In the early days Newcastle was much less important as a centre than Maitland. Early Presbyterian history is not always clear. However, Rev Robert Stewart (1784-1872) worked in the Newcastle area under the Synod of Australia from 1843 until 1847, when he retired to Sydney. The foundation of the original St Andrew's Church, on the western side of Watts Street near Church Street, was laid in November 1847, but the building was only partially constructed 3 years later. Towards the end of 1850, Rev Lorenzo Lodge (1823-1912) was sent to Newcastle by Lang's Synod. He succeeded in gathering a congregation only to have the discovery of gold bring disorganisation. [21] The Synod of Australia sought to gain Lodge by promising to complete the church, build a manse and guarantee him a salary,[22] but Lodge, whose background was United Presbyterian, was not having any. He left in 1853 and went to Tasmania. The same year, St Andrew's was sufficiently complete for use, and Rev James Nimmo, who had arrived from Scotland in March 1854, was settled as the minister by the Synod of Australia until 1861. In April of that year he was succeeded by Rev James Coutts (1800-1884), who continued in the charge until his death.

At the end of 1853, William Chaucer, formerly a probationer with the Synod of Australia whose voluntary views had been rejected by that body, was ordained by Lang's Synod for the Lower Hunter. He had been stationed at Paterson by the Synod of Australia until May 1853, and between then and his ordination on December 12, 1853 he had visited in the Lower Hunter area. At the Synod in April 1854 he was able to report five stations - Ash Island had 3 services a month with 45 regular hearers; Waratah, Newcastle and Borehole [ie. Hamilton] had 2 services a month with 40, 30 and 24 regular hearers; while The Tunnel had a monthly service with 37 hearers. Tomago appears later. A small church was in course of erection at Waratah where Chaucer lived, the site being the gift of C. Simpson. A day school was to operate from the building. In March 1857, he was able to report that a two roomed residence had been erected for the teacher and the cost defrayed by Messrs Gray, McNutty, Russell and Road.

At Newcastle proper, a site was conveyed by Ed. Flood, MP, a friend of Lang's, with power to sell. As it adjoined the existing Presbyterian Church (St Andrew's) it was sold. About $400 was realized for an alternative location. At Pitt Town [ie. Hamilton], where the school room was the usual meeting place, a church building was nearly ready for opening in April 1860. The site was a gift of the A.A.Company (who exchanged it in 1884 for the site on which the present church is built). As the population moved, Chaucer followed the miners to Minmi and Wallsend. A site was granted at the former place by J.&J. Brown in 1863, and at Wallsend by Mr Shaw, the Storekeeper.

21. **Synod of New South Wales Minutes**, p.98 (January 1, 1852)
22. B.J.Bridges, op. cit., p.206.

Meanwhile, in June 1860 William Bain was sent to Newcastle to establish a congregation of the PCEA. Bain was a capable minister and met with considerable success. He was ordained and inducted on June 29, 1861, and a brick church was opened in Hunter Street on September 12, 1863. Previously services had been held in the Odd Fellows Hall. Bain initiated services in Minmi and Wallsend in 1862, and in 1863 J.S.Laing came to further the efforts in these districts. This had the effect of dividing the work Chaucer had sought to build up among the poor and frequently shifting miner and small-farmer population, as the Presbyterian element of the population was inadequate to support two ministers. Some excuse for this may be sought in Chaucer's limitations. He was notoriously careless in marriage matters, and in 1861 had served 2 months of a twelve months sentence with hard labour for making false statements in a marriage certificate.[23] His ministry showed devotion and earnestness yet was to come to an end in 1868 with deposition due to intemperance. On the other hand, considering union was very much in the air, the intrusion appeared unseemly.[24]

THE NORTHERN DISTRICTS

Manning River

During the late 1840s settlers were moving into the Manning Valley then covered with dense bush and rain-forest. Occasional visits were made by the Presbyterian ministers stationed at Port Macquarie - William Purves (1840-1849) and William McKee (1849-53). On December 2, 1849, McKee baptised the infant son of Samuel and Mary Anne Gibson of Redbank (now Pampoolah).[25] McKee founded the Redbank Presbyterian School Board with himself, Samuel Gibson and High Polson as the foundation members. In November 1850, Dr John Dunmore Lang visited the area and found the school in operation with William Small as teacher. A school house 26' x 15' was in course of erection to accommodate the nearly 30 pupils, not all being Presbyterians. The plan was to use the building for church services too.[26]

The first Christian minister of any denomination resident on the Manning was James T. Carter (1819-1858). Carter was of Congregational background and had come out from England through Lang's invitation. He was ordained in Sydney on December 25, 1850, and proceeded to the Manning. At first he

23. B.J.Bridges, ibid., p.227.
24. Chaucer left the Lower Hunter in 1866 for Wollongong where his ministry closed.
25. A.J.Eipper, The History of the Port Macquarie Charge of the Presbyterian Church [1946] p.9. Purves first began visiting the Manning in 1847.
26. J. Ramsland, The Struggle Against Isolation - A History of the Manning Valley, (1987) p.128; J.D.Lang, An Historical Account of New South Wales, Vol. 2 (1852) p.212.

lived at the 'Old Wharf,' where his was the only house, but later obtained land at Purfleet near to Carters Island (which perpetuates his name). It appears his first service was held on February 2, 1851.[27]

Carter's ministry was an evangelical one, though he was deficient from an educational viewpoint according to normal Presbyterian standards.[28] His connection with the controversial Lang was no help, given Lang was a deposed minister, and less than reputable in the eyes of most. His opposition in the Legislative Council to denominational schools was well known. Perhaps it is not surprising that Carter did not receive adequate financial support. In 1852 he was persuaded to seek admission to the Synod of Australia, which was state-aided. On April 7, 1852 his resignation was before Lang's Synod. He advanced as reasons for this step, 'the inefficiency of the Voluntary Principle among a population so scattered and so sectarian as that around him, the questionable source of some of the contributions, advice of friends, and the general desire of the people.' Carter was in due course received by the Synod of Australia as a ministerial candidate - his licence and ordination by Lang's Synod being ignored.[29] He continued his labours in the district and was the preacher at the opening of the Wesleyan building at Glenthorne late in 1857. He died on December 1, 1858.

Migration of Presbyterian settlers to the Manning gained momentum during the 1850s. Many or even most of them had spent 15 or 20 years on the Hunter, Williams or Paterson Rivers as tenant farmers, and moved north as land was opened up to engage in agriculture. A large proportion were Highlanders who needed a bi-lingual pastor. Areas near Wingham were almost entirely Scottish with such families as the McDermids, McDonalds, and Stewarts in evidence. James Murray and Alexander Lobban were Lowlanders (Roxburghshire and Banffshire respectively) who came to the Manning as early as 1851. Joseph Robinson and Samuel Martin arrived with their families from the Hunter about 1856 the former to settle at Dingo Creek and the latter at Dumaresq Island. These men were from Northern Ireland. There were very many others of course, including some who had lived through the Disruption times in Scotland - men like Hugh Cameron of Mount George, and the Jacksons. The Ramsays came from the Paterson about 1858.

On October 2, 1853, Arthur Sherriff conducted a service on the Manning at McLeod's, Mondrook with about 200 persons present. Following a petition from 25 males, mainly property owners, the PCEA Synod recognised the

---

27. G.Dennes, 'Education in the Yesteryears 1850-1870' **Northern Champion,** 5/6/1948.
28. The rather cursory examination is evident from the minutes of the Synod of New South Wales, p.36.
29. B.J.Bridges, op. cit., p.207.

Manning as a congregation on November 3, 1853. No doubt there were occasional visits from Rev Alexander McIntyre of the Hunter until Rev Allan McIntyre (1798-1870) arrived at Wingham in the company of Rev Alexander on November 18, 1854. The next day Rev Allan preached his first sermon in a barn belonging to Alexander Lobban of Parkhaugh near Wingham. He was a single man and resided with Mr Lobban for some time. Allan McIntyre had witnessed the Disruption in Scotland, was a firm exponent of Free Church principles, and was a man of real piety. He was a very awakening preacher and bi-lingual. He could also be somewhat narrow in outlook.

The congregation was soon organised. Three timber churches were erected. The first was planned for Duvegan (owned by the MacLeods) but Tinonee (proclaimed a village reserve in 1854) was settled on. The building was situated on Lot 5 of Section 2 in Winter Street, cost $546 and appears to have been opened in July 1856. The second building was of more basic slab construction. It was situated in Isabella Street, Wingham, between Mrs Black's boarding house and the old School of Arts. It cost $313 and was opened on August 17, 1856, if we read the old records correctly. The third building was on a ½ acre site at Redbank, a short distance from the old Pampoolah School. It cost about $340. The date of erection is not known, but was probably 1857.[30] The site was private property.

On January 7, 1858, Allan McIntyre was formally inducted to the now flourishing charge. The church at Tinonee was literally crammed. As it was 32' x 18' this indicates a crowd of 150 plus any outside. A few months later the first elders were chosen. As the early congregational records have been lost, precise details are hard to come by. There were at least 10 elders and deacons in 1864,[31] and during Allan McIntyre's ministry it appears there were at one time or another no less than eleven elders. These seem to have been Alexander Lobban (1803-1876) and his son, Thomas Lobban; Samuel Martin (1809-1889) and his sons, George and Joseph; James Murray (1827-1893), who was prominent in the Tinonee congregation; Alexander Cameron of Marlee and Donald McMaster of the same place - men who had both known the preaching of Alexander McIntyre in Scotland; and Lachlan McDonald, David Brown and Alexander McMillan.[32]

30. The dates and costs of the early places of worship are taken from the few minutes and papers of the Building Committee which survive, for copies of which I am indebted to Mr Keith Longworth, the present Session Clerk. The location of the first Wingham Church is as given by J.C.Robinson, The Free Presbyterian Church of Australia (Melbourne 1947) p. 110. The date of opening given above differs slightly from the date inferred by Robinson.

31. Presbyterian Magazine, June 1864, pp.172,173 in referring to a call by the Manning to Rev William Grant.

32. Source material on early elders includes J. C.Robinson, 'Allan McIntyre and the Early Manning' in Our Banner, February 1935, and obituaries in church magazines.

The existence of such a sufficiency of elders in a largely Highland congregation is striking. However, several had been participants in revival blessings in Scotland. Principal John Macleod refers to one revival of religion at Lochaber under Rev Alexander MacIntyre . 'The generation that saw these things were made ready to stand the hardships of Disruption days, but many of them after the failure of the potato crop emigrated to Australia, and on some of the northern rivers of New South Wales the tradition of these days was kept alive.'[33] Among those involved were Hugh Cameron of Mount George, and Donald MacMaster of Marlee,[34] and there were others. From 1857 to 1860 there were conversions taking place under Allan McIntyre's ministry, particularly in the latter year at the communion thanksgiving service. On this occasion, McIntyre preached for 2 hours on Zechariah 12:10 to the evident spiritual benefit of those who heard him.[35] Extensions were made to the Tinonee Church, and a new building was erected at Wingham on the present site in Canget Street in 1862. It was 32' x 18' plus a session room 7' x 10' (similar to the Tinonee building) and cost $352 - $200 being received from sale of the first building.

Meanwhile, following James Carter's death, Lang introduced Rev William Ridley, BA, to the Manning in April 1859. He remained only a short time before returning to Sydney (probably because of a demanding spouse). Lang still regarded the Manning as a promising field, and he and Ridley arranged to send Vincent G. Williams, a licentiate of the Synod of New South Wales. He reported to Lang's Synod on April 4, 1860 that there was as yet no organised action for his support. He was instructed to go back for a further three months, and if a call was received he would be ordained. However, the truth was put by H. Richardson of Tinonee in a letter to Lang dated April 14, 1860. Richardson pointed out that Williams was 'a complete babe' in Christianity, and many a Sabbath School child was better fitted to expound the Scriptures. [36] Moreover, his grammatical ability was very poor. Consequently, later in 1860 Williams is found at Murrurundi, so from that time until he left for the Clarence River at the end of 1862, Allan McIntyre was the only Presbyterian minister on the Manning.

33. John Macleod, **By-paths of Highland Church History** (Edinburgh 1965) pp.46,47.
34. J.C.Robinson, 'Allan McIntyre and the Early Manning' op. cit., p.215 (Cameron); W.MacLean, **In the Footsteps of the Flock** (Gisborne, NZ c1968) p.28 (McMaster), and compare J. Macleod, ibid., pp. 67-77 for McMaster's life after he returned to Scotland about 1868.
35. The testimony of George Martin, who was converted under Allan McIntyre about 1857, is to be found in **Free Church Quarterly,** March 1903, p.275 & June 1903, pp.295. Martin also records that it was the practice to preach on alternate Sabbaths at each of the three centres.
36. B.J.Bridges, op. cit., p. 217

Lang tried again at the end of May 1863, when James Martin arrived on the Manning from his Synod. He received a call dated July 20, 1863 from 'Presbyterian and other Evangelical Protestants'[37] in Wingham, Bow Bow, Dingo Creek and Upper Manning, and was duly ordained on August 27, 1863. His education was regarded as inadequate by some while he was also ill in the early months. He remained until mid 1864 and then removed to Queanbeyan on a call promising a stipend of $400 a year.

At this point there was no Presbyterian minister resident on the Manning as Allan McIntyre had concluded his ministry on December 28, 1862. The Presbytery allowed a year for the congregation to obtain a bi-lingual minister. In January 1864, the bi-lingual William Grant of Shoalhaven visited. He reported to the Presbytery that there were about 113 Presbyterian families - which suggests a Presbyterian population of 500/600. Grant had become a late convert to Presbyterian Union as then proposed, and addressed the people accordingly. At the April meeting of the Presbytery of Maitland, a call to Grant was presented accompanied by a letter from Thomas Lobban, Lachlan McDonald and David Brown, elders. The call was said to be 'most unanimous' and was signed by 10 officebearers, 12 communicants and about 100 adherents. It was declined.

The fact that the congregation sent a call to Grant suggests that the people were more concerned to have a bi-lingual minister than to oppose the union. This hypothesis has to be modified however since the need for Gaelic was passing. In September 1864, James McCulloch, who could not preach in Gaelic and was strongly opposed to the projected Union, visited the Manning, and in February 1865, after the initial union had taken place, received a call from the Manning. He declined the call, and the choice of the people was then set on Allan McIntyre and he returned to the Manning in August 1865 living at Wingham at first. He remained until near his death in May 1870. The consistency of the congregation in their calls to Grant and then McCulloch is to be found (a) in maturing views about the projected Union which led to more decided opposition, and (b) the congregation's concern for a minister they could identify with as a conservative and as a man evidently equipped to preach the word 'in demonstration of the Spirit's power' (I Cor 2:4).

Allan McIntyre had married Jemima Pilcher of West Maitland towards the end of 1862, so a manse was needed. A brick home was buit at a cost of $1,008 plus $60 for 11 acres of ground by the river at Little Tinonee (Lots 1 & 2 of Section 2), and was first occupied mid-September 1868. Meanwhile, the union Synod sent William Dron to the Manning in December 1864 with a

---

37. **Synod of New South Wales Minutes,** p.304

view to establishing a foothold, but he left after 9 months. After a brief time at Tumut he went to Ireland and joined the Church of Ireland. Rev J.S.Laing (1833-1905) was settled by the PCNSW in 1866 and was successful in organising the work of that church. The first Session was formed in 1867 and comprised John Cameron (died 1874), Joseph Robinson (Upper Manning) and Samuel Gibson. St Paul's, Taree was erected in 1869 and a manse also provided.

Barrington

The Barrington district is situated on the inland route between Maitland and Taree, west of the latter and about 90kms from it. The Barrington lands were originally part of the Church and School Lands - the one seventh of each County reserved in 1825 for the Church of England. After the repeal of this Act in 1829, the land was leased by the Australian Agricultural Company, which controlled the land until 1899/1900. It then became homestead selections.

The McInnes and McDonald families were the first settlers on the Barrington in 1856.[38] They were followed by the Beatons, Shaws, McQueens, McLennons, McSwans, McKinnons, McRaes, McSweens, John Grant, Norman Belle and the Chisholms. They cleared the land they had selected (the river flats), and got their first crop of wheat in 1857. It was carted by bullock teams to Stroud to be ground, and then carted back again over dirt tracks with no bridges to aid in crossing flooded streams. It was a hard day's work for any man to reap by sickle an acre of wheat which was then threshed by hand.

For a number of years John McInnes (1808-1890) gathered the people together on the Lord's Day and conducted a Gaelic service in his own home about 1.6 kms down the Barrington East Road (river side) from the present village. The first school house was built in 1864 about 2.8 kms down this road, and services were held there. No doubt there were occasional visits from the PCEA ministers on the Hunter or on the Manning. The vast majority of the original pioneers were Free Church and stayed out of the Union of 1864/65. The PCEA Synod of November 1868 approved a request by the Manning Session to ordain an elder on the Barrington, and this was fulfilled by the ordination of John McInnes.

38. For most of the information about the Barrington I am indebted to Mr J.J.(Jim) McInnes, JP., an elder of the Manning PCEA and grandson of John McInnes.

Hastings/Macleay

The earliest Presbyterian ministry on the Hastings was that of William Purves (1811-1870). A licentiate of the Church of Scotland, he had arrived in New South Wales in 1839. After a period as a squatter he was received by the Synod of Australia, and ordained on December 14, 1840 for Port Macquarie. On January 28, 1841, a meeting was held to take steps to provide a place of worship and a manse. 'Those attending the meeting included Mr William McKenzie of Wilson River, Captain R.A.Wauch of Wauchope House , King's Creek (from whom Wauchope takes its name), Alexander Thomson, Peter Sime, J.R.Middleton of Rolland's Plains, Lt. Donald McPhee, Dr McIntyre, Robert Ackroyd, Dr Fattorini (a reputed son of Napoleon Bonaparte), John Dillon, Daniel McInnes, Maxwell Thomson and Mr Irving.'[39] A site bounded by William, Murray and Munster Steets, Port Macquarie, was obtained from the Crown. Dr Fattorini organised the erection of church and manse for a total cost of $2,408. The Crown paid half the cost and the buildings were completed in February 1843.

It is difficult to ascertain details of congregational life. Purves made a number of visits to other districts. In April 1844 he journeyed to New England to solemnize the marriage of Andrew Wauchope and Miss Anne Boyd, and baptised 17 children on the way. He was thus the first Presbyterian minister to visit the Glen Innes and Inverell districts. From 1847 he visited the Manning. However, it is doubtful if there was a great deal of life and spiritual energy in Purves' ministry. Lang accused him, with some justification, of scampering around the colony to further his business interests. Allegations of scandalous conduct arose in August 1844,[40] and there were other questions about his claim for stipend. Shielded by McGarvie, he was transferred to East Maitland at the beginning of 1849. In this centre, with its closer contact with ordered society, Purves got on better. He became a leader in the church and community, and was involved in the University and in the founding of St Andrew's College. He was Moderator of the Assembly of the PCNSW in 1866.

William McKee succeeded Purves as Synod of Australia minister at Port Macquarie. He was ordained on May 1, 1849 and served the district with visits to the Manning until 1853. In that year he moved to Campbelltown where he was suspended from the ministry in 1867. Edward Holland, a man of Congregational background, came about September 1853. He was inducted on May 3, 1854 and continued until 1869. Thereafter, the lack of state-aid meant heavy weather.

39. C.A.White, **The Challenge of the Years** (Sydney 1951) p. 307
40. B.J.Bridges, op. cit., pp.165,166.

The work of the PCEA on the Hastings/Macleay arose in the early 1850s. Alexander Bain (1810-1892) arrived in Australia in 1839 and settled at Cooley Camp (ie. Woodville) on the Paterson River with his wife, Catherine Mackay. Their three children - Duncan, Mary and Annabell - were baptised by William Ross, the Gaelic minister at Paterson. Bain cleared land with a ship-mate, Alexander Mackay, and did labouring and shearing work for the McIntyres as far as Aberdeen and New England. It is said he walked from Maitland to Inverell for the shearing season. In 1846 he adhered to the newly-formed Synod of Eastern Australia, and in 1852 moved to the Hastings. He and a friend from Scottish days, Donald Cameron, purchased 'Crosslands' estate of some 1,960 acres and divided it between them. They doubted the propriety of casting lots so decided who would have each piece this way: Bain said to Cameron, 'Which piece do you want?' Cameron said, 'I to the hills will lift mine eyes', (the first line of Psalm 121 in the Scottish Metrical Version). So he took the hills and Bain took the flats, which then, and for many years after, were covered with bush. This was the first of extensive holdings built up over the next 20 or so years. The main property, which included part of the later town of Wauchope, was called 'Letter Ewe' (the bank of the Ewe) after a property on Loch Maree where Bain had worked as a shepherd before coming to Australia.

When Bain arrived on the Hastings there were only a few other white families. He maintained family worship in his home, and open air services were held under a giant fig tree on Letter Ewe which may still (1988) be seen on Beechwood Road .5 kms from the Bain Bridge. It appears the first of these services was held in 1862, the year two nephews came out from Scotland to join the Bains, and that several children were baptised. [41] Doubtless the preacher was Allan McIntyre of the Manning. A communion service was conducted by McIntyre in 1865. It began in the morning and it was near sun down before the finish, but such was the value placed on the services and the blessing attending the preaching, that this was not thought of as burdensome. The Lindsay family came in 1860 and purchased the 'Huntingdon' estate of 1,552 acres. Of the six sons, three had issue: David, William S. and James. A third prominent family arrived in 1863. This was the Andrews family, originally from Coleraine in Northern Ireland. There were three sons: Joseph (who purchased Wauchope House), and Isaac and Samuel (who were twins). In these two families some were for the Union and others not. The prevailing sentiment on the Hastings was in favour of the PCEA. Language was only a minor factor although Bain had a preference for Gaelic. The first Presbyterian building on the Hastings (excluding Port Macquarie) was the PCEA building erected at Letter Ewe in 1871.

41. So James Bain (1882-1973) in   Hazel Suters, History of Duncan Bain, Esq. (Wauchope c.1983) p.54

Nambucca/Bellinger

Apart from occasional services by ministers on the Hastings, organised Presbyterian work on these rivers commenced after the Union of 1865, and was initiated by the Synod of Eastern Australia.

Clarence River

Land in the Clarence Valley began to be taken up on a permissive occupancy basis in the late 1830s. The first sale of town blocks in Grafton took place in 1851. The lower Clarence developed later especially from 1862. [42]

Presbyterian activity began early. In May 1850, John Gibson, a Congregationalist who had joined Lang's (second) Synod of New South Wales, came to Grafton. Land was purchased and a manse erected at Wilson's Hill, South Grafton in 1851. Losing his wife and three children by death, Gibson removed to Sydney in February 1853. He had found the going difficult as most of the people refused to have any connection with Lang and adhered to the Church of Scotland. They also wished him to take state aid.[43] On June 28, 1854, Robert Miller was ordained by Lang's Synod for Grafton. He was of Church of Scotland background but declined to have connection with the Synod of Australia because of sympathy with Robert Boag, a defector from that Synod. He joined Lang's Synod but was no more acceptable than Gibson. He then applied to the PCEA but was rejected. He died at Grafton in April 1855. Lang sent James Collins in May 1857. He gained a few supporters in North Grafton and held early services in the Court House. He accepted the invitation of his adherents to become the minister. The old manse was sold. Samuel Avery gave a ½-acre site fronting Fitzroy and Mary Streets and a timber church 35' x 25' was erected towards the end of 1858 with a slab manse adjoining. After 1859 Collins ministered part-time. He died in 1864.

Meanwhile, Free Church settlers began coming to the Clarence, especially after the severe floods on the Hunter in 1857. Their strict church views and generally Highland background kept them apart from Collins' group. In mid 1859, Macintosh Mackay visited Grafton to organise a PCEA congregation and preached in Collins' pulpit. If Collins had been paid a sum he had advanced towards the cost of the building, the property would have transferred to the PCEA, but this did not occur. The PCEA organised separately and looked to get a minister from Scotland able to preach in Gaelic. A simple timber church was erected on one of three ½-acre sites purchased on the SE corner of Villiers and Hoof Streets, Grafton, probably

---

42. At various points of Clarence history I have had assistance from and interaction with Mrs Eleanor McSwan, a local historian and member of Maclean PCEA.
43. **Synod of NSW Minutes,** p.112 (April 7, 1852; for other references to Grafton see p.201,205 (April 8, 1858) and p.215 (April 13, 1859).

in 1859 or 1860. The major portion of the worshippers came to services by boat from Ulmarra, Clarenza, Great Marlow, South Grafton and Southampton. Some travelled ten miles in adverse conditions. In July 1861 a call signed by 104 men and one woman was made out to Alexander McIntyre. He declined as he believed his call was to itinerant evangelism from his main base at Geelong. At a later meeting in Grafton village, a call was made out to Allan McIntyre signed by 129 persons and dated June 29, 1862. It was accepted. McIntyre arrived from the Manning in January 1863, and was based at Grafton. Here he conducted an English service as well as a Gaelic, broken by lunch. Those who stayed for both services had a 3 or 4 hour spell on hardwood forms without backs.

Many Scottish settlers were coming to the lower Clarence around Maclean (then known as Rockymouth). James McDonald selected three blocks († 43, 44 & 45) in 1863, and on one of them he built a slab hut about 20' x 14' with a shingle roof. This served as a temporary place of worship for the PCEA. The present PCEA site in Wharf Street was purchased at auction on August 31, 1863 for $80 by J.McRae and D.Black as trustees. At the Synod meeting in November 1863, Allan McIntyre was able to report that a modest brick church was in course of erection, and on November 6, 1863, Maclean was disjoined from Grafton to become a separate charge.

However, the same 1863 Synod approved a Basis of Union which was not acceptable in Maclean. A meeting of the congregation on December 4, 1863 declared for separation forthwith, and proposed to seek supply from Rev Alexander McIntyre, then supplying at Ascot near Ballarat in Victoria. Alexander did not approve the stance: 'I think myself they should have remained as they were until the union had been consummated.'[43] Allan McIntyre continued to care for Maclean. The usual practice was that every third Lord's Day volunteers rowed him from Grafton to Maclean and back - a round trip of nearly 100 kms. The anomalous position of the Maclean congregation ceased upon union being concluded in November 1864, but during 1864 there must have been an element of dissension. In that year application was made for a Government site to be held by the PCEA and Lots 1, 2 & 3 of Section 33 were duly gazetted in 1865. This site was held by the pro-union minority, but it was not until the 1880s that numbers were sufficient to establish a PCNSW parish and even then the action was possible largely because of divisions at the time in the PCEA congregation.

43. Letter Alexander McIntyre to P. Macpherson January 22, 1864 in **MSS Correspondence of Rev Peter Macpherson 1861-67** (State Library of Victoria). Other movements of McIntyre have been traced through these letters.

The Maclean PCEA building was nearly ready for opening at the end of 1864,[44] and presumably was in use early in 1865. The persistent requests for Alexander McIntyre's services obtained a favourable response in the latter half of that year about the time (August) that Allan McIntyre left Grafton for the Manning. Alexander resided at Grafton and it appears that he remained on the Clarence until the end of 1866 or early 1867. He regarded Maclean in particular as a unique field for a Gaelic preacher, and a lasting spiritual work was done. He kept the congregation united with only 2 or 3 lost to the union.

In 1867, when the area was without regular PCEA ministry, the PCNSW intensified their efforts, though where they would have obtained a bi-lingual minister from is anyone's guess. When James Kinross of the PCNSW visited Maclean early in 1867 he was able to gather 70 or 80 hearers, but he said: 'If all the Highlanders would join the United Church, I have no hesitation in saying that the Presbyterian congregation at Rockymouth would be the largest out of Sydney.'[45] Dr William Grant of Shoalhaven, a respected Gaelic-speaking minister who had joined the union, visited the Clarence in July 1867 to see if he could bring in the Highlanders. Some of his own parishioners in Shoalhaven had moved to the district. However, though the people respected him as a man, they were not prepared to move. So strong did he find the influence of Alexander McIntyre that he soon returned saying, That so long as Sandy McIntyre lived there was no use trying to bring in the Highlanders. [46]

Richmond/Brunswick/Tweed Rivers

Organised Presbyterian work on these rivers began about the end of 1865 following a visit by Dr Lang. Rev John Thom acted as an ordained missionary and preached at such places as Woodburn, Lismore and Coraki, where he was drowned in September 1869. A good number of the early settlers were from the Shoalhaven River parish of Rev William Grant. Consequently, he visited the Richmond in July 1867 and opened the first church of any denomination on the Richmond on August 11, 1867 at Woodburn.[47] Real expansion did not occur until the 1880s.

44. Letter Alexander McIntyre to P. Macpherson, January 5, 1865 in op. cit.. McIntyre had been invited to take the opening services.
45. C.A.White, op. cit., p. 262.
46. J.C.Robinson, Rev Alexander McIntyre (Melbourne 1929) p. 23.
47. C.A.White, op. cit., pp. 441-442 provides a useful account of Grant's visit.

9: ACTIVITY IN VICTORIA

The first European settlement in what is now Victoria had been founded by the Hentys at Portland in November 1834, with Melbourne being established the following year. Rev James Clow was the first Presbyterian minister to arrive in Victoria. A retired Indian Chaplain, he visited from Tasmania and conducted a service on October 24, 1837 at Dr Thomson's station on the Barwon River. Later that year he settled with his family in Melbourne, and conducted a service on Sunday afternoon, December 31, 1837. However, on January 28, 1838, Rev James Forbes arrived from Sydney having been appointed to the District of Port Phillip by the Presbytery. He became the first Christian minister settled as such in Melbourne, and made the formal commencement of his ministry on February 3, 1838. Clow assisted Forbes in every way during the early years of strenuous exertions to extend the church and in August 1845 Forbes married Clow's daughter, Helen, at Tirhatuan, the station Clow ran in the present Rowville/Ferntree Gully, now an eastern suburban area of Melbourne. [1]

Scots Church, Melbourne

In June 1836 the settlers had taken up a collection for a church building, and early in 1837 a simple timber building which could hold 80 persons was erected on the south side of Bourke Street just west of William Street and north of Little Collins Street (now AMP Centre). Clow secured the use of it between 2 and 4 on Sunday afternoons. Bishop Broughton considered his church had exclusive claims and gave notice that it would not be available

---

1. Anne Hamilton, **Personal Life of James Clow** (Melbourne 1937) is a primary source for Clow as the author was Clow's granddaughter (daughter of Rev William Hamilton and Margaret Clow).

to other than the Church of England once a permament clergyman was appointed. This event occurred in October 1838, and was followed by the formal grant of the site to the Church of England. The Presbyterians accelerated their plans and the first Scots Church was erected on the south side of Collins Street near William Street. The location was about where the Olderfleet Buildings were later built (now incorporated in the Rialto). It was 29 feet long and 15 feet wide and cost eighty-eight pounds. No window glass was available so sliding shutters were used. This building was also used as a school, but was intended to be temporary. Services began in it in July 1838. A two-acre site was obtained from the Government on the corner of Collins and Russell Streets - a position then regarded by many as too far out of town! - and a brick building called Scots School was erected in Collins Street where *Georges* store now stands. It was opened in September 1839 and served for worship until Scots Church was built on the corner of the site in 1841. Within 12 months it had 150 scholars and a reputation as the most efficient school in Melbourne. Its two rooms, even when opened into one, were insufficient for the growing congregation, hence the erection of the 500 seat Scots Church, the first on the present site, and the fourth place of public worship for Presbyterians. It was a plain building without a spire and was not fully finished inside. Forbes built a two-storey manse between the church and the school but through oversight it was some time before he was paid for it. Early in the 20th century it was demolished to make way for the *Assembly Hall* of the PCV. The population of Melbourne was about 4,000 in the early part of 1840 and increased five-fold in the following year.

Early years

At the formation of the Synod of Australia in 1840, Forbes had desired to sign the Bond of Union with the reservation that he and his fellow-labourers claimed the right of forming Synods and Presbyteries independent of the

138

Synod of Australia. This was denied although 'the Synod at the same time express their cordial wish to assist   Ministers at Port Phillip to establish such Courts according to the rules of the Church, and will have no hesitation in taking up the subject when brought before them in the regular order.' [2]
The first meeting of the Presbytery of Melbourne was held June 7, 1842 with Revs Forbes, Mowbray and Gunn present together with Dr Patrick, elder. Forbes was greatly interested in education and produced two important reports on the subject in his capacity of Convener of a Presbytery Committee. His position on the Scottish Disruption has already been made clear. He was not able to be present in Sydney at the Synod of October 1846 but was in full agreement with those who protested and withdrew under the leadership of William McIntyre. He addressed the Scots congregation on October 25, and summed up his case as follows:

For these reasons, and for others, which cannot now be mentioned, I renounce, from this time forth, all connection and communion with 'the Synod of Australia in connection with the Established Church of Scotland,' and I relinquish all privileges and advantages of a temporal kind which I enjoy as a member thereof. ..I am constrained to it by a desire to maintain the principles and testimony of the Free Church of Scotland - principles which I believe to be the olden principles of the National Church of Scotland - principles which I vowed to maintain, when ordained to the office of the ministry - principles for which many blessed martyrs in other days shed their blood - principles which I am firmly persuaded are taught and inculcated in the Word of God. As long as there was a shadow of a hope that the Synod of Australia would be faithful to these principles I continued in it, though there was much in it I lamented, and much wanting that I desired to see. I am not one of those who regard religious dissensions as slight matters. I believe that the maintenance of the unity & peace of the Church is a duty second only to the maintenance of purity and truth, - of fidelity to her only King and Head. That I may be faithful to Christ, I separate from those I consider disloyal to him, who in words acknowledge him as pre-eminent, but in works deny him.[3]

A written Protest dated October 29 was issued by Forbes. At a meeting of his Presbytery on November 17, 1846, he submitted the protest and desired that certain amounts due him be granted and that he have some weeks to vacate the manse. Gunn derided him and the requests were denied. Forbes formally withdrew from the jurisdiction of the Synod and from presbyterial relation with the three remaining ministers (Love, Gunn and Laurie) in the Presbytery of Melbourne.

On November 22, 1846, Forbes commenced services in the Mechanics' Hall, 100 metres from his old church where the Atheneum now stands. Forbes

---

2. **Minutes of the Synod of Australia**, January 7, 1841 (Printed copy, Sydney 1841).
3. **Supplement to the Port Phillip Christian Herald**, November 7, 1846.

James Forbes 1823-1851

was the Secretary of the Mechanics' Institute which had held its initial meetings in Scots School. About 50 members and adherents of Scots Church followed Forbes and there were some 200 at the inaugural services of his Free Presbyterian Church. The collections for the day amounted to ten pounds two shillings and one penny. [4] Forbes was considered a fool by many since he gave up a stipend of $700 a year when he left Scots Church ($400 from the state and $300 additional from the congregation). This was the highest amount any Presbyterian minister received at that time and indicates the wealth of the congregation and their appreciation of their minister.

4. Minutes of the Free Presbyterian Church Melbourne [John Knox] 22/11/1846-1/08/1865, p.1 (MSS in possession of Rowland Ward)

John Knox Free Presbyterian Church 1848

In 1847 Matthew Orr offered the deeds of an excellent allotment of 1901m2 in Swanston Street (cnr Little Lonsdale Street) for $1 to be paid by each of five trustees, and on November 17, 1847 - the anniversary of his departure from Scots church - the foundation stone of John Knox Church was laid. The building was situated lengthwise along Swanston Street with the entry on Little Lonsdale Street. It was opened in an unfinished state and with temporary fittings on May 8, 1848 - Rev Thomas Hastie preaching at 11am and Rev John Huie at 3pm. There were then no made paths or streets in Melbourne nor were there street lamps. The land in the vicinity of the church was open land and boys used to split chips for kindling off the tree stumps in the roadway. [5]

Free Presbyterian educational work

On July 3, 1848, *John Knox' School* began in the church building under the direction of T.J.Everist, the supervising engineer of the Town Council. and an elder in the congregation. From July 1, 1849, James Robertson was in charge with three assistants and 120 pupils. November 1848 saw a timber schoolroom erected as a temporary measure, while in mid August 1850 a brick schoolroom containing two rooms came into use. It cost some $700, all of which was raised by private subscription. George McMaster succeeded Robertson on September 30, 1850. The school continued until 1862.

McMaster had arrived unexpectedly from Scotland in February 1850 with a commisssion from the Free Church of Scotland to place himself under Forbes' direction. Difficulty was found in obtaining suitable premises for McMaster to commence teaching but at length a lease was secured of a school room with two small cottages attached between Lonsdale and Little Lonsdale Streets at what is now 257 Spring Street. Here *Chalmers' Free Church School* commenced on June 4, 1850. Up to 200 children could be accommodated and there were 100 on the roll by the end of September. The school had the 'advantage of having for a playground, the large Government Reserve fronting St Peter's Church.'[6] Thus the pupils played where the Parliament Gardens are now situated. McMaster became Head Master of John Knox School on September 30, 1850. He was succeeded by George Knox who had an attendance of 57 in October. However, Chalmers' School was overtaken by other events, not least the death of Forbes in August 1851, and it does not appear that it long survived.

5. An interesting account of early conditions is in J.A.Allan, **The History of the John Knox Glebe in Swanston Street** in The Victorian Historical Magazine, June 1944, pp.85-101. A few inaccuracies occur so variations in the following paragraphs are intentional.
6. **PPCH**, July 1850, p.56, col. 2. Other important references to early FPC schools include **PPCH** October 1850, p.79 and November 1850, p.87. The financial responsibility for Chalmers' School was borne by James Forbes, W.M.Bell (an early Mayor of Melbourne) and John McDonnell.

Forbes was anxious to see an Academy for instruction of young men in the higher branches of learning as a first step towards the training of a colonial ministry. On October 6, 1851, in the building of Chalmers' Free Church School, the *Melbourne Academy* commenced with Robert Lawson from Scotland in charge. The Melbourne Academy obtained more adequate leased premises at what is now 99 Spring Street (the southern corner of Little Collins Street) and commenced there on January 19, 1852. On January 10, 1854, the Melbourne Academy began its occupancy of purpose-built premises on the corner of Grey and Lansdowne Streets, East Melbourne, adjoining Adam Cairns' Chalmers Church. From 1855 it was termed variously Scotch College or Scots College, with the former name the accepted title after 1866. So was born the oldest of Victoria's private schools. It was a specifically Christian school seeking to carry on the highest educational traditions of Scotland. What was said by Forbes at the laying of the foundation stone for John Knox School on March 5, 1850 might be said of Scotch also:

Its objects are, to provide sound and solid instruction for youth of both sexes in sacred and secular knowledge. Its projectors regard, with the fathers of the Scottish Reformation, whose principles they aim at upholding and maintaining in their adopted country, 'the virtuous and godly upbringing of the youth' to be one of the highest duties of any community. They aim at supplying their own children, the children of their neighbours, and the children of generations to come, with an education based on the Word of God, and in harmony with its spirit. They desire that all within reach of their influence may know, from childhood, the Holy Scriptures, which are able to make them wise unto salvation, through faith which is in Christ Jesus.[7]

Scotch College remained a school for boys only, and was regularly supervised by the Free Presbyterian Church. In 1875 a school for girls, Presbyterian Ladies' College, was commenced by the Presbyterian Church of Victoria. Later there were other schools, but the two mentioned were the ones secured by the PCV which continued apart from the Uniting Church in 1977.

It is worth adding that the John Knox premises housed a lending library of several hundred volumes. The membership rate was four shillings a year. As well there were classes from 4pm to 6pm for adult females , as well as evening classes in subjects ranging from the Classics to Practical Book-keeping. It has been said with justification that James Forbes, who was behind all these projects, was Melbourne's first public educationist.

7. **Port Phillip Christian Herald,** April 1850, p.32 col. 2

Presbyterianism in Geelong

Rev Andrew Love arrived in Geelong on April 12, 1840 and soon organised the work. The first service was held in Mr Fischer's woolshed. A church was built on a site already secured from the Government. It was opened on July 3, 1842 in Yarra Street, between McKillop and Little Myers Streets and was known as *Scots Church* until October 1859 when it was renamed *St Andrew's Church*. In 1912 the congregation moved to East Geelong and the original building is now a Lutheran Church.

There were quite a large number of Presbyterians in Geelong and a part of the town was called 'Little Scotland.' The Disruption of the Synod of Australia in 1846 saw a significant proportion of Geelong Presbyterians casting in their lot with the Free Presbyterian Church. On June 2, 1847, Rev John Zeigler Huie arrived at Melbourne from Scotland and became the minister of a Free Presbyterian congregation at Geelong which met in the Temperance Hall. A church building which doubled as a day-school was erected in Little Malop Street west of Bellarine Street. It was opened in 1848 and was known as the *Scotch Free Church*. Huie was an energetic preacher and soon had the largest congregation of any in Geelong. Dr Learmonth of Batesford, John Armstrong of Bush Station and Messrs McLean and Williamson of the Barrabool Hills were key supporters. Huie submitted his resignation on March 5, 1850 on account of health and left for Scotland in April. Rev John H. McLachlan, a recent arrival from Scotland, gave supply for 12 months from March 1850, and Rev John Tait became the second inducted minister in 1851 when the average attendance was 280. A manse at 1 Skene Street was purchased the following year. In 1862 a new church was opened in Gheringhap Street, between Little Ryrie and Myers Street. It was known from its elevation as the *High Church*, but was later renamed *St Giles* (now disused Uniting Church).

The increasing numbers of Gaelic-speaking Scots led to the formation on April 25, 1853, of a *Gaelic* congregation of the Free Presbyterian Church. with pulpit supply from Rev Allan McVean for about 9 months from September 1853. Some early services were held in the Baptist Church, and in May 1854 the erection of a sandstone schoolhouse was commenced on the site obtained from the Government on the corner of Myers Street and Latrobe Terrace. A church was added in 1859. Both these buildings still stand as part of the property of the Geelong PCEA congregation. In March 1856 Rev John McDougall was appointed to supply the congregation which was of fair size (132 seat holders) and considerable substance. It was said to be the largest Gaelic-speaking congregation in the Southern Hemisphere.[8] McDougall was inducted later in 1856 and continued as minister until his

8. So Gladys Seaton in **The Investigator** Vol. 8 †1 (Geelong 1983)p.9; see also I.H. Touzel, **I Will Build My Church - A History of the Geelong Congregation of the PCEA** (unpublished BD thesis, Reformed Theological College, Geelong 1980, p.8.

death on May 29, 1858 at the early age of 36 years. His health had been poor for some time so that on February 10, 1858, Rev Alexander McIntyre was appointed to supply. McIntyre declined a call but continued to supply and also visited other areas as well. There were 200 regular attenders at this time and the congregation opened the new church on May 1, 1859.

The congregation supported the Minority in the stand against union but the failure to secure recognition in Scotland led to disorganisation and decline. McIntyre moved to Ascot, about 20 kms north of Ballarat, where he had opened a church in July 1859. Here he had a congregation of some 300 Highlanders. However, on April 10, 1861, the FP Synod received Rev J.Z. Huie, who had returned to the Colony, after satisfying itself as to the integrity of his family relations. He was appointed to supply Geelong, soon gathered a numerous congregation, many or most being Lowlanders, and received a call signed by 152 persons. This was accepted but the induction appointed for September 18, 1861 was delayed pending further investigation of persistent reports of bizarre behaviour associated with excess use of alcohol. [9] Huie resigned 3 months later. Rev William Dron was appointed early in 1862. He was unsatisfactory ('a drone') and resigned in June to join the PCV. He soon went to NSW and eventually to Ireland where he joined the Church of England. Huie continued an independent work in Geelong but died early in 1864. aged 41. None of this helped the stability of the congregation. Rev Alexander McIntyre resumed oversight, but the attendance was weak. McIntyre was often away in other centres. He died in Geelong on June 9, 1878.[10]

The *United Presbyterian Church* was on the scene in Geelong as early as 1851. On May 18 of that year, Rev Alexander McNichol was inducted to Geelong. After using the Masonic Hall in Union Street the congregation erected a building in McKillop Street in 1853 which cost over $2,000. During the construction the building was destroyed in a gale. This set back efforts and McNichol resigned. However, in May 1855, Rev John Cooper was appointed to supply and was inducted on August 29, 1855 following a call signed by 139 persons. On July 5, 1857 what became known from its architecture as the *Steeple Church* was opened at what is now 35A Ryrie Street (part of the Performing Arts Centre). The land and building cost $8,300. Cooper left at the end of 1858 and was succeeded by Rev James Henderson (inducted May 17, 1859).

9. For details see P.Macpherson, The Free Church Principles of Rev Allan MacVean (Melbourne 1866) pp. 5-8.
10. For life see J.C.Robertson, The Rev Alexander McIntyre (Melbourne 1929) 60pp, but note the date of death is incorrectly stated as April 9, 1878.

The last branch of Presbyterianism to be noticed is the *Reformed Presbyterian Church*. There were some families of Reformed Presbyterian background in Melbourne and in Geelong, but it was not until 1857 that a minister was sent out. Rev A.M.Moore arrived at Melbourne from Belfast and almost at once proceeded to Geelong where he met with a few friends for prayer on the Lord's Day, December 27, 1857. He soon gathered 50 or 60 persons who met in various places (including the Free Church School). The present church building was opened on August 10, 1862 by Rev J.G.Paton and the adjoining manse in Fenwick Street in 1869. Mr Moore died in 1897. His was the only congregation of the Reformed Presbyterian Church of Ireland in Australia.

We now look at each of the three main streams of Presbyterian witness.

Synod of Australia (Established Church)

The three members of the Presbytery who adhered to the Synod of Australia in 1846 processed a call from Scots Church to Irving Hetherington of Singleton which he accepted. Hetherington had sympathised with the Free Church, taken a neutral stance in the Disruption crisis, and found division in his parish. Hetherington was quite well off as he had business interests. His administrative gifts were his best asset. He was not a very effective preacher though warmly orthodox. Some did not think too kindly of his acceptance of a pulpit made vacant by Forbes' departure because of consistency to principles Hetherington himself professed. His biographer tells us that he 'found himself unable to work along with his co-presbyters who were all of the old school, and strongly attached to the Church of Scotland.' Faced with an acute shortage of ministers - apart from Gow in 1847 there were no additions until 1852 - Hetherington was able to organise assistance from the Irish Presbyterian Church, and virtually all the ministerial recruits were from that source. The significance of this will be discussed later.

So far as state-aid was concerned, this was continued after the Port Phillip District was separated from New South Wales to form the Colony of Victoria. Indeed, the discovery of gold wrought a revolution in the society. The average annual value of gold produced in Victoria for the 8 years ending in 1861 was nearly $20 million. In the 30 years to 1881 the Victorian production was some $400 million while New South Wales produced about $27 million. There was an astonishing population growth. Victoria's population rose from 80,000 to 300,000 by the close of 1854, while in New South Wales the figures increased from about 197,000 to 300,000 over the same period. There was plenty of money to continue aid on a generous basis, and also plenty of opportunity for the spiritual work of the churches. The Victorian work of the Synod of Australia achieved independence as the Synod of Victoria in April 1854, but the moral and legal tie to the Established Church of Scotland continued.

Free Presbyterian Synod

When James Forbes had been joined by a sufficient number of like-minded men, 'The Free Presbyterian Church of Australia Felix' was constituted with a Synod as its initial assembly. The date was June 9, 1847 and the first members were Rev James Forbes (Moderator), Henrie Bell, an elder of Scots who had left with Forbes, Rev Thomas Hastie of Buninyong and The Leigh, and Rev John Z. Huie of Geelong. Hastie had been colleague to Rev John Anderson of Launceston but resigned as a consequence of the failure of the Presbytery of Van Diemen's Land to break its connection with the Established Church. He came to Victoria and commenced his ministry in January 1847 at The Leigh (out of Geelong). He established his main centre 100 kms to the north at Buninyong (south of Ballarat) where a church building was opened by Forbes on June 13, 1847. Huie arrived on June 2, 1847.

Forbes took the view, as did his brethren, that assistance would not be sought from the Government for sites, buildings or stipends. There was no formal minute to this effect but it was well understood. The inaugural minute of the Synod stated, inter alia, 'A full statement of our distinctive principles shall be forthwith prepared, with the view of being adopted as the Fundamental Act of this Synod. On May 9, 1848, after very careful consideration, the Fundamental Act was adopted. It was a quite full constitutional declaration and a statesmanlike endeavour to lay a sound basis for the Presbyterian Church in this country. As generally indicative of the Free Church of Scotland's understanding of the constitution of the Church of Scotland it is an interesting document. It shows the master hand of Rev James Forbes, who was an able man in church law and procedure. The same basis was adopted by the Free Presbyterian Church of South Australia upon its formation in May 1854. Forbes was one in purpose with McIntyre and his brethren in New South Wales, but formed a separate church because

Experience has painfully convinced me of the undesirableness of the Church here being under the rule of a body meeting in Sydney. The objections felt by every colonist to a political connexion with New South Wales, apply with ten-fold force to an ecclesiastical connexion of Presbyterians. Australia Felix is in every way sufficiently important to constitute a field for an independent Synodical body, and Providence appears to be opening up the way for its formation at a period not very remote.[11]

On February 1, 1848, the Synod adopted formally the rules for discipline and government used by the Free Church of Scotland pending the drawing up of rules adapted to the special needs of the Australian situation. A digest of the rules adopted to the close of 1850 was duly published. This attention to ordered forms adapted to local conditions was not so evident in the PCEA.

11. **PPCH**, November 7, 1846 p.98; similarly Forbes to Bonar 30/6/1847 in **Home and Foreign Missionary Record of the Free Church of Scotland**, January 1848, p.295. The text of the **Fundamental Act** may be found in works by R.Sutherland,p.84, J.C.Robinson, Appendix VIII, and Rowland Ward (1978:pp.79-81).

The two most prominent ministers of the FPCV after Forbes' death in 1851 were Dr Adam Cairns (1802-1881) and Dr Macintosh Mackay (1793-1873). Both these men had 'come out' of the Established Church at the Disruption, and were men of experience specially chosen for Australia. Cairns arrived in Melbourne in September 1853, and Mackay in December of the same year. Subsequent chapters sufficiently indicate their contribution to the union debate, but some other details may be appropriate at this point.

Adam Cairns had been commissioned by the Free Church to establish a congregation in Melbourne as well as to promote education and further union. Prior to leaving Scotland he arranged for an iron church and manse to be shipped out as the cost of labour in Melbourne was very high due to the gold rush. Shortly after his arrival, a temporary timber church was erected in Gipps Street, East Melbourne, adjoining the site where Scotch College was subsequently located. It had no floor but the natural turf of the site, and was erected in 17 days and could seat 1,000. It was opened on November 20, 1853. A numerous congregation attended on Cairns' earnest and evangelical ministry. The iron manse arrived but the iron church was delayed, and it

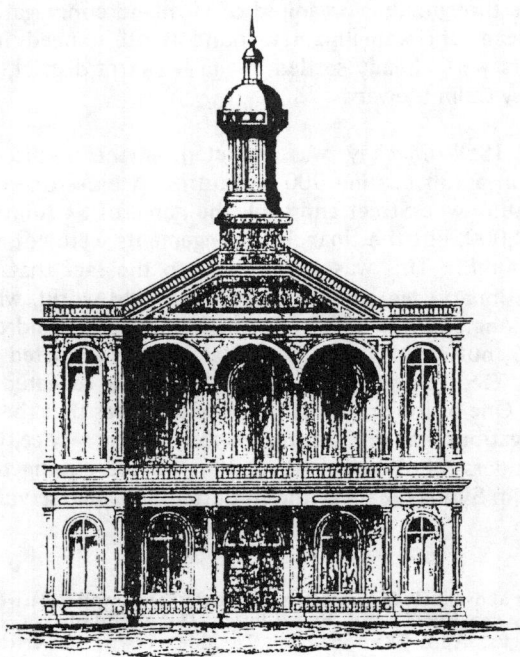

The Iron Church intended for Melbourne

147

was decided to erect a permanent church in stone. This was done by the end of 1855 at a cost of over $20,000, all but $6,500 being paid by the time of opening. The building bore the name Chalmers' Church. The iron church arrived about October 1854. Apart from having a single spire rather than a double one, it was a twin of the iron church imported by the Macquarie Street PCEA congregation at the same time (see page 102). It was 73' x 46', fitted with galleries. Various misunderstandings having arisen, the congregation did not accept delivery and the parts of the building languished in storage in St Kilda until 1863. The building was then sold at auction and became a mechanics' institute at Invercargill, New Zealand. Chalmers' Church did not long survive Dr Cairns' retirement in 1876, as a suitable successor was hard to find. A section of the congregation formed *Cairns' Memorial* Church nearby in the early 1880s, and the original congregation was later wound up.[12]

Macintosh Mackay was the most learned of the Scottish ministers of the colonial period. He had made his name as a Gaelic scholar through the editorship of the Highland Society's Gaelic Dictionary published about 1828. He had also been actively involved in the welfare of Highlanders. He seems to have thought that organised of Highland congregations in Australia could be a means of channelling new-found wealth to needs in Scotland. Two of his brothers were already settled in the Illawarra district, and a sister was married to Rev Colin Stewart.

On April 3, 1854, Mackay was inducted to the Gaelic congregation in Melbourne on a call bearing 900 signatures. A bluestone church was soon erected in Rathdowne Street and took the name of St Andrew's, Carlton. It cost over $20,000, but the financial arrangements were not as satisfactory as in Cairns' Church. This was in part due to the fact that Mackay was an impractical visionary. He also belonged to the old world, while his sermons were far too long and not delivered with animation. St Andrew's was opened May 12, 1855, but on May 13, 1856, Mackay was inducted to what became known as St George's PCEA, Sydney, where he repeated his Melbourne performance. One of the problems Mackay faced was that the English portion of his congregations was not satisfied with only one service, while there were many Highlanders who were 'ashamed to be seen going to hear a Gaelic service.' Thus, in Sydney Mackay did not attempt Gaelic services.[13]

12. Sources for above include 'Statement by Mr James Cowan Relative to Iron Building Sent to Melbourne For Use of Free Church There' (Edinburgh, December 1859); Melbourne Argus, April 18, 1863; and Dr Miles Lewis, University of Melbourne.
13. J.C.Robinson, Alexander McIntyre, op.cit., p.47 (letter by McIntyre dated July 27, 1857).

St Andrew's remained an influential congregation which retained the older Presbyterian views and practices until close to the end of the 19th century under its able and popular minister, Rev D.S.McEachran, inducted 1868.

United Presbyterian Church

United Presbyterian origins in Victoria are described on page 165, and the spread of the church is indicated in the table of ministers on pages 153-155. The significant influence of *Relief* ministers Ramsay and Hamilton may be noted. Both of these men were particularly strong opponents of state-aid to the churches. Ramsay was a very popular preacher in the early years of Melbourne, and gained support from the well-to-do middle class. There was a certain influence of democratic ideals among the UPs together with a tendency to be less rigid on doctrinal points. The situation in Victoria was not as bad as in Lang's second Synod of New South Wales, but there were similarities. Some UPs from the Secession branch in Scotland were more solid, and this contributed to the split in the Synod referred to on page 187 of this book.

The most outstanding of the United Presbyterians after Ramsay was James Ballantyne (1817-1896), who arrived with his brother John in February 1855. He was the minister of Lonsdale Street UP Church, on the south side of the street between Swanston and Russell Streets. From 1858 known as *Erskine Church*, the congregation relocated to the corner of Rathdowne and Grattan Streets, Carlton in 1874. Ballantyne resigned in 1877 on account of ill-health. However, he continued with work as editor of the church magazine for many years. Of conservative theology, he was an able and attractive writer and a popular preacher.

149

ORDAINED MINISTERS CONNECTED WITH THE SYNOD OF AUSTRALIA (FROM 1854, THE SYNOD OF VICTORIA)
IN CONNECTION WITH THE ESTABLISHED CHURCH OF SCOTLAND
1837-1859

†	Name	Ordination	Details of service
1	James Clow	CS- 1815	At Port Phillip October 1837. Held no charge. Died 1861.
2	James Forbes, MA	CS- 1837	Scots, Melbourne 1838-46; to FPC.
3	Andrew Love	CS- 1839	Scots, Geelong 1840-67 and died.
4	T.Mowbray, MA	CS- 1841	Scots, Campbellfield 1842-1844; Sydney 1845-47 (withdrew in 1846); to Qld. '47.
5	Alex Laurie	CS- 1841	Scots, Portland 1842-3; Port Fairy 1843-45; Portland 1845-48 & deposed (drink).
6	Peter Gunn	CS- 1841*	Melbourne (Gaelic) 1842-43; Bulleen 1843 -45; Campbellfield 1845-64 & died.
7	I.Hetherington, MA	CS- 1837	Ex NSW; Scots, Melbourne 1847-75.
8	John Gow	SA- 1847	Colac /Cressy etc. 1847 & latterly at Smythesdale; died 1866.
9	John Reid	US- 1829	Ex CS; Melbourne (Temp Hall) 1853-53; Essendon 1853-54; Nth Melbourne 1854-12/1855; to UPC.
10	John Low	CS-	Chewton (goldfields) 1852-53; then Castlemaine 1853-59; Guildford 1861- died 1877.
11	Thomas Heron	PCI-1849	Arrived 7/1852; East Melbourne (Albert Street) 1853-54; resigned.
12	Thomas Craig	PCI	Arrived 10/1852; Port Fairy 1852-56; Essendon 1856-61; died 1878.
13	David Boyd	SA- 1853	Arrived 1/1853; Heidelberg 1853-69.
14	Samuel Corrie	PCI	Windsor 1853-57; Kilnoorat 1857-91.
15	Peter McLaggan		Colac 1853-54 & left colony.
16	A.Grahame	PCI	Kalkallo 1853-57; Longwood/Mansfield/ Benalla 1857-69 & died.
17	T.McAnlis	PCI	Alberton/Tarraville 1853-57; Skipton 1857-58 & killed in accident.
18	John Martin	PCI	Arrived 1853; chaplain at Ballarat gold-fields; resigned August 1857.

SYNOD OF VICTORIA FORMED APRIL 1854

†	Name	Ordination	Details of service
19	Hugh Blair MA	PCI	Arrived 4/1854; Colac/Ondit 1854-66; returned to Ireland & died 1889.
20	Alex Duff MA	SV- 1854	Cranbourne/Dandenong 1855-76; Cranbourne 1876-88; died 1891.
21	J. Parker	PCI	Arrived 5/1857; Port Fairy 1857-59; resigned from the ministry 1860.
22	G.M.Reed	PCI	Arrived 11/1857; Nth Melbourne (Union Memorial) to 1861 then Ipswich Q.
23	Robert Hogg MA	SV - 1858	Arrived 11/1858; Horsham 1858-60; to India.
24	W.J.Taggart	PCI	Skipton/Carngham 1858-60; injured by bushranger; returned to Ireland.
25	James Megaw	PCI- 1857	Windsor 1858-60; Ararat 1860--92.
26	Samuel Kelly	PCI- 1856	Arrived 8/1858; Alberton/Tarraville 1858-60; supply at Richmond 1860; to Qld.
27	Samuel Kelso	PCI	Arrived 1/1859; Portland 1859-68; Stawell 1869-91; died 1902.

NB: It appears that all but ministers †1 to 10 were of Irish background. The 19 ministers in April 1859 joined the union (entries in bold type). An asterisk means Gaelic-speaking.

ORDAINED MINISTERS OF THE
FREE PRESBYTERIAN CHURCH OF VICTORIA 1846-1867

†	Name	Ordination	Details of service
1	James Forbes,MA	CS- 1837	John Knox, Melbourne 1846-51 & died.
2	Thomas Hastie	CS- 1842	Ex VDL; Bunninyong 1847-91; died 1898 aged 85 years.
3	J.Z.Huie	FCS- 1847	Geelong (L.Malop Street) 1847-50 to Scotland; returned 1861.
4	John H. McLachlan	FCS- 1849	Arrived 2/1850; Geelong 1850-51; Hopkins River (Wickcliffe) 1851-56; Brighton 1856-57; Amherst 1861-63.
5	John Tait	CS- 1837	Ex PCEA 1851; Geelong 1851-61 & died.
6	John Hume	FPC- 1851	Kilmore (St George's)1851-55 & died.
7	William Miller	FCS- 1851	John Knox, Melbourne 1851-65; to England.
8	D.M.Sinclair	FPC- 1852*	Ex NSW; Melbourne (Gaelic) 1852-53 & resigned; various non-ministerial positions & joined C of E in NSW 1873; died 1887.
9	Allan McVean	FCS- 1852*	Arrived 11/1852; supply inc. Geelong & Williamstown; Brunswick 1854-95.
10	Donald McDonald	FPC- 1853*	Bulleen (Gaelic) 1853-54; Sth Melbourne 1854-87 and retired.
11	John Barnet	FCS-	Bellarine 1853-57; Camperdown 1857 and drowned that year.
12	Adam Cairns,DD	CS- 1828	Ex FCS; Chalmers', East Melbourne 1853-76; died 1881 aged 79 years.
13	Wm Henderson	FCS- 1853	Williamstown 1853-58; Ballarat (Sturt Street) 1858-1884 and died aged 57.
14	Arch Simpson	FCS- 1853	Supply 1853-54; The Leigh 1855-82; died 1883.
15	Alex Adam, MA	FCS-	Burnbank district 1853-1899 (resided at Beaufort from 1866).
16	M. Mackay LLD	CS- 1825*	St Andrew's, Carlton (Gaelic) 1854-56; to PCEA Sydney (St George's) 1856-61; to Scotland; died 1873 aged 79 years.
17	George Divorty	FCS- 1853	Sth Yarra (Punt Road) 1853-1861; to Scotland; Sec of Scottish Reformation Society; died 1887 aged 68 years.
18	W.S.Logm	FCS- 1844	Gippsland (based at Sale) 1854-85 and retired.
19	James Nish	FCS-	Bendigo (St Andrew's) 1854-90; died 1892 aged 66 years.
20	R. Sutherland MA	FCS-	Batesford 1854-57; Casterton 1857-61; Allansford 1862-76; to Scotland.
21	Arthur Paul	FCS- 1853	Ex NSW; Richmond (Bridge Road) 1854-55; St Kilda 1855-1910 & died.
22	James Baird	FCS-	Ex Tas; Ballarat (Sturt Street) 1855-57 & resigned due health.
23	Wm McIntosh	FCS-	Ararat 1855-60 & died.
24	John McDougall	FPC- 1856 *	Geelong (Gaelic) 1856-58 & died.
25	Dugald McCalman	FPC- 1856*	St Andrew's, Carlton supply 1856; Narra-coorte,SA 1856-80 & retired; died 1881.
26	Andrew Maxwell	FCS- 1852	Ex PCEA; Kilmore (St Georges) 1856-66 and died .
27	Robert Fleming	FCS-	Port Fairy 1856-58; Lethbridge 1858-62 deposed (drink).
28	John Grant	FCS-	Beechworth 1857-58; Maldon 1858-59 and deposed (drink).

EXPULSION - APRIL 8, 1857 (MAJORITY SYNOD 18 MINISTERS; MINORITY 5)

The names printed in bold type in the above list are those of men in service at the time of the union on April 7, 1859 when 15 of them were in the Majority Synod and 4 in the Minority Synod. An * means a minister able to preach in Gaelic.

MAJORITY SYNOD 1857-59

(Comprised of 18 ministers of whom 2 died and 1 transferred to the Minority but which was increased by 12 ministers as follows making 27 in all who entered the 1859 union.)

1	Angus McDonald	FPC- 1857*	Hamilton 1857-68 & killed in riding accident.
2	William Fraser	FCS- *	St Andrew's, Carlton 1857-59; Bulla 1859-1873 and died.
3	Charles Moir	FCS-	St Kilda (rival to Paul) 1857-72 and returned to Scotland.
4	George Mackie	FCS- 1848	Ex PCEA; Learmonth/Burrumbeet 1857-60; Horsham 1860-62; Sth Yarra 1862-71 and died.
5	Alex Proudfoot	FCS-	Batesford 1857-66; Gladstone, Q 1866-1873.
6	F.R.M.Wilson	FCS-	Camperdown 1857-77; Kew 1877-1903 and died.
7	Evan Macdonald	FPC- 1858	Kyneton 1858-61 and died.
8	John Storie	FCS	Castlemaine (Templeton Street) 1858-60; St Andrew's, Hobart 1860-79.
9	John Clark	FPC-	Williamstown 1858-
10	J.S.Moir	FCS	Ex FCS & FPCSA ; Brighton 1858-61; Alberton/Tarraville 1861-63; Meredith 1863-67; teaching; died 1877.
11	J.K.McMillan	FCS-	Beechworth 1858-69; Hamilton 1869-
12	J.M.Strongman	Cong	without charge.

NB: Some cases have not been sufficiently researched to be certain of ordination dates or whether by the FCS or the FPC.

An * marks a minister able to preach in Gaelic.

MINORITY SYNOD 1857-67

Comprised of 5 ministers (Miller, McVean, Paul, Maxwell and McDougall). McDougall died in 1858 and Maxwell in 1865, while Miller returned to the UK in 1865. With other changes as noted below this left two ministers (McVean & Meiklejohn) to unite with the Presbyterian Church of Victoria on November 19, 1867, and three ministers (Paul, McIntyre & Macpherson) to continue the Synod on the basis of the Fundamental Act in line with their Protest of May 25, 1864. Union with the PCEA was effected 1953.

1	A.W.Sinclair	PCEA- 1854	Bellarine 1858-64; to PCNSW; Windsor 1866-67; Bowenfels 1867-71; to PCV; Bendigo (Golden Square) 1874-76; d 1889
2	Alexander McIntyre	Can 1847 *	Ex PCEA; received 2/1858; oversight of Geelong 1858-61 & various including Grafton NSW 1865-66; died at Geelong 1878 aged 71 years.
3	Robert Fleming	FCS-	Ex Majority Synod 12/58; Lethbridge 1858-62; deposed (drink).
4	John Z. Huie	FCS- 1847	Received 4/1861; supply of Geelong 1861 forced resignation as minister 12/61; had independent congregation in Geelong for a period; died of alcoholism.

5	A. Murdoch	FPC - 1862	Coburg 1862-64; to PCV with congregation 1863; Yea 1864-68; Benalla 1868-82; died 1893.
6	William Dron	FCS- 1851	Received 2/1862; supply at Geelong; to PCV 6/1862; to PCEA 1863; Illawarra 1864; Manning 12/64-8/65 (joined union) Tumut 1866; to Ireland; joined C of E.
7	Peter MacPherson MA	FPC - 1862	Meredith/Lethbridge 1862-74; to PCEA Raymond Tce 1874-78; resided in Sydney died 1886 aged 60 years.
8	John Gardiner	FPC- 1863	Coonewarre 1863-66 (residing in Geelong from mid 1865); leave of absence overseas 1866-67; nothing further known.
9	Donald Meiklejohn	FCS-	Ex NZ; St George's Kilmore 1866-72; lost leg in accident and resigned charge 1872.

ORDAINED MINISTERS OF THE
UNITED PRESBYTERIAN CHURCH OF VICTORIA
1847-1870

†	Name	Ordination	Details of service
1	A.M.Ramsay	Relief 1833	Arrived January 1847; Collins Street, Melbourne (St Enoch's) 1847-69 & died.
2	T.E.Richardson	UPCS-1848	Arrived October 1848; Portland 1/1849-5/1852; thence to journalism.
3	Lachlan McGillivray	† Jan 18, 1848	Ordained by Cong. Bapt, Meth & Relief ministers after resigning from FPC; Burnbank district 1848; Port Fairy/Warrnambool 1849-53; returned to Scotland.
4	William Jarrett	Cong - 1832	Teacher; commenced 2nd Melbourne congregation (later Lonsdale Street) 1850. Resigned 10/1856; to UPCA 1858; joined PCV 1859; Daylesford 1862-65.

SYNOD FORMED January 22, 1850

5	Alex McNichol	UPCV-1850	Bacchus Marsh/Mt Macedon 1850-51; Geelong 1851-55; Bacchus Marsh 1855-59; to PCV 1859; Rushworth/Murchison 7/1859-61; Kalkallo/Wallan 1861-72; Piggoreet 1872-76; Bright 1876-78; Moulamein NSW 1878-80 & retired.
6	David Chapman	UPCV-1851	Broadmeadows 1851-71 & retired (formed Pres of UPCS in Vic 1856; returned to UPCA 1862 & joined PCV 1870.
7	Robert B. Scott	UPCV- 1851	itinerant ministry Macedon area & settled at Carlsruhe; joined PCV 1870, retired 1877.
8	D.H.Ballantyne	UPCV- 1851	Albury 1851-69; formed UPCA 1858; joined PCV 1859; Brighton/ Cheltenham 1869-87 & retired.
9	Andrew Ross	US- 1838	Portland 1851-6/1856 & resigned (poor eyesight) died 1883.
10	William B. Miller	? Ire US	Received ex Sth Aust 9/1851; held no charge; declared no longer minister 9/53.
11	Robert Hamilton	Relief 1840	Received 9/1851; Collingwood (Napier St) 1852-83 & retired (joined PCV 1870).
12	J.R.Dalrymple	US - 1837	Received 5/1853; Warrnambool 1853-58 and died aged 48 years.

13	John Ballantyne	UPCV- 1851	Arrived 2/1855; Sth Melbourne (Howe Crescent) 1855-59; formed UPCA; joined PCV 1859. Died in Scotland 1860.
14	James Ballantyne	UPCV- 1848	Received 2/1855 (brother of John); colleague to Ramsay at St Enoch's 1855-8/1856; Lonsdale Street (later known as Erskine Church, Rathdowne Street) 1856-77 and retired; formed UPCA 1857 & joined PCV 1859; edited church magazines for many years. Died 1896.
15	A.D.Kininmont	US - 1843	Arrived 2/1855; at Melbourne; formed Presbytery of the UPCS 10/1856; moved to McKenzie Street 8/1858 but resigned same year and went to Scotland; returned 1861 to PCV Nth Melbourne (Union Memorial) 1861-78 & died 1881.
16	Hugh Darling	US- 1845	Received 4/1855; supply at North Melbourne; to Phillip Street, Sydney UP Church 5/1855-59 and to Scotland. Later (1861-1877) at Sth Melbourne PCV.
17	John Cooper	UPCS- 1849	Received 5/1855; Geelong (Ryrie Street) 1855-58 & left starting independent cause. Joined UPCA then PCV 1859; Rokewood 1859-66; Coburg 1866-85 & died.
18	Andrew Pringle	UPCV- 1855	Received 12/1855; supply at Gisborne to 5/1856 & at Portland 12/1856-5/1857.
19	John McIlrea	?	Received 4/1856; (with Lang's Synod of NSW 1854-55) no settled charge.
20	Francis Sherlock	Cong	Received 5/1856; supplied at Gisborne 1856 & dropped from roll (intemperance).
21	William Ridley MA	SNSW- 1850	Portland 6/1856-12/1858 and returned to Sydney; joined PCEA 1861 and entered unions 1864/65. Died 1878.
22	John Reid	US- 1829	Ex Synod of Victoria, admitted with congregation of Nth Melbourne 10/1857 but demitted 2/1858 and to Scots, Sydney (Colleague to Lang) 1858-62; Mariners' Church, Sydney 1862-67 (joined Synod of Australia 1863). Died 1867.
23	John Meek	UPCV-1859	Gisborne 1859-1907 & retired; joined PCV 1859.
24	Hugh S. Seaborn	Cong - 1834	Geelong (Ryrie Street) 7/58-1860; joined PCV 1859; Chiltern 1860-62; to NSW and joined PCEA 8/63 and 1864 union but resigned 6/65 and joined C of E.
25	James Henderson	UPCS- 1850	Arrived early 1859; Geelong (Ryrie Street) 5/59-5/66; to PCSA 1866: Port Adelaide 1867-71; St Andrew's Wakefield Street Adelaide 1871-81 & deposed for moral offence.

UNION FORMING PCV - APRIL 7, 1859:

Ex United Presbyterian Church of Australia: †4, 13, 14 & 17.

Ex United Presbyterian Church of Victoria: †5, 8, 23 & 24.

Continuing United Presbyterian Church of Victoria: † 1, 11 & 25 with 6 & 7 in loose connection/independent.

| 26 | Robert T. Walker | US- 1837 | Arrived 3/1859 Armstrong Street Ballarat 1859-67; joined UPCV 3/1861; Doveton Street Ballarat 1867-83 (congregations re-united 1876); joined PCV 1870, died 1890 |

154

27	William (or H.) Duncan	UPCS- ?	Admitted 1/61; supply at Whittlesea 1861; Ballarat (Neil Street) 1861; joined PCV 11/1863; nothing further known.
28	James Dick	US- 1846	Arrived 5/1863; received 6/1865; supply then Neil Street Ballarat (later Lydiard St) 10/65-1880; joined PCV 1870, died 1888.
29	Daniel McKenzie	UPCS - 1862	Arrived 2/1868; Geelong (Ryrie Street) 1868-71; joined PCV 1870; Footscray 1871-78; Collingwood (St George's) 1878-1904.

THE 6 REMAINING UPCV MINISTERS (†6,7,11,26,28 & 29) JOIN PCV, NOV 9,1870.

PRESBYTERIAN CHURCH OF VICTORIA
Constituted April 7, 1859

The first assembly consisted of 53 serving ministers - 18 from the Synod of Victoria, 27 from the Free Presbyterian Church and 4 from each of the two United Presbyterian Synods. Clow, the first Moderator, was retired without charge. William Hamilton, who had been working independently in western Victoria since 1847, joined the PCV after it had been constituted, thus there were 54 serving ministers in the PCV, 7 in the continuing FPCV and 5 in the continuing UPC - ie. the PCV embraced 82% of the serving ministers in the three streams.

Two ministers from the continuing FPCV joined the PCV in November 1867, and the remaining 6 UPCV ministers joined in November 1870. These moves left 3 FPCV ministers outside the PCV. There was also 1 Reformed Presbyterian minister and several Welsh congregations.

ORDAINED MINISTERS SERVING PCV 1859 TO 1865 WHO WERE ADMITTED AFTER THE UNION OF APRIL 1859

NB. This listing has been compiled from the volumes on the PCV by Hamilton, Sutherland and Stewart with a few corrections noted by the writer. But it has not been checked against primary records and is less than complete and will have some inaccuracies. However, it does enable some idea of the growth and spread of the PCV and the background of ministers.

†	Name	Background	Details
1	William Hamilton	CS-1837	Goulburn 1837-1846 & withdrew from S of A; Kilnoorat 1847-57; Mortlake 1857-73; died 1879 aged 72.
2	John Steele	PCI-1858	Heathcote 1859-63; Bellarine 1866-86.
3	A.J.Campbell	FCS-1843	Geelong 1861-1884.
4	John Anderson	FCS	Maryborough 1859- ,Warrnambool 1862 Taradale/Malmsbury 1866-68; Wangaratta/ Oxley 1868-78 and died.
5	Robert Anderson	FCS	Eaglehawk 1860-62; Kyneton 1862-75.
6	William Smyth	PCI	Miners Rest 1860-72.
7	D.H.McMurtrie	PCI	Smeaton 1860-62; Lake Hindmarsh '62-64
8	J.McL.Abernethy	PCI	Towerhill 1860-62; Eaglehawk 1862-69; Port Melbourne 1869- ;died 1904.
9	Edward Blair	PCI	Wickliffe 1860-62.
10	Patrick Simpson	FCS	Port Fairy 1860-62; Horsham 1862-68; (father of Rev P.Carnegie Simpson)
11	Andrew Begg	FCS	Warrnambool/Woodford 1860-61.
12	James Caldwell	PCI	E.Collingwood 1860-67; Maryborough 1870; Mornington 1874; died 1907.

13	Samuel A.Hamilton	PCI	Mernda/Janefield 1860-63; Tarnagulla 1863-66; Rushworth/Murchison 1867- .
14	J.McRoberts	PCI	Barrabool Hills/Duneed 1860; Branxholme Eumerella 1863-75; died 1876.
15	A.Robb	FCS	Maldon 1860-69; Albury 1869-74; Koroit 1874-87; died 1896.
16	John B.Steele	FC/PCV	Creswick 1860-67; Windermere 1868-81
17	James Treadwell	FCS	Balmoral/Harrow 1860-65. [to PCSA
18	James Adam	FCS	Castlemaine 1860-62 and died.
19	James Scott	UPCS/PCV	Bacchus Marsh 1860-70.
20	John Sutherland	FCS	Newstead 1861 died 1866.
21	W.T.Whan	PCI	Skipton 1861 Port Fairy 1885 d.1901
22	Hugh Darling	US-1845	Sth Melbourne 1861-77.
23	W.A.Lind	Cong	Lancefield 1861-79.
24	A.D.Kinninmont	US-1843	Nth Melb (Union Memorial 1861-78,d'81.
25	George Adam	FCS	Brighton/Cheltenham 1861-67; Koroit 1868 Horsham 1873-79;d.1901.
26	T.M.Fraser	FCS	Geelong (Gheringhap Street)
27	Peter Mercer	US-1846	ex FPSA; Fryerstown/Taradale 1861-62; Richmond 1862-64; Echuca/Deniliquin 1864-65; Ulupna/Deniliquin 1865-68; Divinity Prof. 1868-83; d.1902 aged 81.
28	David Moore BA	PCI-1847	Inglewood 1861 To Sy of A (NSW)'63.
29	John Downes MA	OS Ire 1826	ex Tas;Learmonth/Burrumbeet 1861 Clunes 1862-66 & died aged 63.
30	John Nicol	CS	Talbot 1864-1908.
31	William Leishman	FCS	Maryborough 1861 Heathcote 1863-65; Mariners' Church Sydney 1867-70;d1872.
32	Hugh McKail	FCS	Carngham/Linton 1862; St Arnaud 1863; The Richardson -1870; Bacchus Marsh 1872; Bulla/Sunbury 1873; d.1900.
33	William Mitchell	CS-1843	Kilmore (St Andrew's) 1862-63; to Sn of A (NSW) died 1866.
34	J.S.Boyd	UPCS	Essendon 1862-72.
35	W.Matthew	/PCV	Stawell 1862-68; Bright 1870; Murchison 1883.
36	Andrew Robertson	US-1838	Castlemaine 1863-65; West Melb 1865-75.
37	Duncan Fraser	PCEng-1859	Ballarat (St Johns) 1862; Heidelberg/ Janefield 1869-97.
38	Mark Dixon	Cong	FPCSA Penola 1859-63; Smeaton/ Bullarook 1863-74; Scarsdale 1874-76; Wangaratta 1877-78; to Q as Cong.
39	Robert Hamilton MA	FCS	Learmonth & Springs 1863.
40	David Renton	UPCS	Carngham/Linton 1863; Heathcote 1868.
41	David Kay DD	FCS	Wickliffe/Chatsworth/Hexham 1863-74.
42	W. Robertson	FCS	Port Fairy/Towerhill 1863-67; Trentham /Tylden 1870-72.
43	G.Minty	FCS	Chiltern 1863; Newstead 1867-70.
44	W.Graham	FCS	Casterton/Coleraine 1863-67.
45	James Don	FCS-1856	FPCSA; Mt Gambier 1858-64; Penola 1864-72; Miners Rest/Coghills Creek 1872 -75; Kyneton 1875-81; died 1884.
46	James Lambie	UPCS	Melton/Sunbury 1864; Werribee/Melton 1868; Wyndham/Little River 1873-81; assistant at Scots, Melb; died 1884.
47	Donald McRae	FCS	Kilmore (St Andrew's) 1864-67.
48	J.W.McCutcheon	/PCV	Woods Point 1864-65; Majorca 1865-69; Sebastopol 1870; Lwr Woodburn '78-79.
49	A.Murdoch	FPCV-1862	Ex FPCV; Yea 1864-68; Benalla 1868-82.
50	Wazir Beg MD	FCS/PCV	Alberton 1864; to NSW 1864.

51	John Bagley	Ind Ire	Richmond 1864-76; Portland 1877-91.
52	W.Soutar	/PCV	Janefield/Mernda/Whittlesea 1864-84;Lake Rowan 1884-89.
53	A.McGregor	FCS/PCV	St Andrew's Carlton 1864-67.
54	J.W.Inglis	/PCV	Port Melb 1864; Ballarat (St John's) 1869; died 1893.
55	J.Brownlee	FCS/PCV	Barrabool Hills/Duneed 1864;d.1878.
56	C.J.Baird	Wesleyan	Inglewood 1863; Scarsdale 1868; St A's Geelong 1874-1907.
57	H.H.Findlay	PCI	Dunolly/Bet Bet 1864; Penola 1873-80; Carngham/Linton 1881; Mooroopna -92.
58	Archibald Crawford	FCS	Burrumbeet/Windermere 1864-69.
59	W.C.Wallace	/PCV	Staffordshire Reef/Pitfield 1864; Branxholme 1880-1906.
60	R.Falconer	Can/PCV	Penshurst/Dunkeld 1864-69.
61	R.A.Caldwell	PCI	Mt Gambier 1864-
62	John Service MA	CS/PCV	Lower Avoca 1864-65; to Hobart.
63	J.D.Robertson	UPCS/PCV	Wangaratta/Oxley 1864; Horsham 1869; Ryrie Street, Geelong 1872; Yarrawonga 1879 -
64	J.Greig MA	FCS	Yackandandah 1864-80; died 1893
65	H.Thompson	/PCV	Bright 1864-1865.
66	John Menzies	/PCV	Maffra/Stratford -1865.
67	L.Dobinson	Wesleyan	Alberton 1865 died 1869 at Rushworth.
68	M.R.Battersby	UPCS	Maryborough 1865-66.
69	J.F.Hill	CS/PCV	Rushworth 1865-66; Meredith 1868-71.
70	D.Galloway	CS	Avoca/Bung Bong 1865-67; Piggoreet/ Staffordshire 1868-71.
71	W.F.Main	/PCV	Daylesford 1865; E.Collingwood 1868- Bairnsdale 1877-
72	John Henderson	FCS	Ex Tas; Balmoral/Harrow 1865-1907.
73	W.Cullen	CS	Bright 1865-67.
74	R.W.McCully	PCI	Benalla 1865-67.
75	John Roberts	Cong 1854	Ex S.Aus 1865; Stratford/Maffra 1865-98.
76	Peter Brown	Relief 1825	Hawthorn 1/65-71.

FREE PRESBYTERIAN CHURCH OF VICTORIA

Continuing in terms of Protest May 25, 1864

1	Arthur Paul	FCS-1853	East St Kilda 1855-1910.
2	Alexander McIntyre	FCS-1847	Geelong Gaelic (oversight) died 1878.
3	Peter MacPherson	FPCV-1862	Meredith 1862-74 then to PCEA

REFORMED PRESBYTERIAN CHURCH OF IRELAND

Congregation of Geelong

A minister was ordained on August 18, 1857 for missionary work in Australia, and arrived in December 1857, holding a meeting for prayer on the 27th of that month. On August 10, 1862, the present building in Fenwick Street was opened by Rev John G.Paton, and the adjoining manse was built in 1869.

| 1 | A.M.Moore, MA | RPCI-1857 | Geelong 1857 to 18/02/1897 & died. |

WELSH CALVINISTIC METHODIST CONNEXION
IN VICTORIA   BEGAN 1853 GYMANFA (ASSEMBLY) 1863

| 1 | William M.Evans | USA-1861 | Happy Valley 3/63; Sebastopol 5/64 Latrobe Street, Melbourne 1871-81. |

NB: See page 207.

157

10: TASMANIA, SOUTH AUSTRALIA & QUEENSLAND

Considerations of perspective preclude any detailed discussion of the Tasmanian church. In any case, the main factors in the 19th century have been indicated on pages 169, 177 and 223-224. A self-explanatory table of ministers is appended. It is worth noting that the Scottish interest in Tasmania peaked with the opening up of Victoria. Among the 20 settlers who joined together to provide a church, manse and stipend for Rev Thomas Hastie in the Ballarat district were members of the Learmonth family who had earlier resided in Tasmania, but who led in the pastoral settlement of Port Phillip.

Patronage in Tasmania!

One other interesting note could be made. The central Tasmanian parish of Kirklands, which erected a small building in 1836 which still stands, had three trustees for its property in whom was vested the right to appoint the minister. When an Act of Parliament was secured some time later to regulate the holding of Presbyterian property, the Kirklands property was not included. The Acts of Parliament since which have varied the trusts to allow property to be held on different trusts, including in connection with the Uniting Church formed in 1977, have thus had no legal effect on the Kirklands property. For some time prior to 1987 there was unhappiness in the Kirklands parish over the changes brought by church union. The trustees discovered and asserted their power of patronage, dismissed the Uniting Church minister and sought supply from the Launceston PCT. In this case it appears patronage will be for the benefit of the Presbyterian cause - an ironic twist. However, it is a striking and probably unique example for the colonies of the way the rights of the people could be over-ridden in the Established Church of Scotland 150 years ago. [1]

1. This case was drawn to my attention by F.M.Bradshaw and reported in **The Presbyterian Banner**, April 1987.

PRESBYTERY OF VAN DIEMEN'S LAND
CHURCH OF SCOTLAND

Constituted November 6, 1835. In 1878 by the Presbyterian Church Act the name 'Church of Scotland' was changed to 'Presbyterian Church of Tasmania' and in 1880 the Presbytery became a Synod supervising two Presbyteries. On March 18, 1896, the Free Church Presbytery of Tasmania was received into union.

MINISTERS 1835-1865

1	John Mackersey	CS	Scots,Macquarie River (Kirklands) 1829-1854.
2	John Anderson MA	NSW	Scots, Launceston (later St A's) 1832-54.

PRESBYTERY FORMED BY ABOVE PLUS LANG - see page 40.

3	James Garrett	US	Scots, Bothwell 1829-40; Scots, L'ston 1841-42; West Tamar 1846-74 & died.
4	John Lillie MA	CS	St Andrew's Hobart 1837-58.
5	Robert Russell	CS	Evandale 1839-72.
6	Thomas Dugall	SUls 1824	Ex NSW; Sorell 1839-64.
7	James Bell		St John's, Hobart 1840-52 & died age 50.
8	Charles Simson		Glenorchy 1841-70.
9	Alex McKenzie		West Tamar 1842-45; to Scotland, Free Church, Islay, 1847-71.
10	Thomas Hastie	CS -1842	St A's, L'ston 1843-46; to FPCV.
11	John Robertson		Bothwell 1843-65.
12	Thomas Dove MA	OS/VDL	Oatlands 1837; Flinders Is. 1837-42; Maria Is 1842-44; Swansea 1844-82.
13	R.K.Ewing	Cong 1847	St A's, L'ston 1848-68; to PCV.
14	Robert McClean MA	Ire	St John's, Hobart 1853-70; d.1884 age 91.
15	Adam Turnbull MD	VDL	Macquarie River 1854-74; died 1891.
16	John Downes MA	Ire	Supply St A's, Hobart 1855-56; Harrington Street Chapel 1857; to FCT.
17	J.G.Mackintosh	FCS	St A's, Hobart 1858-60.
18	John Storie	FCS	St A's, Hobart 1860-79.(ex PCV)
19	J.Henderson	VDL-1861	Evandale 1861-63; Hagley 1863-64; PCV.

Note: At the close of 1865 there were 8 ministers.

FREE CHURCH PRESBYTERY OF TASMANIA

Instituted on March 18, 1853; dissolved on union with PCT March 18, 1896

1	James Lindsay	FCS	Chalmers' Launceston 1850-85.
2	W. Nicolson, MA,DD	CS-	Chalmers' Hobart 1851-1878; died 1890 aged 95.
3	Robert McClean MA	Ire	Arrived 3/1853 to Pres of VDL 10/53.

PRESBYTERY

4	Lauchlin Campbell	FCS-1852	Oatlands 1853-89.
5	James Baird	FCS	Missionary 17/1/55-4/7/1855; to FPCV.
6	John Downes MA	OS Ire 1826	Ex Pres VDL; Knox, Hobart 1858-61; to PCV.
7	R.M.Webster	FCS	Chalmers' Hobart 1876-1889; d. 1890.
8	John G.Mather	FCPT	Scottsdale 1887-91 (lay agent 1876-87).
9	Alex Hardie MA	UP-1868	Ex PCNSW; Oatlands 1889-92; to Hagley PCT.
10	C.H.Talbot		Ex PCV; Chalmers' Hobart 1890-99.
11	David Matthew	FCS	Oatlands 1896.

Note: From 1934 Chalmers' Hobart was worked jointly with St Andrew's under the name Scots Church, and the congregation entered the Uniting Church in 1977 using the St Andrew's premises. Chalmers' Church was demolished in 1956.

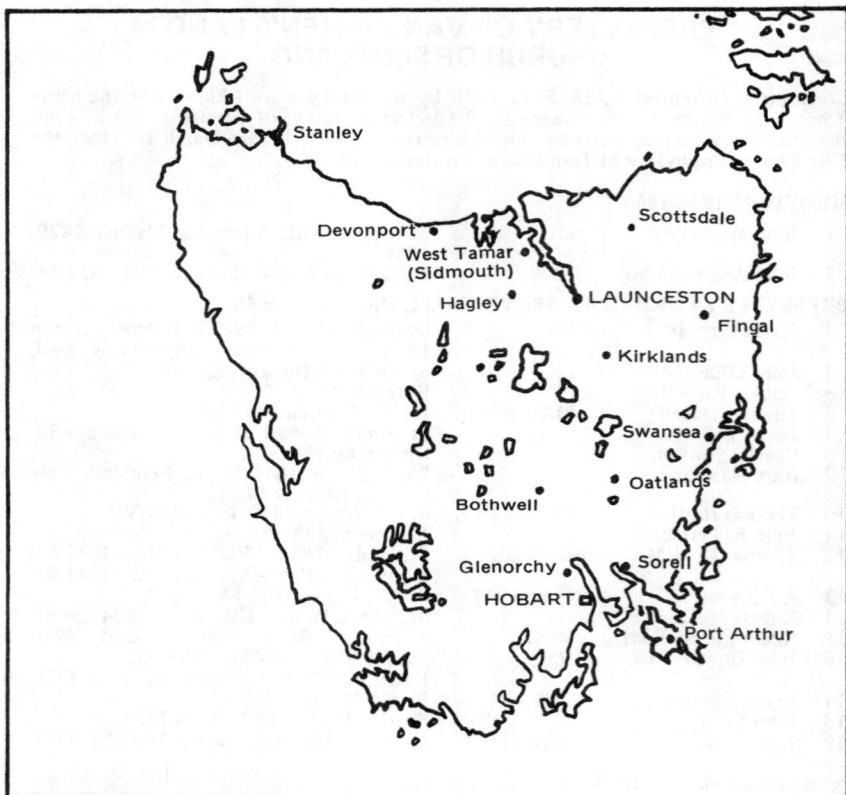

Stanley

Devonport

West Tamar
(Sidmouth)

Hagley

Scottsdale

LAUNCESTON

Fingal

Kirklands

Swansea

Oatlands

Bothwell

Glenorchy

Sorell

HOBART

Port Arthur

↑

TASMANIA

Scale: 50 kms

THE KIRK AT KIRKLANDS (1836)

South Australia

South Australia has been called 'a paradise of dissent.' It had been founded on the principle of freedom of religion without state aid. English and Scots from churches endowed by the state in Britain did not find it easy to adjust to this situation. The smaller Presbyterian groups coped much better but were overshadowed by the much larger Methodist element and hampered by an excessive dependence upon ordained ministers. For union see page 225.

SOUTH AUSTRALIAN PRESBYTERIAN MINISTERS
FROM 1839 TO UNION MAY 10, 1865

UNITED PRESBYTERIAN STREAM

1	Ralph Drummond	US-1821	Adelaide: Gouger St 1839-55 d.1872 aged 79.
2	W.B.Miller	?Ire US	Murray Vale 1851; to UPCV 1851.
3	Peter Mercer MA	UPCS-1846	Gouger St 7/1855-11/1855; to FPCSA
4	James Lyall	UPCS-1857	Gouger St (from 1865 Flinders St) 1857-1898; d.1905 aged 77.
5	William Davidson	UPCS-1859	Burra 1860-62; Clare 1862-71; Wallaroo 1871-82; d.1909 aged 91.
6	Alex Law	UPCS-1861	Stirling Nth 1861-63; Mt Barker 1863-1877; Monarto 1877-1902;d1911 age 90

CHURCH OF SCOTLAND STREAM

1	Robert Haining	CS-1841	Adelaide: Grenfell St from 1859 Wakefield St) 1841-71; d. 1874 age 71.
2	John McBean MA PhD	CS-1841	Inverbrackie 1852-54; Ceylon 1854-61; Inverbrackie (Woodside from 1878) 1861-84. Stayed out of union 1865 with congregation but joined PCSA 5/68.
3	Wm Ross MA PhD	CS-1848	Inverbrackie/Mt Crawford (Springfield) 1856-61; Wentworth,NSW 1861

FREE PRESBYTERIAN CHURCH OF SOUTH AUSTRALIA

1	John Gardner	CS-1840	Adelaide: Chalmers' Nth Terrace 1850--68; St A's, Launceston 1868-74; Queenscliff PCV 1874-88;d.1899 age 90.
2	John Anderson	FCS-1843	Strathalbyn 1851-71 & demitted (intemp); supplied for FPCSA 1877-1889; d.1891 age76.
3	John S.Moir	FCS	Smithfield/Gawler 2/1854-8/1858; to FPCV (Brighton).
4	James Benny	FPCSA-1854	Morphett Vale 1854-1904; deposed 1858 without grounds and continued FPCSA after union; d.1910 aged 86.
5	Peter Mercer MA	UPCS-1846	Ex UP; Port Adelaide 1856-1861; to PCV (Fryerstown/Taradale).
6	James Gordon	FCS-1856	Mt Barker 1858-63; Smithfield/Gawler 1862-82; Gawler 1882-99;d.1905 age 83.
7	James Don	FCS-1856	Mt Gambier 1858-64; Penola 1864-72; to PCV 1872 (Miners' Rest).
8	Mark Dixon	Cong	Penola 1859-63; to PCV (Smeaton).
9	Thomas Smellie	FPCSA-1861	Port Adelaide 1861-65 & resigned previous to the union; to Scotland 1871.

Note: †7 % †8 transferred to jurisdiction of PCV in 1863. D.McCalman of Edenhope(V) and Naracoorte (SA) has been classed as FPCV (†25 on page 151).

Queensland

Work in Queensland was rather limited prior to 1865. Early PCEA work is discussed on pages 95-96, while the progress to union is recorded on page 206.

PRESBYTERIAN MINISTERS IN QUEENSLAND
1847 TO UNION NOVEMBER 25, 1863

PRESBYTERIAN CHURCH OF EASTERN AUSTRALIA

1	Thomas Mowbray MA	CS-1841	Ex Sydney; arrived Brisbane 1847; held no charge but looked for ministers to PCEA and member of first session 1856.
2	W.R.McLeod	SEA-1851	Brisbane 1851-52; d.in Scotland c1855.
3	A.W.Sinclair	FCS-1853	Brisbane 1854-56; to Richmond,NSW.
4	Charles Ogg	SEA-1855	Ex Gerringong,NSW; Brisbane 1856-95.
5	A.C.Smith MA	FC -1855	Gladstone 1863; Rockhampton 1864-68; Scots, Sydney 1869; John Knox, Melb., 1870-72; Wangaratta/Oxley 1873; Daylesford 1875-85; died 1902. (Father of Profs. A.C. & T.J.Smith of Ormond.)

UNITED PRESBYTERIAN STREAM

1	Thomas Kingsford		Arrived 1849; Warwick 1851-66; Allora 1873-78.
2	Thomas Bell	SNSW-1856	Ex United Evangelical Church, Brisbane; Brisbane (Creek Street) 1857-59 & died.
3	John Love	PCI	Brisbane (Wickham Tce) 1862-71.
4	Matthew McGavin	UPCS	Brisbane (Creek Street) 1863-74.

NB: Kingsford joined PCQ in 1864, McGavin in 1866.

CHURCH OF SCOTLAND STREAM

1	W.L.Nelson LLD	CS	Ipswich 1853-60; Toowoomba 1863-74; Drayton & Western Downs 1876-87.
2	G.M.Reed	PCI	Ex PCV; Ipswich 1861-62; Maryborough 1863-64.
3	Samuel Kelly	PCI-1856	Ex PCV; Rockhampton 1861-64.
4	Samuel Wilson	PCI	Ipswich 1863-66.
5	John Wilson	PCI	Sth Brisbane 1863-66.

NB: Nelson joined the PCQ in 1864.

162

Part Four

CONSOLIDATION

11: THE DYNAMICS OF UNION

A comprehensive union of the different branches of the Scottish Presbyterian family was accomplished first in Victoria in 1859 and became something of a model for other colonies. For that reason it will receive greater attention than New South Wales. The story is somewhat involved for ordinary readers, but this chapter will outline some of the considerations which operated to push the churches towards union and which led to the compromise of the older distinctives. Some overlap with other chapters may be found.

The period to 1850

As we have seen, few additional ministers were obtained by any of the churches in Australia for five years or so after the division of 1846. One new factor, however, was the entry of a third stream of Scottish Presbyterianism - the United Presbyterian Church. This church had resulted from a union in 1847 of the two major bodies which had sprung from the 18th century secessions from the Established Church of Scotland - the Secession Church and the Relief Church. The Relief Church was much influenced by English Non-conformity and was not interested in national recognition or establishment of the Church. The Secession Church had at first been the virtual custodian of Church of Scotland orthodoxy but it too had become influenced by 'new light' and in general opposed an alliance between church and state. The general view in the UP Church was that *any* role by the state in relation to the church would be intolerant and involve persecution. The logic of this in a secular, atheistic state was anathema to those of the older school. Both Secession and Relief showed signs of innovation in other areas also. Long left to voluntary means of support from their adherents they were against state support in Australia, some more stridently than others.

165

State Aid in Australia

Aid in the two old colonies of Van Diemen's Land and New South Wales had long operated and enabled ministers to be stationed in rural districts which might otherwise lack Gospel preaching. However, the aid was given to the major churches whether Protestant or Roman Catholic, and on this ground was refused by those Presbyterian bodies representing the Free Church stream. The practicalities in the new and sparsely settled colonies modified the views of a good number. In Victoria, some Free Presbyterians accepted Government sites from 1853 on the grounds that adherence to principle 'was to throw all the best situations for churches into the hands of others and to prevent the Free Church from taking her rightful position in the eyes of the community, and doing justice to her own principles and the interests of her people.'[1] Although a formal motion has not been located the same situation applied in the PCEA from 1856 when a site was applied for in Sydney. The expense of sites given the boom in population was a factor. Even Lang felt at liberty to accept Government sites. Aid for stipends was more sensitive and was not accepted by the PCEA although ministers of the FPCV were free to receive such aid from 1854, and it was also taken by some in the Free Church of Tasmania. South Australia had been founded on the basis that there would be no state aid to religion, but in 1846 a small amount was made available. It was accepted by the Church of Scotland there but not by the United Presbyterians. A number withdrew from the Church of Scotland in protest and this contributed to the forming of the Free Presbyterian Church of South Australia, the first minister arriving in March 1850. It can thus be seen that the three views on the state aid question were modified in practice so that a union which allowed reception of aid to be a matter of individual action could be contemplated. The obstacle would be agreement on the doctrinal issue of church-state relations, and on this the unions involved a compromise. Aid ceased in South Australia in 1851, in New South Wales in 1862 (with existing recipients' rights preserved), in Victoria in 1870 (fully effective 1875) and in Tasmania in 1869 when aid was commuted.

Early concern for unity

There was another reason why those of Free Church sympathy at first declined state aid, and that was the hope of minimizing disunity among Presbyterians. Many United Presbyterians had a bee in their bonnet about state aid but were not really opposed to the state having a role in the countenancing of the Christian faith. And even if they had some theoretical

1. Adam Cairns to Convener of Colonial Committee, October 19, 1853 in **Home and Foreign Record of the Free Church of Scotland,** March 1854, p.218.

problems, if the practical obstacle was removed they could fit in quite well with the Free Church brethren.

Thus, Dr James Buchanan encouraged William McIntyre to look into the possibility of co-operating with Presbyterians other than from the Establishment, and a meeting of the Presbyterians of Maitland on October 26, 1846 resolved:

This meeting recommends that the Synod of Eastern Australia should take steps with all convenient speed to carry out the views expressed in Dr Buchanan's letter, with regard to uniting all bodies of Presbyterians who do not go along with the Established Church as in connection with the Government.[2]

It is not to be supposed that a sacrifice of principle was to be involved, but clearly there was potential to minimize division. The initial point was the position of Thomas Mowbray and his Sydney congregation. McIntyre sought to encourage connection with the Synod of Eastern Australia:

The erastian ground is already occupied, and the ground of spiritual independence and entire freedom from transmarine connexion and control is already occupied; we have already a Presbyterian Church which receives support from the State, and a Presbyterian Church which does not receive such support; we do not, therefore, see that there is any vacant position for a new body...If therefore the Presbyterian Church of Eastern Australia is a rightly constituted Church - if it is, in respect of constitution, what a Presbyterian Church ought to be - any Presbyterian congregation in the Colony that is now in an isolated state, is bound to seek admission into its communion; and is none the less under this obligation, though the Church in question was but recently organized, and organized by *others*.[3]

The Voluntary Churches

After the United Presbyterian Church commenced in Victoria in 1847 under A.M.Ramsay, a rabid voluntary with Relief background, the Basis of the Synod formed by Ramsay and three others in 1850 dropped the Westminster Standards and substituted what James Forbes called an 'extremely meagre' summary.[4] Given that the first Synod included one

2. **Voice in the Wilderness (hereafter Voice)**, November 2, 1846 pp. 169, 172.
3. **Voice**, December 15, 1846, pp. 190-191. It is of interest to note that Mowbray was later a member of the Brisbane PCEA Session.
4. **Port Phillip Christian Herald**, July 5, 1850 p.54. Forbes adds: 'We may be met with exclamations about forbearance, brotherly love, and 'that variation of sentiment on minor points, which seem to be incident to our present imperfect state.' But all our reading of history, and our observations of religious professors and religious sects, only deepen us in the conviction that to witness for and maintain the *whole Truth* is the first duty of the Christian Ministry and the Christian Church.'

avowed Congregationalist plus a former student of the FPCV who could not or would not qualify for a licence, it is understandable that not too much was going to develop on an official level. It is also evident that there was potential for division in the UPCV because of the weak Basis.

Similarly, Lang, who had been behind the coming of the early UP ministers to Victoria, had a Synod from 1850 to 1864 which was even more loose in practice despite its formal acceptance of the Westminster Confession and Catechisms. It was enough if an applicant for ministry was evangelical in sentiment. And Lang himself had been deposed by the Synod of Australia, those who later formed the PCEA being most forward in this act. So it is understandable that the professedly voluntary Presbyterian Synods would have a secondary role in any union negotiations.

The Gold Revolution

The gold discoveries in 1851 in New South Wales and Victoria led to an astonishing population growth. In Victoria the population increased from 77,000 to 409,000 by 1857. In New South Wales the growth was not so great but still substantial - from about 178,000 to 351,000 over the same period. In 1850 Australia's population was 405,000, in 1860 1,145,000 and in 1870 1,648,000. The Presbyterian element of the population was about 10% in New South Wales and 15% in Victoria, but when divided three ways only the few major centres could contemplate supporting a church of each persuasion. In the average country district much depended on who was first in the field. Ministers were in short supply so a reasonably able man would be accepted by all and congregations were nominally what their minister was. In other words, the division of Presbyterians became a territorial one not an ecclesiastical one.

This may not have been a major problem at the local level but it was not good administratively. An area which contained sufficient congregations for one Presbytery was administered by three different Presbyteries which, in order to have sufficient members, embraced larger areas than could be efficiently supervised given the then means of transport and communication. Co-ordination of church extension was thus hindered as well as the furtherance of educational enterprises which needed maximum support. We can also imagine tension in some local settings arising from the fact that the minister represented, or was popularly thought of as representing, one particular stream of Presbyterianism. There would be a natural tendency to wish for a neutral ecclesiastical position if a man of one's preference could not be supported without the co-operation of others. Additionally, there was the fear that the social prestige and influence of the Presbyterian Church would be adversely affected by continued disunion so that losses to other denominations would result. True, the Methodists were also divided, but they made much greater use of laymen to get work going whereas Presbyterians tended to wait until a minister arrived.

Presbyterian statistics

An analysis of Scottish marriage statistics of the time by the present writer shows that 55% of Scottish Presbyterians associated themselves with the Established Church, 27% with the Free Church and 16% with the United Presbyterians. Many nominal people classed themselves as Established Church and there is reason to believe that the Established Church and the Free Church had a similar number of active adherents, thus attendance rates of 30% and 60% respectively would be appropriate to produce the 40% overall attendance rate then existing. The Free Church had major support in the cities and in the Highlands, while the Established Church following was higher in the rural districts.Non-Scottish Presbyterians in Australia were chiefly from Ireland and an overall 50% attendance rate might be possible as the Irish Presbyterians tended to be more active.

We now propose to apply this data to the Australian situation with a view to assessing the composition of the congregations. It is true that the attendance rates stated are somewhat arbitrary, especially in the Australian setting. In fact, H. Mol's studies show Presbyterian attendance rates a little over 20% in 1861, although doubling in Victoria to about 40% in 1871 while remaining almost constant in New South Wales.[5] Why this was so need not concern us now. The point is that even if the assumed attendance rates of 30% for the Established Church and 60% for the Free Church are over-stated, it is unlikely that the basic relationship between the streams was significantly different.

Tasmania

In the 1850s and '60s the Tasmanian population was 55-65% Anglican and about 9% Presbyterian. There was no United Presbyterian work and no scope for it because of strong Free Churches in the main towns of Hobart and Launceston. The colony was well established and was not rapidly expanding. There were some 10 Church of Scotland parishes and 3 Free Church ones. The 1861 Tasmanian census gave the Church of Scotland 73.6% and the Free Church 26.4% of the 9,000 'census' Presbyterians.

Based on knowledge of the size of a number of congregations and guesses about others, I estimate that the average attendance in the Free Church totalled 1,000 or 42% of its census adherents, while the Church of Scotland

5. Hans Mol, **The Faith of Australians** (Sydney 1985), pp.52ff.

had perhaps 1200 or 18% of its adherents. While the proportions attending are less than expected from the Scottish experience, the basic ratio between the two streams is much as expected: 55% of attenders went to Church of Scotland congregations and 45% to Free Church congregations. Tasmania does not provide a good sample because Free Church work was in the major centres and not in rural areas, but the pattern is evident.[6] Given the minimal scope for expansion in the next 40 years despite the doubling of the population, the good quality of the Free Church ministers, the internal disarray and lethargy of the Church of Scotland Presbytery until the 1880s, and the location of the chief Free Churches in the main towns allowing homogeneity, it is understandable that pressure for union was not a major factor until late in the 19th century. Union occurred in 1896. Of the total communicant membership of the united church of about 1,500 some 560 (37%) were in the four former Free Church parishes.

Victoria

The 1857 census of Victoria showed nearly 16% of the population or 65,182 persons claimed to be Presbyterian. Of these 13% claimed affiliation with a non-Scottish church, 42.7% with the Church of Scotland, 29.7% with the Free Presbyterian Church and 14.3% with the United Presbyterian Church. Eliminating for the moment the non-Scottish element, these claimed affiliations show 49% Church of Scotland, 34% Free Church and 16% UP. Compared to the Scottish marriage statistics it is clear larger numbers of Free Church people had come to Victoria compared to Church of Scotland people while the UPs were about as expected. This corresponds with the fact that more Highlanders came to Victoria than, for example, New South Wales, and that the economic opportunities in Victoria appealed to the rising middle class who were well represented in the Free Church in Scotland.

Applying the attendance rates to the census figures we find that a typical sample of 1,000 Presbyterians would show 128 Church of Scotland, 178 Free Church, 86 United Presbyterian and 65 non-Scottish - an overall attendance of 457. Of the attenders, 28% would be Church of Scotland, 39% Free Church, 19% United Presbyterian and 14% non-Scottish. Probably well over 50% of our hypothetical sample would be Free Church in orientation.

It thus is evident that the United Presbyterian stream was not going to be dominant but could anticipate strong congregations in the major centres

6. In January 1852 Rev James Lindsay of Launceston FC considered church-goers were about 10% of the population - 'the rest sink in vice and in indifference to Divine things;' while William Nicolson's average congregation in Hobart FC at this time was 500 compared with a total of about 170 in the two C of S congregations in Hobart. - Vide **Home and Foreign Record of the Free Church of Scotland**, August 1852, pp.21-22.

such as Melbourne and Geelong, with gold towns such as Bendigo and Ballarat also possible. The same would be true of the Church of Scotland, but somewhat less so given the more progressive and democratic nature of colonial society.

New South Wales

The proportion of Presbyterians in New South Wales in the 1850s was consistently around the 10% mark. The 1863 *Statistical Register* of New South Wales estimated one-third of Presbyterians supported the PCEA, but helpful statistical data has not been researched. The 1864 *Statistical Register* gave an average attendance of 10,414 in the 176 places of Presbyterian worship. The Highland proportion of Scottish Presbyterians was probably less than in Victoria and the Highlanders were concentrated in a limited number of areas. This accounts in part for the continuation of a significant Highland section of the PCEA outside the union of 1864/65, and it also suggests that the average non-Highland PCEA congregation may have had a less conservative tone. There was a certain war weariness, while the divisive activities of Dr Lang together with a lack of quality leadership encouraged congregations to see in union the necessary precondition for effective advance of the church despite the Synod of Australia having its ministerial strength in Scots who had associated with the Established Church after the disruption of 1843. The territory to be covered was more extensive and the funds available less plentiful than in Victoria, while the relative strength of Presbyterian following was much lower too.

The ministers

To many Presbyterians the ministers and elders were the church though in truth they were only the governing body of it. Certainly the leadership (or lack of it) by ministers was significant. Accordingly, it will be found that the ecclesiastical background of the ministers was influential in union moves.

Irish Presbyterian ministers were not always well regarded by Scots since their training was thought deficient (as it may well have been until the 1850s),[7] while Ulstermen were not seen as standard-bearers for Scottish ways and identity. For such reasons the Colonial Committee made a policy decision on January 11, 1848 that it would only send Scottish ministers to the PCEA.[8] Perhaps for similar reasons and his antipathy to evangelicals, John McGarvie of the Synod of Australia does not appear to have sought help from

---

7. Cf. Robert Allen, **The Presbyterian College Belfast 1853-1953** (Belfast 1954) for details of early training arrangements.
8. The Free Church Colonial Committee rejected an application from an Irish minister at this time, cf. B.J.Bridges, **Presbyterian Churches in New South Wales 1823-1865** (PhD Thesis 1985) p.173.

Ireland. In March 1850, the FPCV resolved to approach the Irish Presbyterian Church for help, but the request was accompanied by some criticism of Irish ministers in the Synod of Australia (presumably Gilchrist, Blain and Fullerton) who had not acted consistently and 'come out' in 1846. The Irish Church does not seem to have taken the criticism too kindly and support did not come from this source.[9] Meanwhile, Rev Irving Hetherington, the key administrator in the Victorian section of the Synod of Australia, had 'found himself unable to work along with his co-presbyters who were all of the old school, and strongly attached to the Church of Scotland.'[10] He therefore developed contacts with the Presbyterian Church in Ireland. He was able to secure a stream of recruits from 1852 onwards, and he had the money to pay them from state aid.

The result of this situation was that there were few recruits from Ireland in any of the Synods in New South Wales - a couple who came via Victoria to the Synod of Australia in the 1860s being regarded as failures in Victoria. At the same time, the Synod of Australia had many post 1843 Church of Scotland men as well as a larger and more established presence. This would add to the difficulties of achieving union in New South Wales whereas Victoria had a much more homogeneous group, the Irish ministers being generally of Free Church sympathies.

If one summarises data from the lists of ministers provided earlier,[11] it may be seen that 50% of the 54 ministers who entered the PCV in 1859 were Free Presbyterian, 15% UP and 33% Synod of Victoria (Church of Scotland). But when the Irish ministers are separated out only 9% of the ministers in the PCV were Church of Scotland and 24% were Irish. Victoria's ministers were heavily weighted in favour of the thorough-going Presbyterianism of the Free Church tradition, and we have already seen that the same was true of the membership. The situation in New South Wales was quite different as 48% of the 48 ministers at the forming of the PCNSW in 1865 were Synod of Australia (Church of Scotland), 31% PCEA and 21% UP or equivalent. When the Irish element is distinguished, the Church of Scotland proportion drops 6% to 42%. While it remains that subsequent years wrought changes since few Church of Scotland men were secured after 1865, the best men went to Victoria so that New South Wales languished somewhat and was certainly more broad and tolerant than her Victorian sister.

9. Free Presbyterian Synod Minutes p.68 (March 5, 1850: letter to be sent); pp.157/8: December 14, 1852: noting Irish response); F.R.M.Wilson, Memoir of the Rev Irving Hetherington (Melbourne 1876) p.115.
10. F.R.M.Wilson, ibid., p.115.
11. See pp. 110ff (New South Wales and pp. 150ff (Victoria).

It is hardly relevant to speak of the other colonies at this point since numbers were low. Queensland was to become the recipient of Irish ministers in the latter part of the 19th century, while Tasmania and South Australia came under Victorian influence.

The Congregations

It has already been stated that especially in rural areas congregations were nominally what their minister was. One should add that congregations were often not unwilling to change allegiance if ministerial supply would be available by doing so. This was the case with Clare and Mt Barker in South Australia in 1861 and 1863, the change being from Free Church to United Presbyterian. In Portland, Victoria, the Church of Scotland congregation founded in 1842 had a vacancy in 1848 which could not be supplied. The Interim-Moderator suggested T.E.Richardson, who had left the Presbytery of Van Diemen's Land in 1846 and become a United Presbyterian. He became minister to the congregation although a new church was erected and the Church of Scotland building not used. Another example is the transfer of J.T.Carter, sent to the Manning by Lang's Synod in 1851, to the Synod of Australia in 1852. This move gained him sufficient income to continue his ministry to the scattered groups of settlers. These few illustrations, and others which may be gleaned from earlier chapters indicate something of the flexibility in congregations: they wanted capable ministers and the distinctions which loomed large on a Synod level were less important than the pressing practical needs.

Duplications?

It is commonly alleged that there was 'frequent duplication of buildings and clergy in city and country areas.'[12] This claim needs to be heavily qualified. Portland can be taken as an extreme example. In this town, of which great things were expected, a very simple timber building was erected by the Church of Scotland in 1842 (Percy Street). When the people accepted a UP minister a new stone building was erected (1850), while a further building was erected in Palmer Street for the Highland Free Church congregation formed in 1853 and ministered to for a period by a Gaelic catechist. Here then were three buildings when perhaps one would have sufficed. However, after union the stone church was enlarged (1860) and the Palmer Street building housed the Sabbath School until a new hall was opened in 1901.

12. Thus, Keith R. Campbell, **Presbyterian Conflicts in New South Wales 1837-1865** (Journal of Religious History, Vol. 2 †1, June 1962) p. 245. Note, however, that there was significant duplication in Methodism where three or more branches existed prior to the unification completed in 1902. For examples see A.D.Hunt, **This Side of Heaven** (Adelaide 1985) pp.210ff.

There was no under-utilizing of these properties, while we are told that the original building was a 'miserable makeshift' and of no account. While at one point there were three buildings there was never more than one settled minister, except for a collegiate ministry in 1851-52.[13] So even in this extreme case the claim is too simplistic.

On the northern rivers of New South Wales there was some duplication because of the large Gaelic population, and Lang's activities at Grafton and on the Manning complicated matters. There was poor siting of church buildings in the major centres of Geelong, Melbourne and Sydney, but most were well supported and union did little to change the position. Indeed, Geelong had four Presbyterian buildings in the central area - Scots (Yarra Street), the Free Church (Little Malop Street), the Gaelic Free Church (Myers Street) and the United Presbyterian Church (Ryrie Street) opened in 1857. The Gaelic and UP churches stayed out of the 1859 union, but the Free Church moved to Gheringhap Street in 1862 to become the High Church (later St Giles) at the same time as a new parish was created on La Trobe Terrace, a short distance away.[14] Even an appeal to the Assembly was dismissed. So here was activity after the union which (certainly with hindsight) made worse the previous position.

While it is not denied that the original disunity contributed to poor siting in the city areas, there is no real evidence that the result would have been different if the church had been united. Sometimes - often - the motive for starting a new work arises from a dispute in a congregation (as in the case of St George's PCEA), but essentially the problem of too many churches in the major cities arose from a failure to realize the tremendous expansion which would occur which would denude the city centres of residents and create the urban sprawl.

Scottish influence

One further factor worthy of note is the influence of the parent churches in Scotland over events in Australia. This has already been seen in the division of 1846, and it continued to be so because of the dependence on Scotland for ministers. The Synods in fellowship with the Free Church of Scotland were avowedly independent of any overseas church, but it seems clear that the views of McIntyre and Forbes disappeared from view to some extent after the influx of Scottish ministers in 1853. The PCEA and the FPCV

13. W.Huey Steele, Scots Church Portland 1842-1942 (Brunswick 1942).
14. One Hundred Years - St George's Presbyterian Church from 1860 to 1960 (Geelong 1960) pp.6-7. When the Ryrie Street Church came into the union in 1870 there were three PCV churches within 5 minutes walk (p.51). Some rearrangement occurred forty years later.

were treated as extensions of the Free Church. The minutes of the FPCV at its Geelong meeting in November 1856 were written 'Synod of the Free Church of Scotland' and similar thinking applied quite generally among the people as well. The Synods allied with the Church of Scotland were somewhat ambiguous in their independence from the Church of Scotland - there was certainly a legal and moral connection. In November 1854 the Established Church suspended further aid to the Synod of Australia because of consternation at the prospect of union, while in May 1856 it demanded the names of members who were advocating union. In August 1856, with the prospect of union without Church of Scotland approval past, relations were more relaxed.[15]

The Established Church was not very missionary minded and was not very concerned about Australia. The Free Church, as a church of enthusiasts for the principles of the Reformed Faith, was much more interested, and after a slow start was much more likely to be able to provide suitable ministers. Up until 1857 the Free Church supported the sister churches in the colonies, but then her policymakers changed their approach so as to favour comprehensive unions, partly because the mood among the leaders was towards union with the United Presbyterians, a mood which resulted in formal negotiations in Scotland in 1863. The attitude of Scotland was the vital factor in achieving union in Victoria in 1859, and made the unions in other colonies a certainty once any special problems were overcome.[16]

Considering the way in which the anti-unionist minority FPCV was cast out of communion with the Free Church of Scotland in 1860/61, it says something that the minority PCEA (27% of the the 1864 ministerial strength) stood firm. They faced a very uncertain future with no assured supply of ministers and all the difficulties of contending with a larger church which did not seem to care much about principle in its contacts with the continuing PCEA.

15. Cf. B.J.Bridges, op. cit., p.277. M.D.Prentis, The Scots in Australia (Sydney 1983) p.248 misleadingly states 'The Established Church always wanted reunion.'
16. The decisive change in the FCS in favour of comprehensive union occurred in 1857. Keith R. Campbell (footnote 12 above) has incorrectly quoted his source [R.G.Balfour, Presbyterianism in the Colonies (Edinburgh 1900)] and from him the error has passed into other literature. When Victorian union came in 1859 it does not seem that special notice was taken by the Established Church until the Assembly of May 1861 which judged its ministers had 'done nothing wrong which merits censure.'

Conclusion

A review of factors relevant to understanding union moves has now been given and shows the strong pragmatic arguments for union. In Victoria there was little dissent after the decision of the Free Church in 1861. The Gaels were more numerous than in New South Wales and probably felt secure in the united church, while many of them did not want to identify with Gaelic culture since it was regarded as backward. New South Wales proved more difficult for reasons outlined. In comparing 1846 and 1859/64-5, one is forced to conclude that the issues had not changed. If disruption was right in 1846 because the majority were prepared to state good principles but in practice ignore them by a special connection with and preference for the Established Church, then staying out of the unions was likewise right because the practical position of the union church was acceptance of the Established Church on an equal basis. On top of this was an actual deviation from the Confession by making its teaching on church-state relations an open question.

Nevertheless, if one has the outlook of the earlier Scottish writers on the church there were two points to keep in view: first, the church's catholicity which meant that one must seek to accommodate differences for the sake of the church's peace and edification through the maintenance of unity;[17] second, the duty to maintain purity of testimony, doctrine and life. The separatist idea which made each member responsible for every defection or failure even though he did what he could in his place to rectify it, was a competing principle. On a scale, William McIntyre was nearer the catholic view of the old Reformed Church and Allan McIntyre nearer the separatist view. As a consequence, William was at first more favourable to union than Allan, but in the end stayed with Allan and sought anew to testify to the whole counsel of God upon which the Reformed Faith stood.[18]

17. The following extract from George Gillespie (1613-1648) on toleration is of interest. 'Hath not the Mediator (whom the Father heareth always) prayed 'that all His may be one'? Brethren it is not impossible; pray for it, endeavour it, press hard toward the mark of an accommodation. How much better is it that you be one with the other Reformed Churches, though somewhat straightened and bound up, than to be divided, though at full liberty and elbow room! Better is a dry morsel and quietness therewith, than a house full of sacrifices with strife.' - cited from the stimulating and valuable volume by James Walker, The Theology and Theologians of Scotland 1560-1750 (Edinburgh 1982) p.103.
18. Note the name of the PCEA magazine 1865-70 was The Testimony.

12: UNION MOVES: THE FIRST PHASE 1853-1855

While at the Synod of Australia meeting in October 1847, K.D.Smythe moved and Robert Blain seconded 'that the present designation be changed', all the other members voted against it. Malcolm Prentis has gone beyond his source in saying that the Synod made an approach to the Free Church.[1]

Tasmania 1853-54

The first approach with a view to union was made in Victoria about the beginning of 1853 by the United Presbyterian Synod, but the first actual response arose from an approach by the Presbytery of Van Diemen's Land to the newly formed Free Church Presbytery of Tasmania.

At its meeting on April 5/6, 1853, the Presbytery of VDL agreed to propose a conference to the Free Presbytery with the aim of promoting union of the two bodies. On May 24, 1853, the Free Presbytery responded:

'that full and authentic information should be furnished by each Presbytery regarding their present state and condition whereby the way may be prepared for a more effectual understanding of the matters that may require to be discussed in conference.'

The five questions suggested asked the number of congregations, number of regular hearers, communicants and elders in each, and the frequency of observance of the Lord's Supper. Clearly, the Free Presbytery had a pretty good idea that the answers would show a very disordered and poor state of affairs. There is no reason to suppose they were wrong.

1. **The Scots in Australia** (Sydney 1983) p.246 based on Keith R. Campbell. For James Forbes' negative view, see **Port Phillip Christian Herald**, November 5, 1847, p.40 col.2.

However, the response of the Presbytery of VDL was to propose that the question of union be discussed in principle before matters of detail were taken up.[2] But the Presbytery also noted that correspondence had been received from the Colonial Committee of the Free Church of Scotland which led them to expect a Free Church deputation would arrive soon, and so discussion could be deferred.

From this response it appears Dr Lillie of Hobart was negotiating behind the scenes. He was personally very sympathetic to the Free Church. However, the deputation did not come, and in 1854 the Free Presbytery was formally recognised by the Free Church of Scotland. Whatever its sympathies, the Presbytery of VDL was the legal representative of the Church of Scotland, and thus there was a bar to union.

Synod of Australia - January 1854

John McGarvie, the dominant figure in the Synod of Australia, died in April 1853, and this event opened up some possibility of a change in the position of the Synod.[3] Men of Free Church sympathies, such as Irving Hetherington of Melbourne, began to move to that end.

In January 1854, at the same meeting of Synod which noted the death of McGarvie, it was proposed by C. Atchison and seconded by Peter Gunn of Melbourne, and unanimously agreed to, that a Committee be appointed to consider and report to the Synod during the present session on the best means of effecting a union of the Presbyterian Churches in the colony holding the Westminster Standards. The Committee consisted of J.B. Laughton (Convener), J. Coutts, Dr Fullerton and T.W.Robinson (elder). In supporting the motion it was stated by the Moderator (Laughton) that

'he had no hope of any union being effected without an entire dissolution of all connection, nominal or real, with any of the existing churches of Scotland. It would be unreasonable that those who approved of the position of the Established Church of Scotland should be required to maintain even a nominal connection with any seceding body; and he was willing to admit that it was equally unreasonable to expect members of seceding bodies to unite with a body maintaining even a nominal connection with the Scottish Establishment.'[4]

2. Free Presbytery of Tasmania Minutes, pp,6,7,9,10
3. McGarvie was described as 'King Log' by an anonymous writer in The Presbyterian Magazine of 1862. See Keith R.Campbell, Presbyterian Conflicts in New South Wales 1837-1865 (JRH, June 1962) p.239.
4. Minutes of the Synod of Australia January 26, 1854 as reported in the press. See Presbyterianism in Victoria [a collection of cuttings by P.MacPherson in the State Library of Victoria] Volume for 1843-57, p.130

At the same Synod of Australia meeting, the Presbytery of Melbourne was authorised to take the steps necessary to effect separation so as to form a Synod in Victoria and for Victoria. We now look at union moves in New South Wales (which then included Queensland) and in Victoria.

New South Wales 1854-55

Excluding ministers in what became Victoria in 1851, the Synod of Australia had grown from 13 ministers following the division of 1846 to 15 at the close of 1853 when there were 14 in the PCEA.

Although duly appointed Committees of both Synods agreed unanimously on a six-point basis of union, the Synod of Australia declined to accept its Committee's recommendations and substituted another basis of three points. The first was the same as †2 in the original basis but with the deletion of the bracketed words in the text reproduced below. This modification removed the unambiguous anti-erastian interpretation, perhaps naturally, since the Synod of Australia did not admit the Church of Scotland was guilty of erastianism. The second point gave liberty to accept or reject state aid - something that might have been conceded for the sake of union. The third point covered the name of the United Synod. There was a further declaration - that union should not be effected without the sanction of the Church of Scotland. For those enamoured of the Established Church - and nine new ministers were obtained in 1854 - the supposed independence of the Synod was token only.

In summary, as at November 1854, an essentially Free Church basis had been prepared, accepted unanimously by the Synod of Eastern Australia but rejected by a majority of the Synod of Australia; in turn, a basis which merely listed the Standards without any explanation of the parts in dispute (ie. which passed no criticism on the position of the Established Church) had been proposed. One further conference was held in December but there was no progress, though in 1855 each Synod reappointed a union committee to receive proposals the other might make in accordance with the respective basis each had approved.

It was thought by the Synod of Eastern Australia that the Synod of Australia did not really desire union on a basis showing any consistency with the principles professed in 1844. An account of negotiations was published towards the end of 1855 by the former Synod.[5] It is quite clear there was a significant minority of the Synod of Australia keen for union and not slavishly subservient to the Established Church - men such as Laughton, Blain and Carter, for example. Just as certainly there was strong opposition.

5. History of Negotiations anent union between the Synod of Eastern Australia and the Synod of Australia in connection with the Established Church of Scotland, (Maitland 1855) 16pp. Alex. Salmon appears to have drafted the Basis.
179

This was not due simply to enjoyment of state stipends, since these were increasingly inadequate[6], and moves to abolish state-aid were developing strongly. Indeed, William Purves, a great supporter of the Established Church, had no need of his state stipend judging from his numerous business ventures in New South Wales, Queensland and even New Zealand.[7] But perhaps this indicates the point: in general the Synod of Australia men were not enthusiasts for the Gospel. This is not to say they preached unorthodox sermons, but they were more interested in a life of respectable comfort and social acceptance. They would choose rather to enjoy the pleasures of connection with the Established Church than to endure affliction with a band of seceders. And if the pleasures were passing they would replace them by the advantages of a larger and more influential united church even if doctrinal views had to be somewhat relaxed.

PROPOSED BASIS OF UNION 1854

1. The two Synods at present known by the respective designations of the Synod of Australia in connection with the Established Church of Scotland and the Synod of Eastern Australia shall be united under the designation of -

2. The basis of union shall be subscription to the Westminster Standards, in their integrity [and in their true and original import,] viz: The Confession of Faith, the Larger and Shorter Catechisms, the directory for Public Worship, and the form of Presbyterian government agreed upon by the Assembly of Divines at Westminster, and the Second Book of Discipline; [and for the purpose of avoiding all possible doubt and dispute as to the interpretation of the doctrine laid down in the standards, concerning the spiritual independence of church courts, and the rights of the Christian people to elect their own pastors, the United Synod shall hold and declare that there is only one tenable sense in which the said doctrines can or ought to be received, namely, that the civil power has no right, on the ground of granting temporal support, or on any plea or pretext whatsoever, to interfere with the spiritual independence of the church in the settlement of ministers, in the administration of ordinances, or in the infliction or remission of church censures.]

3. The United Synod desires to cherish friendly relationships with every faithful and evangelical church throughout the world, adhering to the same standards, and maintaining the same form of worship and discipline, that has no denominational connection with any church now existing in the United Kingdom.

4. Ministers, probationers and students of any communion holding the Westminster standards shall be deemed eligible for admission into the United Synod, on satisfactory evidence being produced as to their character and qualifications, and on their signing the articles of union.

5. Whereas the system of civil endowments existing in this colony is sinful on the part of the State, and inexpedient on the part of the Church, the Synod of Australia in connection with the Established Church of Scotland, before uniting with the Synod of Eastern Australia, shall relinquish those stipends which her ministers at present receive from the Colonial Government.

6. That if, at any future period, the United Synod shall see fit to accept of temporal support granted by the State on Scriptural grounds; and if the civil power, on the plea of giving that support, shall encroach on the rights of the people and the independence of the Church as above declared; and if a majority of the Synod shall submit to these encroachments, then the Church property of all kinds vested in the Synod shall belong to the ministers and people resisting such encroachments, and faithfully maintaining the Westminster standards as explained in the Basis of Union.

6. A ceiling was placed on the total state-aid allocation, so that as the roll of ministers rose there was less available per head. Aid was so allocated by the Synod that by 1862 18 of the 27 ministers received state-aid and 9 did not. See B.J.Bridges, **Presbyterian Churches in New South Wales 1823-1865** (PhD Thesis 1985) p.158
7. D.W.A.Baker, **Days of Wrath** (Melbourne 1985) p.453.

Victoria 1853-55

In January 1853 there were 24 Presbyterian ministers in active service in the colony. Ten were United Presbyterians, whose work in Victoria had commenced in 1847 through impetus given by Dr Lang.[8] A union of two bodies in Scotland that year favoured the availability of ministers for the colonies, and the rising economic importance of Australia not only stimulated migration of those highly motivated to better themselves but also made self-support by congregations - the UP distinctive - more attainable. The other 14 ministers were divided between the Free Presbyterian Synod (6) and the Presbytery of Melbourne of the Synod of Australia (8), although in the course of 1853 there were nett additions to these churches of 6 and 3 respectively.

United Presbyterian approach 1853

The United Presbyterians made the first official approach by a brotherly epistle dated January 24, 1853 addressed to the Free Presbyterian Synod. The thought expressed was that as the two bodies were agreed in the practice of rejecting state-aid they might be able to achieve a union though they differed in their theory of the magistrate's duty in relation to religion. The letter [9] suggested that a union 'which required no compromise on either side and secured unimpaired liberty to both' would enable an 'unspeakably greater' measure of good to be accomplished than could be done while separate bodies. The intention, as stated by Robert Hamilton, a participant in the matter, was to achieve a two-way union, and from a position of strength negotiate a further union embracing the Church of Scotland, once state-aid had been abolished.[10]

The Free Presbyterian Synod did not take up the approach until January 1854, and meantime changed the previous policy so as to accept sites from the government,[11] though still objecting to the principle on which the aid was

8. The best source is F. M. Bradshaw, **Scottish Seceders in Victoria** (Melbourne, 1947)
9. Referred to by Robert Hamilton, **Jubilee History of the Presbyterian Church of Victoria** (Melbourne 1888) p.118. Hamilton drafted the letter but neither in his history or that of Robert Sutherland (p.129) are the key terms precisely quoted. I have quoted from a typescript made after the original letter was found in the Presbyterian Church of Victoria offices in 1947.
10. R. Hamilton, ibid., p.119, 122
11. **FP Synod Minutes**, September 27, 1853. The vote was 8 to 4, but as the result was to change the practice maintained from inception and reaffirmed by Synod resolution on December 4, 1850, the proposal should have been sent down to Sessions first [there were no Presbyteries until 1854] under the Synod's version of the Barrier Act - Act VI passed December 3, 1850, revising an enactment of February 1, 1848. This was not done. Conversely, the 1850 decision was slightly revised and passed as a temporary Act on March 5, 1851, but returns under the Barrier Act were never made or followed through, undoubtedly due to the death of Forbes in August 1851. Consequently, technically there was no rule against reception of state-aid, and Tait's further motion rejecting indiscriminate endowment, passed December 17, 1852 (**Minutes** pp.163-166), was the only legislation with a claim to validity. The niceties were not recognised at the

181

given - ie. to truth and error alike - and seeking its abolition. This added a further obstacle to union with the United Presbyterians, but there is no doubt that the Free Synod was not interested in a union which did not fully maintain the duty of the civil power, existing under the light of Scripture, to support and further the Christian religion in appropriate ways. The response of the Free Synod on January 4, 1854 was:

That the Moderator be instructed to convey to the Synod of the United Presbyterian Church of Victoria their high satisfaction with this communication, and the great importance which they attach to the Union of the different sections of the Presbyterian Church in this Colony, and to request information especially with reference to their Standards, and their course of education for the ministry, and to forward to them a copy of the Acts of this Synod.

This response hit on two significant points already referred to in the previous chapter. Although Robert Hamilton tries valiantly to avoid the implications, the fact is that while using the Westminster Standards, the UP Synod had not adopted them. To say that 'the practice of a Church must be the best interpreter of her principles'[12] sounds good but is hardly valid when, to use Maxwell Bradshaw's words, 'those principles are already unambiguously set forth in a written instrument.'[13] For the present the UP Synod would have little or no involvement in union talks.

Church of Scotland approach 1854

Meanwhile, Irving Hetherington of Scots Church, Melbourne, was working behind the scenes with a view to a union of his Presbytery with the Free Presbyterian Synod. He broached the subject in the Presbytery of Melbourne in October 1853, and obtained approval to approach other Presbyterian bodies at the meeting of Presbytery in the following January. In that same month, as we have already seen, the Presbytery of Melbourne obtained approval from the Synod of Australia to take the steps necessary to become an independent Synod. Approach was made in January 1854 to the Free Synod and was at once taken up. Negotiations proceeded rapidly with a detailed Basis agreed by the Presbytery (which became the self-governing *Synod of Victoria* in April 1854) and the Free Presbyterian Synod by September 1854. The speed and harmony of the negotiations was due to the readiness of the Synod of Victoria to adopt a basis consistent with the profession of principles back in 1844. It was quite a detailed basis, and had been drafted by John Tait. To all appearances it maintained unimpaired the

time. Hamilton, op. cit., pp.123, 132, 136, wrongly asserts 'no state-aid' was part of the fixed constitution while A.J.Campbell, **Fifty Years of Presbyterianism in Victoria** (Melbourne 1889) p.53, rightly recognises it was not, but wrongly states the first protest against it was March 5, 1851. J.C.Robinson, **The Free Presbyterian Church of Australia** (Melbourne 1947) p.229, confuses the fourth part of the 1850 resolution with Section 4 of the Fundamental Act of Synod which has nothing to do with it.

12. R. Hamilton, op. cit., p.157
13. F.M.Bradshaw, op. cit., p.107

principles of the Scottish Church as vindicated by the Free Church of Scotland.[14] Adam Cairns and Macintosh Mackay, experienced ministers who had 'come out' in the Scottish Disruption of 1843 and who arrived in Victoria in September 1853 and January 1854, were leaders from the side of the Free Presbyterians, while Irving Hetherington was the key man from the Synod of Victoria. The fact there were few diehard Church of Scotland men in the Synod of Victoria was a help, while the acceptance of state-aid by the Free Presbyterian Church, which was extended to stipends on November 2, 1854 [15], not without opposition, did not hurt either.

BASIS OF UNION AS AGREED SEPTEMBER 19, 1854

We, the undersigned ministers and elders of the Synod of Victoria and of the Synod of the Free Presbyterian Church of Victoria, constituting the supreme judicatories of our respective Churches, and being, as such, free and independent, and under no external jurisdiction or control whatever, having resolved, after long and prayerful deliberation and repeated friendly conferences, held on the motion and instigation of the former Synod, to unite together in one Synod and one Church, being satisfied that there is no longer any impediment or hindrance to the same, and that we hold the same Standards and Formularies - namely, the Westminster Confession of Faith, the Larger and Shorter Catechisms, the Form of Presbyterial Church Government, the Directory for Public Worship, and the Second Book of Discipline - do now, in the name of the Great Head of the Church, and with solemn prayer for His guidance and blessing, join and unite in one Synod, to be called 'The Presbyterian Church of Victoria,' having superintendence and jurisdiction over all Presbyteries and Kirk Sessions and Congregations that homologate and agree to this Union, in the same way and with the same powers and authorities as the aforesaid Synods; and resolve and determine that the following be the fundamental principles and articles of this Union, and be subscribed by each of the members of the new Synod, namely:-

I. That the Westminster Confession of Faith, the Larger and Shorter Catechisms, the Form of Presbyterial Church Government, the Directory for Public Worship, and the Second Book of Discipline be the Standards and Formularies of this Church.

II. That according to the views and principles laid down in the said Confession on the duty of the Civil Magistrate in regard to religion, he is bound and required to use his official power and influence for the maintenance, protection, and support of the truth, and the restraining and putting down error and ungodliness, but that that is to be done only in accordance with the requirements of the Word of God, and within the sphere to which mere Civil authority is by that Word restricted; and that, in subscribing to the said Confession, the ministers and elders of this Church are not to be understood as encouraging or countenancing persecuting or intolerant principles, or as professing any views inconsistent with liberty of conscience and the right of private judgment.

III. That according to the views and principles laid down in the said Confession in regard to the sole Headship of Christ over His Church, and the authority with which He has invested her rulers, they have an independent and exclusive jurisdiction in the government of the Church in all spiritual things; that it belongs to them alone to admit or exclude members and officebearers, and to license and ordain ministers, to induct and settle them over congregations, and to suspend or depose them; that with these and the like functions, it is equally presumptuous and unwarrantable in the Magistrate to interfere, and faithless and sinful in the Church to permit or submit to such interference, and that from any of the decisions of her judicatories in reference to such spiritual matters, there can be no appeal to any civil authority whatsoever.

14. According to Tait's letter September 22, 1854 to Arthur Paul, the Basis was intended to condemn the condition of things at that time existing in the Established Church, **The Presbyter**, September 1884, p.69; J.C.Robinson, op. cit., p.244,245 passes unwarranted strictures on the Basis itself.

15. This is the correct date. R. Sutherland, op. cit., p.165 gives the date as April 1855, but this was the date of a further debate on the subject.

IV. That according to the views and principles laid down in the Confession of Faith and in the Second Book of Discipline in regard to the Headship of Christ over the members of the Church individually, they have rights and privileges secured to them which may not be interfered with, and that the rulers are to exercise their authority so as to have respect to these, and take care that no elder or minister be intruded on any congregation contrary to their will; and, in particular, that it shall be a fundamental rule of this Church that the election of ministers, ruling elders, and deacons belongs to the members of each separate congregation in full communion, the judicatories of the Church superintending and regulating the same.

V. That this Synod, while holding itself at liberty to maintain communion and correspondence with all other faithful Presbyterian Churches throughout the world, has yet of right, and is determined to maintain, a separate and independent character and position, and to preserve unimpaired a supreme and independent jurisdiction over its subordinate judicatories and congregations and people, irrespective of any other Church or body whatsoever; and that all privileges, whether ecclesiastical or temporal, held by any of the ministry, office-bearers, or other members, in virtue of their office and membership respectively, are and shall be possessed and enjoyed free from the interference or control of any ecclesiastical body foregn to itself.

VI. That the foregoing principles be summed up in the subjoined formula, and be signed by every licentiate before receiving license, and by every minister previous to his reception into the Synod, or induction into any of its congregations.

FORMULA

I do hereby declare that I do sincerely own and believe the whole doctrine contained in the Confession of Faith, approved by the General Assembly of the Church of Scotland in the year 1847, to be the truth of God; and I do likewise own the purity of worship presently authorized and practised in the Presbyterian Church of Victoria, and also the Presbyterian government and discipline thereof; which Doctrine, Discipline and Church Government, I am persuaded, are founded on the Word of God and agreeable thereto. I likewise sincerely and heartily hold the principles respecting the supremacy of Christ over His Church, and her subjection to Him as her only Head, and the freedom from secular control in the management of the affairs of Christ's House, belonging to her in virtue of His institution, which are set forth in the Articles of Union agreed on and subscribed by the ministers and elders constituting the Synod on.....I approve of all the other declarations and provisions of the said Articles; and I promise that, through the grace of God, I shall firmly and constantly adhere to the same, and, to the utmost of my power, shall, in my station, assert, maintain, and defend the said Doctrine, Worship, Discipline and Government of this Church, together with its exclusive and final spiritual jurisdiction, and its independence from all external control and interference. And I promise that I shall follow no divisive courses from the principles and constitution of this Church, renouncing all doctrines, tenets and opinions whatsoever contrary to or inconsistent with the same.

All looked very promising. Two matters remained to be adjusted: (1) the source of ministerial supplies until locally trained ministers were available; and (2) the adequacy or otherwise of the Act of Parliament regulating the property holdings of the Synod of Victoria to secure the property of the United Church.

As to the first point, it was generally agreed in the Free Presbyterian camp (Tait being the exception) that the Synod of Victoria was prepared to refuse all correspondence and communion with the Established Church, and that a consistent application of the Basis would require this. The reference in Para. V to 'all *other faithful* Presbyterian Churches' - the italicized words being inserted on the motion of Dr Cairns - was intended to make this plain. It was not intended to exclude individual Church of Scotland ministers as such: they might be received if they could honestly subscribe the Basis.

As to the second point, it was found in November 1854 that the Synod of Victoria Act had merely invested the Synod of Victoria with the same powers, privileges and advantages of the parent Synod of Australia, and thus a new Act would be necessary to effect separation from the Established Church and safeguard the property of the United Church. There were delays obtaining the new Act due to illness and also the new constitution granted Victoria in 1855 which created a bi-cameral system. During this time doubts arose from the Free Presbyterian side as a result of views expressed in Committee which showed that the Synod of Victoria did not regard the Articles of Union as expressing disapproval of the position of the Established Church of Scotland. However, on November 6, 1855, Dr Cairns reported to the Free Presbyterian Synod that the documents which had led to the contention, together with other letters based on them, had been withdrawn as not sanctioned by the Committee. This was taken to mean that the Articles of Union remained in their integrity and so, subject to the new Act of Parliament, union seemed assured.[16]

There was another positive note at this November meeting of the Free Presbyterian Synod. The Presbytery of Van Diemen's Land had a letter in reporting on a recent decision in which the Presbytery had declared its agreement with the Free Church position on the principles involved in the Scottish Disruption of 1843; that the name *Church of Scotland* was used by the Presbytery because it held the principles of the true Church of Scotland (ie. the Free Church); that all ministers would be received subject to due enquiry but that the Presbytery felt warranted in looking chiefly to the Free Church of Scotland because of its identity of principles and the likelihood of able and faithful men from that source; and that a locally trained ministry should be aimed at. Dr Lillie of Hobart was present and spoke to the Synod. He expressed the desire for union of his Church with the Victorian, and assured the brethren the legislature of Tasmania would pass whatever Act they asked for, ie. an Act to remove all real or supposed connection with the Established Church.[17]

16. Mackay had drawn up a 'memorial' for the assistance of legal counsel, which he shared with Hetherington who provided 'annotations' which caused concern. A 'statement' on the annotations was prepared by Arthur Paul at the request of the Free Presbyterian Union Committee and approved in June 1855 against the opposition of Tait. F.R.M.Wilson, writing Hetherington's life in 1876, wrongly attributes the 'statement' to Tait, his father-in-law who had died in 1860, Memoir of the Rev Irving Hetherington, p. 115 and has been followed by others. See The Presbyter, 1884, pp.29, 195 for Paul's position.
17. See Presbyterianisn in Victoria [MacPherson papers] op.cit.,p.136, also R.Hamilton, op. cit., 145, 146.

If all was looking rosy between the Synod of Victoria and the Free Presbyterian Synod, what about the position of the United Presbyterians? Several meetings were held, the most significant being on November 19, 1855. The Synod of Victoria was ready to delete the first part of the second Article and combine what remained with Article one. In the Free Presbyterian Synod the same attitude was taken by Dr Mackay and John Tait, but the rest of the Synod opposed such a modification on the grounds that the original articles preserved the obligation of the civil magistrate to countenance and cherish the truth of God, whereas the change proposed would in practice abandon this doctrine. Consequently, while friendly relations should be cultivated, further negotiations with the United Presbyterian Synod should cease for the time being. The Synod of Victoria was disappointed, but jointly resolved with the Free Presbyterian Synod that as both Synods 'adhere to the Articles of Synod in all their integrity as formerly agreed upon', arrangements be made to obtain the approval of congregations and consummate a two-way union. This was the position at the close of 1855.

Summary of the first phase

Reviewing the first phase of union negotiations (1853-55), it is evident that the proposed Basis in each of New South Wales and Victoria was a pretty clear statement of the Free Church understanding of the principles involved in the Disruption. As such, each Basis had the unanimous support of the Synods representing the Free Church position - the Synod of Eastern Australia and the Free Presbyterian Synod. In New South Wales there was a majority in the Synod of Australia opposed to anything suggestive of criticism of the Established Church and so there was no change in the status quo. The Colonial Committee of the Established Church was also against union at this stage. In the Synod of Victoria the majority of ministers were not from the Established Church but from Ireland, so there was not the same contact with and attitude towards the Established Church by the ministers. Hence good unanimity appeared though the Basis proposed was more detailed than that in New South Wales rejected by the Synod of Australia. The Synod of Victoria even seemed somewhat easy-going on the Basis from its willingness to allow modifications to accommodate United Presbyterian views. In this one sees reflected the attitude expressed in April 1854 when the Synod was instituted - that it was 'exceedingly desirable' that the Synod be as 'free as possible from anything likely to prevent Presbyterians in general from uniting in one large and influential body.'[18] In other words, the Synod was ready to be elastic.

18. R. Hamilton, op. cit., p.126

13: UNION & DISUNION IN VICTORIA 1856-1859

New South Wales

Soon after Dr Macintosh Mackay accepted a call to Sydney to pastor a new congregation of the Presbyterian Church of Eastern Australia, he sought to advance the cause of union as he had in Victoria. An overture to the Synod in 1856 was granted and a Committee appointed to confer with a Committee of the Synod of Australia. But the upshot was that the same basic problem remained. The PCEA Synod declared that no Basis would be acceptable that did not explicitly set forth the spiritual independence of the Church and the Headship of Christ over his own House.[1] There the matter rested until 1862.

Stresses and strains

Back in Victoria, the concerns about the interpretation of the Basis of Union by the Synod of Victoria came to a sharp focus in the Free Presbyterian Synod early in 1856. An attempt at the April meeting to have the Union Committee minutes and associated documents tabled failed, since the majority could see that to do so would set the cat among the pigeons. The ministers of John Knox (Swanston Street), Brunswick and St Kilda remained deeply concerned. The minister of St Kilda, Arthur Paul, had come from New South Wales at the close of 1854, after the Basis was in place, and had first sat in the Synod in April 1855. At that time he was made a member of the Union Committee, and later became its Clerk. He held the minutes in question and so had ground for concern.

1. James Cameron, **Centenary History of the Presbyterian Church in New South Wales** (Sydney 1905) p.69. Ordination questions identical to those in the Free Church of Scotland were adopted in May 1857, and in May 1858 incoming ministers were required to concur in the Protest of 1846.

While the Synod had unanimously supported union on the Basis proposed, Arthur Paul, Allan McVean (Brunswick) and William Miller (John Knox) came to the view that Dr Cairns had misled the Synod in November 1855 when he said certain documents had been withdrawn by the Synod of Victoria Committee. They had inferred that the sentiments expressive of approval of the position of the Established Church had been withdrawn. In fact, the withdrawal was an arrangement by Cairns and Hetherington, the respective Conveners. In what has been described as 'an adroit move of Mr Hetherington's',[2] the Union Committee of his Synod simply declared that all the discussion was based on documents which had not in a formal way been brought before it, and therefore it had no responsibility for them. Accordingly, the Conveners (not the Committee) agreed that all the documents should be considered as entirely set aside and of no authority - this despite the fact that the main items had been held as authoritative for many months.

As well as this problem, the United Presbyterians were somewhat unimpressed with the Free Presbyterian attitude to union. On April 29, 1856 the following minute was recorded:

'The Synod yet further submit that they cannot entertain the belief that, at the opening of the negotiations, the Free Church Synod were actually of opinion that the second Article in the basis must be retained in its integrity, inasmuch as this would have required on the part of the United Presbyterian Church the surrender of a great principle, which they have ever held,and a conversion to a principle of an opposite kind; and that had the members of the United Presbyterian Church known this in time, no step would have been taken with a view to union, and much time and trouble saved to all parties.'[3]

One can certainly say that the United Presbyterians had from their first approach in January 1853 talked of a union with the Free Synod 'which required no compromise on either side and secured unimpaired liberty to both.' But the ecclesiastical mind was at work in Messrs Mackay and Cairns, and their policy was to deal first with the Church of Scotland so as to argue from a position of strength and force a UP capitulation on terms which maintained the Free Church principle. From 1856, with Cairns the main driving force, the object aimed at was seen as so desirable that it was

2. Aeneas Macdonald, One Hundred Years of Presbyterianism in Victoria (Melbourne 1937) p. 41.

3. Robert Hamilton, A Jubilee History of the Presbyterian Church of Victoria (Melbourne 1888) p. 151. Compare Lord Robertson's comment in the House of Lords case, Free Church of Scotland v Overtoun (1904): 'It is honourable in the United Presbyterian Church, that in good times and in bad, it has never used ambiguous language or nicely balanced phrases about this matter, and has never sailed under false colours.' cited by J. C. Robinson, Free Presbyterian Church of Australia (Melbourne 1947) p. 290.

to be achieved at risk or even at any price. No doubt Cairns consoled himself in the thought that whatever happened the bulk of the ministers would in fact be Free Church in sentiment, so that any divergent elements could be swamped by superior numbers. At any rate, this is the kind of assessment that stands up in the light of subsequent developments.

United Presbyterian division

The United Presbyterians were further restricted in negotiations by reason of a three way split which occured in 1856/57, soon after there had been several additions to the ministerial roll. It was hard to find places for these men. An arrangement by which Rev James Ballantyne became colleague to Rev A.M. Ramsay of St Enoch's, Collins Street soon broke up and divided the congregation, the former man being a strict Presbyterian whereas Ramsay was less committed though a strong voluntary. The inadequate basis of 1850 came into it,[4] as well as the consistency or otherwise of entering into a United Church while state-aid continued. The upshot was that some United Presbyterians remained out of the union accomplished in 1859 until 1870, when state-aid was in principle terminated.

Free Presbyterian division

As for the Free Presbyterian Synod, the concerns of Paul and his brethren resulted in Paul publishing a pamphlet, *A Coalition of Interests not the Unity of the Faith*, at the time of the Synod in November 1856. Utilizing some of the material that had been in Paul's possession as Clerk of the Union Committee, it was a well argued tract which in polite terms 'intensified the conflict'[5] in the Free Synod. Although several writers give the impression it was written by a pen dipped in corrosive,[6] apart from several unguarded expressions which Paul acknowledged, the only corrosive aspect to it was that it destroyed the dream of unanimity in the Synod in favour of union. Paul was a man of ability in debate, and he certainly could descend to vitriol as some of his latter writings show. But the strong feelings caused by the tract were not due to excessive language but to the fact he showed plainly that men in the Synod of Victoria had not changed their opinions despite giving that impression by approving the Basis. He also showed that Free Church men like Mackay and Cairns had formerly held back from supporting union on the very same ground of opposition that Paul and the minority were still holding to! In 1854, when the Synod of Victoria had been formed,

4. One recalls Forbes' reference to the 'extremely meagre' basis. Invariably, chickens come home to roost.
5. F.M.Bradshaw's phrase in article 'Presbyterian Church' in **Australian Encyclopaedia** 2nd edition (Sydney 1958).
6. Compare A.Macdonald, op. cit., p.44. Robert Sutherland, **History of the Presbyterian Church of Victoria** (London 1877) is more accurate when he speaks of 'great severity' (p.171) in the pamphlet's argument, and 'fine flourishes of rhetoric' (p. 309).

the words 'in connection with the Established Church of Scotland' had been dropped from the name though the connection had continued. Said Paul: 'To change a name without changing the thing designated by it, is simply fitted to mislead the uninformed.' [7]

As if to confirm Paul's criticism, Rev Andrew Love of Geelong, a minister of the Synod of Victoria belonging to the old school, wrote on February 26, 1857 to the *Geelong Advertiser,* that the change of name

was never intended, neither was it implied, that, by the omission of the words, 'in connection with the [Established] Church of Scotland' which is still part of the designation of the Synod of New South Wales [ie. the Synod of Australia in New South Wales], we should break with or repudiate in the slightest degree, the venerable church of our fathers. [8]

However, by this time, Paul had been censured by a special Synod on January 14, 1857 following a 13 to 5 vote, the five opposing brethren standing up with Paul when he received the censure.

The anti-union campaign was now fairly under way and this caused a great deal of concern to Dr Cairns. When the Synod met for its normal meeting on April 7, 1857, the Synod went into closed session and resolved:

I That this Synod did solemnly and deliberately, and unanimously resolve to go into Union with the Synod of Victoria on the terms laid down in the Articles of Union; that having solemnly and deliberately come to this decision, they entered into a covenant or agreement with the other Synod to consummate the Union on these terms that they are still impressed with the conviction of the importance and safety of Union on this basis; and both on this account, and on account of their solemn engagements, they are determined to go forward with it.

II That there being a minority now opposed to going forward with this Union, and threatening to resist it, the brethren, still adhering to their convictions of the necessity and importance of this Union, and feeling their obligation to adhere to their covenant, are shut up by the very nature of Presbyterian constitution to require of the minority that, while retaining their own sentiments and views, and recording their dissent so far as they see necessary, they do not actively resist and oppose the carrying out this deliverance and this covenant, or they can no longer be permitted to remain within the Body; and if they conceive they are shut up by their convictions of duty still to resist and oppose, there is no other course possible in the circumstances without utterly setting at nought the fundamental principles of Presbytery than that they retire at once and form a Church according to their own views, or that the painful necessity will be laid on this Synod to assert the authority of the Synod and exercise discipline on those persisting in the divisive and rebellious course.

William Miller, on behalf of the minority, proposed a pacific arrangement, but

7. A Coalition of Interests....pp. 12/13.
8. Presbyterianism in Victoria [a collection of cuttings by P.MacPherson in the State Library of Victoria] Volume for 1843-57, p.173.

this was held over, the motion above passed and the meeting adjourned until the evening to give the minority an opportunity to think things over. In the evening, the minority submitted their proposal as follows:

The undersigned members of the Free Presbyterian Synod of Victoria, having under consideration a proposal for a pacific arrangement between them and the members of the said Synod who are resolved to promote Union with the Synod of Victoria, resolve and propose as follows:

1. That adhering as they do to all the provisions of the Fundamental Act of this Synod, they do not concur with, but on the contrary, repudiate the general views of Presbyterian Church government which the proposal submitted to them assumes.

2. That being desirous, nevertheless, equally with the brethren opposed to them, of a pacific arrangement, they concur in the proposal made in the close of the paper, to the effect that the minority withdraw peaceably from the majority of the Synod

3. It being provided that all questions with regard to the property of the several congregations shall be equitably determined by a joint-committee composed of members derived in equal proportions from the majority and minority respectively.

(Signed)   Arthur Paul, St Kilda   Joseph Thomson, elder
            William Miller, John Knox   W.M.Bell, elder
            Andrew Maxwell, St Georges,Kilmore   Roderick MacLeod ,el der
            Allan McVean, Brunswick
            John McDougall, Gaelic Church, Geelong

The next day the subject was taken up again when Dr Cairns read a motion of 26 paragraphs [9] which set out the grounds on which it was proposed to expel the minority. The substance of the motion was in the words of the resolution of the previous day, together with a rejection of the pacific arrangement on the ground that the fundamental principle of Presbyterian Church government is that a minority should submit to a majority, whereas in fact the minority were not doing this but asserting for themselves 'a right and power, as an independent party, to make terms and conditions with the majority.'

It is of course true that a minority must submit to a majority but subject always to the constitution, and to the allowance of those avenues of opposition and disssent within the constitution. But Cairns' motion, seconded by Thomas Hastie, ignored the provision of the Fundamental Act of Synod, proceeded on the basis that a majority could competently overturn the constitution, and professed to expel men against whom no charge in regular form had been made and who had not been guilty of actions in the meeting of the Synod which would justify summary action without a trial.

9. Text in R. Sutherland, op.cit., pp.177-186 also R.Hamilton, op.cit., Appendix B.

Adam Cairns

Irving Hetherington

SOME OF THOSE INVOLVED IN THE UNION STRUGGLE

Arthur Paul

James Ballantyne

On the evening of April 8, the motion was put and carried unanimously by the majority, as the minority would not agree to cease opposition to the union nor were they prepared to withdraw on a basis which conceded the legality of the majority's views. The expelled ministers - Miller, Paul, Maxwell and McVean - lodged a Protest[10] which incorporated an adjournment of the Synod to April 14 in John Knox Church.

On that date, the minority duly met and followed up their claim to be the true Free Presbyterian Church by appointing a new Moderator and Clerk and requesting the Clerk to write to John Tait of Geelong requiring him to give up the records and papers of the Free Presbyterian Church. While the minority did not gain the records, their action was consistent with the whole thrust of their position. Until the majority entered the union achieved two years later, the government recognised two Free Presbyterian denominations.

The majority were at first quite confident that they had acted properly. Robert Sutherland records that Dr Macintosh Mackay of Sydney, who had been present at the Synod, rose and said

'that his sympathies were entirely with the Synod. He was the oldest minister present, and never in his lifetime saw or heard of such conduct as was manifested by the dissentient brethren. They, a mere minority, tried again and again, and repeatedly, to resist and thwart the solemn and deliberate resolution of the Synod. Their divisive and rebellious conduct they carried on in the very Synod, and daringly and insolently in the face of the very court. It would be mere waste of time to proceed against them by libel; their guilt and wrong-doing was plain and patent in the face of the court.[11]

One can at least say that Mackay touched on the principle that would have justified some kind of summary action such as took place, but he also shows how judgment can be swayed by personal views. To speak of a *mere minority* makes one wonder if he had forgotten those who left the Established Church in 1843 - a minority which included himself and Dr Cairns! And had he forgotten the 'Ten Years Conflict' which had preceded that event as the constitutionalists sought to maintain the true position? Mackay returned to Scotland in 1861 and became minister of Tarbert Free Church. He lived to regret his part in promoting the Union,[12] and died in 1873.

Reference to Scotland
The Joint Union Committee prepared extracts of the proceedings and they were sent to Scotland. It was important to avoid being seen as unfaithful to Free Church principles, so that future ministerial supplies were adequately

10. The text of the Protest is found in Sutherland (p.487), Hamilton (Appendix C) and Robinson (Apendix X). John McDougall was absent from the evening session.
11. R. Sutherland, op.cit., p.188
12. Principal John Macleod, 'Dr Macintosh Mackay' in **Our Banner**, September 1933.

assured.[13]A meeting of some 100 Free Church ministers examined the Articles of Union in August 1857, and found them satisfactory, while several prominent leaders (Drs Guthrie, Begg, Duff and Nixon) gave strong support to colonial union.[14]

There was nothing particularly surprising about the Scottish approval of the Articles of Union. Even the Victorian Minority did not object to them as such but only to the practical effect the Established Church sympathizers said they would make of them in receiving without reservation ministers of the Established Church. Of course, Scotland could hardly be aware of all that was occurring in Victoria, though the very able *Narrative*[15] prepared by the Minority did not leave much in the dark. However, there was a new attitude developing in the policy of the Colonial Committee which favoured general union of Presbyterians who were still separated in Scotland. Indeed, in 1863, [16]official moves were made for the union of the Free Church of Scotland and the United Presbyterian Church of Scotland.

Clearly, divisions in the colonies were hurtful to developments where united action was desirable - educational institutions, missions and church extension, for example. But union attempts based on a mere veneer of agreement are hurtful to the spiritual influence and task of the church. Still, the 1857 message from Scotland was clear enough: the Majority Synod has support, and an even wider union of Presbyterians is desirable. Armed with this, correspondence with a view to reconciliation began in November 1857. The famous *Edinburgh Letter,*[17] written by Dr Candlish and signed by Drs Candlish, Cunningham, Begg, Guthrie and William Nixon, arrived in February 1858. While it supported union it was also critical of the expulsion as un-Presbyterian.

The Majority Synod appointed John Tait of Geelong and Macintosh Mackay of Sydney as deputies to the Free Church of Scotland. At the May 1858 General Assembly, on the motion of Dr Candlish, the Majority was recognised as maintaining her principles and in close connection with her. The hope of reconciliation was expressed and that the past would be blotted out, but the Minority could not and would not be recognised as occupying the position of the sister church of the Free Church of Scotland in Victoria.

13. **Extracts from the Records of the Synod of Victoria and the Free Synod of Victoria on the subject of Union between the Two Churches** 59pp. There were two editions, in the second of which some material was suppressed.

14. Portions of the letters are given in R. Sutherland, op. cit., pp.189-192

15. **The Free Church Narrative: an account of negotiations for union from October 1853 to April 1857** (Melbourne, September 1857) 96pp. Paul was the primary author.

16. G.N.M.Collins, **The Heritage of our Fathers** (Edinburgh 1974) p. 71

17. The text of this letter is in R. Sutherland, op. cit., pp.492-501

In addressing the Assembly, Macintosh Mackay stated that the Presbyterian Church had to be drawn into one compact body. 'The plain truth was, in their present divided state they could do nothing' - an absurd statement.[18] Tait also spoke, very properly noting that 'but for a special connection, recognised and sanctioned by civil statute, in which they early placed themselves to the Established Church of Scotland, in the full conviction that it was both an honour and a security, they might have been spared the necessity of a disruption' in 1846. But Tait incorrectly asserted that the Synod of Victoria had in 1854 come out of the special and statutory connection with the Established Church.[19]

Tait also noted that 'the universal feeling of those living in the same district was to receive with open arms whatever Presbyterian minister first settled among them' - a true statement which undermines the common argument that the small colonial towns were over-churched while country districts were left bereft.[20] He made the valid point that if the three churches remained separate, the congregations would eventually partake of the character of the denomination to which their first minister belonged. This is as much as to say that at the local level union was not greatly impaired by the existence of three churches, but that division at Presbytery and Synod level brought weakness for the overall cause.

Concessions to the United Presbyterians

In January 1858, the Synod of Victoria proposed to the Majority Synod that the first and third Articles be reworked in a similar though less definite way than that rejected by the Free Synod in December 1855 as voiding 'a necessary part of divine truth' to which they had 'solemnly pledged' themselves. But the Synod of Victoria was anxious to bring in the United Presbyterians, and it was known that the alteration proposed would satisfy them. This time, the Free Presbyterian Majority Synod agreed unanimously to the change thereby effectively abandoning clear testimony to the duty of the civil magistrate. One assumes Tait and Mackay were aware of this concession, but they did not speak of it at the General Assembly of the Free Church in May. If they had, more than eyebrows would have been raised.

18. R. Sutherland, op. cit., p.202. My copy of this book was formerly owned by Professor Robert Miller of the Presbyterian Theological Hall, Melbourne. He has written 'nonsense' against Mackay's words at this point.
19. For summary of Tait's speech see R.Sutherland, ibid., pp.202-203.
20. Compare the comment of Dr Lillie of Hobart who says this was the view of the Free Church leaders he had spoken with in Scotland when visiting [in 1856], R. Sutherland, op. cit., p.187. Melbourne and Geelong were hardly 'small colonial towns' but the argument reflected popular mythology (and inadequate knowledge of geography) rather than significant reality, certainly as far as Victoria and Tasmania are concerned.

Concession to the Synod of Victoria

The Synod of Victoria also had difficulties with the Basis of Union. At the meeting of the Free Synod at which the concession to the United Presbyterians was agreed (January 6, 1858), 'a statement was made showing that the harmony supposed to exist between them and the Synod of Victoria was more nominal than real.[21] This is what the Minority had been saying all along. Scots, Melbourne, and Scots, Geelong, which were congregations of mostly Church of Scotland people (natural enough given the presence of churches of the other branches in these large centres), were the congregations desiring changes.

Objection was made to three parts of the Basis of Union considered critical of the Established Church of Scotland. These were the clause in Article 3 which stated it was 'presumptuous and unwarrantable for the magistrate to interfere in the spiritual affairs of the church and faithless and sinful for the church to permit or submit to such interference'; the statement in the fourth Article which made it a fundamental rule that election of office-bearers belongs to the members of the church; and the section of Article five which referred to holding communion and correspondence with all other *faithful* Presbyterian Churches - the part that Dr Cairns had had inserted and which to his mind excluded communion with the Established Church.

Understandably, Dr Cairns was not at all keen to accept any modification, and strove manfully to have the Synod of Victoria abide by what had been solemnly agreed.[22] However, his proposal was rejected in favour of appointing a Committee to provide an explanation of the points in dispute, which was done by letter dated April 12, 1858. The letter stated that the Articles were not held as pointing at Scottish churches as such, nor the present state of the Established Church.

'we rather regard it as language in which you and we can heartily join, whatever our opinion of the present state of the Scottish Establishment may be, because it is language rendered venerable to us all by the Presbyterian association of centuries.' [23]

Translated, this meant: we have used fine and orthodox phrases, and any interpretation you please can be put upon them which does not imply any criticism of the Established Church.' Considering that the Established Church

---

21. R. Hamilton, op. cit., p.167
22. See the (lengthy) text of Cairns' motion in R. Sutherland, op. cit., pp. 223,224, or R. Hamilton, op. cit., p.169.
23. Rev D. McDonald of Emerald Hill was Convener. The text is in Sutherland (p.225, 226) and Hamilton (p.170). The argument is pure cant in the light of the original intent (compare note 14 in the preceding chapter).

had not changed its position since 1843, except perhaps for the worse,[24] the Committee was saying that the basis contained no testimony against erastianism. One compares this with the provision of the Fundamental Act of the Free Presbyterian Church as drawn up by James Forbes in 1848:

'And this Synod do condemn, and by God's help, resolve ever to testify against all interference of Civil Magistrates with the spiritual affairs of Christ's House, and against all Ecclesiastical bodies countenancing or submitting to such interference, either directly or indirectly; and against all tenets, principles, practices and acts by which such interference on the part of the Civil Magistrate, or such submission on the part of Ecclesiastical bodies may be countenanced.'

The Free Presbyterian Committee also stated that it was understood in the Synod that ministers of sufficient education and good standing prepared to sign the Formula would be admitted to the proposed United Church, whatever denomination they had belonged to previously. This meant that Established Church ministers would be admitted without question if their education was sufficient and they were in good standing at the time they demitted their previous connection. No questions would be asked concerning their involvement in the erastianism of the Established Church.

A completely new basis

However, the insertion of an explanatory clause that would have the effect of explicitly placing the Established Church on the same footing as the Free Church was difficult for the FP Synod. By the same token, the Synod of Victoria found difficulty in proceeding without changes, although the extent of opposition in the Synod of Victoria was really rather limited - Mr Love not being able to find a seconder for his proposal on June 2, 1858 to proceed no further for the present.[25]

The formal recognition of the Majority Free Synod by the May 1858 Free Church of Scotland Assembly was known in Victoria later that year and appears to have helped in the resolution of the situation. In December, the Committee of the Synod of Victoria proposed a completely new and simplified basis, and both Synods accepted it on December 8, 1858. Including a few unimportant verbal amendments adopted later, the Basis of Union was as shown on the following page. It was approved by all the congregations of the Synod of Victoria, and all the congregations of the Majority Free Synod except St Andrew's, Carlton (which joined the Minority), and by a majority of the United Presbyterians.

24. Much of the legislation passed in the years before the Disruption was repealed or ignored. Not until 1866 did those who desired reunion seriously push for the abolition of patronage. Cf. J.H.S.Burleigh, A Church History of Scotland (London 1960) p.394
25. R. Hamilton, op. cit., p. 171

BASIS OF UNION CONSUMMATED APRIL 7, 1859 FORMING
THE PRESBYTERIAN CHURCH OF VICTORIA

We, the undersigned ministers and elders of the Synod of Victoria, the Free Presbyterian Synod of Victoria, the United Presbyterian Synod of Victoria, and the United Presbyterian Synod of Australia, having resolved, after long and prayerful deliberation, to unite together in one Synod and one Church, do now, in the name of the Lord Jesus Christ, and with solemn prayer for his guidance and blessing, unite in one Synod, to be called the Presbyterian Church of Victoria, and resolve and determine that the following be the fundamental principles and Articles of the Union, and be subscribed by each member of the new Synod:

I That the Westminster Confession of Faith, the Larger and Shorter Catechisms, the Form of Presbyterial Church Government, the Directory for Public Worship, and the Second Book of Discipline be the Standards and Formularies of this Church.

II That inasmuch as there is a difference of opinion in regard to the doctrines contained in these Standards relative to the power and duty of the Civil Magistrate in matters of religion, the office-bearers of this Church, in subscribing these Standards and Formularies are not to be held as countenancing any persecuting or intolerant principles, or as professing any views inconsistent with the liberty of personal conscience or the right of private judgment.

III That this Synod asserts for itself a separate and independent character and position as a Church, possesses supreme jurisdiction over its subordinate judicatories and congregations and people, and will receive all ministers and preachers from other Presbyterian Churches applying for admission on an equal footing, who shall thereupon become subject to its authority alone.

FORMULA
I do hereby declare that I do sincerely approve and accept the Standards and Formularies enumerated in the foregoing Articles as the confession of my faith, with the declarations and provisions contained in the second Article; and I promise that, through the grace of God, I shall firmly and constantly adhere to the same, that I shall follow no divisive counsels, but, in my station, and to the utmost of my power, shall assert, maintain and defend the Doctrines, Worship, Discipline and Government of this Church as therein defined, renouncing all doctrines, tenets and opinions whatsoever contrary to or inconsistent with the same.

In comparing the second Basis with the first, it is clear that the second really amounted to a coalition of interests rather than unity based on agreement on the matters in dispute. Hetherington described it as going back to the 'fundamental principles on which as representing the home Churches, we were severally agreed' and that the second Article was not a repudiation of any doctrine of the standards adopted in the first Article but merely a disavowal of an offensive interpretation of which some thought a particular doctrine was susceptible.[26] But this is not what the Basis says. It gives liberty in the area of the power and duty of the civil magistrate in matters of

26. F.R.M.Wilson, **Memoir of the Rev Irving Hetherington** (Melbourne 1876) p.183. The words quoted were written in February 1861.

religion. Some held there was no particular duty though the Confession taught there was. At least some of the United Presbyterians held as a distinct principle a view subversive of the establishment or national recognition principle which had been a fundamental principle of the Church of Scotland since 1560. By the Basis of Union no clear testimony is given to any view of church-state relations. In this sense the second Basis is a marked departure from the first Basis approved in 1855, and represents a significant departure from the full-orbed testimony of historic Presbyterianism to the *whole* counsel of God. Individual office-bearers had liberty to retain their original views, but no binding church voice was given.

In many ways the climb-down in the second Basis was unnecessary or could have been avoided in large measure if there had been a more careful approach in the latter stages of negotiation. However, by then union was so much in the air that men were intoxicated by it, and even Cairns' attempt to apply the brakes when modification of the first basis was desired in 1858 was swept aside. Adam Cairns (1802-1881) has not yet gained a biographer. Dr Chambers describes him as 'hasty of temperament, firm of conviction, doctrinally rigid but withal warm of heart and sincere in his attempt to bring men to reconciliation with God through faith in Jesus Christ.'[27] His policy appears to have been to achieve union on an explicitly Free Church basis but the difficulties were greater than anticipated and he sought to sweep them away in a 'high-handed, utterly unconstitutional way'[28] in the expulsion of opponents from the Synod. Having gone so far and further difficulties arising he really had little room to manoeuvre, and ended up with major concessions and an open-ended Basis. Even so, such was his influence as the most popular and orthodox preacher in Melbourne, and as a major figure in the church courts, that he nearly did succeed in making the Presbyterian Church of Victoria Free Church in sentiment. Certainly, for a decade or more after the union there was in practice not too much to complain about, although there was a lack of discipline, a worldly approach to fund-raising, and weaknesses in the areas of worship and polity. These were straws in the wind which suggested troubles ahead.

27. D.Chambers in entry 'Adam Cairns' (**Australian Dictionary of Biography** 3:329)
28. A. Macdonald, op. cit., p.53

14: THE SCOTTISH CONNECTION

When the Free Church of Scotland Assembly in May 1858 recognised the (Majority) Free Presbyterian Church of Victoria and refused to recognise the Minority, a decisive statement was being made about the eventual outcome of union moves in the various British colonies.

The Synod of Eastern Australia had hitherto taken a consistent line of opposition to a compromising union. William McIntyre and Alexander Salmon, Highlander and Lowlander respectively, were agreed on this, though pro-union sentiment fostered by Macintosh Mackay was increasing. The numbers were such that in May 1859, the PCEA recognised the Minority in Victoria as a sister church by an 8 - 6 vote. The pro-union element, fearful that McIntyre and Salmon would move to take the Minority in to the PCEA, succeeded in rescinding the resolution in November 1859 by 12 votes to 9.[1]

The Minority Synod was not without grass roots support. Some $2,400 was raised[2] to send Rev William Miller to Scotland to represent the Minority 'before the courts of the Free Church of Scotland as he may have opportunity and see cause.' The May 1860 General Assembly heard Miller, but only in the capacity of 'a Free Church minister who has laboured devotedly for several years in a distant land.' The Assembly refused to recognise the (continuing) Free Presbyterian Church of Victoria as in

1. B.J.Bridges, Presbyterian Churches in New South Wales (PhD Thesis 1985) p.280
2. The amounts raised up to the meeting of the FP Synod on November 29, 1859 were: John Knox (Swanston Street) - $560; Geelong Gaelic -$460; Bellarine - $280; Gaelic Carlton (St Andrew's) - $260; Ascot Gaelic (near Ballarat) - $240; Sandhurst (Bendigo) - $204; St Kilda - $180; Brunswick/Coburg $146; Meredith/Lethbridge $66; Kilmore (St George's ie non-Highland) - $62.

ecclesiastical fellowship with the Free Church of Scotland, but expressed the hope that the Presbyterian Church of Victoria would adopt competent measures to remove 'any obstacles existing in previous deliverances of the Free Synod of Victoria.'

The upshot was that in September 1860, the (continuing) FP Synod proposed union negotiations on the basis that 'no connection shall be formed, and no correspondence held, with any Church which admits in its doctrine, discipline or practice, the right of the civil magistrate to interfere in the licensing of preachers, the call from a people to a pastor, the ordination of a pastor, or in any other act strictly ecclesiastical in its nature.'

The Presbyterian Church of Victoria Assembly of November 1860, purported to rescind the expulsion act of 1857 'without sitting in judgment on the necessity or propriety of the said act of excision.' Apart from the question of the competency of the PCV to rescind an act of the former FP Synod, this measure hardly satisfied the (continuing) FP Synod. It left untouched the principle behind the expulsion - namely, the right of a majority to act contrary to the constitution, and it did not provide a response to the question of communion with the Church of Scotland. Thus it appeared pointless to proceed further with local negotiations. It was planned to seek a further hearing in Scotland with a view to receiving recognition and thus a source of ministerial supplies.

Considerable support was generated in Scotland when it became known more generally that the 1859 Union had taken place on a different basis to that before the Free Church Assembly in May 1858. Miller himself, as representing the (continuing) FP Synod, did not press this home as well as he might since 'his tongue was paralysed by the circumstance that he himself had expressed a preference for the second basis over the first.' [3] Nor did he bring the matter of ministerial supplies into the debate sufficiently.[4] However, the subject was handled at length in the May 1861 Assembly, with about 24 of 36 overtures calling for recognition of the Minority. The two most significant speeches were those of Dr James Gibson of Glasgow and Dr William Cunningham of Edinburgh. Dr Gibson was for recognising the Minority 'as a Church in ecclesiastical fellowship with the Free Church of Scotland.' The great Dr Cunningham supported young Robert Rainy's lengthy motion which declined any recognition unless there was abandonment of the FP Synod's claim to be the faithful exponent of Free Church principles over against the Presbyterian Church of Victoria. Cunningham's stature and oratory resulted in a crushing defeat for the Minority - 341 votes to 64.[5]

3. Robert Sutherland, The History of the Presbyterian Church of Victoria (London 1877) p.277.
4. This was Arthur Paul's view: Address on the present position of the Free Presbyterian Church of Victoria, 18th April 1865 (Melbourne 1865) p.9
5. R. Sutherland, ibid., pp.279-299 provides accounts of the major speeches.

Robert Sutherland observes that Dr Cunningham did not attempt to deal adequately with the constitutional claim of the Minority: 'Had he tried to meet them fairly on logical grounds he would have failed, but meeting them on practical grounds, where he was more at home, he was successful.' And Sutherland also states:

The minority refused to enter a general Presbyterian Church. They said, 'We belong to the Free Synod of Victoria; we have come out here to advocate the distinctive principles of the Free Church of Scotland; and we refuse to unite with Erastians and Voluntaries.' This position, in itself narrow, no doubt, was logically unassailable; and the leaders of the majority, able men, and the still abler leaders of the Free Church of Scotland, failed to overthrow it.[6]

Cunningham's speech certainly seized on some expressions in the very able letter dated March 15, 1859, which was sent by the Minority to the Free Church Assembly.[7] This letter only came before the Assembly in May 1861 since it was held back by the Colonial Committee and only brought forward when the Committee's action was exposed by the Synod of Glasgow and Ayr. Cunningham ridiculed the claim that the new basis was one 'from which every vestige of Free Church testimony had been eliminated,' and scorned the statement that 'there is as much expression of Free Church principles in it as there is in the Standards of the Church of Scotland.' It is true that in form the Standards of the Free and Established Churches were more or less identical, but in fact the Standards of the Established Church had been newly interpreted by the legal decisions of the civil courts.

William Cunningham   James Gibson

6. R.Sutherland, op. cit., p. 310, 309.
7. R.Sutherland, ibid., pp. 501-508 provides the text of the letter.

The truth was that Cunningham's concern for a united Australian Presbyterian Church over-rode other considerations. In effect he took the fallacious position that a form of words which was acceptable to all was an adequate basis and testimony of Free Church principles, when he of all people should have known that once a disputed sense is given to a previously acceptable form of words, clarification is necessary if there is to be a distinct testimony. The more was this so, since the Church of Scotland always insisted it was not guilty of erastianism.

In the next place, the Free Church Assembly was guilty of applying standards to Australia that they would not apply at home. In 1863 the United Presbyterian Church and the Free Church of Scotland engaged in negotiations with a view to union. Cunningham was dead by then, but men like James Begg and William Nixon now took a stand against unionism. However, in the earlier years it is evident that there was a change of mood and emphasis which took hold of most when the consequences did not touch them personally. The firm position of the Minority was an irritant and even more than that. Sutherland, writing in 1877, has strong criticism for the 'unmitigated abuse' he alleges was put forth in *The Standard* - a monthly magazine published in the interest of the Minority position from January 1859 to 1861[8] A careful examination of this publication fails to sustain the charge made, especially having regard to the literary standards of the time. Much of the material was not controversial, and there is valuable historical matter preserved. Some of the articles and comments on Scottish church affairs were critical, particularly the subject of the Cardross case which provoked wide discussion in Scotland in 1859/60.

The Cardross case concerned the minister of the place, one McMillan, who was deposed by the Free Church in circumstances where it is hard to see much sympathy was due to him. McMillan took action in the civil courts for redress on the grounds that the proceedings were irregular. This action was regarded by many in the Free Church as *ipso facto* an erastian act. Further, the Free Church was not disposed to hand over her minutes in the case to the civil court. Leaders such as Candlish, Nixon, Buchanan and Cunningham - all conservatives - seem to have taken the view that Free Church principles included a claim to an independent spiritual jurisdiction which precluded any consideration by the civil authority if the matter involved spiritual interests. This was a widespread opinion, but fails to do justice to Chapter 23:3 of the Confession of Faith which asserts that certain

8. The editor was not named nor were articles signed. Rev Peter MacPherson is believed to have had the chief involvement. It was not officially endorsed by the Synod: 'yet the Synod is in no way responsible for the sentiments which may, from time to time, be set forth in our pages.' (Vol. 1 No. 1 (January 1859) p.2. It appears to have ceased with Volume 3 No 7 dated June 20, 1861.

responsibilities rest on the civil magistrate, short of jurisdiction, for securing the proper exercise of discipline within church courts. Thus the great George Gillespie (1613-1648) of Westminster Assembly fame, provides a good statement of the position in his *Aaron's Rod Blossoming; or, the Divine Ordinance of Church Government Vindicated.* [9] Eventually, the Free Church produced the documents necessary for the civil authority to assess the contract between McMillan and the Church and the validity of the process. While the Free Church of Scotland, and most other churches, are not 'established' churches in the eyes of the civil law but merely voluntary associations, British (and Australian) courts have jurisdiction to hear cases based on alleged failure to maintain the rules and procedures, so long as there is a property or money interest involved. Courts will not interfere in the internal affairs of such organisations except to protect a property interest lost because of breach of the rules and procedures. As far as it goes the civil law is admirable and consistent with true Presbyterian principles and the equity to which all should have access. However, the quite sober and discriminating criticism in *The Standard* obviously cut deep, and contributed to the warmth of the opposition by the Free Church leaders.

The break-up of the Minority Synod

The defeat at the Free Church of Scotland Assembly resulted in the break-up of the Minority FP Synod of Victoria. By May 1864 there were 7 ministers and one probationer, but the majority were moving towards abandonment of the principles fought for over the previous period. Arthur Paul sought assurance that the Fundamental Act of 1848 would remain as the bond of ministerial communion but was suspended for his pains. Accordingly, he and two other ministers with an elder withdrew. The unionist section was reduced to three ministers when it joined the Presbyterian Church of Victoria on November 19, 1867. An Act declaring the sense in which the PCV understood

---

9. Cf. the following extract from Book 2, Chapter 8, Answer 3 (cited from **The Standard,** February 1860): If it is asked, what remedy shall there be against the abuse of church discipline by church officers, except there be appeals from the ecclesiastical courts to the Civil Magistrates; which, if it be, church officers will be the more wary and cautious to do no man wrong, knowing that they may be made to answer for it; and if it be not, there is a wide door opened that ministers may do as they please?......Ans. 3: Although the case be merely spiritual and ecclesiastical, the Christian magistrate (by himself and immediately) may not only examine by the judgment of discretion the sentence of the ecclesiastical court, but also when he seeth cause (either upon the complaint of the party, or scandal given to himself) interpose by letters, messages, exhortations, and sharp admonitions to the Presbytery or Synod, who, in that case, are bound in conscience, with all respect and honour to the magistrate, to give him a reason of what they have done, and to declare the grounds of their proceedings, till, by the blessing of God upon the free and fair dealing, they either give a rational and satisfactory account to the magistrate, or be themselves convinced of their mal-administration of discipline.

some aspects of its Basis was passed to facilitate this union.[11] However, the provisions of this Act by the church were essentially cosmetic, the more so as the legal basis of the church in the relevant Act of Parliament was unchanged. The Free Presbyterian Church of Victoria, consisting of Messrs Paul (St Kilda), MacPherson (Meredith) and Alexander McIntyre (Geelong) continued, and was absorbed into the Presbyterian Church of Eastern Australia in 1953.

United Presbyterian Church of Victoria

The death of the senior minister, Rev A.M.Ramsay of St Enoch's, Melbourne, on December 31, 1869 was not insignificant for this body. The congregation had a crushing debt of some $8,600, and dispersed after disposal of its property to the PCV for use as an Assembly Hall. In 1870, state-aid was abolished in Victoria on the basis that sites already given would be vested in fee simple and aid for stipends continued for existing recipients for 5 years more. The six ministers then comprising the UPCV accepted the Basis of the PCV and united with that church on November 9, 1870.

Thus, by 1870, Victoria had two Presbyterian denominations. The Presbyterian Church of Victoria with some 121 ministers, more than double the number in 1859; and the Free Presbyterian Church of Victoria. The latter body had congregations at St Kilda, Geelong and Meredith (between Geelong and Ballarat), as well as a newly organised work at Hamilton. There were also scattered groups of adherents, but overall the cause was not compact and was weak. In addition to these two bodies there was the single congregation of the Reformed Presbyterian Church of Ireland at Geelong. There were also several Calvinistic Methodist (Welsh Presbyterian) congregations who had friendly contacts with other Presbyterians but whose distinct language and origin in the 18th century Methodist movement (Whitefield's theology not Wesley's) kept them apart. [12]

11. A Protest was lodged by Rev Peter Macpherson (text in J.C.Robinson, The Free Presbyterian Church of Australia (Melbourne 1947) Appendix XIII). The text of the Declaratory Act is in R.Sutherland, op. cit., pp.304-305; useful background material on it includes the item referred to in footnote 4 above.
12. Regrettably the history of the Welsh Presbyterians in Victoria has not been written and materials for doing so are now somewhat meagre. It appears that in the 1870s there were six chapels - Latrobe Street Melbourne, Ferguson Street Williamstown, Carmel Church Sebastopol, Armstrong Street Ballarat, Eaglehawk and Castlemaine. The last two seem to have closed before the first World War, Ballarat in the 1930s, and Williamstown about 1971. There were other Welsh churches but they were Baptist or Welsh Independent.

15: UNION IN QUEENSLAND & NEW SOUTH WALES 1862-1865

Queensland 1863

The separation of Queensland from New South Wales in 1859 together with the practical concerns and the union in Victoria, gave impetus to union in Queensland. Neither the Synod of Australia nor the Synod of Eastern Australia could provide effective jurisdiction over the Queensland congregations, nor assist adequately in church extension. A move to unite in Queensland came to a head in 1863. The PCEA had two ministers in the colony - Charles Ogg of Ann Street, Brisbane, and Alex Smith, ordained missionary at Gladstone, 400 kms north of Brisbane. On November 11, 1863, on the motion of William McIntyre, the Synod of Eastern Australia authorised Ogg and his Session and Smith to negotiate a union in accordance with the principles and standards of the PCEA. On November 25, 1863, a union of seven actively serving ministers was formed, though the Basis, being very similar to that in Victoria, was not uncompromising but composite. Still, the Church of Scotland influence in Queensland was low, the other five ministers being from the Presbyterian Church in Ireland. In addition to these seven ministers, Rev Thomas Mowbray participated as an emeritus minister. He found in the inclusive basis the counterpart to what he had desired back in 1846. Three further ministers joined the union to make it complete: 1864 saw W.L.Nelson (Church of Scotland) and Thomas Kingsford (UP) received, and two years later Matthew McGavin joined. The Synod formed in 1863 was designated a General Assembly in 1868 with three presbyteries.[1]

1. For ministers see p.162. For general history see Richard Bardon, **The Centenary History of the Presbyterian Church of Queensland** (Brisbane 1949) pp.29-33.

New South Wales 1862-1865

Although the union in Victoria ensured eventual union elsewhere, there were special factors in New South Wales which retarded progress. In the first place, it was not until 1862 and the arrival of Rev Robert Steel that the pro-union element in the PCEA obtained a leader of stature and a clear majority. In the second place, there was the difficulty created by Lang. He had been deposed by the Synod of Australia in 1842, and thus was not in the good books of that Synod, especially as a running battle had continued since that time. At the same time, there were those in the Synod of Eastern Australia who were most reluctant to recognise Lang. McIntyre himself had been among those who had voted for Lang's deposition back in 1842, and Lang's conduct since hardly had been becoming of a Christian minister. Yet Lang was such a significant figure in political and church life, that a union which did not embrace him was going to be difficult to achieve. The final factor was the complication of state-aid. However, the abolition of this with effect from January 1863, with rights of existing recipients preserved, removed this obstacle. This (leaving aside Lang's deposition) had been the major barrier to union for Lang's small Synod of New South Wales.

By the 1860s, sentiment among the congregations was running strongly in favour of union. The Church of Scotland had lost its power to coerce the Synod of Australia, since the supply of ministers from that source had pretty well dried up, and there had been less and less reliance on state aid for some years past because the total aid budget was fixed and inflation and additional ministers reduced its role. In fact, the well structured Sustentation Fund system of the Synod of Eastern Australia meant that PCEA ministers commonly received a larger stipend than those in the Synod of Australia.[2] The Synod of Australia was therefore ready for union, so long as no reflection on the position of the Established Church was involved, and so long as Lang was not included.

The aftermath of Lang's deposition

The position of Lang himself was complicated. Some time after he had been deposed, and with the aim of destroying his influence in the colony, the Synod of Australia had sent the sentence of deposition to Scotland to be confirmed by the Presbytery of Irvine, which had ordained Lang. In this way, Lang would cease to be a minister of the Church of Scotland itself and his connection with Scots Church, which had a trust deed specifying the minister be of the Church of Scotland, would be ended. Without telling Lang or giving him an opportunity to defend himself, the Presbytery of Irvine declared Lang no longer a minister of the Church of Scotland on September 9, 1851.

2. In the early 1860s the PCEA stipend was over $400 pa. compared with $300 pa. as a usual figure for the Synod of Australia and even less (except for Lang) in the SNSW.

John McGarvie seems to have recognised the futility of acting against Lang's possession of Scots Church,[3] but after his death in 1853, James Fullerton persuaded the Synod of Australia to institute legal proceedings. The Synod was not unanimous in the matter, but succeeded in the action in 1859 and won an appeal in 1860. Lang and his congregation then took the matter to the Privy Council and the verdict in his favour was given in February 1862. But the process left a legacy of bitterness. Meanwhile, Lang had been seeking to have his deposition rescinded. In 1860 he proposed a negotiated arrangement to the Synod but was rebuffed on the basis that confession was the way to restoration. Lang then decided to seek recall of his deposition by the Church of Scotland. A petition to the May 1861 Assembly of the Church of Scotland was dismissed unanimously. However, a legal action against the Presbytery of Irvine claiming damages of three thousand five hundred pounds produced the desired result by scaring the Presbytery into rescinding the deposition on March 12, 1863. When the verdict was given in the case, Lang lost, but he had got what he wanted.

The rescission did not alter Lang's relation to the Synod of Australia, and he continued attempts in this direction, twice demanding the sentence be revoked under threat of legal action for heavy damages if refused.   In November 1862, three arbitrators (Robert Steel, Adam Thomson and N.D.Stenhouse , elder,) were approved, and they advised Lang to write in a certain way to the Synod of Australia. On December 8, 1862, Lang did as he was advised but was refused his request for a special Synod to consider his application. Against Lang's wish not to appear a supplicant,[4] in November 1863 the Synod of New South Wales sent a deputation to enquire as to progress, but the Synod of Australia refused to recognise the Synod by receiving the deputation, and the deputation rejected the opportunity of being received as individual ministers of the Gospel.   When Lang's letter was dealt with on November 6, 1863, the Synod of Australia rescinded the deposition by one vote on the motion of J.B.Laughton against a motion to reject the application moved by James Fullerton.[5] Laughton's five-part motion rescinded the deposition of October 11, 1842, so far as it was a sentence of deposition, continuing it in force so far as it deprived him of the status of a minister of the Church under the spiritual superintendence of the

3. B.J.Bridges, Presbyterian Churches in NSW (PhD Thesis 1985) p.233.
4. Synod of New South Wales Minutes, p.311 (November 4, 1863): 'For his own [Lang's] part he was strongly desirous of seeing an incorporating union of the Presbyterians of the Colony effected forthwith; but he would do nothing even in order to effect that most desirable object that would compromise either his own character or that of the body to which he belonged: he would never appear as a supplicant before the Synod of Australia. It was simply an act of justice he demanded from that body and he could accept of nothing less.'
5. B.J.Bridges,ibid., p.305; also The Presbyterian Magazine, December 1863, p.372.

Synod. It stated that the charges of schism, slander and contumacy were such as inferred the highest censure of the church, that the charges had been fully proved, and the act of deposition had been fully in accordance with the laws of the church. It noted that Lang's letter contained no expression of regret for the offences of which he was proven guilty and that the Synod had no evidence whatever that Lang had purged himself of these offences.

The decision was somewhat illogical. A Presbyterian Church ordains a man to the ministry of the church of Christ, and deposition is deposition from that ministry. To recall a sentence of deposition involves granting status of a minister, even though it be only the status of a minister under jurisdiction without a charge. In effect, the Synod was saying, you deserved to be deposed but we will be lenient and substitute a declaration that you are no longer a minister of our Synod though we do not remove your status as a minister of the church of Christ. Thus, there was an endeavour to remove something of the slur against Lang's character. Bridges very properly notes:

Lang's Colonial deposition was therefore annulled, somewhat fortuitously, [the Moderator was opposed but had no vote] most grudgingly and in terms which conceded nothing to his demands for 'justice'. While he had a very strong case against the Presbytery of Irvine that against the Synod of Australia was doubtful at best and only the desire to make possible an all embracing Presbyterian union won him any concession. [6]

From the viewpoint of those who took church discipline seriously, the position was more difficult than ever. Some of Lang's appeals to civil tribunals for redress went beyond proper limits and virtually amounted to a belief the civil authority had jurisdiction in the spiritual affairs of the church - erastianism, in other words - while yet Lang was the great advocate of no statutory connection according to voluntary principles! The same is true of his desire to regain status with the Church of Scotland. Moreover, to unite with those who had thus acted in the matter of Lang's deposition, would be to unite with those who seemed to lack due concern for the purity of the church. It was admitted that he was guilty and that he had expressed no repentance or even sorrow. Clearly the united church would hardly be consistent if, having embraced an unrepentant offender like Lang, it sought to maintain a Scriptural discipline over its members in the future.

6. B.J.Bridges, op. cit., p.305

Union negotiations begin - November 1862

Meantime, there were no negotiations with Lang's Synod, but the Synod of Australia and the Synod of Eastern Australia continued negotiations. These had commenced in November 1862, following an approach by the Synod of Australia, and a draft Basis was immediately prepared and submitted to the PCEA Synod. The pro-union men in the PCEA were led by Dr Steel, who had arrived in 1862 to be minister of the Macquarie Street Church, and was a man of stature; Archibald Geike, an ex-Congregationalist who saw no justification for the disruption of 1846 and was a 'somewhat quarrelsome, discontented individual'[7] with sufficient ruthlessness to push for union; and John Kinross, a quiet but influential man who had arrived in 1858. James Cameron, who had arrived much earlier (1853) was also among the leaders.

The draft Basis was in the same terms as the Basis adopted in Victoria in 1858 and on which the Presbyterian Church of Victoria had been formed. It was therefore subject to the same criticism as that Basis. There was no clear statement of the spiritual independence of the church, although the Second Book of Discipline, which asserts this strongly, was one of the Standards. No clear testimony was given to any one of the diverse views on church-state relations held among the negotiating churches, and there was no criticism of the position of the Established Church of Scotland. Nor was the question of the supply of ministers settled.

The pro-union element had no fears of objection in Scotland, and were for pressing on, while McIntyre was for hastening slowly. By a 14 to 5 vote (with 1 abstention), the PCEA Committee was given authority, on Geike's motion, to continue in negotiations without first referring points of disagreement in the Committee back to Synod. It had already been agreed by a 11 to 7 vote that the Committees should confer with a view to final terms of union, and that the question of the supply of ministers be kept in view as the main point of real difficulty. On November 10, James Cameron, the Convener of the PCEA Union Committee, reported that the Basis and Formula were agreed but the method of obtaining ministers from overseas had been deferred at the request of the Synod of Australia and Adam Thomson, the UP minister also involved in negotiations.

---

7. B.J.Bridges, op. cit., p.294.

210

The Presbyterian Magazine

In 1862 Rev Robert Steel commenced *The Presbyterian Magazine* in the interests of an inclusive Presbyterianism. It was of considerable influence and reported on all the churches. It remains a valuable source for early congregational history to this day.

William McIntyre's position

William McIntyre was not in the easiest position. He knew what awaited him if he stood out of union: he would be cast out of the Presbyterian world, there would be no supplies of ministers from overseas, and there would be the loss of the larger current of church life and the opportunity to participate in those measures near to his heart which reflected a church rather than a sect mentality. Yet in his heart he knew that the makeup of the proposed union church would be anything but ideal, while if union occurred without some reasonable testimony against the erastian Church of Scotland, it would be a denial of what the PCEA had stood for since its foundation. McIntyre was a man of stature and experience, a scholar and a leader. At the close of 1861 he had left Maitland to take the charge of St George's, Castlereagh Street, Sydney. He was well abreast of the trends and currents of the day, and the mood of most Presbyterians in favour of union without fuss.

The pressure for union was virtually irrisistible by the early months of 1863, especially on the local level. But no solution acceptable to all was found to the vexed question of supplies of ministers, a special Synod meeting in May achieving nothing on this point. McIntyre was in Melbourne for the opening of the rebuilt John Knox Church on July 26, 1863. A newspaper report of a meeting connected with this event records that he said the matter of supplies was the great point of difficulty, and that 'unless such arrangements were made for the procuring of ministers as would not place him in relation to the Established Church of Scotland, he could not agree to union.'[8] The following month, McIntyre wrote in the *Sydney Morning Herald* that, to quote Bridges summary, 'he objected to the proposed union on the grounds that it was not acceptable to obtain ministers from the Established Church of an equal basis with others because it was erastian and guilty also of innovations in worship and tendencies towards prelacy.'[9] The innovations included the use of instrumental music in six Synod of Australia congregations, and unspecified 'ominous' indications towards prelacy in the Established Church - apparently a reference to the 'high church' views and practices of Dr Robert Lee of Old Greyfriars Church, Edinburgh.

8. The Age (Melbourne), July 29, 1863.
9. Sydney Morning Herald, August 24, 1863; also reproduced and discussed in The Presbyterian Magazine, September 1863, pp.285, 286.

Innovations in worship

At this point it is perhaps worth noting that while the matters of worship were not insignificant, it is very doubtful if these loomed so large as has been suggested by some writers. [10] Such matters did not find a place in the reasons included in the Protest eventually lodged by McIntyre and others against the union, and in fact were considered to be of far less importance than the involvement through union with the erastianism of the Established Church. Thus, after the union had been effected, James McCulloch, who if anything was more adamantly opposed to the union than William McIntyre, wrote in the official magazine of the continuing PCEA:

Some admit, as indeed they cannot deny, that the parties who have united hold different views [about the position of the Established Church of Scotland]; but add, that even in the Free Church there are different views held - for instance, in regard to the using or not using of paraphrases and hymns in public worship. But surely this is not a difference that can for a moment be compared with the difference between Popish principles on the one hand [as Purves of the Synod of Australia described Free Church principles], and Erastian principles on the other. [11]

10. Keith Campbell, **Presbyterian Conflicts in New South Wales 1837-1865** (JRH, June 1962) writes: 'For example, echoes of the 'organ controversy' were heard in the **Voice in the Wilderness**. In the late 1840s Rev Dr Fullerton of the Synod of Australia introduced an organ into his services to improve the singing. The Voice deeply lamented his action on the grounds that the use of organ music in church was nowhere mentioned in the Bible, and was therefore neither necessary nor beneficial. The organ controversy continued until the mid-1860s, those remaining outside the union in 1865 continuing without the use of organ music and hymns in church.' Campbell's authority for this is J.C.Robinson, **The Free Presbyterian Church of Australia** (Melbourne 1947) p.96.

However, the reality is that the **Voice** contained little on instrumental music in its years of publication (1846-52). There is a short note on Fullerton's use of an organ in his church in the issue for December 1, 1846 p.186 - use which was discontinued because of opposition in his congregation. At least part of McIntyre's concern was the unilateral action of one minister which was un-Presbyterian. Apart from this there is a 5 part article totalling about 5 pages which was published between June and September 1850. It is a straightforward presentation without any references to contemporary events in Presbyterianism. So far as the exclusion of hymns is concerned, there appear to be no articles of that kind in the **Voice**, and what little there is of related interest could be taken the other way. Thus, a short article by Ralph Erskine (1685-1752) is printed in the issue of July 15, 1846 in which he advocates the addition of 'hymns' to the psalms of the Bible; a piece by R.M.McCheyne (1813-1843) on singing praise is printed in the May 15, 1847 issue and cites the Moravian composition of hymns without disapproval; and an article on teaching children to sing psalms, reprinted from a Scottish paper, in the issue of August 2, 1847 but without 'exclusive' references. Apart from a sermon on John 4:23 and one or two articles on the Presbyterian view of liturgies, the foregoing is the sum total on the subject of worship.

Keith Campbell's reference to J.C.Robinson's book presumably should be to p.139 not to p. 96 (which does not bear on the subject). However, Robinson's analysis, in which he states Article IV (1) of the Basis of Union was objected to because it made questions of worship open questions, is not fully satisfactory. There was a loose approach to worship and concern about the incipient ritualism associated with Dr Lee's 'high-church' movement in Scotland, but the Article of the Basis was in fact based on an 1851 Act of the Free Church of Scotland.

11. The Testimony, p.218 (April 1867).

212

It is probable that William McIntyre would no more have left the Synod and started another because of hymns and organs than did the strict Free Church of Scotland men later in the century when these things were brought in to the Scottish Church (hymns: 1873; instrumental music: 1883). Just as did these men, I think McIntyre would have contented himself with a Protest so long as his own conscience was not coerced. An Australian example of this is Dr William Nicolson of Hobart. Nicolson (1796-1890) was a particularly strong opponent of instrumental music in public worship, yet remained in the Tasmanian Free Church even though an organ was used in the Oatlands parish at least as early as 1874,[12] and also in the Hobart charge from 1884 (after Nicholson's retirement). At least part of McIntyre's concern was that even if instrumental music was held to be lawful in public worship, presbyterian order required synodical consideration, and this had not occurred. [13] So we conclude that McIntyre was concerned about worship questions, and was himself opposed to innovations. He found reference to such matters useful in debate, but retained a sense of proportion. The rather common idea of more recent times that the worship distinctive was the main reason the minority of the PCEA refused to enter union is a reading back of a later emphasis.

Union negotiations - November 1863

The PCEA Synod began on November 4 and concluded on November 12 (Thursday). The pro-union majority defeated (17 to 12) McIntyre and Grant's proposal for a conference in favour of considering the report of the Union Committee. This report stated that various proposals for an agency had been discussed but none had been found satisfactory to all parties. It was suggested that no agency to obtain ministers was necessary.

Geikie then moved 'That the Synod adopt the Report, approve of the basis of Union, declare that it protects the doctrine, worship, government and spiritual independence of this Church, and the rights of the Christian people, and agree to union in terms thereof.' Geikie held the basis was satisfactory, that an agency would not modify it, and that if an agency was to be 'an ecclesiastical filter to get men of a certain class only,' he did not wonder that it was refused by the Synod of Australia. Geikie's motion was seconded by Dr Steel, who delivered a lengthy 12 point speech in favour of union. The reasons adduced were (1) consistency with the course adopted in November 1862; (2) the refusal of the Synod of Australia to become an independent

12. Rowland Ward, **Presbyterianism in Tasmania 1821-1977** (Ulverstone 1977) p.26. Hymns were used in Hobart from 1883, and perhaps some 10 years earlier in Launceston and Oatlands.
13. **The Testimony**, 1866 p.126.

213

church in 1846 was now to be reversed, thus removing (in his view) the original cause of division; (3) to conserve the honour and dignity of the Presbyterian Church by preventing discreditable avenues to its ministry; (4)efficiency and furtherance of evangelistic activity; (5) if agreed on the time honoured standards uniformity in minor points as the relation to Scottish churches should not be insisted upon; (6) the wishes of many congregations; (7) the wishes of the Free Church of Scotland; (8) the appeal of the Synod of Australia; (9) the general tendency to union among Presbyterians throughout the world; (10) the prayer of Christ for the visible union of his people; (11) 'We are so ripe for union that we are in danger of becoming rotten for the want of it'; and (12) the expected blessing and success which would follow union.

William McIntyre proposed an amendment designed to give another opportunity of reaching unanimity. The motion was to receive the report but reconsider the Basis. He was seconded by William Grant of Shoalhaven, an able minister who had been disgusted by the Free Church of Scotland's defection from principles formerly insisted upon,[14] and whose position on union only now became clear. McIntyre stated he wanted 'a more definite and unequivocal assertion of the Church's spiritual independence' in the Basis. He was for 'maintaining the ground that had been gained.' He thought he might have gone too far in the course the Synod was now following, but his justification was that 'I expected arrangements which, taken along with the Basis, might indicate the sense in which it was to be understood, so that it should be less definite than it is.' He repudiated hostility to union as such, citing the endeavours to prevent the disruption in 1843/46, and his efforts in regard to the union of 1840. He considered inconsistency to be a duty on some occasions, 'for we are all by nature walking in the broad way, and our Christian character begins with a great act of inconsistency.' He regarded the Basis as defective in the circumstances in which it was to be adopted. The two points mentioned were the provision for declarations of independence by both Synods when only the Synod of Australia was not independent, and the source of ministers. As for the Basis, it was good as far as it went, but the Established Church of Scotland did not admit it had surrendered her spiritual independence in any way, and an unequivocal statement in the Basis was therefore essential. He considered the Free Church of Scotland had never understood the position in Australia in 1846, looking upon it as more an imitation of Scotland's Disruption than necessitated by the local situation. They should not attempt to combine by leaving out what were called 'non-essentials.' He thought the union would be like that of Siamese twins - a sort of mechanical connexion, mere juxtaposition, rather

14. B.J.Bridges, op. cit., p.281 citing Grant's letter to Kinross, August 19, 1861.

than a symmetrical union, union in the truth for which Christ prayed. McIntyre closed with an appeal:

I appeal to my brethren; I put it to them whether they do not owe it to us to grant this re-consideration. If there be one chance in ten that it may serve a good purpose, we ought to use it. If only as a farewell, give us this consideration. Do not thrust us out. Do not render it impossible for us to continue in union with you. I have made more sacrifices for this Church than any of you have had an opportunity to make. I feel a deep interest in this Church from all I have had to do with its movements. I claim it as a right that you do not thrust me out at this period of my life, after what I have done, without giving me a fair opportunity of arriving at unanimity with you. [15]

William Grant's brief speech as seconder indicated he was prepared to go into union on the Basis, but he was anxious they move unitedly. He also 'regretted they had been so facile as to undertake to declare that they had no connection with the Free Church of Scotland. They were in no way connected with it except by correspondence. What need was there to declare a fact so well known. Nine years ago [1854] they were nearer Union than they were thirteen months ago.'

Allan McIntyre then spoke. He was for union in the truth. But would those they were preparing to join be willing to repudiate the acts of the civil power and of the Established Church by which the Free Church was driven out? He would gladly accept the Basis if there were none but United Presbyterians involved. But because he had to do with other people, he could not accept it, unless they said 'we leave the Established Church because we disapprove of its principles.'

The debate was resumed on Monday and was opened by a motion from Geike and Steel which was carried unanimously in the following terms:

That whereas this Synod has hitherto judged a conference on the subject of Union to be unnecessary, nevertheless, since, in the course of the present debate it has become more apparent that, without danger to the cause of Union, such a conference may be held, the Synod, in deference to respected brethren, agrees to confer privately at this sitting, previous to the resumption of the debate appointed for this evening. [16]

The conference occupied the afternoon, and what transpired was not recorded in detail. At the evening meeting it was reported that words expressing the spiritual independence of the Church and that it was not

---

15. **Synod of Eastern Australia Minutes,** November 1863 (as printed) p.12. Quotations in the preceding and following text which are not footnoted are also from the printed minutes.
16. SEA Minutes, ibid., p.13

215

subject in its own province to the interference of the civil power, had been proposed for insertion in Article 3 of the Basis. The conference had agreed to propose such insertion to the other parties, considering that it did not affect the Basis but was an improvement of it. Geike therefore sought and obtained leave to reword his motion to read:

That the Synod adopt the report, approve the basis, agree to unite in terms thereof, resolve that no agency is necessary for the supply of ministers, and appoint a standing committee to arrange for final union - instructing said Committee to submit to the negotiating parties, with a view to secure greater harmony among the members of this Synod - certain suggestions with regard to the third article of the basis.[17]

McIntyre and Grant then obtained leave to withdraw their amendment to approve the report but reconsider the basis. On McIntyre's part this was because the majority was resolved on union whether or not improvement of the basis was obtained, whereas he had decided he could not unite on the present basis.

The Synod then resolved in terms of Geikie's amended motion, William McIntyre and James McCulloch dissenting for reasons to be given in. But they were not under the necessity of seceding at this stage since Geike's motion allowed for a further attempt to obtain modification to the basis that might satisfy them. A union committee including William McIntyre was then appointed. It met in conference with the Synod of Australia committee and Rev Adam Thomson, United Presbyterian minister, on Tuesday November 10. Although Lang's Synod had approached the PCEA to confer on union, it was not considered competent to receive a deputation from it pending the outcome of the negotiations with the other parties.

When the PCEA Synod reassembled on Tuesday evening there was an encouraging report. Not only was all that was held to be essential by McIntyre agreed, but also all other matters held to be desirable. At the session on Wednesday morning (November 11), Rev John McSkimming (who had been a member of the union committee) moved as follows:

The Synod learn with peculiar satisfaction that various emendations on the Basis of Union, whether independently suggested by certain members, or submitted by the express sanction of Synod, by its committee to the other negotiating parties, have been agreed to by all concerned, accepts these emendations, and orders the Basis, as it now stands, to be engrossed in the minutes, expressing its great thankfulness at the happy result. [18]

17. SEA Minutes, p.15
18. SEA Minutes, p.16

216

Geikie seconded the motion. William McIntyre said he thought the motion fully met the case. It was then carried unanimously with the exception of four members who dissented for reasons to be given in if deemed necessary. James McCulloch, who had not been on the union committee, said he wanted more time to consider. Elders John MacDonald (St George's), Hugh MacDonald (Ahalton) and Allan MacDonald (Clarence River) joined in the dissent. Rev Allan McIntyre was not present at this point, but had previously insisted on positive disapproval of the Established Church, and the amended basis did not provide this. However, it appeared that unanimity was in sight.

BASIS OF UNION AGREED UPON NOVEMBER 10, 1863 UPON WHICH THE PRESBYTERIAN CHURCH OF NEW SOUTH WALES WAS FORMED

1. That previous to the consummation of the Union the Synod of Australia shall dissolve its connection with the Established Church of Scotland, and omit from its designation the terms expressive of that connection.

2. That previous to the consummation of the Union the Synod of Eastern Australia shall formally declare that it has no ecclesiastical connection with the Free Church of Scotland.

3. That previously to the consummation of the Union the Rev Adam Thomson shall formally declare, on behalf of himself and his congregation, that they have ceased to be ecclesiastically connected with the United Presbyterian Church of Scotland.

ARTICLES OF BASIS OF UNION

I. That the designation of the United Church shall be 'The Presbyterian Church of New South Wales,' and that the Supreme Court of the Church shall be designated the 'General Assembly of the Presbyterian Church of New South Wales.'

II. That the Word of God, as contained in the Scriptures of the Old and New Testaments, is held by this Church as the supreme, and only authoritative rule of faith and practice.

III. That the Westminster Confession of Faith, the Larger and Shorter Catechisms, the Form of Presbyterial Church Government, the Directory for the Public Worship of God, and the Second Book of Discipline, are the subordinate standards of this church.

IV. The subordinate standards above enumerated are received with the following explanations:
1. That, while the Confession of Faith contains the Creed to which as to a confession of his own faith, every officebearer in the Church must testify in solemn form his personal adherence, and while the Catechisms are sanctioned as Directories for catechising, the Directory for Public Worship, the Form of Presbyterial Church Government, and the Second Book of Discipline are of the nature of regulations rather than of tests, and are not to be imposed by subscription upon Ministers and Elders.

2. That in adopting these standards, this church is not to be held as countenancing persecuting or intolerant principles, or any denial or invasion of the right of private judgment.

3. That by Christ's appointment, the Church is spiritually independent, and is not subject in its own province and in the administration of its own affairs, to the jurisdiction or authoritative interference of the civil power.

V. That this Church asserts for itself a separate and independent position in relation to other Churches; and that its highest Court shall possess supreme and final jurisdiction over its inferior judicatories, office-bearers and members.

VI. That this Church shall receive Ministers and Probationers from other Presbyterian Churches applying for admission, on their affording satisfactory evidence of their qualifications and eligibility, and subscribing the formula.

FORMULA

I do hereby declare, that I do sincerely own and believe the whole doctrine contained in the Confession of Faith, as adopted in the foregoing articles, to be in accordance with the Word of God, and I do own the same as the confession of my faith; as likewise I do own the purity of worship presently authorised and practised in this Church, and also the Presbyterian government and discipline thereof; which doctrine, worship, and government, I am persuaded are founded on the Word of God, and agreeable thereto. And I promise that, through the grace of God, I shall firmly and constantly adhere to the same and to the utmost of my power shall in my station assert, maintain, and defend the said doctrine, worship and discipline of this Church and the government thereof by Sessions, Presbyteries, and provincial and general Synods, together with the liberty and exclusive jurisdiction thereof; and that I shall in my practice, conform myself to the said worship, submit to the said discipline, government, and exclusive jurisdiction, and not endeavour, directly or indirectly, the prejudice or subversion of the same. And I promise that I shall follow no divisive courses from the doctrine, worship, discipline, government, and exclusive jurisdiction of this Church, renouncing all doctrines, tenets, or opinions whatsoever contrary to, or inconsistent with, the said doctrine, worship, discipline, and government, or jurisdiction of the same.

RESOLUTIONS

1. That no official application for the supply of Ministers be made from the United Church to any of the Churches in the United Kingdom.

2. That no agency for the supply of Ministers shall be appointed in the United Kingdom for the United Church.

3. That so soon as the necessary preliminary arrangements are effected, the Union shall be consummated.

Examination of the 1863 Basis shows that it is much more carefully worded than the 1859 Victorian Basis proposed in 1862. The assertion in Article IV (3) of the spiritual independence of the church had satisfied McIntyre that the Basis inferred disapproval of the erastian positions adopted by the Established Church of Scotland, even though this was not spelt out in as many words as it had been in the 1854 Basis.

Highland opposition

However, the satisfaction McIntyre had in Committee and Synod was not shared by many in his natural constituency. There were the four dissenters at the Synod, and immediately after the meeting there was a considerable Highlander back-lash against Grant and McIntyre. The Highlanders in McIntyre's former congregation of Maitland withdrew because they considered the preliminary declaration of independence accompanying the Basis placed the Free Church and the Established Church on the same level. On the Manning views were not fully settled: Grant declined a call extended to him early in 1864; then McCulloch was called but also declined; finally Allan McIntyre was settled towards the end of 1865. St George's was not unanimous and there was dissension in Grant's congregation at Shoalhaven.

Allan McIntyre at Grafton was anti-union, while a congregational meeting at Maclean on December 4, 1863, chaired by James McDonald, resolved on the motion of D.Shearer and W.McKinnon: 'That this meeting learn with much regret the decision of the Synod of Eastern Australia, in forming a union with the Synod of Australia, consequently this congregation declare themselves a separate body from the said union hereafter.'[19] The meeting further resolved to seek ministerial supply from the Free Presbytery at Geelong, that is, from Rev Alexander McIntyre. The people at Ahalton on the Hunter likewise declared their opposition on January 6, 1864, while for a period to March 1864 the Highland element of the Maitland congregation also withdrew. Thus it can be seen that the areas of dominant Highland feeling were the areas of opposition to union but opposition in Sydney was weak.

The Gaelic backlash must have been stronger than McIntyre, a man of some urbanity and culture, anticipated for all that he was the leader of the Gaelic community in New South Wales. Grant, who was not a Highlander but was fluent in Gaelic, continued in favour of union. His large congregation at Shoalhaven was not exclusively Gaelic, but would hold together given Grant's excellent pastoral work. McIntyre did not have a very large congregation at St George's, and a section were all for union. If McIntyre went that way too, the strict Free Church element in the congregation, with whom the minister had most affinity, would be left high and dry with the union group retaining the debt-ridden building. If he did not unite, he would have a reduced but homogenous congregation and would provide a city outlet for the full-orbed Presbyterianism that would be represented in other centres by rural parishes associated with his kith and kin.

No doubt the atmosphere in discussions with those opposed to union was somewhat different than in the union committee and the Synod. McIntyre decided that he had indeed made a mistake to go so far on the union road. Bridges writes:

In the early months of 1864, McIntyre attempted to sabotage the agreement by insisting that only the Synod of Australia make the statement of independence, humiliating itself by the implication that it alone had a disreputable connection to slough off.[20]

However, the fact was that the Synod of Australia *was* the only body with a disreputable connection, indeed the *only* one with a legal connection to an overseas church. It was the fact of that connection that had been the cause of the division back in 1846. At a union conference in May 1864, McIntyre pressed for modification. Whilst the declaration to be given by the PCEA was

19. **Presbyterianism in Victoria** (a collection of cuttings by P.Macpherson in the State Library of Victoria) Volume for 1863, p.378 [**Clarence River Examiner**, Dec 29,1863]
20. B.J.Bridges, op. cit., p.300

not quite in the same terms as that for the Synod of Australia, McIntyre was satisfied that the object of the Committee of the Synod of Australia in insisting upon its retention was to offset what was otherwise the natural inference - that the Synod of Australia no longer regarded the position of the Established Church with approval. In short, in agreeing to dissolve its connection with the Established Church, the Synod of Australia required the PCEA to declare that it had no connection with the Free Church of Scotland, so warding off any adverse reflection upon the Established Church. Thus, though no agency was provided for securing ministers, the arrangement ensured that ministers of the Established Church would be received by the united body without any question.

There is no doubt in my mind that McIntyre's analysis was perfectly sound. Perhaps the question is, why was he not more particular at an earlier stage? As McIntyre's private papers have vanished, we have no insight into his thinking as we do for others involved in negotiations. My guess is that his own basic stance as a 'churchman' not a sectarian, and his realisation of the value of union and its inevitability on some basis or other, led to him putting aside his instinct that told him a genuine union in the truth could not be achieved. He started on the negotiating road and was drawn in further than was wise. Men like Allan McIntyre and James McCulloch were men of less vision and not so concerned to even attempt to find a way to bring greater unity in a situation which they saw as black and white.

McIntyre's attempts to rework the 3-fold declaration with a view to a more clear and honest understanding failed, as did Adam Thomson's attempts to find a *via media*. It was thus clear to McIntyre that while the Synod of Australia would dissolve her Scottish connection at the time of union it would not be so as to assume an independent position before the union. Rather, it would be a means to the formation of a united body in which the former Synod of Australia men could maintain the same approval of the position of the Established Church. I suspect McIntyre might have worn this if it had come to the crunch and there had been no continuing PCEA. He knew the Established Church had little ability to influence the future of the Australian Church and little capacity to send men. But given all the circumstances, and despite the cost, he would throw his weight behind the continuers, and if an unambiguous Basis could not be achieved he would continue apart from the union.

Union achieved

The final mechanics of union required two steps. Such was the hostility to Lang in the Synod of Australia that this Synod would not unite directly with Lang's Synod. However, if his Synod had lost its identity by a preliminary union with the PCEA to form a General Synod, then the Synod of Australia was willing to unite with the General Synod even though it included Lang. Accordingly, the General Synod of the Presbyterian Church *in* New South Wales was constituted in St George's Church, Sydney, on November 15, 1864. Fifteen serving PCEA ministers, 4 SNSW ministers and two United Presbyterian ministers were embraced. [21] William McIntyre and James McCulloch lodged a Protest as reproduced below. Messrs McSkimming and Greig protested on the grounds that there should have been further negotiations with a view to gaining greater unanimity. Elder John McDonald protested on the ground of the levelling resolutions accompanying the Basis. S.F.Mackenzie of Maitland protested that the Synod's action had prevented proper negotiations with the Lang Synod. William Bain, the Moderator, dissented, resigned as Moderator but participated in the union. Allowing for Allan McIntyre (absent) and W.S.Donald (unattached but opposed to union), there were thus 8 ministers opposed to the Basis for one reason or another. Eight out of 22 is a high proportion considering all that had happened, and the known views in Scotland. While several men had reasons which were essentially pragmatic, this fact indicates the extent of unhappiness with the politicking involved. It also explains why the pro-union majority allowed William Ridley to deliberate and vote despite the fact that he received no employment from the church and thus could not come within the category of an acting ordained missionary. As Bridges remarks: 'it was obvious that he was included solely for the purpose of providing the unionists with another vote.'[22] There is reason to suppose the anti-unionist tactic in wanting actual negotiations with Lang's Synod was designed to highlight the differences rather than to promote union, hence it was rejected by the unionist majority who gave Lang's Synod the option of accepting the basis negotiated by the larger Synods or staying out of union.

The second stage was accomplished in the Masonic Hall on September 8, 1865 when the 24 ordained ministers of the General Synod and the 23 serving ministers of the Synod of Australia, together with those representative elders present, united to form the General Assembly of the Presbyterian Church *of* New South Wales. Rev S.F.Mackenzie was admitted immediately thereafter. The union was not a success, being a union of diverse elements, and the progress of the church would not compare favourably with that in Victoria.

21. See lists on pp.110ff. An analysis of voting in the 1864 PCEA Synod is in the **Presbyterian Magazine**, 1864, pp.371-372.
22. B.J.Bridges, op. cit., p.200

221

THE PROTEST OF THE REV. WILLIAM McINTYRE AND THE REV. J. M. McCULLOCH, ON TUESDAY, NOVEMBER 15, 1864, TO THE UNION OF THE PRESBYTERIAN CHURCH OF EASTERN AUSTRALIA WITH THE SYNOD OF NEW SOUTH WALES AND SOME UNATTACHED MINISTERS.

We, the undersigned ministers, members of the Synod of Eastern Australia, considering that, by the admission of the Rev. William Ridley to deliberate and vote as a member of this Synod, while he is neither a settled minister nor an acting ordained missionary, and only such ought to be so admitted, the constitution of this court has been vitiated. And considering that inasmuch as while the basis prepared by the conference on union, conveys, with the exception of the last article of it, an anti-erastian testimony, that article and certain resolutions which accompany the basis and are hereto appended, have the effect, by placing as they do, the Established Church of Scotland, charged by this Church with Erastianism, on precisely the same footing with the Free Church of Scotland, whose protest against the Erastianism of the Established Church of Scotland, this Church has deliberately adopted, of neutralizing and contradicting that testimony: the Synod, by resolving that this Church shall unite on said Basis and Resolution in the first instance with the Church under the spiritual superintendence of the Synod of New South Wales, and with certain Presbyterian ministers not attached to any Colonial Church, and that the United body thus preliminarily formed shall unite on the same Basis and Resolutions with the Synod of Australia in connection with the Established Church of Scotland, has removed this Church from the position which it occupied as testifying against the Erastianism of the Established Church of Scotland, and has involved it in connivance with that Erastianism.

And further considering, by refusing to endeavour by further conference to obtain such change of the Articles and Resolutions objected to above, that the anti-erastian testimony which, with the exception of the last article, conveys, should remain uncontradicted; and also such explanations, if such could be given, as might evince that notwithstanding that the Synod of Australia in connection with the Established Church of Scotland still regards the position of the Established Church of Scotland with approval, which its connection with that Church implies, the concurrence of the said Synod in an anti-erastian testimony might be held to be satisfactory: the Synod has necessitated a disruption which might otherwise have been averted, and has thus pursued a virtually schismatic course: We, therefore, the ministers aforesaid, do protest, on the grounds now set forth, that the majority have forfeited their rights, powers, and privileges as members of the Synod of Eastern Australia: and that all ministers, elders, and congregations who shall enter into the proposed Union, or either of them, shall forfeit all rights powers, and privileges as ministers, elders, and congregations of the Presbyterian Church of Eastern Australia.

And we protest further, that it is and shall be lawful for us, and such as may concur with us, to exercise all the rights, powers, and privileges of office-bearers and congregations of the Presbyterian Church of Eastern Australia, to administer the affairs of that Church, and to take all necessary and legitimate steps to maintain and extend in the land the dispensations of Gospel ordinances.

16: TASMANIA & SOUTH AUSTRALIA

Tasmania 1861-1896

In 1844 the Church of Scotland Presbytery of Van Diemen's Land entered upon a period of controversy connected initially with the subject of baptism. It extended in due course to the doctrine of the Lord's Supper, and was aggravated by the fact the Presbytery lacked a clearly recognised book of procedure. Personal matters entered into it, for example, the deposition of John Storie of St Andrew's Hobart in 1864 for slander and misrepresentation, and his subsequent successful court action. In these circumstances it is understandable that the pro Free Church outlook earlier expressed by Dr Lillie did not develop into union.[1] The loss of Lillie in 1858 did not help.

As for the Free Presbytery, it was deeply embarrassed by the appointment of J.G.Mackintosh as Dr Lillie's successor in 1858, since Mackintosh was a Free Church minister commissioned to the Church of Scotland congregation by the Free Church! While there was no formal repudiation of the Free Presbytery by Scotland, its position was undermined. Mackintosh left in 1860 and was followed by Storie, a stormy petrel, who publicly denied that there was a true Free Church in Tasmania. Still, the Free Church continued on in a positive way despite these difficulties. The equal dividend for the three ministers [William Nicolson (Hobart), James Lindsay (Launceston) and Lauchlin Campbell (Oatlands)] was $493 for the year to September 30, 1860, a very satisfactory figure.[2] Dr Nicolson's congregation was the largest Presbyterian congregation in Tasmania.

1. The 1844-70 period in the history of the Presbytery of VDL is deserving of further research. J. Heyer, **Presbyterian Pioneers of Van Dieman's Land** (Launceston 1935) devotes pp.45-57 to the 'church crisis' but does not spell out the nature of the doctrinal part of the dispute.
2. This figure is as reported in **The Standard,** March 1861, p.39.

In 1878, the Church of Scotland Presbytery became the Presbyterian Church of Tasmania, following the passing of the Presbyterian Church Act by the legislature in December of that year. Mr Storie resigned St Andrews in 1879, and the following year rules and forms of procedure sustained by the authority of law were adopted. The same year the original Presbytery became a Synod controlling two presbyteries. By this stage the congregations of the Free Presbytery were not adverse to union but considered it preferable not to proceed further for the time being. Dr Nicolson had retired in 1878, and his successor was from the Free Church. But only after Nicolson died in 1890 was union actually taken up strongly. Unlike the PCEA or the FPCV, the Free Presbytery seems to have regarded itself as virtually a part of the Free Church of Scotland. Permission was obtained in 1891 from the Free Church of Scotland to transfer properties to a united church, and on March 18, 1896 - 43 years to the day from its formation - the 'Free Presbytery of Tasmania' united with the Presbyterian Church of Tasmania. It contributed two ministers, four charges (Chalmers, Hobart; Chalmers, Launceston; Oatlands and Scottsdale), and nearly 600 communicants to the united body so that it totalled 13 ministers and 14 charges with about 1,600 communicants.

South Australia 1860-1872

In this colony the several branches of Presbyterianism were present but weak in numbers. The only Presbytery formed before the general union of 1865 was the Presbytery of the Free Presbyterian Church of South Australia. It was constituted on May 9, 1854 by 3 ministers and 2 elders in terms of a Fundamental Act identical to that of the Free Presbyterian Church of Victoria. A sketch of procedure in church courts was approved in April 1855. In 1856, a discipline case arose in the Morphett Vale congregation, and when reference was made to the Presbytery on one aspect of the matter (what to do with the man in a morals case who had left the colony), the Presbytery sought to take over the whole case and handle the discipline of the female member also. This was contrary to the rules adopted by the Presbytery, and was therefore resisted by the Session. The up-shot was that Rev James Benny, the minister, was deposed for contumacy and rebellion on January 5, 1858, though this quite unjustified action had little practical effect.

The union moves in Scotland were a concern to Benny, a capable man with a legal background. He took the initiative in writing to the Adelaide Session of the United Presbyterian congregation asking for a conference to discuss a union of all the Presbyterian bodies. The elders at Gouger Street expressed interest but nothing came of it. The precise nature of the negotiations is unclear. The writer has two scraps of minutes of the elders and deacons of the Benny group, covering meetings at Aldinga on February 24, and May 4, 1860. At the first meeting it was reported that negotiations for union had failed, and it was agreed to write to Dr Alexander Beith of Stirling seeking his assistance in obtaining ministers from the Free Church of Scotland. This was 'on the understanding that if the Free Church should adopt the same course pursued toward the minority in Victoria the officebearers assembled agree to return to Mr Gardner's party [ie. the FPSA] provided they rescinded their whole proceedings which resulted in the division.' It was also agreed to raise $160 to be sent to Scotland to cover travel costs for ministers, and a guarantee was offered of stipend for the vacant charge of Aldinga-Yankalilla. The meeting on May 4 discussed the propriety and expediency of attempting a union of all bodies and a committee was appointed with instructions. Provision was made, if the effort failed, for approaches to be made to Dr Beith.

Discussion between the FPCSA and the UP Church later in 1860 broke down over personal antipathies, particularly the action of the FPC in receiving a UP minister and congregation in 1856. Benny's position was clearly influenced by the practical need of ministerial supplies. He probably considered that a union with United Presbyterians on a Free Church basis was possible, given the absence of state-aid, and that some arrangement could be made with the other ministers. But it was not to be, and Dr Beith could not help with ministers either.

The union in New South Wales in 1864 brought matters to a head. Early in 1865 a Basis of Union was drawn up, similar to that adopted in New South Wales, and union took place on this Basis on May 10, 1865 forming the Presbyterian Church of South Australia. The churches in the South East, which had been linked to the Presbyterian Church of Victoria in 1863, did not enter this union, nor did James Benny and the congregations with him. Instead they published a Protest against the course adopted by the FPCSA in 1856/58. Inverbrackie with its minister, John Macbean, remained in fellowship with the Church of Scotland but joined the united church in 1868.[3]

Those who entered the union in May 1865 totalled 8 ministers (3 UP, 3 FPC and 2 CS) and 1077 communicants. There were 29 preaching places altogether, and 938 scholars in 17 Sunday schools. Benny trained several men himself, and they proved acceptable ministers. In February 1872, Benny's FP Presbytery responded to overtures from the PCSA by appointing

3. See table on page 159. R.J.Scrimgeour, Some Scots Were Here (Adelaide 1986) gives an attractive account of the Presbyterian Church in South Australia. The Benny group is fully discussed in Rowland Ward, The Free Presbyterian Church of South Australia (Melbourne 1984) iv + 91pp.

a Committee of three ministers re union. However, the Formula of Subscription by officebearers was different. Accordingly, on May 7, 1872 the FP Presbytery found there was a 'bar to union' on doctrinal grounds. The inclusive and composite nature of the PCSA Basis was the objection. At this point there were some 165 communicant members in the three congregations of the (continuing) Free Presbyterian Church of South Australia. [A union was never effected and the Benny group became, through deaths and some legal complexities, incapable of presbyterial action with the death of the last minister in 1921.]

Part Five

COMPREHENSION AND TRANSITION

1865-1901

17: THE SPIRIT OF THE TIMES

Major questions had to be faced by all Christian denominations in the latter part of the 19th century: questions related to the new scientific hypotheses, especially in geology and biology, as well as the undermining of the inspiration of the Bible through literary criticism of a rationalistic kind. This chapter reviews responses by Australian Presbyterians to the pressures and challenges.[1] Later chapters take up the particular problem of Charles Strong as well as Protestant/Roman Catholic tension, and also provide clearer focus on theological education.

Geology

As early as 1804, Thomas Chalmers (1780-1847), a minister of the Church of Scotland and later the first Moderator of the General Assembly of the Free Church of Scotland,   stated in a lecture at St Andrews:

It has been alleged that geology, by referring the origin of the globe to a higher antiquity than is assigned to it by the writings of Moses, undermines our faith in the inspiration of the Bible...This is a false alarm. The writings of Moses do not fix the antiquity of the globe.[2]

In 1814, Chalmers published his views on the relationship of Genesis and geology as that science was then understood. In brief, he advocated a form

1. For an excellent general survey see Walter Phillips, The Defence of Christian Belief in Australia 1875-1914: The Responses to Evolution and Higher Criticism in Journal of Religious History, December 1977 pp.402-423; also H.R.Jackson, Churches and People in Australia and New Zealand 1860-1930 (Wellington 1987) pp.125ff.
2. Hugh Miller, The Testimony of the Rocks (Edinburgh 1857) p.107. For a study of Chalmers see W.M.Mackay, Thomas Chalmers: A Short Appreciation (Edinburgh 1980).

of what has become known as the 'gap' theory. He supposed a period of un-determined length between the original creation (Genesis 1:1) and the condition of formlessness described in Genesis 2:2, and considered that verse 2 referred to a condition into which the original creation had been brought. The narrative then described how God renewed the creation in six 24 hour days. With various refinements this became a popular view.[3] It seemed to allow the periods of time the geologists wanted while enabling the traditional understanding of the creation days to be maintained.

However, as geology developed as a science, the idea that ancient deposits could be separated from recent ones by a gulf of emptiness and death had to be given up. Hugh Miller (1802-56), the famous apologist for the Free Church of Scotland and a brilliant self-taught geologist, popularized the idea that the creation days are to be understood as vastly extended periods of time. The more cautious and conservative were not satisfied that this view did justice to the foundation of the fourth commandment,[4] but even they held it to be unsatisfactory to take no notice of geology and resolve all into the power of God. Macpherson adds: 'Perhaps no science is better calculated to exalt the glory of the Creator than the science of geology.'

Whatever one thinks of the interpretation put forward, it is clear that Christian thinkers were committed to a unified view of knowledge: God's book of nature could not contradict his revelation in the Bible. As far as I know, no Presbyterian minister in Australia in the latter part of the 19th century adopted a position of hostility to geology as such. Contrary to R.B.Walker, there was no 'notable victory for liberal views'[5] so far as the interpretation of the days of creation was concerned, for a diversity of view had long been recognised in Scotland, to say nothing of earlier times. By and large the subject was non-controversial for Australian Christians last century.

3. A recent defence of geological ages prior to the first day is in A.C.Custance, Time and Eternity (Grand Rapids 1977) pp.78-118. Custance argues that this view goes back to early Jewish interpreters. The Jewish commentator Umberto Cassuto, Commentary on the Book of Genesis (ET, Jerusalem 1961), does not refer to it, and it is generally rejected by conservative writers on exegetical grounds, eg. Noel Weeks, The Sufficiency of Scripture (Edinburgh 1988) p.96; H.Blocher, In the Beginning (Leicester 1984)p.43.
4. So J.S. (or Peter) Macpherson in The Free Churchman, July 1883, p.78. It is open to exegetical and scientific difficulties, for example, the creation of the sun on the fourth day, and has lost support among conservative writers although it is with some hesitation accepted by Derek Kidner, Genesis: An Introduction and a Commentary (London 1967). Alternatives include (a) the straightforward narrative view providing the chronology of creation and usually associated with a young earth and 'Creation Science' and (b) the literary view which sees the days as a framework for the narrative designed to show the logic and orderliness of creation rather than its chronology , and able to fit in with a young or old earth theory. Alternatives are discussed in H.Blocher, ibid., who argues for (b), while N.Weeks, ibid., goes for (a) with cautions for 'Creation Science.'
5. R.B.Walker, Presbyterian Church and People in the Colony of New South Wales in the Late Nineteenth Century in Journal of Religious History, June 1969, p.53.

Evolution

When we turn to evolution, the position is somewhat different. To quote Phillips:

There was little acceptance of evolutionary thought in either scientific or theological circles in Australia around 1875, as Ann Mozley has shown in the article *Evolution and the Climate of Opinion in Australia 1840-76*.[6]

Evolution made inroads in the 1880s. At first it had been regarded as atheistic or deistic - as denying God or making him an absentee landlord. Yet creation and evolution, properly speaking, are not opposites: creation is origination and evolution modification. By the later 1880s, it was held that the all-embracing philosophical concept of evolution, which presupposed the eternity of matter and traced all phenomena including thought and emotion to evolution from that matter, was indeed atheistic and to be condemned. However, if the origination of the material of creation was seen as the free work of God, and if subsequent evolution was seen as God directed and God controlled at every point, then such a view, it was held, was hardly antagonistic to the Christian faith, particularly if allowance was made for the direct creation of the human soul.

This approach seemed to provide a harmony of the conclusions of scientific investigation and the teaching of the Bible. At any rate, it proved satisfactory to many, and not just those who were 'liberal' on other matters. Such teaching is found in the work of the most influential and orthodox Calvinists of the time at Princeton Theological Seminary in Philadelphia, the bastion of Presbyterian orthodoxy.[7]

The character of God

In the Victorian period many rejected belief in God's wrath. The emphasis fell on the love of God, perhaps partly in reaction to inadequate presentation of God's character in some pulpits. The tendency was to deny the forensic categories as if love and law were mutually exclusive.[8] We are not told why

6. W.Phillips, op. cit., p.407
7. Reformed theology distinguishes the first-created primary material made with time, before which nothing existed save the eternal God. But creation includes also the giving of form, making use of what has already been created (as in the forming of man in Genesis 2:7). The initial act of creation of necessity is instantaneous, as also the stage at which anything passes from inanimate to animate, but there is room for the passing of time during which forming may take place. In this sense 'evolution' has a place in the Christian view of the world. It is probable that the positions espoused by A.A.Hodge (1823-86) and B.B.Warfield (1851-1926) of Princeton, were a little too concessive to the then popular evolutionary approach. Of course they did not deny the unity of the human race in Adam nor an historical fall - matters of far greater moment than the method of God's post-primary creative activity. However, the vast ages propounded by popular evolutionary theory involve a significant metaphysical stake themselves, and it is not surprising that in popular thought evolution and creation are seen as opposites. See also, Mark A.Noll (ed), The Princeton Theology 1812-1921 (Grand Rapids 1983).
8. Note that love is an imperative: 'You shall love the Lord....and your neighbour...'

one should respect a God who makes no distinction between good and evil, but the self-confidence and optimism of the age favoured the spread of such views.

The doctrine of eternal punishment came under criticism in the mid 19th century and spread along with the evolutionary views. In Australian Congregationalism rejection of eternal punishment surfaced in the mid 1870s and was quite general by 1888 among ministers.[9] The same trend among the Presbyterians was evident at the same time. Rev William Ridley (1819-1878) moved away from the orthodox position in the 1870s, and in 1887 W.G.Maconochie of Mudgee, writing in *The Presbyterian*, explained hell in terms of missing out on blessings rather than the infliction of punishment. That rather noisy and strictly Protestant Presbyterian, W.M.Dill Macky (1849-1913) warned against such lax views in the same publication four years later.[10] But by the turn of the century they prevailed.

Naturally enough, Christ's sufferings were reinterpreted to fit the new idea of God. The teaching that Christ was punished in the believer's place 'the just for the unjust to bring us to God' (1 Peter 3:18) was played down, 'reinterpreted' or rejected. A common alternative was to suppose Christ's atonement was designed to work a moral influence on men, leading them to return to God through the impression wrought in them by consideration of the Saviour's love. There is truth in this, but it is not the heart of the atonement. The older teaching spoke of the righteousness of God in redemption, and the covenant bond between Christ and his people by which their sins were laid on him and his righteousness placed to their account (imputation). This was now dismissed as an imposed legal framework, yet it was not explained how the new views were consistent with a worthy conception of God. After all, where is the morality in one who is innocent being made to suffer so shamefully simply in order to make an impression on others? What kind of God would do such injustice? At least the older teaching was consistent with the Scripture explanation of the substitution of Christ so that God might be just and the justifier of whoever believes in Jesus.[11] The newer views were evident in Australian Presbyterianism in the mid 1870s, but more common ten years later.[11]

9. H.R.Jackson, op. cit., pp.128-130.

10. R.B.Walker, op. cit., p.53.

11. Similar moves in professedly Calvinistic bodies occurred elsewhere about this time, usually without a formal split. Two exceptions could be noted. In 1887 the great Calvinistic Baptist preacher, C.H.Spurgeon (1834-92), withdrew from the Baptist Union in England as a result of the 'Downgrade' he rightly perceived as prevalent; for details refer I.H.Murray, **The Forgotten Spurgeon** (London 1973). In Scotland, the Free Presbyterian Church of Scotland was formed in 1893 by those who withdrew from the Free Church because of slackening in the Confessional position.

Biblical criticism

God gave his word through men of his choosing. Inspired by him they wrote what he intended. In seeking the fullest possible understanding of God's message, it is necessary to be sure of the words he used, since changes and copyists' mistakes of greater or less importance may have found a place. The science by which one attempts to compare the surviving manuscripts and ascertain the exact words used in the original is called lower criticism, or better, textual analysis. Having restored the original text, the next step is to ascertain the intended meaning. In doing so, questions of date, authorship, background, literary form and so on are relevant in reaching the most adequate interpretation. This science is called higher criticism, or better, literary analysis.[12]

Textual analysis

The analysis of surviving texts in Hebrew and Greek of the Biblical books has a long history. As we do not have the originals and the surviving copies differ from each other, it is the task of the textual critic to ascertain which variant reading is the original. From the point of view of those holding a high view of inspiration, such a task is specially important. God did not miraculously preserve exact copies of the originals, but the true readings are dispersed in the multiplicity of copies. Recovery of the original is therefore not beyond the reach of the church in the course of the use of textual comparison and analysis. Such work should be pursued just because God inspired the original words and not merely the general thoughts.[13]

Of course, it should be borne in mind that the nett result of the careful assessment of variants in the manuscripts is not very dramatic. No doctrine of Scripture is left inadequately supported, and most of the variants are in matters of spelling or word order which disappear in translation anyway. The effect is in general to sharpen what is already clear.[14]

12. It is worth noting that as early as 1839, the Church of Scotland Assembly passed an Act anent the Establishment and Endowment of a Professorship of Biblical Cristicism, under Barrier Act procedure so as to be a standing law. It embodied the concern expressed by Thomas Chalmers in his Institutes of Theology Vol.1 Chapter 9, and was designed to ensure all students for the ministry had lectures in the subject for two years of their course.
13. It should be hardly necessary to note that the KJV translators, in their Preface (in library editions) acknowledged the principles of textual analysis, noting that to include marginal notes was not wrong but only unsettled those who were over presumptuous. An annotated edition of the Preface to the KJV under the title The Translators to the Reader, was published the the Presbyterian Reformed Church of Australia in 1984.
14. See, for example, B.F.Westcott, Some Lessons of the Revised Version of the New Testament (London 1897) 239pp.

The Revised Version of the Bible was issued in 1881 (NT) and 1885 (OT). In the NT it was based on a consideration of far more manuscripts than had been the case with the King James Version, and, as a consequence, there were quite a number of variations. Naturally there were proponents of a different assessment of the Greek manuscripts which would have produced a text rather closer to the text underlying the King James Version, but by and large there was no outcry among Australian Presbyterians at the basic approach. The new translation was welcomed though a clear distinction was drawn between its value as an accurate edition and its actual use in public worship. Dr George Sutherland of the PCEA in Sydney was rather critical of some of the new readings, but was taken to task by his rival, Rev Peter MacPherson, in a pamphlet entitled *'The Champion Scholarship of the Australian Colonies Exposed'* issued in 1881. It was actually a quite sound argument which vindicated the basic principles by which the Revisers had tackled their task. Most Presbyterians continued to use the KJV in the pulpit, but the RV was valued as an accurate version to use in careful study. In some respects this reaction was surprising since the suspicion in the churches because of doctrinal trends away from orthodoxy could have been expected to rub off on the RV. No doubt in some respects this was so, but it was surprisingly little. It would not be until the spate of newer translations in the 1950s and later that major upsets would occur, and perhaps this was in part due to the fact that only then did the KJV begin to be displaced in a significant way from its place in public worship. [15]

Literary analysis

In the middle of last century, the major area of controversy as a result of literary criticism was the Old Testament, particularly the books commonly ascribed to Moses and thus dating from 1,400 BC, on the common reckoning. The major source of the critical theories was Germany, where rationalistic anti-supernaturalism was rife, and it made itself felt in the English-speaking world from about 1860. It dissected the Old Testament, and found diverse

15. The objections then would be on two main grounds: (1) the literary superiority of the KJV and its universal acceptance by Protestants; and (2) the superiority of its textual basis in the Hebrew and Greek manuscripts. As to (1), the KJV was superior to the RV in literary grace, but did not meet the need for clarity by the 1960s, and thus the Protestant principle of Scripture in the language of the people was at risk. The issue in (2) was more serious, and frequently went well beyond an extreme conservatism as regards textual analysis, and was bolstered by arguments such as had been advanced against the Protestant position by the Roman Catholics and Anabaptists of the 16th and 17th centuries - a rather ironical twist. There was also at stake the Protestant principle of translation from the providentially preserved manuscripts, and the correction of all translations by them. For the history of the formulation of Chapter 1 of the Westminster Confession (Of the Holy Scripture) see B.B.Warfield, **The Westminster Assembly and its Work** (Oxford 1931, New Jersey 1972) pp.155ff. For an exposition of the subject contemporary with the Westminster Confession see Francis Turretin (1623-87), **The Doctrine of Scripture** (ET, Michigan 1981).

strands which were assigned to different authors and different ages. It denied predictive prophecy and explained away the miraculous. New Testament books were dated in the second century, long after the events, and difficulties in the Biblical text were turned into contradictions, and contradictions were found which had not been noticed before. In general, the critics treated the Scripture as a progressive revelation - not in the proper sense of a gradual unfolding from bud to full bloom, but in the wrong sense of from error and misconception to the true and ideal. The inspiration of the human writers was denied in the interest of a naturalistic development of the religion of Israel. 16

The attitude of Presbyterians to these new views was mixed. Few accepted the methods and results of the critics to the extent of jettisoning the supernatural. As Andrew Harper put it in an address before the Federal Assembly of the Presbyterian Church in 1892:

'Now I don't think *we* need discuss what the results of such a denial of the supernatural are certain to be. To all of *us* it means a maimed and mutilated Christianity so feeble for good, that though it has always existed alongside of the true, warm, supernatural Christianity, it has never succeeded. It has never inspired a great cause, nor a great man, nor has it permanently uplifted any state or race which has adopted it. It has only lowered and ultimately killed spiritual life. So far, therefore as the critical results rest upon a denial of the supernatural, *we* don't need to discuss what their effects on life and doctrine are certain to be. In regard to both they mean *Death*. The experience of ages has taught us that, and we have learned the lesson, once for all.[17]

Harper proceeded to ask,

'what would be the effect upon Christian life and doctrine of a general acceptance of the view that the Mosaic law was not the work of Moses, that he only planted the germs of it; that it was an age-long growth' completed in the 6th century BC?

He answered the question in a strikingly frank way. He admitted that acceptance of the critical method and conclusions without denial of the

---

16. For an interesting account of the conditions in Germany see R.L.Dabney, 'The Influence of the German University System on Theological Literature' in his **Discussions: Evangelical and Theological**, Volume 1 (1890 reprint London 1967) pp.440-465. Dabney (1820-98) was a great exponent of Reformed Theology in the Southern Presbyterian Church in the United States. For an account of the history of the literary criticism of the Pentateuch see E.J.Young, **An Introduction to the Old Testament** (London 1966) pp.107-154, and for an exposition of critical views from a recent Roman Catholic author see Peter F. Ellis, **The Men and the Message of the Old Testament** (Minnesota 1975) and note the colour outline of the (alleged) sources of the Pentateuch on pages 57-73. But increasingly studies are revealing the intricate literary structure and artistry of Genesis in developments similar to those in Homeric studies.
17. **The Presbyterian Monthly** [PCV Magazine] December 1892.

supernatural would 'do much harm.' But he argued that 'no great movement fails to do some harm.' There is the inevitable shock to those on the edge of unbelief anyway, and there is the shock and confusion of the minds of pious Christians 'who have been accustomed to treat their Bible as being, in a direct and straightforward way, the very word of God to them.' As to the first class, one must be temperate in advancing the new views and 'no step forward should be taken unless the critic feels that he takes with him the presence, the power and the benediction of our blessed Lord.' As to the second, the end result will be good in that the Christian will be 'forced back upon the real grounds of certainty in things of faith,' this certainty being the testimony of the Spirit. The inspiration of the Scriptures consisted in their moral and spiritual character which brought sincere readers who yielded to their influence nearness to God not otherwise to be attained. What defects they had, literary or otherwise, could not alter this fundamental fact, and thus Christian life would be delivered from any risk of harm by critical enquiries, and it could hardly fail to be deepened by the growth of the conviction that it is only by a real connection with Christ, a life more or less completely hid with Christ in God, that unshakeable certainty in the things of God can be obtained or kept. Harper went on to acknowledge that the change in the doctrine of inspiration, though he considers it to be a reversion to the doctrine of Luther and Calvin, was not unimportant.

...the change in the doctrine of inspiration does not end with itself. In a system of doctrine so carefully articulated and wrought out as that of the Reformed Churches is, no one doctrine of importance can be modified without insensibly modifying all the others.

Nevertheless, he was confident that all the cardinal doctrines of the Reformed faith would still remain, particularly as the main points about God, Man, Sin and Redemption had not been altered by criticism, and even the late dates given by critics to Messianic passages still left these passages written well before Christ came:

To me, therefore, it seems that while a crisis is upon us, which will try all our wisdom, there is no reason to be panic stricken and despondent. Viewed dispassionately and calmly the new teaching may be judged to be wrong, certainly is in some respects extreme, but it is not fatal to the Christian faith. Doubtless, if it be true, much wise mediating will be necessary before the Christian people find themselves at home in all of it, but all that we value may be conserved for the Church and the individual on the new terms as on the old.

Such a viewpoint became general. In 1894, as discussed on pages 238-239, the Moderator of the PCNSW spoke quite scornfully of the earlier position. It would seem that openness to literary criticism was general soon after, though there was more orthodoxy in Victoria and Queensland. The absence of a strong leadership opposed to the new views, the toleration of them in the Scottish churches and a lack of willingness to appear obscurantist, must be considered relevant factors. The fact that leading proponents of the new approach had been in the forefront of the opposition to a rationalist like Charles Strong, must also have encouraged people to feel secure in taking a tolerant line.

There was a third reaction to the new views. If some swallowed them and others accepted the method if not all the conclusions, others were content to hold the doctrine set out in the Westminster Confession. They were ready to grant the human element in Scripture but they held that the divine inspiration of Scripture excluded errors. They granted the word 'inerrant' was not used in the Confession in reference to the Scriptures, and that questions of date, style and authorship were open for discussion within limits which did not impute inaccuracy to the original manuscripts. But they were not prepared to accept a humanistic reconstruction of Israel's history which denied the historicity of the events as recorded any more than they were prepared to accept a reinterpretation of the miracles of Christ which robbed them of their factuality. In a response to Harper's paper 'A Reader' wrote and included quotations from Rev Dr James Stalker, who had responded to Harper in the pages of the *British Weekly*. Stalker wanted to oppose the notion that the authority of the Bible is independent of every kind of criticism. [18]

I believe, on the contrary, that there are views of the Bible, which, if their implications were perceived, would compel honest men to leave the pulpit, and, if diffused in the community, would speedily empty the pews.

Stalker cited the condition of the churches on the Continent where critical views prevailed and added:

If we are reckless in circulating the views which have wasted other churches, what right have we to presume upon immunity from the misfortunes which have befallen them?

Stalker, no arch-conservative, then refers to Harper's views, and states:

What astonishes me is his faith in the virtue of the 'blessed word inspiration.' No matter how untrustworthy a document may be historically, only say it is 'inspired' and you are all right. Is it not an extraordinary superstition to be able to believe that inspiration could so fill a man's mind with divine light that his thinking on moral and spiritual subjects was infallible, while it did nothing for him when vigilance, consistent thinking and love of truth were required in the narration of facts?

'A Reader' asked: 'Does Professor Harper not create the difficulty he proposes to meet by unnecessarily assuming the acceptance of such views to be inevitable?...If Professor Harper has to hold fast the supernatural in

18. **The Presbyterian Monthly,** February 1893, pp.57-58.

spite of these views, why not the whole pre-critical Bible in spite of them as well? The mass of true Christians will certainly reject them...Indeed, it is only a question of time and a little patience; for there can be little doubt that believing scholars will demonstrate a post-critical Bible corresponding with our pre-critical one, while the critical Bible of Kuenan and Wellhausen now sought to be substituted will have died a natural death.

There is reason to suppose that many shared the outlook of 'A Reader' and believed the present deviations were but a temporary aberration. While the shift of subsequent critical opinion has gone a long way to vindicate the reliability of the Scriptures, the rather ready tolerance of the new views was certainly destructive. The 1890s mark the shift to the new views of the Bible as merely a sufficient witness to the self-evidencing Christ. The Spirit's testimony to Christ was divorced from a fully reliable objective witness in Holy Scripture, and the old doctrine was scorned. It was even alleged that the Confession did not teach verbal inspiration. In 1894 the address of Rev George McInnes as Moderator of the PCNSW is scathing in rejecting what he calls the 'Verbally Inspired Code of Rules' theory:

It has been the ally, the vantage ground and the trenchant weapon of the infidel. It has banned enquiry, and 'loved darkness rather than light.' It has narrowed, perverted and bewildered theology. It has cramped the energies of the Church, checked her development and growth, and made the faith of many only a wretched half-faith. It has turned many to indifference or to unbelief, who but for it would have believed and followed Christ. The greatest gain from the disappearance of the 'Verbal Code of Rules' theory is that Christ is thereby restored to His proper place and authority. Strange it is, that Christ has been hidden from men through all the ages, and is hidden still...Among Protestants a tradition of the Scribes has robbed Him of His due. It is a marvel to think that Christian men, Fathers and Reformers, orthodox theologians and evangelical Churches, have been, and are, humble followers of the Scribes and Pharisees whom Christ denounced and renounced, - the very Scribes and Pharisees who crucified the Son of God. The 19th century has been fertile in discoveries and inventions, almost miraculous. But its chief discovery, that which will make it an epoch in the world's history, is the discovery of Christ, the real Christ, whom men are beginning to perceive face to face and to know better than ever before.[19]

McInnes, ordained in 1875, had come from the Church of Scotland in 1880 to be minister at Ashfield. His scornful caricature of the Biblical doctrine, a doctrine largely common to the Christian Church in all ages, was received with applause. At the close of the address we are told that the choir broke in unannounced with the Doxology, with striking effect. The next day when the

19. Text of the address and report of Assembly in **The Presbyterian**, of which McInnes was Editor, March 10, 1894. Rev Duncan McInnes of Maclean PCEA was a cousin but with orthodox views.

minutes were to be confirmed it was moved by Rev R.S.Paterson and seconded by Rev W.S.Frackleton, that the word 'suitable' in the minute 'the Moderator delivered a suitable address' be omitted. Only 8 were found to vote for this and 53 against. The eight were the mover and the seconder with Rev W.M.Dill Macky, J.S.Laing, J.Paton, J. Macaulay, G. Stewart with J.K. Morice, elder. Of the 53, 31 were ministers, including Dr Cameron and Dr Kinross. While not necessarily indicating precisely the theological complexion of the NSW Assembly, it was a reasonable indication. Rev George Grimm (1833-97), not present at the time, later replied to McInnes, but from now on evangelical and Reformed men adhering to the Confession were a tolerated minority. In Victoria there was more orthodoxy and greater circumspection in expressing viewpoints, but a liberal mood. The disastrous fruit would be seen in the 20th century.

18: LONGER CORDS BUT WEAKER STAKES

VICTORIA

By 1865, significant unions had been achieved in each colony other than Van Diemen's Land. In Victoria, there had been an amazing influx of ministers between 1859 and 1865 as the lists on pages 155ff show. The result was a doubling of active strength from the 53 at the time of union in 1859. As there were about 200 Presbyterian ministers in Australia at the close of 1865, Victoria had about 55% of these and New South Wales 25%.

Presbyterian Church of Victoria

The high proportion of Presbyterians in the Victorian population (circa 15%), the prosperity of the people, and the availability of State-aid until 1870, made Victoria the most attractive field for many ministers. However, there was no Central Sustentation Fund to cushion difficulties which an unpopular minister might face, hence there was an incentive to perform well. The result of these factors was that Victoria was able to secure the best qualified candidates and the less satisfactory drifted elsewhere. Of the 74 new entrants into the PCV from 1859 to 1865, at least 15% had Irish backgrounds and at least a further 30% were from the Free Church of Scotland. Only 6 or 7 of the recruits can be identified as from the Established Church of Scotland. Of these, four (Mitchell, Service, Hill and Galloway) pastored only for a short time. Service was a man of intellectual gifts but was an early liberal with similar views to Charles Strong whose assistant he became in Glasgow in the early 1870s. So the PCV continued as a relatively homogenous church of Free Church flavour. It did not have or develop significant extremes.

The number of PCV church buildings increased from 89 in 1861 to 256 in

1871 to 421 in 1891 as the church consolidated its position and kept up with the increase in population. The estimated number of communicant members was 16,500 in 1881 when there were 152 charges (parishes) and 147 ministers in charges. Over the next 20 years the number of charges and ministers in charges rose about 15%, the general population increased by 39% and communicant membership rose 53%. Despite quite significant losses of large land-holders in the Western District to the Church of England, the PCV was a power and influence in the land. The PCV in 1901 embraced about 45% of the ministers and 50% of the members of the Australian Presbyterian churches.[1] As the preceding and subsequent chapters show, this advance was not all it may have appeared. There was pride in one's success, there was the cultural substituting for real conviction, and there was a steady movement with the times rather than a constant heed to the faith once delivered to the saints. Still there was much that was good, and many fine men who served their generation by the will of God. All of us are children of our time, and if the wind is blowing in one direction it is hard not to bend with it.

Mission work began early. In 1862 the PCV Assembly secured the services of a Moravian minister, Rev F.A.Hagenauer, to take charge of work among the Aboriginals. Hagenauer was based at Ramahyuck near Stratford in East Gippsland and activity continued until 1909.[2] Hagenauer became Government Inspector for Aborigines in Victoria, and is also remembered through his son of the same name, also a minister. In 1866, the PCV appointed Revs J.G.Paton and James Cosh as its missionaries in the New Hebrides. Paton, a Reformed Presbyterian in background, had already given service in the island group. A second field, that of Korea, received Rev J.H. Davies late in 1889. His support was pledged by the Young Men's Sabbath Fellowship Union of the PCV. Within six months, at the early age of 33, he was dead of small-pox. But it was a beginning of the costly effort of the Victorian Church to bring the Gospel to Korea, though sadly, too many of those who went out subsequently had little of the Gospel to give.

Free Presbyterian Church of Victoria
Union had become almost total in Victoria by 1870. The continuing FPCV had logic and adherence to principle on its side, but little else. It had no regular supply of ministers, little in the way of resources, and could hardly raise a quorum for Presbytery and Synod meetings, thus necessitating a complicated Act of Reconstruction in April 1876.[3]

---

1. Statistics are given in GAA Reports.
2. R.S.Miller, The Romance of Australian Presbyterian Missions (Melbourne 1978) p.8.
3. Text in The Presbyter , (ed A.Paul) November 1878 & January 1879. The doctrinal aspect has been discussed by the present writer in Our Banner August 1977, pp.6-11.

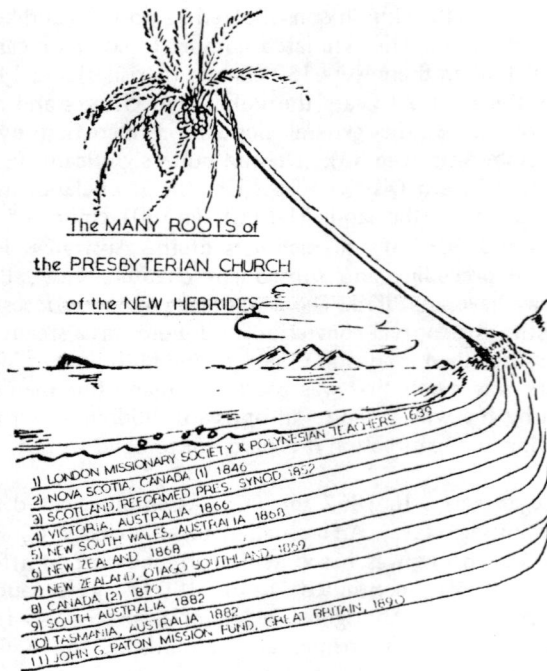

The MANY ROOTS of

the PRESBYTERIAN CHURCH

of the NEW HEBRIDES

1) LONDON MISSIONARY SOCIETY & POLYNESIAN TEACHERS 1839
2) NOVA SCOTIA, CANADA (1) 1846
3) SCOTLAND, REFORMED PRES. SYNOD 1852
4) VICTORIA, AUSTRALIA 1866
5) NEW SOUTH WALES, AUSTRALIA 1868
6) NEW ZEALAND 1868
7) NEW ZEALAND, OTAGO SOUTHLAND 1869
8) CANADA (2) 1870
9) SOUTH AUSTRALIA 1882
10) TASMANIA, AUSTRALIA 1882
11) JOHN G. PATON MISSION FUND, GREAT BRITAIN, 1890

The coconut palm symbolises the Presbyterian Church of the New Hebrides.
The roots symbolise the missionary churches and agencies which helped to
plant the Church, 1839-1890.

[Taken by permission from LIVE Book 1 page 148 by Rev Dr J.G.Miller]

East St Kilda and Geelong were the only centres of significant population
for the FPCV. In these areas the church had unencumbered property and
survived with small congregations. Geelong grew in the 1880s under the
energetic and spiritual ministry of John Sinclair. There was also positive Free
Church sentiment in rural areas. Indeed, in 1871, 12 years after the main
union, nearly 18% of Presbyterians (20,160 persons) described themselves as
Free Presbyterian in the census. Such work as was done was chiefly in the
country districts and among the older people. As the nature of the rural
economy changed the children dispersed into other districts and viable,
organised FPCV work was not possible. Thus the PCV became more and more
dominant. A notable exception was in the Hamilton district where there was
a significant Gaelic settlement. A Free Presbyterian cause was established
there in the 1860s (after union) and has continued to the present.

242

NEW SOUTH WALES

Presbyterian Church of New South Wales

At its commencement in 1865, this church had 45 regular charges and about 2,000 communicant members. Some parishes were very extensive. In 1868, it was reported that Armidale and Walcha had 25 preaching places each, Cooma 22 and Mudgee 20. Elders were scarce: Armidale had only one.[4]

Ministers were in short supply too. The Union agreement forbade any official application to any of the British churches and a proposal to remove this limitation was defeated in the Assembly of 1871. In any event, New South Wales did not attract the best candidates. The basic stipend in NSW was $400 pa compared with $600 in Victoria, there was little in the way of regular provision for training men for the ministry, and financial provisions were often insecure.

The New South Wales Church muddled through with a mixture of recruitment sources, including more than its fair share of rag-tag and bobtail. Queensland coped, with Irish help and some local recruits. The Victorian Church, with its early start, continued to have a guaranteed market for high-quality Scottish recruits, along with an efficient Theological Hall, with full-time staff, which turned out a steady and widening stream of ministers from the 1860s.[5]

Taking Dr Prentis' figures, 26.4% of ministers who served in NSW 1822-1900 had a Free Church of Scotland background, precisely the same percentage as in Victoria. The figure for the UPs is also much the same (c.12%) in each case, although the Established Church figures vary (19.7% in NSW and 11.1% in Victoria). But this does not alter the fact that the theological complexion of the NSW church was more variegated, less confident, and more open to compromise for the sake of peace and unity than the Victorian church. The seedbed was in the discordant elements in the 1864/65 Union which E.A.Rennie, one time Auditor General in New South Wales, called 'nothing more than an incorporation of exceedingly diverse and heterogeneous elements, that could not be called in any proper sense of the term a union in spirit and sentiment and designs - however well it might look in statistics.'[6]

Educational work was limited in the 19th century, and Scots College, Sydney was not founded until 1893.

4. C.A.White, The Challenge of the Years (Sydney 1951) p. 25
5. M.D.Prentis, The Presbyterian Ministry in Australia, 1822-1900: Recruitment and Composition in JRH, Vol. 13 †1 (June 1984) p.55. The statistics following are derived from Prentis' article pp.58,59, but more analysis is needed as to the duration of pastorates as well as the background of men in the influential pulpits. I am quite sure such research will confirm Free Church dominance.
6. The History of St George's Church (Sydney 1881) p.14

Communicant membership of the PCNSW grew from 5,101 in 70 charges in 1879 to 9,751 in 140 charges in 1893. This period covered the reign of Rev J.Miller Ross as General Agent of the church. His duties most nearly corresponded to those of both General Secretary and Home Missions Superintendent of a later time, except he had more tasks and more powers. He was to organise congregations, assist in establishing a Sustentation Fund and generally to promote the extension of the church and its financial prosperity. Ross had held a similar position in the Presbyterian Church of England. During the 1880s about 124 ministers were received (two-thirds from Scotland or Ireland) compared with 46 in the 1870s.[7] In 1880, the NSW Assembly gave Ross 'a seat *ex officio* in the Committees on Church Extension, Heathen Missions, Sabbath Schools and Sustentation Fund, while he was also empowered to sit as a member in every Presbytery of the Church.'[8] He was a strong personality and there were many clashes. There was influential opposition to his having a seat in all Presbyteries, but the Assembly regularly refused to alter the arrangement. Colonel J.H.Goodlet (1835-1914), a foundation elder of the Ashfield congregation and a major benefactor of the church, resigned from all Committees in 1889 because he could no longer work with Ross.

Ross was certainly an indefatigable labourer and commanded the confidence of the Assembly, but his methods were not always to be commended. For example, he had no scruple about going into areas already occupied by the PCEA, although the PCEA held no doctrine which the PCNSW could condemn without condemning itself. This occurred at Wellington in 1882 (with little success at the time), and on the Macleay, Nambucca and Bellinger Rivers in 1883. On the Macleay Rev John Davis of the PCEA gave regular services, all but 2 or 3 of the Presbyterian families worshipping with him though in total a small congregation. A PCNSW congregation could not be formed without drawing people away from the PCEA congregation. Despite the needs in other parts of NSW without any ministry, this is what was done the following year. Similarly, at Bellingen the PCEA had a neat building where up to 80 gathered to hear the Word of Life. This building was placed at the disposal of Mr Ross for one service when a PCEA conducted meeting was not scheduled. At the end of the service Ross calmly announced that a further service would be held the following week. Isaac Greer, one of the PCEA Trustees and a fine Christian of Ulster background, pointed out that permission would have to be obtained first. Ross, 'stamping his foot in the pulpit, said, 'The Free Church must be stamped out,' and denounced the Free Church which had generously granted him the use of the building.'[9]

7. M.D.Prentis, op. cit., p.58
8. C.A.White, op. cit., p.31; on Goodlet, ibid., p.38 and see L.M.McKinnon's article in **Australian Presbyterian Life**, October 1983.
9. W.N.Wilson (who married one of Greer's daughters) in **Australian Free Presbyterian**, July 1917, p.24; similarly, **The Witness**, September 29, 1883.

The $60,000 Berry bequest in 1890 gave a major boost to the Sustentation Fund as the PCNSW gradually consolidated. In the 20 years 1881-1901, membership increased 142% while the general population rose only 80%. Although in 1901 the communicant membership was not much more than half that of the PCV the number of preaching places was slightly more. This reflected the much larger area to be covered, a fact that did not help in unifying the sentiment of the church.

Presbyterian Church of Eastern Australia

On the same day that the first stage of Presbyterian re-union was achieved (November 15, 1864), five ministers and one elder constituted a meeting of the Synod of Eastern Australia continuing on the original basis. At this meeting, held in St George's Church, the adherence of Rev Allan McIntyre and the elders at Grafton, Maclean and Inverell was recorded. Rev S.F. Mackenzie and a section of his congregation at West Maitland joined the final union immediately after its consummation on September 8, 1865.

At the PCEA Synod meeting on November 1, 1865 the position of the PCEA was somewhat as follows: *Presbytery of Sydney* - St George's (Rev William McIntyre); Bombala (Rev Colin Greig); *Presbytery of Maitland* - Raymond Terrace (Rev James McCulloch); Maitland (D.McInnes, student supply); Singleton (vacant); Manning (Rev Allan McIntyre); Barrington (vacant station); Grafton (vacant - Rev Alexander McIntyre supplying); Maclean (vacant); Inverell (vacant station). John McSkimming was without fixed charge, was inducted to Singleton in 1866 but resigned from the ministry the following year. In mid 1868 Rev W.S.Donald was received and was settled in the Clarence Town district.

The major problem faced by the PCEA was the shortage of ministers seeing that the Free Church of Scotland disowned her. The possibilities were transfer from other churches in Australia or overseas and training by the PCEA - something William McIntyre had long advocated. The difficulties were aggravated by the death of Allan McIntyre (May 1870), William McIntyre (July 1870) and the poor health of James McCulloch leading to his death in 1873. Further, Colin Greig resigned in 1872, some question of stipend arrears entering into it, while John Macleod, a former student of the PCV who had transferred to the PCEA in 1868 and become minister in Grafton, also resigned in 1872. Both these men joined the PCNSW. Thus, all the ministers who had continued in 1865 were gone by 1873. Humanly speaking the cause seemed hopeless.

However, Duncan K.McIntyre completed studies for the ministry and succeeded his older brother on the Manning in 1872, while Rev George Sutherland of Dunedin, New Zealand was inducted to St George's in

November of that year. Sutherland was an exceptionally gifted preacher and teacher and well suited for a city congregation. At once he began a weekly newspaper called *The Australian Witness and Presbyterian Herald*, the first issue being dated November 2, 1872. This was a well-conducted paper with religious news as well as general news viewed in a Christian light. It displayed a generous spirit towards other churches while advocating the evangelical Calvinism and simple worship of the PCEA. The publisher was John Lutton, an elder of the PCNSW. In January 1874 Lutton concluded an arrangement by which the paper was transferred at short notice to the editorship of three PCNSW ministers, Dr Steel being the most prominent. If, as seems likely, the major reason for this was to limit Sutherland's impact and the credibility of the PCEA, it did not succeed. The energetic Sutherland changed the name of his paper to *The Witness and Australian Presbyterian* (abbreviated to *The Witness* in 1877) and continued weekly production. There were nearly 1,000 subscribers in 1875 when E.A Rennie was handling the financial side.[10] It ceased publication in 1884.

Isaac Mackay, a capable minister with Gaelic, was received from the PCQ in 1873 and was settled at Grafton. Like Sutherland he had a background in Canada. Sutherland undertook the training of a number of men for the ministry who were subsequently ordained in the years indicated: Hugh Livingstone (1875), John Davis (1877), John S. MacPherson (1878), John A. Nicol (1878) and S.P.Stewart (1879). With the probable exception of Nicol, these men were all capable. Sutherland was able to fire the imagination of his students but he had his own way of doing things and did not find it easy to take counsel of others.[11] Rev Peter MacPherson (no relation to J.S.) was received from the FPCV in 1874 but retired to Sydney late in 1878 due to poor health. He was a man of great ability and a controversialist of note. A brother was Chief Secretary of Victoria. Sutherland and MacPherson were a bit like chalk and cheese. They clashed over the reception and training of students in 1880, and MacPherson was so foolish as to go into print prior to a Synod meeting where matters were to be discussed. He was never a man to mince his words, and it was not long before the church which had made such definite progress since 1865 was split in two.

The position of the PCEA in early 1884 may be summarised thus: *Presbytery of Sydney* St George's (Rev G.Sutherland); Parkes (Mr Moss, catechist); Wellington (James Marshall, catechist); Rev D.K.McIntyre (without charge) and Messrs G.Sutherland and P.MacPherson, Professors. *Presbytery of*

10. **Synod of Eastern Australia Minutes**, p.220 (November 8, 1875).
11. On Sutherland see R.S.Miller's sketch in **Evangelical Presbyterian** (NZ), January 1961, pp.18-22, but note Miller has not referred to the friction between Sutherland and his office-bearers reported at the time in the **Otago Witness** (copies in 'Presbyterianism in Victoria' (a collection of newspaper cuttings by Peter MacPherson), State Library of Victoria).

Maitland Raymond Terrace/East Maitland (Rev J.S.MacPherson); Aberdeen/ Singleton (W.N.Wilson, catechist); Namoi (Rev H.S.Buntine); Clarence Town (Rev W.S.Donald). *Presbytery of the Manning* Barrington (vacant); Manning (Rev S.P.Stewart); Hastings/Macleay (Rev John Davis); Nambucca/Bellinger (Robert Allen, catechist). *Presbytery of Grafton* Grafton (Rev Isaac Mackay); Brushgrove (Rev William Grant); Maclean (Rev Duncan McInnes); Richmond River (Rev Hugh Livingstone).

According to the statistics supplied to the *World Alliance of Reformed Churches* for their 1884 publication, there were 273 communicants, 3,150 adherents, 12 ministers (including two without pastoral charge), 11 regular charges, 5 stations or preaching districts and 19 sabbath schools.

At the Synod of May 1884 party feeling had become such that a majority of Synod members was prepared to sign a document expelling the three ministers who had opposed the action of the majority over the preceding 3 or 4 years. The argument was that they had become an irreconcilable minority who had obstructed the lawful and proper activities of the Synod and vilified the majority in the public press, including by the insertion of paid advertisements. The Synod did not depose or suspend the ministers involved (the two MacPhersons and Livingstone) but expelled them from the Synod while leaving their connection with their congregations undisturbed. This was hardly the regular way of action although precedents were produced.[12] From examination of the rather unedifying literature it is difficult to see what other options there were for the majority.

The expelled men raised an action at law to be restored to their seats in the Synod, but during the case proposed to reconstitute the Synod on the ground that the old one had become defunct. Understandably, the judge did not find this very consistent. The reconstitution was therefore abandoned in June 1885. The judge then gave his verdict for the defendants on the ground that the Court of Equity had no jurisdiction since there was no substantial right of property involved, and such rights as existed had been protected. An appeal to the Supreme Court was dismissed unanimously. The plaintiffs had, to pay costs which amounted to over $900 - a large sum in a time when a reasonable stipend was $500 a year.[13]

12. See **An Authentic Statement of the Equity Suit** (Sydney 1886) pp.86ff; compare the review in **The Free Churchman** (the Macpherson party's paper) April 1886 p.36, and opinion on the judgement in the December 1885 issue.
13. **The Free Churchman**, July 1886, p.77. The judgements were also reported in the **Sydney Morning Herald**, July 15, 1885 and November 28, 1885.

The expulsion did not affect the legal existence of the Synod for it did not involve abandonment of its constitution. At worst the expulsion was an act of improper administration. The MacPhersons thought otherwise and on April 20, 1886, they along with Rev W.N.Wilson and Samuel Porter, elder at East Maitland) organised what they called *The Reconstituted Synod of Eastern Australia*. But not all opposed to the expulsion agreed with this. Livingstone went to Victoria where the FPCV sympathised with the expelled men but did not recognise officially the Reconstituted Synod. Buntine joined the PCNSW. Peter MacPherson died in July 1886 and the Reconstituted Synod broke up in 1904 with the removal of J.S.MacPherson to South Australia, and the healing of wounds associated with the repeal of the expulsion Act unconditionally by the PCEA Synod on February 10, 1903.

Church extension was impossible during the time of the dispute. The PCNSW made headway in areas where the PCEA had been established. The original Synod had a majority of ministers and survived, but the ground that was lost could never be recovered and something of a shadow was cast over the church for a generation. It was a hard way to learn the truth of Galatians 5:20-23. It appears that the bulk of the people did not support the Sutherland section because they distrusted him and with a measure of justification regarded him as sitting loose to PCEA principles. His previous involvement in a union church in New Zealand and his attitude to union in Australia which surfaced early in 1884 (see page 270) were also relevant, and these were exploited to some effect. Also, one should not overlook the situation in Scotland where defection from sound doctrine was becoming prevalent and causing alarm to the lovers of truth. The negative spirit of the times contributed to a rigidity and narrowness of vision on the part of some even as it led others to stray into the bog on the other side. By the close of 1908, the PCEA was reduced to only three ministers able to sustain a pastorate (Stewart on the Manning, Wilson on the Hunter and McDonald at St George's), although there was immediate work for a further three, viz: Hastings, Grafton and Maclean.

QUEENSLAND

Of the 137 ministers who served in Queensland from 1847 to 1900, only 17 (12.4%) were of Church of Scotland origin. A high 21.2% were from the Irish church, the same proportion as was from the Free Church of Scotland. The popular belief was that Irish ministers were second rate although there was some prejudice by Scots in this assessment. The Irish ministers were not always as precise as those with Scottish training, but their training in Belfast was orthodox for a longer period than in Scotland, and many Irish ministers combined an attractive blend of effective, open-hearted preaching of the Cross with warm evangelical fervour which gave colour to the Queensland church. The PCQ grew to 5,053 members in 1901 when there were some 52 charges and 34 settled ministers.

SOUTH AUSTRALIA

The main characteristic of the PCSA worth noting during the period 1865-1900 is the lack of city and suburban extension work and the patchy results in rural areas. The state population more than doubled in this period, reaching 344,000. While communicant membership nearly doubled to about 2,000, the work was not securely based. The distances, the low proportion of Presbyterians in the population (5.2% in 1901), the dominance of Methodism (25% in 1901), poor leadership and a problem of identity were relevant factors. The 3 city ministers drew members from the suburbs and were reluctant to promote suburban extension work out of fear and jealousy. An ineffective attempt was made in North Adelaide in 1877-78. In 1880, Goodwood originated as a result of several Scottish migrant families settling in the area, while in 1883, Norwood began as a mission church through local initiative as well as encouragement from the then minister of Wakefield Street Church. But this was the sum total of suburban activity prior to the 20th century. Many losses occurred to the Methodists and to the Anglicans since the role and style of the PCSA was ill defined and there was no dominant Scottish church tradition. The rural efforts in a developing colony, which were also characteristic of the FPCSA [which began at Kingston SE, 1872; Robe, 1875; Strathalbyn, 1877; and Spalding, 1877], were not adequately supported by leadership and organisation in the major centres, and were subject to shifts of population as mining or pastoral activity rose or fell. The separation of the churches in the south-east in 1862 and their attachment to the geographically more proximate PCV Presbytery, did not help either. By 1901 there were about 20 charges and 13 ministers, and reasonable penetration had occurred. Over 22% of census Presbyterians were on Sunday School or communicant membership rolls - more if the churches in the south east are allowed for. This compares with about 33% for Victoria and Tasmania and 24-25% in NSW and Queensland.

WESTERN AUSTRALIA

In 1858 application for a minister was made to the Church of Scotland via the Synod of Australia,[14] but nothing came of it. In the 1859 census 207 of the 15,000 European inhabitants returned themselves as Presbyterian. In 1891, when the population was near 50,000, there were 1,997 Presbyterians, and 14,707 in 1901 when the population had leapt to near 184,000. Rev David Shearer of the Free Church of Scotland was the first settled minister in Western Australia, founding St Andrew's Perth in 1879. By 1901, there were 19 charges and 13 ministers with about 19% of census Presbyterians on Sunday School or communicant rolls.

---

14. B.J.Bridges, Presbyterian Churches in NSW 1823-1865 (PhD Thesis 1985) p.155.

19: THE STRONG CASE

Whatever theoretical qualifications might be argued for, in practice the terms of Presbyterian union in the Australian colonies involved agreement to receive any minister of reputable personal character who came from a Presbyterian denomination. Inevitably, therefore, the colonial churches would be subject to broadening influences from these other churches. These were not without significance even as early as the 1860s. The chief areas of concern would be Scripture and the doctrine of the atonement.

These issues were of wider concern also. For example, in 1860 seven Anglicans published *Essays and Reviews* in London. It pushed a liberal view of Scripture. It also argued that eternal punishment could not be reconciled with worthy views of God - a tendency of thought that undermines the reality of the love of God and the meaning of the death of Christ. The book created an amazing furore and was condemned by the Church of England Synod in 1864. Nevertheless, a more lax form of subscription by Anglican clergy to the *Thirty-nine Articles* was introduced the following year. In 1862 J.W.Colenso, Anglican Bishop of Natal, issued the first part of his studies of the first six books of the Old Testament which called into question the historical accuracy and traditional authorship of these books. There was great opposition, but his essentially rationalistic views gained an increasing foothold in the following years. These were signs of the times for all the churches. The particular background for Scottish Presbyterians will now be outlined.

Scripture

The very popularity of the Free Church of Scotland and its desire to justify its stand for spiritual independence, contributed to the aim of eminence in scholarship. The better students therefore often completed some of their studies in the German theological schools. These had great reputations in the academic world but were hotbeds of rationalism. Christianity was seen as a product of reason and religious development rather than divine intervention. The onslaught of Hegelian philosophy on the one hand and the new scientific theories on the other led to major shifts in thinking by many teachers and students. Charles Darwin's *Origin of Species* (1859) and, more especially, his *Descent of Man* (1871) were significant. The Free Church had a large stake in the scholarly defence of the faith because of her emphasis on doctrine and her confidence that the facts of the Bible had nothing to fear from the facts of nature. Perhaps it is not surprising, if we recall that pride goes before a fall, that one of the Free Church Professors, the brilliant A.B.Davidson (1831-1902), pioneered destructive Biblical criticism in the church after he took office in the Free Church of Scotland College in Edinburgh in 1863. Davidson's most famous student, William Robertson Smith (1846-94) became Professor in Aberdeen in 1870 and furthered rationalistic criticism in a less cautious way than his teacher. Public controversy over Smith's teaching arose in 1875. He was removed from his teaching post in 1881 for reasons of church politics - the loss of the man being the price to secure the principle of toleration of higher criticism in the church.[1]

Atonement

In 1831, John McLeod Campbell of Row, Dunbartonshire, was deposed by the Church of Scotland. Campbell taught that the atonement of Christ was universal and not for the elect alone; moreover, that the essential message of the gospel was to convince hearers that they had already been forgiven and that they should realize and enjoy the Divine Fatherhood. In effect, Christ's atoning work was held to be the provision of an adequate repentance and there was no infliction of the Father's wrath involved. Campbell's teaching was set out in his *The Nature of the Atonement* in 1856 and was influential in modifying attachment to belief in the substitutionary and sacrificial nature of the atonement, even if not all who abandoned that doctrine embraced Campbell's position fully.

Another influence was in the Secession Church. James Morison (1816-93) of Kilmarnock was deposed in 1841 for denying that Christ's atonement was definite, that is, intended for and made for the elect alone. He affirmed it

1. So P.C.Simpson, **The Life of Principal Rainy** (London 1909) Vol. 1 pp. 399-400. A.C. Cheyne's **Transforming of the Kirk** (Edinburgh 1983) provides a candid survey of the Biblical, Confessional, Liturgical, Social and Life-Style revolution in Victorian Scotland, although some judgements on theological points do not seem fully correct.

was universal and subsequently went further and further down the Arminian path in other areas. He founded the Evangelical Union which became quite a movement. Some who did not follow Morison fully did take a half-way position in which the emphasis on the sufficiency of the atonement for all and the free offer of the gospel to all, positions which any sound Calvinist admits, were regarded as implying a general aspect to the death of Christ of a kind that required the particularism of Christ's saving work to be modified. This view was held by the Secession Synod to be consistent with subscription to the Confession of Faith in that Dr John Brown (1784-1858) of Broughton Place Church, Edinburgh, escaped any censure for views of this kind when tried by the Synod in 1845. When the Secession Synod joined with the even less strict Synod of Relief in 1847 to form the *United Presbyterian Church*, the UP position on the atonement was at least ambiguous. Indeed, Dr Andrew Marshall of Kirkintilloch refused to participate in the union for this reason.[2]

Summary

As early as 1872, Principal A.M. Fairbairn of Mansfield College, Oxford, reviewed the Scottish scene in an article entitled *The Westminster Confession of Faith and Scotch Theology*. This is part of what he recorded:

The continuous earnest struggle of Scotch thought to escape from the harsher points of the Confessional theology has been nowhere without result. Years ago the Secession Synod stamped with its approval a double reference theory of the atonement, which reduced their theology to a modified Calvinism such as the Westminster Divines detested and meant their Confession to condemn. That theory the United Presbyterian Church has never repudiated...The Free Church, long distinguished by its antagonism to eclectic theologies and double reference theories, has, though duly warned by certain of her own Doctors and Professors, repeatedly [since 1867] declared by great majorities that the modified Calvinism of the sister church was no bar to Union... Within the Established Church a circle of men of broad and genial culture has been formed, whose beliefs, influenced by the higher criticism...have not very much in common with the Westminster theology. [3]

This assessment is all too accurate. If we add to it the fact that the colonial churches were also subject to other influences tending to laxity in doctrine, we will have a reasonable background against which to discuss the major conflict which erupted in Victoria in 1880 over the views of Charles Strong, minister of Scots Church, Melbourne. These influences included peculiarities in colonial society.

Church life in Victoria

There were obvious peculiarities in church life in colonial society whether in town or country. In the rural areas mateship, tolerance and co-operation

2. John Macleod, Scottish Theology (Edinburgh 1946), pp. 242-245, 257-258.
3. The Contemporary Review, Vol. xxi (1872) p.80 cited from A.C.Cheyne, op. cit.,p.71

were part of the survival skills needed in primitive conditions. In Melbourne there was a strong tide of rationalistic thought in the prosperous and rapidly expanding metropolis. This was not only among the labouring class but also among the leading and influential capitalists and business people. The position of the Presbyterian Church as only one among several Protestant groups also encouraged a fall back to the common Protestant consensus which existed in Melbourne (then an evangelical Anglican diocese) and in Sydney. A relatively large and united Roman Catholic Church was also relevant.

Capital City Populations 1861 - 1901 [4]

	Melbourne	Sydney	Brisbane
1861	123,000	56,000	6,000
1871	191,000	135,000	19,000
1881	262,000	221,000	37.000
1891	474,000	383,000	102,000
1901	484,000	482,000	119,000

The Presbyterian Church of Victoria had strong Free Church leanings because of the background of many of its ministers. Further, its Theological Hall was dominated from its inauguration in 1866 by Dr Adam Cairns (1802-1881), who took a strict and orthodox view of the vows to maintain the doctrines of the Confession of Faith. A.J.Campbell (1815-1909), another early Professor, was also a man of the old paths, though less able. There were some in the church of more liberal outlook. William Henderson (1826-84) of Ballarat, who had done part of his training as a Free Church minister in Germany, was one of these. Joseph Hay (1847-1921) of Elsternwick was another. However, the general position was the maintenance of orthodox positions along with a natural enough reluctance to appear obscurantist in reference to the issues raised by new trends of thought. Not every i was dotted or t crossed in subscribing the Confession in the 1870s but doctrinal views were pretty uniform all the same, though weakening a little from the earlier period before union. New South Wales was more diverse and less rigid.

Charles Strong (1844-1942) came to Scots Church in August 1875 from the liberal. wing of the Church of Scotland. He had been much influenced by Professor John Caird (1820-98) during his divinity studies in the University

---

4. Statistics (rounded to nearest 1,000) taken from **Australians: Historical Statistics** (Sydney 1987) p.41.

of Glasgow. Caird had become Professor of Divinity in 1863 and taught theology from the standpoint of Hegelian philosophy. As a result, Caird rejected Calvinism and resolved facts into ideas. Strong was not interested in accepted orthodoxy but he was a theist and he had a message. He rejected the offer of a Unitarian pulpit in England from James Martineau (1805-85), and then received an offer from Scots Church.[5] Martineau took the view that any written revelation was subject to a higher truth in man's mind and conscience. He affirmed the inherent goodness of man, embraced evolutionary concepts, and was left with a system of ethics with few ties to traditional beliefs and much stress on human efforts to remedy the ills of the world. This was also essentially Strong's position, but as he used the traditional language it was not necessarily immediately obvious to his hearers that he rejected the deity of Christ or his sacrificial atonement. He was an attractive preacher and gathered a large and influential congregation in Melbourne. His stipend was one thousand pounds - three or four times the average for a Presbyterian minister at that time.

Rumours began to run in 1877 with the publication of an anonymous pamphlet called *Presbyterian Apostasy.* [6] This alleged that there was within more than one Presbytery of the Presbyterian Church a denouncing of the creeds and confessions ministers had vowed to uphold, a scoffing at orthodoxy, a denial of the supernatural and a general avoidance of emphasis on the cardinal truths of the historic Christian faith. Though no names were given Strong was the obvious target. Arthur Paul argued in his pamphlet published at this time under the title, *Twenty Years Ago,* that such an attitude to the sanctity of truth was the natural outgrowth of the disrepect for truth shown by the adoption of a Basis in 1859 which gave the appearance of orthodoxy while allowing diverse expositions on some points. The lax control over admission of ministers was also noted.

Strong was under suspicion by the more conservative ministers in Melbourne, but they were not sure whether or not he was like the former minister of Scots Church, P.S.Menzies. Menzies had been of rather liberal outlook and had attracted large congregations prior to his sudden death in 1874. He had

---

5. C.R.Badger, **The Reverend Charles Strong and the Australian Church** (Melbourne 1971) pp. 158-160. Badger's book is an overly sympathetic study of Strong. It is too dismissive of the Presbyterian opposition and does not give sufficient of the orthodox argument against Strong for the reader to follow the debate for himself. It thus tends to give an impression heavily slanted against the historic Christian position. Thus the book, though not without value, needs to be read with discrimination.

6. C.R.Badger states that Strong identified the author as a Presbyterian minister turned journalist (ibid.,p.36). If this is correct, the author may well have been David Blair (1820-1899) who was brought to New South Wales by Lang in 1850 but came to Victoria early in 1852 following a falling out with Lang. He was involved in journalism and was a member of parliament.

wavered but it seems not abandoned the central facts of the Christian gospel. If Strong was of similar views, he would be left alone. However, the key men became convinced Strong did not hold the basic facts of redemption and that his actual beliefs were subversive of them. A leader in the moves against Strong was J.Laurence Rentoul (1846-1926) who had come to Australia in mid 1879 to pastor St George's Church, East St Kilda. Prior to leaving Britain he had tried to find out Strong's position but was not certain of anything other than Strong's liberal outlook.[7] This was not conclusive since Rentoul was not an old school conservative himself. However, as an Irishman who had done post graduate work in Leipzig and served a parish in Southport, Lancashire (1872-79), he was fully aware of what full blown rationalism could do. If Strong was of this persuasion then Rentoul would give no quarter. Rentoul's nickname of 'Fighting Larry', though earned later, was applicable enough from his early years in Melbourne. On the other hand, if Strong merely wanted to adjust to meet modern trends in biblical criticism and the like while holding the main dogmatic conclusions of the theology of the Confession, Rentoul would leave him alone for that was his own position too.

Strong and the Atonement article 1880-1881

A number of conservative ministers became concerned over essays by Strong published in 1878 and 1879 in the semi-official *Presbyterian Review* edited by William Henderson, and it lost support and was closed. The key conservatives included J.L.Rentoul, D.S.McEachran (1828-1915) of St Andrew's, Carlton,[8] Murdoch Macdonald (1832-1906) of Toorak and F.R.M. Wilson (1832-1903) of Kew. In October 1880, an article on the Atonement under Strong's signature was published in the *Victorian Review*. It was not extravagantly written,[9] but its general tendency as an historical outline of views on the subject suggested that there was no consistent theology of the atonement if the narratives of Scripture were taken at face value, and that the historical facts were only 'temporary drapery' about the real meaning. The truth of the Atonement was to be found in the idea and ideal behind the dogma. This article was brought under the notice of the Presbytery of Melbourne at its December meeting, and in March 1881 a Committee was appointed to examine the article and report to a subsequent meeting.

When the report was presented to the Presbytery on April 26, 1881, a decision was arrived at by which Strong was required to change the emphasis

---

7. C.R.Badger, op. cit., p.39 though Badger's date of 'early in 1878' should probably be 'early in 1879' as Rentoul arrived in Melbourne in June 1879.
8. This was the original Gaelic congregation. The stone building was taken down and re-erected in smaller format in 1940 as St Andrew's, Gardiner (now Uniting Church).
9. Text (without footnotes) is in C.R.Badger, op.cit., pp.239-248.

in his preaching. It was moved by James Ballantyne and seconded by Samuel Robinson and carried:

The Presbytery having considered the paper on the Atonement, published in the Victorian Review for 1880 and signed Charles Strong, and having also considered the Committee's report on the same, express their sincere concern and pain at the negative character of the teaching in Mr Strong's paper, the absence from it of all direct mention of the Divine person of the Lord Jesus Christ as the Mediator, and Reconciler, working out the Atonement, as well as the omission of all reference to the supernaturally given revelation: and inasmuch as the Christian faith rests upon and the Christian consciousness takes hold of, certain objective supernatural historic facts, especially the incarnation, the atoning life and death and the resurrection and ascension of our Lord, the Presbytery earnestly, and in a spirit of brotherly kindness, urge upon Mr Strong that, in his future utterances, he make these essential facts prominent. [10]

This decision rested upon a correct insight into the true nature of Strong's theology as subversive of the historic Christian faith. It may be doubted whether the article itself was sufficient basis, and Strong's supporters, who were few in the Presbytery and seem not to have realised Strong's true position, so argued. Strong himself declined to offer any words of explanation of his views so doubts could be set at rest at once. Still, it was a mild enough decision, and remains of interest since certain of the phrasing ended up in the Scheme of Union of the Presbyterian Church of Australia, constituted in 1901.

J.C.Stewart's assault on the Confession of Faith 1881
Feeling the pressure of the passionate public argument, though much of the press coverage was favourable to him, Strong indicated his intention to resign at a meeting of Scots congregation in August 1881, but agreed to take 6 months leave of absence and to return for at least a further 12 months. At this congregational meeting, J.C.Stewart, an elder and supporter of Strong as well as the law agent for the denomination, assailed the honesty of Strong's accusers, and criticized the Confession of Faith at several points in an intemperate manner. As a result of press reports 'no small sensation' resulted throughout the church. Stewart's speech was reported as follows:

That in the Confession of Faith he found it stated that the world and all things therein, whether visible or invisible, were created in six days of twenty-four hours each; that in order to satisfy the justice of God, millions on millions of God's people had been sent to perdition, simply because they never knew of Christ; that there are elect and non-elect, and that the elect

<hr>

10. R.Hamilton, *A Jubilee History* of the Presbyterian Church of Victoria (Melbourne 1888) p. 403.

will be saved whether they like it or not, and that the non-elect, do what they can, cannot be saved; that there is such a thing as the eternal damnation of infants who had never lisped a name; and further, that the men who pretend to assert, maintain, and defend all the doctrines contained in the Confession are dishonest men. [11]

McEachran's defence of the Confession

Such gross misrepresentation of the teaching of the Confession could not go unchecked. D.S.McEachran was in print in the *Argus* on August 18, and the next day Stewart responded with what seems to be somewhat of a climb down. McEachran followed up on August 20 with a concise summary of what the Confession did teach on the four points raised. He pointed out that the Confession simply uses the language of Scripture in reference to the creation in six days, and did not further define their length. 'Whether we have yet hit upon the right interpretation may be doubted; but certain it is that there can be no opposition between the teachings of science and the teachings of the word of God.' He noted that 'the Confession teaches that all men are guilty before God, that there is no salvation out of Christ, that God will render to every man according to his deeds, and that the punishment of the wicked will be in proportion to the light they have enjoyed.' On the third point, he stated that while the Confession teaches the doctrine of election, 'it teaches at the same time, that no man will perish but for his own sin, and that the door of mercy is thrown wide home to all, so that whosoever will may enter in and be saved.' Stewart's position was fatalistic rather than predestinarian in the Calvinistic sense. As to the salvation of infants, 'the truth is that the aim of the Confession is to show that, if infants are saved, they owe their salvation to the free electing love of God. But anyone is at liberty to believe that all children dying in infancy have been elected, and Presbyterians all the world over believe that.' The expression 'others not elected' in its context does not refer to infants but to persons capable of being called by the ministry of the word.

McEachran's approach was fully in line with full commitment to the doctrines of the Confession. The Editor of the *Argus* was unsympathetic. He noted, 'Mr McEachran's letter is certainly the weakest apology for the Confession we have ever read. We shall give our readers an early opportunity of judging what the Westminster Confession really does teach.' This note indicates not only the ignorance of Reformed Theology on the part of the Editor, but also the changing intellectual climate which was dismissive of dogma of any kind other than the dogma of man's inherent goodness and inevitable progress. The *Argus* published the text of the Confession in three instalments the following week.

11. R. Hamilton, op. cit., p.409.

Charles Strong

Adherence to the Standards

At this point a matter that had concerned some brethren for several years was brought into the debate. At the time of the 1859 union, the Basis had not differentiated the Confession of Faith from the other historic standards of the Scottish Church - the Second Book of Discipline of 1578 (relating to the government of the church) and the other formularies of the Westminster Assembly. The Basis of Union in New South Wales was more carefully drafted and placed these other standards in their correct position as not imposed by subscription but binding in their basic thrust and principles. It was now sought by those opposed to definite adherence to the Confession, to show that as no one accepted adherence to every proposition of the Second Book of Discipline therefore no one was obliged to accept every point of doctrine in the Westminster Confession. Because of the sloppy drafting of the 1859 Basis, which was also the basis on which the church held its property, this was a useful argument but did not deflect the majority from dealing with the issues raised by Stewart.

Stewart censured

The Presbytery of Melbourne, which comprised about one third of the ministerial strength of the church, dealt with Stewart on September 8, 1881. The debate as reported in the *Argus* the following day makes informative reading. The Presbytery resolved 18 to 8 to censure Stewart, to express deep regret that Strong, who had been present at the meeting when Stewart had made his incautious speech, had done nothing to correct the misrepresentations, and to request Stewart's apology. This was not forthcoming and Stewart was suspended from his seat in the Presbytery. By the time the suspension was lifted some 2 months later, Stewart had resigned his connection with the Presbyterian Church of Victoria. At the Presbytery Strong defended Stewart. Others who took a soft line included a number who were not satisfied that there was any direct evidence of gross doctrinal error. Thus, Rev W. Groundwater Fraser said 'if it could be shown there was anything like an approach to Unitarianism by any minister or elder of the church, he would be one of the first to join the brethren in framing a libel direct against such an individual.' Joseph Hay argued, 'the question is not between Christianity or no Christianity, but between Mr McEachran's interpretation of it and the interpretation of others.' [12] Hay was wrong. Strong's theology and historic Christianity were incompatible as Strong's subsequent ministry was to show. Perhaps the best speech was that given by Rentoul which appears to have been reported in the *Argus* in full from a written manuscript. It gives a very fair view of the issue and is deserving of record (see pages 264-269).

The end of the Strong case 1883
The Strong case was not quite over. Strong was absent from Victoria from March to October 1882. After his return he supported the opening of the Public Library and Art Gallery, an attitude to Sabbath observance which shocked Methodists as well as Presbyterians. The Presbytery expressed 'deep regret' at this violation of an earlier decision (February 1883) on this issue. But the final round in the saga arose from his failure as Chairman to oppose views of an essentially Unitarian character by Anglican layman, Mr Justice Higinbotham, which were embodied in his lecture to the Scots Church Literary Association on 'Science and Religion' delivered on August 1, 1883. The Presbytery made some enquiries, McEachran gave notice that he would prosecute a formal charge against Strong and this was taken up at a meeting of Presbytery on September 18, 1883, at which meeting Strong's resignation from Scots Church was submitted. By the law of the church it could not be accepted while the charges were outstanding.

The Presbytery faced some difficulties because of a hostile press and wide popular support for Strong. The procedure also left something to be desired since no formal statement of charges was drawn up and served on Strong in the approved manner. Strong should have been ready to state his views on the

---

12. Speech of Rev Joseph Hay to the Presbytery of Melbourne September 8, 1881 in the **Argus**, September 9, 1881 (text conveniently in C.R.Badger, op. cit., p.173-181.) For a classic statement of the radical differences see J.G.Machen, **Christianity and Liberalism** (1923). J.G.Machen (1881-1937) was an outstanding American apologist for the Reformed Faith, and led in the founding of Westminster Theological Seminary (1929) and of the Orthodox Presbyterian Church.

fundamental doctrines if he was a man with nothing to hide. However, the upshot was that the Presbytery decided to refer the subject to the Assembly convened to meet in November. Strong was booked to leave for Britain on November 15, so his case was taken up on the second day of sitting (the 13th). The reference was approved but the Assembly had some difficulty in knowing how to proceed. McEachran's motion 'that there is good ground for enquiring into the teaching and conduct of the Rev Charles Strong' was not ideal since much of the basis of suspicion was inference rather than direct statements. Some were reluctant to enter into protracted procedure knowing that Strong was going anyway. The result was that the following day Strong was invited to attend the Assembly (he was absent) and 'disavow all complicity with the erroneous doctrines of Mr Justice Higinbotham's lecture and also to declare his faith in the true deity of the Lord Jesus Christ, the propitiatory character of his death and the real resurrection of his body from the dead.' The vote was 143 to 42.

Strong was at a farewell in the Town Hall with over 2,000 of Melbourne's leading citizens. At a late hour he sent a letter claiming the procedure was unconstitutional but that in any event he could see no good in attending the Assembly. The next day the Assembly resolved that as Strong '....has now left the Colony while his case is still before the supreme court of the Church, the General Assembly hereby declare him to be no longer a minister of the Church, dissolves the pastoral tie between him and the Scots Church congregation and directs the Presbytery to declare the church vacant.' This decision was carried 136 to 6 against an amendment proposing further investigation. No doubt the brethren heaved a sigh of relief, even though they would still have to face a concerted attempt by the managers of the Scots Church to remove the congregation and its property from the denomination, an effort which failed in November 1884, and an attempt to settle Rev George Dods, Strong's assistant at Scots since 1883 and a man of like views. Dr Morrison appealed against the call, and was upheld by the Presbytery in March 1886. In May 1886, Dods' resolute refusal to produce the manuscripts of certain sermons resulted in a declaration of his contumacy, and an appeal to the Assembly was dismissed. Failing to clear his contumacy, Dods was suspended by the Presbytery in March 1887 and returned to Scotland. Slowly, the weakened cause was rebuilt, many leaving to join Strong in the church he began on his return to Melbourne in October 1885.[13]

13. D. Scott, The Halfway House to Infidelity - A History of the Melbourne Unitarian Church 1853-1973 (Melbourne 1980) p. 24, acknowledges that Strong was close theologically to the Melbourne Unitarians. Strong's Australian Church prospered only for a few years and was in difficulty in the 1890s. In his later years, Strong did not retain belief in life after death [personal communication to R.S.Ward by C.R.Badger, July 1988]. While Badger regards Strong as 'the major religious teacher and thinker Australia has ever had' [letter Badger to Ward, July 23, 1988], it seems difficult to avoid the conclusion that Strong was an earnest liberal thinker who found, like many others, that the facts of human history and experience were against him.

Assessment of the Strong case

The Strong case is sometimes seen as a struggle between Free Church and Established Church elements in the PCV. The voting and the personalities do not bear this out. However, it is certainly true that the inlfluence of the Free Church heritage of concern for the maintenance of evangelical truth was more pervasive than in New South Wales, and that a public controversy may not have occurred in its absence. When the battle came it was not a partisan fight between strict former Free Church men and liberal former Church of Scotland men. Further, the fight was not over Presbyterian distinctives but over the common heritage of Christendom. It thus united most men against Strong with most of the minority being personally opposed to Strong's views but being unsure of whether or not he held them or else unwilling to make an issue of them.

It was argued in the 1880s, and Badger continues the tradition, that Strong was the subject of 'bitter persecution.' Badger even characterises McEachran as 'incapable of intellectual effort' and Rentoul as showing 'a kind of malevolence which is possibly pathological,' though he has to admit that Rentoul was 'both intelligent and well informed.'[14] The facts do not sustain such criticisms. The simple truth is that Strong did not assert, maintain and defend the doctrines of the Confession to which he had subscribed, nor did he comply with a directive of the Presbytery in April 1881 to give emphasis to the basic doctrines of redemption. The Presbytery did not seek to get rid of Strong because of his views on other matters.

Badger's book is itself ample evidence that McEachran and Rentoul were right to oppose Strong. Their difficulty was that Strong avoided unambiguous denials of orthodoxy and sinned more by omission than commission. Thus, a Scots Church elder so well informed as Dr Morrison of Scotch College should have been, felt confident in asserting that Scots Church was not Unitarian, did not intend to become so, and in fact accepted as well as Rentoul the great essential doctrines.[15] Consequently it was not easy to deal with Strong.

14. C.R.Badger, op. cit., p.84.
15. Report of the proceedings of the Presbytery of Melbourne in the Argus, September 9, 1881. Compare also A First Christian Catechism (Melbourne 1882), undoubtedly intended for use in Scots Church Sunday School. Note Arthur Paul's review in The Presbyter, February 1884: '...there is not a line to indicate the doctrine of the Trinity, or the divine character of Jesus Christ, or his incarnation, or his relation to such as he redeems or to the law they had broken. There is not a syllable which lifts the life or the death of Jesus above the level of a useful example, or which invests either of them with a vicarious character. There is no breath of information to explain the cause of Christ's death, or to justify it as an event in consistency with the rectitude of God's government. We must conclude, therefore, that all these things were regarded by the framer of this catechism as not essential to be known for the ends of salvation - if, indeed, they were not rather repudiated by him as "old wives' tales".'

The reason just stated contributed to the use of irregular procedure against Strong by the courts of the church. The only regular way of removing a Presbyterian minister for heresy is by a form of process called a libel. The objects of this time-honoured procedure are to ensure that charges are not prosecuted unless the allegations are in fact, if proved, deserving of censure, and that the accused receives a fair trial. Strong was not in fact found guilty by any judicial process, so the finding, which purported to be a judicial act and declared him no longer a minister of the church, was quite irregular.[16]

This is not to say Strong was not guilty and did not fully deserve deposition. However, even a guilty man is entitled to a proper trial and this Strong did not receive.

The general unwillingness to proceed by libel was in part connected with a reluctance to use a legal procedure which might backfire. A libel begins with a recitation of the controverted doctrine as a doctrine of Scripture and the Confession of Faith, goes on to state that the denial of or failure to maintain it warrants censure, and then states the accused to be guilty of the offence and specifies the witnesses/evidence to be adduced. Arthur Paul of the St Kilda Free Presbyterian Church made some very pertinent comments at the beginning of the Strong case:

In this movement against the teaching of serious religious error in the union presbyterian church it is impossible not to feel a lively interest. Whatever the issue may be, it can hardly miss exercising a considerable influence on the interests of religion in the colony. The two manner of people which the union church contains have been brought into direct conflict over the question of Mr Strong's orthodoxy; and whichever side prevails, there will be disappointment at the working of the union. It cannot please the orthodox party if it shall appear that unsound teaching must be put up with in the union church; and it will grievously disappoint the advanced thinkers and teachers of the other party if it be found there is no scope for their liberalized opinions in the body which they have helped to establish. So closely is the movement shut up between these two alternatives, that no doubt the more wary leaders of the union church will lay out their endeavours to bring the inquiry to a stop altogether. Nothing is more essential to the continuance of the union than the avoidance of everything that would sift the foundations on which it has been settled.[17]

In this connection it could be noted that the legal basis of the church tied it to

16. Thus also A.Paul, The Presbyter, January 1884: 'There could not be a sentence where there was no judicial process;' also the opinion of the Procurator of the Church of Scotland (W.Mackintosh) dated September 27, 1884, stated the course of action was incompetent - see text in C.R.Badger, op. cit., pp. 196-198. See also below p.346.

17. A.Paul, The Presbyter, April 1881. Paul considered that the Basis of Union in 1859 not only compromised church-state views but also other matters of difference between the Scottish Presbyterian churches. He held that the Confession was modified in its

the doctrines of the Confession. Property was held on this basis. A judicial process which focussed on the constitution was therefore fraught with dangers for the stability of the union. Paul was too pessimistic in his assessment of the church's willingness to deal with Strong, but he did point to a significant issue. Fear of extended adverse publicity in a hostile press seems also to have been a factor. However, the resolution of matters of a judicial kind by an administrative procedure was part and parcel of a changing mood as the grip on the faith once delivered to the saints weakened. Thus, a very similar case in the United Presbyterian Church of Scotland resulted in 1879 in the deposition of David Macrae for heresy (the denial of eternal punishment) on the mere report of a Committee. Macrae admitted his disagreement with the Confession so maybe this was a special case, yet the significant point was that the UP Synod refused to libel him. Perhaps they were thinking of the previous year when Fergus Ferguson had been libelled, found guilty but had no penalty imposed, not even a rebuke. The age of deciding matters according to politics had arrived as Robertson Smith found at the hands of the Free Church in 1881. In other words, if you were discreet you would be tolerated, but if you were rash you would be out on a mere majority vote without formal trial. [18]

operation as a Standard by the provision of the Basis which granted ministerial status in the PCV 'on an equal footing' to ministers of other Presbyterian churches applying for admission. In his view the 'equal footing' was not agreement in the doctrine of the PCV but the possession of a respectable personal character and a certificate of ministerial status from a Presbyterian church. Paul overstates the case but by and large it had been the practice. The Strong supporters opposed moves to test the soundness of ministers in the faith coming from overseas rather than to rely on a certificate from the overseas presbytery (Proceedings of the Presbytery of Melbourne November 6, 1883, as reported in the Argus the following day.)

18. For Macrae see A.Paul, The Presbyter, October 1879 and on both Macrae and Ferguson see J.H.Leckie, Secession Memories (Edinburgh 1926) pp.230-232. It seems likely that the only case in Australia of a Presbyterian minister being libelled for heresy (as distinct from immorality) was that of E.S.Turnbull by the PCEA in 1979. His error was not in the same league as Strong's. In the constituent churches of the PCA doctrinal questions have rarely been the subject of investigation let alone disciplinary action.

On March 7, 1899, the Presbytery of Melbourne North dealt with a complaint by Rev D.S.McEachran against the teaching of a book called Spiritual Law through the Natural World by Rev Hector Ferguson of Northcote. Ferguson had adopted the leading views of the Swedish scientist-theologian Emmanuel Swedenborg (1688-1772). Swedenborg's followers formed The New Church in 1787 and the church extended to Australia in the 1840s. There were 347 members in the four Australian churches in 1899. Fergusson admitted he had adopted the anti-trinitarian views of the New Church even before he had subscribed the Presbyterian Confession about 1891, and he had subsequently adopted other views which involved rejection of creation ex nihilo, the resurrection of the body, the atoning sacrifice of Christ, and justification by faith. He admitted that he had concealed the source of his views so as to get a better hearing for them and, while he could not now subscribe the Confession, if he was deposed his congregation would support him. It is perhaps not surprising that faced with these admissions the Presbytery did not need to proceed to libel but unanimously declared that Ferguson was no longer a minister of the PCV. For details see The Presbyterian Monthly, 1899, pp. 109-110, 160, 186.

SPEECH OF REV J.L.RENTOUL BEFORE THE
PRESBYTERY OF MELBOURNE, SEPTEMBER 8, 1881
As reported in the **Argus** the following day.

It will be remembered that when 'the Strong case' was first spoken of, the newspapers were deluged with anonymous letters, attacking the Confession of our church, and its teaching about predestination, infant salvation, and so forth. That is an old method. Those same attacks have been made in the old country time out of mind, and those questions have been thrashed out to weariness. The object of the outcry was, of course, to divert attention from the real and vital questions at issue. But now this same outcry is raised, and in more vehement language, by an elder of our church, who is also is law agent. I cannot help asking myself, 'Why this outcry just now about the church's standards?' I do not like to believe that Mr Stewart's deliberate object could be, by assailing thus what he deems the weak points in the church's Confession, to blind the public eye to what is really the one solemn question - a question of life or death to the Christian faith - in all this 'Strong controversy.' But whatever his object was, his words could only have this practical result - to divert attention from the one thing we are all concerned about, or to hide that in a cloud of quite irrelevant matters.

Sir, in the Presbytery's finding in 'the Strong case,' the Confession of Faith, or any matter peculiar to Presbyterianism, was never mentioned. These were the matters mentioned, matters vital to the faith of every Christian church - 'the divine person, the atoning life and death, and the resurrection and ascension of our blessed Lord.' And in the conclusion of my speech, in moving that finding, I said, 'the question is not between 'broad churchmen' and 'evangelicals' at all, but between those of all shades, 'broad' or 'narrow,' who hold the supernatural Lord and Redeemer as the church's Saviour, and those on the other hand who, 'ignoring' any supra-natural Christ, find the root and essence of religious doctrine in the human consciousness.'

Mr Strong on Tuesday said, 'If one thing was to be more desired than another in the church it was that men should be outspoken.' I applauded that statement, though I marvelled at hearing it fall from the lips of Mr Strong. Is it only on such questions as 'creation days' and 'predestination' that it is good for men to be 'outspoken'? Should they not be courageously outspoken also when asked frankly to say what their real opinions are regarding the person and redeeming work of our Lord Jesus Christ, regarding his resurrection from the dead? Or is 'outspokenness' good only for 'elders?' Ought it not be good for ministers also? Mr Strong and his church may be quite sure of this - if he and the leaders of his church will say to this presbytery, 'I believe in our Divine Redeemer, the Lord Jesus Christ, as the mediator and reconciler who worked out the Atonement; I believe in His resurrection from the dead, and his ever-living as our King and intercessor,' this presbytery would be right glad to welcome him, honour him as a brother beloved and reverenced, implore him to stay, and strive together with him for the hope of the gospel. But if neither he nor his people will say one word of outspokenness about that - the centre facts and faith of the gospel - then to apply the term 'outspokenness' or courage to a violent outcry about creation days and so forth, is a sorry travesty of language.

Further, so far as I know, the 'Latitudinarian' party have never asked for or sought simplification of the standards. Quite the contrary. I have been long anxious for a shorter, more simply worded, more symbol-like declaration of our church's *credo* and faith. But I have never found any of the extreme broadish school willing to join me. Nay, more, in presbytery debate on a former occasion I said to Mr Strong and his friends, 'If it is a simpler and shorter Confession of our Faith you want, I am with you as far as you like to go. But if it is a question about the supra-natural in our Lord's life, and about his resurrection from the dead, then I am against you.' But they have never asked for a shorter and simpler Confession. Quite lately Professor Knight, editor of *Scotch Sermons*, that volume which the Unitarian organ claimed as Unitarian sermons, wrote defending these Confessions, and said they would soon be the bulwarks of liberty. Why? but because, on Mr Stewart's principle, men can sign them but believe the opposite. But suppose we had a simpler creed to-morrow, would it help you, gentlemen? I can imagine all about predestination, all about days cut out of the church's Confession; but there would still stand fronting you what can never be cut away from any creed - the Divine Lord, His atoning efficacy, His resurrection in the body, His ever-living to save. This cry about the Confession, at this juncture, whatever its object, is a cry that never touches the church's difficulty.

But Mr Strong, they say, is going home because he has not elbow room here. 'He is watched and hampered.' Where will he have more elbow room? I believe there is more liberty for diverse views in this Presbyterian Church of Victoria than in any church in British Christendom. Is the recent vote in the Assembly of the Church of Scotland encouraging? - that little minority who, to save the minister of Lenzie, proposed a motion condemning his views as one-sided, incomplete and creating alarm, and cautioned him to be careful in his future teaching. Yes, his own friends did that - a far more sweeping motion than was passed by this presbytery. But that would not satisfy the Church of Scotland. It demanded of the minister of Lenzie that he should stand and explain his teaching, and he did stand and explain. This is the Church of Scotland, Mr Strong's church. Yet irrational and misinformed men here will fling mud at this presbytery for simply telling one of its ministers that a paper of his made no mention of the central redeeming facts of Christianity, and for earnestly asking him in future to make these facts prominent. Well, I say, if Mr Strong has not freedom enough here, where will he find it? No church in British lands is going to ignore its own faith and abandon its own jurisdiction.

Further, I will venture to say that the tumultuous feelings of Mr Stewart and others over the question, 'Who is responsible for Mr Strong's action in resigning?' are rather unnecessary. I venture to believe, on such good ground that nothing could shake my belief, that Mr Strong's going home has not been expedited by a single day by this presbytery's action. It will be remembered that in pleading that no action should be taken regarding Mr Strong's paper, I stated (and I had good reasons for stating) that Mr Strong was returning home in any case. It seems also to have escaped the notice of those fiery and outspoken orators at the Scots Church meeting, that Mr Strong said, 'There are other reasons, besides those which I have now assigned, for my wish to be relieved of my charge, and which I could better explain to you in private.' Yes, of course there are; and in the name of honour and truth, let Mr Strong's would-be friends, who are doing him so much injury, be done with their womanish clamour.

I come now to Mr Stewart's language. I wish it could be explained away. Unfortunately it cannot. Mr Stewart's explanations have not touched or removed a single difficulty. Mr Stewart's language has unfortunately been quoted in newspaper editorials all over this colony, and his atrocious representations of the creed of our church accepted and quoted as the church's real creed. And when, again and again, our ministers have had to write to these journals explaining that Mr Stewart's representation of our standards was wholly erroneous, those journals answered (I quote the words of the most influential organ in Melbourne) - 'Mr Stewart is a lawyer and a Presbyterian of note, and the meeting - including the Rev C. Strong - agreed to his views; we took it for granted we should make no mistake in accepting the views as correct.' That is the painful and humiliated position in which our law agent and elder has, by his wild travesty of our standards, involved our church and all of us today.

I deeply regret the language for many reasons; for this among others, that it hinders that very simplification of our creed's language which I for one am earnest after. But it does more. Sir, there is, I understand, but one high school for young gentlemen in this colony in which the Shorter Catechism is taught. It is a Church of England School. The Episcopalian Catechism is taught to Church of England boys. Our catechism is taught to Presbyterian boys. But conceive the feelings of those high-spirited lads that morning, when they were taunted with these dreadful charges - 'Oh, your church teaches infant damnation;' 'your church teaches that the God made the world and all things in six days of 24 hours each, and Mr Stewart, your own law agent, says it.' Mr Stewart and Mr Strong's other friends often talk of Mr Strong's feelings - his feeling ill under misconception. I wonder do they ever think that other men, other churches, other clergymen have feelings too that can be wounded and shamed, when they are travestied, and their church and its creed held up to ridicule and laughter in the midst of our wealthiest congregation. Canon Bromby told us not long ago, in noble words, that he is a dastard who is not in the main loyal to the flag he marches under.

The days of creation

Now let me take one or two of the rash and wild assertions of Mr Stewart. He affirms that our Confession asserts that 'the world and all things therein, visible and invisible, were created in the space of six days of 24 hours each' Sir, in every Church of England in this town it is printed, every Sunday its people and clergy say, 'In six days fhe Lord made heaven and earth, the sea and all that in them is, and rested on the seventh day.' But will Mr Stewart or any man force into their mouths the interpretation Mr Stewart chhoses to put upon these words of Scripture? Will anyone affirm that the Church of England means days of 24 hours each? And why will Mr Stewart twist and strain to his own forced views the language of our church?

Besides, Mr Stewart has here made a great blunder; the facts of scholarship are all against him. Long before the science of geology arose, and solely on such grounds as exegesis, the view prevailed among the fathers that the word 'day' was not a temporal day in the common sense at all. That view was held by Gregory of Nyssa, by Augustine, by Ambrose, by many another. Augustine says:- 'Of what kind these days are it is exceedingly difficult or even impossible for us to conceive how much more to say.' And Calvin held that the first verse in Genesis speaks of the world's creation; the rest of the chapter speaks of its fashioning and forming. Now, sir, the Westminster divines were Augustinian scholars - versed in him as Mr Stewart in some legal handbook. They knew the question about creation-days quite as well as Mr Stewart. But, as Augustine said, they would not dogmatize about it. They did not define it at all. If Mr Stewart had but turned the page of his own Bible he would have found the whole creation period termed 'day.' 'In the day that the Lord God made the earth and the heavens.' Had he read further, he would have found that the period of 40 years in the wilderness is called a day. Again, 'a thousand years are in God's sight as a day.' The Puritan, Mede, quoted in Poole, says - God's days are vast years. But Mr Stewart says the reference to the Sabbath proves *his* interpretation. Well, Augustine did not think so. He deemed *that* argument absurd as long ago as the beginning of the 5th century. The present Professor of Mathematics in Cambridge University, says, 'A certain class of persons maintain that, in the Scripture account, the world was created in six successive days, that is, intervals between sunrise and sunset. It never seems to me that this is a necessary interpretation of the Mosaic account. I see in the Mosaic account a testimony wonderfully correct as to the order of development, whose correctness strikes me with surprise.' But while an eminent scientific layman writes thus, our elder and law agent is pouring scorn on our Confession for using that same Bible word 'day,' and he is the less excusable here, because Mr Yule told this presbytery, in a former debate, that in the Westminster Assembly the question about 'day' was perfectly understood.

Infant salvation

Let me take the question of infant salvation. Mr Stewart has used the horrible words - 'In the Confession there is such a thing as the eternal damnation of infant babies who have never lisped a name.' In his statement on Tuesday, Mr Stewart makes that assertion, if possible, worse, for he tells us it follows 'as a logical and necessary inference' from the whole Calvinistic system. That is, of course, an unintentional, but a no less awful, falsehood. The very opposite is the fact. For it is an inherent principle of Calvinism that every one shall be judged according to his works. But infants are taken away before works, and are saved. Mr Stewart says, 'No sound Calvinist will maintain that every heathen child who dies in infancy will be saved.' Well, then, Dr Candlish and Dr Hodge were not sound Calvinists, for they maintained it.

Sir, if Mr Stewart had read into history for the reason why that phrase 'elect infants' was used, he would never have uttered the awful language of his speech. Canon Farrer - who is a bitter foe to Calvinism - confesses that until the Reformation 'the entire mediaeval Church held the doctrine of the damnation of infants dying unbaptized.' And he quotes Dante's *Inferno*. And who broke for ever out of Christendom that awful doctrine? It was Calvin and Calvinism. They get so much vulgar abuse, let us at least be just to them. Calvin and the Presbyterian reformers said, what at least they had Scripture warrant for - that all the elect are saved. And under that blessed name all dying infants, in heathen lands or Christian, are gathered - safe in Christ. That is our Confession's doctrine, if a man can read right the story of the times that formed its careful phraseology. Here is Calvin's grand language, in a book from which (as Calvin was a trained lawyer as well as theologian) Mr Stewart might learn some law, and a great deal of gospel - the *Institutes*. Calvin is battling with two parties - the Romanists and Ritualists on the one hand, the Anabaptists on the other. The Anabaptist view (says Calvin) that children are only to be regarded as Adam's sons, 'is directly opposed to the truth of God.' He goes on - 'This plainly explodes the fiction of those who consign all the unbaptized to eternal death...If (says Calvin) baptism be necessary to salvation, then they that have withheld baptism from infants have consigned them to eternal death. Let them now consider what kind of agreement that has with the words of Christ, 'Of such is the kingdom of heaven.'' And he goes on to say, 'Every one whom Christ blesses is exempted from the curse of Adam and the wrath of God. But infants are blessed by Him; therefore it follows that they are freed from death.' Such are the glorious words over 300 years ago of John Calvin.

But Mr Stewart says - 'The other phrase, 'others not elected,' includes non-elect infants.' But I answer it is absolutely certain it does nothing of the kind. For the proof from the New Testament set down in the Confession for that expression, 'others not elected,' is, stange to say, the very proof that the Anabaptists had urged against Calvin (the expression found in John 3:36; I John 5:12), viz, that 'they who believe not in the Son, or have not the Son, have not life.' But Calvin grandly answers, 'Scripture does not there speak of the general guilt of Adam's posterity, but only of those who spurn the grace offered to them. *But this* (he adds) *has nothing to do with infants.'* [Inst. 4:16.3] Our Confession, in appending that Scripture to the phrase, 'others not elected,' proves that 'it has nothing to do with infants.' All infants that die are elect and safe; so are all other elect persons, like many heathens and others 'incapable of being called by the ministry of the Word.' The phrase 'others not elected' is contrasted with 'other elect persons;' it has no reference to infants.

Sir, Dr Twisse, head of the Westminster Assembly, said:- 'God will condemn all such as finally persevere in sin.' But infants have done no sin, therefore they will not be condemned. Turrentine, regarding infants universally, says, 'Christian love commands us to hope well for their salvation.' Dr Hodge says, 'All infants that die in infancy are elected.' Dr Candlish says, 'On account of the Atonement the salvation of dying infants is sure. All dying in infancy are elect, and therefore saved.' These are the great Calvinist theologians. Yet Mr Stewart, not content with misrepresenting horribly our church's creed, affirms now that no sound Calvinist would maintain that every heathen child who dies in infancy is saved. His language is rash and bad; but what might surprise one most in these gentlemen who lay claim to light, is its ignorance of facts. But what presses on me most today is - if Mr Stewart believed that our Confession teaches all these awful things, why did he, how could he, sign it? He believed it taught that infant babies were damned, yet he signed it, and drew money by signing. What a light that sets Mr Stewart in! 'Honesty!' Impeach our clergy of dishonesty! And he has signed that, believing it taught all those things. Sooner than sign it, had I believed that, I would have burnt off my right hand in the fire.

The charge of dishonesty

Sir, I have listened patiently to Mr Stewart's explanation, but his charge stands unchanged - that not a man of us believes the doctrines in that book, that not a man of us is an honest man. And another, and, if possible,worse charge of dishonesty is in his speech. He says sneeringly, 'This, then, illustrates the sincerity of Mr Strong's brethren in the presbytery.' Sir, if we are not sincere, that is the darkest and most repulsive kind of dishonesty; and that is the charge levelled at all of us by our law agent.

Predestination and free will

But let me come back. I care comparatively little about these questions regarding the non-essentials of the Confession. Only this I would say - When you cut the problem of predestination and free will out of the Church of England creed and out of ours, you have still got to reckon with it in Paul and the Scriptures. Arnold regrets that 'Paul in Romans falls into Calvinism.' Principal Cairns told the Rev David McRae, in a debate similar to this, that the Arminian theory of God's foreknowledge raises darker and more numerous problems than our doctrine of predestination.

The centre-point

But I want to come away from all those metaphysics of theology to the centre of theology and Christianity. Mr Stewart says:- 'Mr Strong came to Melbourne owing to representations as to the kind of teaching they (in the Scots Church) wanted.' and others spoke of being 'broad and liberal.' Sir, these are vague and empty phrases. In politics, Mr Gladstone is 'broad and liberal'; but Mr Cowan also calls himself 'liberal.' Mr Berry, again, says he is a 'liberal.' In religion, Norman Macleod was a 'liberal.' Peter Menzies was a liberal. I am a liberal. But Page Hopps, the extreme Unitarian, calls himself 'broad and liberal.' Strauss, who flung away all supranatural religion, called himself 'broad' or 'liberal.' Will these gentlemen tell this distracted town what is just the 'broadness and liberalness' they want? We are anxious that this dreadful clamour and division should cease. Will they, like manful men, meet us, and say outspokenly what they mean, that, if possible, we may be at peace?

Sir, let me quote the following words of Peter Menzies, for whom the Scots Church was built, defining the broad-churchism that can be permitted in our church:- 'If by broad-churchism be meant a deviation from the old Catholic form of Christianity - if it be insinuated that Dr Macleod set loosely by the High Priesthood and Divine Sonship of the Lord Jesus Christ - the atoning value of the sufferings of Christ - if it be said that these things were not precious to him, beyond life itself, then I repudiate the slander.' Sir, in 1719, when some Presbyterian Churches of England were wealthier, greater, stronger than the Scots Church, this same cry arose about confessions, these same words, 'broad, liberal,' 'new light,' 'resurrection of our Lord from the dead,' were flung about in the city of Exeter. And now all those churches are mostly empty, fallen, dead - the name Unitarian written upon them. No wonder I, an English Presbyterian, who care little for non-essentials, am concerned about this centre-point of the battle - the divine ever-living person of our Lord Jesus Christ, risen with redemption from the dead. If Mr Strong can tell out those things why should he go? But if he cannot, or will not, then, in God's name, let our church, if necessary be poor; let it be assailed with obloquy; but let it be true to the centre-faith of Christendom, bearing Christ's reproach.

Paragraphing/headings provided for this printing.

20: THE ROAD TO FEDERAL UNION

A consultative *Federal Assembly of the Presbyterian Churches of Australia and Tasmania* was formed in 1886 as a means of drawing the constituent churches closer together. It consisted of the Presbyterian Church of Victoria, [1] the Presbyterian Church of New South Wales, the Presbyterian Church of Queensland, the Presbyterian Church of South Australia, the Presbyterian Church of Tasmania and, from 1890, the Free Church of Tasmania (which united with the Presbyterian Church of Tasmania in 1896). The Presbyterian Church of Eastern Australia was not a participant although Rev Dr George Sutherland of St George's PCEA, Sydney, made moves in that direction but could not obtain the support of his brethren. [2] On July 24, 1901, the Presbyterian Church of Australia was constituted on a basis drawn up by the Federal Assembly and approved by the constituent churches. It remains the basis of the PCA which continued after the formation of the Uniting Church in 1977.

1. The Presbytery of Western Australia was constituted on December 7, 1892 as a part of the PCV. It was disjoined in 1900, and the General Assembly of the Presbyterian Church of Western Australia was formed April 10, 1901. The Basis of the Federal Assembly is most readily found in R. Hamilton, **Jubille History of the Presbyterian Church of Victoria** (Melbourne 1887) Appendix K.
2. Sutherland had written to Rev Dr Donald Macdonald of Melbourne, Convener of a Committee dealing with the subject, and after referring to other matters indicated a change in his personal views on federal union. In March 1884 the PCNSW discussed a proposal on the motion of Rev G. McInnes to open negotiations with the PCEA but this was defeated 26 to 15 in favour of an amendment which instructed the committee to receive and consider any overtures from the Synod of the PCEA. On May 14, 1884, the PCEA Synod, on the motion of elders D. Lobban and S. Martin, unanimously resolved not to entertain union with the PCNSW until it adhered to the principles held by the Free Church in 1843, and abandoned innovations, especially uninspired hymns and instrumental music in the public worship of God. On February 15, 1890, Sutherland moved a motion that the PCEA seek a federal union 'in which Union all our principles of doctrine and worship remain as they are,' but was supported only by Alex Macleod, elder at Wellington. Sutherland resigned various offices because of this defeat.

In considering the period up to the 1901 union, the following points may be noted.

1. To make the union acceptable common standards of ministerial training would be required. As Victoria had the most satisfactory training arrangements it was not surprising that the insistence on high standards came from that state.

2. There was never any real doubt that the doctrinal basis would be the Westminster Confession of Faith, but the way the church would relate to this Confession would be modified. A Declaratory Statement largely derived from the experience of the PCV in handling the Strong case would be incorporated. No powers of change existed in the state constitutions but limited powers of change would be provided in the PCA constitution.

3. The union of the state churches would be a federal one, not an organic one. The state churches were different in size, background and development, and an organic union was not feasible. Each state church surrendered certain powers in clearly defined areas to the General Assembly of the PCA, but retained its own identity and all other powers not surrendered. The General Assembly was to meet normally every three years.

These points will now be taken up in turn.

THEOLOGICAL TRAINING

Presbyterian theological training in Australia had had its advocates before the unions which were formed from 1859. Dr Lang [3] and Rev William McIntyre [4] were the most conspicuous advocates of local training despite the fact that for a generation thereafter there was a general preference for Scottish born and Scottish trained ministers. The same vision for an Australian ministry was shared by James Forbes in Melbourne. Accordingly, the infant Free Presbyterian Synod requested the Free Church Colonial Committee

to send out an accomplished Teacher to take charge of an Academy for instruction in the higher branches of science and literature, and in which

3. Lang's early interest is evident from the Australian College founded in 1831 onwards.
4. McIntyre supervised the training of J.S.White (1822-1902), the first locally trained Presbyterian minister in Australia (ordained by the Synod of Australia early in 1847). In the report of the PCEA Committee on the Training of a Native Ministry to the Synod of 1863, McIntyre lamented the lack of local facilities, stating 'it endangers the adaption of the ministry to the people'...and overcoming the problems of a ministry not derived from the local community 'is not a happy arrangement for a settled church.'

young men might pursue their preparatory studies with a view to the office of the ministry. [5]

With the arrival of Robert Lawson in the Colony on September 11, 1851, what was to become Scotch College had its first Rector.

In the 19th century the only really effective work in theological education on the Scottish model of an institution staffed by full-time professors was that of the Presbyterian Church of Victoria, though a commencement had been made in New South Wales. Before considering the facilities in Melbourne and Sydney, a glance at other areas will be in order.

South Australia

In South Australia, the Presbyterian Church entered into co-operation in theological training through Union College. This began in June 1872 with lecturers from the Presbyterian, Baptist and Congregational churches, and graduated 23 ministers (7 Baptist, 2 Bible Christian, 6 Congregational and 8 Presbyterian) mainly in the 3 or 4 years before it closed at the end of 1886. The secular subjects which were included in the original curriculum were taken over by the University of Adelaide upon its commencement in 1873. The cause of the demise of Union College was the withdrawal of the Presbyterian Church in 1886 in order that it might support the Theological Hall of the PCV.[6] The Free Presbyterian Church of South Australia which had continued after the union in 1865 was led by a remarkable man in the person of Rev James Benny (1824-1910) of Morphett Vale.[7] He was well equipped to train men for the ministry. Three men passed through his hands into useful ministries: George Benny was ordained in 1867, John Sinclair in 1868 at the tender age of 17,[8] and William Buttrose in 1875. Benny was of very orderly mind and efficient in pastoral visiting. His influence on his students was considerable.

Queensland

No university was established in Queensland until 1909. Presbyterian theological training was unorganised until March 1876. At that time a *Presbyterian College and Divinity Hall* was opened in the grounds of the Wickham Terrace Church in Brisbane of which Colin McCulloch was minister.

---

5. **Minutes of the FP Synod of Victoria**, March 6, 1850. Scotch College (the title given in 1855) was at first called 'The Melbourne Academy' and commenced on October 6, 1851 in the building of Chalmers School in Spring Street.
6. Robert J. Scrimgeour, **Some Scots Were Here** (Adelaide 1986) pp. 97-99.
7. Rowland Ward, **The Free Presbyterian Church of South Australia** (Melbourne 1984)
8. See the memorial volume, **The Rev John Sinclair** (Melbourne 1939) 97pp.

It was a kind of university in embryo for all young men and also provided for those preparing for the ministry. However, in the early years the church was not fully behind the project which was not directly controlled by the PCQ anyway. The institution was closed in 1891, but did provide for the training of a number of ministers.[9]

Victoria

Ormond College, Melbourne, was established as a denominational college affiliated with the University and opened in its present location in 1881.[10] The aim was to provide residential accommodation, tutorial services and a spiritual environment to students living in the college while attending university courses in any of the various faculties. The Theological Hall of the PCV had been inaugurated in 1866 with an address by Dr Adam Cairns, its first Principal. From this time on it operated with evening lectures, initially in the manses of the temporary professors and from June 1871 in the former St Enoch's United Presbyterian Church in Collins Street, opposite Scots Church, which was used for the Assembly Hall from 1870 to 1911. The course was of four years duration, with sessions of about four months per year. The Confession of Faith was the Standard and 'a warm evangelical ardour for the salvation of men'[11] was characteristic. In 1881 the Theological Hall was moved to the buildings of Ormond College. In this way the College became linked with theological studies while retaining its original functions to which reference has already been made.

In 1884 the first two full-time professors entered on their work, and the next year the course was extended to six months for each of three years. Systematic Theology and Church History were taught by Murdoch Macdonald, formerly the minister at Toorak. In 1875 he had published a well received volume on the Covenanters.[12] A.A.Hodge's *Outlines of Theology* was used for over 30 years as a basic text, while Charles Hodge's multi-volume *Systematic Theology* was also employed.

J. Laurence Rentoul was the second professor. He was responsible for Apologetics and for both Hebrew and Greek language and exegesis, but in

9. Richard Bardon, **The Centenary History of the Presbyterian Church of Queensland** (Brisbane 1947) pp.34-42.
10. Don Chambers, **Theological Teaching and Thought in the Theological Hall of the Presbyterian Church of Victoria 1865-1906** (Melbourne 1967) p.5. On Ormond College generally including the Theological Hall to 1939 see Stuart Macintyre (ed), **Ormond College Centenary Essays** (Melbourne 1984). Ormond College was named after its chief benefactor, Francis Ormond (1827-89), who invested some 112,000 pounds in Ormond College. Ormond's wealth was gained from careful pastoral investments. His estate was valued at over two million pounds (say $200 million in 1988 terms).
11. Don Chambers, ibid., p.18.
12. **The Covenanters of Moray & Ross** (Edinburgh 1875; 2nd edition Inverness 1892).

1889 the Hebrew and Old Testament section was given to the third full-time staff member then appointed, Andrew Harper. Rentoul was something of a middle way between the old and the new as has been indicated in the previous chapter. While personally suspending judgement on the documentary hypothesis which professed to separate various conflicting sources in the early books of the Bible, Rentoul was open to biblical criticism. However, his own conclusions were generally rather conservative, especially in his latter years which terminated with his death in 1926.* Rentoul sought to face the challenges of his day and was, as we all must be, a child of his time. His definite commitment to the central facts of redemption was a significant factor in bringing the church into the 20th century without a major division between liberals and conservatives. A many-sided man, he was on the border of genius with the idiosyncracies often accompanying that gift.

The third professor was Andrew Harper (1844-1936). He attended Scotch College and the University of Melbourne and went to Edinburgh in 1868 to train at the Free Church College. There he was much influenced by A.B.Davidson. He also studied under Dillman in Berlin and came to doubts such as led him to give up thought of the ministry. In 1883 he wrote:

I returned to Melbourne [in 1873] a convinced believer in the methods of critical study since made so popular by my friend and fellow student, Dr Robertson Smith, and a follower of McLeod Campbell and Maurice as to the atonement. Some time afterwards I wished to know whether my views would be tolerated in the church. I accordingly asked some five or six leading members of the presbytery to hear a statement of my belief, and to consider whether they could receive my signature to the standards with such explanations as I gave them. The late Dr Cameron, a Free churchman, consented; others were more or less doubtful; but Mr Hetherington, though on the best of terms with me personally, would not consent, and by his fervid rigour carried it against me. I consequently had to turn my back upon the ministry of the Presbyterian Church then, though I have very little doubt that no man of a similar theological complexion would be rejected now.[13]

13. Letter to the Editor, Argus,. November 7, 1883. The procedure indicated is quite improper, since no presbytery can relieve a man of the obligations of subscription in terms of the formula, although a difficulty can always be referred to the highest church court. When Harper was ordained an elder the Session took the view that a less stringent adherence to the Confession was allowable: 'the only matter about which there was doubt was whether he was bound to sign our standards as holding all our traditional views of interpretation, especially as to imputation, and the session decided that an elder-elect should not be pledged to theories of interpretation.' [Argus, November 7, 1883 being letter from the Moderator of Cairns' Memorial Session, Dr D. Macdonald]. This approach is reminiscent of that in Lang's Synod of New South Wales 1850-64. Note the distinction between belief in the atonement and rejection of the Biblical interpretation of the atonement as a penal substitution. Thus in his Christian Essentials (Melbourne 1914) p.50ff, Harper rejects the substitutionary 'theory' and states 'the essence of the atonement is contained in the simple belief that whatever was necessary in order that the sin of man might be forgiven was done by God in Christ.' This begs the question.*I am aware of S.McIntyre's different assessment in his ADB article on Rentoul.

274

Harper joined Presbyterian Ladies College in 1875 as English Master, and became Principal in 1879. At this time he also assisted at the Theological Hall in his field of chief interest. He was an elder of Cairns Memorial Church when he wrote the letter of which the above is an extract. He had an international reputation in Hebrew and Old Testament studies by the time he entered on the lectureship in 1889. His critical attitude to Scripture brought considerable criticism upon him and on Rentoul who supported his right to maintain such a position. He addressed the Federal Assembly in 1892 on the subject, and became Professor of Old Testament in 1893.

His insistence that the religious revelation of Scripture and the Christian faith were not dependent upon the historical infallibility of biblical statements became acceptable: his staunchly evangelical teaching and practice, and overseas standing, overpowered his critics. In 1895 the Presbyterian Church also appointed him editor of the *Messenger*, whose columns had previously carried many attacks on his ideas.[14]

Harper's first wife died in 1885, and in 1892 he married the daughter of Dr Robert Rainy, the noted architect of the union between the United Presbyterian Church and the majority of the Free Church of Scotland, which was accomplished in 1900. In 1902, Harper removed to St Andrew's, Sydney.

New South Wales

The PCNSW was more tolerant theologically and less influenced by the zeal and evangelicalism of the Free Church than the PCV. A system of theological training by tutors operated from 1873, but lack of finance to provide full-time staff was a major problem. St Andrew's College, the equivalent to Ormond College, opened in temporary premises in March 1874,[15] but it was not until 1901, when the bequest of J.Hunter Baillie became available, that two full-time professorships were endowed at St Andrew's that were related to the needs of the Theological Hall. The two chairs funded were those of Systematic Theology and Hebrew. As already noted, Andrew Harper filled the latter chair in 1902. John Kinross (1833-1908), who had been Principal of St Andrew's since 1875 and a tutor in the Theological Hall, occupied the chair of Systematic Theology. He resigned as Principal in 1901 and was replaced by Harper, but stayed as Professor until his death in 1908. Of Free Church background, Kinross was a good classical scholar and an earnest man who had moved with the times. His major published work was *Dogma in Religion and Creeds in the Church* (Edinburgh 1896).

14. 'Andrew Harper' in Australian Dictionary of Biography 1891-1939.
15. A.A.Dougan (ed), The Andrew's Book (Sydney 1964) p.11

DOCTRINAL POSITION

The controversy which arose in August 1881 as a result of Stewart's speech in support of Charles Strong had what Aeneas Macdonald calls 'one good outcome.'

It had revealed how widespread and deep were the perplexity and the concern throughout the Church with regard to the Confession of Faith and the duty of signing it which was laid upon ministers and elders.[16]

The PCV Assembly which met in November 1881, made the following decision:

....That for an elder to make serious charges against the teaching of the Confessional Standards of this Church, in presence of the congregation, over which he has been appointed to rule, is in the highest degree inconsistent with the engagement, under which every office-bearer comes, to assert, maintain and defend the whole doctrine contained in the Standards, and deserves grave censure...[17]

In regard to the question of modifying the Standards, preparing a compendium of them, revising them, or simply authorising a declaratory expression of the meaning attached to difficult and disputed passages, there was full deliberation and the following resolution was adopted:

That the General Assembly appoint a Committee to draw up a Declaratory Act setting forth the sense in which the Church understands the statements in the Confession of Faith respecting the Divine decrees, the salvation of children dying in infancy, the dealing of God with the heathen, and the creation of the world in six days, and requires them to be received, as also the sense in which the Church regards the formula as having binding force; and report to the Commission, in order that said Act might be submitted to Presbyteries, and be dealt with at next Assembly.[18]

Declaratory Act 1882

A draft Declaratory Act, largely prepared by Murdoch Macdonald from the decision in the Strong case and a rather similar Act passed by the United Presbyterian Synod of Scotland in 1879, was considered by the Commission of Assembly in May 1882 and remitted to Presbyteries. In November 1882, returns to the remit were to hand. One Presbytery (Hamilton) made no return, one (Macedon) disapproved, five approved (Geelong, Gippsland,

16. Aeneas Macdonald, One Hundred Years of Presbyterianism in Victoria (Melbourne 1937) p.130. Aeneas was a son of Murdoch Macdonald.
17. Text most conveniently in R. Hamilton, A Jubilee History of the Presbyterian Church of Victoria (Melbourne 1888) p.410.
18. R.Hamilton, ibid., p. 410.

Melbourne, Mortlake and Seymour), one (Murrumbidgee) did not think it was necessary and in any event suggested some improvements in the phrasing, while Castlemaine approved the Act so far as it went but thought it did not meet all difficulties, and that it might be better to defer since its adoption might conflict with negotiations for a Federal Union then being mooted. The last two of the 11 Presbyteries (Ballarat and Wimmera) also recommended deferral in view of the prospect of a Federal Union. The Presbytery of Melbourne included about one third of the ministers, and there was no doubt the larger part of the church was in favour of the Act and so voted at the Assembly to approve it in the following terms:

That the Assembly approve of the Declaratory Act as explanatory of the mind of the Church, with respect to the statements in the Confession of Faith to which it refers, and the meaning and binding force of the Formula; but agree to defer its adoption in the meantime, in order to afford an opportunity of considering whether any change of form may be required to adapt it to the purposes of the proposed Union of the Churches of the Australian Colonies.[19]

The legal position

There are several misunderstandings which have grown up about this 1882 Act. The first point to note is that it was not adopted in a formal way for the reason stated and also, doubtless, for legal reasons as will be shown. Secondly, even if it had been adopted in a formal way 'no change whatever was made by the Act in the doctrines of the Confession,' to use D.S. McEachran's words in the debate.[20] This view follows from the nature of a Declaratory Act in Presbyterian law, that is, it is an Act purporting to declare what is the *existing* law of the church in a disputed matter. It also follows even if the Act is regarded as having expressed an actual change in doctrine, for the PCV held her property on the basis accepted in 1859 and enshrined in an Act of Parliament. That basis included no claim to a power to change; therefore, until the consent of Parliament was obtained, any purported change in adherence to the Standards lacked validity.[21]

The position in practice

The Declaratory Act was not without significance as indicating views then current. It was popularly regarded then, as now, as giving some measure of relief in subscription and adjusting the church to the current mood, as well as clarifying some disputed points. Mind you, the Act was not without its

19. Text most conveniently in R.Hamilton, op cit., p.417; debate in **Argus**, November 24, 1882, p.9.
20. A.Macdonald, op. cit., p.130 is mistaken when he says the Act was adopted and that the PCV thus became the first church in the Presbyterian family to give such relief.
21. The legal position was recognised in **The Free Churchman**, June 1882, p.45.

own inconsistencies. The liberty granted in non-essential matters appears inconsistent with the reiterated commitment to the whole doctrine. If one tries to specify what is not essential to the system of doctrine in such a well-matured statement as the Confession of Faith, one sees the difficulty. If, as we have seen, the quibble on the 'six days' is a red herring, then other 'non-essentials' likewise appear similarly, especially when it is borne in mind that the subscription is the whole doctrine of the document, not to the document itself as if its very phrasing is perfect. Again, 'the Calvinistic or Reformed system of doctrine' is finely embodied in the Confession with the peculiarities which individuals holding that system may adopt not finding a place in it.

Observers from outside the PCV regarded the Declaratory Act as legally incompetent and likely to be pernicious in practice because of its perceived equivocation.

It appears to have been composed with a design to soothe opponents, as well as to satisfy friends...Quite possibly, the Act will be ignorantly applauded by one section of the public, as if it were a solid exposition of the great doctrine, and a vindication of it against the exceptions of sceptical and irreligious critics. Another section will see it as a triumph for these very critics and their criticisms, and will read the Act as a surrender of the Westminster doctrine. Practically, we believe, the latter will prove to be in the right. [22]

Interestingly, no specific criticism was made of the liberty of opinion clause, probably because it was so qualified by the adherence to the Reformed system of doctrine, that the liberty granted was theoretically minimal, and only what the practical good sense of the church had always recognised.

Some men of liberal outlook, such as the talented William Henderson of Ballarat, (1826-1884), considered the liberty in non-essential matters important. Henderson added:

There are statements in the Confession that contradicted each other, and there were times when he could only satisfy his own conscience by comparing one passage with another, and drawing his own deduction...The Declaratory Act will satisfy conscientious scruples within the church, and on that ground he would support its adoption. [23]

One supposes that it was natural enough for those who found real contradictions in Holy Scripture to find them also in the Confession. Their philosophical outlook, the presuppositions drawn from rationalism, meant contradictions would be found where there are none. Thus, in writing to

22. The Free Churchman, June 1882, p.46.
23. Report of Assembly debate in Argus, November 24, 1882.

Charles Strong on March 12, 1881, Henderson refers to the Confession as full of inconsistencies. In Chapter 3, concerning the Decrees of God, he states two statements there concerning the unchangeable will of God and the freedom of man 'are evidently quite irreconcilable; but then we are at liberty to take which side we like. And so all through.'[24] A few years later, Charles Strong commented on the subscription vow in a way which shows he had come to a more honest position.

Others speak of 'essentials' and 'non-essentials'. The Act of Parliament, however, knows no such distinctions, and this distinction really abolishes the Standards as Standards, opening the flood-gates to endless diversity of opinion...Many accept the Standards 'historically,' regarding them as the old forms of ever new truth. But while this may be the most rational and honest way of regarding them, it does not satisfy the 'law,' and it were better that there should be no appearance even of equivocation or of unreality to the popular mind.[25]

The decision about the Declaratory Act attracted 9 simple dissents. Judging from the record of the debate, Allan McVean believed in 'maintaining the Standards of the Church in their strict simplicity;' J.M.Abernethy thought the Act 'might bar the way to a much required revision of the Confession of Faith;' while Samuel Robinson thought it divisive. So there were differences on the negative side as well as the affirmative.

Liberal evangelicalism

At least one thing is clear about the 1882 Declaratory Act: it was certainly specifically intended to require a chief place be given certain objective supernatural facts on which the Christian Faith rests, 'especially the Incarnation, the Perfect Obedience and Expiatory Death, and the Resurrection and Ascension of our Lord, avoiding such forms of teaching as might be fitted to weaken or destroy the faith of the people in the same.'

Over the next ten or twenty years, the characteristic teaching from Presbyterian pulpits might be described as 'liberal evangelical.' In other words, the main truths about God, including the deity of Christ and his miracles, his suffering for our sin and real resurrection from the dead, were taught but a high view of Scripture as verbally inspired was increasingly abandoned, and many variations on other doctrines existed. The spirit of the times has already been indicated in an earlier chapter. Harper's address to the Federal Assembly of 1892 and George McInnes' address as PCNSW Moderator in 1894 are indicative as previously discussed.

24. The letter is in C.R.Badger, **Charles Strong and the Australian Church** (Melbourne 1971) pp. 169, 170.
25. Charles Strong, **The Westminster Assembly of Divines**, p.12. This is a printed copy of the lecture. (Joint Theological Library at Ormond College reference is MW64 P186(9).

The lack of really effective opposition to the new theology indicates both lack of leadership and confusion of issues. The liberal evangelicals were not secularists, and were opposed at this time to that radicalism which denied the historical character of Christ's deeds. They had undermined the foundation but the building had not yet collapsed. The orthodox minority did not have the leadership and the mood of the church was against them. Instead of making a stand on principle they opted to continue in the church. Thus, they accepted the principle of comprehension which had been very obvious in New South Wales all along. They justified their position to their conscience by an unjustified appeal to the invisibility of the church of the redeemed. That there is an aspect of invisibility to the church as stated in the Confession is true: the church on earth always imperfectly reflects the membership of those who are Christ's redeemed. However, so far as human responsibility is concerned there is no invisible church but rather a visible one which one can see and join. This capitulation was general in the Protestant churches and resulted in many non-denominational mission agencies and the like coming into existence to channel the efforts of those who retained membership in the liberal churches. One's assessment of their action should take account of the common belief that the liberal dominance was a passing phase. However, it was to be a long time passing and havoc would be wrought in the church meanwhile.

There was certainly no prospect that the Westminster Confession would be dropped or significantly altered: there was too much sentiment against such a course. Some shrank from tampering with such a significant document which they regarded either as adequate or adequate until the real value of the new theology had been found from experience. Others did not want a new creed because it might end up requiring a very tight adherence albeit to fewer doctrines, and they would rather keep their options open and treat the Confession as an historical document rather than a binding creed. In November 1898, an overture supported by Dr Rentoul was discussed in the PCV Assembly. It sought to prevent confusion and remove difficulty in relation to the creed of the church in the proposed federal union by either altering the Declaratory Act or by drawing up brief Articles of Religion such as had been adopted by the Presbyterian Church of England in 1890. While not wanting to call these Articles unorthodox, they were in a form which would not provide an effective counter to the divergencies from orthodoxy then current, and Scripture was certainly not given a place of prominence in them.[26] As it turned out the suggestion of a shorter and simpler statement was not adopted, but the 1882 Declaratory Act was suitably reworked and incorporated in the Scheme of Union.

26. The text of the Articles is most conveniently in P.Schaff/D.S.Schaff, **The Creeds of Christendom** (6th edition, New York 1931) Vol. 3, pp.916-919.

DECLARATORY ACT 1882 OF THE PRESBYTERIAN CHURCH OF VICTORIA
(Not formally adopted but in practical effect.)

WHEREAS questions have been raised as to the meaning of certain statements in the Confession of Faith, relative to the divine decrees, the salvation of children dying in infancy, the dealing of God with persons beyond the operation of the ordinary means of grace, and the creation of the world in six days; but, also, as to the meaning and binding force of certain statements in the Formula, by which the ministers and elders of the Presbyterian Church of Victoria profess adherence to the Standards of the Church, and whereas it is desirable, in order to remove such doubts, authoritatively to declare the sense in which the Church understands these statements, the General Assembly resolves to declare, and does hereby declare:-

1. That the doctrine of God's eternal decree, including the doctrine of election to eternal life, is held as defined in the Confession of Faith, chap. iii, section 1, where it is expressly stated that, according to this doctrine, 'neither is God the Author of sin, nor is violence offered to the will of the creature, nor is the liberty or contingency of second causes taken away, but rather established;' and, further, that the said doctrine is held in connection and harmony with the truth, that God is not willing that any should perish, but that all should come to repentance, that He has provided a salvation sufficient for all, adapted to all, and offered to all in the gospel, and that every hearer of the gospel is responsible for his dealing with the free and unrestricted offer of eternal life.

2. That while none are saved except through the mediation of Christ, and by the grace of the Holy Spirit, who worketh where and when and how it pleases Him; while the duty of sending the gospel to the heathen who are sunk in ignorance, sin and misery is imperative, and while the outward and ordinary means of salvation for those capable of being called by the ministry of the Word are the ordinances of the gospel, in accepting the Standards it is not required to be held that any who die in infancy are lost, or that God may not extend His grace to any who are without the pale of ordinary means, as it may seem good in His sight.

3. That, in accordance with the practice hitherto observed in this Church, liberty of opinion is allowed on such points in the Standards as are not essential to the system of doctrine therein taught, as the interpretation of the 'six days' in the Mosaic account of creation, the Church guarding against the abuse of this liberty to the injury of its unity and peace.

4. That the Church does not regard subscription to the Formula as binding the person subscribing to anything more in respect of doctrine than the Formula requires expressly and in terms, viz:- To own and believe the whole doctrine contained in the Standards of this Church as an exhibition of the sense in which he understands the Scriptures, and to acknowledge it as a confession of his faith, meaning by the 'whole doctrine contained in the Standards,' the system of doctrine in its unity, formulated in the Confession of Faith, catechetically exhibited in the Larger and Shorter Catechisms, implied in the statements of the Directory for Public Worship, the Form of Presbyterian Church Government, and the Second Book of Discipline, and historically known as the Calvinistic or Reformed System of Doctrine; but that the Church has always regarded, and continues to regard, those whom it admits to the office of the ministry as pledged to profess, defend, and teach this system in its integrity, and, while giving due prominence in their teaching to all the doctrines it includes, to give a chief place to the central and most vital doctrines thereof, with those objective supernatural facts on which they rest, especially the Incarnation, the Perfect Obedience and Expiatory Death, and the Resurrection and Ascension of our Lord, avoiding such forms of teaching as might be fitted to weaken or destroy the faith of the people in the same.

NOTE RE SOURCES

Preamble	Murdoch Macdonald
Section 1	Taken from Section 2 of UPS Act 1879 except 'doctrine of God's eternal decree' substituted for 'doctrine of the divine decrees'.
Section 2	Taken from Section 4 of UPS Act 1879 with omission, possibly accidental, of 'clear and' before 'imperative'.
Section 3	Taken from Section 7 of UPS Act 1879 except 'as are not essential to the system of doctrine therein taught' substituted for 'not entering into the substance of the faith' so being more precise.
Section 4	Murdoch Macdonald with the 8 lines beginning 'but the Church' derived from decision of the Presbytery of Melbourne in the matter of Charles Strong on April 28, 1881.

The text of the Declaratory Act is taken from the printed minutes of the PCV.

BASIS OF UNION FROM THE SCHEME OF UNION, JULY 24, 1901

I. THE SUPREME STANDARD of the united church shall be the word of God contained in the Scriptures of the Old and New Testaments.

II. THE SUBORDINATE STANDARD of the united church shall be the Westminster Confession of Faith read in the light of the following declaratory statement:-

1. That in regard to the doctrine of redemption as taught in the subordinate standard, and in consistency therewith, the love of God to all mankind, His gift of His Son to be the propitiation for the sins of the whole world, and the free offer of salvation to men without distinction on the ground of Christ's all-sufficient sacrifice, are regarded by this church as vital to the Christian faith. And inasmuch as the Christian faith rests upon and the Christian consciousness takes hold of certain objective supernatural historic facts, especially the incarnation, atoning life and death and the resurrection and ascension of our Lord, and His bestowment of His Holy Spirit, this church regards those whom it admits to the office of the holy ministry as pledged to give a chief place in their teaching to these cardinal facts and to the message of redemption and reconciliation implied and manifested in them.

2. That the doctrine of God's eternal decree....(as per section 1 of the 1882 Victorian Declaratory Act).

3. That while none are saved...(as per section 2 of the 1882 Victorian Declaratory Act except for the substitution of 'subordinate standard' for 'Standards').

4. That in holding and teaching according to the Confession of Faith, the corruption of man's nature as fallen, this church also maintains that there remain tokens of man's greatness as created in the image of God, that he possesses a knowledge of God and of duty - that he is responsible for compliance with the moral law and the call of the Gospel, and that although unable without the aid of the Holy Spirit to return to God unto salvation he is yet capable of affections and actions which of themselves are virtuous and praiseworthy.

5. That liberty of opinion is allowed on matters in the subordinate standard not essential to the doctrine therein taught, the church guarding against the abuse of this liberty to the injury of its unity and peace.

6. That with regard to the doctrine of the civil magistrate and his authority and duty in the sphere of religion as taught in the subordinate standard the church holds that the Lord Jesus Christ is the only King and Head of the church, 'and Head over all things to the church, which is his body.' It disclaims accordingly intolerant or persecuting principles and does not consider its office-bearers in subscribing the confession as committed to any principle inconsistent with the liberty of conscience and the right of private judgment, declaring in the words of the confession that 'God alone is Lord of the conscience.'

III. Any proposed revision or abridgement of the subordinate standard of the church or restatement of its doctrine or change of the formula shall before being adopted be remitted to the local assemblies and through them to the presbyteries, and no change shall be made without the consent of a majority of the local assemblies and three-fifths of the presbyteries of the whole church and a majority of three-fifths of the members present when the final vote of the General Assembly is taken.

IV. On any change being made in the basis of union in accordance with section III, if any congregation thereupon refuses to acquiesce in the change and determines to adhere to the original basis of union, the General Assembly is empowered (1) to allow such Congregation to retain all its congregational property, or (2) to deal in such other way with the said property as to the assembly may seem just and equitable.

V. Any proposed change in either of the two preceding sections III and IV shall be made only under the provisions contained in section III.

VI. Formula to be signed by ministers and elders at their ordination or induction and by probationers on receiving licence:-

I own and accept the subordinate standard of this church, with the explanations given in the articles contained in the declaratory statement, as an exhibition of the sense in which I understand the Holy Scriptures, and as a confession of my faith. I further own the purity of worship practised in this church and the Presbyterian government thereof to be founded on the Word of God, and agreeable thereto, and I promise through the grace of God I shall firmly and constantly adhere to the same, and to the utmost of my power shall in my station assert, maintain, and defend the doctrine, worship, and government of this church.

THE SCHEME OF UNION

The Scheme of Union upon which the Presbyterian Church of Australia was constituted on July 24, 1901 in the Sydney Town Hall is divided into three parts: a Preamble, being a short recital of the churches entering union and with what end in view, the Basis of Union, containing the key doctrinal matters with limited powers of alteration, and the Articles of Agreement, covering administrative matters with more general powers of amendment. The Basis of Union is reproduced on the preceding page.

Section I: Supreme Standard - errant or inerrant?

The first section affirms the Word of God contained in the Scriptures of the Old and New Testaments to be the supreme standard. This wording is very similar to that in the Basis of the PCNSW adopted 1864/65, which basis certainly did not intend to draw a distinction between the Scriptures and the Word of God as if only some of the former was the Word of God, a distinction which is a modern one. The Westminster Confession I:2 states: *Under the name of Holy Scripture, or the word of God written, are now contained all the books of the Old and New Testaments...all which are given by inspiration of God, to be the rule of faith and life.* The Shorter Catechism of 1647 uses the form: *The word of God, which is contained in the Scriptures of the Old and New Testaments, is the only rule.. ,* while the Larger Catechism is actually shorter at this point but also unambiguous for modern readers: *The Holy Scriptures of the Old and New Testaments are the Word of God, the only rule of faith and obedience.* Thus section 1 in any interpretation which is consistent with the Confession is fully orthodox and upholds the full inspiration of Scripture.

The difficulty is that section two states the subordinate standard is the Westminster Confession of Faith read in the light of a 'declaratory statement' which includes paragraph 5 allowing 'liberty of opinion' on matters in the subordinate standard not essential to the doctrine therein taught. As it is known that the majority of those most involved in framing the Basis did not regard verbal inspiration as essential to the Reformed doctrine and some thought it a positive hindrance and in fact affirmed that it was not in the Confession anyway, it may be held that the meaning section one would otherwise bear is compromised. Against this is the consideration that the intention of the framers ought to be found in the words they used not the views of parties. It could also be argued that the 'liberty of opinion' clause is a liberty to hold certain opinions but not to teach them - although this does not seem satisfactory given that the natural sense appears to be that the abuse guarded against is not the abuse of teaching as such but the abuse of teaching of a certain kind, namely such as disturbs the unity and peace of the church.

If section two is held to interpret section one, then a doctrine of Scripture which allows inerrancy is acceptable so long as 'certain objective supernatural historic facts' are emphasised in the message of redemption, and any other matters essential to the doctrine contained in the Confession are maintained. It should be noted that there is no power to change section one.

Section II: Subordinate Standard - one only

It has sometimes been said that there are two subordinate standards, the Confession of Faith and the Declaratory Statement. This is erroneous. There is only one subordinate standard and that is the Confession of Faith read in the light of the Declaratory Statement. 'Thus what is declared essential by the Declaratory Statement must be treated as essential; where the Declaratory Statement gives a meaning or interpretation to the Confession it is to be read as having that meaning or interpretation.'[27] There is no separate standard of worship or government, the other Westminster Standards having been discarded, although the Confession does state some principles in these areas.

Section II (1): Doctrine of redemption

The first sentence is taken with small alterations from the United Presbyterian Act of 1879, while the last sentence is derived through the Victorian Act from the decision about Charles Strong by the Presbytery of Melbourne in 1881. These declarations of what is 'vital to the Christian faith' and what ministers are 'pledged to give a chief place' to in their teaching are on this account not subject to the liberty of opinion. In short, every minister is bound to teach and maintain the great truths summed up in the Apostles' Creed and has no liberty to reinterpret these to destroy their objective, supernatural and historic character. The point of uncertainty lies in whether the references to the 'love of God to all mankind, His gift of His Son to be the propitiation for the sins of the whole world, and the free offer of salvation to men without distinction on the grounds of Christ's all-sufficient sacrifice' are to be regarded as modifying or qualifying in any way the 'doctrine of redemption taught in the Subordinate Standard.' If they are not to be so regarded then the quoted words merely highlight important truths and state they are held consistently with the doctrine of redemption in the Confession. In this case there can be little objection.

However, there is every reason to believe that there is an intention to do more than merely highlight some truths held consistently with the doctrine of the Confession. There is no preamble to give clues as to the motivation, nor is there a corresponding section in the Victorian Act of 1882. Yet as taken directly from the the United Presbyterian Act of 1879, with the

27. F.M.Bradshaw, **Basic Documents in Presbyterian Polity** (Melbourne 1961) p. 92 n 4.

substitution of 'all-sufficient' for 'perfect' in reference to Christ's sacrifice, it is evident there is a twist in it so that some weakening of the straightforward Calvinism of the Confession results. There is certainly no clarification - the true function of a declaratory statement. False issues are suggested as if all pledged to the Confession were not thereby pledged to John 3:16 and I John 2:2 or as if to suggest that the doctrine of the Confession in theory and/or practice leaned to hypercalvinism. While capable of a good sense the inherent ambiguity in the wording allows an Arminian infiltration which undermines the nature of the atonement as a penal substitution of Christ for his elect people. This was the intention in the United Presbyterian Church of Scotland and it appears to have the same motivation in the Australian version. It should be noted that the fact of the atonement but not its nature is referred to in the Statement. At the time of the Strong case and later, diverse views of the nature of the atonement were openly held and accepted.

This paragraph of the Statement declares essential doctrine and therefore the liberty of opinion clause does not apply to it. Nevertheless, the ambiguity in the paragraph itself does give considerable liberty although the ill-defined bounds do not allow a wholesale jettisoning of the historic basis of the faith.

Section II (2): God's eternal decree

This paragraph is derived from Section 4 the United Presbyterian Act of 1879 via Section 1 of the Victorian Act of 1882. The preamble of each Act varies and in construing the meaning it is appropriate to refer to the preamble of 1882 with its background in the Strong case rather than to that of 1879 which appears more definite in offering relief from the teaching of the Confession.

The paragraph may be considered as (1) an assertion of certain truths with a view to repudiating the fatalistic construction of J.C.Stewart and others, and (2) from 'and, further,' it is a statement that the doctrine of the Confession is held in connection and harmony with certain other truths. The end result might be regarded as innocuous and in fact valuable, though one does not need the paragraph to guarantee the free offer of the gospel.[28] However, the statements in the last half, though true in themselves and in context, lack a full context in the paragraph. In other words, it may well be considered that parts of an harmonious whole have been isolated as abstract propositions to which the doctrine of the Confession must harmonize. Thus those who considered the strict Calvinism of the Confession irksome or who, like Rev William Henderson, considered the doctrine in the Confession to be riddled with inconsistencies, would be able to hold a modified doctrine of

28. Compare also Shorter Catechism 31 which refers to 'Jesus Christ freely offered to us in the Gospel.' On the effect of somewhat similar changes by the PC in the USA in 1903 note B.B.Warfield's article in **Selected Shorter Writings - II** (New Jersey 1973) pp. 370-410. Warfield did not regard the changes as having the effect of introducing heterodoxy. There was no liberty of opinion clause however.

the decrees so long as it included the propositions in the last part of the paragraph. Further, a scripture reference such as 'God is not willing that any should perish' (2 Peter 3:9) is a faithful saying but isolated from the context of a carefully constructed doctrine of the divine decrees it brings confusion. The 'will' of which the text speaks is not God's will of purpose or determination at all, otherwise all would be saved, or, if it is thought the Greek word rendered 'willing' in the Scripture context implies purpose, then it refers to God's love for those of the elect who have not yet repented. The last possibility is no relief for those with scruples about the doctrine in the Confession, and the first view does not assist either unless the Arminian understanding of God's purpose is adopted, and that was probably intended, albeit the doctrine of the Confession is not unambiguously contradicted.

Section II (3): Infants and those outside the reach of ordinary means

This section permits the belief that God may save through Christ and by his Spirit some or all those who are beyond the reach of the ordinary means of the preaching of the Gospel. This would include the mentally incapable as well as those who have never heard the Gospel. Whatever may be said for this in the abstract it is really putting the focus on the speculative for what God may or may not do in such cases is not revealed in Scripture. It is also allowed that one is not bound to believe that any who die in infancy are lost, and the background in J.C.Stewart's remarks is evident although the wider restlessness with the Confession's perfectly sufficient statement of the *way* infants are saved and leaving the *number* to one side, is evident in the derivation of the paragraph from the United Presbyterian Act of 1879. The paragraph could be constructed more logically[29] but of itself is not destructive though suggesting and perhaps encouraging a tendency away from the robustness of Reformed doctrine and practice.

Section II (4): Man's fallen nature

This paragraph is taken from the 1892 Declaratory Act of the Free Church of Scotland with the deletion of 'whole' before 'nature as fallen' and three other small stylistic changes. The matters of which it treats are covered in the Confession VI: 1-6 [Of the Fall of Man, of Sin, and of the Punishment thereof] and XVI: 1-7 [Of Good Works].[30]

The motivation for this paragraph may be simply to disavow erroneous conclusions drawn by some from the teaching of the Confession concerning man's sinfulness and utter inability in spiritual things. The last line or two seems to involve a softening of Confession XVI:7, although the teaching

29. See, for instance, the suggestion of the Presbytery of Murrumbidgee in **Returns on Remits** of PCV Assembly, November 1882 p. vi-vii.
30. The criticism of the Free Presbyterian Church of Scotland on this clause as well as others in the 1892 Act is too sweeping, **F.P.[of S] Magazine**, October 1896 [1896-97 Volume reprinted circa 1987 in Inverness].

expressed by the words of the paragraph is not seriously astray even if not fully precise. It provides some complementary statements while affirming the Church holds and teaches according to the Confession of Faith 'the corruption of man's nature as fallen.' It thus appears that the liberty of opinion clause does not apply to this doctrine and the Formula requires it to be asserted maintained and defended.

Section II (5): Liberty of opinion

In assessing the meaning of this famous paragraph it will be helpful to state what we have thus far found to be essential and vital, and teaching to which the church and its office-bearers are pledged.

The following are essential doctrines:

a) the Word of God contained in the Scriptures, the meaning of this phrase being determined by the Confession read in the light of the Declaratory Statement. The possibility/probability verbal inspiration is compromised by the liberty of opinion paragraph has been canvassed above.

b) the love of God to all mankind, God's gift of his Son to be the propitiation for the sins of the whole world, the free offer of salvation to all without distinction on the ground of Christ's all-sufficient sacrifice - these points being held in consistency with the 'doctrine of redemption' as taught in the Confession.

c) certain objective supernatural historic facts, especially the incarnation the atoning life and death and the resurrection of our Lord and his bestowment of the Holy Spirit to be given a chief place together with the message of redemption and reconciliation implied and manifested in them. There is no liberty on these points except to the extent that there are interpretations or explanations in the Confession which are regarded as not essential to the doctrine of redemption implied and manifested in them.

d) the doctrine of God's eternal decree as defined in Confession III: 1 and in connection and harmony with the truth that God is not willing that any should perish, but all should come to repentance, that he has provided a salvation sufficient for all and adapted to all and offered to all in the gospel, and that every hearer is responsible for his dealing with the free and unrestricted offer of eternal life.

e) salvation only through the mediation of Christ and by the grace of the Holy Spirit; the imperative duty of missionary work; the ordinances of the Gospel and calling by the Word.

f) the corruption of man's nature as fallen according to to the teaching of the Confession together with certain complementary truths.

Leaving aside all questions of motive and intention not determined from the context and words used, it thus appears that there is no liberty on any of the above points, nor on any other matters that are 'essential to the doctrine' taught in the Confession. But what is essential is not defined.

In seeking the meaning of the liberty of opinion clause we may note its antecedents. In the United Presbyterian Act of 1879 it reads:'...liberty of opinion is allowed on such points in the Standards not entering into the substance of the faith, as the interpretation of the 'six days' in the Mosaic account of creation...' In the Victorian Act of 1882 it is liberty 'on such points in the Standards, as are not essential to the system of doctrine therein taught, as the interpretation of the 'six days'...', and the system of doctrine is later in the Act defined, inter alia, as the Calvinistic or Reformed system of doctrine. In the Free Church of Scotland Act of 1892 liberty is 'on such points in the Confession as do not enter into the substance of the Reformed Faith therein set forth.' An earlier draft of the Australian Declaratory Statement was in the same form as the Victorian Act of 1882 but was amended in 1900 to the present form.

What are matters 'not essential to the doctrine'? At first glance it might appear that this is a less precise term than 'system of doctrine' since it lacks the inference of logical completeness and consistency. But while it may have been the intention to weaken the requirement of adherence to the Reformed system of doctrine in its completeness, the substitution of the word 'doctrine' does not have this effect. For reflection shows that 'doctrine' is another word for 'teaching' and thus the single word commits to the whole teaching of the Confession. But as the intention evidenced from the words is to make some relaxation of commitment to the whole teaching we are left to give 'doctrine' a meaning equivalent to 'system of doctrine' (ie. the whole teaching minus matters not essential to the Reformed system eg. prohibited degrees of marriage) or perhaps the more vague 'substance of the Reformed Faith.' Notice the liberty is not a liberty on matters not essential to the Christian Faith as if the nature of that Faith is left to oneself, but it is a liberty in matters that are not essential to the system of teaching set out in the Confession. One is not bound to such elements. They would include a particular interpretation of the 'six days' although the Confession uses only the language of Scripture at this point and does not state 'six *literal* days.'[31] It would include the reference to the Pope as Antichrist, prohibited degrees in marriage, and some matters of worship, although

31. As erroneously stated by Rev R.H.C.Crowe in an address on 'The Declaratory Statement' on September 28, 1962 reprinted by the Presbyterian Church of Queensland in 1980. Crowe cited Robert Swanton as providing this illustration. Crowe's address takes the view that the Declaratory Statement was designed to strengthen the Calvinistic position by removing misconceptions. Similarly, the address by Robert Swanton on March 11, 1975 'Our Heritage and Destiny' [Hawthorn, Victoria 1975] does not

most items relate to the imperfection of expression of a doctrine rather than the doctrine itself and hence, seeing subscription is to the doctrine not the document, one does not need the liberty of opinion clause to gain relief.[32]

One final point is the provision for guarding against the abuse of the liberty granted. This provision perhaps suggests that a wider variance from the doctrine of the Confession was envisaged than has been suggested, since it is hard to see abuse coming if the liberty granted is so minimal as a proper construction of the language suggests. At any rate, assuming the liberty is a liberty to teach as well as to hold certain opinions, the church claims the right to guard against abuse that might disturb her unity and peace. This provision may be criticised because in the absence of clarity on what is or is not 'essential' it permits a somewhat fluctuating creed, and also seems to suggest that it is not the church's duty to earnestly contend for the *whole counsel* of God. Still, the provision offers some scope to clarify the doctrinal commitment of ministers and elders. While the Declaratory Statement cannot be changed,[33] it would be possible for the Assembly to declare or clarify the meaning of certain disputed matters in an unambiguous way and require adherence to this in the teaching ministry. The obvious areas for attention would be Scripture and the nature of the atonement. If the Assembly declared that the doctrine of the Confession on Scripture was such that teaching which did not maintain the verbal inspiration of Scripture in the original writings fell short of including an essential element of the doctrine of the Confession, and similarly in reference to the covenant-conditioned substitution of Christ, the testimony of the church on these vital matters would be less ambiguous, and the logical coherence of the truth would tend to ensure that variations from other doctrines of the Confession were not major. Such a declaration has not yet (1989) been made.

concede an attempt to give a wider liberty of opinion other than a private personal liberty, but neither address adequately discusses the background. In my judgement the only question is whether or not the Basis gave the liberty away from historic Calvinism that was the clear intention of many, and my conclusion is that the Basis was treated as giving quite wide liberty but from a strictly legal point of view gave much less liberty than most supposed. Professor Crawford Miller's article in **Australian Presbyterian Life**, December 1977 is a more accurate assessment even if its doctrinal conclusions [general atonement along McLeod Campbell's line, radical Biblical criticism] are less palatable to those holding the classic Reformed theology. Rev Paul Cooper's article in APL, March 1987 is succinct but denies the desire to dilute some distinctives of the Confession while retaining the historic basis of the saving work of Christ. The moves for wider union among Protestants at the inaugural GAA in 1901 are indicative of a widespread view of what was 'essential' and will be discussed in a following chapter.

32. John Murray (1898-1975), one of the ablest Reformed theologians of the 20th century, notes several 'blemishes' in his valuable article, **The Theology of the Westminster Confession of Faith** in **Collected Writings**, Volume 4 (Edinburgh 1982) pp.241-263.
33. The power of change in Section III of the Basis is in respect of the subordinate standard and the formula and not the Declaratory Statement in whose light the subordinate standard is read. This is Bradshaw's position, op. cit., p.93, n 5.

FEDERAL BASIS

The 1901 Basis is distinctly federal in its nature as already noted on page 271. The GAA has supreme authority in regard to doctrine, worship and discipline by Article IV of the *Articles of Agreement* but does not have powers in respect to the government of the church.

The supreme power of government is vested in the state assemblies. What is more, it is this supremacy in government that is the source of the continued separate identity of the state churches. It is because of this that a presbytery, a session or a congregation is primarily such in relation to the relevant state church, not the Presbyterian Church of Australia.[34]

It is for this reason that the matter of women elders is a matter for state assemblies and not the GAA (as noted by the 1985 GAA). As the GAA does have power in respect of admission to the ministry, the ordination of women to the ministry comes within its powers.

MODERATORS OF THE GENERAL ASSEMBLY OF AUSTRALIA

Rev John Meiklejohn was by common consent the great architect of union and he was the first Moderator. The full list is as follows:

1901	John Meiklejohn, MA, DD, Melbourne
1902	Alexander Hay, DD, Rockhampton, Q
1903	David Bruce, DD, Sydney
1905	P.J.Murdoch, MA, Melbourne
1906	Thomas E.Clouston, DD, Sydney
1907	Peter Robertson, Ipswich, Q
1909	John Ferguson, Sydney
1910	W.S.Rolland, Melbourne
1912	J.Laurence Rentoul, MA, DD, Melbourne
1914	George Davidson, MA, DD, Adelaide
1916	R.G.McIntyre, MA, DD, Sydney
1918	John Walker, DD, Ballarat
1920	James Gibson, DD, Brisbane
1922	John Mathew, MA, DD, Melbourne
1924	James Crookston, Melbourne
1926	R. Scott-West, DD, Sydney
1928	Alexander Crow, Perth
1930	Donald A. Cameron, MA, Melbourne
1933	G.R.S.Reid, MA, DD, Sydney
1936	John Mackenzie, MA, DD, Melbourne
1939	John Flynn, OBE, DD, Sydney
1942	R. Wilson Macaulay, BA, DD, Melbourne
1945	A.C.Greive, BA, Sydney
1948	J.R.Blanchard, BA, Adelaide
1951	Richard Bardon, OBE, BA, Brisbane
1954	F.W.Rolland, CMG, OBE, MC, MA, Melbourne
1957	D.J.Flockhart, MA, Sydney
1959	Alan C. Watson, MA, DD, Melbourne
1962	Hector Harrison, OBE, MA, BD, Canberra
1964	William Young, BA, Brisbane
1967	Norman Faichney, BA, Melbourne
1970	J. Fred McKay, OBE, MA, BD, Sydney
1971	J. Fred McKay, OBE, MA, BD, Sydney
1973	G.A.McC.Wood, BA, Hobart
1974	G.A.McC.Wood, BA, Hobart/Neil MacLeod, MA, BD, Sydney
1977	K.J.Gardner, OBE, Brisbane
1979	James Mullan, BA, Dip.RE, Sydney
1982	Norman Monsen, Sydney
1985	E.R.Pearsons, Melbourne
1988	A.C.Stubs, BA, BD,MTh, Dip.RE, Cert.Ed, Adelaide

34. F.M.Bradshaw, op. cit, p. 99 [in 1984 edition, p.101]

21: PROTESTANT & BRITISH

Despite some charitable relationships in the early years,[1] strife between Protestants and Roman Catholics in Australia was significant from the 1840s. Three powerful factors - religious, political and social - combined to express Protestant concern. The religious differences at their root were (a) the Papal claim to turn bread into God (the Mass), (b) the Papal claim to be pastor of all Christians, and (c) the Papal claim to infallibility.[2] These resolved into the question of authority: the Bible was the authority for Protestants and the Pope the authority for Roman Catholics. In popular Protestantism much was made of the superstitions of the Romanists and their belief in all manner of absurdities borrowed from paganism.[3] This fact should not obscure the fundamental question of the truth or falsity of the Roman claims. If they

1. F.Engel, Australian Christians in Conflict and Unity (Melbourne 1987) p.47. Much depended on the individuals involved. Father Geoghegan in Melbourne was on excellent terms with James Forbes and they were always to the fore in community projects.
2. The Infallibility Decree was not made until 1870 but in practical terms was in virtual operation. Similarly, while 'infallibility' is limited and carefully defined, in practice the formal utterances of the Pope must be taken as binding if Papal authority is to be of real significance.
3. The Immaculate Conception of Mary (ie. her sinlessness) was decreed in 1854. Popular Protestant literature often focussed on sexual scandals. In 1860 Rev William McIntyre delivered an address with the plain title, 'The Heathendom of Popery Proved and Illustrated.' There was a riot by an Irish mob prior to this lecture in which McIntyre's brother Donald was injured and subsequently died. Charles Chiniquy (1809--1899), the Canadian priest who left Rome with a large number of followers in 1858 and joined the Presbyterian Church, lectured in Australia 1878-80. Rev George Sutherland of the PCEA, who had ministered in Canada, had a good deal to do with Chiniquy coming to Australia.

are true they have profound implications; if they are false they are monumentally so and derserve to be treated as such.

The political factor was connected with Catholic Emancipation, granted in 1829, and the fear that a large influx of Irish into the Australian colonies could lead to domination by Irish clerics owing allegiance to a foreign power who claimed secular supremacy (the Pope). Over 40% of assisted immigrants to Australia in the 1840s were Roman Catholics, and in 1850 the proportion was 79%.[4] Most of this was due to problems in Ireland following the potato famine, a disaster which London may be accused with justice of doing little to alleviate. Dr Lang supported equality of civil rights for Roman Catholics but wanted the balance of immigration changed so as to ensure a preponderance of God-fearing Protestants, hence his tract, *The Question of Questions! or, Is this Colony to be transformed into a Province of the Popedom?* issued in 1841.[5]

The social factor, linked with the other two, was the concern that the quality of Roman Catholic settlers was poor and thus poverty, superstition and crime would result. Whether adequate weight was given to the depressed conditions in Ireland might well be a question, though the complaint noted was made before the famine as well as after it. Clearly there was concern that British institutions should not be undermined by a rabble element from Ireland. Multiculturalism as discussed in Australia in the 1980s has its precursors!

The Orange Order

The Irish background contributed to the formation of Orange Lodges in the Australian colonies. The first was a military lodge formed by soldiers in Sydney in 1830, but the real step was taken in 1843 with the formation of an Orange Lodge in Melbourne hard on the heels of the closely fought election for the Legislative Council in that year. The contest was between a Roman Catholic and a Protestant, and was narrowly won by the Protestant.

The Orange Order was formed in Ireland in 1795 by Protestant small farmers and labourers, chiefly of Church of Ireland (Anglican) background. They banded together to preserve the Protestant constitution which had been secured by William of Orange. The landed gentry identified with the Order in the face of the United Irishmen movement (which included Presbyterians

4. See F. Engel, op. cit., p.59; also Michael Hogan, **The Sectarian Strand** (Melbourne 1987) p. 63. Hogan is a former Roman Catholic priest turned Senior Lecturer at the University of Sydney.
5. D.W.A.Baker, **Days of Wrath** (Melbourne 1985) p. 192ff. Lang was acutely aware that a (united) Catholic minority could be stronger than a (divided) Protestant majority.

and Roman Catholics), but the failure of the 1798 rebellion resulted in the Orange Order declining into a body of little significance for some years. Its fortunes ebbed and flowed with the political situation. Catholic emancipation in 1829 was a live issue but of far less significance in England itself. The Home Rule Bill of 1886 was also a tension point and marks the entry of the largely urban and middle class Presbyterians into the Orange Order which then became the common voice of Irish Protestantism.[6] Officially the Order objects only to the papal system not individual Roman Catholics, but it has always had an element of rowdy Catholic-haters at one extreme and earnest praying Christians at the other. Certainly as a movement the Order had men of repute in its ranks. Lord Hopetoun, Australia's first Governor-General, was Deputy Grand Master of the Orange Order in Scotland when appointed to the Vice-Regal office in 1901.[7]

Real growth was stimulated by the attempted assassination of the Duke of Edinburgh by an Irish-born settler in New South Wales in March 1868. In New South Wales membership rose from less than 1,000 to 2,500 in 28 lodges by 1869. In 1876 there were 19,000 in 130 lodges and the peak was about 25,000 members in 1882. In Victoria the Orange Order grew to 73 lodges and some 4,000 members in 1882.[8] and there was some further expansion during 1882-1904 when Senator Sir Simon Fraser was Grand Master. Many Protestants regarded it as their bounden duty to belong to the Order to counter the threat of Roman Catholicism. Presbyterians were well represented.[9] Rev John McGibbon (1828-1882), Presbyterian minister at Woolloomooloo, was editor of the *Protestant Standard* until his death.

The religious colour of the Orange Order inevitably levelled off to at best a general evangelicalism since all 'Protestants' were welcome on an equal footing. The religious test was sufficiently general to allow Rev Charles Strong of the Australian Church to be a member.[10] McGibbon resisted

6. I am indebted to a book by British sociologist Steve Bruce, **No Pope of Rome** (Edinburgh 1985) pp.147-152 at this point.
7. Tas Vertigan, **The Orange Order in Victoria** (Melbourne 1979) p.82. This is an official history and rather brief. There is no official history of the Order in New South Wales, but an important source is Mark Lyons, **Aspects of Sectarianism in New South Wales circa 1865 to 1880** (PhD thesis, ANU, 1972). See also Patrick O'Farrell, **The Irish in Australia** (Sydney 1986) p.100ff.
8. T.Vertigan, ibid., p.38. It was considered that there were then up to 80,000 Orangemen in Victoria not attached to lodges. In 1903 lodges for ladies began and 35 were formed in that year (p.99).
9. The meetings of about 90 lodges were advertised in **The Witness** (Edited by George Sutherland) in 1884. The lodge identification numbers suggest about twice that number of lodges had existence at one time or another in New South Wales to that date. Between 1861 and 1868 (when assisted migration was cut) 59% to 69% of assisted migrants in New South Wales were Roman Catholic (mostly Irish) - vide M.Hogan, op. cit., p.141.
10. T. Vertigan, ibid., p.110. Strong was one of the Lodge officers invited to the opening of the first Parliament of the Commonwealth of Australia in 1901. Strong was also a Freemason (vide C.R.Badger, October 1988) and the foundation stone of his Australian Church was laid in 1887 with Masonic ritual: note the regalia in the picture on p.101 of C.R.Badger, **Charles Strong and the Australian Church** (Melbourne 1971).

efforts by fellow Orangeman, Rev Dr George Sutherland of the PCEA Sydney to use Sutherland's paper *The Witness* as a vehicle for furthering sound religious views among the Lodge membership.[11] From this viewpoint the Lodge could be regarded as detrimental to the long-term Christian interest although it is undoubted that its work in checking some less happy features of Roman Catholicism was of value. It has been said that Rev Archibald Gilchrist (1843-96) was an active Orangeman more to defend access to the Bible than to oppose Romanism. Gilchrist was Grand Master in Victoria in 1880 and President of the Grand Council of the Orange Order in Australia in 1882.

The Order progressively declined in influence and numbers in the 20th century, and today numbers some 44 lodges and 2,000 members in Victoria with similar numbers in New South Wales.[12] The drift from some of the original principles of Protestantism has been and is evident in a secularising tendency which sees Protestantism in terms of freedom of inquiry and a separation of Church and State of such a kind as undercuts the responsibility of the State to further the Christian faith.

Freemasonry

Another stream of generally anti-Roman feeling is seen in Freemasonry. Its modern origins are much older than the Orange Order and it appears to have supplanted that body in influence by the 1920s with its high point coming after the second World War when many returned servicemen joined it. Numbers have declined in Victoria from about 120,000 in 1946 to about 50,000 today, and a similar proportionate drop has occurred elsewhere in Australia so that current Australian membership is about 170,000. Allowance must be made for those holding membership in more than one of the 2,800 lodges. Of recent decades service clubs such as Rotary and Apex have taken in many who might otherwise have found mateship and business contacts through Masonry.

In the medieval period there were guilds of stonemasons as well as those who were free to travel in the carrying on of their occupation. The decline

11. See the exchange of correspondence in Peter Macpherson, **Presbyterianism in Victoria** (a collection of cuttings in the State Library of Victoria) volume for 1881.
12. Vide Jeffrey S. Davis, Grand Secretary of the LOIV, August 1988.

of masonry work after the rebuilding of London following the great fire of 1666 led to some of the 'free' masons banding together to maintain a symbolic masonry in a self-improvement society bound by oaths of secrecy. Four local lodges formed a Grand Lodge in London in 1717.

In religion, however, they are non-sectarian, and profess only that faith in which all men of honour agree. Doctrines going beyond that are tolerated as private opinions, but no one is permitted to make propaganda for them. The characteristics of masonry are, therefore, humanistic morals, the cultivation of fraternity, and a deistic belief. It was the outcome of English deism and latitudinarianism, and was soon adopted in Germany in radical religious circles. In those Roman Catholic countries where no Protestantism existed, masonry even obtained the importance of an opposing church..[13]

In the early period there was little Protestant/Roman Catholic friction, probably in large measure because Protestantism and British institutions were not under threat. 'Governor Macquarie, a Freemason of long standing, personally laid the foundation stone of St Mary's Cathedral in Sydney on 29 October 1821. Protestants of all classes contributed to building funds and offered hospitality to the travelling priests as they sought out the Roman Catholic flock.'[14] But with the greater organisation of the Roman Church - Bishop John Polding was appointed in 1843 - and the influx of Irish, the position changed. On the one hand the main Protestant churches seem to have identified Masonry with goodness and virtue if not with Protestantism itself, while on the other the Church of Rome asserted its exclusive claims.

The foundation stone of the Grenfell Street Church of Scotland in Adelaide was laid in February 1844 with Masonic ritual and the minister (Robert Haining) leading the singing of 'To Heaven's High Architect, All Praise'. 'When the event was reported in the Adelaide papers, a number of letters to the Editor appeared, one of which stated that Jesus was neither a Mason or an Oddfellow.'[15] The problems arising from the English involvement in Ireland were also reproduced as migration from Ireland increased, and a rabble element existed on both sides. But there were other matters too. The Melbourne Benevolent Asylum was financed by general contributions, but the Roman Catholic Bishop forced the withdrawal of the Roman Catholic members of the Committee on the stated ground that a 'Clergyman of another denomination' was to read prayers at the laying of the foundation

13. P.Tschackert, 'Freemasons' in New Schaff-Herzog Encyclopaedia of Religious Knowledge (Grand Rapids 1977 reprint) Vol. 4, p.430.
14. F. Engel, op. cit., p.65 (note 61).
15. R.J.Scrimgeour, Some Scots Were Here (Adelaide 1986) p.24; similarly in the case of St Andrew's, Launceston in 1849: see Vera M.Edwards, The Old Kirk and St Andrews (Launceston 1969) p.14.

stone. James Forbes notes: 'An objection might have been taken to the prayers...because they do not plead the mediation of Christ; but on this ground the Romanists objected not. And though reference was made to the fact that the Masonic Institute is under the Papal bann, the chief prominence was not given to this ground of offence. The presence of the Protestant clergyman was the intolerable thing. Surely this is bigotry.'[16] Forbes also refers to priests forbidding their adherents even to join in the family devotions of Protestants, and rejecting the validity of Protestant marriages. (These were not regarded as valid by the Papacy until 1908 and the decree *Ne Temere*.)

It is difficult to know the extent of Masonic influence in Presbyterianism in the 19th century. Rev Wazir Beg (c1827-1885), an Indian convert and remarkable linguist, was Grand Chaplain to the Freemasons of New South Wales as well as an Orangeman. He was a strict Presbyterian Protestant and edited *Freemason* (of which he was the proprietor) and *Orangeman*. William Ross (1803-69) of Goulburn was a leading Freemason and founded the Lodge in Goulburn in 1849. He was a very public-spirited man involved in many worthwhile community projects. A Masonic memorial was placed in the grounds of his church after his death. Rev J.S.White (1805-1902) of Singleton was also a prominent Freemason who was especially known for his many scholarly and scientific interests. He was orthodox but more in the 'Moderate' line. The same mixture of types is seen later in the century. W.M.Dill Macky (1849-1913) arrived from Ireland and became minister of Scots Church, Sydney in 1887. He was a prominent Freemason and was also Grand Chaplain of the Orange Institution in New South Wales soon after his arrival. Richard Broome says his sermons were of 'high calibre - both impassioned and quietly sensitive, powerful yet humble and left a marked impression on his hearers.'[15] However, his militant Protestantism was also noteworthy. He was the first President of the Australian Protestant Defence Association, which he formed in June 1901, and within 3 years it had 22,000 members and 135 branches. Despite his Masonic connections Dill Macky was a strict and uncompromising conservative evangelical of the rather noisy kind.

On the other hand, there was opposition of various kinds. About 1858 the arrogant and opinionated Rev R.K.Ewing of St Andrew's (Church of Scotland) Launceston resigned his position as Grand Master of the Masonic Lodge apparently because a section of his congregation considered his

15. In ADB (1891-1939) p.305

16. **Port Phillip Christian Herald**, August 1850, p. 62. The account differs from that recorded by 'Garryowen' (Edmund Finn), **Chronicles of Early Melbourne 1835-51** (Melbourne 1888) pp. 243-245 cited and accepted by F.Engel, op. cit., p.48 in which the Masonic involvement was the cause of offence. Forbes is less biased and more reliable on such matters than the ardent Roman Catholic historian writing years later.

involvement was inconsistent with with his primary commitment.[17] The Reformed Presbyterian Church had theological objections of such weight that church membership was not open to members of secret societies, but was represented in Australia by but a single congregation. Continental Calvinists were commonly opposed, but few Dutch and German folk were involved in Presbyterian churches in Australia last century.[18]

In the absence of more adequate research into the denominational background of Australian Masons one assumes that the influence of its religious outlook was indirect in the 19th century. People were members for a variety of reasons but did not intend to compromise their beliefs by their membership. Masonry's origins in an anti-Christian outlook which substituted morality for Christ was not considered by many since Masonry had become a vehicle for expressing 'Protestant' solidarity against Romish pretensions, especially in their bearing on freedom of inquiry and British institutions, and also provided a network of social and business contacts. In the 20th century the same was the case with the difference that the idea of salvation through decency and respectability took over in the mainstream churches as liberal theology advanced. Thus there was a better logical fit between the underlying philosophy of Masonry and the views in the mainline denominations. As churches moved toward a more Biblical emphasis on the centrality of Jesus in the 1970s, Masonry itself would come under attack just as would liberalism. This would be quite an acute issue for the Presbyterians in the 1980s.

Summary

This survey of the two leading 'societies with secrets' in 19th century Australia has indicated the strong social forces which fostered their growth. Apart from what has been stated already the existence of the lodges raises questions as to the adequacy or otherwise of church life. Granted that the fragmentation of Protestantism compared to the unity of Romanism suggested an inter-denominational Protestant counter, it remains that the fellowship and mateship fostered by the lodges was something one should have expected in the churches themselves. Perhaps the churches did not adequately meet the needs of the men or harness their energies and interests into explicitly Christian work. Perhaps the churches were seen to be bickering too much among themselves and the lodges were a form of escape and protest. The fellowship of the lodge was generally a fellowship among those

17. V.M.Edwards, op. cit., pp.21-22. The Presbytery's pastoral letter to the pro-Masonic faction in the congregation is in J.Heyer, Presbyterian Pioneers of Van Diemen's Land (Launceston 1935) pp.234-237, and states that the holding of office [as Grand Master] 'is a thing unprecedented in our Church, and as far as we know, in any other.'
18. For an example of controversy among Dutch settlers in America see E.J.Bruins, The Masonic Controversy in Holland, Michigan, 1879-1882 in P.De Klerk and R.De Ridder (eds), Perspectives on the Christian Reformed Church (Michigan 1983) pp53-72.

of Protestant outlook yet in Freemasonry the name of Jesus was kept out and perhaps without realizing it members were likely to substitute morality for Jesus Christ who said, 'No man comes to the Father but by me' (John 14:6).

Further, the secrecy and the benevolence of the lodges raised questions. Should a Christian be involved in any society whose secrecy can appear to cast doubt on his integrity and avoidance of partisanship? And are the oaths of the lodges proper since one should not use an oath lightly nor bind a person without him knowing the full nature and extent of what he undertakes?[19]

It is evident from what has been said that Protestant-Roman Catholic relations were a problem in Australia because of the social and cultural factors - the one British and the other Irish. The conflicts with the English in Ireland were imported into Australia. Consequently relations were confrontationist. Although there was plenty of intermarriage and there is evidence of Catholic women preferring Protestant men as husbands, in general there were two distinct camps. It would await the 1960s and following for real freedom to relate across the boundaries to come.

Having said this, the religious divide remains because the opposing claims cannot be reconciled. The Westminster Confession sets out the views of the Reformed Church so clearly that it is impossible to marry its statements on such matters as the Scriptures, the nature of faith and the power of the Church with the positions adopted by Rome at the Council of Trent (1545-63) and subsequently. This is so even if the famous clause in the 25th chapter of the Westminster Confession, which relates the papal institution to the antichrist, did not appear.

---

19. Note the following conclusion to the report on Freemasonry presented to the PCV Assembly in 1958 (pages 159-161 of **Assembly Reports**):

'Because of the danger, freely acknowledged by both sides in the debate between Church and Lodge, that members may come to regard Freemasonry as a legitimate competitor with the Church of Christ for their loyalty and service, the Committee concludes its report by affirming strongly the following three points -
(1) Christian Masons are urged to remember that the supreme revelation of God is in Jesus Christ, and that such titles as the Great Architect of the Universe do not make this plain. There can, therefore, be no idea of a super-religion above Christianity.
(2) Salvation is in and through Jesus Christ alone: not in some mystic understanding or by our own merits.
(3) Freemasonry is sub-Christian and must never be accepted by members of the Church as a substitute for Christian belief, worship and service. It asks the General Assembly to lay it on the hearts of all Church members to recommit themselves to Jesus Christ as Lord and Saviour, so that there can be no rival with Him for their devotion and service.'

The Assembly ordered that a pastoral letter be prepared and read in all churches along the lines of the Committee report.

Part Six

CONFUSION AND TREASON

1901-1945

22: ASPECTS OF CHURCH LIFE & TEACHING

The constituent churches of the PCA in 1901 were of varied size and background and totalled about 540 parishes, 2,040 preaching places, 380 settled ministers and 47,600 members in full communion. Only in Victoria and Tasmania was there an adequate number and spread of parishes. NSW with 170 parishes actually had more preaching places than Victoria (907 compared with 879) although Victoria had about 250 parishes. The average number of communicants per preaching place in NSW was just short of 15 compared with 20 in WA, 26 in Tasmania, 28 in Victoria, 45 in SA and 55 in Queensland. The high figures for the last two states reflect the fact that sparse population and large distances limited the ability of one man to serve numerous centres, whereas NSW had many centres of population which were close enough to be worked by one man and had to be since the proportion of Presbyterians was so much lower than in Victoria.

PRESBYTERIANS AT THE 1901 CENSUS & ON COMMUNION ROLLS

State	Census ppn of total pop.	Census Number	On Rolls	Ppn of census Presbyterians
VIC	16.2%	191,427	24,749	12.93%
NSW	9.8	132,617	13,071	9.85
Q	11.7	57,442	5,053	8.80
SA	5.2	18,357	2,060	11.22
WA	8.2	14,707	1,023	6.96
TAS	6.8	11,523	1,670	14.49
Total	**11.46**	**426,073**	**47,626**	**11.18**

Progress in New South Wales

Twenty years later (1921), the World War in the past, the Australian population had risen 44%. Presbyterian growth in NSW, according to the census figures, was 55% (the proportion of Presbyterians in the population rising from 9.8% to 10.4% largely through Scottish migration), while in Victoria it was only 27.5%. Accompanying this solid growth were improved congregational, financial and educational arrangements in the PCNSW. The number of parishes in NSW grew by 25% in the first decade of the 20th century, and there was a rise of 91% in the communicant membership 1901-1921, whereas the increase in Victoria for the same period was only 42%. The PCNSW benefited from large bequests - the Hunter Baillie gifts funded two professorships at St Andrew's in 1901, and the success of a special appeal enabled a third appointment to be made in 1910. J.H.Goodlet (1835-1914), a stalwart of Ashfield parish and a leading businessman, left 93,000 pounds in 1914 (say $6 million in 1988 terms), while the McCaughey Bequest of 150,000 pounds was received in 1920/21. These developments brought greater optimism to the PCNSW, weakened the practical arguments in favour of wider union among Protestants, and brought the PCNSW nearer to the benchmark maintained with some pride by the PCV.

Liberalism

While the smaller states lagged somewhat, the overall outward prosperity of the PCA was somewhat of an illusion. Its spiritual roots were being sapped by a subjective and increasingly liberal theology. Liberal evangelicalism, which maintained the supernatural elements in our Lord's saving work while discarding verbal inspiration, was itself an unstable position. The confidence in human reason which underlay it triumphed in the overthrow of the supernatural and the reign of liberalism pure and simple which is associated with the name of Professor Samuel Angus. The Angus Affair demoralised the PCNSW and further polarised it, while the PCA at large was not unaffected.

The Outback

In 1894 a mission to the far north of South Australia was established by the PCSA using a bequest by a Free Church of Scotland lady, Mrs Smith, who had intended the money for aboriginal education and evangelisation. Rev Robert Mitchell was the driving force behind the 'Smith of Dunesk Mission' which was based on Beltana, 150 miles north of Port Augusta. The missioners sought to overcome 'the tyranny of distance' and to bring Christian ministry, help and friendship to the isolated settlers. An account of the experience of one Smith of Dunesk missioner, Rev H.E.Carey (1881-1955), who served 1916-19, will convey some idea of the work done.[1]

1. R.J.Scrimgeour, **Some Scots Were Here** (Adelaide 1986) pp.106-118 provides useful material on the Smith of Dunesk Mission. Rev H.E.Carey was the present writer's grandfather, and the following four paragraphs draw on material provided by my mother.

Life in the inland was fraught with difficulties and dangers of many kinds. The loneliness and isolation were incredible and the dangers in case of illness or accident were appalling. The visit of a minister, especially when there were children in the home, could be something never forgotten. Carey would go on his travels in a hooded buggy drawn by two horses, the vehicle being loaded for the long trips of perhaps 4 or 5 weeks at a time with a magic lantern and sheet, drum of carbide, slides, perhaps the gramophone, camp sheet and blanket, literature, coloured pictures for those unable to read, some dental equipment, quart pot, eating and cooking utensils, a little food and water, chaff for the horse and personal effects.

Carey would visit every station except those known to be occupied by Roman Catholics, isolated huts, fettlers' camps on the railway, especially those at the time engaged in building the East-West Railway to Perth, and anyone camping by the track. It was easy to lose your way because roads were often ill defined and there were so few landmarks. Often places where no minister had been before were visited, and places where the manager's wife had not seen a white woman for several years. Carey would always endeavour to hold a service at each station if possible, probably in the dining-room or kitchen or in the men's quarters. There could be only 3 or 4 present, but there could be 20 or more depending on the number of people employed and whether they were all at the head station. Most loved the lantern pictures with slides of the life of Christ and of favourite hymns. The lantern was worked on carbide. Sometimes there were hymns on the gramophone, but music was rather difficult as so few knew any but the most familiar hymns. Often he gave simple Gospel addresses.

Many of those met could not read or write. If there were children with nobody to teach them, the missioner would give them some help with the alphabet as well as teaching them Bible stories and giving them coloured Bible pictures. Sometimes there were children to be baptised. At huts where lonely old men lived, perhaps unable to read or write, he would put up a big coloured picture illustrating a Bible story. Carey was concerned at the lack of educational opportunities for underprivileged children. He arranged for one particular family to receive correspondence lessons from a teacher in Beltana, and eventually the Education Department provided correspondence lessons more generally for those in the outback.

Some dental work was done. It was rather nerve-racking for the 'dentist' who had few and rather inadequate instruments and little knowledge, but was usually successful. Living in a barren and desolate area without company, church, school, medical attention, shops, reading matter or beauty, and often with difficult, drunken husbands, life for many of the women was extremely difficult, and yet one met examples of 'the Women of the West' (as George

303

Essex Evans' poem describes them) who endured great hardships and showed great courage, and who are among the unsung heroes of Australia's development as a nation.

John Flynn and the Australian Inland Mission

John Flynn (1880-1951) - 'Flynn of the Inland' - was Smith of Dunesk missioner 1911-1912. His experiences contributed to his dream of 'making Christ known throughout the Australian Bush; of fighting the forces of evil, and of improving the conditions of life across half a continent' - to use the terms he employed in 1912 in a Report to the GAA. The AIM was the result. It was based on outback patrols by itinerant padres with associated hostels and nursing homes. In the 1920s Flynn was pushing the use of aeroplanes to bring pastoral and medical care to isolated locations, but he needed effective wireless communication. Afred Traeger solved this problem by producing a compact transmitter with pedal-driven generator. What was to become the *Royal Flying Doctor Service* made its first flight in 1928 from Cloncurry, and soon spread to other centres. In 1939 the Flying Doctor Service was transferred by the AIM to a new organisation as part of the evolution to a government supported service to the outback. The medical service had cost 47,000 pounds up until that time.

Work projected in 1920
From *The Inlander* of that year.

EVENTUALLY— WHY NOT NOW?

304

Flynn was a remarkable man. He was a dreamer of dreams who got others to work them out. He was both a simple man with practical skills and a man of vision who spent a good deal of time analysing statistics and the trends they indicated. A Victorian, he trained at Ormond College. He was not obtrusively liberal although he joined with Samuel Angus in opposing church union in 1922 (see page 333). He was not logically consistent on many things and he cannot be categorised precisely. He considered the existing Methodist work at Darwin should be supported by Presbyterians rather than starting a rival work. This and his general freedom in working among people of all backgrounds, seem to have led many to think he was in favour of a wider union on a national level. This does not appear to be the case. Indeed, near the end of his life he called on F.M.Bradshaw in Melbourne to urge him to fight the church union movement which was then developing. After all, it is one thing to co-operate heartily in frontier situations; it is another to vote for the end of the Presbyterian Church as an institution. In this one may note the example of Rev Chris Goy, also an AIM patrol padre from 1937-42, who continued after 1977 with the PCA.[2]

2. Rev W.S.McPheat published two volumes on Flynn: John Flynn: Apostle to the Inland (London 1963) and John Flynn: Vision of the Inland (London 1977). Australian Presbyterian Life, November 1980, includes several articles about Flynn. The Bradshaw family had known Flynn from his early years.

The use of the name 'Australian Inland Mission' was contested by the Uniting Church. However, the case was settled by negotiation in 1979 when the PCA and the UCA agreed not to use the AIM title except as a subtitle which would indicate succession but not exclusively, eg. 'The Presbyterian Inland Mission (successor in the Presbyterian Church to the Australian Inland Mission founded 1912).' The Uniting Church paid the costs involved. (See GAA Minutes, 1979, pp.70-71).

Free Presbyterian Church of Australia 1913

We left the PCEA on page 248 as a small and scattered remnant. As at September 1911, the position of the different sections of the Free Church movement in Australia was as follows:

Presbyterian Church of Eastern Australia (NSW)

Presbytery of Manning and Clarence

Manning	Rev S.P.Stewart since 1879
Barrington	vacant station
Hastings/Macleay	vacant since 1897
Bellingen	vacant station
Grafton/Brushgrove	vacant (supply by H.W.Ramsay, student)
Maclean	Rev James Henry, BA (supply ex FCofS)
Richmond/Brunswick	vacant

Presbytery of Sydney and Maitland

St George's, Sydney	Rev William McDonald since 1901
Raymond Tce/E Maitland	Rev W.N.Wilson since 1904
(without charge)	Rev W. Grant (retired 1908)

Students in Scotland: I.L.Graham and J.C.Robinson.

Free Presbyterian Church of Victoria

Presbytery

East St Kilda	vacant since 1910
Geelong/Drysdale	Rev John Sinclair since 1881
Hamilton/Branxholme	Rev John D. Ramsay since 1911
Camperdown	vacant station

Free Presbyterian Church of South Australia

Adelaide	Rev W.R.Buttrose since 1892
Morphett Vale	Rev J.S.Macpherson since 1904

A closer relationship between the different state churches was deemed highly desirable for the good of the work as a whole and to facilitate relations with the post-1900 Free Church of Scotland. A Conference was held in Sydney on September 18/19, 1911 at which all the ministers were present except J.S.Macpherson who maintained an isolated position until his death in 1921. There was excellent unanimity at this Conference which agreed:

that it is desirable that the aforesaid Churches, holding as they do the same doctrines and principles, which are identical with those which the Free Church of Scotland held in 1843, and also does at the present time, federate under one supreme ecclesiastical court; possessing the powers and full jurisdiction of a Presbyterian Assembly in all spiritual matters; but without in any way interfering with the rights and titles of each State Church to its own properties and funds; and the Conference also agreed to reaffirm what these Churches aforesaid have always maintained, and to recommend that the following brief summary be the basis of union, viz.: -

1. The Scriptures of the Old and New Testaments are the Word of God, and the only infallible rule of faith and practice.

2. The Lord Jesus Christ is the sole King and Head of His Church, and the Head of the Nations, in opposition to erastianism on the one hand, and voluntaryism on the other.

3. The Confession of Faith agreed upon by the Assembly of Divines, which met at Westminster in the year 1643, together with the Larger and Shorter Catechisms, which is the Confession of Faith in the aforesaid Churches, as being founded on the word of God and being agreeable thereto, shall be the Confession of the uniting Free Churches.

4. The Form of Presbyterian Church Government and Discipline of the aforesaid Assembly of Divines shall be obligatory on the office-bearers of the uniting Churches as a pattern for the right-ordering of the Church of God.

5. The Directory for Public Worship of the aforesaid Assembly as containing "the substance of the service and worship of God," is to be regarded as the Directory of the uniting Churches, its leading provisions being held to be the following as concerns the Divinely prescribed method of worship, viz. :—1. The disallowing of liturgies. 2. The singing of inspired psalms only without instrumental music in the praise of God. 3. The assigning of the principal place in public worship to the preaching of the Word. And 4, the non-observance of religious days except the Lord's Day and days of humiliation or thanksgiving that may be found proper as heretofore in the uniting Churches.

THE CONFERENCE ON UNION, APRIL 1911

Front row (L to R): Samuel McKay, Geelong elder; Rev W.R.Buttrose, Rev William Grant, Rev S.P.Stewart, Rev William McDonald, Rev John Sinclair. Back row (L to R): Rev J.D.Ramsay; James Robinson, Manning elder; Rev James Henry; D. McLachlan, Maclean elder; Rev W.N.Wilson

Clauses 4 and 5 are abbreviated from the *Act of Reconstruction* of 1876 drawn up by Arthur Paul of the FPCV (see page 241). Clause 5 is interesting because it indicates what were regarded as the leading features of the *Directory*, and in this is consistent with the intent indicated by the preface to that document.

The union had to be a federal one because it was felt the legal difficulties of an organic union could not be overcome. However, the federation created its own difficulties and an organic union was eventually effected in 1953. The same Conference in 1911 considered the proposal for a complete union with the Free Church of Scotland advocated by Rev (later Professor) Donald Maclean, who had visited Australia in 1910.[3] In May 1912, the Assembly of the Free Church of Scotland agreed to receive the Australian brethren on the basis of the constitution of the Free Church in 1843, but this was not taken up in Australia. Men such as John Sinclair were in favour since it would provide a supply for ministers, but others opposed it. The students then training in Scotland (Messrs Graham and Robinson) wrote to Australia in the latter part of 1912 voicing their opposition. Their main concern was the practical impossibility of having representation in the Scottish Assembly because of the distance and the cost, and thus the Australian Church would be left a colonial outpost under the maternal care of the Free Church. They were also concerned that hymns were used in some Sabbath Schools and slum work, and that 'sales of work' were common in Scotland as a means of raising money. They also noted that it was unlikely that there would be ministers surplus to Scottish needs for 10/20 years. Although some of these arguments were not substantial,[4] it was fortunate the proposal was not accepted in Australia. There were discussions in after years, and some diversity remained,[5] but it was settled that the Australian Church would continue independent but with close fraternal links with the Free Church of Scotland.

On April 9, 1913, there was a further Conference at which it was reported that the PCEA and FPCV had approved unanimously the proposed basis,

3. See his **Travels in Sunny Lands** (Edinburgh 1911); also **Free Church Quarterly**, January 1911, pp.213-217. Rev S.P.Stewart had visited Scotland in 1908.
4. The letter dated October 24, 1912 , is in the possession of R.S.Ward. 'Sales of work' and hymns in Sabbath Schools may not be desirable but of themselves ought not to be a barrier to union. Hymns in Sabbath Schools were quite common in the PCEA itself a generation before. Eg: in May 1883, the children of the East Maitland PCEA Sabbath School had their annual outing at Pitnacree, the home of elder Samuel Porter, and were each presented with 'a new and enlarged edition of a hymn book for use in S. schools' - The Free Churchman, June 1883, p.72.
5. In April 1927 the Assembly of the FPCA resolved in similar terms, considering that a union without preservation of autonomy was the great difficulty. Rev William Archibald, a former PCEA minister who died in 1941, left his property to the Free Church of Scotland for missions and not to the PCEA, probably considering that union was the appropriate outcome of negotiations.

which was therefore implemented the following day in terms of the following five resolutions.

(1) That the name of the federating Churches be the "Free Presbyterian Church of Australia."

(2) That the Supreme Court of these federating Churches be the Assembly of the Free Presbyterian Church of Australia, and have the jurisdiction and powers proper to a Presbyterian Assembly in all Spiritual matters.

(3) That the properties and funds of each State shall remain under the complete control of each of the Churches in each State as hitherto.

(4) That the Basis of Union above referred to, as submitted to and approved by the State Church Courts and Congregations, be now formally adopted as the Basis of Union by the Churches now federated under the name of the "Free Presbyterian Church of Australia."

(5) That any Free Presbyterian Church or congregation or adherents in any other State of Australia who may desire to join in this union of the Free Presbyterian Churches shall be cordially received on the same basis.

It should be noted that the FPCSA was not represented at the final Conference owing to the death of Rev W.R.Buttrose. Individuals in South Australia were in favour but the church courts had been rendered inoperative by legalism among some relatives of Rev James Benny.[6]

An important event occurred in 1918 when the property of congregations in New South Wales was conveyed to a trust corporation incorporated at the request of the Synod by Act of Parliament, and of which the Moderator, Clerk and Synod Treasurer were members. This provided more adequate security for church property, and eliminated the complications and expense of electing local trustees. The measure cost the Synod $371.03.

FPCA consolidation to 1945

The small denomination with a big heritage consolidated over the next 25 years. Ministers were obtained from the Free Church (Neil Macleod in 1929 and M.M.MacDonald in 1931), but also from the membership (I.L.

---

6. The FPSA became incapable of effective action and as the trust deeds did not allow the transfer of the properties to the management of the sister church in Victoria, they remained in limbo. The PCSA obtained appointment as custodian trustee in a number of cases and considered it had a good claim. After 1977, the Uniting Church in South Australia considered it incorporated the PCSA, and therefore had a claim too, while the PCEA believed it had a moral claim. The legal principle is the cy pres (as near as possible) principle, the PCEA having similarity of doctrine but the PCSA being more proximate in location. However, leaving aside all the legalities, on December 2, 1987 an agreement was reached between the three denominations on an approach to the South Australian Parliament for legislation to enable the sale of the properties, then having a probable value of $200,000, with the PCEA to receive 20% of the nett proceeds of the sale, with the balance after expenses be divided thus: one third to the PCSA and two thirds to the UCSA. Enabling legislation by private member's bill is hoped for in 1989.

Graham of the Hastings, ordained 1918 at Hamilton; J.C.Robinson of the Manning, ordained 1921 at Melbourne, M.C.Ramsay of the Macleay, ordained 1921 on the Hastings, James A.Webster of St George's, ordained 1933 on the Hunter, and Joseph Harman of the Hastings, ordained in 1934. Arthur Allen of Sydney and Dudley Trotter of the Hastings were ordained in 1938. All these men were trained in the facilities of the Free Church of Scotland College. Considering the lack of facilities for regular training in Australia in Reformed theology, this provision was of great value in ensuring adequate training and exposure to something more than the relatively insular experiences of Australian church life. Of course it ran the risk of continuing an over-Scottish outlook in the Australian scene, but it was hard to avoid this. The church also benefited from visits by ministers of the Free Church. Rev James Henry made several visits, the last in 1926. Principal John MacLeod from the College came in 1928 as did Rev George Mackay of Fearn. Mackay supplied St George's pulpit during 1929 and made a lasting impression on the young Marcus Loane, later Archbishop Sir Marcus Loane, and thus indirectly on the Anglican Diocese of Sydney and beyond.[7] While nothing much could be done in South Australia, the other centres were maintained and there were 8 or 9 ministers in parishes for most of the period into the 1950s.

Theological Education in the PCA

Victoria and New South Wales were the significant centres of theological training for the PCA 1901-1945, and a review of this follows.

Victoria

Rev A.C.Smith succeeded Harper as Professor of Old Testament studies in 1902. A son of Rev A.C.Smith (1823-1902) of the PCQ (originally FCS/ PCEA), Smith died the following year. T.Jollie Smith (1858-1927), his younger brother, acted as tutor in 1904 until Rev Alex Skene was appointed. He was not a radical but was not as conservative as the talented but ageing T.J.Smith, who became lecturer in Hebrew in 1921 and Professor in November 1922 in succession to Skene. Smith was a ripe and versatile scholar whose strictly conservative conclusions in theology, especially Scripture, could never have been said to be due to ignorance.[8]

7. A tribute by Marcus Loane to George Mackay is in See (the Anglican news magazine) October 1981, reprinted in Our Banner, May 1982. Loane's book Sons of the Covenant (Sydney 1963) is dedicated to Mackay's memory, and another (Makers of Religious Freedom in the Seventeenth Century, Grand Rapids 1961) is dedicated to Dr Helen Ramsay, then medical missionary of the PCEA to Central India and daughter of Rev M.C.Ramsay. The Ramsays and the Loanes were close friends.
8. T.J.Smith was minister at Narracoorte 1889-1903 and at East Malvern 1905-1922. He lectured at the University in Logic, Psychology and Ethics 1911-1921, initiated Japanese studies at the University and lectured 1919-1921, and wrote for the Argus 1907-1922 as well as lecturing (chiefly in Apologetics) in the Deaconess Institute. Smith was involved in the Bible Union formed in Melbourne in 1923. Cf. David Parker, The Bible Union: A Case Study in Australian Fundamentalism, JRH Vol. 14 †1 (June 1986).

J.Laurence Rentoul continued as Principal and Professor of New Testament until his death in 1926. In the stormy union debates of the first decades of the 20th century he defended Presbyterian distinctives. The prospect of union with the Methodists sharpened his thinking and contributed to a rather more conservative stance on doctrinal questions. He gave strong support to T.J.Smith's election to the Professorship of Old Testament.

Murdoch Macdonald, Professor of Systematic Theology and Church History, died in in 1905. David S Adam from the United Free Church of Scotland was his replacement and served from 1907 until his death in 1925. Adam was a rather definite liberal though not provocative. He was considerably influenced by Hegelianism which he regarded as coming nearest 'to finding a satisfactory rational basis for the affirmations of religious faith.'[9] In church matters he was anti-Free Church as a result of the 1904 legal decision, and he was an enthusiastic supporter of a wider church union in Australia.

The death of the three incumbents within a short time (1925/27) meant a completely new faculty. Rev John Gillies filled the New Testament chair from 1928 until his retirement in 1938. Gillies (1870-1952) had a strong background among the Free Church constitutionalists in Scotland before he came to Victoria in the 1890s. He was a thoroughly orthodox Calvinist, a penetrating and intellectual preacher. He provided much of the intellectual resources employed to try to keep the church on the lines of the Westminster Confession, although the spirit of the times was against him. He was quiet and hard to get to know at first. He wore a white tie rather than a clerical collar, and while a Professor only gave out Psalms when he led the College devotions. He used to say that in all the world the church he most loved to preach in was St George's PCEA and after that the Free Church at Geelong.[10]

F.E.Oxer, who had studied at Ormond with Gillies, was appointed Professor of Systematic Theology in succession to Adam. He was not so conservative, but was more a plodder. Gordon Powell remembers him as 'a grandfatherly figure.' He went to Western Australia to help in theological education there and so the chair was vacant in 1938, the same year Gillies retired. Gillies was succeeded by Alex Yule. He was orthodox on Scripture and the Trinity but was not a five point Calvinist. He was too old at the time of his appointment, his lectures were more like sermons and he was not taken seriously by the majority of students for their theology was quite liberal.

9. D.S.Adam, Cardinal Elements of the Christian Faith (London 1911), p.264.
10. Gillies was a particular friend of Rev Arthur Allen, who was minister of St George's PCEA 1944-58 and of Geelong FPCV 1938-44. Gillies, Allen, F.M.Bradshaw and others were involved in the forming of the 'Calvinistic Society of Victoria' in 1939, Allen giving the address at the first public meeting of the Society, see Our Banner, November 1939.

Smith was replaced by Hector Maclean (1885-1968). He was capable and, while committed to the critical approach to Scripture study, he was not destructive. Possessed of very considerable mental powers he had strong conservative streaks. His students often thought he appeared as the epitome of a Hebrew prophet as he opened up the Old Testament.

Oxer was replaced in Systematic Theology by Norman McLeish (1898-1949). He was a definite liberal but friendly, sincere and a man for peace and harmony. His teaching on the Trinity appears to have been Sabellian[11] and he held a moral influence theory of the atonement. He was a philosopher more than a theologian, a thorough gentleman from whom one could learn quite a lot even if it was not the Reformed Faith.

New South Wales

As noted on page 275, Andrew Harper filled the Old Testament chair in 1902 and he continued in this position until 1924 when he returned to Scotland. Harper was also Principal of St Andrew's College from 1902 to 1920. His influence was very significant, and St Andrew's became well established during his time. In theology Harper did not change his position. He was the recognised leader of 'higher criticism' in Australia but his students somewhat outran their master in many cases, and Harper was not without concern for its possible effects on future generations.[12] Harper's major published work in the period included *The Song of Solomon* (Cambridge 1902), *Christian Essentials* (Melbourne 1914), and the life of a leading Victorian Presbyterian *The Honourable James Balfour MLC* (Melbourne 1918)

John Kinross (1833-1908) continued as Professor of Systematic Theology until his death in 1908. A replacement was found in Robert G.Macintyre (1863-1954), who held the chair from 1909 to 1927. Macintyre had been minister of the Free Church of Scotland at Maxwelltown in 1900. It had been expected that he would side with the minority against the union of that year but, like Ephraim, he turned back in the day of battle.[13] This

11. By this meaning that McLeish thought of the persons as only modes or aspects of the one person, God, in the sense of an actor who plays different roles in a play. Gordon Powell set forth this position, which he assures me was what he was taught at Ormond in the 1930s, in his book of Christian doctrine, **The Blessing of Belief** (1956). It was also set out in the Bible Class Handbook '**I Believe**' published by the Joint Board of Religious Education, which led two members of the Albert and Middle Park Session to overture the PCV Assembly of 1951 (see p. 208 of proceedings). A dismal picture of the state of theological teaching is evident, a similar emphasis affecting much mainstream 'Protestant' writing to the present. There is, of course, much to be said for the view that only in the orthodox Reformed theology does Trinitarian theology come into its own.
12. Cf. D.Maclean, Travels in Sunny Lands, op. cit., pp.111-113.
13. G.N.M.Collins, The Heritage of our Fathers (Edinburgh 1974) p.100.

action is suggestive of his eye for the main chance. At any rate, Macintyre was to become the arch ecclesiastical politician of the PCNSW almost until his death. He was a liberal evangelical along Harper's line.

The chair of New Testament and Historical Theology, endowed in 1910, was occupied by Thomas Clouston who had tutored at the Theological Hall since 1894. He was a prominent churchman but a pastor rather than a scholar. His theology was not markedly different from that of Harper and Macintyre and, like them, he was a prominent supporter of a wider union among Protestant churches.

Upon his death in 1913, the PCNSW was keen to appoint a replacement who would further the image and standing of the church in the eyes of the world. By a vote of 102 to 55, Samuel Angus, who had been licensed by the United Free Church of Scotland in 1911 and was engaged in literary studies in Edinburgh, was chosen over Daniel Lamont of Hillhead UFC, Glasgow. Angus lacked significant pastoral experience - not a good sign - but had high testimonials as an up and coming scholar. He also had a testimonial written in 1912 from Professor James Orr (1844-1913), a liberal evangelical of great distinction and more conservatism on biblical criticism than Harper, which stated:

I know from himself and his writings that his theological standpoint is that of evangelical Christianity in his acceptance of the great cardinal doctrines of the Divinity of Christ, the Incarnation and the Atonement. [14]

This was in fact far from the case and Orr, who had befriended Angus and urged him to publish his first and best book [*The Environment of Early Christianity*, 1914][15] should have been far more perceptive. Indeed, Professor H.A.A.Kennedy had given Angus' name to Professor H.R. Mackintosh, who was the head of a Selection Committee in Britain appointed on behalf of the PCNSW. Angus knew all these men and his autobiography tells us of the following incident after attending worship in Edinburgh some time before coming to Sydney:

I frankly confessed to him [Kennedy] a difficulty I had experienced at the service when the officiating minister announced: 'Let us confess our faith in the Apostles' Creed.' I told Kennedy that, as this venerable Creed did not represent my Christian faith and was not to my mind the Christian faith, I stood up with the others in reverence to the divine service but refused to join in repeating the Creed. Kennedy thereupon informed me that he experienced exactly the same difficulty and that he never repeated the Creed as an act of worship, though neither of us could object to this Creed as an historic

14. Alan Dougan, A Backward Glance at the Angus Affair (Sydney 1971) p.8.
15. S.Angus, Alms for Oblivion (Sydney 1943) pp.158ff refer to his friendship with Orr. Rev Dr Neil Macleod affirmed to me on July 28, 1988 the statement made. Macleod knew Angus.

document of what had once been regarded as the Church's faith...Kennedy was himself an earnest and thoughtful preacher and under no suspicion of unorthodoxy.[16]

It will thus be seen that from his own mouth Angus was a radical, rejecting the fundamental facts of redemption affirmed by the church. But whereas Strong had been forced out Angus was invited in. While his appointment was not made unanimous in the usual manner, which seems to indicate some disquiet among some of the brethren, Angus accepted the offer of the Professorship, and was ordained and inducted to his post in March 1915. He continued without open accusation of unorthodoxy until 1923. The rest of his career has a separate chapter devoted to it. He died in 1943.

What the above says for Angus' oft lauded integrity will not be overlooked by the candid reader. It also says something for the situation in Australia and in Scotland that key teaching posts could be given to those who denied not mere Presbyterian distinctives but the common faith of Christendom. The Scriptures say the teaching office is given to build the church up in the unity of the faith and to protect from the deceitful scheming of false teachers (Ephesians 4:11ff). Here was the reverse. Mind you, it appears that the true nature of Angus' radicalism was not clearly known at the time of his appointment. Harper, who had been the chief one pushing for his appointment, presumably did not suppose he was supporting other than someone open to mainstream scholarship and committed to the supernatural facts of redemption. To what degree Angus fully disclosed his beliefs at the time remains an unanswered question.

Angus differed from Harper and Macintyre in his radicalism and also in that from 1919 he publicly opposed a wider church union. His own religious interest did not focus on the external organisation of the church but on individual commitment to following Jesus as Angus saw him, while he was also quite a typical Ulster Scot in many aspects of Presbyterian practice and heritage (eg. a centrally placed pulpit).

Harper's retirement led to the appointment of E.E.Anderson as Professor of Old Testament. He held this chair from 1924-1937. Kenneth Edward succeeded Macintyre in the chair of Theology and held it until his death in 1941. Neither of these two Scots were men of great prominence in the church but both had a good relationship with Angus, and Edward wrote a book in 1934 [The Creeds and the Living Church] in defence of his friend. So it will be seen that by 1928 the NSW senatus (faculty) was essentially liberal whereas the Victorian faculty was more conservative.

16. S.Angus, op. cit., pp.152, 153.

23: ATTEMPTS AT WIDER UNION 1901-1924

The fact that Presbyterian union was achieved in the same year (1901) as the political federation of the Australian colonies contributed to a general feeling of optimism as regards further union among Protestants. This was especially so among the more liberal-minded ministers. The 1901 GAA sustained an overture in the following terms which sought a Federation of Protestant Churches.

WHEREAS there are many Protestant Churches working in Australia for the advancement of the kingdom of Christ:

AND WHEREAS they are preaching practically the same Gospel, and the theological differences which have hitherto separated them have ceased to have a living interest, and they now differ from each other mainly in matters of Church government and forms of worship, which none of them regard as essentials of the faith:

AND WHEREAS of late years there has been a marked advance in the friendly relations of many of these Churches, so that interchange of pulpit services have become frequent, to the mutual satisfaction and profit of the congregations concerned:

AND WHEREAS in the country districts especially, the pastoral work of the Ministry could be more effectively overtaken if parishes were more compact and of less extent:

AND WHEREAS it would be an immense gain to the Christian Church if a united front could be presented in this land to the forces of sin and unbelief:

IT IS THEREFORE humbly overtured by the Presbytery of Sydney to the Venerable the General Assembly of New South Wales to overture the General Assembly of Australia to take these premises into consideration, and to appoint an influential Committee to devise a scheme for the federation of as many as possible of the Protestant Churches of Australia, with power to confer with the representatives of other Churches, so as to promote closer fellowship and organised co-operation, with a view to the ultimate formation of one grand Church of Australia, or to deal otherwise with the premises as to your Venerable House may seem fit.

The GAA resolved 'to sustain the overture in so far as to express sympathy

315

with the great ideal of a United Evangelical Christian Church in Australia' and set up a Committee 'to consider the principles on which the Presbyterian Church of Australia is prepared to consider the question of a larger union.'[1]

A premature move

As is now generally recognised,[2] this was a premature move. The Presbyterians had only just formed their own union and had not stabilised after the debate of previous years. Moreover, the powers of the GAA were limited. The Methodists did not achieve union among themselves until 1902, and their first General Conference was not held until 1904. The Congregational Union formed in 1888 held its second meeting in 1902 and only gained stability at its third meeting five years later when a constitution was adopted. The Anglicans were legally part of the Church of England and would not obtain autonomy until 1962. The Churches of Christ were too busy proselytising for their distinctive restorationist view of the church to even respond to an invitation to discuss union,[3] while all the Protestant bodies were still in their expansionist phase and not keen to act in a way which might be detrimental to the prospects of denominational growth.

Then there were the theological difficulties. The Methodists were Arminian rather than Calvinistic in orientation, and the Congregationalists, while originally Calvinistic, were no longer a confessional body and did not desire to enforce subscription to a confession of faith. The Baptist position (or lack of position) on children of believers was obviously a major question, and the Church of Christ position was different again. The Anglicans included an element who had moved well away from the earlier Protestant evangelicalism of the Thirty-nine Articles and who maintained a ritualism approaching Rome. This, together with other doctrinal fears associated with the spirit of the times, contributed to the demise about 1892 of the 'Church of England and Presbyterian Church Pastoral Aid Society' formed by members of both churches in 1872 to provide funds to supply religious ordinances in thinly-populated areas of Victoria.[4]

1. GAA, 1901, Minute 107
2. C.Uidam, **Why the Church Union Movement Failed in Australia 1901-1925** in JRH, Vol. 13 †4 (1985) p.393; J.S.Udy, **Australian Negotiations Towards Union: An Historical Survey 1901-1977** in **Church Heritage**, September 1978, p. 3.
3. F.Engel, **Australian Churches in Conflict and Unity** (Melbourne 1984) p.169 states he found no record of response and such would have been most unlikely at that time for the reason I have given. For Church of Christ background see T.J.Gore (ed), **That They May Be One** (Melbourne 1909); also D.Roper, **Voices Crying in the Wilderness** (Adelaide 1979).
4. F.Engel, ibid., pp.80-83.

The question of church polity was also significant. The Congregationalists, Baptists and Churches of Christ held that each congregation was independent, and the position of elder in these churches was also uncertain. The Methodists were connectional with a Conference appointing ministers to circuits (a group of congregations) for a limited number of years, whereas Presbyterians worked on the call system without a fixed term in the generality of cases. Methodists did not have elders as such but did make extensive use of lay preachers. This may have ensured the longer continuance of evangelical views but it did not safeguard the Presbyterian standards of ministerial education. These were much higher than usual in other churches and any threat to them was a cause of concern as has already been shown in reference to Presbyterian union.

The period 1901-1914

In September 1902 the GAA received a report from the 'Committee on the Federation of the Protestant Churches' which set out the Committee's understanding of those elements of doctrine and polity which could not 'be surrendered without disloyalty to Him who is the Head of the Church' and expressing 'all contained in the subordinate Standard which the Assembly regard as essential to the Church as a Divine Institution, or as necessary as matters of belief, for those connected with it.' The Committee's articles were as follows:

DOCTRINE

1. That the Supreme Authority in Doctrine and duty is the Holy Spirit speaking in the Old and New Testaments.
2. That God is personal, transcendant and immanent.
3. That the Godhead is essentially triune.
4. That Jesus Christ is God manifest in the flesh, and is truly God and truly man.
5. That God is love, and that His love is holy and sovereign.
6. That the Divine Fatherhood expresses an eternal relationship, which has been revealed most clearly by Jesus Christ, through whom the children of men come into possession of the Spirit and the privileges of sonship.
7. That sin is universal in the human race, and implies lawlessness and alienation from God, and unless repented of and forgiven, involves death eternal.
8. That Salvation is wholly of God, having the Father as its source, Jesus Christ as its Mediator, the Holy Spirit as its Agent, and is appropriated by faith.
9. That the active and passive obedience in the life and death of Jesus Christ is vicarious and propitiatory.

THE CHURCH

1. That Christ instituted a Church upon the earth of which His people are the members.
2. That Jesus Christ is the Supreme Head of the Church, and that He calls men to the ministry of teaching and ruling.
3. That the people, under the guidance of the Spirit of Christ, recognise and choose those whom He calls and who are thereupon, in Churches already constituted, officially set apart by those in office.

317

4. That the Sacraments of Baptism and the Lord's Supper are effectual means of grace appointed by Christ, and should be regularly and orderly celebrated.

5. That the efficacy of the Sacraments does not proceed from any virtue in the mere administration of the elements, or in Him [sic] who administers them, but depends upon the Spiritual presence of Christ with believing participants.

6. That those who administer the Sacraments have no priestly function save that which is shared by all believers.[5]

This rather diluted list of articles did not receive the hearty endorsement hoped for by the Convener, Dr Meiklejohn. The Assembly rejected the proposal to 'approve generally of the Articles contained in the Report on Doctrine and the Church as fairly setting forth the mind of the Church on the matters with which they deal, and as fitted to form a basis of negotiation for union with other Churches.' Rev Alexander Stewart sought various amendments. The first article in form was part of the Westminster Confession (1:9) but, taken out of its context of a well-defined, inspired canon of Scripture, the wording seemed to open the door to that kind of rationalistic higher criticism which found the message of God in a limited part of Scripture only. Thus, Stewart proposed as an amendment: 'The Scriptures of the Old and New Testaments are the supreme standard of doctrine and duty for mankind.'[6]

As explained by one who sympathised with Stewart, S.G.McLaren of Presbyterian Ladies' College, Melbourne, the first article would render it possible for one to hold that the Spirit of God does not speak in Genesis, for example, or that he speaks only in the actual words of Christ in the New Testament. McLaren held that the higher critics had a right to operate in the church but that the conclusions of the extreme variety were not yet 'assured results' which should be given recognition.[7] The result at the GAA was that the article was amended by prefixing the words: 'That the supreme and full revelation of God to men is the Lord Jesus Christ.' This did not solve the problem, but the GAA went on to resolve: 'Without taking the Articles in the Report into detailed consideration, or expressing final approval of them at this stage, agree to forward the same to the other Churches for their consideration and as affording a basis for further discussion.' A 17-man Committee was then appointed, with Dr Clouston of Sydney as Convener.

The next year the Committee reported at length and indicated useful discussions had been held with the Methodists and Congregationalists.

5. GAA, 1902 Reports, pp.71-72.

6. The GAA Minutes do not record the words of Stewart's amendment but see S.G. McLaren's letter in The Messenger (PCV), October 3, 1902.

7. S.G.McLaren to the Editor, The Messenger (PCV), October 3, 1902.

Organic union rather than a federal union was advocated in the report. The original articles had received some changes, in particular to include reference to the life to come and final judgement, but were essentially the same. It was quite obvious that matters were not yet ripe for major advance, and the Assembly resolved to this effect, appointing a large Committee to continue discussions with a view to formulating a basis of union.

At the Fourth GAA in 1905 the Committee was reappointed, and in 1906 reported considerable progress in drawing up a a Basis in conjunction with the Methodist and Congregational Churches. There had been some useful discussion with the Anglicans but their lack of autonomy would render further progress abortive. The Baptists had earlier indicated they could not contemplate a union which left infant baptism · an open question. The Committee indicated its readiness to modify the call system 'for life or until blame' to a call with 5 year tenure for self-supporting parishes. Non-self-supporting parishes would be on an appointment system. The major doctrinal point was predestination. Unanimity had not been possible and the question was left an open one for the present. The Committee in 1903 had suggested that there not be 'rigidity' in the subscription to a doctrinal basis. An attempt by Rev T.R.Cairns to have the GAA proceed no further was unsuccessful, and the Committee was instructed to proceed with further consideration of the Basis.

By 1907, the 16 point 'Proposed Basis of Doctrine' prepared by the New South Wales section of the Committee had been reviewed by the Victorian section and with a few amendments now supplanted the brief list of principles drafted earlier. In the form in which it was submitted to the 1907 GAA the Basis was almost entirely derived from the 'Brief Statement of the Reformed Faith' approved in 1902 by the Presbyterian Church in the United States of America. It had been drawn up by that Church for the purpose 'of giving information and a better understanding of our beliefs and not with a view to its becoming a substitute or an alternative of our Confession of Faith.' [8]

The 1907 proposal followed the order of the 1902 Statement, except it combined the paragraph on Election with that on the Grace of God, omitting the positive teaching of election in the process, and split the section on the Church and the Sacraments into two, so retaining 16 Articles. Other significant changes included the addition of reference to the progress of revelation and to the authority of the Holy Spirit in the Article on Revelation, the omission of 'our first parents' in the Article on the Sin of Man, and a reworking of the Article on the Law of God.

8. Text in P.Schaff, The Creeds of Christendom (6th edition 1931) pp. 922-924.

The GAA resolved to send the Basis of Doctrine to Assemblies and Presbyteries for information and suggestions. However, few were received by the next GAA in 1909, most regarding any major comment premature until a complete Basis of Union was drafted. The 1909 GAA directed the Committee to 'continue vigorously' the negotiations (Minute 80), and the following year the Scheme of Polity was submitted, received 'general approval' (Minute 102), despite opposition which led to the recording of 13 dissents, and was sent to State Assemblies and Presbyteries for comment.

At the next GAA (1912) it was reported that more time was needed to consider the comments from State Assemblies and Presbyteries. By a narrow margin (36 to 32) the GAA defeated a proposal by Rev John Gray and Rev T.J.Smith which would have ended negotiations with a view to organic union, and authorised the Committee to proceed to further revision and to report to the next GAA in 1914. However, the reactions of 15 Presbyteries and 3 State Assemblies as reported in 1912 should have been a fair warning of major problems. Several Presbyteries (Melbourne North, Wagga Wagga, Hobart and Toowoomba) and the Tasmanian Assembly opposed the Basis of Doctrine and Scheme of Polity; there was evident support for co-operation and federation rather than organic union (Presbyteries of Mortlake, Bendigo, Hamilton, Hobart and Hastings); and there were major concerns about the Scheme of Polity. The Basis of Doctrine attracted little criticism at this stage, the only major addition requested being a reference to the Return of Christ. However, as the Scheme of Polity did not provide a place for Boards of Management, did not retain the status of the elder as a spiritual office, and replaced the call system by an appointment system in which the call of the congregation was not determinative, there was a strong focus of opposition on these practical matters which could be expected to show among the other 30 or so Presbyteries which had not sent in reports.

The Committee's report to the GAA in 1914 made amendments to meet some of the objections but it was too little too late. Only the casting vote of the Moderator saved the Union Committee. It was accordingly instructed to send its proposals to lower courts if the other negotiating churches were happy with them. However, the Methodist Conference of 1913, apparently frustrated by the slow progress, discharged its Committee, and so the first chapter in progress towards a wider union was closed.

*

Considering that the Scheme of Union adopted by the Presbyterians in 1901 did not envisage formal departure from the doctrine of the Confession of Faith,[9] or union with churches of a different tradition, it might be wondered why negotiations with the Methodists and others began at all, and why they continued despite growing opposition. The origin in the optimism of the era on the part of the more liberal churchmen has already been indicated. However, another factor in the pro-union push seems to have been confidence that the Church could act in the discharge of her obedience to Christ as she conceived it without risk of consequences before the civil courts. This subject is worthy of some attention.

The Free Church Case

In 1900, 98% of the Free Church of Scotland united with the United Presbyterian Church of Scotland to form the United Free Church of Scotland. Having thought there was little to fear, the shock when the minority Free Church won their appeal to the House of Lords in 1904 was considerable. The principle in the case was simple: in the absence of a power of change in the trust instrument, a dissenting minority can enforce the trust for the benefit of those adhering to the original principles and prevent the transfer of assets to a body holding different principles. If the minority was unable to effectively administer the trust some court or parliamentary sanction for a scheme of allocation would be appropriate. Put more simply, any church which has not expressly claimed a power of change in its constitution and then changes its beliefs is exposed to forfeiture of its property to a dissenting minority. This was not new law (as often supposed) or law made by English judges with no understanding of Scottish Presbyterian ways, although this was often said.[10] It was merely the eminently equitable

9. Note the following from the Report on Union to the PCV Assembly in November 1899: 'The proposal of the Presbytery of Melbourne North to limit the power of changing the Basis so that the change will go no further than a revision or abridgment of the Subordinate Standard of the Church, or a restatement of its doctrine, gives all the liberty that the Church is at any time likely to seek, and while the clause as it stands in Article III, viz., 'Any proposed change in the Basis of Union,' seems to the majority of the Committee perfectly safe, and on the whole preferable to the other, they do not object to the clause being so altered...' (page xcv).

10. The FCS based its claim upon the leaving of the establishment principle an open question and upon the revised relationship to the Confession brought about by the new Formula of 1900. UFC writers often said that if Lord Shand had not died before giving his judgement the decision would have been against the FCS 2-3 instead of 5-2 in favour in the re-hearing with an enlarged bench. It is probable that Lord Shand's view was actually favourable to the FCS. This was the understanding of Rev John Sinclair of Geelong FPCV when he made enquiry of Scotland over a [false] press report [Argus, November 8, 1904] which alleged a FCS minister had told his people to be thankful for the death of Lord Shand. This aside, the relevant aspect of the law of charitable trusts in England is the same as in Scotland; at the re-hearing (but not the first hearing) the judges had copies of all the historical documents relied upon; and the decision, so far as it related to the establishment principle, was consistent with opinion of eminent counsel obtained by the FCS in 1873. See also F.Lyall, **Of Presbyters and Kings: Church and State in the Law of Scotland** (Aberdeen 1980) p.109.

application of existing law. The property involved was many millions of pounds sterling, and the handful of Free Church ministers were ridiculed as the 'Wee Frees'[11] or even the 'Legal Frees' by those hostile and contemptuous at their success.

In Australia the sentiment was naturally mostly with the United Free Church. There was some concern that the union negotiations then occurring in Australia could be imperilled, but in general there was an attitude dismissive of an apparent 'aberration' in British justice. It seems likely that some were stimulated to see in the planned union an opportunity to obtain a more flexible constitution. The theory behind the need for such flexibility is the belief that Scripture is not so clear in its main principles that they can be stated in a form which can stand the test of time. Put in its most attractive form by the GAA Moderator in 1905, Rev P.J.Murdoch, the argument was that all the freedom the Church can properly seek is freedom to obey, but who is fit to judge whether she is obeying Christ or not? Thus, the only earthly judge of the Church's obedience was held to be the Church itself.[12]

The Frackleton Case

In 1907, Rev W.S.Frackleton, minister of Ann Street Presbyterian Church in Brisbane, issued a writ to restrain proceedings against him by the Presbytery of Brisbane which would have terminated the pastoral tie. The Queensland Assembly regarded Frackleton's action as subversive of his ordination vows, suspended him for six months and declared the pastoral tie dissolved. The right to appeal to the forthcoming GAA was denied and a petition to that body in September 1907 was refused. Frackleton then took legal action against the Queensland Assembly and the Presbytery before the Chief Justice. He was successful and also obtained a favourable result when the decision was appealed to the Full Court and then to the High Court in 1909. The basic issue was that his suspension and removal from his charge were not in accordance with the constitution and rules which the church had adopted. As his civil rights were touched the civil court had jurisdiction. It was the same issue as in the Cardross Case discussed earlier (pages 203-204).

11. 'Wee Frees' was not employed in reference to the Free Church of Scotland in 1843 although 'Wee Kirk' was sometimes used as in the rhyme: The Wee Kirk, the Free Kirk, the Kirk without the steeple! The Auld Kird, the Cold Kirk, the Kirk without the people! It had relevance in the post 1900 position in Scotland since only 26 ministers out of more than 1,000 continued to adhere.
12. See Murdoch's address 'The Liberty of Christian Churches' in The Messenger (PCV) September 22, 1905 and September 29, 1905. In 1905 the United Free Church passed legislation concerning spiritual independence which asserted the liberty of the church to 'alter, change, add to or modify her constitution' subject to the Word of God and the fundamental doctrines of the church of which the church was to be the sole judge. The Church of Scotland secured Parliamentary sanction to act similarly and such a position became part of the Church of Scotland constitution in 1926. The PCA has a rather more limited power of change (compare footnote 9 above). The PCEA claims no power of change hence any change places the property trust at risk if a dissenting minority take legal action.

It might have been thought that the PCA would pause a little. However, so worked up did the generality of ministers become that an assertion of the spiritual independence of the church which would have excluded protection of the civil rights of ministers and members was mooted at the GAA in 1909. In vain did men like Dr Rentoul, Dr Dill Mackay, Revs A.Stewart, T.J.Smith and F.A.Hagenauer point out that the Presbyterian position was not at risk from the decision in the Frackleton Case. That position does not include a claim to be the sole judge of what is spiritual and what is civil, nor does it exclude the civil tribunal in civil consequences attached to ecclesiastical decisions. While the civil law might regard the church as a voluntary association for its purposes, this did not mean that the church itself was created by civil statute or mere human decision. As the creation of Christ in the call of his Word and Spirit, Presbyterians held the church to be a divine institution, but this did not imply that the property trust of a church may not be tied to civil enactments or that the civil rights of ministers are not a province for Caesar.[13]

GAA Reaction

However, the GAA blithely and blindly pushed ahead with somewhat fatuous legislation which reached its final form in 1914 as the 'Declaration and Rules Relative to Spiritual Independence.' This purported to exclude recourse to civil courts, on pain of contumacy, against any decision of the church in doctrine, worship, discipline and government, and asserted a *nobile officium*, that is, the power of a General Assembly in matters in which it is supreme to supply a provision for handling a matter for which no provision existed, or for modifying in certain cases the existing provision in the rules.

As to the exclusion of recourse to civil courts, this was not effectively and fully prohibited although the impression is there that such an act is a heinous sin. As to the nobile officium, this implies that the polity of the Presbyterian Church is inadequate - something that was never admitted until Robert Rainy advocated such a power in 1880/81 as a means of handling the Robertson Smith Case administratively rather than judicially. In other words, there was appropriate power to deal with Smith judicially but to serve political ends the fiction of a nobile officium was claimed. The principles of Presbyterian polity are such that an analogy from an existing provision can always be made to apply to a case somewhat different from those previously handled. But Smith did not get a fair trial.[14]

13. Thus the Cardross Case discussed previously. To similar effect note †32 & †44 in **Catechism of the Principles and Constitution of the Free Church of Scotland**, which received the approbation of the Assembly of the Free Church in June 1847.

14. The nobile officium is a provision of Scots law not English law. It is the power of the Court of Session (the highest civil court in Scotland) to provide a remedy on an

The reactions to the Free Church Case and the Frackleton Case indicate a trend of thinking that was relatively unconcerned with legal consequences of ecclesiastical acts. The Frackleton Case did lead to more careful formulation of rules and indirectly it may have tended to help the anti-union cause since it stimulated clan loyalty and encouraged members to rally to the defence of their church.[15]

Renewal of negotiations 1916-1918

A second chapter in the union saga began in 1916 when the GAA of that year noted that the War gave fresh urgency to the union project and that the Congregational, Methodist and Presbyterian Churches in Canada were planning to unite. Accordingly, the Committee was instructed to prepare a revised Basis in consultation with the other churches and, if agreement was reached, to send same to State Assemblies and Presbyteries for approval or otherwise.

The 1907 Basis of Doctrine had been expanded in 1914 to 17 Articles - that on the Resurrection was combined with that on the Last Judgment, and two new Articles (Of the Ministry and Of Church Order and Fellowship) were added. The 1914 Basis was now revamped by the addition of Articles X and XII and a Preface together with some other changes. These included removal of reference to the eternal punishment of the finally impentitent (Article XVII), a fuller statement on the sacraments (Article XV), contraction of Article VI, and changes to Article XI which appear to concede something of the Methodist 'sinless perfection' doctrine.

As for the Scheme of Polity, this remained as revised in 1914 except that it conceded the expressed wishes of the ministers and congregations should operate as much as possible in the appointments of ministers. The councils and courts of the church were to be: (1) Board of Management; (2) The

equitable basis where there is an inadequacy in the law. A rather abstruse account of the nobile officium in Scotland is in GAA Reports for 1912, pp.130-132. However, Gibb & Walker's standard work, **Introduction to the Law of Scotland** (5th edition 1952) p.8 stresses it is a power to supply some lack due to statutory informality in non-contentious procedures. Three points may be made: (1) the application to a Presbyterian assembly is far-fetched and it would need to be shown that the assembly has or needs such a power; (2) it is an extremely limited provision and must be even less in Australia seeing that our law is English in origin not Scottish; (3) in the PCA the constitutional basis is merely an Act of the GAA and is not part of the binding constitution. Interestingly, the Practice of the Free Church of Scotland (1964 edition page 96) and the Practice of the Free Presbyterian Church of Scotland (1969 edition page 93) retain the claim of nobile officium although its exercise is another thing. In the PCA the provision does not appear to have had formal use either, but it remains an influence which encourages a wrong outlook, such as the handling of a judicial matter administratively.

15. So S.Emilsen, **Samuel Angus and the PCA in the State of NSW** (PhD Thesis, University of Sydney 1985) p.50.

Elders' Meeting; (3) The Circuit Council; (4) The Presbytery; (5) The Conference; (6) The General Assembly. As the interchange of nomenclature suggests, the polity was an amalgam of Methodist and Presbyterian elements. Changes to the constitution of the proposed church would require the approval of a majority of Presbyteries and Conferences reporting on the change (Para. 25b) - a much less onerous requirement than in the 1901 Presbyterian constitution.

The Canadian connection

As early as 1902 the Methodist Church of Canada appointed a Committee to formulate a Basis of Union with the Congregational and Presbyterian Churches. Each of the Churches took the matter up and a Joint Committee met in 1904. After failing to gain support from the Baptist and Episcopal Churches, a proposed Basis was submitted. Based upon the American 'Brief Statement' of 1902, it received the approval of 71.4% of the Presbyteries (50 out of 70). When voted on at the local level in 1912, 68.9% of the 155,033 votes cast were in favour, although only 53.8% of the 287,944 eligible voters (communicant members) voted. Union could have taken place at this point, as the constitutional provisions had been met. However, it was decided to delay with a view to gaining wider support, and to that end make a few amendments to the Basis. The Methodists had voted 86.1% in favour (150,841 votes out of 175,198 cast), although there was only a 59.6% turnout from the 293,967 on the voting roll. The Congregational voting roll was less than 11,000, but the 35% who voted were 78% in favour. When the Presbyterians took a further vote on the slightly revised Basis, 69.7% of Presbyteries (53 out of 76) voted in favour. However, while the turnout of voters at the parish level was higher (176,447 compared to 155,033 in 1912) the number approving union actually declined (106,534 compared to 106,775) and the proportion in favour dropped to 60.4%. However, the 1916 Presbyterian Assembly, by a vote of 406 to 90, resolved to proceed to union after the War. Meantime, local unions, especially in the prairie provinces, continued.[16]

There was a truce on agitation from 1917 to 1921, when something like a war broke out. Elders in particular provided support to preserve the Presbyterian Church as an institution from what they considered an unwarranted attack upon it. This support came chiefly from the urban congregations in Ontario which were well established and had little to gain from the union. However, by 1921, when the truce ended, there were more than 1,000 union congregations and 'there could be no turning back.'[17] In 1924/25 a further

16. The statistics on voting and the Basis of Union are in P.Schaff, op.cit.,pp. 934-938.
17. Alan W.Black, Church Union in Canada and Australia: A Comparative Analysis in Church Heritage, September 1983, p.109.

vote was taken which showed 113,773 in favour and 114,367 against. This indicates the success of anti-unionists in rallying support from the previously uncommitted. This support was not on the basis of re-creating a new church or adopting a new or an old theology. Concerning the anti-union movement:

It had no desire to turn the clock back, it had no great plans for the reconstruction of the church or society and it was not opposed to change within the Presbyterian Church. All it opposed was any change which would involve the elimination of an historic institution. Consequently, its defence of the Presbyterian Church was simply a point by point rebuttal of all the unionists' arguments in favour of merging the Presbyterian Church into another institution.[18]

The 1924/25 vote had no direct relevance to the validity of entering into union, only to the disposition of property, and the United Church of Canada was duly constituted on June 10, 1925 with about 3,750 ministers, 8,691 congregations and 600,000 members. About 25% of Presbyterian ministers and 35% of the membership remained Presbyterian. Thus after the 1925 union there were 558 ministers, 1,140 congregations (including 434 self-sustaining charges) and 154,000 full members. In the light of the Free Church Case of 1904 there was provision for congregations not in favour of union to retain their property, and an equitable share in denominational property was granted the continuing Church.

The significance for our purposes of the Canadian experience lies in the great similarity of the Basis as well as the increase of opposition over the years. However, the result was different since the constitutional requirements to enable union were not achieved in the Presbyterian Church of Australia, and the union move came to an end in 1923. The following paragraphs will review the progress to this result.

The period 1918-1924

Despite opposition, the 1918 GAA adopted the Basis of Doctrine and Scheme of Polity as one on which it was prepared to unite, and ordered a vote to be taken of the members. This was done by each of the three denominations.

The evangelistically minded Methodists accepted the Basis to the extent of 86% of the 71,538 votes cast. The lowest figure was 74% in New South Wales where there was organised Methodist opposition. The Congregationalists - as in Canada a very small group - cast 10,841 votes of which 84% were in favour. However, the Presbyterians with their background in a definite confessional

---

18. N.Keith Clifford, **The Resistance to Church Union in Canada 1904-1939** (Vancouver 1985) p. 2. Clifford's book is the best one on the subject that I have seen. He is a United Church member but writes with understanding and objectivity. A more popular study is N.G.Smith et al, **A Short History of the Presbyterian Church in Canada** (Toronto 1964).

position and Scots-Irish traditions recorded 45,251 votes of communicant members, of which only 58% were in favour. The chief opposition was in Victoria with Tasmania and South Australia, which were largely dependent on Victoria, not far behind. The following table summarises the voting and includes corrections to September 1920 as reported to the 1920 GAA which are commonly overlooked in published accounts (eg. 1924 GAA Reports p.87; also D.E.Hansen's paper in *Church Heritage*, September 1979).

COMMUNICANTS' VOTE ON UNION 1920

State	Members	Votes cast	% vote	'Yes' vote	% yes vote	% of members
NSW	22,936	15,761	69	9,983	63	44
VIC	34,972	21,794	62	10,443	48	30
SA	2,574	1,345	52	764	57	30
QLD	9,316	4,356	47	3,535	81	38
WA	2,156	1,289	60	926	72	43
TAS	1,476	706	48	383	54	26
AUS	73,430	45,251	62	26,034	58	35

Note: The votes of 31,371 adherents were also recorded, 64% in favour of union.

The constitution did not require the consent of congregations before union was effected, but did give dissenting congregations certain rights. Further, the Free Church Case of 1904 had relevance since without a proper measure of opinion and reasonable provision for minorities standing out, the sanction of the various Parliaments to changes in the basis on which Presbyterian property was held would be unlikely.

Of greater significance was the voting in State Assemblies and Presbyteries. At the GAA it was reported that all State Assemblies approved and 28 of the 49 Presbyteries (57%).[19] A gain of two Presbyteries would be necessary to meet the constitutional requirement of 60%. The 1920 GAA viewed the results with some optimism and instructed the Committee to press on in the expectation that more discussion and a few amendments would increase support. A new vote was ordered on the Basis as finally revised. This revision included a reference to 'the Word of God in the Scriptures' as the supreme rule, and an acknowledgement of 'the faith of the Ancient Church, as expressed in the Apostles' and Nicene Creeds.' However, at the State level three of the six Assemblies disapproved thereby killing church union and rendering further voting pointless. The voting in State Assemblies as reported to the GAA is shown in the following table and indicates that the anti-unionists had been successful in rallying opposition particularly through the activities of the Melbourne-based *Presbyterian Church Defence Association*, formed in 1919, which had a lot of influence among elders.

19. GAA Reports, 1920 p.124 show 28 approved and 20 opposed with one (Goldfields) not submitting a return, and this has sometimes (wrongly) been taken as an approval.

STATE ASSEMBLY VOTING ON UNION

	1920			1923		
State	Yes	No	Total	Yes	No	Total
VIC	123	48	171	140	148	288
NSW	41	23	64	114	83	197
QLD	26	13	39	31	26	57
SA	30	0	30	10	11	21
WA	15	11	26	14	16	30
TAS	11	5	16	8	4	12
AUS	246	100	346	317	288	605
	71.1%			52.4%		

The failure of union

As was also the case in Canada, opponents of union were not united theologically. Anti-unionists included such solid Calvinists as John Gillies, formerly of Hawthorn, South Australia but latterly of Victoria; Allan McKillop of Lismore, New South Wales and later of Clayfield, Brisbane; and R.J.H.McGowan of Ashfield, Sydney. These men were of Free Church type. Gillies had come to Australia in the 1890s to complete his training for the ministry at Ormond. His background was with the constitutionalists in the Free Church of Scotland. He did not at first know of the continued existence of the FPCV which was then at its lowest ebb. Gillies was later Professor of New Testament at the Theological Hall and was a rather typical Highland divine. McGowan wrote against the union, particularly in reference to the weakness he perceived in regard to the doctrines of Scripture and the Trinity. Among some others who could be mentioned was Rev John Gray of Warrnambool, a very orthodox man but not controversial. There was also that rough-hewn Calvinist and pulpit orator, F.A.Hagenauer, son of a minister of the same name. Of him many tales are told. A former champion boxer he was a colourful figure and forthright in his defence of the faith. He was for a good period minister of Cairns' Memorial Church, East Melbourne.[20]

Alongside such men there were others whose commitment to the robust doctrines of the Confession of Faith was perhaps less obvious although they would not have admitted it. Rev Donald Cameron, the driving force in social service work in the PCV, was not aggressively orthodox, but he was a very

20. A motion proposed by Rentoul at the GAA in 1920 (Minute 40) went to a division was lost 74 to 128 and the names were recorded (Minute 45). I owe a debt to F.Maxwell Bradshaw for recollections of several of these men which though they do not find a place in the narrative have certainly helped appreciate them as individuals. McGowan's main work against union was A Doctrinal Landslide or the Union Basis in the Light of the Creeds and Confessions (Ashfield, July 1920).

shrewd tactician. He worked with 'Fighting Larry' Rentoul to organise effective opposition to union. Rentoul, having trained so many for the ministry, was very influential although he appeared less than relevant to some of the younger men. The union debate and the failure of the liberal approach contributed to him furthering conservative views on doctrine although he had never been a radical. Rev Peter Foster, a rather excitable man, was also prominent with Cameron and Rentoul in the Presbyterian Church Defence Association.

If many or even most opponents of union fell in the middle ground there were also opponents from the radical liberal side too. Although Samuel Angus was not yet widely known for unorthodox views, he was an advanced liberal and from 1919 he came out strongly against union, criticising the Union Committee and its two prominent members - fellow Professors Andrew Harper and R.G.McIntyre - and accusing the Committee of exceeding its powers in its education campaign, and criticising the whole idea of selling the Presbyterian birthright for a mess of pottage. But to Angus and other liberals like John Edwards of Rose Bay, the Basis was too specific and too dogmatic. The Basis was in general a summary of doctrine as in practice accepted by most ministers about 1900. It was therefore neither strictly orthodox nor radically modernist. It was neither one thing nor the other, hence was criticised by McGowan and by Angus from their particular perspectives. The actual subscription required was vague, and the Basis was not treated like a subordinate standard had been in historic Presbyterianism.

The following words in reference to Canada also apply to Australia:

The later 19th century had witnessed a steady erosion of the Calvinistic orthodoxy with which Presbyterianism had traditionally been identified. In part, this was in the direction of a Methodist type of pietism which placed the primary emphasis on feeling and experience rather than on purity of doctrine. In part, it was in the direction of theological liberalism with its confidence in progress, its optimistic assessment of human nature, and its faith that enlightened human effort would usher in the Kingdom of God on earth. In such an atmosphere the sombre creed of Calvinism seemed an alien intrusion, and many Presbyterians were induced, consciously or unconsciously, to dilute it or adapt it to altered circumstances. Some were coming to believe that all creeds were in essence pretty much the same, that they complemented rather than contradicted one another, that they should no longer be allowed to keep Christians apart, and that the practical needs of the Church in Canada must take precedence over denominational peculiarities.[21]

21. N.G.Smith, op.cit., p.70. For Angus' views on church union see Susan Emilsen, op. cit., pp.203-218. For liberal criticism of the similar Canadian basis see E.L.Morrow, Church Union in Canada (Toronto 1923) especially pp.214ff and pp.405-434. C.N. Button, D.J.Flockhart and John Flynn dissented with Angus, GAA, 1922, p.42.

Criticism which suggested a decline in the Presbyterian standard of ministerial training, or alleged that union 'would be a gross violation of our historic memories, and Ordination Vow, and a forfeiture of the place of our Presbyterian Church of Australia within the Brotherhood and Community of the Presbyterian Churches of the British and other English-speaking lands' (J.L.Rentoul 1920) had a powerful effect. The ordered way of operation and the ethnic dimension were very much part of the birthright to Ulster Scots as diverse theologically as Rentoul and Angus.

If union had proceeded there would have been a sizeable continuing church, more conservative theologically, initially at least, which would have continued to claim to be the heir of the traditions and culture of Scots-Irish Presbyterianism. It would have had significant funds since the wealthy Victorian church was anti-union, and its geographical spread, judging from Presbytery voting as recorded in the 1920 GAA Reports, would have been widespread and not localised. As it turned out, while attempts to delay did not achieve much, the increasing strength of sentiment against union killed any prospect of real progress, the Angus controversy did not help, and a survey requested by the 1933 GAA showed lack of support.

Approach to Australian Free Church 1923

In the light of the preceding context it is of interest to note that the Assembly of the Free Presbyterian Church of Australia meeting in Sydney in February 1923 received a letter from the GAA requesting the appointment of a Committee to confer re union. The following resolution was recorded by the FP Assembly on February 20, 1923:

In reply to the overture from your Assembly regarding Union, we wish to state very respectfully that whilst appreciating your commendable desire for a closer union of the Christian Churches, we deeply deplore that the differences in doctrine, worship and practice between you and us are becoming increasingly great.

The inspiration, inerrancy and supremacy of the Old and New Testaments and the essential Deity of Our Lord and His vicarious atonement as declared in His own Word we regard as fundamentals of the Christian faith and any divergence from them as fatal to the purpose for which Christianity exists.

Our Assembly is unanimously agreed that until your General Assembly has declared its unqualified belief in these vital doctrines no good purpose can be served by conferring about the subject.

And that seems a courteous and appropriate response. It is also worth noting that the same FP Assembly received advice from its solicitors that an organic union of the PCEA, FPCV and the South Australian folk 'cannot be effected' in their opinion. So the federal Assembly structure continued for a further 30 years until the FPCV was in fact absorbed into the PCEA.

APPENDIX: PROPOSED BASIS OF UNION 1918

The following is the doctrinal part of the Basis agreed to by the Joint Committee of the Presbyterian, Methodist and Congregational Churches, September 1918. Subsequently a few small amendments were proposed, the most significant perhaps being the omission of 'Last' from the title of Article XVIII. See also page 327.

GENERAL.

1. The name of the Church formed by the Union of the Presbyterian, Methodist, and Congregational Churches in Australia and Tasmania shall be "The United Church of Australia."

DOCTRINE.

We, the representatives of the Presbyterian, the Methodist, and the Congregational branches of the Church of Christ in Australia, do hereby set forth the substance of the Christian Faith, as commonly held among us.

In so doing we build upon the foundation laid by the Apostles and prophets, Jesus Christ Himself being the chief corner-stone. We affirm our belief in the Scriptures of the Old and New Testaments as the primary source and ultimate standard of Christian Faith and life. We maintain our allegiance to the evangelical doctrines of the Reformation, as set forth in common in the doctrinal standards adopted or held by the Presbyterian Church, by the Congregational Churches, and by the Methodist Church. We present the accompanying statement as a brief summary of our common faith, and commend it to the studious attention of the members and adherents of the negotiating Churches as in substance agreeable to the teaching of the Holy Scriptures.

ARTICLE I.—OF GOD.—We believe in one only living and true God, Who is Spirit, the Father of our Spirits; infinite, eternal, and unchangeable in His being and perfections; the Lord Almighty, just in all His ways, glorious in holiness, unsearchable in wisdom, and plenteous in mercy, full of love and compassion, and abundant in goodness and truth. We worship Him, Father, Son, and Holy Spirit, three persons in one Godhead, equal in power and glory. To Him be the glory for ever. Amen.

ARTICLE II.—OF REVELATION.—We believe that God has revealed Himself in nature, in history, and in the heart of man; that He has made clearer revelation of Himself through men of God, who spoke as they were moved by the Holy Spirit, and that this revelation, gradually advancing in clearness and grace, reached its fullness in Jesus Christ, the Word made flesh, Who is the brightness of the Father's glory and the Express Image of His Person. We receive the Holy Scriptures as given by inspiration, to be a faithful record of God's gracious revelation and the sure witness to Christ; and we reverently acknowledge the Holy Spirit speaking in the Scriptures to be the Supreme Judge in questions of faith and duty.

ARTICLE III.—OF THE DIVINE PURPOSE.—We believe that the eternal, wise, holy, and loving purpose of God embraces all events, so that, while the freedom of man is not taken away, nor is God the author of sin, yet, in His providence, He makes all things work together for the fulfilment of His sovereign design and the manifestation of His glory. Wherefore, humbly acknowledging the mystery of this truth, we trust in His protecting and guiding care, and set our hearts to do His will.

ARTICLE IV.—OF CREATION AND PROVIDENCE.—We believe that God is the creator, upholder, and governor of all things; that He is above all His works and in them all; and that He made man in His own image, meet for fellowship with Him, free and able to choose between good and evil, and responsible to his Maker and Lord.

331

ARTICLE V.—OF THE SIN OF MAN.—We believe that man, being tempted, chose evil, and so fell away from God, and came under the power of sin, the penalty of which is death; and we confess that by reason of this disobedience, we and all men are born with a fallen nature, that we have broken God's law, and that no man can be saved but by His grace.

ARTICLE VI.—OF THE GRACE OF GOD.—We believe that God, out of His great love for the world, has given His only-begotten Son to be the Saviour of Sinners, and in the Gospel freely offers His salvation to all men.

ARTICLE VII.—OF THE LORD JESUS CHRIST.—We believe in and confess the Lord Jesus Christ, the only Mediator between God and man, Who being the eternal Son of God, for us men and for our salvation became truly man, yet without sin, being conceived by the Holy Ghost and born of the Virgin Mary; unto us He has revealed the Father, and made known the perfect will of God; for us He fulfilled all righteousness; by His perfect sacrifice of Himself upon the Cross He manifested the love and showed forth the righteousness of God, and became the propitiation for the sin of the world; for us He rose from the dead and ascended into heaven, where He maketh continual intercession; in us, united to Him by faith, He abides for ever; over us and over all He rules; wherefore, unto Him we render love, obedience, and adoration, as our Prophet, Priest, and King.

ARTICLE VIII.—OF THE HOLY SPIRIT.—We believe in the Holy Spirit, the Lord and Giver of Life, who moves upon the hearts of all men, to restrain them from evil, and to incite them unto good, and whom the Father is ever willing to give unto all who ask Him. We believe that He has spoken by holy men of God in making known His truth to men for their salvation; that through our exalted Saviour He was sent forth in power to convict the world of sin, to enlighten men's minds in the knowledge of Christ, and to persuade and enable them to obey the call of the Gospel; and that He abides with the Church, dwelling in every believer as the Spirit of truth, of power, of holiness, of comfort, and of love.

ARTICLE IX.—OF REPENTANCE AND FAITH.—We believe that every one who through the grace of the Holy Spirit repents and believes the Gospel, confessing and forsaking his sins, and relying upon God's redeeming love in Christ for salvation, is, through Christ's perfect obedience and atoning sacrifice, freely pardoned and accepted as righteous in God's sight.

ARTICLE X.—OF REGENERATION.—We believe in the necessity of regeneration, whereby we are made new creatures in Christ Jesus by the Spirit of God, Who imparts spiritual life by the gracious and mysterious operation of His power, using as the ordinary means the truths of His word and the ordinances of divine appointment in ways agreeable to the nature of man.

ARTICLE XI.—OF THE NEW LIFE.—We believe that those who are regenerated and justified grow in the likeness of Christ through fellowship with Him, the indwelling of the Holy Spirit, and obedience to the truth; that a holy life is the fruit and evidence of saving faith; and that the believer's hope of continuance in such a life is in the preserving grace of God. And we believe that in this growth in grace Christians may attain that maturity and full assurance of faith whereby the love of God is made perfect in us.

ARTICLE XII.—OF PRAYER.—We believe it to be our duty and privilege to draw near to God, our Heavenly Father, in the name of His Son, Jesus Christ, and on our own behalf and that of others, to pour out our hearts humbly, yet freely, before Him, as becomes His beloved children, giving Him the honour and praise due to His holy name, praying that His Will may be done on earth as in heaven, confessing unto Him our sins, and seeking from Him every gift needful for this life, and for our everlasting salvation. We believe also that, inasmuch as all true prayer is prompted by His Spirit, He

332

will, in response thereto, grant us every blessing, according to His unsearchable wisdom and the riches of His grace in Jesus Christ.

ARTICLE XIII.—OF THE LAW OF GOD.—We believe that God requires of every man to do justly, to love mercy, and to walk humbly with his God; and that only through this harmony with the will of God shall be fulfilled that brotherhood of man wherein the kingdom of God is to be made manifest. We believe and acknowledge that the Lord Jesus Christ has laid His people, by His grace, under new obligation to keep the perfect Law of God, and has by precept and example enlarged our knowledge of that Law, and manifested the spirit of filial love in which the Divine Will is to be obeyed.

ARTICLE XIV.—OF THE CHURCH.—We acknowledge one Holy Catholic Church, the innumerable company of saints of every age and nation, who, being united by the Holy Spirit to Christ, their Head, are one body in Him, and have communion with their Lord and with one another; further, we receive it as the will of Christ that His Church on earth should exist as a visible and sacred brotherhood, consisting of those who profess faith in Jesus Christ and obedience to Him, together with baptized children, organized for the confession of His Name, the public worship of God, the upbuilding of the saints, the proclamation of the Gospel, and the administration of the sacraments. We acknowledge as a part of this universal brotherhood every particular Church throughout the world which professes this faith in Jesus Christ, and obedience to Him as Divine Lord and Saviour.

ARTICLE XV.—OF THE SACRAMENTS.—We acknowledge Baptism and the Lord's Supper, the two Sacraments instituted by Christ to be of perpetual obligation as signs and seals of the blessings of the new covenant, and as means of grace, made effectual only by the operation of the Holy Spirit, and always to be used by Christians with prayer and praise to God.

(a) Baptism with water into the name of the Father and of the Son and of the Holy Spirit is the Rite of Initiation into the Visible Church of Christ. The proper subjects of Baptism are believers, and infants presented by parents or guardians in the Christian faith, upon whom shall be enjoined their duty to train their children in the nurture and admonition of the Lord.

(b) The Lord's Supper is the Sacrament of Communion with Christ and with His people, in which the bread and wine are given and received in remembrance of Him and His sacrifice upon the Cross; and they who in faith receive the same do, after a spiritual manner, partake of the Body and Blood of the Lord Jesus Christ, to their comfort, nourishment and growth in grace.

ARTICLE XVI.—OF THE MINISTRY.—We believe that Jesus Christ, as the Supreme Head of the Church, has appointed therein a Ministry of the Word and Sacraments, and calls men to this Ministry; that the Church, under the guidance of the Holy Spirit, recognizes and chooses those whom He calls, and ordains them to the work of the Ministry.

ARTICLE XVII.—OF CHURCH ORDER AND FELLOWSHIP.—We believe that the Lord Jesus Christ is the sole Head of the Church; that its worship, teaching, discipline, and government should be in accordance with His will, and that the Church alone has supreme authority and jurisdiction in all matters pertaining to its doctrine, worship, discipline, and government.

ARTICLE XVIII.—OF THE RESURRECTION, THE LAST JUDGMENT, AND THE FUTURE LIFE.—We believe in the Resurrection of the dead, through the power of the Son of God, Who shall judge the world in righteousness, and render to every man according to his works, and we believe in the life everlasting.

ARTICLE XIX.—OF CHRISTIAN SERVICE AND THE FINAL TRIUMPH.—We believe that it is our duty as servants and friends of Christ to do good unto all men, to maintain the public and private worship of God, to study the word of God, to hallow the Lord's Day, to preserve the sanctity of the family, to uphold the just authority of the State, and so to live in all honesty, purity, and charity, that our lives shall testify of Christ. We joyfully receive the word of Christ, bidding His people to go into all the world and make disciples of all nations, and to declare unto them that God was in Christ, reconciling the world unto Himself, and that He will have all men to be saved, and to come to the knowledge of the truth. We believe that by His power and grace all His enemies shall finally be overcome, and that the kingdoms of this world shall become the Kingdom of our Lord and of His Christ.

THE RELATION OF A MINISTER TO THE DOCTRINES OF THE CHURCH.

1. The duty of final enquiry into the personal character, doctrinal beliefs, and general fitness of candidates for the Ministry presenting themselves for ordination shall be laid upon Conferences.

2. In the ordination service these candidates shall answer the following questions:—

(a) Do you believe yourself to be a child of God through faith in our Lord Jesus Christ?

(b) Do you believe yourself to be called of God to the office of the Christian ministry, and your chief motives to be zeal for the glory of God, love for the Lord Jesus Christ, and desire for the salvation of men?

(c) Are you persuaded that the Holy Scriptures contain all that is necessary for eternal salvation? Do you accept the Statement of Doctrine of the United Church, as in substance agreeable to the teaching of the Holy Scriptures; and are you resolved out of the said Scriptures to instruct the people committed to your charge, and to teach nothing which is not agreeable thereto?

24: THE ANGUS AFFAIR

From March 2, 1915, when Samuel Angus took up his post as Professor of New Testament, until early in 1923, there was no public comment of significance expressing concern about Angus' teaching.[1] These years included the War as well as the debates on Church Union, and one way or another, Angus did not stir controversy. Although his class teaching reflected the views he was later to express in print, it does not appear that the radical nature of these views was widely known.

There was theological controversy in the immediate post-war period. In the first place, Professor R.G.McIntyre published *The Other Side of Death* in 1920 in which he presented a modified form of conditional immortality. It earned him an Edinburgh DD, but also brought criticism from orthodox ministers. A number of Methodists were concerned since Methodist, Presbyterian and Congregational students shared in a United Course of theological study which had been organised in 1918.

In May 1921, the Moderator of the PCNSW Assembly, John Edwards of Rose Bay, delivered an address entitled *Theological Reconstruction: A Plea for Freedom*. Edwards expressly linked his address to the inspiration he had received from hearing George McInnes' address in 1894 to which reference has been made on pages 238-239. Following out the method advocated by McInnes to its logical conclusion, Edwards rejected the authority of the Bible, Creeds or the Church, insisting there be freedom to follow the truth as one saw it in his own conscience and reason. In the published edition of

1. Angus was one of those in view when the FPCA Assembly framed its response to the overture on union in 1923 as recorded on page 330 , **Our Banner**, July 15, 1933, p.105.

335

this address Edwards acknowledged his debt to his friend Dr Angus at several points. The controversy over this provocative address was laid to rest by Professor Harper who secured a re-assuring *Declaration of the Church's Faith* at the 1922 NSW Assembly (Minute 94). However, it is significant that Angus himself took no part in the debate, while Professor Adam of the PCV was not certain that Angus held similar views to Edwards.[2]

Episode One 1923

In January 1923, Angus addressed a Student Christian Movement Conference at Parramatta on 'The Bible' and a summary of what he said appeared in the *Daily Telegraph* on January 9, 1923. His remarks were enthusiastically defended by John Edwards and there was considerable controversy in the columns of the papers. However, a brief statement of Angus' views published in June 1923 [*Faith in God through Jesus*] excited little comment. Private concerns were expressed, as by Professor Rentoul,[3] but there was no organised opposition, no real willingness to take effective action. Orthodox Calvinists were few and far between, most ministers relied on some liberty in adherence to the Confession, while Angus expressed great devotion to Jesus which satisfied most. Moreover, Angus was overseas from August 1923 to March 1925, when he, along with the American Modernist, Harry Emerson Fosdick (1878-1969),[4] received a DD from Glasgow University. When he returned, Angus settled into a busy life. He was well-positioned socially, and was the friend of the wealthy and influential. He and his somewhat humourless American wife had no children.

Episode Two 1929-32

In the issue of the *Sydney Morning Herald* for November 9, 1929, a critical review of Angus' recent book *Religious Quests of the Graeco-Roman World* appeared. It was written by Emeritus Professor R.G.Macintyre, and led to considerable public debate. Macintyre considered the book 'a polemic, pure and simple, against sacramental religion' because of its presentation of early Christianity as a development from pagan religion. Angus, of course, accepted a distinction between the religion *of* Jesus and the religion *about* Jesus in the creeds and many of the practices of the Christian Church.

---

2. Susan Emilsen, **Samuel Angus and the Presbyterian Church in the State of New South Wales** (PhD Thesis, University of Sydney, 1985) p.231, citing Adam's letter to Harper dated October 19, 1921.
3. Susan Emilsen, ibid., p.243, citing Rentoul's letter to Angus dated August 21, 1923.
4. Fosdick was ordained a Baptist minister in 1903, but later supplied the pulpit of First Presbyterian Church, New York from which he was excluded in 1922 as a consequence of his sermon 'Shall the Fundamentalists Win?' since he refused to subscribe such doctrines as the Virgin Birth. Sponsored by John D.Rockefeller,Jr., he became pastor of Riverside Church and exercised an influential ministry, including by radio and through his many books. He and Angus were essentially in the same theological camp.

336

Again there was concern among some influential Methodists who did not want their students exposed to such teaching. The efforts of Rev J.Ward Harrison of Botany Methodist Church in circulating a series of pamphlets in the last half of 1931 eventually resulted in the NSW Methodist Conference taking up the matter in 1932 and 1933. In the latter year, and until 1937, Methodist students were withdrawn from the United Course.

The Presbyterians showed more reluctance to act while in any case Macintyre was only aiming a warning shot across Angus' bow to remind him of the need for caution in public utterances. However, in May 1932, Rev Joseph Fulton (1861-1934), an elderly Ulsterman, petitioned the NSW Assembly alleging heretical teaching in the Theological Hall. Conservatives were unfortunate in that, while Fulton had the root of the matter in him, he did not have the ability to prosecute a case of this kind successfully. At least he tried, but the wily politician, R.G.Macintyre, mindful of Angus' recent change to a pro-church union stance and mindful too of the financial health of the church in the event of a heresy case, gained the support of the Assembly for a pious affirmation:

that the Assembly reaffirms the adherence of this Church to the doctrines of the evangelical faith as laid down in the Basis of Union (1901), and expects all its Ministers and Teachers in their preaching and teaching to conform thereto, giving chief place to those doctrines of Redemption which the Church has declared to be vital to the Christian Faith.[5]

Susan Emilsen rightly observes:

There was little interest in policing the Assembly's 'expectation' that ministers and teachers conform to the doctrines of the evangelical faith. What the Assembly demonstrated by its action was that it required of its ministers and teachers discretion...If Dr Angus could maintain a suitable measure of discretion within and outside the Assembly, the implication was there, he need expect little opposition from within the Assembly.[6]

Episode Three 1932-33

In March 1932, J.T.H.Kerr, a graduate of the Sydney Missionary and Bible College and an elder in the flourishing Ashfield congregation, began his course at the Theological Hall. He made no secret of the fact that he prepared transcripts of Angus' lectures and passed them to his minister, the able and orthodox Robert McGowan. McGowan was a Victorian who had trained at Ormond and been ordained in 1899. McGowan came to the view that Angus' growing influence and heretical teaching had to be addressed, and he overtured the NSW Assembly through the Presbytery of Sydney.

5. NSW Assembly, 1932, Minute 57.
6. Susan Emilsen, op. cit., pp. 326,327.

along with Rev Hugh Paton of St Stephen's, Macquarie Street, asking for an enquiry into the doctrinal views of Professor Angus. However, when the Assembly met in May 1933, Paton was out of the country and McGowan was under stress through the death of his mother the previous day as well as a threat of civil action from some unknown person if he continued open opposition to Angus. So he withdrew his overture (Minute 38).

Early in 1933, Fulton and McGowan had complained to the Presbytery of Sydney about Angus and a Committee of seven persons was appointed to confer with him about his teaching. The Committee included John Edwards, Professor Kenneth Edward, R.G.McIntyre and C.A.White. Only White was strongly opposed and he was persuadable.[7] The Report which was produced was conciliatory and impressed the 1933 NSW Assembly to which it was sent for information. The Assembly resolved 245 to 19 to the effect that while not identifying itself with Angus' teaching, it received with satisfaction his assurance of adherence 'without mental resrvation' to the doctrine of the church, and expressed its confidence that Angus did not hold views on the person or work of Christ which were contrary to the faith of the church. Seven members appealed to the GAA against this vote of confidence in Angus. They were Rev A.J.Carter of Ebenezer/Portland Head, Rev J.B. Fulton (retired), Rev James Gillespie of the Middle Clarence, Rev Dr William Gunn (retired medical missionary to the New Hebrides), R.J.H.McGowan of Ashfield and Rev J.A.R.Perkins of Eastwood. McGowan's reasons of appeal take seven pages in the Assembly *Proceedings*, and amount to a quite lucid statement of Angus' deviations from orthodoxy - perhaps the substance of the speech prepared in support of the overture he had withdrawn.

The GAA met in Melbourne in September 1933, the same month Angus' *Jesus in the Lives of Men* came off the press. The GAA found that a case for proper inquiry had been demonstrated and the matter was remitted back to the Presbytery of Sydney. It was provided that if the decision of the Presbytery was appealed to the NSW Assembly, and if the Assembly's decision was appealed, that the Judicial Commission of the GAA hear such appeal and conclude the matter (Minute 102). The GAA also passed a motion authorising the preparation of a restatement of the church's creed (Min. 122).

Episode Four 1934
Back in New South Wales, the Presbytery Committee of Preliminary Inquiry, which included McGowan, White and Macintyre, commenced its work early in 1934. Angus now went on the attack with a polemical volume entitled

7. In the 1934 NSW Assembly White said that Dr Angus' faith 'is much stronger than his intellectual statement of it' which was not very flattering to the learned Professor. Note also White's cursory handling of the Angus affair in his **Challenge** of the Years (1951).

Truth and Tradition published in April 1934, which the foreword indicates had developed from his preparation for the expected confrontation at the NSW Assembly. The publication of this assault on Biblical doctrines made any likelihood of peace returning to the church out of the question. Angus had broken Macintyre's dictum of discretion, and the Presbytery referred the case to the Assembly of May 1934. Other literature was issued at this time. Macintyre came out with *The Theology of Dr Angus*, which was good as far as it went. Macintyre asserted that Angus rejected the most fundamental doctrines. This was true and Angus' writing at least was unambiguously clear. Of course Angus maintained he retained the essence of the faith while only discarding its theological form. John Edwards and Professor Kenneth Edward also wrote in defence of Angus. There were many anti-Angus pamphlets from writers otherwise as far apart as Rev H.K.Mack of the Reformed Presbyterian Church in Geelong and Dr Rumble of the Roman Catholic Church.

The NSW Assembly of 1934 was, for once,   not loyal to 'King Ronald' Macintyre. [8] By a vote of 174 to 83 a mediating decision was reached. The Assembly accepted Angus' assurance that he taught the 'essential substance' of the church's faith, and that the Declaratory Statement made the church wide enough to hold men of different views. An attempt by McGowan to have the Assembly proceed by judicial process was lost 79 to 154.

McGowan thereupon appealed to the Judicial Commission which heard the case in September 1934. The point at issue was the lawfulness or otherwise of the NSW Assembly refusing to allow judicial process. As is common in such matters, the substance of Angus' position was entered into, Angus was substantially upheld, all parties were counselled to unity, and the commitment of the church to the 'historic faith' was reaffirmed. The appellants dissented, reserving all rights, but this fourth episode was at an end, the more so as Angus was sick. His wife died in November 1934.

Episode Five 1936

At about the time Angus resumed teaching (March 1936), both Carter and McGowan advised him they proposed to resume investigation of his teaching. In March, Carter alleged before the Presbytery of Sydney that Angus did not

8. The Assembly Moderator in 1934 was Rev Joseph Lundie, an Irishman, who reminded the members of the case of J.E.Davey, Professor of New Testament in the Presbyterian College, Belfast, who was charged with heresy in 1927 but acquitted. His views were not far different from those of Angus. Davey was subsequently Principal of the College and Moderator of the Irish Presbyterian Assembly. A small secession, now known as the Evangelical Presbyterian Church, resulted. Rev W.J.Greir was a well known minister of this church. Cf. Robert Allen, **The Presbyterian College Belfast 1853-1953** (Belfast 1954) pp.256ff; W.J.Greir, **The Origin and Witness of the Irish Evangelical Church** (Belfast 1945). An interesting eye-witness account of the 1934 NSW Assembly is in **Our Banner**, June 1934, pp.275-279.

hold to such vital doctrines as the Trinity, the Deity of Christ, Christ's atoning sacrifice and bodily resurrection. He was prepared to produce evidence and asked the Presbytery to deal with the charge according to the laws of the church. On the motion of Rev John Edwards, the Presbytery refused to hear Carter, who then appealed to the State Assembly on the ground that the Presbytery was wrong in law in failing to investigate the charge. This appeal was sustained.

When the Presbytery took up the matter once more in June 1936, Carter was not given the opportunity to present his evidence, and in fact was subject to a grilling by the intellectually superior Angus. The Presbytery then resolved 28 to 11 that Angus had no case to answer. Both Carter and McGowan sought to appeal against the Presbytery's finding direct to the GAA due to meet in September. Their argument was that an appeal to the next State Assembly (1937) would in all probability be appealed to the GAA anyway, and it was best to deal with the matter finally in 1936 rather than have to wait until the 1939 GAA. This appeal was refused by the Presbytery which seems to have had the rules of the church on its side, but both men petitioned the GAA against the refusal. The GAA did not allow these, but the Angus matter came up in other ways, so that over one third of the decisions made at the 1936 GAA related to Angus.

Episode Six 1936
The most significant document before the GAA which met in Sydney in September 1936 was a petition signed by 111 ministers (79 from Victoria, 12 from South Australia, 10 from Western Australia, 7 from Tasmania and 3 from Queensland) and some 250 elders from all states except New South Wales. The petitioners considered that *Truth and Tradition* was a denial of the Supreme and Subordinate Standards of the church to which every office-bearer was pledged. They noted that the Presbyterian Church of New Zealand had refused to allow its students to attend St Andrew's Theological Hall because of the teaching of Dr Angus, and it sought 'such decisive action as will vindicate our position as a Church holding the common Christian faith in Jesus Christ....'[9]

McGowan was not a member of the 1936 GAA but three motions, representing the three chief views, were proposed. R.G.Macintyre, liberal evangelical, proposed that in the interests of the unity and peace of the church, the Assembly affirm its adherence to the evangelical faith, instructing that teaching and preaching conform to it. The wording looked good but did not deal with the subtleties of modernism in an unambiguous way. Rev F.A. Hagenauer of Cairns Memorial, East Melbourne, evangelical, proposed a much

9. The petition is in 1936 **GAA Proceedings**, pp.191-197.

tighter wording which specifically rejected Angus' views on the incarnation, atonement and resurrection, and proposed no further action if the Basis of Union was adhered to subsequently. Rev A.D.Marchant of Turramurra, the congregation of which Angus was an elder, proposed to affirm adherence to the historic Catholic faith in Jesus Christ as God manifest in the flesh, recognise diversity of theological outlook and expression was allowed for in the church's constitution, and to exhort the church to get on with its 'real' business of moral and social action.

After discussion by a small committee, a resolution was adopted unanimously by the GAA. It was moved by Hagenauer, to whom was owed clauses 3 to 7, seconded by Marchant, who had contributed clauses 1 and 2, and supported by Macintyre. The text of the decision was as follows.

DECISION ON SEPTEMBER 11, 1936 RE TEACHING OF PROF. S. ANGUS

1. That this Assembly, in view of the theological unrest within the Church, and for the assurance of those who have expressed deep concern, as well as for the strengthening and peace of our whole Church, hereby affirms its adherence to the historic Christian faith;

2. That this Assembly hold that the real function of the Church is to be found in the teaching, preaching and practice of a vital religion which seeks to express the mind and spirit of Christ, and affectionately enjoins all members and adherents of the Church, through fellowship in worship, witness and life, to work and pray for the fulfilment of the Church's high vocation, which is the advancement of the Kingdom of God in the lives of man, in the morals and institutions of nations, and in the brotherhood of mankind throughout the world; and;

3. Inasmuch as the Basis of Union in giving liberty of opinion on all doctrines taught in the Subordinate Standard not essential to faith declared that in regard to the doctrine of Redemption, the Love of God to all mankind, the free gift of His Son to be the Propitiation of the sins of the whole world, and the free offer of salvation to men without distinction on the ground of Christ's all-sufficient sacrifice, are essential to faith and the historic facts of Incarnation, the atoning Life and Death and the Resurrection, on which the faith is based, must be taught by all who are admitted to the office of the Holy Ministry, as formulated in the Subordinate Standard, until the formulation is altered in the prescribed manner;

4. And as any denial or discarding of these facts, as so formulated, by any person admitted to the Holy Ministry constitutes a breach of trust with the Church;

5. And as the Rev Dr. S. Angus has frankly and openly, with obvious sincerity, in **Truth and Tradition**, acknowledged himself to be in conflict with the formulations of the doctrine of the Incarnation, the Propitiation and the Resurrection, as they are set forth at present in the Subordinate Standard, and laid down in the Declaratory Statement, claiming that they are at variance with the Supreme Standard, such doctrines, however, being among those parts of the doctrine of Redemption which the Basis of Union has declared to be essential to faith and must be taught as set forth in the Subordinate Standard and laid down in the Declaratory Statement, unless and until altered in the prescribed manner;

341

6. Therefore the Assembly instructs State Assemblies, Presbyteries and all who have been admitted to the office of the Holy Ministry, that the laws of f the Church must be obeyed, and draws their attention in particular to the clause in the Basis of Union declaring that the doctrine of Redemption is essential to faith and must be taught as set forth in the Subordinate Standard, and laid down in the Declaratory Statement unless and until altered in the prescribed manner.

7. The Assembly also draws the attention of Dr Angus, various appellants and petitioners and all other parties directly or indirectly concerned in the case to the above instruction, and feeling confident that it will be obeyed by all, resolves that, unless it be disobeyed hereafter, no further action is necessary.

8. Further, the Assembly does not now consider it advisable or necessary to enter further upon the matter of petitions and appeals in reference to the teaching of Professor S. Angus, and instructs the Presbytery of Sydney and all other courts of the Church in accordance herewith.

This decision was one which in form upheld the position of the church. In general the contribution from Hagenauer and such men as Professor Gillies correctly interpreted the Scheme of Union as discussed earlier (pages 284-288). The interpretation of the liberty of opinion clause is rather wide. The clause grants liberty of opinion on matters not essential to the doctrine of the Subordinate Standard, not liberty of opinion on matters not essential to faith. However, the decision in effect presupposed liberal theology would be tolerated provided it was not presented unambiguously or provocatively. Professor Kenneth Edward (died 1941) and Rev John Edwards (died 1942) and others had made their position of essential agreement with Angus plain but were never threatened with heresy charges. In large measure this must be seen as reflecting concern at the high profile Angus gave his teaching, and his tactless and provocative nature.

Episode Seven 1939

Never one for hiding his views, Angus issued a volume entitled *Essential Christianity*. Prepared by March 1938 (see preface) it was published early in 1939 and was selected as the best book of the month by the *Religious Book Club* of America in March that year. Angus thus 'poured petrol on the embers of the earlier controversy'[11] as he had with *Truth and Tradition* in 1934. Hagenauer, with the support of his Session, petitioned the GAA due to meet in Melbourne in September, as did 26 ministers and 17 elders of the PCV and R.J.H.McGowan. They all complained that the teaching of *Essential Christianity* was an act of open disobedience, and that steps ought to be taken to stop teaching so contrary to the Basis of Union.

Rev George Tulloch of St Andrew's, Perth was for Angus' suspension with

11. I.Breward, 'Christianity Must be Reinterpreted' in **Trinity Occasional Papers**, April 1985, Vol IV †1, p.29. This is a somewhat mediating article on Angus.

possible reinstatement by the 1942 GAA if proof of a complete change of view and withdrawal of *Truth and Tradition* and *Essential Christianity* was provided. Hagenauer was for noting Angus' disobedience and giving him a further injunction to obey in future, this mild proposal reflecting the problems brought about by the outbreak of war. Rev A.R.McVittie of St Philip's, Newcastle was for postponing further consideration until the 1942 GAA due to the world crisis. Rev Harold Perkins of Bega proposed that 'as there is no doubt of Professor Angus' loyalty to the faith as he understands it' (a remarkable statement!) and as there were many others who stood with Angus, that the matter be held over until 1942 with a view to a report being made by the Committee on the Attitude of the Church to its Creed.

Rev C.N.Button of St Andrew's, Ballarat, a former student and great admirer of the Professor, was not a member of the 1939 GAA but pled in *The Messenger* that Angus receive 'a fair go', suggesting that he could not be judged fairly by a 'few extreme passages' taken from his books. In any case, according to Button, Angus' unorthodoxy was a washed out pink compared to the crimson of Albert Schweitzer, whom everyone regarded as one of the very greatest of living Christians.[12]

After six hours debate in private the GAA resolved:
That consideration of these petitions and all matters anent the teachings and writings of Dr Angus be postponed till the next meeting of this Assembly. The division on this resolution was 155 to 100, with names recorded in the minutes. The vote against postponement and thus, it appears, in favour of a further warning or suspension, was surprisingly strong. Macintyre, ever the politician, moved that the dissents lodged by McGowan and Tulloch be not answered, and so the matter rested. Angus himself regarded the GAA as without courage:

What you term the 20th century heresy hunt came to an ignoble postponement in September. Heaven knows what the trembling Church would have done without the excuse of the European War to reprieve the culprit until 1942. The Church displayed no courage, courage being evidently the quality of heresy. Macintyre, openly neutral, worked hard behind the scenes 'to stop Angus denying the vital doctrines of the Church'. By 1942 there may be some promotions that will simplify the procedure for the next General Assembly of Australia...'[13]

12. Schweitzer (1875-1965) interpreted Jesus' teaching in terms of eschatology rather than the mystery religions which Angus supposed had modified Jesus' teaching. But while Schweitzer captured the popular imagination by his rejection of academic and social position in favour of spending 60 years of his life in French Equatorial Africa, he was no more and perhaps no less orthodox than Angus. Schweitzer regarded reverence for all life as the basic ethical principle although his formulation of this seems nearer Indian philosophy than Christianity.
13. S.Emilsen, op. cit., p.429 citing letter January 4, 1940 by Angus to J. Boyall.

Epilogue 1942

Angus suffered a stroke shortly after the 1939 GAA and was off work until March 1941. Further petitions from McGowan, Hagenauer and a group associated with Professor Alex Yule of Ormond were on the agenda of the 1942 GAA. However, the serious war situation and the obvious decline in Angus' health resulted in unanimous support for passing from these without prejudice to the rights of any of the parties. On November 17, 1943, Angus died of cancer and thus the Angus affair proper was concluded.

F.A.Hagenauer   Samuel Angus

Theological setting

At the turn of the 20th century, the theological spectrum included (1) post-Tridentine Roman Catholicism with the Church, headed by the Pope, as authority; (2) Reformation orthodoxy with the Scriptures as authority and the Reformed creeds as statements of Scripture teaching; (3) Liberal-evangelicalism, which had compromised on Scripture, was affected by humanistic thought, but which endeavoured to retain the more important doctrines of Reformation orthodoxy; and (4) Liberalism, which accepted much post-Enlightenment thinking, but regarded the Bible as an imperfect record of human experience and opinion and found authority in human reason and experience. Orthodoxy was widely infected by Arminianism.

In 1920 in the United States of America, the term 'fundamentalist' was first used by some anti-liberal Baptists to describe their stance, and in that country is most appropriately applied to the present to those militantly anti-modernist, white Protestants with a heritage of evangelistic revivalism. Thus the 'fundamentalist' has a somewhat diluted and unbalanced position compared to the full heritage of Reformation orthodoxy, while staunchly maintaining such fundamental Christian teachings as the inspiration of the Bible, the deity of Christ, the virgin birth of Christ, the substitutionary atonement, Christ's physical resurrection and his second coming. In Britain the term 'fundamentalist' is used more generally of evangelical Protestants of various kinds who often lack the excessive interest in unfulfilled prophecy and the anti-intellectualism which are common in the American form. The British use is nearer that applicable in Australia in the 1920s, but in my opinion is not a specially useful term in discussing Presbyterian reaction to the Angus affair.[14]

Angus belonged to the liberal school. He had done part of his training under the historian Adolf von Harnack (1851-1930) of Berlin who was reckoned a chief spokesman of this school. F.F.Bruce tells us that Harnack 'perceived the essence of Christianity to lie in the fatherhood of God, the infinite worth of the individual soul, the higher righteousness and the commandment of love',[15] and the same outlook was held by Angus.

Angus' personal history is of interest. Brought up in the old Presbyterian orthodoxy of Ireland - psalm-singing and all - he had been dedicated to the ministry by his parents who hoped he would be a champion of the old faith. He was certainly a brilliant student and enrolled in Princeton University (MA 1905; PhD 1906) and Princeton Theological Seminary, the greatest

14. A useful discussion of the Angus Case is in David Parker, **Fundamentalism and Conservative Protestantism in Australia 1920-1980** (PhD Thesis, University of Queensland 1982) pp.255-287.
15. **New Dictionary of Theology** (Leicester 1988) p.286 col. 2.

centre of Presbyterian learning at that time. However, his chief interest was the classics and he refused to give the attention to theology the seminary required. In fact, he came to reinterpret Christianity according to the principles of liberalism. He would not have said his presentation of liberal thought was a deliberate slighting of his orthodox upbringing or of the Seminary, although he regarded the earlier dogmas as outmoded and could hardly imagine any thinking person could retain them in the light of modern knowledge. However, he thought he was retaining the substance of the faith despite discarding the intellectual form in which it was expressed, for his Platonistic philosophy was structuring his thinking rather than Biblical norms.

For Angus, Christianity was a life; for orthodoxy it was a life too, but a life based on a message centred in that Jesus whose person and deeds were attested by God in Holy Scripture. Angus discarded the message and presented his own based on what he considered to be the original teaching of Jesus. His theology, such as it was, was dated by the time controversy arose, but Angus dismissed the neo-orthodoxy of Karl Barth and Emil Brunner which arose in the aftermath of an impotent liberalism, shocked by the calamity of the Great War, as readily as he dismissed Reformed orthodoxy. Presbyterian opposition in Australia was not specially effective but the contribution by Hagenauer and Gillies (ever in the background) should not be overlooked just because McGowan was often in the limelight.

Procedures

The Angus affair was one which the church did not find easy to handle. The most striking feature is that a regular judicial process was not instituted against Angus. The case of Charles Strong is analogous in this respect. There were repeated efforts to have the matter dealt with administratively or by the Presbytery or Assembly itself proceeding by judicial process. McGowan did express willingness to make out a charge but this did not occur.

The approved procedure in the event of prejudicial reports or allegations to the discredit of a minister is along the following lines:

(1) friendly remonstrance and timely admonition as a general practice can avert the need of more formal procedure subsequently.

(2) the knowledge and understanding of those who make allegations must be carefully considered before the adoption of action in respect of them, lest superficial allegations are rashly entertained.

(3) serious errors of doctrine or errors spreading among the people may require formal process by libel, whereas small things, especially related to personality clashes etc., can be resolved by less formal means.

(4) a minister is entitled to demand a libel be drawn up and served on him before he will discuss the subject of the allegations with his co-presbyters, although it is more usually appropriate that he should from the first speak frankly and directly with those who propose to deal with him.

346

(5) a libel is a written, regularly arranged statement of charge signed by the parties prosecuting and listing witnesses and documents which will be adduced in evidence. Its general character has been described on page 262.
(6) there are only three grounds which would warrant a presbytery entertaining or framing a libel: (a) a person or court giving in a written complaint against the life or doctrine of the accused with some account of its probability, and undertaking to make out a libel; (b) a person (or court) undertaking to make out a libel containing a charge as in (a), under the penalty of being censured as a slanderer if he fails to do so; and (c) prejudicial reports being so great that a presbytery, for their own vindication, find it necessary to begin a process without any particular accuser.
(7) once a libel has been properly prepared, the accused is summoned with ample notice. At the meeting the presbytery must first consider the relevancy of the libel - that is that the offence specified in the major proposition is truly such and that the libel is logically sound. The accused is entitled to participate in the discussion. If the libel is found relevant, the presbytery then encourage the accused to confess the truth of the charges, since it is his duty to Christ and to others, to save the trouble of adducing proof if the accusation is well founded. If the accused does not admit the charges, the presbytery then order the libel to be served on the accused who thereupon is suspended from the exercise of his functions as a minister until the libel is disposed of. At this point any appeal or complaint made during the process by members of the court or the accused comes into operation. These are disposed of by the higher assembly. No member of a court whose decision is appealed against can judge in the matter of the appeal.
(8) it is competent to the presbytery, once a libel has been served, to refer the case to the higher assembly on the ground that it is not expedient for the presbytery to act as prosecutors and judges, or on the ground that it does not appear expedient for the proof to be taken except in the presence of those who have the power of giving a final deliverance as to its effect.

Now it is abundantly obvious that this kind of procedure with its checks and balances designed to ensure the vindication of truth with the minimum disruption to the life of the church was not followed. It has been said friends of Angus in the church courts 'used their knowledge of procedure with great skill to protect Angus, because a number of influential ministers agreed with his theological position and greatly valued his scholarship and teaching gifts.'[16] There is some truth in this, but it also seems that there was quite considerable ignorance of procedure as well as manipulation of it, which is not the same as being skilful. For example, in 1934 the GAA Judicial Commission of 38 members met to hear the appeal from the NSW Assembly. Admittedly it was the first time this Commission had been called since Union had occurred in 1901, yet several persons who had been involved in the appeal were allowed to sit on the Commission, and when some conservatives tried to have the minutes tabled at the GAA of 1936, the motion was ruled incompetent on the advice of the Procurator. The bad conscience on this is shown in the changes passed by the 1936 GAA which prevented those involved in an appeal in future from sitting as members of the Judicial Commission.

16. I. Breward, op. cit., p.28.

It might be noted here that the Procurator (top legal advisor) of the GAA for 15 years until 1936 was John Ferguson. In 1936 Brian Fuller was appointed and served for 20 years. F.M.Bradshaw was appointed in 1959. Ferguson was engaged in industrial law and was competent enough in his church advice. Fuller was a KC specialising in motor accident cases and his church decisions were not infrequently inadequate or incorrect. Bradshaw has been the only procurator with a profound grasp of the Presbyterian constitution and a practice in trust law. Ordinary members of an Assembly are very much inclined to follow a Procurator's advice. The issues are often not clear to them and the concern for legal consequences is an added incentive, and rightly so, to seek and follow what is thought to be expert advice.

It seems a variety of reasons explain the absence of a judicial procedure. These include the unwillingness to have a divisive heresy trial which would require Angus to be suspended from teaching until the case was finalised; general ignorance of procedure and a belief that a church which tolerated divergent theologies should not or could not do other than tolerate Angus; on the conservative side, a reluctance to have a formal trial lest an adverse judgement weaken the doctrinal position. It is plain the old difference between conservative Victoria and diverse New South Wales was still relevant.

The basic thrust of the conservative case against Angus was correct. Angus himself could see the point. He wrote:

If Presbyterianism is a religious legalism consisting of the letter of the Confession and based on the legislation of the Declaratory Statement, as my opponents contend, then I emphatically repudiate such authoritarian religion and the Church cannot do better than expel me forthwith....I neither plead to be retained by the Church, nor do I challenge the Church to expel me... but it is not in any ecclesiastical hands to expel me from my prophetic calling.[17]

Of course Angus' opponents had not argued on the basis of the letter of the Confession in an inclusive and legalistic way. Rather, they emphasised that the ordination vows, freely taken, committed ministers to certain essential doctrines which Angus rejected. The church courts were really obliged to take up such an attack on the doctrine of the church, since each minister and elder was pledged to assert, maintain and defend them.

17. S.Angus, **Truth and Tradition** (Sydney 1934) pp. 138, 142. Angus made a great impression on many who did not always see the full implications of his position. Alan Dougan, **A Backward Glance at the Angus Affair** (Sydney 1971) went so far as to state 'a greater teacher and more devout lover of the Church's Lord and a more lovable man has not and is not likely to rise among us' (p.28). Compare Professor Gillies' remark that 'the worship of Jesus, unless it involved the belief that Jesus was the Son of God, was rank idolatry' cited in **Our Banner**, October 1933, p.153. Angus rejected Christ's Deity.

Angus was also inclined to appeal to the Supreme Standard (the Scriptures) as a means to avoid statements in the Subordinate Standard which might conflict with his teaching. In 1933 he stated to the Presbytery of Sydney Committee, when questioned as to how he saw his obligation:

My conscience does not accuse me of any violation of my vows. I appeal to the Supreme Standard as of greater importance than the Subordinate Standard. There is none of my teaching which is not found in Scripture, and there is none of it which is not in accord with the teaching of Jesus. From my point of view it is more important to inquire whether my teaching is in accord with the teaching and spirit of Jesus that to inquire whether it is in accord with the Subordinate Standard. Presuming that the only essential in a doctrine is its truth, I have not transgressed the liberty of interpretation allowed even in the Subordinate Standard.[18]

This extract shows both the subtlety of liberalism and a quite improper position. A Presbyterian Church is a creedal church precisely so as to avoid the promulgation of erroneous doctrine under the guise of professions of loyalty to the Scriptures or to the 'spirit of Jesus'. As one said a century ago, 'To appeal from the Confession to Scripture on doctrinal points in the way of repudiating the confessional statement in favour of the scriptural, involves the abandonment of that communion of which the Confession is the bond.'[19] This is true though it be recognised that it is the doctrine of the document and not the document itself which is subscribed.

The Angus affair is sometimes viewed as a crime against the rights of the individual conscience as by Michael Parer. Again, the simple fact is that Angus and every other Presbyterian minister and elder makes a vow freely which commits them to conscientiously maintain certain teachings. On Parer's view, sacred vows and obligations mean nothing or mean only what from time to time your conscience decides they will mean.[20]

The Strong and Angus Cases

There are striking parallels between the Strong and Angus cases. The very provisions in the Basis of Union that were designed to prevent another Strong Case were found inadequate because the church did not have the will to maintain them. There were differences of detail between the two men, but no differences of real substance. As individuals they were rather different.

---

18. The Presbytery Report is in GAA Proceedings 1933, p.98ff.
19. John Macpherson, Handbook on the Confession of Faith (Edinburgh 1882), p.2.
20. Note the preface to M.S.Parer, Australia's Last Heresy Hunt (Sydney 1971). This book (edited by Ernest Vines) comprises the text of a radio broadcast on Angus. Note that there are two factual errors on p.13, paragraph 4.

Angus moved in a high social circle including such prominent laymen as the McIlraths and Gillespies, and was of right-wing views, even pro Nazi for a period. Strong appears to have had a much more real concern for the poor although he too had wide and influential contacts.

Some consequences of the Angus affair

The Angus affair tended to reinforce the dictum of discretion. Many men accepted the basic thrust of Angus' position but they were not as honestly outspoken as Angus had been. Such men did not sound unorthodox, but it was not what they said but what they did not say that was significant. There were some exceptions, most notably Rev Ernest Vines (1888-1979), who was ordained in 1924 and retired in 1959. Vines was a tutor for Home Mission students for many years, and was also active in Christian Education, Youth, and Christian Unity matters.

So far as the church in New South Wales is concerned, the Angus affair was disruptive and there were significant losses of members. Claimed communicant membership in 1926 was 26,837, and rose to 34,483 in 1931 before the main controversy broke out. By 1936 the membership was 29,329, and 10 years later had recovered to 34,991. Thus there was virtually no growth in the 15 years 1931 to 1946, whereas the Methodists grew 16%, the Baptists 20% and the Churches of Christ 23% in the same period. Interestingly, in Victoria both the Presbyterians and Methodists put on about 6.5% in membership 1931-46, while the Baptists added 2% and the Churches of Christ fell.

The position in New South Wales was further complicated by the poor state of the Theological Hall at St Andrew's College. In 1939 Rev W.Cumming Thom of the Church of Scotland became Professor of Old Testament in succession to Professor Anderson. His task was difficult because Edward died in 1941 and Angus in 1943, his administrative burden as Principal of St Andrew's College was heavy, and he was not an effective administrator in any case. He retired in 1950.

Lecturers supplied the vacancies in the faculty until they were filled in 1946 by two Scots - J. Haultain Brown in New Testament and John McIntyre in Theology. Brown was a cautious middle of the road man while McIntyre was an admirer of Emil Bruner (1889-1966), the neo-orthodox theologian, and both were in marked contrast to Angus. Thom was from an earlier period (ordained in 1923) but not provocative. So the NSW church regained an uneasy equilibrium but did not return to orthodoxy. There would be further repercussions and even a split further down the track (1967) as we shall see.

350

Part Seven

THE CONSERVATIVE CHURCHES

1945-1988

25: PREPARATION FOR PROGRESS 1946-1953

By and large orthodoxy continued in decline in the PCA after 1945, although this is not to say that pulpits always sounded very unorthodox. Conservatives in the different states and among the several Presbyterian groups did some things together, and there was some co-operation on a denominational level. The tercentenary of the 1650 Scottish Psalter was observed in March 1950 by the Presbyterian Church of Victoria, the Free Presbyterian Church of Victoria and the Reformed Presbyterian Church.[1]

Reformed Presbyterian Church

The Reformed Presbyterian Church of Ireland ordained W.R.McEwen (1906-89) in 1928 and he arrived in Australia in 1929 to help out at Geelong and then to establish a new congregation in the Melbourne suburb of McKinnon. He became Secretary of the *Bible Union of Australia* in 1942, and was influential through his editorship of *Evangelical Action* 1944-1985. Rev Alex Barkley arrived from Ireland at the close of 1946 to succeed Rev H.K.Mack as the minister of the Geelong congregation. These three RP ministers were men of ability. Messrs Mack and Barkley tutored S.N.Ramsay for the PCEA ministry in accordance with a curriculum established by the Assembly of the FPCA in 1948.[2]

1. See report in **Australian Free Presbyterian**, July 1950, August 1950.
2. The curriculum is set out in printed form in the **Australian Free Presbyterian**, May 1948, pp.5-8.

Free Presbyterian Church of Australia

The federated churches of the FPCA were small - 3 charges in the FPCV with probably none of them having more than 40 people,[3] and seven charges in the PCEA embracing perhaps 1,000 people. Theologically, the FPCA was conservative and Calvinistic although there was some lack of clarity and grasp of Reformed doctrine in some areas. Indeed, copies of the Westminster Confession were imported and made available to office-bearers in 1950, and copies of the Second Book of Discipline were duplicated to further familiarity with the principles of the church. Rev Arthur Allen was particularly to the fore in this.

When Allen had been settled at Geelong in 1938 it was possible to revive the Victorian Synod which required a quorum of three ordained ministers. This was done in December 1939, but Allen then realised that the Victorian church had its own constitution which, while for substance the same, was different from the FPCA constitution, and different again from the PCEA constitution as he discovered after being settled in Sydney in 1944.[4]

Allen brought out the legal, moral and practical issues in a comprehensive report to the PCEA Synod and to the FPCA Assembly in March 1951. In reviewing the constitutional history of the PCEA, FPCV and FPCA, he noted that the property of the federated churches was held in each case on a basis which required the officebearers to recognise the applicable Synod as the supreme ecclesiastical court. The property was held accordingly and could only be dispersed in accordance with the trust deed. Thus, the Assembly could not have the powers set out in the Preamble to the 1913 Basis (see p. 306), and could only be regarded as a Conference without powers. It was also noted that the Assembly itself, after 1922, had gradually taken control of the funds contributed by the two churches. Urgent attention was needed to tidy up the messy situation which had arisen from the well-intentioned but legally inept federation of 1913. Given that there was currently a quorum for the Victorian Synod, it was advisable to proceed at once while this situation continued. While it was not mentioned publicly, Messrs Robinson and Graham in Victoria, while not really anxious to see the FPCV disappear, were ready to act to resolve the situation since they feared the small FPCV could become incapable of constitutional action, as had happened in South

---

3. Cf. K.MacRae, **Diary of Kenneth MacRae** (Edinburgh 1980) pp.404-428. This records MacRae's visit to the Australian church in 1953-54, and indicates the low state in Victoria. Regular statistics have not been kept prior to 1981, but the figures are informed estimates.

4. Rev James Cameron was Clerk of the PCEA Synod at the time of union in 1864. The minute book covering 1846-64 was purchased on a bookstall by J.A.Ferguson (1881-1969), the great bibliophile, and is now held in the Ferguson Library, Presbyterian Church Offices, Sydney. See also, **Australian Free Presbyterian**, April 1951, p.3.

UNION NOVEMBER 1953: Front (l to r) Rev I.L.Graham, Rev M.C.Ramsay, H. McPherson [Richmond/ Brunswick], Rev A.Allen, H.C.Nicolson [St Kilda], Rev J.A. Harman. Back (l to r) C.J.Green [Maclean], G.R. Anderson [Grafton], Rev A.D. McIntosh, Rev S.N.Ramsay, A.M.McLean [Geelong], Rev K.MacRae [Stornoway], Rev J.A.Webster, R.Allen [St George's], J.E.Huckett [Hastings], C.A. McMillan [Hamilton] No elders present from Hunter and Manning

Photograph courtesy of Mary Cameron, Harwood Island, NSW

355

Australia with the FPCSA, and thus the property would not be available for effective furtherance of the principles of the church.[5]

A desirable union achieved 1953

Knowing the slowness with which such negotiations normally proceed, there was a remarkable alacrity in dealing with the issue and in less than three years all had been resolved in a most satisfactory way by the PCEA absorbing the congregations of the FPCV. The amalgamation committee met at Melbourne in November 1951, the Victorian Synod unanimously approved union, subject to certain assurances, on January 15, 1952, and the PCEA Synod approved and gave the assurances sought on April 1, 1952 following Barrier Act procedure that day. On May 16, 1952, remits under the Barrier Act were received from the sessions and congregations in Victoria showing complete unanimity. The union was to take place on the basis that the principles of the PCEA are identical to those of the Free Church of Scotland in 1843 following the Disruption, and thus no change was needed on the part of the PCEA except to dispense with the anomalous Assembly. Voting in NSW, other than at Synod level, was not required. After a delay with the legalities, the necessary Act of the Victorian Parliament to vary the trusts so that property might be held for the PCEA was obtained. A special PCEA Synod under Allen's Moderatorship was held in the East St Kilda Church on November 25, 1953, and the congregations and officebearers were received accordingly.

In his address of welcome Allen stated:

During the period of negotiations, and I was present at all the meetings convened, there was not one dissenting voice; opinions may have differed, but the consciousness of Christ's presence led to unanimity without compromise. I doubt if a similar case in church union negotiations can be shown in ecclesiastical history. My voice may not betray my emotions, and I cannot find words to express them; but this is the day I have longed and prayed for.[6]

---

5. Allen's 1951 Report is 22 foolscap pages. The views of Robinson and Graham were conveyed to me by F.M.Bradshaw, who was the key man in advising on the legalities. His reference to the importance of the position of the PCEA and the significance of its stand for ordered government, sound doctrine and pure and Scriptural worship is of note: see his article in **Australian Free Presbyterian**, January 1954, pp.1,2. He states: 'The desire to return to the constitutional position inherited from Scotland is not a question of pandering to Scottish nationalism. Far deeper goes the reason. For of the churches which arose from the Reformation movement - and this has been said by many whose words are entitled to deference - that which was most perfectly reformed according to the Word of God was the Church of Scotland. That is why its constitution is such a priceless possession of the Presbyterian Church of Eastern Australia.'

6. For report and minutes see **Australian Free Presbyterian**, December 1953.

In the run up to the 1953 union, the PCEA Synod of 1952, following Barrier Act procedure, passed an *Act Anent Questions and Formula* which renewed the use of the original questions employed by the Synod at ordinations and inductions prior to some changes in the 1870s, and also clarified the position of the church as to the use of the Scottish Paraphrases of 1781. A formal relationship was also established with the Free Church of Scotland. With these steps it might be said that the PCEA ceased to think of herself as a colonial appendage of the Free Church of Scotland and cast off the accretions to her constitution and asserted it with greater clarity and self-awareness as an indigenous Australian church. It was not an immediate transformation of thinking, nor is it yet quite universal, and each generation must be vigilant not to fall back into mere tradition, but it was a very significant development which set the stage for more effective operation.

The worship question 1947/1952

The position of the Reformation Church of Scotland in its subjection to the teaching of the word of God as regards the praise portion of public worship, may be summarised in the terms expressed by Professor John Murray and Dr William Young in the *Minority Report of the Committee on Song in the Public Worship of God*, presented to the Assembly of the Orthodox Presbyterian Church (USA) in 1947: [7]

(1) There is no warrant in Scripture for the use of uninspired human compositions in the singing of God's praise in public worship.

(2) There is explicit authority for the use of inspired songs.

(3) The songs of divine worship must therefore be limited to the songs of Scripture, for they alone are inspired.

(4) The Book of Psalms has provided us with the kind of composition for which we have the authority of Scripture.

(5) We are therefore certain of divine sanction and approval in the singing of the Psalms.

(6) We are not certain that other inspired songs were intended to be sung in the worship of God, even though the use of other inspired songs does not violate the fundamental principle in which Scripture authorization is explicit, namely, the use of inspired songs.

(7) In view of the uncertainty with respect to the use of other inspired songs we should confine ourselves to the Book of Psalms.

The constitutional position of the Church of Scotland in 1840 when the Bond of Union was signed in Sydney (see pp. 51,52) was that the said church claimed no constitutional power, nor had any, to introduce in the praise portion of public worship other than 'inspired songs' - this expression allowing the Psalter, other songs embedded in Scripture, and probably singing versions of prose Scripture, but it excludes songs whose text is not Scripture.

7. Cited from my **Psalmsinging in Scripture and History** (revised edition 1985), p.2.

It might be argued that the statement in the Confession 21:5 says otherwise:

The reading of the Scriptures with godly fear, the sound and conscionable hearing of the Word, in obedience unto God, with understanding, faith and reverence, <u>singing of psalms</u> with grace in the heart; as also the due administration and worthy receiving of the sacraments instituted by Christ, are all parts of the ordinary religious worship of God: beside religious oaths, vows, solemn fastings, and thanksgivings upon special occasions, which are, in their several times and seasons, to be used in a holy and religious manner.

However, the Scottish church has not regarded the term 'psalms' in that section and elsewhere in her subordinate standards as necessarily equivalent to the 150 songs of the Psalter.[8] The Church of Scotland had the power from time to time, following due process, to authorise the use of songs coming within her constitutional powers. Prior to 1840 such authorisation had been given only to English and Gaelic psalters, thus adhering to points 1 to 7 in the Report quoted above.

All is not quite so straightforward, however, since in 1781 the General Assembly had given approval for the use of 67 paraphrases and 5 other hymns where the minister regarded it as edifying pending receipt of comments by the General Assembly in 1782. But nothing seems to have been done in that connection. The use in some Lowland congregations of the Free Church, which continues on occasion to this day, is therefore not adequately supported by legislative sanction.[9] In Australia the same anomalous practice occurred in some post-union 'Free' congregations. James Benny used them at Morphett Vale, and had a choir as well, while George Sutherland employed them in St George's. Use this century died away.

It appears that Rev D.G.T.Trotter of Maclean considered that the fact he had liberty to use the 1781 Paraphrases in Scotland, meant that he should have the same liberty in Australia, but in 1947 the Assembly declared otherwise. Holding that 'there are undoubtedly inspired psalms in the Word of God other than the 150 in the Book of Psalms',[10] Trotter disagreed with the interpretation placed on the 1913 Basis, and resigned from the ministry in 1948 to take up farming. Other factors entered into this unfortunate situation. It may well be that some of those who opposed him did not have the best grasp of the issues, but it is also evident there was some disproportion in Trotter's position. In 1952, as part of the *Act Anent Questions and Formula*, the PCEA Synod made the following Declaration.

---

8. **Psalmsinging**...op.cit., pp. 41ff gives the history and constitutional position.
9. In any event, many of these Paraphrases are so loose as to be nearer what are commonly called 'hymns,' while if one compares them with the earlier edition of 1751, which was approved only for private use, the influence of the 'moderate' strain of teaching becomes very evident in the changes introduced in the 1781 edition.
10. Letter from D.G.C.Trotter to Clerk of Northern Presbytery, August 16, 1948.

The Synod declare that the expression 'purity of worship presently authorised and practised in the Presbyterian Church of Eastern Australia' as used in the formula of this Church is held to require, *inter alia* the exclusion from public worship of instrumental music, and from the praise portion thereof, of all compositions other than the Psalms of the Word of God.

Trotter should not have had difficulty with this declaration since it falls within the constitutional powers of the Synod. What is 'practised' in the church does not mean that what may be found being done at any particular time is sacrosanct, but the clause means practice that is legislatively sanctioned, ie. is in harmony with the doctrine of the Confession of Faith and the principles of the Directory for Public Worship. Use of a particular Psalter, being an application of the unchanging 'purity of worship presently authorised and practised', comes under the general legislative power of the church, and so may be varied from time to time.

Further, the Declaration does not entangle the conscience of the person who accepts the regulative principle of worship but personally regards it as Scriptural to apply it a little differently than the church has authorised, so long as he heartily accepts and is willing faithfully to uphold the worship principles of the church in practice. Someone who believes that some extra songs are permissible does not have his conscience coerced if he abides by the PCEA constitution. Thus, ministers of the Free Church of Scotland are (in theory at least) permitted to use the 1781 Paraphrases, yet are automatically recognised as ministers of the PCEA upon signing the PCEA formula of subscription.

There are several reasons which may persuade one that the position of the PCEA is a Scriptural one: its consistency, spirituality, ecumenicity, and sufficiency, as well as its securing of freedom of the conscience from the doctrines of men, are some of these.[11] The declaration does not go into these but exacts a pledge that one 'owns' (ie. accepts) the worship in such a way that one will not seek to overthrow it and make it of a different kind, but rather will uphold it and reject worship based on principles other than those in the Confession and the Directory.

Again, the propriety of singing uninspired hymns in connection with the worship of other churches is not determined. The formula of subscription requires one 'in my station to assert maintain and defend the said...worship,' but the church has wisely, as I think, not concerned itself to legislate about

11. The Synod of 1984 dealt with this issue in regard to a man seeking a licence, and the opinion of the Procurator is on p.60 of the 1984 Reports, and see Minutes, pp.6,7 & 23.

the participation of officebearers in Christian worship where uninspired material is used in praise. Obviously one can have competing claims because of the communion of saints, and each man must be persuaded in his own mind.

Finally, the declaration covers public worship. For myself, I consider that the same principle should apply in family worship though not of course excluding the singing of uninspired hymns at other times, and it is obviously desirable that the Psalter be employed in Sunday School and Youth groups of the church. Still, the formula does not require this, and we have already noted an example in one of the strictest PCEA congregations where such was not the case (see note 4 on page 308), and similarly in Benny's church at Morphett Vale where Bateman's Sacred Melodies was used in the Sunday School as early as 1858.[12] Thus, there needs to be a proper balance in handling this subject so it is always related to Christ as the one through whom alone our worship is accepted.

Federal Relations with the Free Church of Scotland 1952/54

The final important matter in this period was the passing of an Act by the Free Church of Scotland Assembly of May 1952, and a similar Act by the FPCA Assembly of 1953, duly re-enacted in 1954 by the PCEA Synod, by which fraternal relations involving mutual eligibility were established. The self-explanatory Act is as follows (an error noted in 1983 having been corrected in 1984):

The Synod of Eastern Australia does now enact that there shall be established between this Church and the Free Church of Scotland such a relationship as shall maintain and manifest the unity of the Churches, their separate and independent jurisdiction being always preserved. This relationship shall be carried out as follows:-

(a) This Church shall henceforth recognise the status of the office-bearers and ministers of the Free Church of Scotland as if they were its own, and the ministers and probationers of the Free Church of Scotland shall be eligible for calls by any congregation of this Church as if they were ministers and Probationers of this Church.

(b) In the event of a Theological College being established by this Church, Students of the Free Church of Scotland attending such a Theological College shall be recognised as Students of this Church under regulations to be framed by the Training of Ministry Committee, and approved by the Synod of Eastern Australia.

(c) In the event of a Mission Field being established by this Church, Missionaries of the Free Church of Scotland in such a Mission Field shall be recognised as if they were our own.

---

12. R.S.Ward, **The Free Presbyterian Church of South Australia** (Melbourne 1984) p.4 (citing Session Minutes, June 25, 1858). It would be a serious mistake if one erected barriers because of such differences or even because of the use of a different Psalter. Such action would in effect be adding to the terms of communion solemnly agreed, for it does not have valid basis in the constitution of the church, to say no more.

(d) A corresponding member appointed by the Supreme Court of the Free Church of Scotland shall be admitted to the Synod of Eastern Australia to attend its meetings with a right to deliberate but not to vote, and the Synod of Eastern Australia shall appoint a corresponding member to the Supreme Court of the Free Church of Scotland on similar terms, but any failure in the appointment or attendance of these Commissioners shall not invalidate the proceedings of these Courts.   [Enacted April 12, 1954]

Formula

Reference has already been made to the *Act Anent Questions and Formula* passed by the Synod in 1952. which set out the formula used prior to the formation of the Assembly in 1913. This Formula is the same as that approved by the General Assembly of the Church of Scotland in the year 1711 (see page 19), but with the necessary modification to relate it to the post-Disruption situation. A disclaimer of intolerant or persecuting principles along with the maintenance of the doctrine of the civil magistrate set out in the Confession of Faith, was also made, so that the doctrinal position is the same as that of the Free Church of Scotland in 1846, which in turn was the historic constitution of the Church of Scotland back to 1560. The wording of the formula is as follows:

I,...................................., do hereby declare, that I do sincerely own and believe the whole doctrine contained in the Confession of Faith, approven by General Assemblies of the Church of Scotland, to be the truths of God; and I do own the same as the confession of my faith; as likewise I do own the purity of worship presently authorised and practised in the Presbyterian Church of Eastern Australia, and also the Presbyterian government and discipline thereof; which doctrine, worship and church government, I am persuaded, are founded upon the Word of God, and agreeable thereto; I also approve of the general principles respecting the jurisdiction of the Church and her subjection to Christ as her only Head, which are contained in the Claim of Right, and in the Protest, referred to in the questions already put to me; and I promise that, through the grace of God, I shall firmly and constantly adhere to the same, and to the utmost of my power shall, in my station, assert, maintain and defend the said doctrine, worship, discipline and government of this Church, by Kirk Sessions, Presbyteries, Provincial Synods, and General Assemblies, together with the liberty and exclusive jurisdiction thereof; and that I shall, in my practice, conform myself to the said worship, and submit to the said discipline, government and exclusive jurisdiction, and not endeavour, directly or indirectly, the prejudice or subversion of the same; and I promise that I shall follow no divisive course from the doctrine, worship, discipline, government and exclusive jurisdiction of this Church, renouncing all doctrines, tenets, and opinions whatsover, contrary to, or inconsistent with, the said doctrine, worship, discipline, government, or jurisdiction of the same.   [Enacted April 2, 1952]

This formula may be compared to that of the Presbyterian Church of Australia given on page 282. The position of the Church of Scotland is even more loose. Consequently, the PCEA cannot routinely accept ministers from the PCA or the CS, while the PCA is ready to take men from the PCEA and hitherto has routinely taken men from CS but ought to tighten this if she wishes to maintain her doctrinal integrity. The RP Church until the 20th century required all members and officebearers to acknowledge the Confession of Faith and Catechisms as founded upon the Word of God and agreeable thereto. Officebearers in addition had to give affirmative answers to detailed questions but no formula was signed. Nowadays, there is a quite brief formula of subscription.

26: THE REFORMED FAITH IN THE NETHERLANDS

From 1950 onwards, many Dutch immigrants came to Australia, and a proportion (upwards of 10%) were of positive Calvinistic conviction. To appreciate the position of the two denominations formed by these folk in Australia, it is necessary to know something of the history of the Reformed faith in the Netherlands. This is the more so since there is a lack of good material in English, and this makes an idealistic reconstruction of the past all too easy. For if there is an idealistic construction of Scottish church history (and of Australian Presbyterian history!), there is also such a construction among the Dutch.

Early years of Reformation

At the time of the Reformation, the Low Countries were part of the Hapsburg Empire ruled by Philip II of Spain. Every effort was made to crush the Reformed faith. However, under William of Orange (William the Silent), Spanish domination of the seven northern provinces was overthrown in 1579. The Dutch 'Beggars' who controlled the sea were the key to victory. The area of the 7 provinces is less than half the area of Tasmania or Scotland.

In 1563, the well known Reformed preacher, Petrus Dathenus (1531-1588), pastor of the Flemish congregation at Frankfort before becoming court preacher of the Palatinate, translated the Heidelberg Catechism into Dutch. He also revised the Belgic Confession of Guido de Bres, composed a liturgy, and translated the psalms of Marot and Beza into Dutch. His Psalter preserved the original Genevan metres and tunes, and was published in 1566.

The earliest general Synod of 'the Belgic churches' met at Emden in East Friesland in October 1571 with 29 members. It adopted the French and Belgic Confessions and the Genevan and Heidelberg Catechisms, as some congregations spoke French and others Dutch. A polity was established and a church order modelled on the French one of 1559 was drawn up. The full series of assemblies - consistories, classes, provincial and national synods was included. What with the political changes, the first national Synod on Dutch soil was not held until that at Dort in June 1578 under the presidency of Dathenus. In general, its decisions confirmed those at Emden. A further Synod was held at Middelburg in 1581 and another at The Hague in 1586. The 1586 Synod formulated a slightly revised church order which made some concessions to the civil magistrate so as to give him a share in the administration of the church. This reflected the reality that the local and provincial magistrates were very generally influenced by the pre-Reformation humanist tradition, and by the views of Thomas Erastus (1524-1583), who argued against the church's right to govern its own affairs. A further church order was drawn up by a committee of the States in 1591 and was decidedly Erastian in giving the civil government effective control over the calling of ministers. It was at this time that Andrew Melville was emphasising the doctrine of two kingdoms in Scotland (see p.15).

Due to political factors in the main, there were no general synods of the church between 1586 and 1816, with the exception of the great Synod of Dort in 1618/19, and the rather loose provincial system prevented the development of church-wide policies. It must be remembered also that by 1600 only a small proportion of the people had accepted the Reformed faith wholeheartedly. The shortage of trained preachers was overcome gradually by the founding of universities at Leiden (1575), Franeker (1585), Groningen (1614) and Utrecht (1636). The financial needs of the church were met by the civil authorities, but the degree of independence from civil interference varied in the different provinces. The 1591 church order was proclaimed only in 1612, and was part of the struggle over Arminianism referred to below.

The rise of Arminianism

In the early years of the 17th century, the views of Jacobus Arminius (1560-1609), Professor at Leiden, caused alarm. Arminius was an earnest and pious man, but he moderated the doctrine of original sin and taught that the origin of salvation is based not upon God's sovereign election, of which faith is a fruit, but upon God's foreknowledge of man's faith which leads him to elect those who he sees will have faith. The distinction is vital since, in the last analysis, salvation is placed in the hands of man and not God by the Arminian scheme. The furtherance of these views may have been helped by the high (supralapsarian) Calvinism of Francis Gomar (1563-1641), a fellow professor at Leiden. However, at root they were native to man's sinful heart and had fertile soil in the humanism that characterised influential sections of Dutch life - the politicians and the wealthy merchant class in particular.

Arminius had been less than frank about his views at times. His followers drew up five articles in 1610 called the *Remonstrance*, and received strong support from many influential people. The doctrinal struggle became also a national struggle between the States, under the leadership of Oldenbarne-veldt (the Grand Pensionary), and the Reformed. The States refused requests for a national synod, and only the effective intervention of Prince Maurice, the Stadholder, prevented an extended civil war. So it was that in 1618, a national synod was convened at Dort. At this Synod there was a total of 84 members, and its ecumenical character was shown by the presence, with full voting rights, of representatives of the British, German and Swiss churches. The British members were John Davenant (Bishop of Salisbury), Samuel Ward, Joseph Hall and Walter Balcanquall, a Scot and chaplain to King James. The president was Jan Bogerman, and he had as his advisor 'the learned doctor' William Ames (1576-1633), an English Puritan who was later a professor at Franeker (1622-32).

The National Synod, held at Dordrecht (the Netherlands) in 1618-1619.

The Synod of Dort was remarkable for its learning, and proceeded to draw up several Canons which affirmed the true doctrine on the disputed points and rejected errors. The five points of Calvinism (as they have been called) are thus really only the response to the five points at which the Reformed doctrine had been attacked. They are remembered by the word TULIP:

The Total Depravity of man was affirmed ie. that while he is not as bad as he can be, no part of man's faculties has escaped the effects of sin; thus, he is utterly incapable of himself of any spiritual good.

Unconditional Election was affirmed ie. that God's choice of those who shall be saved does not rest on any good foreseen in man, but solely on his love and mercy.

Limited (or Definite) Atonement was the third point ie. that Christ had made satisfaction for the sins of the elect, those given to him by the Father; nevertheless, it was specifically acknowledged that Christ's sacrifice was sufficient for all.

Irresistible Grace was affirmed ie. that while men can and do resist God's grace, yet in regard to the elect God works in renewal so that opposition is overcome and the elect person freely embraces Christ. Nevertheless, the unfeigned call of God in the Gospel to all who hear was affirmed.

Perseverance (or Preservation) of the Saints ie. that God, having begun the good work continues and perfects it, rendering the means of grace effective so that the elect do persevere in faith and holiness and inherit the kingdom prepared for them.

While one may prefer the more calm setting of the Westminster Confession drawn up a generation later to the polemics of the Synod of Dort, yet the Canons of Dort provide a lucid and fair exposition of the doctrine of grace that is at the heart of the Augustinian or Calvinistic understanding of salvation by God's mercy. The Canons reflect, as does the Westminster confession, an infralapsarian position without condemning the minority supralapsarian position.[1]

About 200 Arminian preachers were removed from the ministry in consequence of the decisions of the Synod of Dort, but the rationalistic thought still remained and reared its head again. The Synod also revised and established a church order. In its 162nd session, Christmas, Easter Day and Whitsunday, and the day following each of them, were prescribed as religious festivals to be kept along with the Lord's Day - a decision which did not please the Scottish church. It was a concession to what seemed practical wisdom, since the days in question had been continued as civil holidays by the magistrates and it seemed fitting to the church to promote a religious aspect to them. It was a decision hard to reconcile with Article 32 of the Confession, as also a prescribed liturgy. Indeed, Jacobus Koelman (1632-95), a capable minister, was deposed by the church at the insistence of the civil authority in 1675 for refusing to use the prescribed prayers other than as guides and for refusing to honour any day as holy except the Lord's Day. This would not have happened in the Scottish church.

1. On the Synod of Dort there is an excellent exposition by the great Scottish theologian William Cunningham in his **Historical Theology** (Edinburgh 1862, reprinted 1970) Vol. 2 pp.371-513 ; while a helpful historical introduction is in **The Bride's Treasure**, Chapter 1 by H.J.Meijerink pp.1-37 (published by the Free Reformed Churches of Australia in 1979).

The Synod of Dort also declared that in the churches only the 150 psalms, the Commandments, the Lord's Prayer, the Creed and the Songs of Mary, Zacharias and Simeon were to be used. There was no reference to instrumental music since such was not used in the worship service of the Dutch churches, and organs in those churches which had them were played outside worship times by authority of the magistrates.[2]

From Dort to the Napoleonic Conquest 1619-1795

While in 1638 the Scottish church cast aside the unbiblical polity imposed on her by the king and struggled to eventually gain liberty in 1690, the history of the Dutch church after Dort was somewhat different. The theory was that only Reformed people held public office, but the lack of a strong central government, plus the strength of non-Reformed sentiment as well as the presence of many religious refugees of various persuasions, meant that the reality was somewhat different. The formal end to the dispute with Spain at the Peace of Westphalia in 1648 did not change the position, and with only a few exceptions, such as by men like Willem a Brakel (1635-1711), there was little opposition to the civil power's retention of control over the placement of ministers.

Preaching in the Reformed church in the 17th century was usually orthodox after Dort, but was often cold and intellectual, and there was ample evidence of worldliness and nominalism in the towns and cities which enjoyed the economic prosperity that continued through the century. The prevailing systems of philosopy had their strengths and weaknesses. The orthodox relied chiefly on an Aristotelian approach although the less scholastic approach of Petrus Ramus (1515-1572), the Frenchman who was killed in the massacre of Protestants on St Bartholomew's Day, was also influential. William Ames at Franeker (1622-32) drew much from Ramus' stress on the practical bearings of belief. The most influential theologian was Gijsbert Voetsius (1589-1676). He was a precise and militant Calvinist, essentially following what might be regarded as a scholastic approach but influenced by Ames and by Willem Teellinck (1579-1629), who has been called a Dutch Puritan. Voetsius opposed Arminianism, and with the rise of the philosophic

2. In 1574 the provincial Synod of Dort resolved on the basis of 1 Corinthians 14 to abolish organ playing from worship, and in 1578 to dismantle all church organs. However, as they were state property and the organists state employees, a compromise was reached: the organs were excluded from the worship services but played at other times, including on the Lord's Day. The national Synod at Middelburg in 1581 resolved to endeavour to have the use of organs in, before or after worship laid aside, but found difficulty in fully implementing this decision. Gijsbert Voet (1589-1676) states that the first use of an organ to accompany congregational singing occurred in 1637 through the private zeal of a state official [**Politica Ecclesiastica** (Amsterdam 1663), Book 3, p.593]. It was at that time absent from the Reformed world. In Scotland, prohibition was lifted by the Church of Scotland in 1865; by the United Presbyterian Church in 1872; and by the Free Church in 1883 (repealed 1905).

method of René Descartes (1596-1650), which he saw rightly as opening the floodgates of rationalism, he upheld the old orthodoxy and emphasised its practical bearings. Voetsius was a staunch upholder of the sanctity of the Lord's Day. He is often remembered because of his opposition to the teaching of Johannes Cocceius (1603-1669), whose version of covenant theology sought to be biblical and anti-speculative but broke the unity of the Old and New Testaments in the process. Two factions developed among the ministers, and wrangling went on for decades. The Erastian situation in the church and its lack of structural unity did not help the resolution of these difficulties.

The difficulties in doctrine and life in the church contributed to a marked increase in house meetings or conventicles for prayer and spiritual exercises. Such meetings had existed from the earliest days of the Reformation, but they now became of greater significance as folk sought to maintain the warm devotion of the older piety and to continue the use of the catechism in the training of their children. Voetsius worked with men like Willem a Brakel among these groups. The meetings provided an outlet for those unhappy with prevailing circumstances in the church without requiring them to withdraw from the church. Stigmatised by many later writers as 'pietistic', it is true that some groups developed peculiarities through the excesses of their leaders, particularly an introverted and experience-centred piety. However, in the main they represented a synthesis of orthodoxy, spirituality and godliness that was a light in a dark place.

The 18th century has many parallels with the Scottish situation. The work of Herman Witsius, who served at Franeker (1675-80), Utrecht (1680-97) and Leiden (1698-1707), contributed to some easing of contention among the ministers. His work *The Economy of the Covenants* first saw the light in 1677, and was translated from Latin to English and published in Edinburgh about a century later.

Separation from the church was not contemplated by orthodox leaders in the 17th and 18th centuries, and the conventicles came to fill the place held in Scotland by the Secession and Relief churches (see p. 21), although there was less uniformity. By the middle of the 18th century, the spirit of the age had become dominant. One of the last who protested against this false tolerance and worldly Deism was Alexander Comrie (1706-1774), the Scottish-born minister of Woubrugge in South Holland. His tract against departure from the Three Forms of Unity (Catechism, Confession and Canons of Dort) was censored by the government in 1761. The older orthodoxy was preserved in the conventicles which savoured the writings of men like Willem a Brakel as well as sermons of the Erskines in Scotland. They found then (and still find) a ready market in the Netherlands, along with other works of English and Scottish ministers.

The period from 1795 to 1834

The establishment by France of the Batavian Republic in 1795 meant also that the Dutch Reformed Church was separated from the state, and the Reformed doctrines were no longer taught in the public schools. It was also expected that all financial support would be phased out. However, to cut a long story short, Napoleon's defeat at Leipzig in 1813 brought the return from exile of the son of the last stadholder. In 1815 he became William I, King of the United Netherlands.[3]

While the separation of church and state was maintained and all existing denominations made equal before the law, the king, who himself professed the Reformed faith, saw it as his role to exercise a fatherly care over the churches. Only the Mennonites were determined enough to resist the imposition of the king's will. On January 7, 1816, a royal decree ordered that the classes and synods be dissolved and that they be replaced by executive boards. Eight classes, notably Classis Amsterdam, raised objections, but all acquiesced in the new situation where church and state were separated in doctrine but linked administratively. This unbiblical situation was contrary to Articles 30/32 of the Belgic Confession, and was a more developed form of the erastianism which had operated during the previous century.

The first general synod (board) under the new rules was held later in 1816. A formula of subscription was appointed for subscription by candidates for the ministry which contained an ambiguity compared with the subscription set out in 1619 by the Synod of Dort. The earlier requirement, which, however, had not been universally accepted or enforced, stated that the subscriber held the doctrines to agree with God's word. The new requirement was acceptance of the doctrine which, 'according to God's Holy Word, is contained in the accepted forms of unity.' This ambiguity reflected the mixed situation then in the church and only J.W.Vijgeboom of Axel made significant protest. In 1822 he seceded and formed the *Restored Church of Christ*, but was suppressed for his pains. However, the 1820s did see increased interest in the truths of Scripture through the influence of the *Reveil* or Awakening which spread from Switzerland to France, Holland and Great Britain. The meeting began with Bible study meetings among the upper classes but came to have a more widespread influence. At the same time, the Groningen theology - an undogmatic religion of feeling and morality, gained ascendancy.

First Secession 1834

What subsequently occurred in the 1830s as the first significant secession

---

3. A helpful and well-documented study is Gerrit J. tenZythoff, **Sources of Secession** (Grand Rapids 1987) and covers the period 1795 to 1834.

from the Dutch Reformed Church has parallels in the Scottish Disruption of 1843, but there are also differences. There were major social factors in that a large proportion of those who seceded represented poorer and less educated people who feared the centralising squeeze of the new order of things. One might see a parallel here in the support of the Free Church by the Highland peasantry of Scotland. The Dutch secession did not involve 30-40% of the church as the Disruption did in Scotland. Effective church-wide government had not been characteristic of the Dutch church, and the first secession began with one minister - Hendrik de Cock of the village of Ulrum, who withdrew on May 29, 1834. He was soon joined by several others, while within two years there were over 120 congregations, many formed from members of the Reformed Church who had been involved in conventicles. For some years fines and penalties were applied against the seceders, but the revival of orthodox preaching stimulated considerable growth. From being perhaps 1% of the total Dutch population in 1840, the seceders rose to 5% by 1880, despite the fact that many went to America, principally for economic reasons. A number of them formed the Christian Reformed Church of North America in 1857 - a large church today.

In the original 'Act of Separation and Return', De Cock asserted separation from what he regarded as a false church in terms of his understanding of Article 29 of the Belgic Confession, and he claimed to return to the Three Forms of Unity as acknowledged by the Synod of Dort in 1619. One can appreciate that the history of the Dutch church, and its retention of one church organisation for so long, was influential in De Cock's sharp antithesis, which would seem to allow no shade of gray between black and white, true and false. There is no doubt that the serious defections in the Dutch Reformed Church justified separation by those who sought to be loyal to Christ, but the orthodox Reformed theologians of the 17th century would not have had difficulty with the Westminster Confession's more pure/ less pure/ degenerated terminology in reference to the visible church.[4]

The first secession also rejected the uninspired hymns which had received approval in 1806, and reverted to the position of Dort on song in worship, but retained organs. The fewness of the early ministers and the lack of organisation meant that there were considerable difficulties in the way of unity among the seceders. However, partial unity was achieved in 1854, the year a Theological College was founded at Kampen, and all but some of the more introspective groups were united in 1869 under the name *Christian Reformed Church*.

4. A strain of teaching which absolutises the language of Article 29 of the Belgic Confession contrary to its original intention has continued evident in Dutch Calvinism. For the historical position see H.Heppe, **Reformed Dogmatics** (German 1861, English 1950, reprint Grand Rapids 1978) pp.657ff; also a more recent survey in P.Y. de Jong **The Church's Witness to the World** (Ontario 1980) Pt. 2 pp.268ff. Note also James Walker, **The Theology and Theologians of Scotland 1560-1750** (Edin 1982) pp.95-126.

Second Secession 1886

In 1886 there was a major secession from the Reformed Church which is associated with the name of a many-sided genius, Dr Abraham Kuyper (1837-1920). A great visionary and organiser,[5] Kuyper was converted to the orthodox faith through the ministry of one of his flock when he was minister of Beesd. Something similar had happened to De Cock. Kuyper devoted all his powers to the furthering of the Reformed faith and a spectacular flowering of Reformed influence occurred 1870-1920. Kuyper dominated his age in his exposition and application of the Calvinistic world and life view, and was Prime Minister 1901-1905.

In the church the seceders had left, liberalism was rife and the administration by the boards was corrupt. However, quite a body of orthodox people remained in the church. In 1867, a measure of participation by church members in the election of elders (they were elected for a term and not for life as in Scotland) was granted. It resulted in many orthodox elders being appointed and liberal dominance was broken in some areas. In seeking to maintain the Reformed doctrines, a clash occurred between the large Amsterdam church (which included the whole city) and the Classis. The Classis deposed 80 members of the Amsterdam consistory who had refused to give certificates of good standing to baptised persons of liberal beliefs. The Synod confirmed the action of the Classis, so the consistory members broke with the corrupt administration on December 16, 1886 at a meeting in The Hague. There were soon about 200 congregations which called themselves the Netherlands Reformed Churches (Lamenting). They had broken with the synodical hierarchy in order to maintain the Reformed confession.

The Secessions unite 1892

Those of the second secession did not say the Reformed Church was a false church since they distinguished between faithful local congregations and the corrupt administration. Kuyper spoke more in the terminology of the Westminster Confession, though at times he seemed to some to go beyond recognising that the church exists in different branches in different degrees of purity to suggest that conflicting statements of Christian truth have validity as a counterpoise to each other. Suggestions of this kind could only confirm those of the first secession in their more rigorous view.

In achieving unity between the first and second secessions, the question of the falsity of the Dutch Reformed Church was left open, provided those of the second secession broke with the local congregation. This they were ready to do and union took place on June 17, 1892, when the first Synod of the

5. A helpful introduction to Kuyper and his life and times is L.Praamsma, **Let Christ Be King** (Ontario, 1985, 192pp). Kuyper's **Lectures on Calvinism** (Grand Rapids 1961) are a good example of the principles of his thought. Francis Schaeffer (1912-1984) might be seen as a populariser of concepts elaborated by Kuyper.

Reformed Churches in the Netherlands (*Gereformeerde Kerken*) met. There were soon 700 congregations in this bond, embracing about 10% of the population. Over against it was the mixed Dutch Reformed Church (*Hervormde Kerk*). Some churches of the first secession remained out of the 1892 union and retained the original name. Their chief cause of concern related to some of the opinions of Dr Kuyper which had wide acceptance but appeared dubious to these brethren.

The Reformed Churches since 1892

Kuyper was a great gift of God to the church, but a man so often right can be too readily followed when he is not right or less than balanced. The disciples can easily outrun their master too. So it was that in 1905 the RCN Synod had to deal with the conflict over Kuyper's teaching on baptism and the covenant. Kuyper said that baptism was a seal of regeneration, and since we do not know whether a baptised child will come to faith or not in later years, we must presume the child is regenerate. If the child comes to faith later, well and good; the baptism was real. But if the child does not come to faith, the baptism had not sealed anything. This subjectivism in place of the sure covenant promise of God caused major concern. Against it, the more correct position is to affirm that baptism is a seal of the covenant promise of God with the baptised obligated to repentance and faith. The baptised person who rejects the covenant promise is a covenant breaker; God's promise was true but he acted in unbelief. In such a presentation there is a refusal to introduce as regulating our practice what is known only to God. A peace was patched up in 1905, but undercurrents remained.

There was concern also over the place given to common grace in Kuyper's theology. He developed this concept rather more than others had done to provide the basis for Reformed involvement in the world. While stressing the antithesis between believers and unbelievers, the recognition of God's gifts to all as distinct from the gift of Christ to the elect was a significant factor in overcoming an excess of pietistic practice in Reformed people, but it seemed at times to overshadow the Gospel with cultural activity. A reaction was seen in America in the rejection of common grace in any sense by some in the Christian Reformed Church. Led by Herman Hoeksema, they organised the Protestant Reformed Churches in 1926, but still held Kuyper's teaching about the covenant of grace referred to in the previous paragraph. When some, partly through the influence of Schilder, who also had reservations on common grace, turned from that teaching about the covenant, a division occurred.

Schilder was also concerned about Kuyper's doctrine of the pluriformity of the church, and had difficulty acknowledging other than the true/false antithesis reflected in 1834. There was much discussion in the 1930s.

The final result of conflict in the RCN was that the Synod imposed Kuyper's views on the covenant and baptism, and deposed those who would not accept the decision, including Professors Schilder and Greijdanus of Kampen. At a meeting in The Hague on August 11, 1944, Schilder read an 'Act of Liberation and Return', being a claim to liberation from the synodical hierarchy and of return to the Confessions. About 10% of the RCN adhered. They continued to use the old name but added 'vrijgemaakt' (liberated) where necessary to avoid confusion. Subsequently, the original Synod modified its position somewhat, but did not change in essence nor recall the depositions. Those who regrouped were concerned particularly over the abuse of synodical power according to their understanding of Article 31 of the Church Order. A formal pronouncement on the disputed doctrines as such has not been made by the liberated churches, but the line taken in practice opposes Kuyper's view.

It might be added that very serious decline into liberalism has become evident in the original RCN - the synodical churches, as they are sometimes called. The very fundamentals of the Gospel as to doctrine and ethics are trampled underfoot. A formal union with the Dutch Reformed Church can be expected. This leaves the other main groups as the Christian Reformed Churches with some 170 congregations and 70,000 members in 1972, the Reformed Churches in the Netherlands (liberated) with 260 congregations and 100,000 members as of 1980, plus some smaller bodies, most with origins in the 19th century. There is a semi autonomous group of orthodox churches (the Reformed League) within the Hervormde Kerk which includes perhaps 20% of the total of about 2,000 congregations.

27: THE COMING OF THE DUTCH

Dutch migrants began coming to Australia in 1950. In the early period to 1954, about 80% of these were Roman Catholics, although they formed only 38% of the total Dutch population of some 10 million. The major religious groups had emigration committees to co-ordinate efforts. Canada was a preferred destination for the Reformed Churches: it was closer and less tainted with socialism and agressive trade union activity.[1]

Mr A.Warnaar Jr. had travelled widely in his business of flower merchant, including to America, and had been involved in co-ordinating emigration of Dutch Christians since the mid 1920s. Such was the post-war urge to migrate that Australia came into the picture. It was Warnaar who first sought contacts with Bible-believing churches in Australia that could be recommended to Dutch Christians. Rev Arthur Allen of St George's PCEA, Sydney was the Australian correspondent of *Calvin Forum*, a publication of the Christian Reformed Church of North America, and thus Warnaar came in contact with Allen, and also with Rev W.R.McEwen of the RPC in Melbourne.[2]

Arthur Allen had been influenced by Dr Donald Maclean, Professor of History at the Free Church of Scotland College from 1920 to 1943. Maclean was an ecumenical Calvinist in the best tradition. His lectures in the Free University of Amsterdam[3] in 1927 were published that year under the

1. For general background see E.Duyker, **The Dutch in Australia** (Melbourne 1987). Sources for the early history of the Reformed Churches of Australia include the series of articles 'Pages of the Past' by John vanderBom in **Trowel and Sword** from September 1984 to 1985; R.VanderNoord, **Reformed Churches in New South Wales 1951-76** (Sydney 1977, 24pp). The Yearbook of the RCA includes a survey of the previous year.
2. Letter A.Warnaar to A.Allen, July 23, 1951 (held by R.S.Ward).
3. Founded by Kuyper in 1880 to further scholarship on Reformed principles. For the first 5 years it was housed in the mission church of the Free Church of Scotland.

title *Aspects of Scottish Church History*, while he edited *The Evangelical Quarterly*, an international magazine of Reformed theology, from its commencement in 1929 until his death. Allen was familiar with the history of the Dutch church, keenly supportive of international co-operation among people holding the Reformed faith, and was an original editor of the *Reformed Theological Review* commenced in Melbourne in 1942. Allen saw in the prospect of Dutch migrants of Reformed persuasion an opportunity for the resurgence of Calvinism in Australia. He spoke of his thanks to God if Holland could give to Australia a similar gift as it had given in the past to North America in the Christian Reformed Church.[4]

Rev J. Kremer of Utrecht was sent out by the Deputies for Emigration of the RCN, and he surveyed the Australian situation in June and July 1950.[5] Some Dutch folk were already worshipping at St George's and others at Wauchope PCEA. Kremer noted the liberalism prevalent in the PCA, and met all the FPCA ministers. He indicated that the Dutch church was willing to send out two ministers. Kremer reported back to Holland, and recommended that the differences on worship did not justify starting a separate church. The RCN agreed to recommend that their people join the FPCA.

On October 16, 1950, the Church Extension Committee of the FPCA resolved to invite two ministers to come to Australia to minister to the needs of people already in Australia and to organise for the expected influx of mainly young Dutch settlers.[6] These men would be stationed in Melbourne and Sydney. There was a chronic shortage of housing in both these cities, but a church flat was available in Melbourne. A single man was suggested for Sydney because of the housing problem. The Dutch deputies suggested that a pre-fab house could be shipped out, and so the FPCA purchased a site in the then new suburb of Chester Hill in anticipation.

There was a certain amount of misunderstanding about some aspects, probably mainly because of language difficulties. For example, was the invitation equal to a call? The FPCA intended that the men should be assistants without status as FPCA ministers until they were ready to subscribe the FPCA position. Meanwhile it would be sufficient to conform to the FPCA position on worship even if disagreeing with it, and no time limit was set.[7]

---

4. Letter, A.Warnaar to A.Allen, July 23, 1951. The formation of the Reformed Ecumenical Synod was something Allen planned and worked for. The FPCA was received as a constituent member at the Amsterdam meeting in August 1949.
5. A brief report is in Australian Free Presbyterian, July 1950, p.5.
6. See report in **Australian Free Presbyterian**, November 1950, p.6; December 1950,p.4.
7. Cf. Letter from Deputies for Emigration of RCN to FPCA, May 5, 1951 and response May 18, 1951.

Rev S. (George) Hoekstra (ordained 1930) arrived in Melbourne in March 1951 and resided at 94A Alma Road, East St Kilda. He was not the easiest man to get on with, nor the most suitable for pioneering work. He was over-awed by the distances, and as homesick as some of the new settlers. The FPC minister, Campbell Robinson, was an elderly bachelor, readily upset by practices at variance with the Free Church tradition, and relationships between the two men did not develop well.[8]

In Sydney, John vanderBom (ordained 1943) arrived with his young family in May 1951. He was much more suited for the difficult work of pioneer, although housing was a problem since he had a wife and 4 children. Allen and St George's were very supportive. Mrs Sutherland, a member of St George's, moved from her two bedroom cottage, part of which she had already allowed for the use of another Dutch family, and the vanderBom's moved in. The main migrant centre being at Bathurst, VanderBom had plenty of difficulties in getting about. Money was short and the FPCA stipend was not at the level customary in Holland.

Forming a distinct denomination 1951

The FPCA had only 7 ordained ministers, all but two outside the capital cities. A small church, it was in the midst of consolidating its structure as described on pages 354/355. It had little in the way of financial resources, although this situation had just improved with the receipt of several legacies, most notably the Patterson Bequest from Geelong of some $40,000. The influx of the Dutch was increasing, but they were settling in the outer areas of the cities where the FPCA was not represented. The two Dutch ministers thought it an unreasonable requirement that they should have to conform to the FPCA position on worship when conducting services in such areas, and they could see that the Dutch would soon outnumber the Australian members. In mid 1951, Rev J.A.Schep arrived to minister in Tasmania where only skilled migrants were allowed to settle. As there was then no FPC in Tasmania, he saw no relevance in being part of it. Soon it was resolved that a distinct denomination should be formed which, however, would maintain fraternal relations with the FPCA.

Lest one suppose that the formation of the Reformed Churches of Australia was merely over the organ or lack of it, the situation needs to be put into perspective. Warnaar put it this way:

The Rev Kremer was very strongly of the opinion that such minor differences did not justify starting a new separate church in Australia. Personally I hesitated....I have learned that in a foreign country you cannot expect every-

8. See Holtrop's report, July 1951; letter, A.Warnaar to A.Allen May 31, 1951; Trowel & Sword, December 1984, p.15.

thing just the same as it is in your own country, and I have learned to distinguish between major and minor points....But I did not feel so sure that this would apply to all our emigrants....I was thinking that a smaller or larger number of our Emigrants, especially the younger people, when they found your church services not very attractive, might try a Methodist or Presbyterian church. Even if the Minister in his sermon would say something that would be wrong according to Reformed standards, they would not understand the English language well enough to find this out. And if the service was 'attractive' and the Minister and the people would be nice to them, the danger would be great that these people would go astray in a modernistic church without knowing it themselves.[9]

Warnaar's personal preference had been to establish a distinct denomination as the surest way of keeping the largest number of the people together, but it was feared the Dutch Government might veto the sending of funds which, in any event, were somewhat short. Thus, the assistance of the FPCA was greatly valued, and Warnaar considered that the subsequent development of the Reformed Churches of Australia would not have been possible if Allen had not been so strongly interested and if the FPCA had not made it possible for the first two ministers to come.[10]

In June 1951, Dr H.Holstrop arrived in Australia as representative of the RCN Emigration Committee to assess the situation at first hand, having regard particularly to the difficulties in Melbourne.

VanderBom wanted to see the Dutch congregations stay under the roof of the Free Church but to have their own form of worship and church government, and to be self-supporting. This was an impossible dream since it would have required an abandonment of the constitution. It was not supported by Hoekstra or Schep. Allen was distressed by the difficulties in Melbourne, but was realistic in suggesting the Dutch form a distinct denomination.

At a meeting in July 1951 attended by Hoekstra, VanderBom, Holstrop and Mr K. Van Egmond of Brisbane, it was agreed that the congregations would not be part of the RCN, although this was Hoekstra's preference. Hoekstra also wished the proposed Australian church to be bound by the decisions of the RCN which had given rise to the division of 1944 (see page 371). Holstrop and Van Egmond agreed, but VanderBom was wise enough to oppose this, as some 'liberated' members worshipped with him and there was

9. Letter, A.Warnaar to A.Allen, July 23, 1951.
10. Letter, A.Warnaar to A.Allen, July 23, 1951 and January 22, 1952.

no sense in creating division. After the meeting, Schep in Tasmania indicated that he agreed with VanderBom, and the RCN Emigration Committee also advised that they were prepared to support the new church even if it did not bind to the disputed views. Thus, despite Hoekstra's reservations, this became the position.

Schep on Tasmania's north-west coast was first off the mark. The Reformed Churches of Tasmania was established on October 13, 1951 according to a protocol signed by about 45 communicant members, and this is the date of the formal institution of the Ulverstone and Penguin congregations. A similar move was made in Sydney on December 16, 1951, 145 members subscribing. This latter protocol differed a little from the former, and included reference to the Westminster Confession as well as the Three Forms of Unity. The Brisbane congregation was instituted on November 25, 1951, Rev Peter Pellicaan becoming its minister, while Melbourne instituted on December 30, 1951.

First Synod of the RCA - June 1952

The first Synod of the Reformed Churches of Australia was held in Hoekstra's flat in Melbourne , June 24/27, 1952, with public gatherings in the Albert Street Baptist Church, East Melbourne, the meeting place of the congregation. The function of the Westminster Confession was discussed at this Synod. Quite a number of Dutch people supposed the Westminster Confession to be not a truly Reformed confession - which indicates perhaps a combination of ignorance and parochialism. The Synod of 1957 decided that the Westminster Confession should be one of the standards of the RCA. This was an aid to identification with the Scottish Presbyterian heritage, but anything in the Westminster Confession which might be distinctive does not bind the individual.[11]

Overseas relations

Another major issue was the relationship to churches in the Netherlands. The close relationship with the RCN (synodical) was not in doubt given the large proportion of migrants from that church. The 1952 Synod offered full correspondence with the CRC and the RCN (liberated). However, it could hardly be expected that the latter church would be able to recognise the RCA. It is true the doctrinal issues that had caused the split were not binding in the RCA, but geography hardly alters principles. How could people deposed by the RCN (synodical) be accepted as in good standing by the RCA? The difficulties have an analogy in the relationship of the Australian

11. An example alleged at the 1988 RCA Synod in connection with the Word and Spirit issue, was the specific rejection of further revelation in WCF I:6. Such a specific statement does not appear in the Three Forms of Unity, although I would suggest such a position is implied.

Presbyterian Synod with the divisions in Scotland at the time of the Disruption, although the position in 1944 was more one of enforcing a position that was open rather than positively heretical.

The RCA is now very much an Australian church. There remain emotional ties among the older people, but the Netherlands is not a source for ministers or money any more, and the relationship with the RCN (synodical) has been reappraised since the RCA began to express concern about the doctrinal moves of the mother church in 1970, and her joining the World Council of Churches. The full sister-church relationship was restricted in 1973, and in 1982 was reduced to one of intensive correspondence.

Progress

By the end of 1958, when the major period of migration ceased, the Reformed Churches were found in all states, particularly Tasmania. There were 20 instituted congregations with 5,770 members, 2,483 of whom were full communicants with the balance baptised but not confessing. As at March 1988, there were 10,256 members in about 40 congregations. Reflecting

The first Synod of the Reformed Churches - June 1952

the lower birthrate and ageing, 5,811 of the members were confessing and 4,445 not confessing. Several congregations have over 400 members. These include Blacktown (with nearly 600) Inala, Q (509) , Kingston, T (535), Box Hill, Dandenong and Mt Evelyn in Victoria, and Canning in WA. Most gain is biological although significant evangelistic efforts are made in some areas. Theologically, the church is conservative with some tension arising from different approaches to Scripture interpretation. Kuyper's emphasis on the cultural mandate is influential, although there is a lack of adequate reading at a solid level in some quarters, a common problem among Australian Christians. . There has been difficulty with pentecostal/charismatic influence. Rev J.A.Schep (1897-1972) adopted Pentecostal views and left the Reformed Churches in his retirement. Kingston and now Narre Warren have been affected for some years through the teaching of their minister, while there have been losses of members to charismatic groups. This may in part be due to the rather formal style of Reformed church life, and a certain cultural nominalism.

Reformed Theological College 1954

The RCA Synod at Ulverstone in 1954 considered that an institution for the training of ministers on a Reformed basis was an urgent necessity. The Synod expressed its readiness to co-operate with and to assist in the maintenance of a theological faculty to be established by an Association for Higher Education on a Reformed Basis, and accordingly the RTC came into being at Geelong. Rev J.A.Schep (retired 1964) became Professor of New Testament, Rev A.Barkley of the RP Church in Geelong served as Professor of History (retired 1980). Professor Klaas Runia was obtained from the RCN in 1957 and became Professor of Theology. He related well to the wider scholarly community and put the RTC on the map, so to speak. Somewhat mediating in his approach, but no liberal, he returned to the Netherlands in 1971. T.L. Wilkinson became Professor of New Testament in 1965. He had served the PCA 1954-58, but left over liberalism, particularly as reflected in Freemasonry in the PCA. He became emeritus in 1982 and subsequently rejoined the PCA. He was succeeded by Rev S. Voorwinde, a local minister, in 1985. Professor Allan Harman filled the Old Testament chair in 1974, which earlier had been served by George van Groningen from the CRCNA. When Harman came, Sierd Woudstra, also from the CRCNA, moved from Old Testament to Theology. He came from the left wing of the CRC, was provocative in his approach and considerable disquiet resulted. After serving 1971-74 he was settled at Hobart for a period and then returned to America.

Rev Raymond Zorn, who trained at Westminster Seminary in Philadelphia, was appointed to the Theology chair in 1976. A man of ability he has been a steadying influence on the College. A disappointment was Dr Van der Laan, who served from 1975-78 as Professor of Philosophy and Christian

Education. He was a follower of the philosophy developed by Herman Dooyeweerd (1894-1977), which aimed to be specifically Reformed but got away from the simplicity which is in Christ to become a kind of new Gnosticism. Van der Laan made known his unhappiness with the RCA, and his rejection of the binding character of the Confessions, and soon returned to the Netherlands. Two local ministers were appointed in 1981: Henk De Waard to succeed Barkley in History, and Keith Warren to the Chair of Practical Theology. Along with Voorwinde and Zorn, plus Alastair McEwen, an RP minister and son of Rev W.R.McEwen, as Professor of Old Testament, a full theological faculty was operating in 1988. An additional appointment to a Chair of Education has recently been made with a view to assisting the Christian school movement.

Involvement of the PCEA in the RTC

On April 14, 1973, the PCEA Synod agreed in principle to effect membership of the Association for a Christian University (which runs the RTC), and subject to this and to a Professor from the PCEA being appointed to the faculty, to recognise the RTC for student training. Some disquiet was evident at the next PCEA Synod (April 1974) on account of Sierd Woudstra's views (there were then 3 PCEA students at the RTC) but the action of the Synod Committee in effecting membership of the Association was endorsed and two College Visitors appointed. Allan Harman was appointed Professor in May 1974 and took up his appointment later that year. At the next PCEA Synod (March 1975) concern was expressed over the appointment of Dr Van der Laan, in which the PCEA had no participation. Internal discipline problems, as well as theological difficulties, were evident in the RTC later in 1975, and on October 3, 1975, the PCEA Presbytery resolved to withdraw the PCEA students 'until such time as this Presbytery considers that their spiritual welfare is in no way jeopardized.' Following a report by the College Visitors (S.N.Ramsay and E.R.Lee), the Presbytery decided to abide by its earlier decision. A special Synod meeting was held in Melbourne on November 12, 1975. It expressed regret at Presbytery's action without prior attempts at an official level to rectify problems, but supported the temporary withdrawal. Student Gadsby completed his course with distinction in 1976. Students Cromarty and Varnes did not return. The May 1976 PCEA Synod resolved to withdraw from membership of the Association. In January 1978, Harman took up the post of Visiting Professor at the Theological Hall of the PCV.

It is unfortunate that the involvement of the PCEA corresponded with a period of difficulty in the RTC, while it is also clear that a step of this kind needs very general support in the church at large if a stable situation is to be developed. In May 1979 the PCEA withdrew its recognition of the RTC for student training but allowed student Bloomfield to complete the course he had begun in 1978. The current situation is that the RTC is not officially recognised but the possibility of training at the RTC is not ruled out. The 1988 Synod considered by a significant majority that an alternative to Scotland should be available and recognised. For various reasons it was thought that the Theological Hall of the PCV would be acceptable and this became the finding by a large majority. The PCV courses are subject to external examination by an independent body, so ensuring impartial assessment. The ecomics of overseas training loomed large. However, taking all things into consideration, including the increased strength of PCEA work in Melbourne, the decision was not difficult.

Christian Schools

The RCA brought the concept of parent-controlled Christian Schools from the Netherlands. Kuyper had championed such and in 1920 they received equitable funding from the Government. The desire for such schools in the alien Australian context was strong, but the fundamental principle that all of life is religious and that life could not be neatly divided into sacred and secular was the key. It was not until 1962 that the dream was realised with the commencement of the first school. There are now about 50 such schools enrolling over 8,000 pupils. This has been the result of considerable sacrifice, principally by members of the RCA in the early days. The availability of state aid since the 1960s, though not on a fully equitable basis, has been of great importance. The schools operate through a Board elected by and answerable to the parents and members of a School Association. The Constitution of the school may vary. It may adhere to the Reformed Confessions or adopt an Educational Creed - the latter method being that preferred by those more influenced by Herman Dooyeveerd's philosophy. In either case, the membership is not limited to members of the RCA but embraces others who can subscribe the basis. Much therefore depends on the faithfulness with which the basis is adhered to. A number of schools have lost something of their distinctive character through a weak basis or else a too ready admission of members who lack the depth of Reformed conviction which is necessary to ensure the proper working of the school and its influence for Christ in the years ahead.

The earlier position of Australian Christians had been to have a state-provided education that was not opposed to Christian values, and to supply religious instruction by outside instructors. As well, the major denominations ran schools themselves, the cost in the Protestant ones being rather much for Christian parents on ordinary incomes unless the child could obtain one of the scholarships available at secondary level. Since the advent of parent-controlled Christian schools in which Christian teaching permeates the curriculum, there have also been Christian schools of a somewhat different type begun in many places. While some Reformed people are inclined to over-emphasise the principle of parent control as appropriate to this sphere of life and thus to regard 'church schools' as anathema, the truth must surely be that the method of control is not the primary concern, but the standards maintained and the content of the curriculum. The writer's own preference, having seen something of the operation of several Christian schools, is a school which is related definitely to the church so as to give stability of doctrinal position, but which is involved closely with the parents but circumstances must dictate what is best. Either way, it appears to this writer that the school can be open to Christians of a variety of backgrounds if the safeguards to maintain a particular position are in place and applied.

Summary re RCA

It is quite evident that the RCA has made a significant contribution to Australian Christian life, and that her distinct position as a separate denomination has been worthwhile. What the future will bring or requires is another question which will require great wisdom to answer aright. The RCA has stood for confessional integrity, emphasis on the calling of the Christian to serve Christ in this world, and the emphasis on learning 'Christianly.' The early use of English is also noteworthy. A deliberate policy, it was helped by the relatively young age of the migrants and their ready adaptation to a new society.

Free Reformed Churches of Australia 1951

Among the migrants in the 1950s were some from the 'liberated' churches in the Netherlands. In general they came together in groups from their home localities (the common Dutch practice) and they concentrated in Western Australia and northern Tasmania. A church was instituted at Armadale on the southern outskirts of Perth on June 24, 1951, a second at Albany, WA, in December 1952 and a third in Launceston on February 15, 1953. Apart from the latter place, there were not significant numbers of RCN (synodical) people in these locations.

As would be expected from the background in the Netherlands, these migrants kept themselves rather much to themselves, and they instituted what they called the Free Reformed Churches. By the close of 1975 they had 651 communicant members and 978 baptized members not yet professing. For a time there were groups in Melbourne and Wollongong, but these were discontinued in order that members might consolidate at the centres already mentioned. School Associations were formed and schools at primary and high school level operate at each centre and also at Kelmscott near Armadale, where a fourth congregation was instituted on January 1, 1981. Growth is almost entirely biological, and two further congregations near Kelmscott have been formed (1985 and 1987), while the congregation at Launceston was divided in 1989. There are now about 1,200 communicant members and 1,300 baptized members in the seven congregations.

The impact of this orthodox and disciplined community has not been as great as might have been expected because of a rather high doctrine of the church which has kept them somewhat aloof and self-contained. The writer has met numbers of very fine people among them. As a result of the writer's friendship with some of the Launceston people when ministering in Tasmania, the PCEA Synod made official contact in 1978, and discussions and contacts are continuing. The PCEA would like to see both the RCA and the FRCA come closer, but it is easier to make a break than to heal it.

Students are trained for the ministry at the Seminary of the Canadian Reformed Churches, the sister-church formed in 1950.

FRCA MINISTERS AT A MEETING IN 1988
From left: W.Hulzinga (Armadale), J.Koelewljn (Port Moresby), K.Jonker (Launceston), C.Bouwman (Byford), A.Veldman (Albany), G.van Rongen (ret'd).

Discussions on some RCA/PCEA differences

The RCA explored differences with the PCEA. Arthur Allen was again to the fore as he was Convener of the Church Principles Committee until his early death in 1958. In a paper read at a meeting with the RCA c 1957, Allen argued against requiring more as terms of communion than a credible profession of faith in Christ. He considered that 'to set up rules and regulations, forbidding certain interests, activities and associations - upon which there are differences of opinion among brethren equally zealous for the faith - and making them tests for church membership is an invasion of Christian liberty.'[12] Applying this to oath-bound societies of the Masonic type, he held that to require a person to renounce all oath-bound societies for a profession of faith to be regarded as credible, was without Scriptural authority. He placed strong emphasis on the effectual teaching of the Holy Spirit through the ministry of the word of God. 'Must the sinner who beats upon his breast and cries, "God be merciful to me a sinner" wait until he has been convinced of the evil of oath-bound societies before he can be a member of the Body of Christ?' he writes, and reminds his hearers that the ministry is given for the very purpose of edifying and perfecting the saints (Ephesians 4:12-13). It might be worth noting that no PCEA minister in 1957 was in favour of Freemasonry, but Allen argues the matter on principle.

The further question of 'open' communion, that is, the practice of allowing to the Lord's Table persons who are members in good standing of other churches, was also addressed. The churches of continental origin commonly hold to closed communion ie. their own members only. Allen argued that both were agreed that the scandalous were to be excluded (Larger Catechism †173; Heidelberg Catechism 82), while he held that the Lord's Table was not open to all in the PCEA but to all, however weak in the faith, who rest in Christ as Saviour and Lord. Fellowship with God, though an individual experience, cannot be separated from fellowship with other believers (I John 1:7). So the sacrament cannot take precedence over the evidence of grace, the love of the brethren, which is the evidence of eternal life. It cannot be right, claimed Allen, that we may walk together in spiritual fellowship until we come to the communion table. If our fellowship is broken at this point, our love postponed, it is because we have added to what the Scriptures lay down. So he concludes: 'If our spiritual experience is sealed by the Word and Spirit and evidenced by our fellowship one with another, there should be no place for a closed communion.' Thus, the practice of the PCEA is not because of a casual attitude to truth but is an acknowledgement of the unity of faith among God's people, and reckons seriously with the problems of several denominations side by side, a situation not faced in such a marked

12. page 38 of the typed submission.

384

way in earlier times. As Allen said to his RCA audience: 'When the sacrament is dispensed in my congregation, I invite you with all the sincerity of my heart, as brethren in Christ, to partake of the sacrament with us. While I differ from you on matters of worship and observance of days, I do not for one moment question your faith in the sufficiency of our Lord's sacrificial death, or your adoption into the family of God.' It must have been stimulating listening to him.

PCEA Ecumenical involvements

The PCEA had been a member of the Pan Presbyterian Alliance in the 1880s, but the troubles of those days resulted in membership lapsing. There was a Sydney Ministers' Union for Protestant ministers from 1886, and Rev George Sutherland of the PCEA was a member.[13] The PCEA was invited to join the New South Wales Council of Churches which was formed by Protestant churches in 1925 but declined.[14] In 1931, a Methodist layman built and equipped a radio station for the Protestant churches (2 CH). After Rev Neil MacLeod came to St George's in 1936, there were contacts with the Council, and the Assembly gave the Synod permission to affiliate with it if desired. This affiliation continued until new regulations on membership were adopted in 1964 which gave the PCEA the right to send an observer but not hold membership. The period of the PCEA affiliation was not without its ups and downs. The theological liberalism was of concern, but the opportunity of joint statements on matters of social concern, such as gambling and state aid to Roman Catholic schools, was sufficient to keep the Synod in membership.

There is always a tension between a truly catholic view of the church and the loyalty one owes to the distinctive position one holds to be Scriptural. The PCEA in general has not been myopic about other churches but has sought to be careful at the same time. Standing broad-based on the full inheritance of the reformation, the PCEA needs to be a good steward by showing its breadth and strength to others from who also the PCEA can learn. To share in the gifts and graces of other believers, and to perform such public and private duties as are for mutual good, is a Scriptural obligation (compare Westminster Confession XXVI). This has been expressed at a Synod or Assembly level by receiving visitors from churches with whom no possibility of union exists. Examples include the visit of Rev A.P.Cameron (son of a Free Church man), when Moderator of the PCNSW in 1929; the visit and address by Rev W.H.Lock, President of the Methodist Conference, in 1941; and Marcus Loane's similar visit in 1944. The PCEA does not seem

---

13. F.Engel, **Australian Christians in Conflict and Unity** (Melbourne 1984) p.110.
14. D.E.Hansen, 'The Origin and Early Years of the NSW Council of Churches' in JRH, June 1981, p.455. This article. covers the period 1925-39. See also, **Our Banner** (PCEA), April 1939, p.1209.

to have reciprocated such visits, and perhaps that is understandable given the small size of the church. The PCEA Moderator in 1982 (Rev Rowland Ward) appears to have been the first from the PCEA to have addressed the General Assembly of Australia of the Presbyterian Church..

Reformed Ecumenical Synod

On the level of ecumenism among those of Reformed conviction, it was natural that the RCA and the PCE both being members of the Reformed Ecumenical Synod (inaugurated 1946) would co-operate together. Apart from the involvement in the beginnings of the RCA, there were discussions and contacts which led to the formation of the *Australian Council of Reformed Churches* at Geelong on April 27, 1964, the churches represented being the RCA, PCEA and the Australian Presbytery of the RPCI. The idea was to develop fellowship and co-operation between the churches. This depends greatly upon the individuals involved, as well as the opportunities available. The RPC was closely involved in the RTC, and the PCEA delegates (E.R.Lee and A.M.Harman) were positive. However, both of them were soon overseas. The RCA and PCEA were joint hosts of the RES meeting in Sydney in 1972, but problems in the RTC 1974/78 (see pages 379/380) so soon after PCEA involvement set back relations. The Council lapsed around 1976.

The PCEA has continued to exchange greetings with the RCA Synod, and in 1985 sought clarification of the relationship, at the same time urging in Christian love, that the RCA try again to reach a better understanding with the FRCA. The PCEA withdrew from the RES in 1981, since the RES appeared unwilling to maintain its own constitution. In particular, the membership of the RCN (synodical) was a problem given that it had joined the WCC against the advice of the RES, and had developed alarming errors in doctrine and practice, including toleration of homosexuality in the church. The RCA continues for the present in the RES, and has downgraded its relationship with the RCN. The situation is to be reviewed at the RCA Synod in 1991.

International Conference of Reformed Churches

The PCEA Synod of 1984 resolved to apply for membership of the ICRC, having been nominated by one of the organising churches - the Free Church of Scotland. The other force behind this move was the Reformed Churches in the Netherlands (liberated). The Free Church had withdrawn from the RES several months after the PCEA, while the RCN had not been a member of the RES. This initiative in Reformed ecumenism among those who profess and practice the faith is an important one. Rev Peter Gadsby represented the PCEA at the inaugural meeting in Edinburgh in September 1985. He was also the delegate to the second meeting to be hosted by the Canadian Reformed Churches in June 1989. The FRCA also became members. The FRCA had formally recognised the FCS but not the PCEA, which seems odd, but reflects the difficulties present in inter-church relations. Time will tell how the ICRC progresses, but it holds much promise.

The PCEA and FRCA have intensified discussions, and a visit by Messrs Ward and Gadsby to Perth late in 1988 was found very profitable, particularly the opportunity of addressing a well-attended public meeting.

28: REACTIONARY REFORMATION - TASMANIA 1961-88

The rationalistic criticism of the Bible and the inroads of modernistic theology contributed to the fragmentation of church life and a depreciation of the importance of the church as a visible body holding fast and holding forth the word of life. The Bible College movement had become an established part of the Australian scene, and provided an alternative to denominational institutions. Conventions and gospel campaigns which by-passed denominational structures were common, but doctrinal understanding was very limited. Evangelicals stressed the reliability of Scripture, the Deity of Christ, his substitionary atonement, bodily resurrection and return in glory, as well as the necessity of conversion, but there was not much depth. Indeed, higher education was sometimes feared because of the thought of its corrupting influence, given the domination of places of learning by those not committed to the historic Christian faith.

The organisation of the World Council of Churches in 1948 was also of concern to evangelicals, and many associated this development with the forming of a world church and the approach of the final conflict. Dancing on church property became evident in some mainstream circles, and the lack of emphasis on repentance and conversion alarmed many. The mass evangelistic crusades associated with Dr Billy Graham in the late 1950s and later had beneficial impact in bringing many to commitment to Christ who had a background in Christian teaching, and other people without any such background were also converted. Yet the tremendous effort expended in these campaigns, and the large number which fell away from their 'decision for Christ', raised questions. In addition, these campaigns operated on the basis of co-operation among the major denominations, and not infrequently included men on the organising committees who did not share Graham's theology and were not evangelicals in any true sense. Further, among those of Reformed convictions as well as some in the mainstream, the methods were objectionable either because of Arminian, man-centred theology or because of the emotional pressure of the well-managed meetings.

Rediscovery of Reformed teaching in Tasmania 1958

In Tasmania, a number of people, chiefly those who moved in Baptist and Brethren circles and had been associated with Ambassadors for Christ, were not only concerned about modernism in the study courses for students for the ministry and in the churches, but were also affected from 1958 by contact with literature which reasserted the faith of the Protestant Reformation. Such literature challenged the superficial and man-centred nature of much Christian witness and practice, and provided the key to understanding the plight of the churches. Much of the literature in question was put out from 1957 by the Banner of Truth Trust, but there were other publishers as well. B.B.Warfield's *Plan of Salvation* was early read by Ian Morgan, a bank officer in Launceston. He became the theological brains of the movement that developed into what is now known as the Evangelical Presbyterian Church. This book stimulated Morgan's interest in systems of theology. Other books included Watson's *Body of Divinity*, an old exposition of the Shorter Catechism, Martin Luther's *Bondage of the Will*, and also the *Baptist Confession of Faith 1689*, which was reprinted in the UK in 1959, and imported in quantity by Rev K.Tuck, a Baptist minister.[1]

Morgan circulated doctrinal papers called 'sputniks' (after the Russian satellite), and it was not long before quite a number of people adhered to the doctrines of grace (that is, to the five points of Calvinism - see pages 364/365). There was a group in Hobart called the 'People's Fellowship, pastored by Hugh McNeilly, son of a Brethren evangelist; there was Charles Rodman, home missionary of the Taroona Baptist Church (10 kms south of Hobart); there was a group associated with Morgan and Robert Gibb at Launceston which operated 'The Evangelical Society' to spread literature; there was Eric Turnbull, home missionary at Penguin Baptist Church on the north-west coast; and there was a group of former Methodists and Presbyterians in the rural locality of Winnaleah in the north east. There were some in other places. McNeilly became pastor at Winnaleah in 1959, and it appears that he there became convinced of the Reformed doctrines through the influence of Claude Lefevre. J.Laurie Lincolne, Principal of the World Evangelisation Crusade (WEC) Training College outside Launceston also had links with the movement.

1. Information re Tuck from E.S.Turnbull, April 20, 1989; see also the report in Free Grace Record (UK), April/June 1959, pp.181,182, which includes Tasmanian detail. Morgan and Gibb were removed as deacons of Elphin Road Baptist in May 1958.

Baptist Union reaction 1959-60

The Baptist Union held a special Assembly on November 28, 1959 to discuss the Calvinistic teaching. Considering that Australian Baptist work had originated from Calvinistic English Baptists, the level of understanding of this Assembly was poor. Hyper-calvinism and Calvinism pure and unmixed were confused, and it was asserted that Calvinism was completely out of harmony in many ways with such Baptist giants as William Carey and Andrew Fuller.[2] Several resolutions were passed which showed that the Assembly was more interested in evangelism than clear doctrine, despite the fact that Biblically one cannot evangelise except by teaching (Matthew 28:19-20). A special sub-committee was set up to further clarify the issues, Rev Ken Tuck (Elphin Road Baptist), Rev Alex White (Latrobe Baptist) and Eric Turnbull being the pro-Calvinistic members.

Before the Baptist Union held another special Assembly on March 26, 1960, there were a number of developments. A *Tasmanian Reformation Fellowship* was formed on February 6, 1960, which included most of the pro-Calvinist people mentioned. (It was renamed the *Baptist Reformation Alliance* on February 15, with the 1689 Baptist Confession as its basis.) An Easter Rally was planned with a view to clarifying the Reformed position, and Rev Edwin Lee of the PCEA Melbourne was to be the main speaker. Ian Morgan had met Lee after he had moved from Tasmania to Melbourne in 1959, and was worshipping in Lee's church.

Four days after the Fellowship (later Alliance) was formed, representatives of the Baptist Union met with Turnbull, and he was told that preaching of the Reformed doctrines must cease. As Turnbull could not in conscience comply with this direction, he wrote his resignation on Sunday February 21, 1960. The portion of the Penguin congregation which adhered to him continued meeting at a hall in Penguin under the name 'Baptist Reformed Church.' They advertised themselves to be what they were - Calvinistic and Missionary.

When the Baptist Union Assembly met again on on March 26, 1960, Messrs Tuck and White submitted a a two page statement of their position in which they affirmed their adherence to Calvinistic teaching in careful terms, rejected certain erroneous constructions put upon that teaching, and stated they were 'prepared to modify our policy' for the sake of unity in the Baptist Union. They discontinued their involvement with the Baptist Reformation Alliance. The Assembly, on its part, came up with a statement that in general took Arminian ground. As a consequence, David Nibbs, a student for the ministry,

---

2. A report of the Assembly is in the Baptist magazine **Advance**, December 1959, p.12. Such great Baptists as Carey, Fuller and Spurgeon were strict Calvinists.

390

withdrew his resignation, and the movement of Rodman, McNeilly and Turnbull continued without the assistance of Tuck and White. This compromise was seen as a betrayal, and it strengthened the view that one must be black and white on every issue, and militantly so, if one was to be regarded as truly faithful to the Reformed position.[3]

The situation did not reflect very well on the Baptist Union, while the zeal and relative immaturity of the Calvinistic brethren was likely to get them into hot water. There was not much patience with any who were slow to agree. In June 1960, Lincolne and about 30 of the 50 students left the WEC College because of their sympathy with the Reformed doctrines. The *Bible College of Tasmania* was set up on a farming property near Latrobe, which was given the name 'Geneva'.

The Presbyterian factor 1960-61

Lee of the PCEA spoke at the Reformation Rally at Ulverstone over Easter 1960. and from then on the influence of the Presbyterian concept of the church was felt. The Reformed Churches of Australia took an interest. Morgan wrote an open letter dated July 19, 1960, cautioning against the idea of a Reformed Baptist Church. He pled for the maintenance of the wider vision of reformation and revival on the basis of the Westminster Confession. He pointed out

All lasting and well founded Reformations and Revivals have been led by men of learning. It is here that great advantage will accrue to our movement by not turning it into a sectarian movement. The Reformed movement in Tasmania has reached such proportions that it is being closely watched by other Reformed Churches, who are ready to assist in any way possible.... However, it needs to be understood that the established Reformed Churches are not greatly interested in ministering within sectarian movements, even though they may be Calvinistic. Sooner or later they must come into conflict with that precept which has been placed in the forefront of all others, so making it a sect.[4]

Later on this wise counsel was abandoned, even by Morgan himself, as the tendency to react against anything which looked like the mysticism or ambiguity of their former theology gathered strength. But for the present there were good contacts with both the RCA and the PCEA. There was a congregation of the FRCA in Launceston but it does not appear that there

3. For Assembly report see **Advance**, April 1960, p.12. The Assembly decision received trenchant criticism in The Evangelical Society paper 'The Articles of the Tasmanian Baptist Remonstrants 1960' (10pp), much of it fully deserved.
4. Open letter, A.Ian Morgan, July 19, 1960, p.4. The present writer has these letters on file together with letters from Morgan to R.L.Gibb from 1960-65, as well as other documents and papers given him by R.L.Gibb in 1977, and others collected by himself. In R.S.Ward, **Presbyterianism in Tasmania 1821-1977**(Ulverstone 1977) pp.36-78 a fuller account of some aspects is provided.

was other than minimal contact with it at this stage. Rev John Heenan, the Home Mission minister of the RCA, visited Tasmania in November 1960. He was keen to see integration with an existing church. On the other hand, Lee of the PCEA was more cautious. Not only was the PCEA only represented on the mainland, there were only seven PCEA ministers in the whole of New South Wales and Victoria. Moreover, new wine cannot well be put into old wineskins, and Lee could see that the zeal and enthusiasm of the Tasmanians could be a disturbing factor if they became part of the PCEA at once.

The Tasmanians themselves seem to have been virtually unanimous in holding that God had raised up the work and that it should be distinct but in friendly association with other Reformed Churches. There was concern that neither the RCA or PCEA was militant enough, and Morgan, in particular, promulgated the view that the established reformed churches were adhering to 'moderate Calvinism'.[5] There was some truth in such charges. The PCEA was weak in numbers, there was a fair amount of traditionalism about it, and the Reformed faith was just now undergoing a reviving. Morgan[6] considered Arminians should be rejected after a first and second admonition. Aside from anything else, he showed a less than Calvinistic regard for the meaning of Titus 3:10 (see Calvin on this passage), while most of the brethren seemed to have forgotten they were true believers while holding Arminian views before they became true believers holding Calvinistic views. Certainly, Arminianism is not to be accepted in the teaching ministry, but it does not follow that Arminian members are to be rejected if they will sit under a true ministry. Nor does it follow that unless a man preaches the 'five points' every sermon he is not a Calvinist. Indeed, the five points are not the whole of the Reformed understanding anyway.

At a Convention in Winnaleah at Easter 1961, the group under Lincolne at Latrobe separated from the others. The temper of most was rather strong. Once they had accepted Presbyterian church government and rejected the

---

5. This is a constant theme in the sources - eg. A.Ian Morgan, Open Letter, November 6, 1960, with its severe criticism of Rev W.R.McEwen for his association with Arminians in the Bible Union. Another example is in the circular letter from the Penguin Church by E.S.Turnbull dated May 25, 1960: 'I want to sound a strong and urgent note of warning. BEWARE of so called quiet, mature, moderate policy in the preaching of Calvinism.' It may be that someone thought union with an existing church was in order, but I have not found such evidence. There was the thought in the mind of some that eventual affiliation might come, but that was not in the forefront. The movement was receiving wide support and the brethren were optimistic that the Lord would use them for a thorough Reformation. There is no foundation for the claim made in a recent paper 'Information on the Evangelical Presbyterian Church of Australia' by Pastor C.Coleborn (Brisbane, February 1988, 14pp) that the Tasmanian brethren 'sought union' with the PCEA but that 'that denomination drew back from receiving those who wished to join'.
6. Letter to R.L.Gibb, February 9, 1961.

'faith' principle in the support of the ministry, those who did not agree were branded as non-Calvinistic. So the Latrobe work eventually became Calvinistic Baptist and affiliated with an English group which tended to hyper-Calvinism. After consideration, integration with the RCA was rejected. There were two grounds: (1) cultural and (2) doctrinal. The cultural factors included such matters as alcohol and tobacco use, and some aspects of life-style. The doctrinal issue was the 'regulative principle'. True to their views in 1951, the Dutch brethren considered instrumental music and uninspired compositions in worship were things indifferent. In fact, both Scripture and the Reformed Confessions are against this interpretation (cf. Articles 7 & 25 of the *Belgic Confession*),[7] as is the history of the Reformed Church in the Netherlands (see page 366), but it is hard to shake off what one has become accustomed to. Of course there are things indifferent in the Scriptures, but it is all too easy to declare indifferent or an open question what God has revealed, as had happened in the Australian unions in the previous century.

There had been some thought of leaving the worship question open to be decided on after a church was instituted,[8] but it was soon seen that consistency required this to be decided first. Lee of the PCEA had consulted with the PCEA Procurator, F. Maxwell Bradshaw, and a constitution was drawn up by him in harmony with the PCEA constitution. This harmony would enable several PCEA ministers to form themselves into a special Presbytery to ordain ministers of the church to be formed in Tasmania without acting inconsistently with their own doctrinal commitment. The newly ordained men could then constitute their own Presbytery in terms of the constitution. It was decided to proceed in this way and a meeting on August 12, 1961 finalized arrangements and issued a Letter of Intention to other Reformed Churches.

A Church Instituted - September 1961

The ground for the ordination of Messrs Rodman, McNeilly and Turnbull rested on a direct request from their congregations (Launceston, Winnaleah and Penguin) per medium of a form of call subscribed by the members under scrutiny of those acting as elders. The institution in this manner conferred legitimacy as far as Presbyterian practice was concerned. The ordinations

---

7. Note also the correct text of WCF XX:2 -' 'God alone is Lord of the conscience, and hath left it free from the doctrines and commandments of men which are in any thing contrary to his word, or beside it, if (not 'in') matters of faith and worship.' So in matters of faith or worship it is not sufficient to say that Scripture does not forbid such and such a belief or practice, but we are to remain content with Scripture alone. The **Belgic Confession** is to the same effect.

8. Criticism of this proposal was made by Morgan in his Open Letter, August 5, 1961.

took place at a meeting on Thursday evening September 28, 1961 in Chalmers' Hall, Frederick Street, Launceston, before a congregation of about 200 persons. The members of the special Presbytery were Revs E.R. Lee, I.L.Graham and J.A.Harman. The following evening the newly ordained ministers met and constituted themselves a Presbytery, adopting the following constitution:

1. The name of the Church shall be, 'The Reformed Evangelical Church'.

2. The Standards and Formularies of the Church shall be, the Westminster Confession of Faith, the Larger and Shorter Catechism, the Form of Presbyterial Church Government, and the Directory for Public Worship as originally accepted by the Church of Scotland.

3. Subject to these articles the constitution and law of the Church shall be the constitution and law of the Church of Scotland in the year 1843 so far as applicable, and the legislative, administrative and judicial power of the courts of the Church shall be those existing in the Church of Scotland in that year.

4. This constitution shall operate from such day as at least three ministers with lawful Presbyterial ordination constitute themselves a Presbytery in terms of this constitution.

5. Until such time as a Synod shall be constituted the Presbytery shall be the supreme court of the Church.

6. The Presbytery at such time as it thinks fit may constitute itself a Synod which shall then be the supreme court of the Church. Any such Synod so constituted may take steps for the convening of a General Assembly to be the supreme court of the Church.

7. The formula shall be, [the same as the PCEA formula on page 361 except for the name of the Church.]

8. The name of the Church may be changed from time to time by act of the Supreme Court.

9. That in owning the purity of worship presently authorised and practised in this Church a minister or elder is deemed to disapprove the use in public worship of God of instrumental music and materials of praise other than the Book of Psalms.

The intention was to establish the REC on the same principles as the PCEA. Later a dispute arose in which it was alleged that the REC was committed to the position of the Church of Scotland in 1843 whereas the PCEA was committed to the position of the Free Church of Scotland which withdrew from the Church of Scotland as established by law in 1843. This is a complete misapprehension. Those who formed the Free Church did so in order to preserve the principles of the Church of Scotland. They regarded themselves, and rightly so, as the true inheritors of the Church of Scotland constitution, and the body they left was very generally described as the Established Church rather than the Church of Scotland. Moreover, the formula refers to the principles in the Disruption documents, while the special Presbytery of PCEA ministers could never have ordained the ministers if they were setting them apart to other than the propagation of the same principles to which they were committed themselves.

Messrs E.S.Turnbull, H.McNeilly, E.R.Lee and C.L.Rodman at the time
of constituting the Reformed Evangelical Church, September 1961.

Crossroads and transition 1962-65

The newly constituted church was concerned for ministerial training. Despite the strenuous opposition of Morgan,[9] it was decided to co-operate with the PCEA in theological training, and the *John Knox Theological College* was established in Melbourne with Rev E.R.Lee, MA and Rev Allan Harman, MA, BD, MTh , along with Rev W.R.McEwen, BA, as the lecturers. Regular instruction began on April 29, 1963, and because of Morgan's attitude, the Tasmanian students (Cameron-Smith, Lyons and Burley) were asked not to enter into discussion with him on College issues. Alan Tripovich was the other student who attended and he was a member of the PCEA. However, this promising start was soon upset by the Tasmanian students, particularly Burley but also Cameron-Smith, who objected to the presentation of the

9. Note the following in letter, Morgan to Charles Rodman, November 15, 1962: 'I appeal to you not to compromise with the moderate Calvinism of Free Church. If you will tolerate their moderation, you must also be counted to embrace it, for tolerance embraces that to which tolerance is given, [a recurring phrase since 1958 - RSW] when you are prepared to make a compact with it....I must inform you, that if the REC is going to compromise with Free Church in her present condition, then you may regard as certain, my resignation as a student.' Morgan worshipped in Lee's congregation. Morgan accepted the relationship in the College in the end, because he could 'see no other way at the moment...What can I do other than this - only create a schism in the Church - I have no such warrant - read Calvin on schism.' - Morgan to Gibb, 12/2/1963.

gospel offer to all men as expounded in a booklet by Ned Stonehouse and John Murray, of the Orthodox Presbyterian Church in America. The REC dealt with the complaints at its meeting on August 12, 1963 and subsequently. The dispute related to the preaching of the gospel to those who do not end up believing. Can it be said that God has a love to all men (of course Murray and Stonehouse answered affirmatively), and, if so, how does one relate this to the fact that God does not decree to give saving faith to all who hear the gospel? Can one speak of a well-meant gospel offer, and how is one to regard the will of God which is one but appears manifold to men? The issues here can become quite complex, and perhaps some matters are best accepted without probing too deeply. Some of the expressions in the Murray/Stonehouse booklet do not appear to the present writer to be the most suitable, but their position was well within the beaten path of balanced Reformed teaching. However, given the background of the REC folk, they found it hard to allow mystery, hard to accept what seemed to be an ambiguous compromise of militant Calvinism.

Morgan thought he had found the underlying principle of 'moderate Calvinism'[10] while the Presbytery called a public meeting for February 15, 1964, which effectively passed the decision to the people. Turnbull, who had sided with the Murray/Stonehouse presentation came in for strong criticism of his position, while McNeilly came under pressure from his congregation because he would not acquiesce in the instant dismissal of Turnbull. Procedure dragged, Winnaleah sacked their minister, but the Presbytery at a visitation in June 1964 resolved that he return to his pulpit. The majority would not accept his ministry since they considered there was a complete breakdown in Presbyterian church government. The upshot was that Turnbull and Penguin applied to join the PCEA in June 1964 and were granted release by the REC in September 1965. Winnaleah was divided and the process of discipline was not carried through against the majority

10. Morgan's 'Exposure' of the Murray/Stonehouse booklet 'as "Modern" or Moderate Calvinism..A modification of the doctrine of decrees by way of the doctrine of Amyraldianism' was issued in August 1983. In simple terms, Amyraldianism (following Moses Amyraut, 1596-1664) teaches that God desired to save all mankind, gave his Son to die equally for all men so that a universal offer could be made on this basis. Since man's sin made him morally incapable of faith, God himself worked faith in the hearts of those he had chosen to redeem. It was an attempt, therefore, to combine universal redemption with particular election, and had torn the heart out of the French Reformed Church. Morgan wrongly interpreted Murray/Stonehouse in this way since, although Murray/Stonehouse did not believe in universal redemption, Morgan considered their emphasis on a universal love of God was equivalent, and he passed over their careful distinctions. In a letter to Gibb, August 28, 1963, Morgan stated: 'The real solution came when I purchased an old set of Systematic Theology in Keswick by Ralph Wardlaw - 3 large volumes for 10 shillings. I bought them thinking them to be orthodox theology, but when I got them home I found them to contain the very thing I was wrestling against.' Wardlaw (1779-1853) was a Scottish Congregationalist, and an Amyraldian.

who continued to meet as an unattached congregation until they approached the PCEA in 1971. McNeilly eventually left the ministry and returned to his trade of carpetlayer. He was remembered as a most arresting preacher. Cameron-Smith resumed ministry at Hobart, was ordained and obtained his BA degree. Lyons was ordained with a limitation to Taranna, while Burley went to Rockhampton where a group who had come to the Reformed doctrines originated about 1961. A preaching station was also organised at Brisbane.

Going it alone

In 1966 the REC changed its name to the *Evangelical Presbyterian Church*. It is perhaps surprising after the upheaval referred to, that there were quite good relations between the PCEA Penguin and the EPC.[11] Various EPC members came to the north-west coast and worshipped with the PCEA. During the vacancy 1967-69, EPC office-bearers assisted with supply. In some quarters there was the expectation that the congregation would return to the EPC. However, in September 1969, shortly after Rev Angus Beaton of the PCEA arrived to supply, the EPC Presbytery visited their members and at length resolved that it had been wrong to grant release in 1965, and so on April 4, 1970 resolved to work separately from the PCEA, and established a preaching station at nearby Burnie.

Doctrinal issue

So far as the doctrinal question was concerned, several publications were issued by the EPC. There was an elaborate 'Vindication' of 50 pages issued on February 13, 1965. Written by Morgan, this sought to argue that the Confession of Faith could not resolve the issue since it had been drawn in such a way as to allow similar views expressed by some, such as Calumy, in the Westminster Assembly. If it was replied that the Confession in the Church of Scotland was accepted in 1647 as being in no way contrary to the previously held doctrine in the Church of Scotland, the EPC response was that before 1647, the Church of Scotland did not hold to any limitation on the extent and intent of the atonement purchased by Christ. Hence, the Acts of the Church of Scotland condemning the 'Marrow' (see page 21) were the first such limitation. The EPC therefore relied on them, and also rejected the Murray/Stonehouse teaching on the ground that its alleged ambiguities and contradictions are inconsistent with the principle that each part of Scripture, seeing God is its author, must be interpreted harmoniously.

11. Note the following: 'Now that your release has been formally granted from the Church I wish to inform you that it is my desire that our past fellowship be restored. This will mean that a grave will need to be dug to bury the past, namely, those things which we have both seen and been disturbed about, and may this grave be covered with love.' -Letter, C.L.Rodman to E.S.Turnbull, September 16, 1965.

The response to this line of reasoning is to reject the claim that the Confession does not condemn Amyraldian views,[12] to reject the allegations against the teaching of the Scottish Church prior to 1647,and to regard the Acts of Assembly in condemning the teaching of the Marrowmen as not relevant since a Declaratory Act declares existing law when some confusion has arisen, and is incompetent to effect the actual change the EPC claim, even if passed under the Barrier Act, which they were not, since the Church of Scotland lacked power to change the Confession of Faith. Consequently, the action of the EPC was constitutionally inept and unlawful, and Maxwell Bradshaw, the Procurator of both churches, so advised. So far as the force the Acts do have as long as they are unrepealed, this is exceedingly dubious because of the peculiàr circumstances under which they were passed. The fact that they were appealed to in the McLeod Campbell case does not prove a great deal (see page 21); twelve ministers (including Boston and the Erskine brothers) tendered a Protest to the Assembly of 1722, asserting it was lawful for them to continue to preach as before, and no action was taken against them. It is irrelevant that the Assembly refused to allow the Protest to be read or recorded, since the Assembly knew the contents, the refusal broke its own law, and Boston was not proceeded against in the future. It is not surprising that a later generation also saw the business had not been handled adequately, so that while not formally repealed, no one would suppose that the Acts had actual effect to cover the issue of the love of God in the free offer. Indeed, it is a libel on the Scottish Church to suppose it ever had any hesitation on that doctrine.

The PCEA Synod of 1971 issued a report on the dispute with the EPC, covering both the Penguin problem and the doctrinal issue, in a total of 28 pages. The EPC opposed the teaching that 'there is in God a benevolent lovingkindness toward the repentance and salvation of those who He has not decreed to save. This pleasure, will, desire, is expressed in the universal call to repentance.' This teaching was supported by Scripture and quotations from Reformed writers. The two chief objections of the EPC were examined, namely, that to teach that God desires the salvation of the non-elect implies a duplicity of wills in God, and to speak of his benevolent lovingkindness or mercy to those he has not purposed to save is unscriptural. The Report was adopted by the Synod as a reply to the issues raised by the EPC in a report re Penguin they had issued in April 1970.

The EPC issued a further paper of 47 pages about June 1972. Entitled, *Universalism and the Reformed Churches*, it went over the subject once more, and stated that the issues were similar to those in the CRCNA which led to the formation of the *Protestant Reformed Churches* in the USA by Herman

12. See the discussions in W.Cunningham, **Historical Theology** Vol.2, pp.323ff; B.B. Warfield, **The Westminster Assembly and its Work** (Oxford 1931) pp.138ff.

Hoeksema in 1926. The argument is developed along the lines that the PCEA position is a system of doctrine in its own right deriving from the principles of self-salvation (!), rather than being a Calvinist variant. The essay shows much human logic, considerable distortion of the exegesis of Scripture and the interpretation of church history, and the EPC position is seen as the key to recovery of the Reformed faith in the world: 'The root problem in the failure of the once reformed churches is not liberalism or Arminianism, but modified Calvinism' (p.2).

Whence and whither?

Having resolved to go it alone by adoption of distinctive views on the free offer and related questions, the EPC had to face the consequences. For a time considerable progress was made. Lyons retired in 1975 but Morgan was ordained to the ministry in view of his services, but held no regular charge. Mr Anthony Fisk, a man of Baptist background, came from South Africa in 1977, and was later ordained and inducted at Burnie. After several not very easy years, he was settled at Rockhampton where a good congregation gathers. Philip Burley went from Rockhampton to Winnaleah in 1979. A student, Chris Coleborn, went to Brisbane about 1975 when about 20 people were meeting. Coleborn was subsequently ordained and his congregation is currently (1989) the largest in the denomination, over 100 people attending. Preaching places in Queensland included Townsville (800 kms north of Rockhampton) and Chinchilla (320 kms west of Brisbane). Later Townsville ceased but a station currently exists even further north at Cairns. At its greatest strength before 1986, there were six active pastors (2 in Queensland and 4 in Tasmania) and a following of about 450 people in all. A Synod had been formed with two presbyteries, the aim being to try and overcome the tremendous barriers of distance.

Division in 1986

However, all was not at peace. The imbalanced approach was still evident and ready to flare up. In 1984, Charles Rodman (Launceston) preached on the subject 'Christ our example to all men' based on Galatians 4:4-5. His argument was that Christ in his human nature showed love to all, and so fulfilled the law of God in this as in other respects. This created strong objection from elders J.Steel, V.Connors and P.Morgan. The Confession notes that Christ acts in both natures, by each nature doing what is proper to itself (WCF VIII:7), but because of the unity of the person of Christ they could see that they were faced with the same difficulty as in the free offer controversy. If Christ the Son of God loved his neighbour, including those God had not purposed to save, the 'moderate Calvinist' was right. In the subsequent flurry of papers, some of which reached considerable length, the truth seems to the present writer to be divided somewhat between the two parties. Morgan, as usual, produced articles against Rodman's position, as did his son Peter. They wished to argue that Christ loved only his elect neighbour and had no love or compassion for the lost. It is surely only necessary to state this for its unscripturalness to be recognised. Rodman still professed to hold to the teaching on the free offer earlier adopted by the EPC, and he got into some difficulties in explaining his position consistently. Some of the arguments he employed imperilled the unity of the two natures in Christ, since Rodman sometimes attributed Christ's love of his neighbour to the human nature in a manner which suggested two persons in Christ rather than two natures in one person. One sees in the controversy the fruit of the false approach taken years before.

There was deep division among the ministers, elders and people. Considering that a state of schism already existed, and in the interest of peace and harmony, Raeburn Cameron-Smith(Hobart) Charles Rodman (Launceston) and the Hobart, Taranna and minority of the Launceston congregations left the Evangelical Presbyterian Church stating: 'We sincerely trust that by this action peace and harmony may be restored within the EPC. It is our hope that good relations and fellowship may be established between us and the members of the EPC.' The date was June 21, 1986. The action may appear to be a failure to maintain vows to uphold Presbyterian government, as was also alleged in the division of 1964. Against this not unreasonable assessment must bè placed the inadequate working of that government because of the polarisation and the small number of presbyters.

The present position

Cameron-Smith and Rodman, together with elders J.Coles and T. Kingston, had signed the document by which they withdrew from the EPC. At a meeting on July 12, 1986 the *Southern Presbyterian Church of Australia* was constituted. The Bible in the 'Received Text' was taken as the Supreme Standard, and the Westminster Confession of Faith was adhered to as the principal subordinate standard. There was no assertion of descent from the Scottish Church, but in general the position adopted is not in practice different. The 'Received Text' historically refers to a 1633 edition of the Greek New Testament published in Leiden. Its textual base is essentially that of Erasmus' edition based on a half-dozen manuscripts, the oldest of which dates from the 10th century, and in about 12 places its reading is not supported by any known Greek manuscript, Erasmus having supplied deficiences from other translations known to him. It is thus not the best form of Greek text which can be constructed from the manuscripts preserved in God's providence. One surmises the SPC saw its significance in the fact that it is the form of Greek text used by the King James and other principal translations of the New Testament prepared by Protestants prior to 1881. No accompanying explanation appears in the constitution, but the SPC constitution does require the use of the King James Version in the reading, preaching and teaching ministry.

The SPC wants to leave the past behind. While a very conservative church, and while having some sensitivity on matters discussed in the past, it does not want to be isolationistic, but simply to be positive in presenting the gospel and responsive to the needs of the people under its care without becoming lords over God's heritage. Rodman died in 1987 aged 68. However, the three congregations are presently stable and growing. Hobart is the largest with about 60 people, and the total is about 120. The SPC negotiated a settlement with the EPC concerning the church property at Hobart in 1988, a fairly nominal amount ($5,000 plus transfer costs) being paid. A church building has been purchased in Launceston. Since the division all the office-bearers have stood down and fresh elections have been made. The perils of smallness and inexperience need to be borne in mind but this group is showing a growing maturity. Coles serves the group at Taranna while Launceston is currently vacant.

As far as the *Evangelical Presbyterian Church* is concerned, those who withdrew were censured as schismatic by the Synod on June 24, 1986, but the parting seems to have been relatively peaceful, all things considered. Ian Morgan also decided he would pull out, and so sometime later he ceased to be connected with the EPC. He still continues his theological interests but did not take a group with him. This probably has taken some pressure off. He was a man to ride a hobby-horse to an extreme, and unfortunately had many who would ride it with him. During the preceding decade contacts had increased with the *Protestant Reformed Churches in America*, and the EPC appears to have moved closer to their position although the constitution is still the same. The EPC has five regular charges: Burnie, Launceston and Winnaleah in Tasmania; Brisbane and Rockhampton in Queensland. However, there are only three ministers: Fisk and Coleborn in Queensland and Burley at Winnaleah. Supply at Launceston was obtained from a minister of the Reformed Presbyterian Church of Ireland for a year 1987/88, which helped settle the congregation. The doctrinal position of the RPCI is in practice no different from the PCEA. Professor H. Hanko of the Protestant Reformed Churches came in 1988 to give supply at Burnie. The EPC differs on worship to the Protestant Reformed, while agreeing with the latter's position on the free offer and against common grace. The Protestant Reformed view of the covenant is also distinctive since the tendency to approach the subject from the standpoint of God's eternal decree has modified the recognised Reformed doctrine. This contributed to a schism in the early 1950s. An information paper on the EPC issued by Coleborn in February 1988 with the knowledge of his brother ministers, indicates a constitutional change is contemplated to tie the church less directly to the Scottish inheritance.

One can only suggest that this group has not yet matured. They mean well but have done what Morgan warned against back in 1961: their novel interpretation arising from an imbalanced approach has made them very much the introverted sect type with some exceptions. So far as the people generally are concerned, the present writer knows a number of them and holds them in esteem, but can only lament at where the immaturity of leadership has led them. He suspects that numbers of them are not happy with the direction of the church, and he hopes balance is recovered. The total following at present is quoted at a little over 300 people.[13]

REFORMED PREACHING OF THE GOSPEL

Space does not allow other than a cursory summary of the balanced approach to the preaching of the gospel by those who adhere to the understanding of Scripture set out in the Reformed Confessions.

The hyper-calvinist denies that men in a state of nature should be exhorted to believe in or turn to God, The underlying thought here is that to press the claims of Christ on unconverted people could imply that they have a natural ability to choose for Christ, which is Arminianism. Among other things, the hyper-calvinist confuses responsibility and inability in a reverse way to the Arminian. The hyper-calvinist reasons that the sovereignty of God is imperilled by any stress on the responsibility of man, whereas the truth is that all are spiritually incapable but remain fully responsible because the inability is self-inflicted. Hyper-calvinism is most notable at present among a section of English Baptists, but wherever there is a reluctance to use means for the spread of the gospel, the essence of hyper-calvinism is present. In popular attacks on the Reformed Faith, Arminians commonly represent hyper-calvinism as true calvinism.

The balanced calvinist believes with all calvinists that the atonement of Christ is sufficient to meet the needs of each and every one who believes, and he affirms that the atonement was made for the elect alone. He holds that the gospel is to be preached to all because the Bible commands it, and because this is the appointed means by which the elect, who are known only to God, are brought to repentance and faith, and thus to know their election.

13. The Protestant Reformed Churches of America have a following of c.4,000 in some 21 churches. Their position is evident from the many books of Herman Hoeksema (1886-1965). The denominational history is G.Hoeksema (ed), God's Covenant Faithfulness (Grand Rapids 1975). On the free offer and related questions they have published D.Engelsma, Hyper-Calvinism and the Call of the Gospel (Grand Rapids 1980), a frustrating book because of its confusion of truth and error. Probably the most helpful accessible treatment of the free offer is K.W.Stebbins, Christ Freely Offered published by the press of the Presbyterian Reformed Church of Australia in 1978 (124 pages). It interacts with the EPC position. A few historical inaccuracies have been noted such as ascribing to Rodman what was the work of Morgan, but this hardly affects its value as a balanced examination and discussion.

The consistent Bible believer holds that God is love, that Christ has suffered for sins, and that redemption is offered freely and sincerely to every person who hears the gospel. A sincere offer can be made because atonement has been made for all who will avail themselves of the offered salvation. The condition to the offer (repentance and faith) is not a condition fulfilled by human ability, but it is a condition fulfilled solely through the unconditioned free grace of God who gives to his elect what he demands of all in the gospel. (Cf. WCF VII:3; Canons of Dort, III/IV:8-10.)

The doctrine of unconditional election is not to be feared as if it blocks the path to salvation for someone who wants to be saved. Rather, this truth affirms that salvation is obtained as a divine gift rather than by human merit, and thus it points out the way and gives hope to the worst sinner. Election is only thought of as arbitrariness on God's part when we have in our thinking a sense of our own virtues. When this is so we are offended at God's mercy and misrepresent it as capricious.

In preaching the gospel the balanced calvinist cannot say to the unconverted sinner, 'Christ died for you', and exhort to repentance and faith on that basis as the popular Arminian preaching does. Nor, to adapt some words of Ebenezer Erskine, is the *first* language of faith, 'Christ died for me' or 'I was elected from eternity', but rather, 'God offers a crucified and risen Saviour, and I take him as my Saviour.' In my taking and embracing of him as offered, I have grounds to conclude that I was elected, and that he died for me, but not before.

In presenting the gospel, the balanced preacher presents the truths of Scripture in appropriate proportion. He must preach about sin and its pervasive effects of the corruption of man's heart; he is to publicise the great facts of redemption; and he is to tell all who hear that Christ promises to be their Saviour if they will come to him in the way of repentance and faith. He is to beseech them to be reconciled to God; to assure them of God's promise of eternal life if they come to Christ, but that if they reject Christ, they reject God's proffered mercy and will die in their sins.

The balanced teacher of truth recognises that God is good to all men, that there is a real sense in which he loves all men, even his enemies, and that he gives many common gifts to men, and even restrains the operation of sin so that the world continues with an environment in which the church may prosper. None of this moves him from upholding that God's redemptive grace is for the elect alone, and he refuses to suppose that what is mysterious to man involves ambiguity or contradiction in God.

Hyper-calvinism is unbalanced calvinism. There is also another unbalanced presentation such as arose in Tasmania. In this presentation the perspective of God's secret purpose dominates the thinking. It holds to the sufficiency of the atonement for all who believe, and also holds that the gospel should be made known to all. In this sense it is not hyper-calvinistic. However, in his desire for consistency this unbalanced calvinist (as we will call him) limits God's favour and love of any and all kinds to the elect alone. This means that common grace (so called) is rejected, and the pleading note in preaching is somewhat muted. It means that in the preaching of the gospel Christ seriously confronts men with the demand of the gospel, but does not express any desire for their salvation, and makes no sincere promise of grace conditional upon repentance and faith. It means that the only purpose in the non-elect hearing the gospel is to confront them with their duty, show them what will be pleasing to God, render them inexcusable, and heighten their damnation.

So far as such a passage as the Messiah weeping over Jerusalem and saying, 'How often I would have gathered you...but you would not' (Matthew 23:37), it is said Christ either weeps for the elect, which is impossible in the context, or that it is Christ in his human nature who weeps and so, it is said, no indication of God's attitude is provided. However, this second explanation strikes at the heart of the meaning of the incarnation. If Christ is the express image of the invisible God, there can be no un-Christlikeness in God, particularly in a passage which shows him as Messiah and Saviour. Thus, Jesus illustrates a longing and yearning for what has not been decreed, and who would dare call this a contradiction?

29: THE TWENTY YEARS 1968-1988

THE PRESBYTERIAN REFORMED CHURCH OF AUSTRALIA

New South Wales Presbyterianism in the 1960s

The 1960s are called by some the swinging '60s; they were also the secular '60s and the uncertain '60s. Australia had troops in Vietnam from 1965 to 1971, and there was quite a ferment of ideas on all kinds of issues as the post World War II baby boom took its place in society. There was radical theology such as John A.T.Robinson's *Honest to God* (1963) and Harvey Cox's *The Secular City*, but there was also literature setting forth the historic Reformed faith. The overall picture in Presbyterianism was one of an entrenched liberalism, intolerant of any definite opposition. Preaching was commonly dead, dry, dull and dreary.

There were pockets of evangelical witness. The Hurstville Church, where ex-PCEA man Neil MacLeod ministered from 1960-1974, had an evangelical tradition. Its strategic position in Sydney's southern Bible-belt suburbs, contributed to its influence. An earlier minister (1943-45) had been J.T.H. Kerr who, when a student, had provided R.J.H.McGowan with lecture notes during the Angus controversy (see page 337). He was a fine man. A subsequent minister (1974-1980) was Dr J. Graham Miller. Evangelical ministers were few and far between. The most active and obvious ones in New South Wales were MacLeod, Donald Campbell (ordained 1939) of Inverell, J.J.T.Campbell (ordained 1959 and no relation of DC) at Hurstville Grove, and A.Graham Kerr (ordained 1959), who succeeded Rev Cam Williamson, a quiet evangelical, at Sutherland in 1961. A son of J.T.H.Kerr, he had spent two years in the New Hebrides.

The Westminster Society within the PCNSW (see page 452) had only a small following, perhaps 50 members in the 1950s, few of them ministers. For a time in the 1960s Kerr was President, and he commenced monthly rallies at Scots Church which attracted up to 100 young people. Raised an Arminian evangelical, Kerr had by now become Reformed. His preaching at Sutherland transformed the congregation. Many left but others came. Straight-out giving replaced the Stewardship Scheme, and church offerings more than doubled. The session resolved that indiscrimate baptism would cease, and that infants would only be baptised if one or both parents professed faith - an eminently Scriptural and Presbyterian position. This brought increased opposition from the Presbytery. Students in the congregation told of the difficulties faced because of a liberal or Scoto-Catholic faculty at the Theological Hall. Home Mission students had Rev E.H.Vines as lecturer, a man who was as bad if not worse than Angus. Some of the students who were simple Arminians had their faith destroyed; those who were Calvinistic stood up better. These factors obviously affected Kerr's outlook. It may be that he carried something of a chip on his shoulder because of the way the church had failed to deal with Angus and had also made life somewhat difficult for his father. However, it appears that he had not contemplated separation from the PCA before about 1964. At that time a visiting American Presbyterian, William Mahlow, sat down with him and went through the Biblical teaching on the church and showed him that the Bible taught a doctrine of separation.[1] What was to be the catalyst was a controversy in the New Zealand Presbyterian Church.

Controversy in New Zealand 1966-67

At Easter 1966, controversy erupted in the PCNZ as a result of an article in the *Outlook*, the PCNZ periodical, on the meaning of the resurrection of Jesus Christ (issue of April 2, 1966). The article was written by Lloyd Geering, the Principal of the Theological Hall at Knox College, Dunedin, where PCNZ students were trained. Geering (1918-   ) had been a good student. In 1937 he moved from agnosticism to what he regarded as the Christian Faith through the influence of the Student Christian Movement. However, in essence he was a liberal, perhaps captured by the ideal he saw in Jesus, but in practice not very different from Samuel Angus in his beliefs. His chief interest was languages and he found theology dull.[2] He was in the parish ministry from 1943-55, but in 1956 became Professor of Old Testament and Comparative Religion at Emmanuel College within the Presbyterian Church of Queensland. He took up a similar appointment at Knox College in 1960.

Geering's 1966 article, which was followed up by others in which such

---

1. Information from Rev R.Kennelly, PRC Sutherland, April 25, 1989.
2. Ian Breward, **Grace and Truth - A History of the Theological Hall, Knox College, Dunedin 1876-1975** (Dunedin 1975), p.73.

questions as the role of the Westminster Confession were discussed, aimed to relate the Resurrection faith to men today. So far so good, but in attempting to do this he jettisoned most of the historical foundation in typical liberal fashion. He argued that the Christian faith does not depend on the tomb being empty nor would that faith be affected if the bones of Jesus were found in Palestine. We would still be able to affirm, said Geering, that 'the Lord is risen indeed!' By this Geering did not mean that Jesus' soul lived on while his body decayed, for Geering did not believe that man had an immortal soul. His views on this subject came to prominence in March 1967, several months after the 1966 General Assembly of the PCNZ had adopted a statement on the resurrection which, although ambiguous, appeared to have brought a measure of unity. When the Geering case (for charges were laid) came before the November 1967 General Assembly, Geering's views on the soul caused some controversy in Melbourne when, in response to Rev G.G. Powell's statement in a sermon reported in the press that the PCA had no doubt about the immortality of the soul, three PCV ministers (R.Creevy, I.Steer and A.Hardie) asserted they rejected such a doctrine, although still believing in some form of future life. They admitted their position was contrary to the Westminster Confession, but claimed Scripture support.[3]

The handling of the Geering case was much less complicated than the Angus affair. Charges of heresy were laid by Mr R.J.Wardlaw and by Rev R.J. Blaikie, the former with a view to censure, the latter with a view to forcing the church to give clear guidance as to what was fundamental. The PCNZ had a similar but less precise Declaractory Statement to that in the PCA. Blaikie needed it to remain in the PCNZ with a good conscience, for he could not accept the Westminster Confession *simpliciter*; but he thought Geering had gone too far.

Although there had been a *Westminster Fellowship* within the PCNZ since 1950 which enrolled 95 ministers and 1,000 lay members in the mid-1960s, the evangelicals lacked leaders able and willing to take on the liberals, and it is doubtful if many would have contemplated a fight to the finish. The continuity of the church's structure took precedence over the doctrine that is fundamental to the meaning and existence of the church.

The case came to a head in November 1967. The Doctrine Committee of the PCNZ Assembly reported, and Geering was exonerated from the charges on the grounds that no doctrinal error had been established. He was simply endeavouring to restate the Christian Faith in modern terms and had not stepped out of the bounds of reasonable liberty of thought and expression.

3. See **The Herald**, 30/11/1967, p.1 and **The Age**, 8/12/1967, p.4. They seem to affirm a form of conditional immortality with a 'demythologised' resurrection. In 1966 Rev C.S.Boyall of the PCNSW, a great Angus supporter and former missionary in India, published **Honest to Christ**, a booklet in which his agnosticism about life after death is plainly asserted along with other heresies. No action was taken and few seemed to care.

Grahame Kerr of Sutherland was familiar with the situation in New Zealand, and in fact represented the *Westminster Fellowship* (NZ) in New South Wales. As early as August 1966, as Rev J.G.Miller recalls it,[4] he had publicly urged at a meeting at Stanwell Tops, 'We have to separate!' Kerr accepted an invitation to preach and lecture in New Zealand at the time of the Geering case, although he was warned by Donald Geddes, who had lived in New Zealand, that he could be trapped.[5] If he told New Zealand evangelicals to leave the PCNZ, he would be under pressure to leave the PCA, for the PCA was as bad, if not worse, than the PCNZ. However, Kerr went and returned to withdraw from the PCA. All the elders and all but 4 of the members (in excess of 80) adhered to him, the property, which had just been paid off, remained with the PCNSW, and the first service of what was to be come the *Presbyterian Reformed Church of Australia* was held in the buildings of the Reformed Church of Sutherland on December 8, 1967.[6]

A catalyst for PCA evangelicals

There was no widespread tide of support for Kerr elsewhere, although a number of younger elders and students were swayed for a time. An influential body of evangelical opinion regarded his action as schismatic or at least unwise or uncalled for. However, his departure was a catalyst for some, like Donald Geddes, to pitch in whole-heartedly to try and change the direction of the church. Geddes and Alan Vaughan made a significant contribution to the Presbyterian Fellowship of Australia (PFA), Geddes giving many addresses at camps and other meetings in his capacity of Visitation and Evangelism Convener, and a significant strengthening of Reformed and evangelical teaching occurred in this circle.[7] Later they were able to publish *Prenewal* (Presbyterian Renewal) which ran for several years prior to 1977 with a circulation of up to 400. It stressed, Theological Education, Christian Education and Youth Work. It rallied prayer support, and it was possible to institute an alternative course of training at Moore College (an Evangelical Anglican institution) prior to 1977. Rev Graham Miller of Hurstville (1974-80) was very helpful in encouragement and guidance. He showed that it was possible to be an evangelical and retain academic integrity, and be a normal, warm-hearted person. Some liberals became evangelicals. Rev C.R.Thomas, ordained 1971 when liberalism was at its height, became an evangelical the following year. He soon became a leader in the battles in the church courts since he knew how the liberals thought and was also a little older than most evangelicals.

4. Information from Dr Miller, Wangaratta, April 1989. The secession of 1967 had been planned for the May 1968 Assembly but was brought forward.
5. Information from Rev Donald Geddes, Albury, April 1989. Geddes learned Reformed theology from Rev Edwin Lee of the PCEA Melbourne when he lived in that city in the early 1960s. A member at Balaclava PCV, he attended St Kilda PCEA.
6. The Protestant Review (PRC periodical) for August 1977 brings together a number of details in connection with the separation.
7. Information from Rev Donald Geddes and Rev C.R.Thomas, April 1989.

The PRC organised 1968

In June 1968, Kerr was joined by Rev D.C.Shelton (1939 -   ), who had been active with him in the Westminster Society. Evangelicals were unhappy with the liberal Sunday School material put out by the Joint Board of Christian Education. It was widely used in Presbyterian and Methodist circles. It gave quite a deal of attention to peace and justice issues, while its coverage of Christian teaching was far from orthodox. Shelton had become minister at Warren in outback New South Wales. The Presbytery made a rule requiring the use of Joint Board material, and Shelton took a complaint against the Presbytery to the Assembly due to meet in May 1968. His Session also overtured the Assembly to give a message of reassurance to the church at large given the publicity given to Geering's views. The overture was sidestepped by merely affirming adherence to the 1901 Basis, but the complaint received a fair hearing. The Presbytery was upheld, and 13 dissents were recorded, one name being that of Rev E.H.Vines, the extreme liberal, who wanted to maintain liberty. It is of interest that Shelton belonged to Vines' congregation as a youth prior to his conversion in 1957. Shelton speaks of Vines as a diligent pastor, and excellent parish minister apart from the fact that he did not believe or teach orthodox Christianity and opposed doctrines such as the Deity of Christ with some passion. Early in 1968, the Westminster Society (NSW) had issued a critique of the Joint Board material under the title 'Thy Children...taught of the Lord?' which was written by Shelton, although the Society decided not to indicate the author. The Joint Board's response was to state that its task was to ensure its materials came within the mainstream of the church's scholarly thinking. The Joint Board being the servant of the church it could hardly be otherwise.[8]

Shelton resigned on June 5, and expected he might have to return to teaching for a time. He joined Grahame Kerr as did John Stafford. Stafford had been a PCEA student at one stage and had a congregation at Ryde of some 30 or 40 folk. The PCEA told Kerr that difficulties could arise with Stafford. Shelton received an invitation to minister to a small group in Brisbane. There had been a *Reformed Literature Information Society* there. It included three families who had been involved in the EPC in Tasmania and a few others of varied background. The EPC people decided to stay on their own, but nine others attended the first service held by Shelton on July 5, 1968. By 1988 the number attending the 3 Brisbane congregations was not far off 200. R.Kennelly, a Home Mission student of the PCA at Dorrigo, and a former member at Sutherland, resigned from the PCA in 1968 and was received by the PRC. An invitation from Wagga Wagga resulted in his ministry commencing there with just two people in September 1968. He had to work

8. See the 4 page 'Statement' issued by the JBCE, May 1968. Shelton's account in 'An End...and a Beginning', 28pp published June 1968, is a very fair one. The 1968 Assembly required the Westminster Society to apologize and unreservedly withdraw the booklet (Minute 62).

full time for 4 years until the work was established. There were young men training or soon to train for the ministry, and centres of witness spread. Adelaide was instituted at the end of 1969, Newcastle in 1970, the year Stafford at Ryde left. Wollongong, Townsville and Toowoomba appeared in 1973. Some ministers came through resignations from the PCA - John Singleton, William Baigrie and John Amos were PCA Home Missionaries. Rev James Cooper of the PCQ joined at the end of 1970. By December 1976 there were 13 ministers, 12 parishes and about 310 full members in Australia, plus 3 missionary couples. Work began in Vanuatu in 1969 and a distinct Presbytery was formed there in 1977 with three centres. Work was also opened up in Papua New Guinea, and for a period from 1983 work extended to Kenya.

PRC PRESBYTERY - ADELAIDE MEETING 1972

BACK ROW: from left: Rev R. Kennelly, Rev G.Kastelein, Rev D.Shelton, Rev E.Kastelein, Mr J.Wyllie (Brisbane), Rev W.Ham, Mr S.Esplin (Wagga). CENTRE: Mr P.McIntyre (Sutherland). FRONT: Mr J.Aikman (Newcastle), Mr G.Mak (Adelaide), Rev J.Cooper.
ABSENT: Rev A.G.Kerr

PRC problems

The PRC began in a somewhat casual way. The Code of the PCNSW was adopted as a guide, but it was not until 1973 that vows for officebearers were settled on.[9] It was then determined that the relationship of the church to the Westminster Confession would be expressed thus:

Do you believe the sixty-six books of the Old and New Testaments to be the inspired and infallible Word of God and the only rule of faith and life?

Do you own and acept the Westminster Confession of Faith as a faithful interpretation of Holy Scripture, and as a confession of your own faith, always providing that if any chapter or sentence is noted apparently contradictory to God's Word, the Church is informed in writing; whereupon the Church shall give satisfaction from Holy Scripture or amendment of that which is proved to be wrong? And do you engage firmly to adhere thereto, and to the utmost of your power to assert, maintain and defend the same?

The aim here was to avoid such a fixity of creed that it might seem to suggest that the Confession was infallible and not Scripture. The words in the first sentence of question two from 'whereupon' were derived from the Scots Confession of 1560. The intention is good but it does raise difficulties. It still gives a power for a majority to legally change the bond of communion, and to declare something to be unscriptural which has previously been declared scriptural. One would think the question of the scripturalness or otherwise of the doctrine of the Confession is decided before one signs it, not afterwards. The PCEA formula is to 'the whole doctrine' not the document as such, as if its very forms of expression were sacrosanct, and there is no power to change the doctrine.

As the PRC developed, two notes were sounded which caused disquiet to others. First, there was a very negative note as regards other churches. In particular, other churches' faults were exposed but positive points overlooked. The PCA was regarded as apostate, and an excessive emphasis on separation from error was evident. One can contend earnestly for the faith (Jude 3) without descending to bitter denunciation and carping criticism. The second note was a heavy discipline upon members. As issues were discussed those who might see things a bit differently were all too readily considered offenders against the authority of the elders. Excommunication, too infrequently employed in other Reformed and Presbyterian churches, was too frequently employed in the PRC. There was a streak of self-righteousness, and a lack of a charitable spirit. There was also a tendency to over-commit the membership in matters of finance. The PRC was certainly a dedicated group. The average offering per member was about $14 per week in 1977, compared to a little over $5 in the PCEA and much less in the PCA. In part

9. See The Protestant Review, March 1973, p.1.

this reflected the city based nature of the PRC and the number of young wage earners and absence of nominal members, but it remains indicative of the kind of commitment.   From about June 1985, attention was given to these matters. Acknowledgement has been made of past sin and reconciliation sought with those wronged. There is a general realisation of changes in the PCA, and so there is cause for optimism concerning this group of churches. In March 1989, two ministers in Brisbane withdrew from the PRC with about 100 followers, chiefly because they considered progress to a more liberated outlook had not been quick enough, and for other reasons. Another minister withdrew in April 1989. However, the partings appear to have been reasonably amicable in the circumstances. Wider and more fruitful contacts with the Westminster Presbyterian Church should be possible (see below).

Rev A.G.Kerr's life came to a sudden close in 1988. He had retired due to ill health back in 1977, and had subsequently fallen out with his brethren and been excommunicated. Perhaps his difficulties were compounded by having lived too long in the PCA when it was not standing firm for the truth. The betrayal one can experience in such a situation, the suspicion one can come to entertain because of the double-talk of those supposed to be speaking the truth in love, 'the vicious laws of survival that operate in the liberal church'[10] - these are factors that have their corrosive effect and even contribute to division among those who have left liberal churches in their endeavour to be Biblical. The PRC had grown to an Australian membership of some 430 by June 1985 when there were 15 ministers, 16 parishes and some 5 ordained missionaries. The position at the close of 1988 was not much different. The largest congregations are in the Sydney and Brisbane areas.[11]

A note re Geering in 1988

As a footnote, Geering's antisupernaturalism   continued after he left Knox for a university post. His lectures under the auspices of the St Andrew's Trust as reviewed in *The Dominion* for February 4, 1989, state in the most unambiguous terms that God has no objective existence. The idea of a Supreme Being is created by the human imagination. Says the reviewer: 'It cannot be too strongly stated that there is room for a bold, imaginative and radical orthodoxy. But if I believed that God was the artefact of human thought, I would not set foot in a church again, and I would express my views, not in churches, but under the auspices of the local humanist society.' But liberal theologians of the modern kind are not usually so honest.

10. Dr Noel Weeks in **The Protestant Review**, August 1972, p.8.
11. The following are some of the more important references to the PRC: David Parker, **Fundamentalism and Conservative Protestantism in Australia 1920-1980** (PhD Thesis, University of Queensland 1982) pp.302-323; **The Protestant Review,1969-1989**: the issue for July 1985 contains statistics of membership and finances 1974-84; the issue for April 1987 refers to errors in discipline; the issue for October 1988 includes the final text relative to this. The PRC position on various subjects is most conveniently found in **Reformation Applied**, published by Covenanter Press, Q. in 1983 (208pp).

THE WESTMINSTER PRESBYTERIAN CHURCH

This denomination began in December 1970 in Western Australia. Its first congregation was organised by Rev David Cross, a missionary pastor of World Presbyterian Missions, the overseas missions arm of the Reformed Presbyterian Church, Evangelical Synod, in the USA. The RPCES was a merger of one of several groups which traced their origin to the withdrawal in 1936 of about 100 orthodox ministers from the PCUSA, during the modernist/fundamentalist controversy. These had continued as the Orthodox Presbyterian Church but two years later a rather less Reformed group withdrew under the leadership of Dr Carl McIntyre, a rabid anti-modernist campaigner, and formed the Bible Presbyterian Church. In 1956, this church divided into two, and the larger and less politicised body changed its name to Evangelical Presbyterian Church in 1961, and in 1965 united with a small 'new school' Reformed Presbyterian Synod to form the RPCES with approximately 20,000 members in some 150 congregations. In 1982 it joined the Presbyterian Church in America, a group of some 400 congregations of conservative position, most of which had withdrawn from a larger denomination in the southern states of America in 1973 when that church pursued a union with another church of liberal character. The Presbyterian Church in America has in excess of 115,000 members, mainly white.

There were two streams of development behind the appearance of the WPC. The first was associated with the work of Miss Mary Jones, an independent missionary to the aboriginals in the wheat-belt town of Brookton, about 130 kms south-east of Perth. She wanted a Presbyterian connection for the mission but the PCWA was in a similar condition to the PCNSW. She opened up correspondence with World Presbyterian Missions, hoping to obtain a missionary pastor who might also establish an evangelical Presbyterian congregation in the suburbs of Perth. As a result of her persistence two ministers representing World Presbyterian Missions visited Western Australia, one in 1964 and the other in 1965. At this stage they also met some Presbyterian families distressed by conditions in the PCWA, particularly the enforcement of the use of Sunday School literature subversive of the doctrinal position of the church. A Presbyterian elder, Andrew Priddle, who also happened to be the state representative for the magazine of the Westminster Fellowship of the PCNZ, added his voice to that of Miss Jones.

One of the US pastors, Rev William Mahlow, who also visited Rev A.G. Kerr in Sydney (see page 406), recommended the formation of a mission organisation to give backing to Miss Jones. It was called 'Evangelical Presbyterian Missions (USA)', the USA being added after a PCWA complaint that the new body's name might mislead the Christian public. Priddle was chairman, and he continued to press World Presbyterian Missions for a missionary pastor. This concern was heightened by the Geering affair.

Western Australia had none of the smaller Presbyterian Churches present in the eastern states. Had any of these been in WA, the WPC would not have been formed in all probability. A congregation of the Reformed Churches of Australia met in Perth, and gave much help and encouragement to Miss Jones and the troubled Presbyterians without proselytising overtones. What was then a strong Dutch ethos, coupled with a firming of the relationship between EPM and WPM, kept the Presbyterians from membership in the RCA.

At last, after years of correspondence and many pleas, WPM assigned Rev David Cross to Western Australia. He arrived in January 1970 and began work in Brookton. Towards the end of the year he began the first congregation in Perth with three familes to begin. No significant additions came from the PCWA, but others came. Cross was an exceptional church-planter. By the time he returned to the USA in 1980, three congregations and a bookshop had been established, and oversight of Brookton was maintained. By 1983, there were 5 suburban congregations in Perth, the same number as at present (1988). There is a bookshop and a quite advanced training programme. In the earlier stages there was co-operation in training with the continuing PCWA, whose ministers were generally evangelical. In 1981, work was extended to Queensland, and three congregations and a bookshop have been established in that state. Oliver Claassen, a South African now naturalised, pioneered the work in Queensland and also in New South Wales where 3 congregations have been established in the western suburbs of Sydney since 1985. A work has also begun in Canberra, although in this connection it does seem there could be more effort to avoid simply taking from other good Christian work, such as the RCA congregation. The total regular involvement as at 1986 in the 12 centres then operating was about 750 persons, 450 of these being in Western Australia. About half of the 12 ministers are Australians. The missionary pastors develop congregations to the point of reasonable maturity and then the congregations call their own pastors.

In the early days there were some links between the PRC and David Cross. However, personal difficulties including Grahame Kerr's dislike of Americans, soon brought the links to an end. The US church repeatedly counselled against establishing a new denomination. However, the Australian elders eventually came to the view they would have to do so. They believed in Biblical separation and were not happy with the Declaratory Statement of the PCA. However, nor were they happy with the polemical note in the PRC attitude to other churches. As they were not convinced on a limitation to psalms in public worship, they therefore organised separately. The quality of leadership and the less tempestuous origin are reflected in the relatively steady progress made.

The WPC does have problems due to the fact that a large number of its members have little understanding of Presbyterianism. Significant numbers of folk from evangelical rather than Reformed background have meant some problems. The ethos might be said to be a little light in weight compared to the more homogenous position of the PCEA, for example. There have been debates on the matter of praise, on the nature of the sabbath, and bible versions.

Given that the WPC holds a high view of Scripture and cordially adheres to the Westminster Confession, some scope for co-operation with other bodies exists.[12]

THE REFORMED PRESBYTERIAN CHURCH

On page 353 it was noted that a second congregation of the Reformed Presbyterian Church of Ireland had been established by W.R.McEwen in the 1930s. In the period now under review, the RP Church first became a distinct Presbytery of the Irish parent church, and later (1974) achieved autonomy as the Reformed Presbyterian Church of Australia. A draft constitution was approved by the Irish Synod at that time. The RPCA operates under this draft but it has not yet reached a final form. It is rather unlike a traditional Reformed Presbyterian document, for these were commonly closely reasoned justifications for the distinctive position adopted from 1690 onwards (see page 18 above) since the RPs were very sensitive to any suggestion of schism. The old distinctives of the RP Church compared with the Free Church (no voting because of the inadequate nature of the civil government, prohibition of membership in oath-bound societies) are not included, consequently one would have thought a union between the PCEA and the RPCA could be readily accomplished. However, Inter-Church Relations are rarely easy, and despite a number of meetings 1983-86, nothing concrete has eventuated. There is a concern on the PCEA side that the RPCA is a bit directionless at present, while the RPs may feel the PCEA is too traditional. Certainly the troubles in the PCEA 1978-81 were not helpful.[13]

12. The section on the WPC is based largely on information supplied by Rev Andrew Priddle, Clerk of the WPC Presbytery in Perth, August 1988. Links with the PRC may be noted in **The Protestant Review**: issue of June 1971, p.10, records Priddle's letter of resignation from the PCWA; the issue of October 1972 indicates it was hoped David Cross' congregation would join the PRC.

13. The fact that the PCEA did not prohibit Freemasons from membership was an obstacle for W.R.McEwen in the 1930s. There have been repeated discussions over the years. To justify continued separation one or other church must be satisfied that the total loyalty due to Christ would be prejudiced by union. If the churches are not so satisfied, then union should occur to remove the reproach implied by separation, and the only question is the practical one of the best method. The historical differences and the possible methods of union were surveyed in PCEA Synod Reports 1986, and printed in **The Presbyterian Banner**, May 1986.

REFORMED PRESBYTERIAN MINISTERS, AUSTRALIA SINCE 1959

AUSTRALIAN PRESBYTERY - RPCI : October 9, 1959

1	W.R.McEwen,BA	5/09/1928	arrived from Ireland 9/08/1929; supply, then McKinnon 1933 - 5/9/1978; d. 1989.
2	Alex Barkley,MA,DD	8/03/1939	arrived from Ireland 31/12/1946; Geelong 1947-11/12/1964; RTC 1954-80, Principal 1958-78. DD - Central School of Religion.
3	Arthur W.Palmer,BD	8/06/1965	Geelong 8/06/1965-9/02/1969; to Mangere Reformed Church of New Zealand.
4	Lynsey Blakston,BD	7/04/1972	Geelong 7/04/1972-1/6/1986; Sunbury/ Melton 1/6/1986-

PRESBYTERY OF THE RPCA : June 12, 1974

5	Godfrey Franklin,BD	20/2/1976	To RPCNA (Selma, Alabama)
6	A.R.McEwen,BA,BD	8/06/1977	(Son of WRMcE) Frankston 8/6/77-1981; RTC (Full time) 1982-
7	Geo M.McEwen,BA	[Ex RPCI]	(Nephew of WRMcE) McKinnon 28/3/80-2/85; returned to RPCI.
8	Robt McCracken,BA	[Ex RPCNA]	Sunbury/Melton 13/3/81-1/86; to RPCNA
9	A.McConaghy,BEc,BD	12/2/1983	Frankston 12/2/1983-
10	Chris Brown,BD	23/6/1985	McKinnon 23/6/1985-
11	Anthony Power,BD	3/08/1986	Geelong 3/08/1986-

CONGREGATIONS:

GEELONG: First congregational meeting held June 22, 1858, church erected 1862 and adjoining manse in 1869. Ministers: A.M.Moore,MA (1857-97), A.Holmes, stated supply, (1897-98), W.McCarroll,BA (1899-1903), A.M.Thompson,MA (1904-1909), H.K.Mack, BA (1909-1946), Alexander Barkley,MA (1947-64), Arthur Palmer,BD (1965-69), Lynsey Blakston,BD (1972-86), Anthony Power,BD (1986-   ).

McKINNON: Work commenced by W.R.McEwen in 1933. A church building was opened in 1940, an adjoining manse in 1949 and hall to church in 1952. Constituted as a congregation on April 11, 1946. Ministers: W.R.McEwen,BA (retired 1978); George M. McEwen,BA (1980-85), Chris Brown,BD (1985-   ).

FRANKSTON: Monthly service in private home commenced March 1965. Preaching place with weekly service from March 11, 1972, and congregation instituted May 9, 1975. Ministers: Alastair R. McEwen,BD,BA (1977-81), Andrew McConaghy, BEc,BD, (1983-   ).

SUNBURY/MELTON: Monthly service in private home beginning October 21, 1979. Chief emphasis is at Sunbury. Congregation instituted November 6, 1982. Ministers: Robert B.McCracken,BA (1981-86), Lynsey Blakston,BD (1986-   ).

The material for preparing this summary was provided by Hugh Wright, **A Brief History of Colonial Mission Work in Canada and Australia** by the RPCI (Belfast 1957) together with data since 1957 kindly furnished by Rev Dr A.Barkley, Geelong.

THE PRESBYTERIAN CHURCH OF EASTERN AUSTRALIA

Following the 1953 Union (see pages 353ff), the PCEA was in much better shape to extend her borders. However, it was not until the 1970s that sufficient new ministers were available, and only slowly did the Sydney and Melbourne congregations come to grips with the need for extension into the populous suburban areas where, particularly in Sydney, many country members came to reside. Meanwhile, there was a not inconsiderable loss of such folk to other churches.

There were seven PCEA ministers serving in Australia at the close of 1960, but only 4 of these were under 65 years of age. A comparison of the next 25 years shows the number in this category rose to 6 at the close of 1965, to 11 at the close of 1970, slipped to 9 at the close of 1975, was 12 at the end of 1980, and 11 five years later. The appendix at the rear of this volume provides detailed information about the ministers.

The increased man-power facilitated the establishment of new centres at Brisbane, Armidale and Sydney Western Suburbs, with the 1980s seeing an additional centre in each of Melbourne and Sydney, and the relocation of the existing Melbourne centre. By 1988 just under 50% of the communicant membership of the PCEA was in the capital cities and the major centres of Geelong and Newcastle. The figure 5 years before was about 42% on a slightly smaller membership. More attention needs to be given to the large metropolitan areas, with a further centre in each of Melbourne, Sydney and Brisbane being a priority.

Stresses and strains - the Turnbull Case 1978/79

The PCEA experienced a number of stresses as it shared in the resurgence of interest in the Reformed faith. New ministers wanted to check out the basics for themselves, and wanted to apply the great principles they found to the needs of contemporary society. Older men were a little uncertain at the prospect and risk of extension lest the purity of the church's testimony be compromised. An element of reaction derived through the Tasmanian experience rocked the boat, and for a time threatened to capsize it. While the PCEA had had personality clashes it had never had a significant doctrinal problem, but this occured in the context of the changes referred to.

The issue arose in connection with the discussion on modern translations of Scripture. The King James Version had been in general use, but the proliferation of modern translations called for some guidance. The Synod of 1972 decided to continue to commend the KJV, but in 1975 a thorough report was presented to the Synod in which the matters of the best underlying text and the principles of translation were discussed. The Synod resolved to -

remind officebearers of the responsibility we have to present the Scriptures in the language of the people, in accord with the teaching of the Westminster Confession of Faith I:8. Synod recommend to our people the NASB and the NIV as being among the most reliable of modern versions. Where an alternative to the AV is desired or considered necessary, it is suggested, in the interests of uniformity, and faithfulness to the original text of Scripture, that either the NASB or the NIV be used.[14]

This recommendation was adopted without recorded dissent. A number of congregations acted on the guidance and introduced the NASB into public worship. However, a number, particularly G.C.Lefevre of Winnaleah, C.P. King of Newcastle and G.A.Neil of Sydney were not very happy with this move. C.P.King had long been connected with the Trinitarian Bible Society. One can fully appreciate that an issue like this touches deep emotions. Questions about the underlying texts were raised, since most modern trans- lations use a Greek text in the New Testament which draws upon many more manuscripts than were available in the 17th century, and thus there are differences. There was a fairly even division of opinion in the Synod, but as no one was wanting to force others to use what they were not happy with, the question seemed destined to settle down. This did not occur, however, in a fair measure because of the advocacy of views in favour of the KJV by the minister at Melbourne, E.S.Turnbull. Turnbull reacted into the false position that the Hebrew and Greek texts underlying the KJV translation were providentially preserved copies of the originals without any variation, and that the KJV translation was also free of mistakes or errors. To hold otherwise was, to Turnbull, to believe in the inspiration of the Bible you do not have rather than the Bible you do have.[15] In addition, Turnbull held that he knew these claims for the Scriptures to be true through the testimony of the Spirit. There was obviously a good amount of confused thinking here, for the testimony of the Spirit is in the way of illumination to receive the truth rather than the communication of certain facts or truths themselves. But Turnbull's claims for the KJV and his rejection of other versions as not 'the word of God' were so zealously promoted that action became necessary.

The bare facts are that a complaint about Turnbull's statements at a public meeting was made to the Geelong Session in September 1978, the subject was

14. **Synod Minutes, 1975, p.27** (March 25, 1975). I have heard it said that the guidance was intended for individuals and not for the pulpit. However, there was no rule for the pulpit other than 'the best allowed translation' (**Directory for Public Worship, 1645**). The 'Authorised Version' was not in fact formally authorised in the Scottish Church, but over a generation or more came to supplant the Geneva Bible of 1560.
15. In writing the two previous sentences I was struck by the way W.R.McEwen had dealt specifically with these points in setting out the Reformed doctrine of Scripture at the St Kilda Conference in December 1961 - **Our Banner**, March 1962, pp.2,3.

raised at Presbytery, Turnbull read a paper at the meeting of Presbytery in March 1979, and the Presbytery resolved unanimously that the differences on the Confession of Faith 1:8 were irreconcilable and referred the matter to Synod. On May 17, 1979, the Synod, anxious to defuse the situation, merely affirmed adherence to the disputed section of the Confession without explaining it. This resulted in a Protest by 9 ministers and 2 elders. The Synod then resolved without dissent to take up the erroneous statements and beliefs made and held by the Melbourne minister. The matter was sent back to the Presbytery which found it necessary to proceed by way of libel (see pages 346/347 for this procedure). The case was appealed to a special Synod meeting, and on October 13, 1979 was found proved. The finding was:

Synod direct Mr Turnbull to desist from teaching that a particular translation of Holy Scripture has been made which is without any mistake or error and that if he concurs with this he be rebuked for disturbing the peace of the church and his suspension be lifted. Failing this that he be given the opportunity to resign from the ministry of this church and failing this he no longer be considered a minister of this church.

The Southern Presbytery met on November 2, 1979, and found it necessary, in terms of the Synod decision, to declare Mr Turnbull no longer a minister of the PCEA. Turnbull lodged a prepared Protest and this was answered by the Presbytery and both documents engrossed in the Presbytery record on December 11, 1979.

There were after-shocks in several congregations, but equilibrium was recovered from 1982 onwards. The controversy contributed to the loss of several ministers. Indeed, part of the problem of adjustment was the lack of vacancies at the time. Men desiring a change had no options in the PCEA, since forward planning to open up new areas had been in abeyance. It is understandable that many who did not hold Turnbull's views did not understand the issue very clearly. Thus over 300 persons in eight congregations signed a petition seeking a discontinuance of action, although this document was never presented to Presbytery or Synod.Turnbull put his views in book form with a dedication to Rev A.D.McIntosh,[16] but this should not be taken as implying anything other than that McIntosh wanted the KJV retained. Many who sympathised with Turnbull were in the same position.

16. E.S.Turnbull, **Mountain of Myths Moved by Faith in the Word of God** (91pp issued early 1983 so far as is known). This work is a mixture of truth and error and certainly vindicates the action taken by the PCEA. Its distinctive claim is rejected by such a conservative organisation as the Trinitarian Bible Society, see **The Quarterly Record of the TBS**, October/December 1984, review by A.J.Brown.

Note Warfield's admirable summary of the Presbyterian doctrine of the Bible in the three points: '(1) the plenary inspiration of the Bible as God gave it, by which it is made the Word of God, trustworthy in every one of its affirmations; (2) the safe preservation of the Bible as God gave it, so as to be accessible to men, in the use of the ordinary means of securing a trustworthy text; and (3) the adequate transmission of the saving truth in every and any honest translation, so that the Word of God is accessible to all at all times for all ordinary purposes.' **Selected Shorter Writings II** (Philadelphia '73) p.594.

To those who said that Turnbull had not contradicted the Confession, it was enough to reply that he subscribed it in terms of the formula and therefore rejected all doctrines contrary to or inconsistent with the doctrine of the Confession. In simple terms, Turnbull's position was to claim for the KJV what the Papacy had claimed for the Latin Vulgate at the time of the Reformation, and the statements in the Confession were deliberately framed in the light of such claims.[17]

Discussion on the antichrist 1974/1977

It probably did not help the calm handling of the Turnbull case that it occurred when other matters of some contentiousness were being discussed. One of these was the meaning of the section on the antichrist in the Confession XXV:6 -

There is no other head of the Church but the Lord Jesus Christ. Nor can the Pope of Rome, in any sense, be head thereof; but is that Antichrist, that man of sin, and son of perdition, that exalteth himself, in the Church, against Christ and all that is called God.

One minister, who subsequently resigned, made some unguarded remarks in which he appeared to reject the identification of the Pope and the Antichrist. He was quite happy to accept that the Papacy was part of a system of error but did not consider the Papacy exhausted the meaning of the Bible passages about the antichrist. There was nothing wrong with this position, but some matters of a personal nature were influencing the situation, as well as some misunderstandings all round. After the air cleared at Synod 1977, a legacy of suspicion remained and flared when opposition was made to Turnbull's teaching. The claim was made that those opposing Turnbull had not adhered to the whole doctrine re the antichrist so were hypercritical in opposing Turnbull. This was very far from the truth. The following two paragraphs are added to try and wring some lasting good out of a rather small affair.

The illustrative texts of Scripture offered in support of WCF 25:6 beginning with the word 'Nor' are Matthew 23:8-9 (concerning religious veneration to teachers), 2 Thessalonians 2:3-4,8-9 (the prediction of apostasy in the church) and Revelation 13:6 (the beast with Satan's power who blasphemes God and persecutes his people). [What is said about the proof texts on page 17, note 6 should be kept in mind.]

Concerning the import of this statement: *First,* it occurs in the context of the doctrine of the Church. Consequently, only as the true doctrine of

17. Cf. the literature cited in footnote on page 234 of this book.

Christ's Headship is grasped is the enormity of the blasphemy of anyone claiming to be Christ's vicar on earth appreciated. *Second,* the Confession does not intend to exhaust the meaning of the texts cited or to commit one to a detailed scheme of prophetic interpretation. Rather, it affirms the seriousness of the Pope's exaltation of himself as if he were the head of the Church. *Third,* 'antichrist' as the term is used in 1 John refers to a movement of heresy represented in individuals professing friendship for Christ but stripping him of his glory, and the 'man of sin' passage fits the same pattern. Such language is not applied to pagans or political tyrants but to those who both profess and contradict the truth, hence the language does not mean we must regard everything the Papacy does is wrong. The danger of the Papacy, and liberal Protestantism too, is that truths are affirmed in one breath but taken away in another: thus, the authority of Scripture is accepted in Rome but not the sole authority - tradition is brought in too and effectively is placed over Scripture. *Finally,* the only serious objection to the Confession is that to those who have little understanding it seems that we are being less than polite to the Pontiff. Still, we doubt it is kindness not to·face him up with the Biblical picture. See also the comments on page 291, and my article 'The Man of Sin' in the *Banner of Truth,* December 1977.

The Service of Praise

A matter of importance in relating the church to 20th century society was the suitability of the version of psalms in use, namely, the 1650 Psalter. As the church moved more into the cities it was imperative it translate its principle into practice. In a debate with the PRC on the use of psalms (1968/71), the PCEA was clearly disadvantaged by the fact that it did not have available the more accurate translation Rev M.C.Ramsay declared it would be ready to adopt.[18] As long ago as 1893, Rev J.J.Stewart of the FPCV had argued most ably for additional version of the psalms, and the matter had been a hardy annual of more recent years. In 1971 it was agreed to participate in the production of a new psalter planned by the RPCI and the Free Church of Scotland, although there was no commitment to use the end result. In 1973 the Convener of Psalmody (Rev S.N.Ramsay) reported: 'For our part we are persuaded that it is our duty as a Church both to preserve the principle of Purity of Worship in using a faithful translation of the Psalms of the Word of God in our public worship, and at the same time to ensure as far as possible that in our worship we employ those versions which are the best available.'

In 1976 a Psalter Revision Committee was appointed of which the present writer was Convener. A rather thorough report of 11 pages was considered by Synod 1978. The Report reviewed the present and alternative Psalters,

18. M.C.Ramsay, **Psalms Only: Objections Answered** (Sydney 1971) p.34. It is probable that poor singing (quite general) and the old translation furthered the move to hymns in the 1860s, and also the bringing in of the organ which was common by 1880, St Andrew's, Carlton being the last PCV Congregation to do so (early 1890s).

discussed translation principles, and suggested a thorough recasting and revision was desirable rather than an annoying tinkering with the 1650 text. After further reference to Sessions and Presbyteries, the Synod of 1981, without recorded dissent (!), authorised the Committee to produce a booklet of alternative versions as a supplement to the existing version, and reappointed the Committee for five years with a view to report being made as to progress and possibilities towards a fresh translation of the whole Psalter which would have acceptance beyond the PCEA as well as in it. In April 1983 a booklet containing about 20% of the Psalter was published in inexpensive format under the title *Psalms for Singing*. This has been found quite acceptable in Melbourne. Interest is continuing both in Australia and overseas, and one would hope that a fresh Psalter which retains all the well loved sections of the 1650 Psalter will eventually be available.

Administration

The PCEA at Synod level has become more effective. Committees have been reduced in number with a view to making their operation more effective. The Synod had little legislation of its own until the 1970s, and tended to follow the practice of the Free Church of Scotland. The Book of Procedure used by that church was also used in the PCEA from 1928, but its poor arrangement and inapproriateness in a number of areas has often caused difficulty. A Book of Procedure drafted by one member was commended as a useful adjunct to the Scottish Practice in 1983, and work continued on an official revision. The first part of this (covering Sessions and Deacons' Courts) was approved by Synod 1989. Along with a regularly up-dated Decision Book, this should streamline business and enable the spiritual well-being of the church to be furthered.

Paying for a minister

The stipend of a minister in the Presbyterian Church is not intended to be a figure that fully represents a professional remuneration, but is intended to enable him to live without undue anxiety. In 1840 a good stipend was $400/500 per year, and was far above the working man's earnings. In 1940, the PCEA still paid a stipend of $500 but it was less than the average worker received, so a fall in relative position had occurred. It appears that stipends as set by Synod from time to time fluctuated between 60 and 70% of average male earnings 1950-1962 and 1980-89, being currently about 70%. During the years 1963-79 they were generally 55-60%. The stipend usually has been 10-20% less than in the constituent churches of the PCA, but the gap has now closed. A manse (or manse allowance) is provided. Some churches, such as the PRC, do not favour the church owning manses, and so they provide a larger stipend related to average earnings, and the minister provides his own manse. A non-contributory superannuation plan was introduced in 1967, and Long Service Leave, currently one week per year of service, was introduced in 1974. These are financed by a levy on all congregations.

Church property

The PCEA is really quite well off as far as property is concerned. Only one congregation has commercial debt as at 1988. Some resources are under-utilised but there is growing awareness of the need to use what we have to the maximum furtherance of the Gospel. The oldest PCEA church building is at Geelong, with St George's a close second and Maclean in third place. The 1960s saw several buildings erected: halls at Broadmeadow near Newcastle, at Port Macquarie and at Byaduk south of Hamilton, and also the purchase of the Macarthur Methodist Church in 1967 by the Hamilton Charge. In the 1970s Lismore erected a church and hall (1972) as did Taree (1977), while Maclean replaced the Chatsworth Church with a hall and book shop at Maclean (1975), Ulverstone built a multi-purpose church centre (1977) and St George's erected a retirement complex of 21 units at Lindfield. So far, the 1980s have seen Brisbane's purchase of the former PCQ church and hall at Kalinga (1983), the purchase of the Anglican Church at Mount Druitt Village in Sydney's west (1986), and the new church at Wantirna in the eastern suburbs of Melbourne (1987) with another planned for Narre Warren by 1990.

At Synod level, the story is not quite so satisfactory. Apart from Missions, the endowments for stipend assistance and church extension are minimal. A small sum is available for Training of Ministry, while Missions has endowments of about $150,000, most of which the donors have said must be invested and the interest only used.

It has often been the case that a legacy has been provided to enable the provision of a building, and in some respects this is more desirable today given that large and prosperous congregations are not easily gathered. The aim set at Synod 1988 was a new congregation every two years, and the almost immediate commencement in the southern suburbs of Sydney and in Narre Warren (Melbourne) is a good beginning.

Youth work

The Free Kirk Youth Fellowship began in 1938 with much of the impetus coming from Rev Neil MacLeod. It provided much benefit of a spiritual and social kind for many years.[19] It fell on hard times in the 1970s, but seems to be reviving. The distances are a problem, but transport today is easier than 50

19. Cf. J.E.Huckett in **Our Banner**, November 1964, pp.8,9 which covers the history from 1938-64; and the April 1988 issue of **The Presbyterian Banner** for the jubilee.

years ago. Every reasonable encouragement must be given the young people so that they meet others of like background, and so that they grow in the faith of the God of the covenant.

Education

The Presbyterian interest in cultivation of the mind is well known. Many PCEA folk have been and are teachers, either in state or private schools. Barry Bridges records:

Presbyterians were the first to introduce university-educated teachers, the first to employ professionally trained teachers, the originators locally of subject specialisation, a broad curriculum and regular use of teaching aids, were instrumental in starting adult education in Sydney and in its spread to important country towns, initiated the public library movement, commenced the first ragged school, and published the first primer for Aborigines in a vernacular. Although not the first with infant schools they espoused and advanced early childhood education. Presbyterian teachers were with exceptions, exponents of teaching for understanding, cumulative assessment and unrehearsed examination.[20]

In the light of this kind of background, one would expect the PCEA to continue to be interested in education. The small size of the denomination limits the possibility of direct involvement in the ownership of educational establishments, although one hopes this may come in God's good time, but the warm-hearted Biblical teaching the PCEA espouses should encourage young men and women not to be afraid of learning but to learn and study for Christ, since it is his world.

Conclusion

The PCEA appears well placed to play a constructive role in the development of the Presbyterian and Reformed Faith in Australia. By the grace of God she has survived down through the years, and is now more aware of her heritage of full-orbed Biblical faith and practice. She is able to relate to other Reformed bodies with an increasing level of maturity (see page 385ff). Despite her frequent failure to grasp the opportunities in obedience to Christ, the bush still burns and is not consumed. The PCEA, considering its trifling size, has had an influence for good out of all proportion. That may be some justification for the stand taken in 1846 and 1864/65 and subsequently. But she cannot look back at a golden age. This history shows there was no such time, although it indicates something of the great revival in the Reformation of the 16th century, the Covenanting period, and the age of the Scottish Disruption and the resurgence of the Reformed Faith in the Netherlands last century. We look back to learn but we press forward to obey. Our heritage is not a Scottish or a Dutch tradition but the everlasting Gospel of our Lord and Saviour.

20. B.J.Bridges, The Presbyterian Contribution to Education in New South Wales (PhD Thesis, 1985) pp.1,2.

30: PCEA MISSION WORK

With the kind permission of Dr Andrews I have made very liberal use of his excellent article on PCEA mission work in **From The Frontiers,** *1987 issue.*

After the unions of the 1860s, a very depleted band of ministers and congregations was left to carry on the full reformation testimony. Nevertheless, the PCEA Synod of 1866 ordered a collection to be taken for 'Missions to the Heathen'. This interest was maintained, and in the 1870s support was given to several Chinese evangelists in Formosa. It appears the interest in Formosa was encouraged by George Soo Hoo Ten (1848-1934). Soo Hoo Ten led a mission to the Chinese in Sydney for some 30 years. He was ordained in the Church of England (deacon 1885, priest 1898) and had a very successful work among market gardeners and later on in the opium dens. It appears that he was officially retired about 1913, but then identified with the PCEA because of its Scriptural principles. He was always in his accustomed place in St George's, and was marked by his tall and stately appearance, silk hat, stick and gloves. A devout man, he maintained a keen interest in his kinsmen until his death.[1] At the Synod of November 1881, it was resolved to support the Chinese Mission of the Presbyterian Church of England, the Indian Mission of the Presbyterian Church in Ireland, and the Jewish Mission of the Free Church of Scotland. Some support was also given to individual missionaries and native helpers in the New Hebrides. In Victoria, the church there began to support the *Spanish Evangelisation Society* in 1893. This was a society formed in 1855 by Mrs Maria D. Peddie, a member of the Free Church of Scotland. Support for this Mission continued into the 1930s, when it is assumed that the Spanish Civil War interrupted operations.

1. For Soo Hoo Ten see S.Judd & K.J.Cable, **Sydney Anglicans** (Sydney 1987) pp.149, 150; the entry in the **ADB**; obituary in **Our Banner,** March 1935, p.427 and picture in J.C.Robinson, **The Free Presbyterian Church of Australia,** (Melbourne 1947) p.163.

The size of the home church

With the establishing of friendly relations with the minority who continued the Free Church of Scotland after 1900, the Australian church began to support the missions of that church, a policy that has continued ever since. In looking at the Australian church's contribution to those missions, two period may be distinguished: 1900-1947 when funds alone were provided, and the years since when funds as well as personnel have been supplied. It must be borne in mind that the Australian church was and is small: in 1915 some 2,500 members and adherents were counted in 10 congregations served by six ministers, and the committed following was possibly only half.[2] Forty years later the number one would count as adherents was down, the number of congregations was the same, and the active following about the same. The expansion since the late 1960s has meant that there are now (1989) 15 or 16 congregations, but the country congregations are weaker today and the overall strength of the church is still not much above 1,000, with communicant membership around the 630 mark since 1971, though beginning to rise. It is obviously important that the support base grow in order to maintain support of mission work. Clearly, home mission work and overseas mission work are both important and the latter cannot be neglected in the interest of the former or vice versa.

The first half of the 20th century

This period embraced a number of notable events in the history of Australia. The attainment of nationhood by the Federation of Australian States, themselves the product of the original British Colonies, into the Commonwealth of Australia in 1900; World War I in which out of a population of five million some half million entered the armed services to sustain more than 350,000 casualties and 65,000 war dead; the Great Depression of the late twenties and early thirties; World War II with its disruption of personal lives and close deliverance from Japanese invasion; the post-war flood of immigration continuing for more than two decades to help swell Australia's population to over 16 million.

In 1904, $36 was forwarded to the Free Church of Scotland for Foreign Missions. The Seoni [Indian] Mission received special mention in 1909. Rev John Sinclair was appointed Treasurer for the Foreign Mission Fund in 1914, and was instructed to send the money in hand to Scotland to be equally divided between the Seoni and South African Missions. In 1916 he reported that $154 had been sent and an additional $106 collected. This also was sent to Scotland. In estimating the value of these givings it could be noted that the minimum stipend for a minister of the PCEA was $500 p.a. during most

2. Figures for NSW congregations are in **The Australian Free Presbyterian**, November 1917, pp. 57,58 and total 2,050 with Maclean (549) at the top of the list. This issue also includes names of some 300 men who enlisted in the War of whom more than 10% died. The basis of the statistics is not known, but it is evident only 10% of the following was in Melbourne and Sydney.

of the half century - about one fortieth of the 1989 level. In 1916 Miss Barbara McLean of Melbourne offered for mission service but was not able to proceed because of ill-health.

In 1918 an annual collection for Missions was appointed. In 1920 the claims of the South African field were commended to church members and thereafter the three fields (India, South Africa and Peru) were supported. Further, it was desired to 'undertake in whole or in part the salary of an accredited missionary on a Free Church field.' In 1924 $304 was remitted to Scotland and in 1927 $562. The amounts sent are not always specified, and it is evident from the records of the Women's Missionary Societies that their contributions to particular fields were not entered in Assembly records but transmitted direct either to Scotland or to missionaries on the field.

Women's Missionary Societies

The work of the Women's Missionary Societies merits special mention. The first was formed in Geelong in 1911 following the visit of Rev Donald Maclean of Edinburgh in 1910. The Society sent to the South African Mission in 1912 a box of dresses made up by its members along with additional materials, needles, cotton etc. so that African women and girls could be taught to sew for themselves. That same year the Geelong congregation gave $60 for the support of 'a Native missionary in South Africa'.

In October 1920 the St George's Women's Missionary Society was formed. In July 1923 another was formed in Maclean followed by Barrington in 1924 and Wauchope in 1927. The Assembly, taking note of the valuable contribution the ladies could make, had resolved in 1925 on the motion of Revs John Sinclair and Malcolm Ramsay 'that Women's Missionary Societies be formed in all congregations'. The Societies met monthly or quarterly. They received and despatched missionary information, adopted orphans in India, sponsored students in training to be teachers, nurses or national pastors, raised funds to help erect school and church buildings, provide hospital accommodation or equipment on the fields, and supply protective foodstuffs such as milk powder and vitamin preparations to combat mal-nutrition. It would be difficult to assess the blessings experienced and the benefits imparted through the activities of these missionary-minded ladies through the years - activities twice blessed like Shakespeare's mercy, 'blessing him who gives and him who takes'.

To illustrate the point reference may be made to Rev Prakash Kumar, adopted by the St George's Women's Missionary Society in 1936 at the age of two and supported through childhood, school and college training to become a pastor to his own people and the senior minister on the Indian field today. Dr Andrews experienced the prayerful and practical support of the

427

same Society which not only supplied medical and surgical equipment for his work in South Africa, but also, through the generosity of one of its senior members, Mrs Margaret Gillies, provided most of the money needed to erect the church and clinic buildings at Jafta, and through friends of Miss Marjorie Davis that needed for the Tyusha church and clinic - some $1,500 in the former case and $1,200 in the latter.

It may also be noted that the same Society initiated Gift Afternoons or Evenings once a year, a practice followed by some other Societies and still carried on by all three Societies on the Manning River. In 1930 the amount thus raised was $56 and in 1950 $800. In the final year of active operation before it was replaced by the Congregational Missionary Society, the St George's WMS handed over $1,100 to the Synod Treasurer. Carefully kept minutes of the meetings of the Societies make stimulating reading.

The years from 1948 to the present
During this period personnel as well as funds were provided. There had been volunteers earlier in the century. Miss McLean has been mentioned. In 1920 Malcom Ramsay, then a student in Edinburgh, wished to open a mission in Russia but the Assembly advised him to complete his preparations for the regular pastoral ministry. Rev Isaac Graham offered for foreign service in 1925 but the need of the church in Australia led to the offer being deferred. Rev Joseph Harman in 1932 applied to serve in Peru but there were insufficient funds to send him. From late 1931 to 1933, Miss Barbara McLean worked as a missionary to aboriginals, first at Baryulgil (90 kms from Grafton) then at Burnt Bridge near Kemsey. Conditions were poor and the finance was not available, so the work was discontinued. Miss McLean married Mr Robert Muir, a widower and elder at Geelong. Miss Sarah Harriss (died 1972) of the Melbourne congregation applied in 1938, trained as a Bible Woman at the Melbourne Bible Institute, but became involved in National Service and resigned in 1943.

South Africa
Rev Dr J.Campbell Andrews became the first foreign missionary of the PCEA. He had been ordained in October 1946 to serve in the South African mission field of the Free Church of Scotland. After delays in securing a passage he sailed with his wife and daughter Elspeth in December 1947 to begin work in the Pirie District of the South African Mission in January 1948.

With the support of his wife, and later Mrs S.A.Colville, he engaged in pastoral and medical work from 1948 to 1964 inclusive. This period saw the increase of preaching centres from 10 to 19 and a proportionate increase in church membership and givings. Seven new church buildings were erected and two old buildings purchased and renovated and equipped to serve as churches, the one at Mngqusha also serving as a clinic. Most of the money required for the new buildings at Jafta, Tyusha, Mxaxo and Izihlahla came from Australia as well as donations towards translating and publishing the Psalms in Xhosa metre, based on J.A.Jalobi's work, in 1964.

Medical clinics conducted weekly in the District made regular use of five church buildings and occasional use of two others. Malnutrition and pulmonary tuberculosis were rife in the early 1950s but were increasingly brought under control by voluntary and government relief agencies, use of BCG vaccine and provision of anti-tuberculosis drugs. Later mobile X-ray teams operated in the area and mobile clinics were formed to treat the follow up positive cases. Patients seen at the Mission Clinics who required hospital treatment were conveyed either to Gray Hospital in King William's Town or to Mt Coke Methodist Mission Hospital. Regular donations from Australia for the 'Milk Fund' made it possible to provide powdered milk and vitamins to malnourished children and treat patients unable to pay.

The Andrews' second period of service was from 1970 to 1975. Dr Andrews was seconded to Mt Coke Hospital which was then in desperate need of doctors and was in process of being enlarged from 150 to 300 beds and transferred to the Ciskei Department of Health. Fully subsidised by the Republic of South Africa's Department of Health, it served an extensive area, including the Pirie and Knox Districts, with its large Out-patients Department, ten outlying clinics and two Health Centres (at Zwelitsha and Dimbaza). Granted a seat on the Mission Presbytery Dr Andrews was able to serve as Interim-Moderator of Burnshill District while Rev Albert Sleip had furlough for one year and of Knox District for three years while Rev Bryce Taho took study leave to obtain a B.A. degree.

Mrs S.A. (Lex) Colville(1902-1987), a stalwart of the Maclean congregation who had been widowed in 1953, offered for missionary service. She was accredited as an honorary missionary of the PCEA and worked in the Pirie District of Ciskei, commencing in July 1955. She later received assistance for transport and travelling but largely maintained herself for 25 years of devoted service. She assisted Mrs Andrews with the work among the women and girls, but also initiated work in the heathen locations of Bulembu, Gwaba, Mamata and Ngcamngeni. In those areas she engaged in Bible teaching, and ministered to needy and under-nourished people with fruit and vegetables purchased in the municipal market. She also visited the sick and transported them to clinic or hospital, distributed clothing from Mission Boxes, and assisted bright but needy children to obtain secondary school and teachers college training. She was primarily a Bible-woman whose greatest concern was to reach the women and girls of the heathen areas. In all four places named above there are today organised congregations with permanent church buildings erected largely with funds provided by Mrs Colville and her Australian friends.

In 1982, when revisiting South Africa, she transferred the property at 22 Maitland Road, King William's Town, which had been left to her by Elizabeth Erskine, to the Free Church of Scotland to be used as a residence for missionaries. Her memorial is the transformed lives of those who came to know Christ through her teaching and example. She exemplified the truth of the Psalmist's words: 'And in old age, when others fade, they fruit still forth shall bring.' (Psalm 92:14)

Mrs Lex Colville

India

Helen Ramsay, daughter of Rev M.C.Ramsay, had from childhood desired to serve as a missionary and studied medicine at Sydney University to that end. Accepted as a missionary candidate in 1949, she graduated in 1952 and proceeded to Scotland for post-graduate experience at Raigmore Hospital, Inverness. She began her work in India in September 1955 and was in the Field for some 24 years until she retired in 1985. (The years 1970 to 1976 were spent in Australia caring for her parents.) Dr Ramsay took up residence in Taree where her father had ministered from 1937 to 1965.

It would be impossible to detail the scope of her services to the Indian people in Chhapara and Lakhnadon Districts. She twice relieved at Lakhnadon for a period of a year or more when she was the only doctor on the field, yet continued to visit Chhapara clinic weekly for the remainder of the time she was in Chhapara. For long periods she was the only European resident there. For eleven years she had charge of the orphans. On her return to India she initiated Community Health Work of a most helpful and imaginative nature in the Chhapara District. TEAR Fund at first fully funded the scheme but it is now substantially aided by the Mission Relief Fund of the PCEA, established through a gift of $85,000 by an anonymous donor in June 1981. The scheme virtually became a model project for similar Community Health Projects in India.

In 1981-82 Dr Ramsay was able to supervise the conversion of the orphanage at Chhapara to a small hospital and then enlarge that with the addition of two private wards, giving a total of 14 beds, and the addition of a well equipped Outpatients Department with large waiting room, dispensary, consulting and treatment rooms and a small emergency theatre. It has been a matter of great thankfulness that the PCEA has been able to provide such a capable and devoted missionary to maintain the noble tradition of other pioneer 'women who laboured in the Gospel' (Romans 16:12).

Sister Heather Beaton, who had applied to work overseas in 1961, served in India from 1963. She gave 13 years valued service in the Lakhnadon Hospital until she returned to care for her parents in 1976. Despite great difficulty in getting permission to resume work in India she was able to return in 1982 and assist Dr Ramsay at Chhapara until 1985. She now resides at Taree.

Peru

Angus Beaton (a distant relative of Heather Beaton) was received as a candidate for missionary service when in his final year at the Free Church of Scotland College in 1957. But he was asked by the Church in Australia to minister to the Richmond/Brunswick Congregation before proceeding to Peru in September 1960 with his wife Jean, herself a trained nurse.

Some missionaries past and present pictured at Taree, March 1989
From left: Helen Ramsay, John Graham, Elizabeth and Bill Graham of the Free Church in Southern Africa, Heather Beaton, Anna Sutherland, Campbell and Ruby Andrews

They served first in Lima, but mainly in Cajamarca, for a total period of eight years. Mr Beaton did extensive evangelistic work in the area involving much travelling, and was pastor of the congregation in Cajamarca where he opened a Bookroom for the distribution of Bibles and Evangelical Reformed publications. He furthered the Presbyterian focus of the work in Peru. Owing to great difficulties arising with the children's education, the Beatons returned to Australia at the end of 1968. Mr Beaton subsequently served the Ulverstone and Maclean Congregations, and accepted a call to a PCA Congregation in 1981.

Mr Hugh Varnes also served in Peru as a teacher. He was a trained Primary School teacher and had completed a course at Melbourne Bible Institute. His wife Roberta was a triple-certificated nurse and had also trained at Perth Bible Institute. They began work in Lima in 1965 where Mr Varnes taught in Collegio San Andres, but in 1968 were transferred to Cajamarca where he was ordained to the eldership of the Evangelical Presbyterian Church of Peru, which had developed from the Free Church Mission , and managed the Bookshop. He opened an Academy of English which was attended by pro-fessionals - teachers, doctors, lawyers, as well as university students who needed to keep abreast of publications in English. The Academy, however, was closed by Peruvian law. This enabled Mr Varnes to spend more time exhibiting and distributing literature at provincial fairs in the region, some 8 to 10 a year lasting for 8 to 10 days. The Varnes family returned to Australia at the beginning of 1975, in order that Mr Varnes might undertake training for the ministry.

A further link with Peru continues at the present since Rev William M. Mackay, who was Headmaster of Collegio San Andres 1966-1978, was appointed Principal of Presbyterian Ladies' College in Melbourne from 1986, and is an elder in the PCEA Melbourne Congregation. The Collegio is a school for some 700 boys founded in 1917 by the Free Church of Scotland.

Christian Witness to Israel

Almost from its inception the PCEA has been interested in what came to be known as Christian Witness to Israel. Visits from Mr Ernest Lloyd from 1953 onwards and from its Director, Rev Murdo MacLeod more recently quickened this interest with the appointment of Rev John Graham and his wife Katie to work in Sydney. They arrived in September 1979. A number of members of the Committee of CWI (Australia) are members of the PCEA, and increasing financial assistance has been voted by the Synod, especially in 1988 with the arrival of Anna Sutherland to assist in this difficult work. Anna has had 17 years experience in Jewish work and arrived in January 1989.

432

Joe Vuki, Leone Tupua and Iliki Kalonmira, 1988

Fiji

In 1976 Mr Sam Tamata, a Fijian residing in Britain who had served in the Army, commenced a four year course of study at the Free Church of Scotland College with a view to missionary service in his native land under the oversight of the PCEA. Completing his studies in May 1980, his British wife and the three children came to Australia and gave supply on the Manning and in Brisbane for a period. Mr Tamata had been ordained in August 1981, and in January 1983 the Tamatas left Brisbane for the Fiji Islands to commence the first indiginous Presbyterian and Reformed work in that land. Encouraging contacts were made and work done, but Mrs Tamata found it very difficult to adjust to such a completely different culture and there were health and family. The illness of her father in Scotland aggravated the situated and she and the children returned to Scotland for rest and recuperation at the end of 1984, and Mr Tamata in January 1985. As a long term commitment to the work was not possible, the first chapter in this work closed. Mr Tamata now serves a charge of the Free Church of Scotland. However, one of those much helped by Mr Tamata's ministry was Mr Leone Tupua. He left Methodism at the end of 1984 and has done an excellent work in conducting services and Bible Studies

433

while continuing in a very responsible position with Fiji Telecom. He has been able to visit the Australian church in 1985 and 1987, and was ordained to the eldership in 1985. He is a man who has imbibed the great Biblical truths and by God's grace we are sure he will continue a blessing. Several visits have been made to Fiji, and it is hoped to apply sound Scriptural principles to the building up of an indigenous church in that land.

Support of Mission work

In the 20 years to 1948 to 1967, the average annual amount given to Missions was 218% of the annual stipend for ministers. It fell back in the decade 1968-77 to about 160% and has continued to fall, no doubt reflecting the lack of personnel in the field of latter years. It ought to be a matter of prayer and planning that the Lord would provide suitable persons for the work of spreading the Gospel and of bringing the compassion of Christ to others.

A footnote

As a sidelight on the work of Missions, Sister Flora Macleod, who had served in India for a number of years to the close of 1975 on behalf of the Free Church of Scotland, soon after married the Missions Correspondent of St George's PCEA, and is now Mrs G.A.Neil of Sydney. The Superintendent of the Indian Mission for a number of years was Rev Ian McKenzie. An Australian, Mr McKenzie was directed to the Free Church of Scotland College by Rev M.M.Macdonald of the PCNSW, and subsequently married a sister of Professor Allan Harman's wife. Mr McKenzie now serves the Asian Outreach work of the Free Church in Glasgow. In early 1989, Barbara Stone, the daughter of a Free Church of Scotland minister, married Keith Schmidt, a member of the Brisbane congregation. Barbara had for some time served as a nurse at the Indian Mission.

Part Eight

MOVES IN THE MAINSTREAM

1945-1988

31: NEGOTIATIONS FOR A WIDER UNION 1945-1971

Moves to reiax the doctrinal basis

As early as 1922 the GAA established a 'Committee on the Church's Attitude to its Creed', but nothing much was done for some years. In 1938 the Committee was instructed to report to the next GAA on the Church's attitude to the Westminster Confession. Hitherto, the GAA had made two amendments to the text of the Confession: in XXIV 4 an exception had been allowed for the deceased wife's sister or the case of a deceased husband's brother (approved 1914), and in XXVII.4 a special provision for non-ordained persons to administer the sacraments was allowed for (1916). These had proceeded on the basis that the Confession was the publicly adopted statement of faith, but it could not be said that it was the personal confession of any but a small minority in the ministry, hence the desire to do something to bring the doctrinal position more into line with practice.

The Committee, under the guidance of Professor McLeish, brought a proposal to the 1945 GAA that a new Declaratory Statement should be adopted drawn in the main from the Articles adopted by the Church of Scotland in 1926.[1] The Westminster Confession would remain the nominal subordinate standard, but the Church's relationship to it would be further modified. It would be defined as containing 'the sum and substance of the Faith of the Reformed Church', and it was to be read in the light of a Declaratory Statement which gave power not only to modify forms of expression in the Confession but power to formulate other doctrinal statements and to define the relation of

1. For the text of the 1926 Articles of the Church of Scotland see J.T.Cox (ed), **Practice and Procedure in the Church of Scotland** (5th edition, Edinburgh 1964) p.366. The text of the Committee's proposal is in GAA Reports, 1945 p.133ff.

officebearers to them. Such statements had to agree with the Word of God and the fundamental doctrines of the Confession, but the Church was to be the sole judge of such agreement. While a positive summary paragraph of Christian belief was included, nowhere were the fundamental doctrines defined. Liberty of opinion on points not entering into the substance of the faith was also allowed.

The general effect was alleged to be definition and simplification so as to remove causes of misunderstanding and dissension, and to give emphasis to the positive message of the Church as well as to provide an effective instrument of discipline. In reality there is no reason to suppose the proposals, if adopted, would have had any significance other than freeing the church further from a fixed creed. McLeish was a liberal, who professed to maintain the doctrine of the Trinity. But from his perspective, the proposal provided the means by which the Church could 'be faithful to the new truth which God has revealed since the Westminster Confession was written' while still retaining the Westminster Confesssion.[2]

The proposal was considered for some years and had general support including from the then top legal adviser to the Church, Brian Fuller,QC. However, there were some who argued that the Church had no constitutional power to alter the existing Declaratory Statement, or, seeing the proposed new wording was not a restatement of doctrine, to make the proposed statement an addition to the Scheme of Union of 1901. This was the position of Wallace Archer and F.M.Bradshaw. In view of the division of opinion the Committee reported in 1951 that it did not propose to proceed further.[3]

Federal Union proposed 1945

In 1945 the Christian Unity Committee of the GAA reported that a conference of Methodist, Congregationalist and Presbyterian representatives held in Sydney in December 1942 had concluded:

That in view of the spiritual union which already exists between the three churches, negotiations be re-opened with a view to ultimate union; that an engagement be entered into to continue such negotiations until that end has been achieved; that, in the meantime, negotiations be opened with a view to the establishment of a Federal Union.[4]

The idea was that certain areas of work could be done co-operatively by means of a federal arrangement which would otherwise leave the polity and property of the participating churches untouched. As a method of growing

---

2. McLeish's address at the GAA was printed and a copy was bound with the copy of the GAA Reports I consulted in the Joint Theological College Library, Melbourne.
3. GAA Reports, 1951, p.79.
4. GAA Reports, 1945, p.130.

successfully into full union the plan had merit. It was approved by the Methodists and Congregationalists, but in 1947 three State Assemblies disapproved and two made no report. Only New South Wales gave approval in principle. Accordingly, the 1948 GAA resolved on a vote of communicant members, but three years later it was reported that nothing had been done, probably because the federal union proposals lacked definition.

Organic Union proposed 1954

The Methodists and Congregationalists decided to negotiate an organic union between themselves and by 1954 had worked out the Basis. It was then proposed in the Methodist Conference that an opportunity be given the Presbyterians, due to meet in GAA in September 1954, to participate. There was a positive reaction, although the following somewhat prophetic motion was proposed by F.M.Bradshaw.

Instruct the Clerk, in consultation with the Committee on Christian Unity, to advise the appropriate authorities of the Methodist Church and the Congregational Churches that the General Assembly, at the present juncture, while appreciating the action of these Churches in approaching the Presbyterian Church on the matter of union, sees no early prospect of a union embracing the Presbyterian Church of Australia being accomplished, and therefore would not feel justified in entering upon negotiations which would have the effect of postponing the further implementation of proposals provisionally agreed upon between the Methodist Church and the Congregational Churches for a union of those two denominations.[5]

The motion was lost 47 to 201, and the GAA resolved to seek a vote of lower courts and communicants 'on the desirability or otherwise of entering into negotiations with the Congregational and Methodist Churches with a view to corporate union on a basis to be agreed upon by the three Churches and to be submitted at a later date.'[6] The chief strategist for the opponents of union was Rev E.Wallace Archer, but he was not a member of the 1954 GAA. Bradshaw submitted a 12-point dissent which was adhered to by 11 others including Rev Robert Swanton of Hawthorn, (of which charge Bradshaw was Session Clerk), and Rev Hector Dunn, then of Tasmania. In theology Swanton was Reformed whereas Dunn was in the mainstream not without influence from Samuel Angus. But they were united in desiring to preserve the Presbyterian Church, and both ended up in the body which continued after the formation of the Uniting Church nearly 33 years later.

The results of the vote taken in 1955 appeared encouraging. Overall, 70% of votes in State Assemblies were favourable although, probably in reaction to Methodist dominance in that State, South Australia registered only 39% in the Assembly. The communicants' vote was 74.6% in favour. On analysis, the raw data in the Report shows a somewhat different picture as indicated

5. GAA, 1954, Minute 67.   6. GAA, 1954, Minute 82.

in the table which follows (the roll figures are for 1954 as stated in the *Year Book*).

1955 VOTING ON BEGINNING UNION NEGOTIATIONS

State	Membership roll	Votes cast	% of roll	% Yes	Yes % of roll
VIC	46,577	25,771	55.3	70.4	39.0
NSW	37,821	17,142	45.3	77.4	35.1
QLD	15,800	7,384	46.7	84.6	39.5
SA	3,301	1,574	47.7	57.4	27.4
TAS	2,263	1,156	51.1	69.3	35.4
WA	2,289	1,191	52.0	91.4	47.6
AUS	108,051	54,218	50.1	74.6	37.4

Draft Basis 1957

A draft Basis of Union was submitted to the 1957 GAA for the proposed 'United Church of Australia'. The existing subordinate standards of the three churches were relegated to 'an honoured place' while the polity was a re-working of the old 1919 Scheme. The key doctrinal section, the first paragraph of which is almost entirely taken from the Church of Scotland Articles of 1926, was as follows:

IV. The Faith of the Church

1. The United Church of Australia is part of the Holy Catholic or Universal Church; worshipping one God, Almighty, all-wise, and all-loving, in the Trinity of the Father, the Son, and the Holy Spirit; adoring the Father, infinite in majesty, of whom are all things; confessing our Lord Jesus Christ, the Eternal Son, made very man for our salvation; glorying in His Cross and Resurrection, and owning obedience to Him as the Head over all things to His Church; trusting in the promised renewal and guidance of the Holy Spirit; proclaiming the forgiveness of sins and acceptance with God through faith in Christ, and the Gift of Eternal Life; and looking for the consummation of the Kingdom of God in the return of Christ and the manifestation of His Glory in the world.
2. The supreme standard of the United Church is the Word of God contained in the Scriptures of the Old and New Testaments.
3. The subordinate standards of the United Church are the Creeds commonly called the Apostles' and Nicene.
4. The United Church holds in honour the Westminster Confession of Faith, the Savoy Declaration, and John Wesley's Forty-four Standard Sermons and Notes on the New Testament.
5. The United Church has the inherent right, as part of the Universal Church wherein the Lord Jesus Christ has appointed a government in the hands of Church office-bearers, free from interference by civil authority, but under the safeguards for deliberate action and legislation provided by the Church itself, to legislate, and to adjudicate finally, in all matters of doctrine, worship, government, and discipline in the Church; to frame or adopt its subordinate standards and doctrinal statements, to declare the sense in which it understands them, to modify the forms of expression therein, or to formulate other doctrinal statements and to define the relation thereto of its office-bearers and members, but always in agreement with the Word

440

of God and the fundamental doctrines of the Christian faith contained in its standards and doctrinal statements, of which agreement the Church shall be sole judge, and with due regard to liberty of opinion in points which do not enter into the substance of the faith.

In the draft Basis the aim of the United Church to foster the spirit of unity was expressed. The eventual inclusion of the Anglican Church was in the mind of some.

A minority raised the competency of the GAA to deal with the report given that the Church had no constitutional power to unite with other churches, but was defeated 56 to 214. Nevertheless, there were others not happy with the form of the proposals. A motion by Rev Alan Dougan unsuccessfully sought to disapprove them. The final result was the acceptance of the report (without approving it) and the appointment of a Joint Commission of not more than 7 members from each of the three negotiating churches to work further on a Basis, and to prepare and circulate relevant study material.

Of the seven Presbyterians appointed in 1957 only two were to continue right through: Rev Professor Davis McCaughey and Rev J.C.Alexander, both of Melbourne. McCaughey was Convener of the Presbyterian section, while A.Harold Wood and J.D.Northey, both of Melbourne, fulfilled a similar role for the Methodist and Congregational representatives. The strong Melbourne influence undoubtedly was a factor in the eventual strong support for union by Presbyterians in Victoria as compared to New South Wales.

First Report 1959

The Joint Commission produced its first report under the title *The Faith of the Church*. It was presented to the GAA in September 1959. The following outlines the contents.

THE REPORT.

Introduction.

PART I: THE FAITH WE HAVE RECEIVED.
A. Concerning Statements of the Church's Faith:
    1. The Holy Scriptures
    2. Creed and Canon
    3. Confessions at the Reformation
    4. Forms of Confession in Evangelical Christianity.
B. A New Awareness of the Church.
    Some factors leading the Churches in the 20th Century to a new awareness of the Church:
    1. A Biblical Perspective
    2. A Secularised Western World
    3. A World Mission
C. The Call to Confess Our Faith.
    1. The Way to Confess Our Faith
    2. What We Must Do

PART II. THE FAITH WE AFFIRM IN COMMON.
A. Where the Church's Faith is to be Found.
    1. The Holy Scriptures
    2. The Creeds of the Ancient Church
    3. The Confessions of the Churches of the Reformation
    4. The Affirmations of the Evangelical Revival
B. Our Confession:
C. Our Commitment:
    1. Our Commitment in Faith
    2. Our Commitment in Love
    3. Our Commitment in Hope

The GAA asked for comments from State Assemblies and Presbyteries. Work was slow and nothing much was heard until March 1963 when a further report was issued together with a proposed Basis of Union which had taken account of comments on the first report, though the nature of the comments has not been preserved.

Second Report and Proposed Basis of Union 1963-1964

The striking thing about this second report was the proposal to introduce bishops into the new church on its formation. The argument ran that bishops were useful on pragmatic grounds such as providing supervision and continuity, but how would such bishops be recognised? The idea of the majority was for a concordat with the Church of South India, formed by a merger of several groups including Anglicans. Assuming the Anglicans recognised the episcopal consecration of the CSI, a wider union in Australia in the future would be facilitated. To those who, like Dr McCaughey, were given to diplomacy, and to those like Professor Alan Dougan of Sydney, who was 'High Church' in his Presbyterianism, this was an attractive scheme, and was supported by George Yule and Colin Williams, Presbyterian and Methodist theological teachers who were consultants to the Commission.[7]

This mad-cap proposal, so full of potential to destroy union, was strongly opposed by Dr Alan Watson, another Presbyterian member. He saw what any clear-eyed Presbyterian should have seen - that any introduction of bishops was the way to guarantee insurmountable objections from Presbyterians. Three Presbyterians, including J.P.Adam, a lawyer and only non-ministerial Presbyterian member and Professor W.Cumming Thom of Sydney - a liberal but not High Church in outlook, signed a reservation on this part of the Report and were joined by four Methodists, including Dr Wood. Surprisingly, the Congregationalists all voted for the idea since, influenced by Dr Northey, they were concerned that union might not be possible if they did not agree to bishops even though they are so alien to

---

7. Personal conversation of the author with A.Harold Wood, 22.12.1988.

Congregational polity. Congregationalists were relaxed on their principles and did not require exact subscription to a creed. Methodists did not claim divine right for their method of church government. However, Presbyterians had ever held that the basic principles of church order are laid down in Scripture and are binding. The modern idea that Scripture is not definite on the subject or approves of radically diverse polities was behind the thinking of those who proposed a virtual sell out to the three-fold order of ministry espoused in episcopacy.

The overall content of the Report, which was received by the GAA in September 1964, is outlined as follows: [8]

SUMMARY OF PROPOSED BASIS OF UNION 1963/64

A "preface" states that broadly the Uniting Churches have:—
(a) Failed to bear full witness.
(b) Despite this failure, God has blessed and preserved them.
(c) "They have been led to undertake together, God helping them, to enter more fully into the Churches' life and faith and worship."

The union is said to be characterised by a justifying faith.

1. DECISION TO UNITE. The Churches enter into a union under the name "The Uniting Church in Australia."

2. CONCORDAT WITH CHURCH IN SOUTH INDIA (C.S.I.). Expressing Unity outside national barriers and an "agreement in faith and order and a membership and ministry mutually recognised and interchangeable." (The C.S.I. will provide the line of episcopal authority.)

3. GENERAL ARTICLES. Stated under sub-headings.

    1. *Doctrinal Standards.* Declares the Holy Scriptures Rule of faith and life; confesses the Catholic faith in the Apostles' and Nicene Creeds and the Chalcedonian Decree; affirms the doctrine of salvation by the grace of God alone and justification by grace through faith; acknowledges the witness borne in certain listed documents.

    2. *Sacraments.* It will recognise the sacraments of baptism and Holy Communion, and include certain listed elemental characteristics. Celebration of communion will be limited to ordained and authorised clergy.

    3. *Church Membership.* The Uniting church will accept into membership all existing members of churches in full standing, thereafter it will be by baptism and some form of confirmation.

    4. *Concerning the Ministry* all existing ordained ministers will be accepted in full standing, but after union terms are set out of the three-fold ministry — preaching, administration of Sacraments, pastoral care.

    4.1 *Presbyters* will be ordained within an episcope by the laying-on of hands by bishops and presbyters and will be known as presbyters (present day Ministers).

8. Taken from **The Other Side** (Melbourne 1965) pp.35-36.

4.2 *Bishops* will be appointed, and within the prescribed episcopate exercise the functions of a bishop as understood for an episcopal church. The C.S.I. will provide the inaugural link with the episcope in consecrating bishops. All subsequent consecrations will be by the laying-on of hands by at least three bishops and three presbyters.

4.3 *Deacons.* Existing elders will be accepted with life tenure as Deacons, but after Union the role of elder will cease. The deacons will be ordained for limited service. They will usually be elected by the congregation, subject to the Council of the Congregation, and may be either men or women. Ordination by laying-on of hands by a presbyter or a bishop.

4.c *Ordination Vows* will be required of all ordained persons who must accept the fundamental Catholic Faith, and the Order of the Uniting Churches.

5. COUNCILS OF THE CHURCH. These are listed briefly.

   (a) *Ecumenical Councils,* expressing the episcope of the Catholic Church, in all walks of life, remain within W.C.C. and other ecumenical movement bodies.

   (b) *The National Council* (equivalent to General Assembly) of bishops (one presiding), presbyters, deacons and others appointed by synods. Will deal with matters similar to our General Assembly.

   (c) *Synods.* A State or Regional Council presided over by a bishop and having jurisdiction over a specified area.

   (d) *The Diocesan Council* replaces the presbytery (broadly).

   (e) *Council of the Congregation* will be frequent meetings of the congregation to foster love for one another, and to share in responsibility for the wider work of the church.

      (i) *The Parish Council* will be a body of the deacons and others assisting the presbyter.

      (ii) *The Church Meeting.* A meeting of all congregational members under presidency of a presbyter.

6. ORDERS OF WORSHIP. To continue as at present until the Uniting Church develops its own forms.

7. REVISIONS OF STATEMENTS OF DOCTRINE. The ruling Council of the Uniting Church may alter or modify or add to the Statements of Doctrine after a 75% vote, in a majority of Diocesan Councils.

4. INTERIM CONSTITUTION. Provision is made for the adoption of an interim constitution and then an eventual constitution, but this is not outlined.

5. A CONFESSING ACT. Upon entering into union there will be established an Act of Confession which is outlined in statement form in the Basis. This will be used at "all services of Inauguration or Recognition."

The GAA resolved to send the Report to lower courts for consideration. Comments or amendments of the Proposed Basis were invited and special attention was requested to the doctrinal implications, to the Concordat with the Church of South India, and to the point of view expressed in the reservation. Five GAA members dissented because they feared delay, and another 33 dissented against the union proposal itself.

A booklet *Towards Understanding* was published by the Christian Unity Committee in August 1965, and circulated chiefly in New South Wales. F.Maxwell Bradshaw, the Secretary of the anti-union Presbyterian Church Association in Melbourne, was the principal author of *The Other Side*, also issued in 1965, and circulated widely.

Rejection of the 1963-1964 Basis 1967

The Report received by the GAA in 1967 disclosed that none of the State Assemblies had approved the Concordat with the CSI and only 5 of the 52 Presbyteries, while 2 Assemblies and 26 Presbyteries clearly disapproved the introduction of bishops. Anglican observers had been present at the Joint Commission meetings since at least 1964, but it is understandable that the Christian Unity Committee had advised the Anglicans that it would not be helpful for them to become participants in the aimed at union.[9] The section on Baptism was heavily criticised, 12 Presbyteries rejected inclusion of the Chalcedonian Decree, there was an 'inescapable demand' for retention of office similar to eldership and for a distinct separation of spiritual and temporal oversight, and the Confessing Act was generally rejected as wordy and outmoded in language and thought forms. The heavy emphasis on confirmation was objected to and there were other lesser matters. All in all, it was a rather devastating criticism of the work of the previous seven years, and reaction in the other two denominations was also not without criticism.

The 1967 GAA disapproved of the introduction of bishops, and each of the three Churches wished reference to the Chalcedonian Decree[10] deleted and the term 'minister' used instead of 'presbyter'. None of the Churches was happy with the section on the Parish Council and the Church Meeting, while the GAA proposed a reworded section on the doctrinal standards and the preparation of a Confession of Faith within six years of the union.

Proposed Basis of Union 1970

The Joint Commission continued the process of revision and in March 1970 published what was to be very close to the final Basis. A well written

9. GAA Reports, 1967, p.96 and 1964, p. 92. The Church of Christ was also recorded as having observers in 1967. The proposal to include bishops in the 1963 Basis was known to some at the 1962 GAA, and Hector MacFarlane, a prominent elder, unsuccessfully moved that any proposed Basis be free of references to episcopacy (Minute 59).

10. In 451 the Council of Chalcedon issued its famous definition of the doctrine of the Person of Christ in opposition to Nestorianism (which denied the real unity of the two natures in the one person), and Eutychianism (which affirmed the unity of Christ's person but denied the distinction of natures). It is regarded as an orthodox Council by Protestants and Roman Catholics alike; however, its reference to Mary as 'Mother of God' [theotokos] has been regarded with some suspicion by many Protestants because of erroneous views about Mary's place in redemption which have been associated with it.

document of some nine pages and 18 sections,[11] the Basis places the Uniting Church within the 'faith and unity of the One Holy Catholic and Apostolic Church' (Sec.2) and thus uses the Confessions known as the Apostles' Creed and the Nicene Creed' as authoritative statements' (Sec.9). Neo-orthodox influence is seen in the statement on Scripture (Sec.5) where the Bible is described as 'prophetic and apostolic testimony, in which she [the Church] hears the Word of God and by which her faith and obedience are nourished and regulated.' There are also references to ministers and teachers studying 'the witness of the Reformation fathers' and listening to the preaching of John Wesley in his Forty-four Sermons (Sec.10). However, the doctrinal side is really rather open as the principles by which Scripture is to be interpreted are not expressed, thus there is freedom to move 'through contact with contemporary thought' (Sec.11). It is to be noted that Sections 11 and 18 are to be regarded as sufficiently protecting the liberty of the Church to change.[12] The revision of 1971 explicitly stated that adherence to the Basis 'allows for liberty of opinion in matters which do not enter into the substance of the faith' (Sec.14). So on the doctrinal side the practical effect of the Basis appears to be similar to that proposed in 1957.

As for the polity, a conciliar system is set out and thus it could be called presbyterian. However, the method of operation is not one which includes the checks and balances at each level of the presbyterianism of Scotland. The lower Assemblies have only the powers and functions committed to them by the highest council, the Assembly. The Appendices to the Basis left matters concerning the celebration of the sacraments and the ordering of the ministry to the first Assembly of the Uniting Church, but in Section 14 of the Basis recognised the various ministries in the participating Churches. Section 16 recognises the right of councils of the Church to 'acknowledge gifts among the members for the fulfilment of particular functions.' In this provision lies the potential to introduce an order of bishops.[13]

The final Basis 1971

The 1970 GAA received the Report. A number of criticisms were made, particularly by Professor Crawford Miller of Sydney. He was concerned about Scripture, the sacraments and ordination in particular. There were no requests for revision from the other two Churches, so the Joint Commission had only to deal with the Presbyterian concerns. A number of amendments were made and the slightly revised Basis was published in April 1971. The GAA of December 1971 received this Basis and remitted it to State Assemblies

11. Dr Davis McCaughey was largely responsible for the writing. His **Commentary on the Basis of Union** (Melbourne 1980) 107pp is helpful.
12. Basis of Union 1971 (Melbourne 1971) pp.7-8.
13. J.D.McCaughey, **Commentary on the Basis of Union**,p.97.

and Presbyteries under Barrier Act procedure and arranged for voting to take place in congregations in accordance with provisions embodied in a revision of the existing constitution which gave power to unite with other churches subject to certain provisions for minorities. In 1977 union was accomplished on the 1971 Basis.

Legal preliminaries to Union

Before looking in more detail to the events following 1971, it is desirable that something be said about the changes necessary to the constitution of the Presbyterian Church of Australia to enable union to take place.

The 1901 Scheme of Union provided safeguards for congregations which refused to acquiesce in any revision, restatement or abridgment of the Westminster Confession, but there was no clause explicitly giving the Church power to unite with other churches. Further, the GAA had final authority in matters of doctrine, worship and discipline, but not in respect of church government. Also, as we saw earlier, there was no power to change the Declaratory Statement and therefore modify the Church's relationship to the Confession.

Of course it was possible for the Church, considered as a company of persons professing and practising the Christian faith, to join any other Christian fellowship. But the Property Trust was subject to the conditions upon which it had been created. In other words, the Church as a divine society had not been incorporated but it had arranged by Acts of Parliament to form corporations to hold property and for similar purposes. Unless the Church was prepared to walk away from its property to enter union with others, it needed to secure a revision of its constitution so as to have power to unite. From at least 1954 there was also a body of opinion in favour of adopting a national structure in which the federal arrangement would disappear, and the six state churches become synods of one church. Some took the view that such a structure would be necessary to enable union, although in this they were mistaken.[14]

The 1963 GAA directed the Code Committee 'to prepare a basis of corporate union of the six State Presbyterian Churches, which basis was to include power to amend the subordinate standard and the declaratory statement, and also, subject to due and proper safeguards, to enter into union with other churches.'[15] A draft was prepared and sent to State Assemblies and Presbyteries for comments and suggestions. There was very general support and in 1967 the GAA sent the proposed constitution to State Assemblies, and through them, to Presbyteries, under Barrier Act procedure for approval or

14. F.M.Bradshaw, **Basic Documents on Presbyterian Polity** (Melbourne 1984)p. 102.
15. GAA Reports, 1970, p.113

447

disapproval. The result, as reported to the 1970 GAA, was that 42 of the 54 Presbyteries and all the State Assemblies approved the proposal. Accordingly, the GAA gave approval and instructed State Assemblies to seek the necessary enabling legislation. This was secured to an extent sufficient to enable union to be competent in 1971, and that section of the new constitution was brought into effect at the close of the year.

We turn now to the content of the legislation.[16] Part I set out the doctrinal constitution in similar terms to the 1901 Basis except that there was a general power of change including amendment or replacement of the Westminster Confession and Declaratory Statement, subject to the same 60% approval level as in the 1901 Basis. Part II set out matters of church government under the national constitution. Part III dealt with union with other churches. It prescribed Barrier Act procedure and 60% approval as previously, and required a vote to be taken of communicant members 16 years of age and over prior to the final General Assembly vote on such union. A procedure was set out, including two questions to be asked of communicants, and provision was made for a Property Commission to handle property matters. As far as congregational property was concerned, if one third or more of voters in a congregation expressed desire to remain in membership of the PCA, they retained the property. As for central funds, the Property Commission was to have regard to the need of a continuing church for a centre for theological training, administration and at least one school for boys and one school for girls in each state where there was more than one at the time of union. These were the major provisions.

An important provision in the Act enabled Part III only to be enacted, thus enabling union with other churches but leaving other matters unchanged. From the unionist side this provision was an advantage since they were optimistic of the outcome of a vote for union about the time the new constitution would be ready. On this basis the other provisions would be redundant. Further, they were concerned about the time element. Should any State delay or refuse to pass the legislation because of concerns related to Parts I or II, this could delay union. On the other hand, Bradshaw, the expert in this field of law and opposed to union, did not want the new constitution since he anticipated a small continuing church would find the national provisions unworkable, nor did he want the continuing church left with a constitution which gave wide powers of change which might be misused in the future. However, he was keen to see union take place lest delay lead to weakening of the anti-union forces, and so long as there were good provisions for minorities he was prepared to go along with the rest of the Code Committee, of which he was a member.

16. GAA Reports, 1970, pp.115-123.

F.Maxwell Bradshaw MA,LLM

It might be worth noting in this connection that Maxwell Bradshaw was descended from an English Puritan family with law as one of its main interests. A member at Hawthorn, a congregation going back to the older solid Presbyterianism,[17] he became an elder in 1941. This was some years after he had been asked by several of the veterans of the the earlier church union battle (Rev D.A.Cameron, Rev John Gray, Rev F.A.Hagenauer and Rev John Gillies) to take a special interest in legal matters bearing upon the Presbyterian Church in anticipation of trouble to come. Bradshaw developed his practice as a barrister in the equity/trust field. He took special interest in the Free Church Case of 1904 and the experience in Canadian Presbyterianism. He was active with John Gillies, Robert Swanton and others, including FPCV ministers Robinson and Allen, in the Calvinistic Society formed in the late 1930s. It was his knowledge and ability which obtained the *Free Presbyterian Church Property Act* from the Victorian Parliament in 1953 so enabling the union of the FPCV with the PCEA. In 1959 the GAA appointed him procurator (senior legal advisor) at which time he indicated he would seek to serve faithfully and well but would not preside over the dissolution of the PCA. Nor did he. It was his legal acumen which was largely responsible for the continuing Presbyterian Church surviving in such good shape as far as constitution and property are concerned. The uniting element did not have anyone with his depth of knowledge in one of the most intricate branches of the law. He is the author of the standard text, *The Law of Charitable Trusts in Australia* (1983).

17. F.M.Bradshaw, **Rural Village to Urban Surge** (Hawthorn 1964) gives the history.

449

Provision for minorities

These provisions were modelled on the combined effect of the Free Church Case and the Churches (Scotland) Act, 1905, but also took into account deficiencies in the operation of the said Act as found by experience and described in *The Free Church of Scotland 1843-1910* written as a vindication of the Free Church by Alexander Stewart and J.Kennedy Cameron.[18] The object was to obtain just and equitable terms. It was thought that generally speaking less than one-third of members would be unable to carry out a congregational trust, and in that event the property would go to the Uniting Church. In Scotland the proportion (including adherents) had been the same, although the fact figures were taken at the time of the union rather than after the victory in the House of Lords was prejudicial. In Canada in 1925 congregational property was retained only if a majority voted to continue. As to central funds, something over 20% of the Free Church of Scotland's central funds were retained by the Free Church minority under the Churches (Scotland) Act. It is thus not very accurate for former GAA Clerk, L.Farquhar Gunn, to state: 'For all practical purposes the report of the Royal Commissioners was a reversal of the House of Lords' decision, while admitting the strict legality of the judgement.'[19]

The questions

In drawing up the amended constitution, the questions to be asked of communicants prior to a final decision to unite were specified.[20] One question could have sufficed but the Code Committee, on which non-unionists were a minority (Bradshaw and Rev Ross Williams) decided two would be best. The first dealt with the general principle: *'Do you desire this congregation to become a congregation of the church which may result from the proposed union?'* The second dealt with the legal consequences: *'Should the required majority vote for union be obtained in presbyteries, State General Assemblies and the General Assembly of Australia, do you desire to remain in membership of any Presbyterian Church of Australia continuing to function on the present basis?'* There was little debate on the subject. Better drafting was possible, but any suggestion of deliberate lack of clarity, whether in the interests of unionists or non-unionists, is without foundation.[21]

18. Alan W.Black, in his generally accurate and valuable article 'Some Aspects of Religion and Law: The Case of Church Union in Australia' in **Religion** (1986) †16 pp.225-247, does not allow for the deficiencies in the operation of the Churches (Scotland) Act, but rightly recognises the Australian provisions were 'if anything, more generous'. (p.229) They were more generous because of the need to aim at equity.

19. Ian Breward (ed), **The Future of Our Heritage** (Uniting Church Historical Society 1984) pp.14,15.

20. As a consequence the second vote (1973) took place on identical questions to the first vote (1972), a point missed in Ian Breward, **Australia: 'The Most Godless Place Under Heaven'?** (Melbourne 1988) p.65.

21. See the GAA Code Committee's statement in **Australian Presbyterian Life** August 12, 1972. I also confirmed this with both F.M.Bradshaw and L.F.Gunn, January 1989.

32: THE CONTINUING PRESBYTERIAN STRUGGLE
   1972-1988

In assessing the union struggle and the subsequent history of the continuing Presbyterian Church, it is important to realize that there was no one unified position among the anti-unionists. The same was true for the unionists except that few evangelical ministers were unionists.[1]

Prominent unionist ministers included Scott McPheat and Professor Ian Gillman in Brisbane, Archibald Grant and C.M.Dyster in Sydney, Gordon Powell of Scots Church in Melbourne and the whole faculty at the Theological Hall of the PCV. The overwhelming proportion of ministers in other states were pro-union.

The articulate anti-unionists were mainly those of a conservative (ie reformed or evangelical) theology. The best researched material was that of the *Presbyterian Church Association* in Melbourne. Maxwell Bradshaw was the intellectual powerhouse of this Association and was himself a Calvinist of the old school and on close terms with the PCEA. In the PCAssn literature, most of which he wrote, he did not aim to dot the 'i's or cross the 't's of the Confession, but his historical and theological skills were employed effectively so that the PCAssn literature gained wide circulation beyond Victoria and rallied people of diverse theology to the defence of the Presbyterian Church.

---

1. The best analysis of the different positions known to this writer is by Helen Clements in The Presbyterian Struggle 1970-1977 (PhD Thesis, University of NSW, 1983)pp215-221. I have also spoken with various people involved including Revs. Norman Monsen, Dr Neil MacLeod, J.J.T.Campbell, Professor Crawford Miller, H.A.Stamp, L.Farquhar Gunn, G.G.Powell, E.R.Pearsons and Mr F.M.Bradshaw. I was myself a member of the PCV only until 1968.

The PCAssn was the best organised anti-union group. Its Public Relations Officer was Charles Homer Fraser, a retired businessman and elder who has been described as 'an armour-plated bull-dozer'[2] because he was ready and willing to take any amount of flak. Sometimes he was even an embarrassment since his enthusiasm easily overstepped the limits of good order. He was the full-time, unpaid advocate of the anti-union cause and had significant influence in the Victorian country congregations which stayed out of union. Financially, the PCAssn was well supported by donations from many ordinary people. There were also others, such as Sir Robert Knox of Toorak, Hunter Patterson of Conargo, and Walter Nixon of Heidelberg, ready to give generous assistance. Sir Lyell McEwin, President of the South Australian Legislative Council, was also an active supporter.

The *Westminster Society* in New South Wales, which had received recognition by the PCNSW in 1948, had contact with the PCAssn. It had been formed to study and encourage Reformed worship, the background being the liturgical and high church influences which had arisen and concerned some. Its early leader was Rev T.P.McEvoy of Wentworthville. Although a small society it was not without influence in the union ferment. The rising influence of Reformed theology in the 1960s strengthened its interest in the whole Reformed heritage. Rev A.G.Kerr of Sutherland was its President for a time prior to the close of 1967 when he and some others left the PCNSW and formed the *Presbyterian Reformed Church*. The remaining members were not all Reformed in theology and many were concerned only for the major evangelical truths. Several publications were produced including several issues of *Presbyterians Today* written by Rev J.J.T.Campbell. There was no clear strategy. Rev George Morrow, President after Kerr, thought that defeat of union would be best for both Presbyterianism and Methodism.[3] He and others wanted to stop the union moves if possible and work for the purifying of the whole church. Others wanted to unload the liberals into the union and get on with reformation. So really the question was over the purity of the visible church. An influential sympathiser of the Westminster Society was Rev Neil MacLeod of Hurstville, a former PCEA minister. He was to play a rather public role in later developments.

The similar *Westminster Fellowship* in Queensland was also active against union. Rev Desmond Blake was its President and Rev G.C.Lake its Secretary. Rev F.W.F.White was an active supporter, while Samuel McCafferty of historic Ann Street Church in Brisbane was another opponent of union from the standpoint of conservative theology as was Hugh Gallagher in Townsville.

2. E.R.Pearsons to R.S.Ward, December 1988.
3. H.Clements, op. cit., p.48 quoting Morrow's letter dated September 27, 1972.

Another rather different element of anti-union opinion was the High Church group represented by two Sydney ministers, Professor Crawford Miller and Principal Alan Dougan. They considered that serious ecumenical effort must reckon with the Anglicans, and they had strongly supported the 1967 Basis with its explicit provision for bishops. Leaving aside that question, they were of the belief that the Basis of 1971, despite amendments secured through Crawford Miller's efforts, did not adequately conserve the Catholic and Reformed elements of the faith. Miller articulated concerns felt by a good number since the Basis of Union did indeed lack a definite creedal commitment such as Presbyterians were used to. The size of the group which supported Miller and Dougan was never tested. In the final washup some supporters entered the Uniting Church.

On the other hand there were those like Arthur Stamp in Melbourne who objected to the provision for bishops that was implicit in the Basis of Union. They believed that in general the Spirit of God was more free to act through the local parish ministry rather than through the episcopal system. Further, they were concerned that the doctrine of Scripture was weak - there being no unequivocal commitment of ministers to the truth taught in Scripture. Any sincere man, whether of liberal or conservative theology, who professed to regard Scripture as containing authoritative revelation, could hardly be content with such an imprecise and cavalier approach.

The largest opposition group might be called 'the silent minority' since they did not do much in the way of circulating printed material objecting to the union. They were variously called the 'Bagpipes and Haggis Brigade', 'the Clan and Club' and similar names although basically they were traditional and cultural Presbyterians of several flavours and emphases who were not convinced there were compelling reasons for organic union and who did not consider the Presbyterian Church had played out its role in the life of the nation. There were many of these in New South Wales.

In earlier times many in this category might have been called 'moderates' and in their general approach they certainly gave attention to good order and traditional procedures, and in their teaching seemed to lay the most stress on respectability and discharge of social duties. Many were members of the Masonic fraternity. They were different from the Scottish moderates in that those were closely tied to the Confession of Faith as a condition of receiving their stipend, whereas the Australians considered themselves to have liberty on most matters of belief so long as nothing outrageous was said from the pulpit. Many of them would have been concerned over the effect on church polity of the Basis of Union, but theological points were not their forte. They relied on arguments put forward by others, plus their deep feeling that it was not sinful, as the unionists said it was, to continue as a Presbyterian, nor was there anything wrong in believing aspects of one's own denomination were superior and worth preserving while always being ready to fellowship with other churches without actual organic union.

Some were not strongly anti-union in principle. They were opposed to union on pragmatic grounds: the time and the method were not right. A union by revolution and upheaval which would leave a trail of damage was not on. Rev E.R.Pearsons, later the very capable Clerk of the Assembly of the PCV, was of this mind. 'The churches prior to the vote were co-operating and given time there would have been a natural evolution towards union.'[4] Pearsons himself was in the theological mainstream. Rev H.Arthur Stamp, a scholarly man describes himself as 'broadly evangelical';[5] conservative evangelicals would respect his sincerity but find great difficulty in regarding his theology as anywhere near orthodox Trinitarian Christianity. Rev Chris Goy, a born raconteur, was, like Rev Ray Russell, Rev Hector Dunn and Rev W.A.Loftus, somewhat influenced by Professor Angus, and gave major emphasis to the humanity of Jesus. Goy gathered big congregations although there were some who thought he was more interested in Freemasonry than the church, judging by his practice and his autobiography - A Man is his Friends'. Loftus had more depth than the others and showed greater conservatism when the heat was on following the stand against union. Yet all these men continued in the PCV.

In reviewing the pro-union arguments, it is evident many followed the leader, and that theology was not a big factor with ordinary people. There had been only rather limited doctrinal teaching for many years, so few knew of battles of long ago or cared to try and grasp the principles in the union discussions. Many took a pragmatic line and followed the lead of their minister. In some rural areas conservatism was overcome by thought of the problems of survival outside union. Many, like Gordon Powell of Scots Church in Melbourne, had a variety of Protestant denominations in the family background. He prepared a pamphlet early in 1982 entitled *How to Avoid a Tragic Split in our Beloved Church*. He sent samples to every parish minister in the Presbyterian Church and eventually some 75,000 copies were ordered and circulated. But apart from a reference to John 17 to establish his point that 'there is no life in a dismembered body', the argument was a pragmatic one and was correctly described as an appeal very much 'to numbers, size, status and the praise of this world.'[6] The Christian Unity Committee pushed union in *Presbyterians and Unity* while the PCAssn came out with a critique of the 1971 Basis and a 1972 edition of *The Other Side*. No one knew what would happen when voting took place.

4. E.R.Pearsons when Moderator General in The Age (Melbourne) November 30, 1987.
5. H.A.Stamp to R.S.Ward, January 20, 1989. Stamp's special interest is Hebrew.
6. Our Banner (PCEA Magazine) May 1972, p.2. Dr Powell kindly provided details of distribution. The first 45,380 were requested by 352 ministers.

The first vote - June 1972

There was a total of 1,447 congregations although, allowing for several congregations in one pastoral charge, there were about 800 parishes, quite a number without ministers. The vote was taken separately in each 'congregation', most ministers lobbying for their particular viewpoint though not necessarily excluding the opportunity for the other side to be heard. Everyone was surprised when the votes were tallied.[7] Several months prior to the vote, Rev Ross Williams in Melbourne had calculated that 60 charges in each of Victoria and New South Wales would continue (say, roughly 20% and 25% respectively), while 40 charges (say 30%) in Queensland would continue and a handful in other states. As it was, 73% of the members on the roll voted, and of these 75% were in favour of union (first question) but 39% of voters wished to stay in membership of a continuing Presbyterian Church. This meant that 50.8% of congregations would retain their property outside union if it occurred. Broken down by states it was evident that Victoria, the jewel in the Presbyterian crown, was strongly pro-union, but even there 30% of congregations would retain their property. New South Wales and Queensland were in a better position, just on half the congregations retaining their property in New South Wales.

The subsequent voting showed all State Assemblies in favour and 40 of the 53 Presbyteries, so there was no legal impediment to the GAA resolving on union. However, the cost would be high and it appeared that the opinion at grass roots was less favourable than in the courts of the Church.

The unexpected result of the congregational voting led many to the view that union was finished because the cost would be too high. Many alleged the questions were confusing, even deliberately framed to favour anti-unionists. But the official guide to voters prepared by the Code Committee had indicated all possibilities. Some professed to see no consistency in people answering in the affirmative to both questions. Rev S.A.Goddard, who entered the Uniting Church, responded to this: 'They express their desire for a union embracing the great bulk of the membership, and their intention, in the event of union by division leaving them with the choice of two viable churches, to remain on the Presbyterian side of the fence.'[7] Some had the aim of encouraging union but remaining in a 'purified' continuing Presbyterian Church.

The unionists generally came to favour the idea of a second vote on the basis that people would be more aware of the significance of the second question and would be aware of the approval of the Basis of Union in the

7. Letter to the Editor, **Australian Presbyterian Life**, August 12, 1972. An official statement from the Code Committee appears in the same issue. The estimates pre-vote of continuing charges are incorporated in the article (unsigned) by F.M.Bradshaw in **Our Banner**, op. cit., p.2.

State Assemblies and Presbyteries.[8] It was considered unlikely that the continuing cause would gain from a second vote. Maxwell Bradshaw saw no legal objection to a second vote since the vote on the second question established no rights until the GAA actually resolved to enter union. Moreover, Bradshaw himself was concerned that the continuing church might have difficulty carrying out the trusts if union took place on the basis of the first vote: there would be too few men to effectively employ the congregational property for the forseeable future and thus the Courts could be called in as had Parliament after the Free Church decision in 1904. But a large body of opinion was hostile to union on a second vote. They held that rights had been established by the first vote and could not be taken away by a second vote. The hope of these people was to force the abandonment of union because of the cost.

The second vote - September 1973

The GAA in Melbourne in May 1973 approved the Basis of Union 242 to 134, but held off approval of union itself. Instead, by a 251 to 100 vote, it was resolved to have a second vote later in 1973. The number who voted was down about 9,000 to 100,525 on this occasion. The percentage of voters who answered Yes to the first question actually declined in all states and Australia-wide was down from 75.6% to 72%. The main difference was on the second question where the percentage desiring to remain in any continuing church was down from 39.3% to 31.3% and thus only 36.8% of the 1426 reporting congregations would continue compared to 50.8% in the 1972 vote. St Stephens, Macquarie Street in Sydney, was the major congregation to change and was now uniting whereas Scots Church in Melbourne, despite its minister's promise to resign if it did not vote uniting, voted as before to continue. Dr Powell kept his word and resigned in 1975. Voting in State Assemblies found only 5 of the 6 in favour as New South Wales voted against. In Presbyteries the result was 42 of 53 in favour.

Again there was no legal impediment against the GAA resolving to unite, as constitutional requirements had been met. The rising opposition in New South Wales and the flurry of overtures seeking a halt, indicating legal opinion in favour of the first vote, and suggesting federal union as an option, might have given cause to reassess the position, seeing that about half the large New South Wales church would continue if union proceeded. However, these considerations were put aside, and on May 1, 1974, the GAA resolved, 230 to 142 (61.4%) to approve the Basis of Union. Rev Rhys Miller of Burwood (Melbourne) records: 'Then with some fence-sitters evidently deciding that the game was up, or casually slipping out to catch trains home,

8. Helen Clements, op. cit, p.51-52.

the actual motion to unite on a date some two years hence carried convincingly by 210 to 82.'[9] However, Miller is in error here. Clause 1 of the deliverance of the Christian Unity Committee which proposed union take place on or about June 2, 1976, was passed 236 to 133 (Minute 26), or by 64%. Time had dragged, there were another 17 clauses to the deliverance, and everyone knew many Queenslanders were booked to return home. It was only against the deliverance as a whole, moved later in the night, that the vote was down. In fact it was 201 to 82 (71%) - see Minute 42.

May 1, 1974 - the day of the break

When the decision on Clause 1 agreeing to unite took place, a Protest signed by 13 ministers (including Norman Monsen, Samuel McCafferty and R.C. Russell) and 14 elders (including R.P.W.Jell of Brisbane) was submitted and read by one of the signatories, Rev K.J.Gardner of Queensland. It was brought on at this point because the Queenslanders had made travel arrangements on the assumption of a one day sitting and time was getting on. They objected to the union on the grounds that it involved a forsaking of the pledge to Scripture as the only rule of faith and practice, a forsaking of the Confession of Faith particularly the covenantal relationship of baptism, a downgrading of the pre-eminent place of the ruling elder, and also a cause of grievous division. They claimed as of right a separate existence henceforth but were willing for the sake of peace and good order to continue to meet in an undivided assembly and not take legal action, so long as no actions prejudicial to the (continuing) Presbyterian Church of Australia occurred.

The object was to safeguard the position of the continuing church against the uniting majority during the two or so years before union actually took place. From that point of view it was deserving of support. However, the objection was that the Protest had one inescapable implication which could not be avoided, namely, that it required the GAA to recognise the continuing PCA before that church actually assumed that position. Accordingly, the Clerk moved its rejection and his motion carried 272 to 83 (76.6%).

Upon the adoption of the whole deliverance dealing with union, the Moderator of the New South Wales Assembly, Rev Neil MacLeod of Hurstville, read the following dissent and protest:

I crave leave to DISSENT and I PROTEST that clause 1 and now clause 3 of this resolution just passed is unacceptable to those of us who in conscience cannot enter this union: and I lay on the table this PROTEST on behalf of those who elect to remain in the Presbyterian Church of Australia.

9. Rhys Miller, Calling and Recalling (Melbourne 1984) p.140. Miller conducted the 'Geneva Gown' question column in Australian Presbyterian Life for many years. He was an ardent unionist. The suspicion remains that the unionists' plan to delay the actual consummation of union was seen by some as a useful tactic to further weaken the anti-unionists, some of whom, however, ended up contributing to the delay by legal action.

In humble dependence on God's grace and the aid of the Holy Spirit, and maintaining the Confession of Faith and Standards of the Church as hitherto understood; it shall be lawful for us to adopt such measures as may be competent to us, for the continuance of the Presbyterian Church in Australia, to the advancement of God's glory, the extension of the Gospel of our Lord and Saviour throughout the world, and the orderly administration of Christ's House according to His Holy Word.

And we finally PROTEST before the Great God, Searcher of all hearts that we, and all that adhere to us, are not responsible for this schism in the Church or for any consequence which may flow from the enforced separation.

In humble submission to His Will we give this our testimony. To Him we commit our cause, and we pray that in the days to come, His richest blessing may rest upon the Church of our fathers, which Church we are resolved by His help to maintain.

And I invite all who adhere to this PROTEST, since there is not room in this place for two assemblies, to follow me to another place, namely, 46 Russell Street, 'The Amethyst Hall'. where we the continuining General Assembly of Australia shall resume the sittings of this House.

Of olden times that Bush flamed - nec tamen consumebatur.

Let no one say that We here stamped on the Ashes of that fire.

(Dissenters may sign at the 'other place' and these will appear in minutes.)[10]

There was ample Presbyterian precedent for this move. Those who voted for union repudiated or abandoned their vows, or at least committed themselves to the step of entering a union on a basis quite different from that to which they were committed as officebearers of the PCA. The Acts of Parliament permitted this step to be taken without loss of property provided a non-concurring minority was not deprived of a proper share in it. However, it was not a step that one who had vowed to 'assert, maintain and defend the doctrine of this Church' could take or vote for without a change in what he had vowed.

Thus, while the vote for union was lawful by Act of Parliament so far as the property was concerned, it did not alter the fact that those so voting were changing the position to which they had previously committed themselves by their ordination vows, and thus, *ipso facto*, they were no longer eligible to be regarded as bona fide officebearers of the PCA as

10. GAA Minutes, 1974, Minute 45. The Amethyst Hall minutes give few names and no record of signatures to the Protest. Estimates of the number who left range from 20 to 40, the probable number being 30. The last two lines were somewhat loosely derived by MacLeod from a passage in Samuel Rutherford's writings. The Protest proper is largely drawn from the Canadian experience of 1925.

constituted in 1901. The statement in the GAA deliverance on union that 'until the PCA enters such union it shall continue to function pursuant to its existing Constitution, its existing Basis of Union and existing Acts of Parliament' (clause 1) could not change what has just been stated. To assert something is green when it is black does not make it green. In any event, the federal nature of the 1901 Constitution gave no power of general government over the member churches to the GAA, and therefore the GAA could not give a valid direction to its member churches in this sphere.

The commitment of officebearers was far more than to abstain from actions hurtful to the Presbyterian interest. The requirement was a positive commitment to assert, maintain and defend. The commitment to union modified this requirement and thus the eligibility of those committed to union to be regarded as lawful office-bearers. The position on this basis was one in which those professing continued adherence to their vows were entitled to be regarded as the true Presbyterian Church with a legal claim to an interest in the undivided property trust, the terms of which they continued to profess in their integrity. The unionists were only nominally Presbyterian but had been granted by Parliament a legal claim to what was otherwise not theirs in order that part of the property could go with them into the Uniting Church and be held on new trusts.

The position was analogous to that in the Free Church of Scotland case in 1900 with this difference: in that case legal capacity to apply the property for the United Free Church had not been obtained by the majority of the General Assembly of the Free Church of Scotland, hence legal capacity to apply the *whole* property of the Free Church belonged to the tiny handful of Commissioners of the General Assembly who had protested against the union, and to them alone.

While there are other opinions, in my judgement anyone approaching the matter from an adequate understanding of Presbyterian law will have difficulty avoiding the conclusion that today's PCA is legally the same church as it was before 1974, just as surely as the PCEA after 1864 was the same church as before the union of that year, and similarly with the continuing Free Church of Scotland in 1900.

An objection to this position would arise if Parliament had made some provision to the contrary. However, it should be noted that the Acts of Parliament enabling union are silent about the authority of church courts between a decision to unite and the consummation of such union. In short, no legal sanction was given by the Acts of Parliament which would extend/entrench the authority of unionist-dominated church courts beyond the moment of the resolution to unite. Thus, the church was left to act in appropriate ways. In the GAA this was through MacLeod's Protest and the continuation of the meeting elsewhere, again analogous to the Free Church case in 1900. MacLeod was elected Moderator-General, E.R.Pearsons became Clerk and Bradshaw continued as Procurator. In the absence of a voluntary withdrawal of the unionists there would be similar action in the State Assemblies. In fact, continuing courts were established in Victoria, Tasmania and South Australia. An attempt to do likewise in New South Wales failed because of the large quorum (16) required under the code in that State.[11] Continuers in Queensland contented themselves with a Protest in the Assembly along the lines of that unsuccessfully moved by Rev K.J.Gardner in the GAA, and so continued to sit in undivided assembly.

As well as the precedents and legalities already mentioned, it should be noted that the rights of continuing congregations came into being at the moment of the decision to unite. Thus it would be wrong for these congregations to take directions from a 'mixed' church court, especially with a unionist majority, just as it would be wrong for them to be governed by a completely outside non-Presbyterian body.

The issue was a pragmatic one for many. In New South Wales the Assembly had voted against union so there was no necessity for a break by continuers nor was the risk of detrimental action by unionists so marked. Besides, there were many in New South Wales who hoped to stop the union by legal means and did not want to withdraw from the unionist element.

Resort to the civil courts

Several legal cases followed the decision to unite. In the resolution to unite provision was made for the prescribed Property Commission, and certain persons, including F.M.Bradshaw and C.H.Fraser were included as representing those opposing union. However, contrary to what had been earlier agreed between the parties, at the last moment a proviso was inserted by which any anti-union representative on the Commission would cease to be a member if he refused to acknowledge that the PCA continued to function pursuant to its existing constitution until union took place. Bradshaw and Fraser had protested with MacLeod and others and refused to make the acknowledgement, claiming the proviso was invalid. Mr K.R. Handley, QC, the Sydney Anglican layman who was independent Chairman of the Commission, would not convene it until the question was settled at law. The Church obtained a declaration in the Supreme Court of Victoria in April 1975 that the proviso was binding, but in November the Full Court unanimously overturned that decision on the grounds that the proviso was in excess of the GAA's power.

11. Those who adhered to J.Boyall's Protest in the NSW Assembly on May 14, 1974 were J.Boyall, N.MacLeod, S.J.Clements, T H.Prisk, R.M.Herriman and J.J.T.Campbell, all ministers. They formed an Interim-Committee but failed to obtain a quorum to constitute a State Assembly meeting.

A second matter was the validity of the second vote. Action was taken by Rev Neil MacLeod and Charles Brierley, elder, in December 1974. MacLeod would have preferred to 'stagger along' in the theologically mixed PCA, and he wanted to stop the union. He sincerely believed that the decision to unite was wrong because he regarded the second vote as invalid. He was not alone in this. Senior counsel such as D.A.Yeldham, T.E.F.Hughes, T.P.Lonergan, C.W.Pincus and R.N.Chesterman held the same opinion. Bradshaw, whose speciality was equity, held the second vote to be perfectly valid since no rights were established by the first vote in the absence of GAA approval of union in consequence of that vote. R.M.Northrop, QC, a uniting member of the Commission, also took this view, and they were vindicated when the case was lost in the Supreme Court of New South Wales and also on appeal to the High Court of Australia, 1976.

Division of property

With these matters out of the way the Property Commission got to work. Apart from the schools, the work was exhausting but straightforward enough. K.R.Handley and I.M.Hunter, two of the three independent members of the nine-man Commission, were evangelical Anglicans from Sydney and good to work with. Allocation of the schools had to have regard to centrality of location and the existence of boarding facilities if the continuing church was to be equitably provided for, since only 2 schools in each of Melbourne and Sydney were to be allocated to it. In Melbourne the result was the allocation of Scotch College (founded by the FPCV in conjunction with the FCS in 1851) and Presbyterian Ladies College. However, without the authority or approval of the Uniting Church, litigation was commenced by the Old Scotch Collegians' Association and a PLC parent with a view to overturning the decision of the Property Commission. The implication of a successful challenge for other decisions of the Commission was obvious, although this did not deter Dr McCaughey, then Vice-Chairman of Scotch College Council.[12] Nevertheless, what the arguments of the Uniting Church officials could not do the mounting costs of the almost hopeless action did. In 1980, the litigation was settled out of court with the Colleges becoming incorporated under the Companies Act, each with 17 council members and the PCV having effective control over the appointment of 12 of these, Scotch and PLC paid $100,000 each towards the PCV's costs of $280,000, and also bore their own much higher costs.

One of Bradshaw's concerns was to ensure an adequate endowment (say $2,000,000) for a fully staffed theological hall. This was achieved in Victoria because the funds were there. However, New South Wales did not have much in the way of assets for this purpose. Reflecting the greater wealth of the

12. Alan W.Black, 'Some Aspects of Religion and Law: The Case of Church Union in Australia' in Religion (1986) †16 p.239.

Victorian church, the PCV (continuing), although having only 15% of its pre-union membership, probably gained about 25% of the undivided central funds. New South Wales with 52% of the people gained about half.

Freedom and reunion June 1977

The small section of the GAA which had continued under MacLeod became known as 'the Camberwell Assembly' because of its association with the Camberwell Church in Melbourne of which Rev W.A.Loftus was minister. Loftus was the Moderator of that section of the PCV Assembly which withdrew in June 1974 in line with the action at the GAA that year. The GAA which did not divide until the inauguration of the Uniting Church on June 22, 1977 was called 'the Collins Street Assembly'. Rev Ray Russell was a leader in this in Melbourne. Upon the inauguration of the Uniting Church the two continuing sections were reunited.

One pre-union GAA decision was repealed on June 23, 1977. This was the modified Formula for elders which had been enacted in 1928. The background was that after the defeat of union in 1923, largely because of the votes of elders who might not have followed every point but did recognise that they had taken vows to maintain and defend Presbyterianism, some ecclesiastics took the opportunity to have the vow modified. This was a change not permitted by the Scheme of Union of 1901 but attention was not drawn to that point. In fact the legislation started off as a Formula for deacons (church managers) but it is hard to avoid the conclusion that Rev George Tait, the GAA Clerk and son of Rev John Tait, by a sleight of hand, substituted 'elder' in the process of enactment.

There was the usual concern to protect the legal interests of the church. As for three years there had been two assemblies in Victoria, the Trusts Corporation of the PCV prior to the re-union obtained legal opinion as to the legitimacy of the PCV Assembly upon the inclusion of the Camberwell group. The Registrar of Titles and the Attorney-General also obtained opinions and there were differences. The continuing PCV was ready to take the matter to court but this did not prove necessary. In 1979 an Act of Parliament was obtained to ensure that the legal security of PCV property was unambiguous, but the legalities of the 'time of break' were not entered into.

The time of break has come to some note subsequently since the 1974 GAA gave approval to the ordination of women to the ministry after the Amethyst Hall group had left. Post-union sentiment has become increasingly opposed to such a course although there are noteworthy exceptions - Rev Stuart Clements in New South Wales and Rev Robert Humphreys in Victoria being examples. But the obvious course on this emotional issue is not to worry about the 'date of break' but to seek the mind of the church as it now is.

This was ordered by the GAA 1988. New legislation need not necessarily be retrospective so as to exclude the 5 or 6 women currently serving in the ministry.

Training of the ministry

For our purposes the training of the ministry is an important point. New South Wales had a large number of students but no money for the regular kind of theological training envisaged in the Scheme of Union. Many students took the Moore Theological College [Anglican] course with additional lectures in areas of concern to Presbyterians. Others continued with the course at the Theological Hall. However, Professor Crawford Miller's term on the theological faculty was not renewed for a further three years by the Assembly, and the right of the Principal of St Andrew's to be ex officio a member of the theological faculty was also terminated. These matters and the associated theological ferment in the PCNSW as it sought to recover its roots, were relevant in the decision of the St Andrew's College Council to ask the Theological Hall to moved from the College premises. Accordingly, in 1983 the hall was temporally located at Ashfield. It subsequently located at Burwood. Rev J.A.Davies, whose wife is a daughter of the Treasurer of the PCEA Synod, is the Dean and a suitable faculty has been obtained, although funds are not adequate for the desirable range of full-time appointments. The Moore College course remains an acceptable option but the Sydney BD was rejected as an approved course of training in 1985.

Queensland reorganised theological training in 1976 and have two full-time faculty - Rev Norman Barker and Dr Nigel Lee. They are assisted by part-time lecturers. These have included ministers of the Brisbane congregation of the PCEA. Theologically the stance in Brisbane and Sydney is conservative and Reformed. It might be apt to describe Dr Lee, a prolific author, as triumphalistically so!

However, it was in Melbourne that the continuing church first organised training. All the staff and all but 2 students (F.G.Graham & T.S.Fishwick) were 'uniting'. Nevertheless, on March 10, 1975, the 110th session of the Theological Hall was inaugurated with a lecture by Acting-Principal, Rev Robert Swanton, in the Hawthorn Church. He taught Theology while Arthur Stamp lectured in Hebrew. New Testament was by means of Dr Leon Morris' lectures at Ridley College [Anglican], while Rev A.Crichton Barr took Practical Training and W.A.Loftus acted as Dean of Students. There were two students (S.Miskimmin and J.Stasse) but there was conflict between them and Stamp on theological grounds. The upshot was that Miskimmin's candidature terminated but Stamp also was phased out at the close of the year. He had taught Hebrew language while PCEA minister, Professor Allan Harman, then at the Reformed Theological College in Geelong, had lectured in Old Testament exegesis and theology With the approval of the College at Geelong, Harman continued to fit into his schedule suitable lectures at the Theological Hall.

When the two streams of continuing Presbyterians united in June 1977, the Hall was more regularly constituted. The Assembly of October 1977 appointed Swanton as Principal and Professor of Theology, while Harman was appointed Visiting Professor of Hebrew and Old Testament with life tenure with effect from January 1, 1978. This meant he remained a PCEA minister and could fully maintain his own position with accountability to his own Presbytery. The idea was that he have the best of both worlds. Those reponsible for this action (Bradshaw, Pearsons, Loftus and Homer Fraser) were particularly anxious to avoid any appearance of poaching from friends. In 1978, Rev Robert Miller, a man with a gift for writing, was appointed Professor of Church History.[13] Miller's family background in New Zealand had derived from the Free Church of Scotland. Rev E.R.Pearsons was sent to Scotland and North America with a view to securing another Professor so as to make up a complete and genuinely Reformed senatus (faculty). As a result, Rev Douglas W.J.Milne, then of Glenurquhart Free Church, was appointed Visiting Professor of New Testament with effect from January 1, 1979, with the same provisions as Harman enjoyed. However, Milne took the view that he was paid by the PCV and he did not intend to hold ministerial status with the PCEA, the sister church of the Free Church. This was somewhat of an embarrassment to Bradshaw and Pearsons at the time as they did not seek this at all. Professor Miller died in 1981, the same year that the Principal purposed retirement. In May 1981, Harman tendered his resignation from the PCEA ministry in order that he might transfer to the PCV. The PCEA Presbytery members may not have agreed with Harman's action but they all spoke of their deep appreciation of his counsel and encouragement, and their desire that his future ministry be owned and blessed of the Lord, when accepting his resignation on July 10, 1981. Harman was subsequently inducted as Principal and Dr S.D.Gill of Canada was appointed Lecturer in Church History.

In 1987 the Theological Hall was transferred from the Assembly Hall buildings in Collins Street, Melbourne, where it had been located in 1978, to premises purchased in the eastern suburb of Box Hill with portion of the endowment. As of early 1989 a replacement for Swanton in the Chair of Theology has not been found but visiting scholars from Australia and overseas have assisted.

13. See Robert Strang Miller - A Tribute by his Family (Melbourne 1983) 68pp. Miller came from New Zealand to St Andrew's Launceston in 1966. He and his brother, J.G.Miller, are among a number of ministers from New Zealand who have exercised a beneficial influence in Australian parishes.

Official relations between the PCEA and the PCA do not exist except in an informal way. From time to time there have been common gatherings as in 1950 to commemorate the 300th anniversary of the 1650 Scottish Psalter still widely used. Although the PCEA was not to be taken as approving the actions of several of her ministers in joining the PCA, relations brightened. At the GAA in 1982, the then moderator of the PCEA Synod, Rev Rowland Ward, took the opportunity to bring greetings to the Assembly, the first time this had happened from the PCEA side.

The continuing Presbyterian Church is still going through a process of change and adjustment. The relative harmony in Victoria from 1977 was broken by 1984 although perhaps is now beginning to return. Differences in approach to the schools as reflected in attitudes to appointment of the School Councils, and something of a power struggle between old and new elements in the church, have been evident.   In New South Wales there has been a more continuous turmoil, partly because of the more entrenched element of liberal and/ or traditional opinion. Among the some 100 new ministers in the PCA since 1977, some have had only a minimal appreciation of Presbyterian polity, and others have had the zeal of the new convert without the wisdom to go with it. What was said of the Canadian experience was certainly true for the post-1904 Free Church of Scotland and is in part true of the PCA:

Many of these men admitted to the ministry of the Canadian Church rendered admirable service. Others were maladjusted malcontents who had not found suitable employment in their own Churches. A few were erratic and eccentric individuals whose behaviour brought discredit to the Church in communities where they laboured. Irreparable harm was sometimes done to the presitige of the Church before a hopeless situation could be dealt with by the regular process of Church discipline.[14]

Freemasonry has been a significant and divisive issue, as has the ordination of women. As might be expected, there is not a uniform approach among those whose theology is by and large Reformed.

However, given that all three training centres in the eastern states are largely or entirely Reformed in their teaching, the continuing church will continue in a conservative theological direction. The danger is that if there is not a good measure of balance and patience shown by the younger men, opportunity will be given for the advance of more liberal teaching based on exploitation of a back-lash from older elders. It will be necessary for the Reformed men to show disciplined and uncompromisingly ethical conduct if discredit to the Gospel is to be avoided.

14. N.G.Smith, et al., A Short History of the Presbyterian Church in Canada (Toronto c.1964) p.96.

The situation is not an easy one, and differs from earlier successful efforts to reform a wayward church as in 19th century Scotland and Ireland because of the lack of pressure for reform from the local congregations. However, no one can contemplate with complacency the unwillingness of the PCA to uphold the basic fundamentals of the Christian faith during much of the 20th century, and no church can prosper if it reaches the point, as happened, where it did not know or did not care what the fundamentals were. This just contributes to the formation of new denominations and the decay of the old. Thus only about 65% of those professing the Presbyterian and Reformed Faith in Australia are regular worshippers in PCA churches, and large sections of major cities are without Presbyterian witness. Adelaide is very weak, while suburbs established since World War II are not well served.

A certain realism is necessary in the missionary situation in which the PCA finds itself after the blighting inroads of non-doctrinal ministry and of liberalism. In God's good providence the PCA has been given an opportunity to recover its heritage. Some aspects of the Declaratory Statement are less than satisfactory and toleration within these limits must be extended unless or until appropriate amendment or clarification is made. But a definite personal ministry in the Reformed tradition is thoroughly legitimate, whereas a definite liberal one is not. At the time of union in 1977 only about 40% of the ministers who continued in parish ministry in Victoria and New South Wales could be described as 'evangelical'. The figures were higher in other states but the numbers in total in those states were not large. Today the percentage of evangelicals in parish ministry is about 80%, with the largest liberal rump in New South Wales, and most of the more than 100 new ministers since 1977 are Calvinistic. Men of ability as future leaders are evident in the PCA ministry today. The leadership they give will determine the judgement passed by an historian another century on. May the PCA be found faithful to her stewardship! May she not fail in the time of testing!

* The estimates in the last paragraph are based on estimates made by Rev Robert Humphreys calculated in 1986 for inclusion in R.Humphreys & R.Ward, **Religious Bodies in Australia**. An interesting comparison of Uniting and Continuing Presbyterian Ministers' views in Victoria in 1969/70 is in Norman W.H.Blaikie, **The Plight of the Australian Clergy** (Brisbane 1979) esp. Appendix B. [It might be added that sociologists are generally more candid and less ambiguous than the mainstream theologians.]

Part Nine

HISTORY OF CONGREGATIONS

PRESBYTERIAN CHURCH
OF EASTERN AUSTRALIA

SOUTH EASTERN AUSTRALIA
Some locations mentioned in the text

Scale: 300 kms

SYNODICAL ORGANISATION

Those who protested and formed the PCEA in 1846 did not establish a church with new or changed doctrines, but renewed their adherence to the standards of the Church of Scotland 'in their true and original import' (that is, as interpreted by that section in the Established Church of Scotland which withdrew on May 18, 1843 to form the Free Church of Scotland), and they erected a new ecclesiastical court to have jurisdiction accordingly. The Synod of Eastern Australia has remained the supreme court of the church. It exercises the powers of a synod and a General Assembly, unless and until such an Assembly is created.

The Synod consists of all the members of all the presbyteries unless and until representation is changed by Synod following Barrier Act procedure. It ordinarily meets once a year. From 1846 to 1882, the meeting was normally in the first week of November. There was no meeting in 1883, and from 1884 to 1903, the Synod was held in the first week of February. Since that time it has varied somewhat between February and May except for 1988. There was no meeting in 1980. The venue was commonly St George's Church, but the larger numbers and lack of catering facilities in the central city place of worship contributed to a move to the Salvation Army camp site at Collaroy in 1977 and 1978, while the 1979 meeting was held in Melbourne. The meetings since 1981 have been hosted by the Manning at Taree, except for 1984 when the meeting was at Maclean.

Moderators of the Synod during its first century are most conveniently listed in *The Presbyterian Banner*, April 1983, page 195. Moderators since are:

Mar 25,1947	Arthur Allen	Apr 03,1968	Alexander D.Campbell
Mar 16,1948	Alvan D.McIntosh	Apr 30,1969	Angus R.Beaton
Apr 05,1949	M.C.Ramsay, MA	Mar 18,1970	Joseph A.Harman
Mar 28,1950	Arthur Allen	Apr 01,1971	E.S.Turnbull [125th]
Mar 13,1951	M.C.Ramsay, MA	Mar 23,1972	E.R.Lee, MA
Apr 01,1952	J.A.Webster	Apr 11,1973	Kenneth MacLeod
Mar 24,1953	Arthur Allen	Apr 03,1974	Alan L.Tripovich
[Nov 25,1953	FPCV received]	Mar 19,1975	S.N.Ramsay
Apr 07,1954	J.A.Webster	May 12,1976	A.M.Harman, ThD,MLitt
Mar 30,1955	Alvan D.McIntosh	May 10,1977	David R.Nibbs
Mar 21,1956	S.N.Ramsay	May 09,1978	Angus R.Beaton
Apr 10,1957	M.C.Ramsay, MA	May 12,1979	R.W.Murray, BA,MTh
Mar 26,1958	Arthur Allen *	May 09,1981	E.R.Lee, MA
Mar 18,1959	J.C.Andrews,MA,MB,ChB	May 08,1982	R.S.Ward, BA,BTh(Hons)
Apr 06,1960	J.A.Webster	May 07,1983	John M.Cromarty
Mar 22,1961	S.N.Ramsay	May 05,1984	Alan L.Tripovich
Apr 11,1962	Alvan D. McIntosh	May 11,1985	Kenneth MacLeod
Apr 03,1963	J.A.Webster	May 17,1986	E.R.Lee, MA
Mar 18,1964	I.L.Graham, MA *	Apr 20,1987	R.W.Murray, BA,MTh
Apr 07,1965	E.R.Lee, MA	July 02,1988	P.J.Bloomfield, BEc,BD
Mar 30,1966	J.C.Andrews,MA,MB,ChB	Mar 28,1989	W.P.Gadsby, BSc,BD
Mar 15,1967	Alvan D.McIntosh		

Those who have filled the important positions of Clerk and Treasurer are as follows (ignoring the occasional pro-tem Clerk):

CLERK OF SYNOD		SYNOD TREASURER	
1846-1847	John Tait,Parramatta	1846-1875	William Buyers
1847-1849	Colin Stewart, Bowenfels	1875-1877	James Buyers
1849-1850	George Mackie, Kiama	1877-1900	E.A.Rennie
1850-1864	A.M.Sherriff, Williams R.*	1900-1905	Rev S.P.Stewart
1864-1867	J.L.McSkimming	1905-1920	Rev William McDonald
1867-1885	D.McInnes, Maclean	1920-1921	W.H.Reid
1885-1900	I.Mackay, Grafton *	1921-1923?	A.Gunn
1900-1904	W.Archibald	1923-1940	James Ross *
1905	S.P.Stewart, Manning R.	1940-1949	Harald C.Nicolson
1906-1922	W.N.Wilson, Hunter R.*	1949-1953	Neil A.McPherson
1922-1941	H.W.Ramsay, Grafton	1953-1971	Harold C.Nicolson
1941-1966	J.A.Harman, Hastings R.	1971-	Neil A.McPherson
1966-1982	S.N.Ramsay, Hunter R.		
1982-	W.P.Gadsby, Armidale		

Note: * = died while in office

From 1913 to 1953 the PCEA and the FPCV co-operated in spiritual matters by means of the Assembly of the FPCA (see page 306ff), a body electing its own Moderator, Clerk and Treasurer.

The Synod is primarily a court of review. Most business is remitted to Standing Committees which report each year with proposals. No matter what the size of a church it requires a number of such committees, but at one stage there were at least 14. Rearrangement, particularly in 1982 and 1988, has reduced the number and seems to have produced greater effectiveness given that it is often difficult to arrange regular meetings and much is done by correspondence. Some brief details of the standing committees follow.

ADMINISTRATION: Known in earlier times as the Bills and Overtures Committee, its chief task is to advise the Synod concerning documents and papers for transmission to Synod and to propose a suitable order of business. It is convened by the Synod Clerk. Since contacts with other churches are often made via the Clerk, and because points of principle or protocol can be involved, in 1982 the INTER CHURCH RELATIONS Committee (formed in 1971) was combined with the Administration Committee. In 1963 a LAW AND ADVISORY Committee was formed with a view, chiefly, to revising the Church Practice and Procedure (see page 422) and obtaining a new Act of Parliament in respect of property in New South Wales, similar to that in Victoria. The latter task has been completed well and truly but awaits approval by several congregations before sanction by Parliament is sought. Conveners since 1963: J.A.Harman (1963-74), A.M.Harman (1974-79), S.N.Ramsay (1979-82), W.P.Gadsby (1982-85), R.S.Ward (1985-   ). The three TRUST CORPORATIONS which hold the property of the denomination also report to Synod, and act on instructions given by the relevant courts of the church.

The Synod has always had a FINANCE COMMITTEE whose task is to co-ordinate finances. Conveners since 1953: I.L.Graham (to 1958), A.M.McLean (1958-77), A.M. Harman (1977-79), N.A.McPherson (1979-85), R.L.Campbell (1985-87), R.W.Murray (1987-88), K.Longworth (1988-   ). Funds for Widows & Orphans and Aged/Infirm Ministers existed from early times, but were fairly nominal apart from a useful bequest from Rev D.K.McIntyre which was used to pay insurance premium for ministers. After many years discussion, in 1967 a Superannuation Scheme was adopted, financed by a levy on congregations. With certain changes this has proved very effective. Long Service Leave (currently one week per year of service) was introduced in 1974. Conveners of this PROVIDENT FUNDS Committee since 1953: I.L.Graham (to 1964), N.A. McPherson (1964-71), C.P.King (1971-78), R.S.Ward (1978-   ).

In 1982 the Church Principles Committee was combined with the Religion and Morals Committee to form the Faith and Life Committee. The Publications and Psalmody Committees were added in 1988, and the combined committee renamed the CHURCH

470

SYNOD 1972 PICTURED IN FRONT OF THE PULPIT OF ST GEORGE'S CHURCH

Back row from left: A.R.Beaton, K.MacLeod, J.D.Heenan, E.S.Turnbull, E.R.Lee (Moderator), R.W.Murray, A.L.Tripovich, K.Kerr (St George's), D.R.Nibbs.

Middle row from left: G.R.Anderson (representing Brisbane), G.C.Alford (Grafton), K.D.Causley (Maclean), J.S.Robinson (Manning).

Front row, seated, from left: J.H.Brammah (Lismore), S.N.Ramsay (Clerk), J.A.Webster, J.A.Harman, M.C.Ramsay, C.P.King (Hunter), J.E.Huckett (Hastings), N.A.McPherson (Treasurer), J.Hill (Hamilton).

Absent: A.D.McIntosh, J.G.Simpson (St Kilda), J.Rathbone (Ulverstone), C.Mackeechnie (representing Geelong)

471

AND NATION Committee in 1989. Arthur Allen had been Convener of Church Principles 1953-58, and A.D.McIntosh from 1959-70, M.C.Ramsay held the reins of Religion and Morals 1954-69, while S.N.Ramsay had convened Psalmody for most of the period to 1975. Conveners since 1988: R.W.Murray (1988-).

The important TRAINING OF MINISTRY Committee has had many changes of convener. In the decade 1951-60, 7 students were received but only 3 were licensed; in 1961-70 five students were received of whom four were licensed; in 1971-80, 8 of the 11 students received were licensed. In 1983 strict regulations governing the acceptance of students and associated matters were introduced. Conveners since 1953: M.C.Ramsay (to 1955), J.A.Harman (1955-56), A.D.McIntosh (1956-62), E.R.Lee (1962-66), J.C. Andrews (1966-69), A.D.McIntosh (1969-70), R.W.Murray (1970-75), E.R.Lee (1975-76), E.S.Turnbull (1976-78), R.W.Murray (1978-81), W.P.Gadsby (1981-82), R.S.Ward (1982-84), P.J.Bloomfield (1984-).

MISSIONS is an important Committee, and for 30 years to 1971 it was convened by J.A. Harman. Subsequent conveners: E.R.Lee (1971-74), A.R.Beaton (1974-77), E.R.Lee 1977-78), A.R.Beaton (1978-81), E.R.Lee (1981-84), K.MacLeod (1984-88), W.M. Mackay (1988-). On the home front the CHURCH EXTENSION AND SUPPLY Committee has regard to the general needs of congregations, receiving reports from Presbyteries on all work being done. Conveners since 1953: S.N.Ramsay (1953-65), J.C.Andrews (1965-70), A.R.Beaton (1970-74), E.R.Lee (1974-75), D.R.Nibbs 1975-

J.C.Andrews (1965-70), A.R.Beaton (1970-74), E.R.Lee (1974-75), D.R.Nibbs 1975-77), R.W.Murray (1977-78), W.P.Gadsby (1978-82), D.D.Heenan (1982-84), R.W. Murray (1984-85), J.S.Graham (1985-86), J.A.Cromarty (1986-). The YOUTH AND FELLOWSHIP Committee was formed by combining the old Welfare of Youth Committee and the Fellowship Committee (formed in 1959) in 1982. 'Uncle Bob' Allen, Arthur Allen's brother, was the convener of Welfare of Youth from 1953-71 while S.N.Ramsay was influential on the Fellowship side (convener 1965-74). Conveners since 1982: J.D.Ramsay (1982-85), J.M.Cromarty (1985-88), H.C. Varnes (1988-).

SYNOD 1989 AT TAREE:Rear row from left: W.M.Mackay, H.C.Varnes, R.L.Campbell, J.D.Ramsay, K.Longworth; next row: G.A.Nell, J.S.Graham, I.Miller, J.B.Louden, R.W. Murray, J.R. B.Webster, J.Pateman; third row: A.Steel, K.MacLeod, T.I.Leggott, P.J. Bloomfield, N.A. McPherson; seated: W.D.Graham, R.S.Ward, S.N.Ramsay, W.P.Gadsby, J.C.Andrews, E.R.Lee; standing, J.M.Cromarty (J.A.Cromarty in front), A.L.Tripovich.

NEW SOUTH WALES-BASED PRESBYTERIES

At its formation on October 10, 1846, the Synod of Eastern Australia exercised also the powers of a presbytery until distinct presbyteries were formed on November 22, 1852. These presbyteries were the *Presbytery of Maitland* with jurisdiction as far north as one could go from the 33rd parallel, and the *Presbytery of Sydney* embracing the rest of the colony as far south as the Murray River.

On May 5, 1859, a portion of the Presbytery of Sydney was brought under the jurisdiction of a new presbytery - the *Presbytery of Illawarra.* However, when the General Synod was formed on November 15, 1864, all the charges in the Presbytery of Illawarra except Bombala (ie. Illawarra, Shoalhaven, Shellharbour and Twofold Bay) joined the General Synod. Similarly, all the charges in the Presbytery of Sydney except St George's (ie. Macquarie Street, Chalmers, Newtown, Richmond, Penrith and Bowenfels) joined the General Synod. Accordingly, on May 3, 1865, the PCEA Synod united the presbyteries of Sydney and Illawarra under the original title of the *Presbytery of Sydney,* with St George's and Bombala as its charges.

Efforts at extension work in the Sydney area and at Parkes and Wellington were not entirely successful, while the minister at Bombala joined the PCNSW in 1872 and the congregation followed some time later. However, the congregations on the Clarence were more readily accessed by sea than by land at this time, and on November 6, 1873 they were taken from the Presbytery of Maitland and added to the Presbytery of Sydney until transferred to the new *Presbytery of Grafton* on November 8, 1878.

Meanwhile, the Presbytery of Maitland lost the charges in Queensland (Brisbane [Ann Street] and Gladstone) upon the formation of the PCQ on November 25, 1863. The formation of the General Synod on November 15, 1864 saw the further loss of Newcastle (Hunter Street) and Wellingrove, but the other charges continued at this point (ie. West Maitland, Clarence Town, Ahalton/Raymond Terrace, Singleton, Barrington, Manning and the Clarence River charges of Grafton and Maclean. West Maitland and its minister were received into the PCNSW on September 8, 1865, while the Clarence charges (then Grafton and Maclean) were taken from the Presbytery of Maitland and attached to the Presbytery of Sydney on November 6, 1873.

The sanctioning of Brushgrove as a charge separate from Grafton in 1874, and the stationing of a minister at Lismore in 1876, led to the formation of the Presbytery of Grafton on November 8, 1878 to have jurisdiction in these areas, and the Presbytery of Sydney reverted to jurisdiction over St George's and several preaching centres.

The Presbytery of Maitland after 1865 lost the Clarence charges in 1873, as recorded above, but extended to the Hastings/Macleay and further north to the Nambucca and Bellinger in the late 1870s, with moves to the Namoi Valley to the west soon after. On November 14, 1881, a fourth post 1865 PCEA presbytery was erected to have jurisdiction 'south to the Barrington inclusive and to the north as far as the Bellinger inclusive.' The *Presbytery of the Manning*, as it was called, included the ministers on the Manning and Hastings and catechists on the Barrington and the Bellinger. The charges then left in the Presbytery of Maitland were divided as a consequence of the Macpherson/Sutherland dispute in the 1880s. Clarence Town and portion of the Upper Hunter was attached to the Presbytery of Sydney on February 5, 1886 to form the *Presbytery of Sydney and Maitland*, Namoi was lost to the PCNSW in 1887, and the balance adhered to the 'Reconstituted Synod.' This Synod faded out in the early 1900s and work was consolidated on the Hunter under the original Synod.

The Presbytery of the Manning does not appear to have held a meeting after February 5, 1894, while the Presbytery of Grafton was defunct in practical terms at an earlier date. On February 7, 1907 the two jurisdictions were combined as the *Presbytery of the Clarence and Manning*.

NORTHERN PRESBYTERY

Formed on February 7, 1907 as the Presbytery of the Clarence and Manning, the first meeting was held four days later, and by late the same year the name 'the Manning and Clarence' was used. The Manning was disjoined in March 1931 and the name 'the Clarence and Hastings' adopted. The present name was given on March 17, 1937, and Synod 1986 defined the boundaries as 'the Hastings Municipality and to the north and west of the same in New South Wales together with the whole of Queensland.'

Presbytery Clerks 1907-1988: Rev W.N.Wilson (1909-1912, 1915-1917); Rev William McDonald (1912-1915); Rev H.W.Ramsay (1917-1920, 1921-1923, 1930-1935, 1937-1938, 1943-1945); Rev T.M.McClean (1920-1921, 1923-1924, 1926-1930); Rev M.C.Ramsay (1924-1926, 1935-1936, 1946); Rev J.A.Harman (1936-1937, 1940-1943, 1945-1946); Mr D.A.MacDonald (1937); Mr Kenneth McDonald (1938); Rev D.G.C.Trotter (1938-1940); Rev A.D.McIntosh (1946-1951); Rev J.A.Webster (13/03/1951-30/04/1964); Rev A.D.Campbell (30/04/1964-24/9/1970); Rev K. MacLeod (18/12/1970-8/12/1972); Rev R.W.Murray (8/12/1972-1/8/1980); Rev W.P.Gadsby (1/8/1980-4/3/1983); Rev P.J.Bloomfield (4/3/1983-12/10/1985); Rev K.MacLeod 12/10/1985-   ).

GRAFTON

As discussed on pages 134-135 the Grafton PCEA Congregation was organised by Rev Dr Macintosh Mackay in mid 1859, and a timber church was erected soon thereafter on the SE corner of Villiers and Hoof Streets. Rev Allan McIntyre of the Manning became the first minister following acceptance of a call signed by 129 persons. He arrived in Grafton in January 1863 and maintained Gaelic and English services. Maclean, then called Rocky-mouth, was included in his pastoral visits and became a separate charge on November 6, 1863. McIntyre left Grafton to return to the Manning in August 1865. He had piloted the congregation through the difficult union period when strong efforts were made to extinguish its distinctive witness. It was at this time that Rev Alexander McIntyre came to the Clarence and he gave supply for about 18 months before returning to his base at Geelong.

Rev John McLeod 1869-1872

A call to Rev James McCulloch in 1869 bearing the signatures of 80 men failed. It should be noted that McCulloch was not a Gaelic preacher but was a trusted and warm-hearted preacher of the whole counsel of God. The choice then fell on Rev John McLeod, a newly licensed probationer who had been labouring chiefly in the Hastings district. This young man was fluent in Gaelic and had actually left the PCV, where he had been a student for the ministry, to join the PCEA in 1868. He gave supply, chiefly on the Hastings, was ordained on November 12, 1869, and was admitted minister of Grafton early in 1870, a call bearing 108 signatures. He preached in English and Gaelic at Grafton and travelled to Brushgrove for an afternoon service. Good progress was made. A fine site was obtained from the Government on the corner of Fry and Prince Streets, and on June 6, 1870, it was resolved to build a manse and church on that site. The manse, the first belonging to the congregation, was of brick and was completed early in 1871. It was built too low on the ground so that it was a rather damp house but it was to serve for the next 60 years. It cost $1,076.

The church building costing $1,100 was next. Also of brick in a simple style, the main assembly area was 44' x 24' and was supposed to seat about 200 persons. It was completed in November 1871, and the first service in the building was held on December 10, 1871. The old timber church (but not the site) on Villiers and Hoof Streets was sold. It was re-erected in Duke Street for business purposes. Soon after, Mr McLeod decided to leave Grafton. Some unpleasantness had arisen the true nature of which is unclear. He left Grafton by sea for Sydney on July 2, 1872, joined the PCNSW and had his resignation from the PCEA accepted July 22, 1872. He returned to Grafton and was farewelled on October 18, 1872, and an appreciation signed by 145 members and adherents was given to him. The same year he left for Canada.

The Fry Street Church

Rev Isaac Mackay 1874-1900

During the vacancy the congregation sought to secure Rev Alexander McIntyre, but without success. However, Brushgrove was separated from Grafton on May 27, 1874, thus making a more compact charge, and Rev Isaac Mackay was inducted to Grafton on July 25, 1874, following a call signed by 59 men, chiefly heads of families. Mr Mackay had a ministerial background in Canada, but had previously served the PCQ at Warwick (1869-1873), and had been Moderator of that denomination in 1873. Mr Mackay commenced the Sabbath evening services at Grafton desired by the people, together with a morning Bible Class and an afternoon Sabbath School. He had the Gaelic and ministered effectively. The average attendance in the mid 1870s was 100. However, he was hampered by the lack of a regular Session and the initial failure to adequately define the boundaries between the Grafton and Brushgrove charges. The synodical dispute in the 1880s broke the harmony and progress otherwise indicated. Mr Mackay was a very even-tempered man and kept on amidst all the difficulties. He died suddenly on March 3, 1900.

476

Rev Herbert W. Ramsay 1915-1945

The acute shortage of ministers plus the blighting effects of the contention in the church meant the situation in the years following Mr Mackay's death were extremely discouraging. The buildings were in disrepair, there was not one male member in Grafton and thus no officebearers, and there was still some dissension and bitter feeling. In August 1911, Herbert Ramsay was appointed to labour in the charge while still pursuing his studies for the ministry. There were then some 80 or 90 in attendance. Late in 1914, the Brushgrove congregation united with Grafton in issuing a call to Mr Ramsay. He accepted and was ordained and inducted on February 15, 1915. He was a good pastor, an able preacher and possessed a ready pen. He continued at Grafton until his death on the afternoon of the Lord's Day, February 18, 1945.

In 1909 the three ½-acre blocks in Villiers and Hoof Streets were sold for $198 and the proceeds used to pay expenses connected with securing the title to the Fry Street property and for repairs to the Fry Street church. The roof shingles were replaced and the building ceiled in 1912, the same year that plates replaced the long-handled collection boxes previously used. The telephone was connected to the manse in 1915, and electricity to the church and manse in 1927. A Model T Ford had been purchased for the minister's use in 1921, although 5 years later he was using a motor-cycle and sidecar. Money was tight in the depression years. However, the manse was quite unhealthy. The old manse was demolished and a seven roomed timber manse was erected and occupied in July 1931. It cost $2,078 and there was still $500 owing four years later. However, two blocks of land facing Prince Street were sold in 1935 for $400, which helped considerably. The Grafton church building was cement rendered in part in 1943 and the balance in 1955. The manse at Brushgrove (but not the site) was sold in 1944. It had previously been let but was in poor order.

Ministers from 1946 to 1988

After a vacancy of little more than a year, Rev Alvan McIntosh, a native of the Clarence, was inducted on July 17, 1846. He was transferred to Hamilton on May 3, 1951. Rev Stewart Ramsay, son of Rev H.W.Ramsay, was ordained and inducted on February 24, 1953 following a call signed by 32 members and 54 adherents, but was inducted to the Hunter on November 11, 1954. Mr McIntosh was again the choice of the congregation, which then had about 40 members. The call was delayed because the Victorian Presbytery considered it could not afford to lose its only regularly settled minister. However, in due time the call was cleared and Mr McIntosh was inducted on August 14, 1957. He continued until he was transferred to St George's, Sydney, on January 19, 1961. The choice then fell on Rev A.D.Campbell, who had returned from theological studies in Scotland in September 1963.

477

He was inducted on January 16, 1964 and resigned with effect from July 26, 1971 to visit Scotland for family reasons. The congregation then called Rev David Nibbs, then in Victoria. He was inducted on May 19, 1972. The average morning congregation was then 30-35 with 20-25 of an evening. There were no services at Brushgrove in Mr Nibbs' time, and the building and the ½-acre site were sold for about $8,000 in 1979. The proceeds were used to renovate the Grafton manse. Mr Nibbs was transferred to Ulverstone on February 11, 1982. Rev R.W.Murray, an Australian, was called from a pastorate in Scotland and inducted on March 29, 1984. The congregation had been financially weak for many years. Mr Murray has undertaken work as Special Religious Education teacher in the High Schools of Grafton. This involves a very significant input into the education of 700 children, and has also meant the Grafton congregation has been able to manage without financial help from the wider church.

Elders 1878-1988: The historical booklet (1971) is inaccurate but records are defective. It appears the first session was formed on October 16, 1878 and the church dispute of the 1880s created difficulties, the Session being in effect inoperative in the 1890s. Samuel Martin (1878-89 & died); Hugh H. McIntyre (1878-85 & suspended), Joseph Martin (1883-85 & suspended). The session was reformed in 1915. Donald Anderson (1915- ? , - the father of Rev Arthur Allen's wife); Angus Beaton (1919-   ); E.J.Harrison (1921-1966 & died aged 93); David McPherson (1926-   , father of N.A.McP); James R.Anderson (1926-1947 & died aged 73, brother of DA); H.Fuller (1930-); Kenneth Reid (1933-   ); Angus Gillies (1936-   ); Campbell P.King (1947-1949); George Alford (1947-   , to Hamilton); Norman Kerr (1955-   , to Sydney); Gordon Anderson (1966-   , from Maclean); W.E.Cowling (1966-); Bob Law (1974-1986); John Kerridge (from Hunter, 1988-   ).

The dates of decease of several of the above have not been secured.

Brushgrove: As indicated in the above narrative, Brushgrove was originally part of the Grafton charge, was separated in 1874 but reunited in 1914. Its history as a disctinct charge is as follows.

The Middle Clarence district erected a timber church at Cowper, opposite Woodford Island, on a ¼-acre given by Robert Young. The contract price of $494 was more than covered by subscriptions by the time the building was opened in 1873. On Woodford Island at Woodford Dale, a timber church costing $350 was erected about the same time on a ¼-acre given by Hugh Munro (part of Portion 77). It was this district with the two main centres which formed the charge commonly known as Brushgrove. Brushgrove is on the southern part of Woodford Island opposite Cowper on the mainland. A ½-acre riverbank site was obtained at Brushgrove from the Government in the early 1870s (lot 8 section 5) and a manse was built on it a little later at a cost of $804.

The Brushgrove charge had the services of William McDonald, catechist and student for the ministry, for a period prior to his departure for Victoria in 1876. There were about 70 in attendance at Woodford Dale and 50 at Cowper, with Sabbath Schools in both centres. In August 1879, Rev William Grant arrived from Canada, and became the first settled minister. The promising situation was soon disturbed by the synodical dispute. Mr Grant, as well as Mr Mackay and Mr Sutherland, were regarded as suspect because of their past involvement with unionist denominations. In January 1865, Mr Grant felt it desirable to withdraw and he went to New Zealand for a time. The majority of the people were unsympathetic to Sutherland. They looked mainly to Rev Duncan McInnes of Maclean for assistance, McInnes taking a middle position. In January 1887, Rev John Finlayson, formerly of Coigach Free Church in Ross-shire, arrived in New South Wales. He was a Free Church constitutionalist whose health had rendered it advisable to seek a warmer climate. While still in Scotland he had received an invitation to take the pastorate of Brushgrove which was then an unattached congregation. As there was no presbyterial organisation he could not be formerly inducted. However, in due time he became a member of the Maclean Session and acted as ordained missionary. He served centres at Woodford Dale, Cowper and Grafton (using the Oddfellows' Hall), and resided at Brushgrove. He was an exemplary minister whose facility in Gaelic was valued. He died of a ruptured blood vessel on October 10, 1890. His widow (nee Nicolson) and infant son returned to Raasay, Scotland.

It was in this situation that Rev J.S.Macpherson sought to gain the allegience of the Brushgrove people to the 'Reconstituted Synod' which some of those expelled in 1884 had set up in 1886. On October 27, 1891, Macpherson addressed a meeting in the Oddfellows' Hall, Grafton, and the meeting resolved to adhere to the 'Reconstituted Synod.' A similar resolution was passed at Brushgrove 4 days later. Occasional supply was given by Messrs W.N.Wilson, J.S.Macpherson and F.MacKenzie. For 6 weeks in July and August 1894 supply was given by Rev Walter Scott of the Victorian FPC, whose Synod counselled Mr Scott to bear in mind the position of the Victorian FPC to the then disorganised state of the PCEA - a position of rejection of communion with the Sutherland party but of neutrality otherwise. Soon after, Mr Scott received a call signed by 65 persons. There were some irregularities in the procedure but the FPCV allowed the call to be 'morally receivable' and Scott accepted it on May 22, 1895 rather than a call to be assistant at Hamilton. He commenced work at Brushgrove on July 21, 1895, and was inducted in the Woodford Dale building on September 23, 1895, the service lasting 3 hours and being followed by a less formal welcome. Scott maintained services as had Mr Finlayson and held a midweek meeting at Laurence. The Cowper building was in poor repair. In 1898 it was re-erected on the manse property at Brushgrove, which was then developing as the commercial centre.

After going to Brushgrove Scott excluded all from communion with him who did not recognise the 'Reconstituted Synod,' and this meant his position was somewhat isolated. He appears to have been an earnest man but not without the infirmities of other mortals. His severely uncompromising nature led him to espouse the position that the use of public transport on the Lord's Day to reach a place of worship was to be condemned while yet he used the river punt himself to reach his preaching centres. With the breakup of the 'Reconstituted Synod' about 1904, Scott was left as the only minister. He

The Brushgrove Church during the 1928 flood

had previously had contact with the Free Presbyterian Church of Scotland, and the success of the minority Free Church in the 1904 made no difference to him. He left his charge in the latter part of 1908 and went to Scotland. Scott sought by correspondence to commit the Brushgrove people to receive supply from the FPCS but they were by no means unanimous about this, especially as the PCEA was getting its act together. Scott was admitted a minister of the FPCS on January 2, 1911. The majority of folk resolved to adhere to the PCEA. In November 1911, a petition signed by three elders (Alex Kidd, James Kidd and Hugh Grant), ten members and a few adherents was granted by the FPCS, and the petitioners were received as a congregation of that church. It has continued until this day, erected a neat church building in Grafton in 1941, but is apparently ignorant of the real reasons for the dispute. Published accounts seen by the present writer are partial and confused at best. Suggestions that the PCEA stole the properties from the 'Reconstituted Synod' are, of course, nonsense, since they were never competently transferred from the ownership of the PCEA. The whole business simply reflects the fruit of dissension and bitterness against which the Scripture warns us. The fate of the Brushgrove property has been described in the Grafton history. The Woodvale Dale property was in poor repair and was rather close to Maclean, while there were also prospects of a church building at Chatsworth. So the structure and its contents were sold for about $220 in 1915 and the land leased to the Munro family for one shilling a year plus rates. In 1978 it was transferred to Colin Munro and the price of $250 paid to the Maclean PCEA.

NB: Settled ministers of the Free Presbyterian Church of Scotland, Grafton have been William MacLean (1973-76) and E.A.Rayner (1976-   ).

480

MACLEAN

The period 1863 to 1867 is covered on pages 135-136. It may be added here that the contractor for the church building was John Davies of Grafton and the cost was $1,134. It still stands but the original shingle roof has been replaced by galvanised iron, a porch and session room have been added and the whole has been cement rendered.

Rev Duncan McInnes 1868-1908

An attempt in 1865 to obtain Rev Alexander McColl of Durinish, Skye, was not successful, but in 1868 a call signed by 108 men was addressed to and accepted by Duncan McInnes, a licentiate who had been trained in the church. He was ordained in the Presbyterian school house/church at East Maitland on July 30, 1868, and took up his duties on the Clarence soon afterwards. He continued the pastor until his death in August 1908. Duncan McInnes has been described as a 'quiet, thoughtful and lovable minister, who, by conscientious adherence to principles, his true Christian characteristics, and unbounded faith, made friends on every side, irrespective of class or creed' (R.J.McDonald). Proficient in Gaelic and English, there were two morning services for some years, one in each language. The first service of the day would occupy about two hours and the second somewhat less. Those who understood usually stayed for both services. An afternoon service was held at Chatsworth the 10km trip being made by rowing boat until the steam ferry commenced at Harwood in 1885 when a horse was used. Mrs McInnes was a very cheerful and capable Christian woman. She conducted Psalmody classes for many years, and also a successful Bible Class for South Sea Islanders engaged in the sugar industry. A brick manse with shingle roof was built next to the church in 1869 at a cost of $1,138.

Mr McInnes took a middle course in the Synod dispute and his congregation held together quite well although the PCNSW established a parish in 1882 following a petition signed by 83 persons. Although cut off from the Synod in 1887, McInnes worked for reconciliation and rejoined after the provisional recission of the expulsion Act of 1884 in 1898. He was deservedly esteemed as a faithful minister of the Gospel.

Vacancy 1908-1916

After the death of Mr McInnes the congregation depended on supply. A call to Professor D.McLean of Edinburgh, signed by 56 members and 222 adherents was sustained on December 30, 1910, and sent off. It was not successful, but at least it had the good result of stimulating interest in the need. Rev James Henry came out from Scotland in September 1911 and gave supply until May 1912, and soon after, Mr Donald McDonald, a student of the FCS, arrived to give supply for an extended period. Mr Henry gave some further supply on a return visit in the latter part of 1914.

481

The Maclean place of worship built 1864

Rev Thomas M. McClean 1916-1936

Rev T.M.McClean, then labouring in the Hamilton district of Victoria, gave some supply early in 1916. Later that year he received a hearty call from the congregation which he accepted. He was ordained and ind inducted on November 9, 1916. When he commenced his new ministry the old manse had been demolished and a new timber dwelling was in course of erection. The 8-roomed house was built by F.J.Robertson, and the bricks from the old building were used to build a front fence for the church and manse. The cost of the project was about $2,000, and it was completed free of debt. Mr McClean was a bachelor and boarded elswhere, using only the study in the manse. McClean was an Irishman who had joined the Free Church of Scotland in her hour of need. Unlike many who did so he was a capable minister and an attractice preacher who did not lack a sense of humour. It is recorded that when the Anglican Bishop of Grafton rang one day and introduced himself in the Anglican way as 'Cyril of Grafton' he was to have returned to him the greeting 'McClean of Maclean here'! He took a year off to visit his home country in 1922. One of the elders, D. McLachlan, was particularly helpful in giving supply during this period. After a very appreciated and successful ministry during which the communicant membership doubled, Mr McClean resigned with effect from January 8, 1936. In that month he married Annie, daughter of Murdoch McPherson, and sailed for Britain. After spending two years supplying FCS congregations the McCleans settled in Ulster.

Subsequent ministries 1936 to 1988
In March 1938, Rev D.G.C.Trotter became the third minister. The following year a timber church was opened at Chatsworth. This building was sold in 1975 as the opening of the Harwood Bridge had made travel to Maclean practical. Mr Trotter resigned in September 1948. The following year Rev J.A.Webster was inducted and he provided a warmly devotional ministry for 20 years. He and his wife were excellent visitors. The fifth ministry was the short one of Rev J.D.Heenan (1970-73) and was followed by that of Rev Angus Beaton (1974-81). Mr Beaton was instrumental in having a hall/book shop built next to the church in 1975. It was built mainly by volunteers under the supervision of Barry Hilberts, a church member and builder from Wauchope. Rev Kenneth MacLeod became the seventh minister in June 1982.

The Maclean congregation has always been strong and is the only congregation (with the exception of Melbourne) which has not required financial assistance from the wider church at some stage.

Elders: The first session was constituted on February 10, 1869. Hector McDonald (1869-1880 & died); Allan McDonald (1869-1875 & died); James McDonald (1869-1883 & removed due church dispute; not related to above McDonalds); Donald Shearer (1869-1882 to PCNSW); William Shearer (brother of DS, 1881-1882 to PCNSW); Francis McKenzie 1881-1897 & died, was with MacPherson faction); Roderick McDonald (brother of James, 1884-1892 & died); Duncan McLachlan (1901-1930 & died); Murdoch McPherson (1901-1927 & died); Alexander Anderson (1904-1922 & died); Alexander McDonald (1907-1922 & died); Duncan Nicholson (1907-1916); James Ross (1915-1923 to Sydney); Donald Gillies (1915-1970); Kenneth McDonald (son of Alexander, 1917-1952); A.N.McDonald (brother of Kenneth, 1917-1945); G.J.Martin (1926-1938); C.J.Green (1935-1956); Gordon Anderson (1935-   to Grafton); Alexander Martin (son of GLM, 1949-1980); Samuel Gray (1949-1973); Alex Ross 1958-   to Sydney); Walter McKinnon (1958-1968); G.Andrews (1968-1973 to Sydney); K.D. Causley (1968-   ); J.Greensill (1976-1981 to Brisbane); R.L.Campbell (1980-   ); J.McPhee (1986-   ).

HASTINGS RIVER

The formative years of Presbyterian work on the Hastings have been described on pages 132-133. The Hastings Congregation, now based on the town of Wauchope, has a well researched history based on the work of J.E. Huckett which was issued in 1979, so this survey can be brief.

Rev Allan McIntyre made occasional visits for services which were much appreciated. It is recorded that the grandmother of Rev I.L.Graham used to walk and ride with a Mrs McGregor from the Hastings to the Manning for communion seasons, having only one horse between them. One can imagine the love for the word of God illustrated by such conduct. Rev John McLeod supplied on the Hastings and Wilson Rivers during most of 1969, while it is recorded that Hugh Livingstone was a catechist in the same area in 1871. On July 16, 1871, the first PCEA building for worship was opened by Rev W. S.Donald at 'Letter Ewe' a little to the north of Wauchope. Previously services had been held in Alexander Bain's new barn. In July 1875 the folk on the Macleay to the north sought monthly services from the Presbytery and guaranteed $80 per annum toward the stipend of a minister. In October of the same year the PCEA people on the Hastings, Wilson and Macleay Rivers approached Presbytery, the document bearing 99 signatures, asking that an ordained missionary be appointed to labour among them. Accordingly, Rev John Davis was ordained on June 6, 1877, his labours were blessed, the charge was sanctioned November 17, 1877, and Davis was called and inducted as the first minister on February 3, 1879.

Macleay

A timber church seated for 100 was opened at Gladstone on March 23, 1879 on land given by Mr McIlwaine. It cost $210 but was destroyed by fire in August 1885. Prior to Davis' settlement, services had been held at the School of Arts at Frederickton on Lord's Day evenings. There were transferred to the Presbyterian schoolhouse which had been opened in 1862. Mrs Smith gave a site in Belgrave Street, Kempsey (allotment 19 of section 1), and a timber church 40' x 24', which could seat 'comfortably' 200 people was opened on April 6,1884 by Rev D.K.McIntyre. The total project cost $815, and the debt at opening was $100. The first trustees were Thomas Marshall, Hugh and Mitchell Mackay and Alex Dornan. The PCNSW entered the field in September 1883, the school was converted into a church and a minister settled in 1884. The inevitable result was that one congregation would suffer. Davis' ill health led to the resignation of the charge and removal to Sydney in February 1891, and PCEA services on the Macleay ceased.

Hastings/Wilson

Davis returned to the Hastings and Wilson Rivers in the early part of 1894. An excellent minister, his services were much valued. Great was the shock when it was learned on November 25, 1897 that he had been killed by a falling tree branch at the rear of the manse at Letter Ewe built in 1879. He was only 43 years of age. After some time his widow and the six children moved to Sydney where Mrs Davis died in 1926.

There must have been some solid piety among the people for they held together through years without a minister. Alexander Bain exchanged the

484

land at Letter Ewe for 3 acres in the rising town of Wauchope, about 5 kms to the south and there the 'Davis Memorial Church' was erected and opened on August 29, 1918 by Rev S.P.Stewart, who had provided quarterly services through most of the vacancy. Several students for the ministry came from this period - the three sons of John Ramsay of the Macleay, and Isaac Graham.

The Wauchope Congregation pictured in 1988

Malcolm Ramsay was to become the second inducted minister, and served from 1921 to 1937. Not without some misgivings, the Kemsey property was sold for $864 to aid in funding the manse at Wauchope which was erected in 1922. A preaching centre was early established at Kindee, in the home of Mr and Mrs Henry Huckett some 30 km from Wauchope, and 2½ years after the opening of the Kindee Bridge a neat timber church was officially opened at Kindee (June 23, 1939) which is still in use. Rev J.A.Harman, a native of the district, became the third minister in 1938. He patiently endured some stormy times and maintained an appreciated ministry until his retirement in 1967. A hall was erected at the rear of the Wauchope church in 1955. A Youth Centre Hall was built at Port Macquarie in 1963 and is used for services. Other centres include Birdwood and Comboyne. There is a lack elders at present although the congregation is quite strong. Obvious potential exists for further development as and when suitable leaders are available, The fourth and present minister is Rev A.L.Tripovich, inducted 1968.

Note re Kemsey: There was a desire for quarterly services at Kemsey in 1939 but war-time petrol rationing would have limited this. In early 1957 services were resumed by Mr Harman, a mid-week meeting being held in the PCNSW building once a month. The focus for this work was A.K. (Ken) Mackay, his family (descendants of Robert Mackay of Rollands Plains) and friends. Mr Harman maintained these services until his retirement, at about which time the late Mr Mackay's family moved to Sydney.

Elders: The Session met first in 1879, and the following is a complete list of elders. Alexander Bain (ordained c.1869 died 1892); David Lindsay, Huntingon (1879-1885 & resigned); Angus Kennedy, Wauchope (1880-1906); Duncan Bain, Wauchope (1880-1925); Robert Mackay, Rollands Plains (1909-1929); Alexander Bain, Wauchope ((1920-1931); John (Jock) Graham, Wauchope (1920-1937 & resigned); Lachlan Campbell, Koree Island (1922-1943); John Warwick, Comboyne (1928-1949); H.D.Andrews Wauchope, 1931-1975); D.L.McLeod, Comboyne (1936-1983); A.M. McKinnon, Kindee (1937-1964 & retired); J.E.Huckett, Kindee (1944-1987); W.J.McKinnon, Kindee (1950-1958); Grant Harman, Wauchope (1956-1970); G.W.Lindsay, Huntingdon (1960-1969); James Bain, Wauchope (1960-1973); A.L.Bosanquet, Wauchope (1974-84 to Sydney); Paul Bearup, Kempsey (1977-1980 resigned).

LISMORE

The organisation of PCEA work on the Richmond River can be dated to 1874, 12 years after large scale settlement began as a consequence of the Land Acts which came into force in 1862 and enabled selection on easy terms. Most of the free river-bank land had been taken up by 1866. Organised Presbyterian work began towards the close of 1865 following a visit by Dr Lang. He brought with him Rev John Thom of the PCNSW who acted as an ordained missionary. Thom's centres were chiefly Woodburn, Lismore and Coraki, where he was accidently drowned in September 1869. Rev Daniel Blue came about a year later and was based at Lismore until he resigned in 1875. There was a lack of organisation and finance at this stage, while many settlers were attached to the Free Church. Some of these had come from the Shoalhaven after the severe flood there in 1860.

Richmond River work 1874-1893

The PCEA people included John McPherson and his 8 daughters and one son. They settled at Oakbank on the North Arm. Hugh Livingstone (1832-1926) of Codrington was another, while Donald McKinnon (1800-1884) of Oakfield near Coraki was also prominent. McKinnon was born on Coll, had been a Gaelic teacher prior to coming to Australia in 1860, and moved from Shoalhaven to the Richmond in 1866 to live on a property selected by two of his sons. It appears that Isaac Mackay of Grafton was the first PCEA minister to visit to establish preaching stations. This was in 1874. In July 1875 Rev George Sutherland came and arranged for Mr J.A. Niçol to act as catechist for 6 months. He resided during this period at the McKinnon home. Rev Hugh Livingstone arrived in June 1876. At first he appears to have resided at the home of his namesake at Codrington, but later lived at Lismore. Work progressing, he was inducted at a service in Lismore on June 20, 1878, the call bearing 83 names. A debt-free church was opened at Wyrallah on July 24, 1880. The cost was $300 and the site was McPherson land 1.5km south of Wyrallah on the Woodburn Road. Casino was also developing. The Campbells and the Cummings were prominent at this centre. 'St Paul's Free Presbyterian Church' opened its doors on February 5, 1881, the same year the PCNSW erected their church in Lismore. St Paul's cost $686, of which $240 was given by Mrs M.M.Campbell, a niece of Rev William McIntyre. She and her husband, a Police Magistrate, also gave land for a proposed church and manse at Wardell.

If circumstances seemed extremely positive the Macpherson/Sutherland dispute soon changed them. The work was divided and it became difficult to maintain a settled ministry. The Casino work in general took the Sutherland side and would not support Livingstone and the folk in other centres, who were anti-Sutherland though not necessarily pro all that the Macpherson faction wanted to do. Mr Livingstone served Wyrallah and Coraki but left in the middle of 1886. He was inducted to the Wimmera charge of the FPCV on July 28, 1886. There was no further supply of significance in these centres for about 20 years. The Wyrallah church was destroyed by fire about 1910, and the site reverted to the McPherson family. Elders known in the early period include Hector McKenzie and Andrew Wotherspoon of Lismore.

From March 1885, James Marshall was stationed at Casino as a student. He was ordained and inducted on November 2, 1885, Casino and district being recognised as a distinct charge by the Sutherland section. Centres supplied included Bexhill and Deep Creek as well as Casino. A manse was erected at Casino late in 1885. It cost about $800, much of which was borrowed. It would appear that Marshall remained until 1888. The following year he joined the PCNSW and served that church until his death in 1930. He was succeeded at Casino by Rev William Archibald who remained about 2 years. The economic downturn, loss of population, lack of ministers and the burden of debt resulted in supply being sought from the PCNSW from August 1893. The PCNSW offered to pay the debt of some $680 if the church and manse were transferred to that church and this is what happened in 1895.

Brunswick River

In March 1881, Angus and James McSwan, N.& J. McInnes, A.McGilvary, McAulay Bros., C.McNeill and A.McKinnon, all of the Clarence, visited the untouched lands of the Brunswick and took up land at Tyagarah. Rev Hugh Livingstone of Lismore made occasional visits, but the opportunity of consolidating an effective witness was lost due to the synodical dispute. The PCNSW formed a parish based on Byron Bay in 1884. It was not until a visit by Rev William Archibald about 1907 that a PCEA minister was in the district. Even after such an interval it was found that a number of families retained their love for the principles of the Free Church. These included such names as McSwan, Gillies and McKinnon. There was also Neil Campbell of 'Inverary' on the Main Arm. He was a 'father in Israel' (to use H.W.Ramsay's words). Although not an elder he acted the part in his concern for the spiritual welfare of the people.

The twentieth century

From about 1907, visits by PCEA ministers were made, particularly by ministers on the Clarence. On February 24, 1914, the Presbytery received a request signed by 11 male residents on the Brunswick River which sought supply of church services. For about 18 months from September 1914, the people had supply from Mr Donald Macdonald, a student of the Free Church of Scotland. Thereafter, the ministers at Grafton and Maclean visited from time to time. For a period prior to proceeding to Scotland in 1929, Mr J. A.Harman gave supply. He lived at Coraki in Mrs Barnett's home. Centres where services were held included Mullumbimby, Tyagarah, Byron Bay, Alstonville, Lismore, Ruthven, Battle Creek, Dyraaba and Coraki. A Sabbath School with 29 children was established at Ruthven in December 1928. Upon Mr Harman's return from Scotland in 1932, he was based at Lismore as a licentiate and ordained (but not inducted) May 17, 1934. The scattered nature of this charge, the lack of a manse and financial difficulties made conditions very difficult. On March 22, 1937, the Richmond/Brunswick was raised to the status of a fully sanctioned charge. About 60 adults were then connected with the work but there was no manse and only an amount equal to about half the normal stipend could be raised. Mr Harman resigned his appointment and was inducted to the Hastings early in 1938.

The past 50 years

The congregation used public halls for the services and relied on what supply could be obtained. By the mid to late 1950s, a group of some 30 folk were meeting in Lismore. Supply was given by a student, John Stafford, and for 2½ years up to September 1960 by Rev Angus Beaton. A modest timber hall was purchased in Keen Street from the Workers' Club in 1959. It cost $3,750 and was sold in 1972 to Woolworths for $10,000. This helped fund a fine modern church in the Lismore suburb of Goonellabah which was opened on December 9, 1972. The land cost $3,500 and the church, the work of Barry Hilberts of Wauchope, but $12,000. A few keen people had moved to Lismore and Rev Kenneth MacLeod, who came from Scotland to work in the area in 1968, by dint of hard work and vision, had proved a great encouragement. He served the congregation until 1973. An adjoining block was purchased in 1973, and an excellent manse was erected in 1975, replacing the Smith Street manse. Rev D.E.Nicholds was pastor from 1976 to 1982, when he left for Victoria. The congregation subsequently received supply from a student, Paul Cornford. He was ordained and inducted as the third

The nearly completed Goonellebah (Lismore) place of worship, 1972

minister this century in March 1985. However, some underlying problems in the congregation flared up, the congregation weakened and the pastor resigned in October 1985. Services are supplied at present each Lord's Day, the minister at Grafton taking a large part in this. It is hoped the congregation can again be settled with a suitable pastor and the work built up.

Elders: Records are exceedingly patchy but the following is approximately complete. Andrew Wotherspoon and Hector McKenzie (died 1887) are elders known in 19th century; J.I.Stewart, Mullumbimby (?   -1924 & died); Lyle McPherson, Ruthven (?   -1942 & died aged 79); Hector McPherson, Tuckarimba (? -1955 & died age 97 different family to L.McP); J.C. Campbell (pre 1934-c1970 & died); A.A.Campbell, father of Rev ADC, (? - 1971 & died aged 82); D.D.Campbell, father in law of Rev A.R.Beaton, (1937-1983 & died age 89); [The Campbells were brothers from Mullumbimby] D.A.McDonald (1937-1937 to Scotland); Cecil Ramsay (c1956-1962 & died, eldest son of Rev HWR); George Martin (? -1968 & died); John Brammah (1962-1981 & died aged 69); Malcolm Moore (1972-1985 & resigned); John D.Ramsay (1972-   ,son of Rev MCR).

BRISBANE

The Brisbane congregation has its roots among those people who came from the Clarence River area of New South Wales to settle in Brisbane in the 1960s. The shortage of ministers restricted the provision of worship services, but things improved as the decade progressed. On June 18, 1967, a service was conducted by Rev Dr J.Campbell Andrews in the (now demolished) Canberra Hotel in Brisbane. Some 35 to 40 were present, including some with backgrounds in the EPC Tasmania. Services were kept up as best possible with visiting preachers as well as services by some in the local group such as Murray Logan, Ken Anderson and Wes Hanna. Formal recognition as an extension congregation was given by Northern Presbytery on February 27, 1969. Throughout that year there was a meeting each Lord's Day and a Bible Study/Prayer Meeting each fortnight. The coming of Mr MacLeod to Lismore in 1968 was a help. In 1971 it was reported by Rev J.A.Harman, who was then giving supply, that average attendances in the morning were 33 and 28 in the evening. Synod 1972 recognised the work as a Church Extension Charge, and on July 21, 1972, Rev R.W.Murray was inducted as the first minister. A manse was purchased at this time in the northern suburb of Kedron. Work progressed steadily. With extra man-power available, Rev Peter Gadsby was inducted on August 18, 1977 as a second minister in an attempt to develop a work at Rochedale, a southern suburb. However, early in 1980 Mr Gadsby was seconded to work in Armidale, while Mr Murray took Long Service Leave later that year and decided to stay in Scotland. However, the services were maintained, and Rev Sam Tamata gave much valued supply which rallied the congregation during the time of tension over the Turnbull issue. Rev Peter Bloomfield arrived with his family at the end of May to work alongside Mr Tamata for a short time before the Tamatas went to Fiji. Mr Bloomfield was ordained and inducted as minister on October 29, 1982.

The congregation has continued to progress in spirituality and numbers. A milestone was the purchase of the Kalinga PCQ property for $65,000 in 1983. The congregation itself contributed liberally and it was possible to finance the purchase within the denomination. Less than $20,000 was outstanding at the close of 1988, and as from January 1, 1990, Brisbane is to be reckoned a regular fully self-supporting sanctioned charge. Consideration is being given to establishing a further centre in one of the developing areas.

Elders: K.G.Anderson (1971-   , son of GRA); W.J.McClean (1971-75, to Manning); W.J.W.Hanna (1971-   ); J.A.Anderson (1974-   , brother of KGA); T.Turnell (1974-82); John Greensill (1984-   ); Ron Lawson (1986-)

The Brisbane Congregation's 'Camp Toowooma' 1989

ARMIDALE

Armidale is a University town of some 25,000 people in the New England district of northern New South Wales, about 110 kms NE of Tamworth. In 1962 the Synod noted the number of PCEA young people studying in Armidale and arranged for a visit to be made by Rev J.A.Harman. There were also members of the Ramsay family at Tamworth. Mr Harman became Moderator of an Interim Session which was appointed to supervise the work. In 1965 Mr John King, formerly of the Hunter, was conducting a monthly service in Tamworth with an attendance of 17, but Armidale was not so promising, and next year it was reported that work in both centres had been curtailed due to lack of ministers. One service was held at

The Manse of the Armidale Congregation

Tamworth in 1967 and none in Armidale. However, the keen witness of two young men who had come to study in Armidale in 1969 - Malcolm Causley of Maclean and Alan Mackay from Kemsey - improved the situation in Armidale. There was an awakening of interest in the Reformed doctrines among some former PCA members and some members of the Evangelical Union at the university. At the beginning of 1972 the McKinnon family moved from Wauchope to Armidale. Rev John Heenan of Maclean was an enthusiastic visitor and he organised what could be regarded as the birthday service of today's Armidale Congregation on February 6, 1972 at 'Rutullah' the home of the Dawson family. There were 20 present. Regular weekly services were conducted thereafter. Synod 1972 recognised the work as a Church Extension charge, and on September 15, 1972 Rev Graham Bradbeer was ordained and inducted as assistant to the minister of Maclean but with responsibility for Armidale. A manse was purchased at this time, and Mr Bradbeer gave a little over 7 active years in establishing the congregation.

When Mr Bradbeer left in December 1979, there was only the shortest of vacancies. Rev W.Peter Gadsby, then working in Brisbane, was seconded by the Presbytery in February 1980. Mr Gadsby's background made him well suited for a work which has a high involvement with students, and sufficient progress was made for the Synod to declare the charge eligible to call a minister. Mr Gadsby was duly called and settled as the first inducted minister on October 30, 1981. The membership fluctuates as there are constant changes as students complete their courses, but a very strategic work is being conducted. The congregation is not yet fully self-supporting but has no debt on the manse. Local halls have been used for services. The Community Pre-School in Allingham Street has been the home of the congregation for about 11 years. Consideration is being given to the purchase of a site for a future place of worship.

Elders: The first Session meeting was held on June 19, 1973. Keith Dawson (1973-   ); J.W.McKinnon (1973-82, 1983-   ); Paul Ridgewell (1984-84, to Victoria).

CENTRAL PRESBYTERY

On pages 473,474 the early history of the Presbytery covering the present bounds of Central Presbytery was outlined. After the Presbytery of Sydney was renamed the Presbytery of Sydney and Maitland in 1886, it continued with this name until 1931, when the Manning was included in the bounds, and the official title became the *Presbytery of Sydney and Manning*. The present name was given on April 3, 1944, and Synod defined the boundaries as the Manning Municipality and south and west of the same in New South Wales. (1986)

Presbytery Clerks since 1870: Rev W.S.Donald (1870-72), John McDonald Jnr. (1872-73); Rev Isaac Mackay (1873-79); Rev J.A.Nicol (1879-81); Rev G.Sutherland (1882-88); Rev G.B.Greig (1888-89); Rev G.Sutherland (1889-93); Rev John Davis 1893-   );   Alex Law (1896-1900); Rev W.Archibald (1900-06); Rev W.N.Wilson (1906-11); Robert Allen (1911-14); Rev William McDonald (1922-27); James Stitt (1927-31); Rev N.MacLeod (1931-32); James Stitt (1933-37); J.H.Cameron (1937-38); Rev J.A.Webster (1938-46); Rev Arthur Allen (1946-58); Rev S.N.Ramsay (1958-76); C.P.King (1976-79); K.H.Kerr (1979-85); D.E.Kerr (1985-   ).

Present charges: Hunter/Barrington (1846); Manning River (1853); St George's Sydney (1856), Hawkesbury/Nepean (Mt Druitt) 1977; Sydney South (1989).

NOTE: As mentioned on page 473, there was extension work last century at Parkes (by Rev Hugh Livingstone), Hay (by S.P.Stewart) and Wellington. At Wellington there had been supporters from at least 1862. Robert Allen, catechist, was supplying in1882, and 'First Presbyterian Church' was opened on March 18, 1883. James Marshall supplied in 1884, in 1885 the PCNSW forcibly took possession and stationed a minister but the arrangement did not hold. William Archibald gave supply, also W.H.Marshall from January 1889 to about March 1891, preaching in 12 centres. However, the weak position of the PCEA led to withdrawal and the property became PCNSW. A new church on another site was built in 1908.

HUNTER RIVER

The outline of Hunter Valley Presbyterianism to 1865 earlier in this volume showed PCEA work was concentrated on Raymond Terrace (timber church on present site opened October 8, 1865) with East Maitland a main out-station; Clarence Town/Dungog (churches in each centre opened in 1856); and at Singleton (brick church opened April 30, 1860). Rev James McCulloch had been minister in the Raymond Terrace district since 1861 having previously (1855-61) served Singleton. He died in harness in May 1873 after a period of poor health. The closure of Clarence Town/Dungog after Donald's death in 1890 has already been recorded.

Upper Hunter 1866-1908

Singleton was ministered to for about 15 months to August 1867 by Rev John McSkimming until his resignation. The shortage of ministers resulted in the suspension of services from 1868 to 1873 when a fortnightly service began. Rev John A. Nicol was settled over the joint charge of Singleton/Aberdeen on October 23, 1878. However, he went to Victoria at the close of 1880, just as the McPherson-Sutherland dispute was brewing. The division in the Synod was reflected in the charge. The Singleton building was closed from 1882 to 1894, while Aberdeen/Westbrook was becoming the more important end of the district. A timber church was built at Aberdeen (near the railway) about 1877 at a cost of $500. The Synod statistics for 1882 show Aberdeen with 15 subscribers, 17 communicants, an average attendance of 50 and a community of 200. There were two services each Lord's Day, two weekday services and occasional cottage meetings at Rouchel, Kayuga, Muswellbrook, Westbrook and Goorangoola. A probationer, Rev Hugh S. Buntine, was supplying the charge in 1881 and in fact was called. A majority of the communicants and contributors opposed the call because they took Sutherland's side in the dispute whereas Buntine took MacPherson's, as did a majority of adherents. In all the circumstances a settlement could not proceed. Buntine was ordained and appointed to the Namoi on February 6, 1883, and each side then obtained a pastor.

A catechist/student, William N.Wilson, replaced Buntine. He was ordained by the MacPherson section in 1886 and resided for about 8 years in Singleton in a house provided by John Fraser of Rouchel. Upon that good man's decease from typhoid in 1895, a manse was erected at Upper Rouchel on a ½ acre block (portion of Conditional Purchase 68/406). The chief centres were at Westbrook, north east of Singleton, where William Fraser, senior, resided, and Upper Rouchel, where a timber church was opened on October 24, 1886, on a site given by Mr Adam. John Fraser, the Adam family, the Cumming and McKinnon families were prominent at Rouchel together with the Burns, McColls and the McPhees at Aberdeen. A monthly service was also held at

494

Scumlow. It was largely through Mr Fraser's generosity that the Singleton building was put in repair and re-opened about 1895. Mr Wilson was much loved by the people of the district. He ministered to all, whether Protestant or Roman Catholic. On his visits he used to take with him Kirk's book of household remedies. He was very good with young people and conducted several Sabbath schools with an overall attendance at one stage of 300.

The Sutherland party, which included the influential and wealthy Rev D.K. McIntyre with family connections in the Aberdeen district, disjoined the section of the Aberdeen congregation which adhered to them and attached it to the Presbytery of Sydney. The use of the church at Aberdeen was continued by this section, since at this stage the site had not been conveyed from D.K.McIntyre, who had given it some years before. The McKenzies of Sandy Creek were a leading family. There was no supply in 1887, but Rev William Grant, originally from Canada and able to preach in Gaelic, was inducted on May 3, 1888, based at Aberdeen. A timber manse on the corner of Segenhoe and Bedford Street (Lots 1,2,3 & 4 of Section 10) was erected about this time. The original manse trustees were William Grant, Kenneth McLeod, Kenneth McKenzie, Murdo McLeod and David Munro McKenzie. Grant was an able minister who covered a wide area and served the whole community.

More harmony occurred as the new century was reached. Wilson left for Raymond Terrace/East Maitland in 1904 and Grant thereafter ministered to all the PCEA people. About July 1908 the ill health of his wife necessitated Grant's retirement to Sydney to care for her (he was then about 70 years of age). He received a testimonial from the Mayor and citizens of Singleton and district and a parting gift of some $130. Local friends appear to have conducted Sabbath Schools at Rouchel Brook and Davies Creek, for Wilson officiated at prize-givings for many years after he left the Upper Hunter. It seems the Rouchel manse was rented out after Wilson left, although it is not clear what happened to the proceeds. In 1922 the Synod accepted an offer to purchase the property for $312 from Mr D.F.Adams, the proceeds to go the the fund to purchase a manse at East Maitland which was already receiving the rent from the Aberdeen manse. The PCNSW got hold of the deed to the Singleton property and in fact entered into a contract to sell it. This was prevented but years later (1926) the property passed to the Council because the rates on the disused building had not been paid. It became a store until it was demolished in the 1970s, some of the bricks being used for a fireplace in the nearby hospital. Aberdeen did not develop as a centre, being overshadowed by Muswellbrook. The church lands in Mount and Queen Streets were of nominal value and were forfeited to the Council for unpaid rates. The Aberdeen manse land was sold for $600 in 1942.

Lower Hunter 1865-1988

McCulloch gave supply to the East Maitland people, being those who had not gone along with the West Maitland charge joining the union in 1865. For a time they had the services of an elder and student for the ministry in the person of Duncan McInnes, but in mid 1868 he accepted a call to Maclean. About a year after McCulloch's death, Rev Peter MacPherson was called from Victoria and was inducted on June 9, 1874. However, in the first year of his ministry at Raymond Terrace he lost his wife and a daughter in a typhoid epidemic, while his own health deteriorated towards the close of 1876. In May 1877 the services of a student, John S. MacPherson (no relation) were obtained and Peter MacPherson was on leave for most of the time until his formal resignation on September 4, 1878. John S. MacPherson having finished his studies was duly called and ordained to the combined charge of East Maitland and Raymond Terrace on October 22, 1878.

The day of John S. MacPherson's ordination was also the day the foundation stone of a brick church building was laid at East Maitland. The building was situated on the corner of Lawes and William Streets, was seated for 300, and cost the sum of $3,000 of which $900 was still owing three years later. A picture appears in J.C.Robinson's church history, page 165. The early trustees included W.T.McDonald, J. Wyllie, John McPhee, Joseph McDonald, William Zuill (died 1890) and Samuel Porter (died 1912). The last two named were elders, the later living at Pitnacree, the property formerly owned by Rev William McIntyre. In 1882 there were two services each Lord's Day, a Sabbath School of 77 scholars and a mid week meeting. There were 18 communicants, 31 subscribers and an average congregation of 60, the same as in 1875. It is a pity the building was over-ambitious. A more modest building and the provision of a manse would have been a better proposition. In 1882 Raymond Terrace was receiving one service each Lord's Day. There were 11 communicants, 23 subscribers, an average attendance of 45 and a community of 140.

During the MacPherson/Sutherland dispute of the 1880s most of the people on the Hunter followed their minister. Moves to restore unity were afoot in the 1890s although Rev J.S.MacPherson and a few others, such as elder Samuel Porter, remained rigid. MacPherson went to South Australia about April 1904, and in August the same year Rev W.N.Wilson moved from the Upper Hunter to take oversight. Ecclesiastical conditions were such that the formality of induction did not occur, but for practical purposes he may be reckoned as the fourth settled PCEA minister in the Raymond Terrace district. The old Raymond Terrace church building was replaced by the present timber structure which was opened on November 23, 1905 by Rev William McDonald of Sydney. Wilson was a kindly man and a good pastor.

The church at Raymond Terrace in 1988 with manse behind

He drove himself everywhere in a two-wheeled vehicle with a folding top. The East Maitland building was still encumbered with debt but was secured to the church when Samuel McQueen of Tomago met the liability. He was repaid over a period of years.

Wilson's death in May 1922 aged 66 years was a sad and serious blow due to the shortage of men at the time. However, in April 1924 Rev Malcolm Galbraith of the Free Church of Scotland arrived in Sydney to help the PCEA for 12 months. Most of his service was spent in the Lower Hunter and Barrington district. Galbraith was from Durinish, Skye, and would have found many people of Skye descent in the district. His quiet and faithful work was of great benefit, especially to the middle-aged folk. Joseph Harman, student, supplied in 1925-26, while another FCS minister, Rev James Henry, late of Burghead, was of great help during his visit to Australia in 1926-28. He was elderly but energetic. His wife used to drive him about in a sulky. Six elders were appointed in the 1920s as the work was consolidated.

After a period of supply while completing his studies 1932-33, Rev J.A. Webster was ordained and inducted on October 31, 1933, and remained until transferred to Geelong in June 1946. Webster was nothing special as a preacher but was an excellent visitor and was much assisted by his like-minded wife. They never complained of shortages or the many difficulties of working the scattered charge, given the poor roads, the depression years

497

and then the problems of wartime. Messrs Galbraith and Henry had boarded, but a manse in William Street, East Maitland (a few doors from the church), was purchased for the Websters' use. This was only the second manse owned by the congregation since that at Ahalton occupied by James McCulloch in the 1860s.

A vacancy in excess of eight years followed. In 1948 the Synod gave permission for the disposal of the properties at East Maitland and in 1952 a timber manse was erected at the rear of the Raymond Terrace church building. On November 11, 1954, Rev S.N.Ramsay was inducted to the pastorate. The principal preaching places were Raymond Terrace, Anna Bay (about 30km east) and Newcastle (about 25km south) as well as Barrington (some 120km to the north), with an occasional cottage meeting at Maitland (15km west of Raymond Terrace). The Anna Bay services had been commenced in 1928 for the ten church families in that locality, the local elders taking the initiative. Services in Newcastle were held in homes or halls with an average 26 attending at the time the 1957 Synod made some financial provision to assist in obtaining a place of worship. In 1960 a ¼-acre block was purchased with the aim of remodelling the existing house into a hall. The location was 142 Broadmeadow Road near the railway station. In the event it was decided to build a hall next to the house. The resultant timber hall was duly opened on December 9, 1961 by Rev M.C.Ramsay. Subsequently, changes were made to the road system which meant the location was. less advantageous, but at least it provided a settled place for PCEA folk and others desiring a Biblical ministry. Mr Ramsay had the extra load of editor of the denominational magazine (1958-66) and Clerk of Synod (1966-82). He retired with effect November 12, 1984, having given 30 years to the charge.

James Cromarty had already given some assistance as a Home Missionary in 1984, and he now gave full supply until he was ordained and inducted on April 11, 1986. The communion roll, which had slipped to 31 at the end of 1983, rose to 62 at the end of 1986. There remains the difficulty of adequately serving such a widely scattered charge. Clearly there is need to make Newcastle a separate charge and Raymond Terrace could then receive greater attention and outreach could be made to Maitland, now a growing centre. There is a high level of commitment and it remains to grasp the opportunities.

Elders: [Session records go back only about 25 years hence this listing, which is a reconstruction based largely on magazine references, may have missed one or two names. Elders residing at Barrington are listed separately. East Maitland and Raymond Terrace had separate Sessions from 1864 to 1904 to the extent of having two representative elders in the Presbytery.] **East Maitland:** Finlay Nicholson (died 1866); William Zuill (1852-1890 & died); Samuel Porter (c1865-1912 & died); Duncan McInnes (c.1865-1868 & to Maclean); John Calman (1887-1906 & died). **Ahalton/Raymond Terrace:** Hugh MacDonald (ex Hinton 1846-c1870 & to the Clarence); William McCloud (18 - 1867 & resigned); William McQueen of Tomago (186 -1882 & died aged 74 years); Malcolm Gillies of Millers Forest (186 -18); Ewen Cameron (1887-   ) ? the same person as J.H.Cameron who was an elder c.1904; **Elders 1906-1988:**   John Matthewson (1906-1909 & died); Robert Galloway (-1918 & died aged 87); James Robinson (ex Manning 1914- 192   & to Sydney); J.R.H.MacDonald (1928- ?   ); George Morris (1928-1959 & died); Samuel McQueen (1928-1943 & died); W.J.Anderson of Bobs Farm (1928-1954 & died); Magnus Campbell (1928-1955 & died); Donald Maclean (1938- ?   ); Campbell C.King (ex Manning 1958-   ); John King (son of CPK 1963-1963); Alisdair Webster (son of JAW 1963-1973); Eric George 1963-1975 & died); John M.Cromarty (1963-1973 to Geelong); Graeme King (son of CPK 1973-   ); John Kerridge (1986-1988 to Grafton); Trevor Leggott (1986-1988 to Melbourne); John Shaw (1988-1988 to Melbourne); Ian Miller (1988-   ); Stewart Upton (1988-   ).

BARRINGTON

The relatively isolated Scottish settlement near Gloucester and the shortage of ministers meant that much depended on the local people. As indicated in a previous chapter, John McInnes was chiefly responsible for organising early services and the Manning rather than the Hunter was the charge to which Barrington was related, possibly because of the presence of Gaelic preachers in the former centre until the 1880s. Catechists/students were able to supply for various periods. Such men included W.N.Wilson (1881-82) and Robert Allen (1886-88), and ministry extended to the Wollamba River. In April 1888 a petition bearing 110 signatures sought that Allen be ordained but this did not proceed, largely because the Synodical dispute had resulted in local divisions which were probably exacerbated by language factors, Allen being less acceptable to some because of his lack of Gaelic. Allen was associated with the Sutherland section but there were many who followed the MacPherson line. In December 1887, a bi-lingual FCS licentiate arrived and was ordained by the MacPherson section on the 23rd of that month with a view to labouring on the Barrington, Manning and Hastings rivers. After six months the Hastings was excluded from regular visits. Thereafter, somewhat more than half his time was spent on the Barrington and the balance on the Manning. Services on the Barrington were held at first under tarpaulins stretched outward from the verandah of a private house. A sawn slab church was soon erected and formally opened on January 20, 1889. An interesting picture of this building appears in *Our Banner*,December 1935.

It was situated on the east side of the Barrington East Road a short distance south of the first school house (1864). [Between these two buildings on John McInnes' house paddock was a block about 1 acre in area reserved for a church in the early 1900s but it was never used and was deeded back to the McInnes family in 1942.] It appears that McKenzie was not very proficient in English while some thought him less than energetic. It seems he concluded his position with the MacPherson section and in February 1894 applied to the PCEA Synod. However, his application was declined, chiefly on the ground that the Synod had no field suitable for him. He returned to Scotland thereafter.

With the turn of the century the population of the district began to increase in consequence of the AA Company's leasholds becoming available for purchase. The PCNSW desired to place a minister in the district. The older Free Church settlers were averse to a unionist minister, but many of the younger people went along with the plan. In consequence, Rev Donald Ross, a Gaelic-speaking minister, began work at the beginning of 1904 when the population of the district was 700, half of them Presbyterian. The village of Gloucester became the centre of the charge and a church was soon built.

The PCEA work continued with supply, especially from Rev W.N.Wilson, who helped heal the division. He would ride up from Maitland, no easy trip, to supply the congregation. From 1932 Rev J.A.Webster came up from Maitland every third weekend. He excelled in visitation and most would say that no one, before or since, has been his equal. The centre of population having moved, it was decided to build a new church in the village of Barrington. On October 9, 1935, a neat timber building was opened on a good 1 acre site on the main road. The cost was $380, of which nearly half was owing at the time of opening. This building is still in good order and continues to serve the congregation.

Prior to 1923 it appears Barrington was linked to the Manning but since that time it has been linked with the Hunter. Today it is a small group which regularly gathers for worship, perhaps a dozen or so people. But over the years the congregation has had its impact in the wider life of the PCEA through the influence of those who have moved elsewhere. Of the Free Kirk pioneers there are few of their descendants left continuing with the church of their fathers in the Barrington congregation. Miss Jean Beaton and Mr Douglas Shaw, deacon, are two present members who are descendants of the pioneers.

Elders: John McInnes (c.1869-1890 & died); John McInnes (son of JMcI 1928-1943 & died aged 81 years); John Beaton (1938-1952 & died); Hugh A. Grant (1938-1962 & died aged 78).

MANNING RIVER

The early history (1853-70) of the Manning River charge will be found on pages 126-131. It is not entirely clear what happened when Rev Allan McIntyre fell ill and died (May 1870). Probably the elders kept up the services, and perhaps Rev W.S.Donald of Clarence Town assisted. About the middle of 1872 Duncan K.McIntyre, Allan's younger brother commenced supply. He had trained for the ministry with a view to filling the blank created by Allan's death. He was a ministerial member of the Synod of November 1872, so it appears he was ordained a little before that time, although a record of the event has not been located. Just what kind of minister he was is also unclear. He was not very robust, for he resigned the charge on April 3, 1878 because of poor health. However, he remained in the district for a further year, although most of the pastoral work in 1878 was carried out by S.P.Stewart, who was licensed in July 1878 and ordained and inducted at Tinonee on February 5, 1879.

Stewart was a tall man, well over 6 feet, and a fearless horseman. He was also a man with a remarkable facility in the English language and possessed of a retentive memory. He was also well known for his wit. He was a firm Protestant, and became the spokeman on things Protestant far beyond the local district. He continued in the pastorate until sometime after his resignation took effect on March 27, 1929 [the memorial in the church states May 2, 1929]. He was then 72 years of age, and had been virtually blind for a number of years. That did not stop him preaching however. His lengthy ministry saw many changes. The church dispute of the 1880s affected the charge, while population shifts resulted in Taree coming into prominence as a centre whereas previously Tinonee had been the main centre. There is some reason to think that the life of the congregation suffered by the lack of adequate involvement by members and the employment of their gifts for the edification of all, though this was not uncommon of churches generally in that period.

Changes in buildings 1880-1920

On March 10, 1880, the foundation stone of a brick church was laid at Tinonee by Rev D.K.McIntyre. The site, the present one, was opposite the original timber church (1856). The cost was $1424, and it was opened on October 7, 1880. The Wingham Church (1862) was replaced on the same site by the present timber building, and opened in March 1899. On December 15, 1907, a modest timber church was opened in High Street, Taree which was to serve the congregation for 70 years. Services had been held in the Protestant Hall before the congregation was of a size to warrant building a place of worship. The Synod of 1920 gave permission for the sale of the manse and acreage at Little Tinonee, and a house was purchased in Wonga

Street, Taree. This was a more suitable arrangement given the difficulties the minister was experiencing with his eyesight.

The fourth man to hold the pastorate was Rev Neil MacLeod. He arrived from Scotland in October 1929 and was inducted on December 17, 1930. Given that he was a young man himself, he very naturally gave attention to the needs of the young. Some of the older members thought him a little brash and tactless, as young men often are, but he did good work in the charge. Services had been held at many centres over the years, but with changes in population and transportation as well as a decline of interest in spiritual things, the outlying centres gradually closed. MacLeod left for Sydney early in 1936, and Rev M.C.Ramsay was settled the following year and remained until his retirement in 1965. The Sunday School work MacLeod had introduced was continued, and a good teaching ministry conducted over a wide area. From 1965 to early 1970, Rev Dr Campbell Andrews gave energetic ministry which was appreciated by young and old alike. Late in 1970 Rev Edwin Lee was inducted and continues as the

SOME ELDERS AND DEACONS 1988: Front from left: K.Longworth, C.Alley, E.Lee; Middle row from left: R.Alley, R.Muldoon, W.McClean, J.McInnes, D.Stewart; Rear from left: B.Semple, J.Milligan. Absent:N.Robinson & R.Weber, elders; A.Weber,deacon.

minister to the present time. He has made a considerable impact through a much appreciated radio broadcast each Lord's Day evening, and through his straightforward and earnest preaching.

On July 11, 1959, a neat timber church was opened in the outlying centre of Bunyah on a site given by the widow of Mr James Murray. It was built under the direct of Mr John Milligan, a member of the congregation and a builder. He was also the contractor for the new brick church on the old site in Taree. It incorporated the facilities of the hall which had been built in 1955, and was opened free of debt on July 2, 1977. More than half the total cost of $49,000 was covered by a legacy from the late Miss C.McKay. The Wonga Street manse had been sold in 1948 and a new manse erected in 1951 on a fine corner site in Wynter Street given by the Stitt family. In 1988, this property was exchanged for an older one adjoining the Taree Church with a view to future extension. For the past several years the minister has supplied his own accommodation, but the congregation have funds put aside for a new manse for the future, and there is also a timber manse next to the Wingham church.

The Manning River is one of the oldest and strongest PCEA charges, and has contributed greatly to the church at large in missionary interest and hospitality at Synod time. It loses many young folk to the cities, as happens in most towns under 20,000 people, but in many cases other centres are thereby enriched.

Elders: Records before 1899 are minimal. Elders in the Allan McIntyre period are referred to on p.128. Elders known to have served the Manning after 1870 include: Alexander Lobban (died 1876), Samuel Martin (to Grafton c1877), George Martin (1862-71 to the Clarence), Lachlan McDonald, Longview (1864-1892 & died), Hector McLean, Oxley Is. (dates uncertain: 1870s), David Lobban (-1898 & died), James Murray, Tinonee (-1893 & died), Alex Cameron (pre 1883 - ?), Hector McLennan (pre 1899-1913 & died), John Robinson (1899-1936 & died), James Robinson, Keppy Hills (?1905-1915 to Hunter), Alexander McLennan (1904-1925 & died), William McIntyre Macdonald (1923-46 & died aged 86), Alexander Cameron (1923-40 & died), James Murray (1923-54 & died aged 86), Donald Frank Robinson, son of John (1932-55 & died aged 73), George Campbell, Nabiac (1932-55 & died), John H.Cameron (1932-61 & died), Francis Longworth (1932-45 & died), George Morton (1932-49 resigned), Duncan Allan McIntyre Murray (1932-38 & died), Duncan Cameron (1941-   ?), John S. Robinson, son of Frank (1941-81 & died aged 73), J.J.McInnes (1949-   ); R.V.Weber (1949-   ); R.Muldoon (1957-   ), J.M.Milligan (1957-   ); C.P.King (1950-58 to Hunter), J.W.Berry (1966-85 & died), F.Neil Robinson (1980-83, 1986-   ), J.A.Cromarty (1975-84 to Hunter), K.L.Longworth (1975-   ), W.J.McClean (1976-   ).

ST GEORGE'S, CASTLEREAGH STREET, SYDNEY

The congregation now known as St George's originated when a section of the Pitt Street congregation memorialised the Presbytery of Sydney to organise another congregation, the minister of which might be able to preach in Gaelic. A deputation consisting of Messrs Peter Stewart, Dugald McPherson, William Buyers and John McKay appeared in support of the memorial and its prayer was granted, February 22, 1854. A call signed by 150 people was addressed to Dr Macintosh Mackay of Melbourne but was declined. Another call to this minister, signed by 100 persons, was accepted in 1856 and Mackay was inducted on May 10, 1856. E.A.Rennie states that on any reasonable view there was no need for the additional congregation, and that the main cause of it was the difficulty of reconciling the Gaelic portion of the Pitt Street congregation to a ministry wholly English in character as was provided by Mr Salmon. But those who formed the congregation thought the name and fame of Dr Mackay would gather a good congregation. The congregation rented a building at the back of the east side of George Street near Hunter Street for $400 p.a., and undertook to pay a stipend of $1,200 p.a. to the learned Doctor. Little success attended the efforts, but this was attributed to the lack of a fine church building. Mackay was somewhat of an impractical dreamer on such matters as was demonstrated in the crushing debt he left on the church built for him in Melbourne. The same occurred in Sydney.

Application for a site was made to the Government in 1856, and land was granted in Harrington Street. However, meantime the congregation purchased the present site of 607m2 at 201a Castlereagh Street for $4,000, and proceeded to construct what was intended to be the finest church in Sydney. It occupied the full width of the site, was in Gothic style, seated for about 900 including the gallery on three sides, and cost the sum of $21,844 for the construction alone, say 1½ million 1988 dollars. At the time the church was opened on February 5, 1860, there was a debt on the whole project of $23,152. That such a building could be erected indicates something of the credibility of some of the leading members of the congregation, but it also shows great folly. A year after the building was opened, the Deacons' Court had to tell the minister they could only offer $800 a year stipend. The annual interest bill was over $1,800 and expenses were exceeding income. Mackay resigned towards the middle of 1861, and the advice of the Synod was sought. The Synod disapproved of the erection of 'so unnecessarily expensive a place of worship' and ordered a church-wide appeal. About $8,000 was raised which reduced the debt to $16,000. In February 1862, William McIntyre was inducted as the second minister. He undertook to serve without stipend and continued as pastor until his death in July 1870. If there had been no interest to pay, the revenue during this period would have been sufficient to allow a stipend of $800 a year. As it was, at his death there was still about $12,000 debt. It was cleared at the end of 1879, when it was calculated that of the total expenditure of the congregation for all purposes from 1856 to 1879, almost 30% or $18,636 had been spent on interest. However, the debt had been met without the aid of concerts, tea meetings or bazaars.

McIntyre was a solid preacher, not a popular figure. He could not compare in the pulpit with Robert Steel, for example, but a rather small congregation found his careful and quiet expositions good fare. He was succeeded by another scholar, Rev George Sutherland, who was inducted in 1872. He was more attractive as a preacher, and was possessed of great energy and abundant literary gifts. The congregation grew steadily throughout the 1870s and the debt was finally liquidated. The 1880s saw the sad quarrel in the Synod and some of the older members left. Sutherland was a man of catholic spirit, and was behind the forming of a branch of the Evangelical Alliance in Sydney. He was also prominent in the Orange Lodge. He collapsed and died at his home at Peenant Hills on July 27, 1893. The pulpit was then supplied by an elderly man, Rev T.S.Forsaith. After he died aged 80, the various ministers did what they could. However, things were at a low ebb, as in the church generally, and all but one of the elders resigned, thinking the cause was a sinking ship.

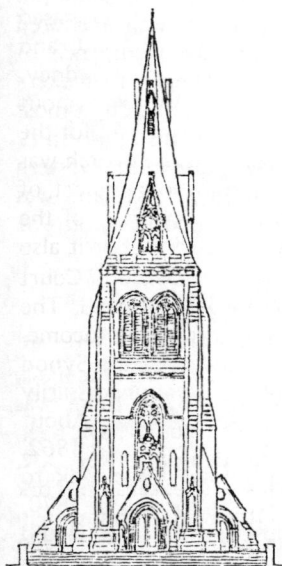

On August 26, 1901, the Presbytery was requested to moderate a call to Rev William McDonald of Hamilton, and an income of $340 per year was thought within the capacity of the congregation. The call was signed by 17 members and 38 adherents, was accepted, and Mr McDonald became the fourth pastor on December 13, 1901. He saw steady growth so that by 1926 there were 75 members and 90 adherents and an income of $1,280. During the latter part of his ministry Mr McDonald lost the power of speech and could only walk with difficulty. Men connected with the Bible College at Croydon were among those who helped supply the pulpit. Rev George Mackay of Fearn FCS came in 1929 for a year. Mr McDonald took great interest in the congregation until his death in 1930 aged 82.

Rev. M. M. Macdonald.

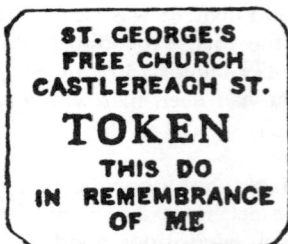

ST. GEORGE'S
FREE CHURCH
CASTLEREAGH ST.
TOKEN
THIS DO
IN REMEMBRANCE
OF ME

Nickel communion token
used 1933 to c.1970.

Rev. N. Macleod.

Ministers 1931 to the present

Rev M.M.Macdonald came from Scotland in May 1931, and was inducted as the fifth minister in March 1932. He was an able preacher whose sermons were well prepared and delivered with perfect diction. After a period of some months on leave he resigned in April 1935 and returned to Scotland. A year later Rev Neil MacLeod was inducted. He stimulated the Youth Fellowship work. He would have had perhaps 140 in the congregation. Mr MacLeod resigned towards the end of 1943 to become a Chaplain in the Forces. On March 1, 1944, Rev Arthur Allen, who had grown up in the congregation, became the seventh minister. Mr Allen was noted for his clear presentation of Reformed doctrine. His catholicity of vision was always well anchored in the Scriptures. He was taken in 1958, just before the resurgence of Reformed teaching for which he had worked and prayed began to make a mark in Australia. The congregation then called Rev A.D.McIntosh, a most generous and warm-hearted man who was known for his expository preaching. A portion of the congregation formed a new cause in the western suburbs during his ministry. Mr McIntosh retired in July 1981, and was succeeded by the present pastor, Rev John McCallum of Scotland, on June 28, 1985.

Extension work

Over the years the building has continued something of a problem. There had been proposals to sell it early in Mr McIntyre's ministry, except that the likely price would not have covered the debt. During the 1870s there was opportunity for extension in the Sydney suburbs which could have been more readily funded if the debt had not been so burdensome. Rev D.K. McIntyre had retired to Sydney in 1879, and sponsored extension work first in Riley Street, but the Synod's sanction of this was withdrawn in 1882 since it became a vehicle for the MacPherson party, and then from 1887 in Newtown. A church was opened in Erskineville Road on February 13, 1887. Some financial support was given by St George's. In the early

506

1890s Rev John Davis was connected with this centre, with which quite a number of families were associated. Robert Allen (father of Arthur Allen) also gave supply. Services seem to have ceased about 1906. No record of location or ownership has been found, and it is probable that the property was owned by D.K.McIntyre who died in 1899.

In August 1921 a gale dislodged one of the three pieces of stone forming the crown of the 100' steeple of the church and sent a 13 kg piece hurtling to the footpath. The street was blocked and repairs cost $294. The country congregations assisted in this. Of latter years the congregations has become well established financially. However, the best use of the property exercised the minds of the officebearers, and Synod 1972 agreed to a proposal that the site be redeveloped with an office block providing 57,300 square feet of floor space. The idea was that the church use a portion of the building and that the rents after mortgage costs would eventually aid in church projects. In the event the plan did not proceed, and the present intention is to endeavour the renovation of the premises, one of the last churches in the heart of Sydney.

The congregation acquired its first manse through the generous help of the country charges   during Mr McDonald's ministry. The present manse at Waverton was purchased in 1961 and replaced a previous manse at Strathfield. In 1978 the Lindfield Retirement Community of 21 units, principally funded by residents on a long-term lease basis, was opened in the northern suburb of Lindfield. An adjoining property was acquired in 1984 with a view to future development.

ELDERS: William Buyers, merchant (1857-60, died 1875); John Macdonald, clothier (1857-died pre 1880); John Moon, surgeon (1857-64 joined PCNSW); Peter Stewart, builder (1857-82 & died); Robert Campbell, merchant (1865-71); Duncan St Clair Maclardy, merchant (1873-79); E.A.Rennie, auditor general (1873-189? resigned, died 1911); Alex Law, auditor general's dept (1876-1914 & died aged 88 [his wife was a sister of Rev S.P.Stewart]); Joseph Knox, merchant (1876-86 & resigned); William Halley, coachbuilder (1878-79 & died); A.W.S.Gregg, real estate agent (1878-1887 & resigned, died 1915); James Bremner, sea captain (1878- ?); Henry T.Page (1887-91 & resigned); Andrew Steel, interior decorator (1887-9? & resigned); William Kernaghan (1887-89 & died); Donald McLean, prison governor (1902-08 & died); Robert Allen (1905-15 & died); Alex Gunn, haberdashery salesman (1913-25 & to Scotland); Alex McLean (from Strathpeffer FCS 1914-16 & died aged 63); Kenneth MacRae (from Strathpeffer FCS 1914-16 to Scotland); Donald McIntyre (1920-26 & died); Murdoch Stewart (1921-   ?); James Stitt, farmer (1922-40 & died); James Ross, farmer/storekeeper (from Maclean 1924-40 & died); James Robinson 1924-31); James Nisbet, water police (1926-31 & died); Colin Mackay, retired (1928-60 & died aged 97); Alex Gillies, prison warden (1930-46); Samuel Cruickshank, farmer (1935-37 & died); Stanley Bateman (1935-50 & resigned); Norman McDonald, mechanic (1935-35 & resigned); Robert Allen, teacher (1938-76 & died); Kenneth Kerr, carpenter (1938-51 & died); Harald C.Nicolson, accountant (1938-47 to Melbourne); Donald Shaw, retired farmer (1941-48 to Scotland); Neil McPherson, haulage contractor (1948-89 to Sydney South); Joseph Harris, builder (1947-   ); Lachlan R.McKinnon, painter (1954-81); Alex Ross, cane farmer (from Maclean (1969-86 to Western Suburbs); Kenneth H.Kerr, engineer (1969-87 & died); Norman Kerr, accountant (1969-   ); Graham Andrews, electrician (1975-77 & resigned); Donald E.Kerr, real estate agent (1975-   ); Alex H.Steel, bank manager (1975-   ).

HAWKESBURY-NEPEAN (MT DRUITT)

On March 23, 1977, St George's Session agreed to overture the Central Presbytery to approve extension work in the western suburbs of Sydney, and to invite Mr Brian Dole, then a student for the ministry, to undertake that work for a period of up to two years under the oversight of the St George's Session. This was agreed to, and accommodation rented for the Dole family at South Penrith which they occupied in July 1977, on their return from Scotland. The first service of the new work was held on October 9, 1977 in the Harold Corr Community Centre at Werrington. Work progressed in an encouraging way, and on June 25, 1978 the first communicants were received. Eighteen of these were by disjunction from St George's congregation and 3 on profession of faith. Mr Dole was ordained and inducted to the charge on August 11, 1978 and served for nearly three years when he resigned. Following a period of supply, Rev H.C.Varnes, the present minister, was inducted on March 5, 1982.

The church in Mt Druitt Road

The congregation knew some years of pilgrimage as more fully outlined in the attractive 10th anniversary brochure issued in 1987. Places of worship were rented in Werrington, Cambridge Park, Mount Druitt and Plumpton, until late in 1985 when a 70-year old Anglican Church with a hall and adjacent land was purchased in Mt Druitt Village for $100,000. The sale in 1985 of the manse in Oxley Park, acquired in 1982, facilitated the purchase of the property, and a manse was built on the vacant land in 1986. Some land held by the Synod at Castlereagh from last century was also sold for $20,000 and the proceeds applied to Mt Druitt. The property was thoroughly renovated to provide a most attractive home for the congregation, and the generosity of the members and friends together with assistance of more than

508

$20,000 from St George's has reduced the amount owing to very manageable levels. The congregation has been well supported and has not needed to seek assistance from the Synod. For several years from 1983 a regular afternoon service was held at Richmond and a radio programme on the local FM station was presented.

Elders: The first elders were inducted on November 12, 1978. G.A.Neil (1978-   ); A.P.Webster (1978-86 & resigned); M.N.McIntosh (1978-81 & resigned); C.A.Barnes (1980-81 & resigned); S.P.Swinn (1985-87 & resigned); L.E.Wells (1986-   );

SYDNEY SOUTH

In 1988 a family in the southern suburbs of Sydney and in membership of St George's asked their visiting elder about the possibililities of a charge being established in the southern area. The matter was brought up at the next Session meeting at which time the Session also had a letter before them from the Church Extension Committee which had been sent to all congregations asking about church planting in the local areas. The Session responded positively to the Committee, indicating there was great potential in the south and south western area of Sydney for a church extension charge. An Interim session was appointed by the Presbytery to arrange a preaching station for six months with a view to then assessing viability. The first service was held in Bexley Congregational Church on November 6, 1988 and attracted 51 people in the morning and 35 at night. The steady average settled down at 35 both morning and evening and 17 at the mid-week prayer meeting, with offerings sufficient to fully support a minister. On January 24, 1989 the Presbytery recognised the new work as a fully sanctioned charge and the a membership roll with about 28 names of those who transferred from St George's was established. The bulk of the supply has thus far been provided by Rev John Graham with Mr Neil McPherson taking the mid-week meeting. On February 5, 1989, services were relocated to St David's Uniting Church in Kingsgrove.

SOUTHERN PRESBYTERY

Messrs Arthur Paul, Alexander McIntyre and Peter Macpherson with Joseph Thomson (St Kilda elder) continued the FPCV in line with the Protest of May 25, 1864 and met as a Presbytery and also as a Synod. The Synod became defunct in 1870 on account of a dispute between Paul and Macpherson resulting in inability to obtain a quorum for the Synod meetings. Macpherson resigned his charge at Meredith in 1874 to go to East Maitland PCEA. At a meeting in Geelong on April 25, 1876, Messrs Paul and McIntyre met and drew up an 'Act of Reconstruction' in which they claimed the power and specified the procedure to reconstitute the Synod when a quorum was available. The Synod was reconsituted on March 28, 1877 upon the ordination and induction of William McDonald to the Hamilton charge, but became unable to find a quorum on March 6, 1902 following the resignation of Rev Hugh Livingstone of the Wimmera. It was next reconstituted on December 12, 1939 and disappeared upon the union with the PCEA on November 25, 1953.

The old Presbytery was also unable to hold regular meetings for some years this century when John Sinclair was the only settled minister. The three congregations of the Free Presbyterian Church of Victoria were received into the PCEA on November 25, 1953, and the Victorian Presbytery erected to have jurisdiction accordingly. The first meeting of the new PCEA Presbytery was on November 30, 1953. In 1965 a congregation on the North West Coast of Tasmania was received, while oversight of South Australia had always been exercised. The Synod of 1977 gave permission for the Presbytery to adopt the current name, while the Synod of 1983 formally declared the Presbytery boundaries to be the States of Victoria, South Australia and Tasmania.

Presbytery Clerks 1953-1988: Rev A.D.McIntosh (30/11/1953-30/07/1957), Charles Mackechnie, ACIS (30/7/1957-18/04/1975), Rev G.L.Weber (18/04/1975-9/12/1977), Rev R.S.Ward (9/12/1977-17/7/1979), Mr J.G.Simpson (17/07/1979-22/02/1980), Rev R.S.Ward 22/02/1980-

Present congregations: Geelong [1853], Melbourne [1855], Hamilton [1869] and Ulverstone, Tasmania [1965].

Former congregations having existence after 1864: Meredith (and Ballarat region) - P.MacPherson minister 1862-74; Nareen - W.R.Buttrose minister 1878-88; Wimmera (Rev J.A.Nicol 1881-84, Rev H.Livingstone 1886-1902) and stations at Camperdown (originated 1880) and Charlton (originated 1881). There was a shortlived work (1930-32) at Woodville, an Adelaide suburb, and a group in Adelaide itself until the 1970s. Drysdale, part of the old Bellarine charge, was revived and linked with Geelong 1883-1935. The building (c.1853) was sold in 1937 and is now RSL Hall. For Winnaleah (1972-79) see under Ulverstone. [For old Victorian work see **Our Banner**, 11.77,12.77.]

GEELONG

The Geelong congregation originated on April 25, 1853 in the formation of a Gaelic congregation of the Free Presbyterian Church. The early history has been outlined on pages 143/144. In May 1854 the erection of a sandstone schoolroom was commenced to the design of John Young, and the first services in this building were held on October 8, 1854. According to the minutes of the congregation for December 3, 1856 the gross cost was the large sum of $3,846 of which half was met by the Denominational Schools Board. There were 132 seatholders and a school was conducted in the premises during the week but was closed about 1859. The site of some 3,370m2 on the corner of Myers Street and Latrobe Terrace was a grant from the Government.

First minister 1856
In July 1856 the congregation called Rev John McDougall to be their pastor. He had been supplying for several months and was duly ordained and inducted. He was dogged by poor health and died on May 29, 1858 at the early age of 36. Rev Alexander McIntyre had been appointed to give relieving supply in February 1858, and he continued after Mr McDougall's death. As the congregation of some 200 persons was too large for the schoolroom, tenders were called for the construction of a church designed by Christopher Porter in a Transitional Colonial Georgian style. The building was completed

The Myers Street/Latrobe Terrace Church as it appeared c.1900

511

for the sum of $3,043 and was opened for worship on May 1, 1859, just a few weeks after the union which formed the PCV. Minus the turret and with the external walls cement rendered, this is the building which houses the congregation today.

Effects of union controversy 1857-61

The congregation had supported the Minority in 1857 against the union, but the failure to secure recognition in Scotland at the Free Church Assembly of May 1860 and May 1861 led to disorganisation and decline. Despite McIntyre's popularity among the Highlanders there were some in Geelong of a type more interested in assimilation to prevailing views and the congregation weakened. About March 1861 McIntyre gave notice that he planned to move to Ascot near Ballarat, where there was a substantial settlement of Highlanders. However, on April 10, 1861, Rev J.Z.Huie was appointed by the FP Synod to supply Geelong. He was well and favourably known from his earlier years in Geelong as minister of the original Free Presbyterian congregation in Little Malop Street. He soon gathered a large congregation, many or most being Lowlanders, and received a call signed by 152 persons. This was accepted but the induction appointed for September 18, 1861 was postponed pending investigation of persistent reports of bizarre behaviour associated with excessive use of alcohol. Huie resigned from the FPCV ministry three months later, but continued an independent work in Geelong for some time. His gifts of oratory were not matched by his sanctification. All of this was unhelpful to the progress of the work.

Work of Rev Alexander McIntyre

Early in 1862 Rev William Dron was appointed supply. In a pun on his name he was said to have been 'a drone' and resigned in June to join the PCV. He soon went to NSW but fared no better there and ended up in the Church of England in Ireland. The upshot was that Rev Alexander McIntyre resumed oversight although he would not accept a call. He managed to hold the work together, although he was often away preaching in other centres of Gaelic settlement. He used to speak of Geelong as 'the hard rocks' that broke his heart, probably because so many Highlanders compromised the faith of their fathers and others who attended his ministry were relatively unresponsive. Upon McIntyre's death on June 9, 1878, the *Geelong Advertiser* [June 12] recorded that 'It was noticeable that during the whole of the [funeral] proceedings there appeared to be no one present to offer up prayer in Gaelic, although it was in that language that Mr McIntyre invariably addressed his congregation.'

McIntyre had no taste for the routine of church courts or the organisational aspects of church life, nor did he do much in the way of visitation. He was pre-eminently a preacher and for the most part had neither session or communion roll. Always refusing a settled pastorate he regarded himself as free to preach to the Highlanders wherever they were to be found. He had named Rev John Sinclair of South Australia as a suitable successor, which indicates his hearers must have understood English well enough, for Sinclair had no Gaelic. A Lord's Day afternoon Gaelic prayer meeting was kept up and occasional worship services. Despite the lack of full organisation and there being but 12 communicant members, there were able Christian men of principle keen to see the Gospel witness maintained.

The ministry of Rev John Sinclair 1881-1932
A call in 1879 to Mr Sinclair was unsuccessful but a second the following year containing 107 signatures was accepted. Mr Sinclair was installed as the second inducted minister on May 3, 1881. Rapid improvement in the congregation's position followed. Mr Sinclair was an attractive preacher, an excellent visitor and an able administrator, although not given to effective delegation. By 1889 there were 80 communicant members.

Mr McIntyre was a bachelor and lived with his brother's family at Ashby. However, the congregation soon made good the lack of a manse by erecting a timber home next to the church in 1881. This served during the period of Mr Sinclair's ministry which terminated with his death on August 18, 1932. A total of eight children were born to Mr and Mrs Sinclair, and a brick home (known as 12 Myers Street) was built next to the manse in 1934 at a cost of $2,677 to provide for the widow. Assistance from the Presbytery by way of short-term loans aided the completion of this project.

A time of difficulty
Mr Sinclair's ministry was a long and memorable one. Ministers were in short supply and he carried on to the last and was 81 at his death. It was not so easy to obtain a new minister. The congregation in 1933 was basically an ageing one of about 70 people with relatively inexperienced elders. There was something of a spiritual and leadership vacuum which seems to have played a part in a serious division over a certain Rev T.Russell Cameron of New Zealand. He was eloquent but seemed to polarize congregations wherever he went. He was of Free Presbyterian Church of Scotland background (trained in Belfast), but came to Australia from Auckland in 1935. The Presbytery resolved in September 1935 to prohibit him from the Geelong pulpit and this was upheld by the Assembly in 1936. Rev Arthur Allen, newly returned from studies in Scotland was ordained and inducted on June 8, 1938, and contributed considerably to the strengthening of the Reformed faith. He helped inaugurate the *Calvinistic Society* in Melbourne and was an original editor (1942) of the *Reformed Theological Review*. He was translated to St George's, Sydney on March 1, 1944. A section of the congregation was for seeking supply from Mr Cameron, but the ban remained on this good but somewhat erratic gentleman. The fourth inducted

minister was Rev James Webster, formerly of the Hunter PCEA, installed on June 29, 1946, when the membership was about 20. He was translated to Maclean PCEA on July 27, 1949, but was replaced by Rev A.D.McIntosh of Hamilton on July 31, 1953. In 1954 the last local elder died and until 1973 the St Kilda Session acted as interim-session of Geelong. Financial assistance from the Synod became necessary in 1956. Mr McIntosh was translated to Geelong on August 14, 1957. The congregation held on with less than a dozen members who were determined that the distinctive PCEA witness be preserved.

The period 1962-1972

Rev Allan Harman became the sixth inducted minister in 1962. Beginning with an attendance of 12 or 14 numbers grew to 30/35 at the morning service. He was on leave of absence in America for nearly two years from August 1964 and then resigned the charge. The services were kept up by Rev Robert Murray, a retired FCS minister and latterly by Mr (later Rev) Alan Tripovich prior to his induction on the Hastings in early 1968. At the close of 1968 Rev David Nibbs commenced residential supply with 12/18 attending an afternoon service. He was inducted as minister on February 11, 1970 following a call bearing 14 signatures. The receipt of a legacy of $10,000 enabled the church building to be improved, especially be replacing the old frosted glass windows. Mr Nibbs was translated to Grafton, May 1972.

The eighth inducted minister - Rev John M.Cromarty

In February 1973, Mr John Cromarty, formerly Vice Principal of Maitland Primary School, entered on studies for the ministry of the PCEA at the Reformed Theological College in Geelong, and supplied the congregation as well. He along with Bruce Webster, a son of the former minister, were installed as elders of the congregation in 1973. The following year, Professor Allan Harman returned to Australia to become Professor of Old Testament at the RTC, and he also became a member of the session. On December 3, 1976, Mr Cromarty was ordained and inducted as the eighth minister of the charge. The cause has subsequently experienced quite a revival of fortunes with current attendances at the morning services around the 50/60 mark. In 1980 the Deacons' Court was re-established by the ordination of 3 men. In July 1982 the original manse which had been used latterly by students and then by the School opposite, was demolished as being beyond useful life. A 200m2 brick manse was erected in its place in 1983, the cost being nearly covered by the sale of 12 Myers Street for $92,000 the same year. A significant improvement to the church was the partitioning of a section to provide a creche, bookroom and vestibule area at a 1982 cost of about $6,000. Concerns remain about the adequacy of the buildings: though the position is central further upgrading is necessary, and some thought has been given to relocation. The congregation is a relatively youthful one with almost everyone from non PCEA backgrounds. There is thus a challenge and an opportunity for the furtherance of God's word among Geelong's 160,000 residents.

Elders 1853-1988:[The first session was formed in 1877.]

John Boyd (1877-1893), Neil McPherson (1877-1881 & returned to Scotland), W.J.Reid (1881-1914), Charles Sach (1883-1904), George Graham 1885-1887 and resigned), John Hensley (1887-1891 - Mr Sinclair's father-in-law), Archibald Hutchinson (1893-1906), Samuel McKay (1899-1919), Robert Hair (1903-1931), James Young (1903-1932), Robert Muir (1919-1955), Donald McDonald (1922-1936), James Paterson (1932-1938 resigned to visit Scotland), Charles MacKechnie (1931-1934 and moved to Melbourne), Alex McDonald (1947-1951), J.R.Bruce Webster (1973-   ), John M.Cromarty (1973-1976 and became minister), Allan M. Harman (1974-1980), Peter J. Bloomfield (1978-1982 and to Brisbane as minister), Cliff Cumming (1981-   ), John Sweet (1983), Greg Cahill (1983-1985).

NB. W.J.Reid was Session Clerk from 1882 to 1912.

Messrs P.Bloomfield, C.Cumming & J.M.Cromarty in November 1981
The old Geelong manse is in the background.

515

MELBOURNE

Melbourne is a large, sprawling city of some 2.8 million people located around Port Phillip Bay with a bias toward the eastern and south-eastern areas. The population in 1901 was about 500,000. During the 19th century, Rev Arthur Paul's congregation at East St Kilda was the only one which stayed permanently out of the union of 1859 which formed the Presbyterian Church of Victoria. In 1986 the principal centre was relocated to Wantirna in the eastern suburbs and in 1989 an additional centre was commenced at Narre Warren, east of Dandenong.

Early Presbyterian work in St Kilda

St Kilda, now a bayside suburb of some 47,000 people, was proclaimed a village in 1842. At that time a bush track connected it to Melbourne via a punt over the Yarra River. The name 'St Kilda' is probably derived from a ship of that name which foundered nearby. There is also an island of the same name off the Scottish coast (now uninhabited) but no 'saint' named 'Kilda' is known.

In May 1855, a number of Presbyterians in the St Kilda district gathered for public worship in an iron building on the corner of High Street (now St Kilda Road) and Alma Road. The Sundays of that month were 5th, 12th, 19th and 26th, so one of these dates was the birthday of Presbyterian witness in St Kilda. The services were under the oversight of the Free Presbyterian Synod, and continued for some months with Rev Arthur Paul of Richmond the principal preacher. Names mentioned in the early days include J.Mathieson, J.Hunter, Patterson, Spottiswoode, Williams, Christie, Miss Jackson, George Urquhart and Joseph Thomson. The building soon became rather crowded by a congregation of about 60 persons. It was also rather primitive - earthen floor and simple wooden forms for seats. When the opportunity came to purchase the timber Congregational Church on the north side of Inkerman Street (about present †70 - between Barkly Street and St Kilda Road), the Presbyterians lost no time in securing the building. It was opened on September 23, 1855 as the Free Presbyterian Church, St Kilda. Arthur Paul was duly called and inducted as the first minister on October 2, 1855. He was but 29 years of age. Then a bachelor, he lived on the Brighton Road. He was to continue as minister until his death in 1910.

Division over church union 1857

As shown in the general history, Paul was the key man in the opposition to union. The very general support of the congregation was a key factor in its survival. All but one of the communicant members supported Paul's stand. However, some adherents, including several wealthy men with Established

516

Church of Scotland sympathies, did not. Financial pressure was brought to bear. The upshot was that it was mutually agreed Paul and his supporters would vacate the premises and the wealthy men would accept liability for the building debt of some $800. This arrangement suited Paul since the Inkerman Street location in the busy market area was not favoured and a government site at the corner of Alma Road and Chapel Street was in course of transfer. However, St Kilda's population of some 2,700 was near the coast and the government site was considered too far from town for a church just yet. Hence, a site at 23-29 Alma Road, now occupied by two office buildings and portion of a service station, was purchased and a temporary wooden church erected about June 1857. It was seated for 200 and the cost was covered by gifts and a loan from Thomas Bailey, an associate of William M. Bell, an elder of John Knox Congregation in Swanston Street and an early Mayor of Melbourne.

The unionist congregation

The one member and the adherents who remained at Inkerman Street were re-organised as an avowedly unionist congregation (though nominally Free Presbyterian for the next nearly two years) in July 1857, details being reported in the Melbourne *Argus* on the 30th of that month. Charles Moir was obtained as minister later that year. This congregation is represented today by the St Kilda Presbyterian Church on the NE corner of Alma Road and Barkly Street - the site to which they moved in 1861.

About August 1857, when Paul's congregation set about erecting a manse for their minister on the government site, strenuous and persistent efforts

The 1858 manse showing the bay-windowed 1868 extension.
Picture taken about 1925.

517

were made by the Inkerman Street congregation to obtain the property. Motions passed at a meeting of Paul's congregation on September 6, 1857 included one claiming to be 'the identical congregation which two years ago with the approval of the government elected three trustees from their own number to hold the land reserved for the Free Presbyterian Church in St Kilda having suffered no change in its ministers or its elders and lost no members in full communion except such as have removed from the district with one exception.' A further one stated, 'That another ecclesiastical body claiming to be the Free Presbyterian Church of Victoria but which nevertheless has abandoned the principles of that church by entering into a covenant of union with a different body, hostile to the Free Presbyterian Church, has not and ought not to have any right of control or jurisdiction over this congregation nor any claim whatever to denude it of its property.' For some years attempts were made to obtain the property, but failed.

East St Kilda church and manse

The 7 roomed brick manse was completed in 1858 at a cost of $1,080. Mr Paul married Miss Janet Moffatt and the growing family (eventually there were 12 children of whom one died in infancy) needed more space. A 3 room extension was therefore added in 1868 bringing the total cost by 1869 to $2,518. These were the days when a builders' labourer cost $1 a day.

The East St Kilda Church as first proposed

518

By 1861 the population of St Kilda was about 6,400, and thoughts turned to erecting a permanent place of worship in Chapel Street adjoining the manse. On August 6, 1862 it was resolved to proceed, and the 160m2 buttressed bluestone building was duly opened on the Lord's Day, January 17, 1864 with Paul the preacher in the morning and Rev Alexander Gosman of the St Kilda Congregational Church in the evening. The architect was Lloyd Tayler, then in the early part of his career. The original design envisaged a longer building with a spire. As erected there was a squat tower over the seession room and seating for 150/200 people. The cost was about $3,050, with a debt in 1865 of only $80. The temporary building in Alma Road was sold at auction for $518 (or 4 cents a square foot of land area). It appears it was used for some years by a Baptist group who subsequently built in Crimea Street what is now a Masonic Hall.

Arthur Paul's ministry

Arthur Paul's ministry was solid and instructive rather than popular. After the union controversy it does not appear that the congregation was large. There were even renewed attempts to 'buy him out' at the time a PCV congregation was projected for East St Kilda (implemented in the building of St George's Church, Chapel Street, in 1877). Paul was a logical thinker, a competent Hebraist, and one who maintained a life-long interest in mathematics. He wrote well but was often quite biting in his attacks in the press. During the last 23 years of his life he took a rather isolated position, but the contraction of his sympathies should not blind one to the contribution he made to the preservation of a testimony to the full-orbed Presbyterian position. His second oldest son, William, was a noted barrister and the author of several standard legal texts.

Most of the records of Paul's ministry have been lost but the marriage register for 1876-1901 is available. It shows that up until 1876 Paul had officiated at 59 weddings and from 1876 to 1901 at a further 34, all but 2 of these being held somewhere other than the church building.

Paul was a competent administrator and a man with an eye for the future. In 1877, somewhat more than one-third of the 2 acre site was sold for $2,310. This together with other monies, including , it would seem, the proceeds of the sale of an unused government site on the corner of Simpson and Grey Streets, East Melbourne [lots 5 & 6 of Section 27], was applied to erect two 9/10 roomed two-storey villas in Alma Road adjoining the manse at a cost of about $8,500 - a sum equal to about $600,000 in 1988 terms. These houses were completed in 1877 and let, with a charge of $600 per annum for Paul's stipend. Hard times came with the collapse of the land boom in 1891, Melbourne lost 10% of her population to other colonies and rents were halved. Late in 1891 a section of the congregation began meeting during the week in the Protestant Hall in Melbourne for a worship service conducted by the Geelong minister. Circumstances in the first decade of the 20th century at St Kilda are unclear, although things were at a low ebb at Paul's death on August 13, 1910, for there were no elders or trustees and only 11 members.

The vacancy 1910 - 1921
The Protestant Hall meeting was consolidated with the St Kilda congregation after Paul's death, and gradually work was organised. For a time the building was made available for the Reformed Presbyterian Church. Supply was given by different men including Rev John Watson Smith, BA. Mr Smith had been connected with John Knox Congregation in Swanston Street in early life and later with Chalmers' Church, Dunedin. He was a licentiate of the PCNZ.

Second minister - J.Campbell Robinson 1921-1952
On August 13, 1921, Rev J.Campbell Robinson was ordained and inducted as the second minister. With family links to Ireland but from a strong PCEA background on the Manning River, Mr Robinson had trained at the Free Church of Scotland College in Edinburgh. He reconstituted the Session in 1921 and did excellent work getting things going. Within a year or two 24,000 sermons by him had been distributed in pamphlet form and the property was put into better order. The actual strength of the congregation was not great for a list of attenders in 1927 has only 40 names, all but 7 being females. The McLean family, Miss Annie, Miss Catherine and Miss Mary among them, were prominent in the membership. They came originally from an old church family in the Hamilton district. Mr Robinson was a bachelor and these ladies, who lived in the villa next to the manse, provided housekeeping services for him. The last of these hospitable ladies died in 1981 at an advanced age.

Mr Robinson founded the *Free Bible Society of Victoria*, which distributed the Scriptures gratis, and for about 6 years before his retirement he prepared the script of a Sunday morning programme on radio 3UZ called *Gems from Holy Literature*. Mr Robinson resigned the charge on February 29, 1952 and died of a heart attack later that year. He had expended a great deal of energy writing the denominational history (published in 1947), and some felt this had permanently weakened his health. He had married Florence McSwan of the Clarence River in 1951, and his widow returned to New South Wales.

Property improvements
When Mr Robinson became minister the rental properties needed quite a deal of attention. The rental value of each was about $400 pa gross. Each was electrified in 1922 and divided into two a little later. In 1932 Mr Robinson

advanced a sum sufficient to enable the extension of 94 Alma Road (next to Alma Park) thus providing 5 flats on that site. The total cost was $3,006, and Miss M.I.Cameron advanced $600 of this and was allowed a one-bedroom flat in return. Mr Robinson was repaid from rentals over the next few years.

His next project was the reconstruction of the manse. This occurred in 1938 to the design of the minister as drawn up by Victor G. Cook, architect. The old manse had been about 230m2 on one level; the new manse was about 280m2 on the ground floor plus 3 attic bedrooms and facilities totalling some 100m2. It was a large home in a form of modern Tudor style, retained the 1868 extension with remodelled roof-line, and cost $4,478 - a modest figure for the size but excessive if viewed in terms of practical usefulness. A report and picture in the Melbourne *Herald* for February 16, 1938 shows that Mr Robinson had in mind a further wing on the east side which accounted for his unwise insistence on the new building extending over the equivalent of two blocks (88-90 Alma Road). The bulk of the funds was borrowed at interest from the Presbytery.

Dutch migrants

Accommodation and some financial help were provided Dutch migrants in the early 1950s, and the first Synod of the Reformed Churches of Australia was held in the upstairs front flat at 94 Alma Road in June 1952.

92 & 94 Alma Road after 100 years

521

Another vacancy 1952-1959

There was a lengthy vacancy following Mr Robinson's death as ministers were still in short supply. Rev Kenneth MacRae, MA, of the Free Church of Scotland, gave valuable help from June 1953 to June 1954. At his first service he had 26 hearers - quite a change from the 1,500 in his home charge of Stornoway. Services were maintained however. Rev Angus Beaton gave 6 months supply up to March 1958 prior to going to Peru as a missionary.

Ministers 1959 to 1979

On October 21, 1959, Rev Edwin Lee was inducted after a short period of supply. Under his energetic Christ-centred ministry a considerable revival of the congregation took place, and membership rose from 24 to 50 during his all too brief ministry. The first deacons in the congregation were set apart in May 1962. The church hall built in 1961 at a cost of $3,931 was a big improvement and enabled *John Knox Theological College* to operate 1963 to 1965. Mr Lee resigned April 17, 1966 to accept a charge in Scotland. During the vacancy major maintenance was done on the church. Rev Ray Murray was called direct from Scotland and ordained and inducted as the fourth minister on December 11, 1968. The congregation was maintained under his earnest ministry, but he was translated to Brisbane on July 21, 1972. Rev E.S.Turnbull became the next minister, and was inducted June 29, 1973 and continued until he was suspended on libel August 31, 1979. During his ministry the membership declined from 44 to 36, but givings improved so that the church was nearly self-supporting without the need for property income.

'By schism rent asunder' 1979-1983

The majority of the active members left with Mr Turnbull in November 1979 and formed an independent congregation nearby. Two elders were involved in the schism and had to be removed. Other members who remained acted very inconsistently and much pastoral care was required but did not produce lasting harmony. At the end of August 1981, Rev Rowland Ward arrived from Tasmania to give 6 months supply. The supply period was extended by invitation of the congregation for a further 12 months, but dissensions soon arose, so that by early 1983 only 4 regular attenders remained plus the Ward family. However, there was an extra service in the eastern suburbs begun by Professor Allan Harman using Chalmers Church in Auburn on February 4, 1979.

Relocation in the eastern suburbs

The Auburn service was attended by up to 30, including the Harman and Milne families. However, for them it was essentially a stop-gap measure pending an improvement in the available ministry in the PCV. Their work and effort in the congregation was appreciated, but Mr Ward was naturally concerned to establish a sound PCEA work and to have it located further out in the eastern heartland of Melbourne. The Auburn service was suspended in October 1982. However, on the Lord's Day afternoon of January 2, 1983, in the premises of St Paul's Lutheran Church, Rooks Road, Nunawading, a regular service began with three families - the Loudens, the Grahams and the Wards. Meanwhile, two services each Lord's Day continued at East St Kilda. Mr Ward became the sixth inducted minister on June 2, 1984. Immediately a strategy plan for the next 10 years was drawn up, unanimously agreed by the Session and congregation, and put into effect. What has occurred subsequently has been in line with the aim of 3 or 4 centres by 1994, and God in his providence has dealt most encouragingly to this end.

The East St Kilda property was sold in three parcels progressively in 1986/87 to institutions in each case. The sale of the manse and adjoining villa was settled in February 1986, and covered 90% of the cost of a new church, car-park and manse at Wantirna. The flats at 94 Alma Road were sold mid 1987, while the church went to the adjoining owner at the close of the year, a large premium above market value having been offered. All the buildings are covered by conservation provisions.

Knox Presbyterian Church, Wantirna
This congregation is in direct continuity with the congregation which began meeting in St Paul's Lutheran buildings on January 2, 1983. Attendances averaged 17 in 1983 and increased by 3 or 4 in each of the next three years. Search for a site in the eastern suburbs was intensified. Vermont South was the general location being considered, but in February 1986 an ideal site adjoining a busy shopping centre with plenty of exposure to passing traffic was located, and contracts signed on the 12th of that month. A brick building of 245m2 in a simple but pleasing design was erected together with a car park for 20 vehicles. The cost was about $224,000 inclusive of $74,000 for the two blocks of land. A manse was built on an adjoining site and was occupied by the Ward family at the end of August 1987.

The opening of the church on December 28, 1987 was an occasion of much thanksgiving. The visiting preacher was Rev Edwin Lee, who had wanted to relocate to the eastern suburbs when he had ministered at St Kilda many years before. The Moderator-General of the GAA was present to bring greetings. Steady growth has occurred, principally from the local area, and the average number of different people in actual attendance at the Lord's Day services had reached 48 by the end of 1988.

The name of the church was chosen because of its position at the time as the only Presbyterian place of worship in the City of Knox. It is of interest that Sir George Knox, after whom the City is named, was descended from a brother of John Knox, the Scottish Reformer, while the first European settler in the bounds of the City was Rev James Clow (see p.137).

North Caulfield

The East St Kilda Church had been leased in August 1986 with a view to funding another minister from the revenue. For a time access for a morning service was retained, but this service was transferred to the Church of Christ building on the corner of Alma and Dandenong Roads on November 30, 1986, a mutually satisfactory arrangement being made with the small Church of Christ congregation. This service continues with a small group of ten or a dozen folk from the local area, the Wantirna minister being the usual preacher. Potential exists to further develop this work.

Berwick City Presbyterian Church, Narre Warren

Once the work at Wantirna was fairly underway, it was appropriate to take steps to establish a further centre in one of the under-churched and growing outer areas. The City of Berwick, to the east of Dandenong, was without a Presbyterian Church, and was predicted to grow from about 57,000 people to 186,000 by the year 2,001. The central part of the city at Narre Warren was a major focus due to the Fountain Gate Shopping Centre and the Civic Offices being lacated there, but no Protestant church building existed in that part despite explosive residential development.

On October 12, 1987, a site on the corner of Narre Warren North and Prospect Hill Roads was purchased from the developer for $75,000, and the normal brick dwelling covenant modified on purchase to remove the reference to dwellings. A Town Planning permit was obtained for a church of similar design to that at Wantirna together with 31 car spaces. A 5 year old home of sufficient size for a manse was purchased for $105,000, and this became the home of the Leggott family from December 1988.

During 1988 the Wantirna congregation sought a suitable man to commence work at Narre Warren from scratch. Mr Trevor Leggott, a home missionary in New South Wales who had recently completed his studies, accepted the invitation extended. He was licensed by the Southern Presbytery on January 27, 1989, and commenced a morning service in the premises of the Education Support Centre, 53 Webb Street, Narre Warren on February 5, 1989. Twenty-seven were present at the first service, and a core group of about 20 continue to gather to worship, praise and work for the extension of Christ's cause. Mrs Leggott gives religious instruction to about 260 primary children each week. Steady progress is being made with the Rickard, Smith and Shaw families the initial members along with the Leggotts. The erection of the place of worship is to commence in 1989.

Elders: (A) Period 1855-1921: Records for this period are lost. However, Joseph Thomson and probably George Urquhart were early elders. Robert Campbell, a teacher and one of the first two elders of Scots Church under James Forbes, was another. Thomas Watson (died 1893) was an elder for many years. David Moffatt and W.G.Murray, formerly connected with John Knox congregation, are other possibilities in the 1870s along with Duncan Niven. (B) Period 1921-1983: The following is a complete listing of the 16 men. Rev ·J. Watson Smith (1921-1928 and died), Samuel Nicolson (1921-1943 and died), A.G.E.Smith (1923-1933 and resigned), Thomas McKay (1928-1934 and returned to Stornoway), Angus McDonald (1929-1935 to Scotland), Donald McLeod (1930-1935 to Scotland), Charles Mackechnie (1933-1980 and died), Alexander MacLeod (1937-1946 and died in Adelaide), Alfred M.McLean (1937-1983), Gilbert H. Brain (1940-1949 and died), Harald C.Nicolson (1947-1955 and 1961-1979 and resigned), J.G.Simpson (1967-1980), David S.Webster (1967-1976 and resigned), William A. Semple (1976-1982 and resigned), Ivor Briggs 1976-1980 and resigned), John D.Nelson (1979-1980). (C) Period from 1984: Mr John B. Louden (1984-   ), Mr Angus A. MacLeod [son of Alexander] (1985-1989 and moved from Melbourne), Rev William M.Mackay (1986-   ).

Knox Presbyterian Church & Manse - Mountain Highway, Wantirna

HAMILTON, VICTORIA

Early Presbyterianism

The town which was to become Hamilton was originally named The Grange. The name was changed in 1851 as the population of the district began to rise following the gold discoveries. An above average proportion of the population was Scottish and Presbyterian. At a meeting in Hamilton on December 8, 1854, it was resolved to form a congregation for the public worship of God in connection with the Free Church of Scotland. Subscription lists were opened for the erection of a building subject to the provision that no minister would be settled who could not preach in Gaelic and English. This was a very necessary provision since the majority of Presbyterians were Highlanders who could not speak English well or at all. On April 14, 1857, Rev Angus Macdonald was inducted and services were held in the Concert Room of the Victoria Hotel until the church building was opened on August 8, 1858. There was a Gaelic service at 11am and English services and 2pm and 6pm each Lord's Day. At a congregational meeting on March 14, 1859 there was unanimous support for the union and the Presbyterian Church of Victoria was duly formed the following month.

The harmony in Hamilton was soon broken.[1] One of the elders was guilty of serious immorality but had retained his status and was allowed to sit at the Lord's Table despite protests. Many of the Highlanders stayed away from Communion on account of this lack of discipline. This was made the occasion of reducing and then cutting out entirely the Gaelic service since those who stayed away were held to have disenfranchised themselves. By September 1863 there were no Gaelic services in Hamilton, a pastorally inept situation, and a breach of faith given the decision in 1854.

Services had been held in the schoolhouse at Branxholme from 1856. The connection with Hamilton was loose given the demands on the Hamilton minister, but there were family connections. The foundation stone of a church building at Branxholme was laid on November 25, 1861 and it was opened on June 15, 1862 by Rev Angus Macdonald (now Uniting Church). Rev James McRoberts was inducted as the first minister on July 2, 1862 despite his lack of acceptability to the Gaelic speakers.

1. The account of the origin of the Hamilton charge which is found in J.C.Robinson's denominational history and in the booklets issued by Hamilton in 1970 and 1979 states that the main Scottish section of the Hamilton Presbyterian Church resolutely stayed out of the union in 1859. This is incorrect. The best source for what really occurred is **The Testimony** (edited by William McIntyre) 1866, p.143 and 1869, pp.601-603.

Withdrawal from the PCV in the 1860s

In this failure to provide for the pastoral needs of the people lies the origin of the present congregations of the. PCEA in the Hamilton/Branxholme district. The Free Presbyterian Church of Victoria which continued after the union of 1859 was not in a position to provide much assistance for some years. However, Rev Alexander McIntyre paid several visits, and one assumes Gaelic prayer meetings were kept up by some of those who later became elders. Rev Angus Macdonald was killed by a fall from his horse in March 1868, and his successor, Rev J.K.Macmillan, did not have Gaelic. At a meeting of the Free Presbyterian Synod on April 21, 1868, an application from Hamilton seeking the services of a minister was received. The following year Alexander McIntyre was able to visit for a period, and he organised the work into a regular charge. On August 11, 1869, at a meeting in Hamilton, it was resolved to proceed to the erection of a brick church on the site in Brown Street obtained as a government grant (part of allotments 7 and 8 totalling 2,530m2). The building was seated for 200 and the opening services on September 18, 1870 were conducted by Rev Alexander McIntyre and Rev Arthur Paul.

Rev William McDonald 1877-1901

It was some years before a settled ministry could be provided. Meanwhile, services were held in the Brown Street building and also at Branxholme in the schoolhouse. On March 28, 1877, Rev William McDonald was ordained and inducted in the Brown Street Church before a congregation of about 180 people. Mr McDonald was born at Dunvegan on the Isle of Skye and was brought up in Geelong. He proved an acceptable pastor and served both Hamilton and Branxholme. In March 1878 elders were ordained in each of these centres and functioned separately until they combined in April 1885. On February 7, 1879, a timber church was opened at North Byaduk on land obtained from Donald McKenzie. It was destroyed by fire about 1907 but was later replaced. On March 30, 1879, a brick church in Monroe Street, Branxholme was opened by Mr McDonald. It cost about $1,000 and was designed by the Shire Engineer, Mr Steward. Like the Hamilton building it is still in use. In 1882 a timber manse was erected next to the Hamilton Church for a cost of about $830, while a few years later a timber church was erected at Hotspur. It was sold in 1920. Services were held at many places where the erection of a building was not warranted. These included Condah and Grassdale, as well as Redruth. A manse was provided at Branxholme, so it would appear from a reference to additions to such a property in 1897, but records for this period are lost. Nareen, 70kms north, had its own FPCV minister from 1878 in the person of William Buttrose. After he left in May 1888 because of ill health and population shifts, the Hamilton minister visited when possible. In 1895 it was proposed to settle Rev Walter Scott as assistant to Mr McDonald which would have led to more services at Nareen, but this proposal did not come into effect.

527

Mr McDonald resigned his charge on October 17, 1901 in order that he might accept a call to St George's PCEA, Sydney. He received splendid tributes from the congregations when he was farewelled in December 1901. He had married Christina McLean of Branxholme, and his continued affection for his first charge is reflected in the name he gave his home in Sydney - 'Hamilton'.

Transitional ministry 1901-1918

During the next five years services were held irregularly due to the lack of ministers. The Lord's Supper was observed twice a year with the help of ministers from South Australia and New South Wales. In December 1906, James Payn Lewis, a student of the PCNSW based at Kyogle, cast in his lot with the PCEA. Through Mr McDonald's influence he came to Victoria and commenced supply at Hamilton/Branxholme early in 1907. He was duly called upon 100 signatures and ordained and inducted on July 25, 1907 at Hamilton. He did excellent work in rallying the congregations. In November 1909 he was called by Maclean PCEA but resolved to decline the call in view of receiving a petition that he remain signed by 175 members and adherents in the Hamilton/Branxholme district.

There was considerable surprise and disappointment in May 1910 when Mr Lewis announced his intention to enter Parliament at the end of the following year. Considering this to be a virtual abandonment of his ordination vows the general feeling was that he should immediately resign. The formal resignation was accepted by the Presbytery on August 18, 1910, some few weeks after Mr Lewis had left to reside in Melbourne. At the close of 1908 a licentiate of the PCEA, John Ramsay, was based at Branxholme and assisted in the pastoral work. Following Mr Lewis' departure he was ordained and inducted to the pastorate on May 10, 1911 in the Hamilton Church. He was a capable minister. However, his wife was not strong physically and died in October 1912. Consequently, Mr Ramsay concluded his ministry in March 1913 and went to Scotland. There he served the Free Church until his death in 1933 aged 54 years. Supply was given for about 3 years by Rev T.M. McClean before he went to Maclean in November 1916.

Rev Isaac Graham

The fourth inducted minister was Rev Isaac L. Graham. He was from the Hastings River, New South Wales and was one of the first Australian students to train at the Free Church of Scotland College in Edinburgh. He was ordained and inducted on January 3, 1918 and obtained Rev A.D.McIntosh as colleague and successor in May 1951. However, Mr McIntosh remained only to July 1953, so Mr Graham continued as senior minister. He resigned with effect from April 16, 1954 but continued to care for the charge until his death on July 10, 1964 aged 76 years.

Mr Graham was a man of business capacity, whose ministry was a teaching one. His pastoral visits were characterised by sympathy and prayerfulness. He was also concerned for the welfare of the Aboriginals. Early in his ministry he got the properties into order and opened a new church at Mt Eccles,1924. In the latter part of his ministry he resided in his own home, and after Mr McIntosh left, the manse was let for a period. Some of the land had been sold at an earlier time and in 1961 the manse was sold to the City of Hamilton, and a modern manse purchased in 1965. It was soon in use as a meeting place for the youth group commenced by Mr Varnes who was then giving supply prior to going to Peru. The same year a multi-purpose hall was erected in place of the old Byaduk church. During most of 1966 Rev Robert Murray, a retired FCS minister gave supply, and for some months in 1967, Rev Joseph Harman did likewise. There was then no settled minister in any of the three Victorian charges. On August 19, 1967, Dr Andrews presided at the opening of a church building at Macarthur. Built of stone in 1878, it had been purchased from the Methodist Church for $1,250. Methodist work had broken up due to modernistic ministry and some of the folk came over to the PCEA. At the opening Dr Andrews was able to announce that Rev Eric S.Turnbull of Tasmania had accepted the call extended by the congregation which then numbered some 34 communicant members and about 20 adherents.

The period 1967 to 1988

Mr Turnbull's ministry (1967-73) was a strong teaching one in which the distinctives of the Reformed Faith were set forth prominently. The building at Mt Eccles was sold in 1975 as it had been superseded by Macarthur. After a vacancy of some 18 months, Rev Graeme Weber became the seventh settled minister and remained 4½ years. The congregation had been maintained under his ministry, but his departure was not easily made up, largely due to the sympathy of many of the people with Mr Turnbull. Successive calls to Messrs A.D.Campbell, B.L.Dole, H.C.Varnes and A.L.Tripovich failed. However, services were maintained and a PCA minister, Rev Peter Swinn, gave residential supply from January 1983 to May 1985. In July 1985, Rev John Pateman of East Kilbride FCS was elected. The call was transmitted and after the usual immigration delays was accepted. An Englishman, Mr Pateman was inducted on April 25, 1986. Some time has been spent in settling the congregation. Once a strong Highland locality, the cause has declined to a faithful few. The challenge is to look forward and to take the Gospel to the needy all about. Some consolidation of the three regular preaching centres is desirable.

Elders 1878-1988: By checking references in the denominational magazine it has been possible to provide the following more or less complete list of elders (30 in all): Lachlan McLean (1878-1899 then to Gippsland), Hugh McInnes (1878-   ), Coll McDonald (1878-1915 when died aged 93), Malcolm Murchison (1878-1897 and died), John McDonald (1878-   ), Dugald McFarlane (30/09/1878-3/09/1900 and died age 76), Hugh McLean of Camp Creek (1879-1899 and died aged 76), Ken Murchison (1879-   ), Roderick McInnes (1883-1892 and died), John McLean (1886-   ), Roderick McLeod (c1891-1898 and died), Angus Nicolson (1892-1933 and died), Lachlan Morrison (1892-1898 and died), Angus Morrison(1894-1921 and died aged 83), John McFarlane (1917-1936 and died aged 64), John Nicolson (c1924-1930 and left district), Lachlan Muir (c1924-1936 - brother of Robert Muir, Geelong), Archibald McFarlane JP (1924-1942 & died), Jack Macpherson (1935-1978 & died), John McLean (1941-45), Joseph R. Jackson (1950-1966 & died), Charles McMillan (1950-1968 & died), Dugald Macpherson (1951-1969 & died), James Hill (1965-1988 & died), William Hutchins (1968-1981 & resigned), John H.C.Cunningham (1969-1988), George Alford (1973 -1984 to Sydney), Doug Hamilton (1983-1986 to Sydney), Mark J.Simpson (1983-1987 & resigned), Donald McFarlane (grandson of Archibald, 1987-   ), Max Hutchins (1988-1989 to Geelong).

OFFICEBEARERS 1970: From Left, Jack MacFarlane, E.S.Turnbull, James Hill, Hector MacFarlane, William Hutchins, John Cunnigham (Dugald MacFarlane, deacon, absent).

ULVERSTONE, TASMANIA

The Ulverstone PCEA congregation had its beginning on September 14, 1965, when the minister (Rev E.S.Turnbull) and congregation of the Reformed Evangelical Church at Penguin were released by their Presbytery and accepted into the PCEA. A change of ministry was indicated, and after some months leave of absence, Mr Turnbull was settled at Hamilton in October 1967. Rev Angus Beaton began supply in August 1969 and was inducted on December 5, 1969 and remained until translated to Maclean early in 1974. The strength of the congregation grew to about 30 members in Mr Beaton's time.

In 1969 the congregation sold on terms the timber manse in South Road, Penguin which had been purchased in 1960. It was no longer central to the work, was in poor order and encumbered to about its full value. In 1970, a manse was purchased in West Ulverstone for $10,500, and paying it off was aided by Mr Beaton taking outside employment. Rev Rowland Ward commenced supply at Ulverstone in October 1975, and was ordained and inducted as the third minister on March 16, 1976 when there was about 16 members. Mr Ward designed a simple place of worship capable of being turned into a dwelling in the future, and at an all-up cost of $20,542, including $2,878 for the land, the building was erected and opened on July 30, 1977. There was only a very small debt at the time of opening. Particular

The opening of the Ulverstone Church, July 30, 1977
From left: R.S.Ward, A.M.Harman, M.R.Hingston, N.G.Triffett

assistance was given by members of the Bosveld family which aided in this provision. For a time Mr Ward also took outside employment as finances were tight. He concluded his ministry in August 1981, and left to supply in Melbourne. Almost immediately a call was issued to Rev David Nibbs, a Tasmanian then at Grafton. It was accepted and Mr Nibbs was inducted on February 11, 1982. He gave a warmly devotional and prayerful ministry which was cut short in his sudden death while in his study at the church on October 5, 1988. Although small, the congregation is characterised by Christian fellowship. Some increase has occurred of late, and it is hoped another minister may be settled in due course. There is good fellowship with brethren in the Southern Presbyterian Church.

Elders:M.R.Hingston (pre 1965-   ); J.Rathbone (1965-1972 & resigned); N.G.Triffett (1970-   ); E.N.Harvey (1980-83 to Hobart).

Note re Winnaleah: A majority of the Winnaleah REC Congregation left in 1964 (see page 396) in circumstances where the blame was not all on one side. This group continued independently until one of them, Mr Don Cairns, wrote to Beaton in 1971. After appropriate reference to Presbytery and Synod, the group was received as a congregation, and local courts were established in 1972. In 1973 Rev G.L.Weber gave residential supply, and from February 1976 to August 1978, Mr H.C.Varnes did likewise. A timber house at Winnaleah was purchased at the close of 1975 for $3,000, renovated and used by the Varnes' family. Towards the close of Mr Varnes' supply period, some of the members indicated they would rejoin the EPC, whose congregation in Winnaleah secured a minister early in 1979. Accordingly, while several folk retained membership in the PCEA, PCEA services were discontinued. Subsequently the manse was sold for $8,500 and applied for the benefit of Tasmanian work based at Ulverstone.

Elders: D.T.Carins (1972-78); G.C.Lefevre (1972-77); T.M.J.Peters (1972-79)

BIBLIOGRAPHY

(A) Denominational histories

Apart from parish histories of varying quality, there are state histories of Presbyterianism as follows:

New South Wales

Cameron, James, *A Centenary History of the Presbyterian Church in New South Wales* (Sydney 1905)

White, C.A., *The Challenge of the Years* (Sydney 1951).

Both of these volumes provide sketches of parishes and lists of ministers but are weak on the pre 1865 period, White particularly. Neither contains much in the way of analysis and the focus is more on the continuity of the institution than the changes which were taking place.

Victoria

Sutherland, Robert, *The History of the Presbyterian Church of Victoria* (London 1877)

Hamilton, Robert, *A Jubilee History of the Presbyterian Church in Victoria* (London 1888)

Campbell, A.J., *Fifty Years of Victorian Presbyterianism* (London 1889)

Stewart, D.Macrae, *The Presbyterian Church of Victoria: Growth in Fifty Years 1859-1909* (Melbourne 1909)

Macdonald, Aeneas, *One Hundred Years of Presbyterianism in Victoria* (Melbourne 1937)

Bradshaw, F.M., *Scottish Seceders in Victoria* (Melbourne 1947)

Stewart's work is not of literary worth, Campbell's is an official history, Hamilton's is written from the UP viewpoint, and Sutherland's from the position of a Free Churchman who entered union. These two older books are rather full narratives but lack analysis. Bradshaw's work fills out the UP history and is exact and well written. The Victorian church histories have little in the way of content on individual parishes. Macdonald's book reads very well but did not sell well.

Tasmania

Heyer, J., *The Presbyterian Pioneers of Van Diemen's Land* (Launceston 1935).

Miller, R.S. (ed), *Presbyterian Church of Tasmania : Triple Jubilee 1973* (Hobart 1973)

Ward, Rowland S., *Presbyterianism in Tasmania 1821-1977* (Ulverstone 1977)

Heyer's work is comprehensive but tantalising also since he does not probe too deeply into some areas. Miller's volume picks up the story where Heyer left off, and includes a good selection of photographs. Ward's volume gives a survey of mainstream Presbyterianism but concentrates on the old Free

Presbytery of Tasmania, the two Reformed denominations of Dutch origin, and provides the first published history of the Evangelical Presbyterian Church (pages 36 to 78).

South Australia

Scrimgeour, R.J., *Some Scots Were Here* (Adelaide 1986)

Ward, Rowland S. , *The Free Presbyterian Church of South Australia: An Account of James Benny and South Australian Presbyterianism* (Melbourne 1984)

Scrimgeour's attractive and well illustrated volume covers Presbyterianism in South Australia to 1977. A good overall coverage although lacks analysis. Ward's volume resolves the tangles in the story of the group associated with James Benny.

Queensland

Hay, Alex, *The Jubilee Memorial of the Presbyterian Church of Queensland* (Brisbane 1900)

Bardon R., *The Centenary HIstory of the Presbyterian Church of Queensland* (Brisbane 1949)

Bardon's work supersedes Hay's volume and is a quite fair effort although lacking theological analysis.

Western Australia

No published history of significance is known to the writer. It is a matter of regret that PCWA records stored in a garage were destroyed by fire.

The Free Church/PCEA stream

Robinson, J. Campbell, *The Free Presbyterian Church of Australia* (Melbourne 1947)

Ward, Rowland S., *The Making of An Australian Church: A History of the Presbyterian Church of Eastern Australia* (Ulverstone 1978)

Robinson's volume is a valiant attempt with masses of material but lacks scientific arrangement, accuracy and due proportion. It preserves many important photographs. Ward's 1978 volume was written in anticipation of division in the church and the desirability of warding this off by a more adequate outline history.

(B) Presbyterian Publications

From the time of the 19th century unions printed reports and minutes of Assemblies are generally available. In New South Wales, early records are in the Ferguson Memorial Library in the PCNSW Offices, in Victoria and Queensland, they are in the church archives, and in Tasmania and South Australia the early records are in the State Government Archives.

Minutes of the PCEA were often printed prior to 1887 but should be checked against the MSS in the 1880s. The book for 1846-64 is in the Ferguson

Library, and subsequent books covering 1864-1880, 1881-1912, 1913-1922, 1937-1955 and subsequently are accessible through the Synod Archivist (Rev R.S.Ward). The book for 1923-1936 has been mislaid, but the minutes of the FPCA Assembly, which was more significant at that time, are in the church archives covering the years 1913 to 1953.

Church periodicals are an important source. The PCV has the most complete series, with a monthly paper under varies titles and with various degrees of status from 1864 to 1899, when the weekly *Messenger* commenced publication. The New South Wales church was served at times by more than one periodical. A weekly paper allied with the PCEA began in 1872 but changed affiliation to the PCNSW in 1874, but a paper with a somewhat different title continued in connection with the PCEA.

Free/PCEA periodicals
The complete list of 'Free Church' periodicals in Australia is as follows:
New South Wales
The Voice in the Wilderness edited by William McIntyre (1846-1852 fortnightly), copy in the Mitchell Library, Sydney. *The Testimony* edited by William McIntyre (1865-70 monthly), copy in ML. *The Australian Witness and Presbyterian Herald* edited by George Sutherland (weekly from 11.72 to 1.74) name changed to *The Witness and Australian Presbyterian* 1.74 and published till 1884; the title was shortened to *The Witness* in 6.1877. In 1882 *The Free Churchman* began as a monthly and continued to 1893 under the direction of John S.Macpherson. In 1905 *The Free Presbyterian Magazine* commenced under the editorship of William McDonald. No perfect set of the irregular issues of this magazine has been located, but the others are in the ML.

Victoria
In Victoria the founder of the FPCV, James Forbes, issued *The Port Phillip Christian Herald* as a monthly from 1846 until April 1851, a short time before his death. *The Free Presbyterian Messenger* was also issued by Forbes for the years 1847 to 1849. Copies in the State Library of Victoria. The Victorian union controversy resulted in a monthly, *The Standard*, being issued from 1859 to 1861, Peter MacPherson having the largest share in its production. Arthur Paul issued two series of a monthly called *The Presbyter* (1878-1881, 1884-1886). In 1889 the *Free Church Quarterly* was begun by the FPCV with John Sinclair as editor.

South Australia
In South Australia the FPCSA published *The Free Presbyterian* from 1875 to 1881 with James Benny as editor. Its circulation brought the FPCSA into contact with the Victorian and NSW churches and the magazine was therefore discontinued.

In 1913 the 'Free' churches began co-operation through the Assembly of the FPCA, and the Victorian and NSW papers were merged into one, which continues to the present after many name changes and with editors as noted:

Title
The Australian Free Presbyterian [1913-1924, Quarterly]
The Free Church Monthly [1924-1928]
The Free Presbyterian Banner [1928-1929, Monthly]
Our Banner [1929-1940, Monthly]
The Australian Free Presbyterian [1941-1954, Monthly]
Our Banner [1954-1982, Monthly]
The Presbyterian Banner [1982 -

Editors

1913-1928	Rev John Sinclair, Geelong
1928-1929	Rev J.Campbell Robinson, St Kilda
1929-1932	Rev I.L.Graham, Hamilton
1933-1940	Rev J.Campbell Robinson, St Kilda
1941-1943	Rev Neil MacLeod, Sydney
1944-1958	Rev Arthur Allen, Sydney
1958-1966	Rev S.N.Ramsay, Raymond Terrace
1966-1970	Rev A.D.Campbell, Grafton
1970-1972	Rev R.W.Murray, St Kilda
1972-1975	Rev E.S.Turnbull, St Kilda
1975-1979	Rev Professor Allan M.Harman, Victoria
1979-1981	Rev E.R.Lee, Taree
1981-1987	Rev R.S.Ward, Melbourne
1987-1988	Rev R.W.Murray, Grafton
1988-	Rev W.Peter Gadsby, Armidale

There is a virtually complete set in the State Library of Victoria.

Other Presbyterian periodicals

The monthly journal of the **Reformed Churches of Australia** is *Trowel and Sword;* the fortnightly journal of the **Free Reformed Churches of Australia** is *Una Sancta*, while the **Presbyterian Reformed Church of Australia** has issued *The Protestant Review* monthly since November 1968.

(C) Journal Articles and Unpublished Theses

The following listing is a tolerably complete record of items since 1960 with significant bearing on the subject matter of the present volume. Items in Presbyterian periodicals are excluded but reference to certain of such are made in the footnotes in the body of this work.

CH = Church Heritage, published by the Uniting Church, North Parramatta.
RAHSJ = Royal Australian Historical Society Journal, Sydney.
JRH = Journal of Religious History, Sydney.

Black, Alan W., *Church Union in Canada and Australia: A Comparative Analysis* (CH, September 1983, pp.97-121).
Black, Alan W., *Some Aspects of Religion and Law: The Case of Church Union in Australia* (*Religion*, 1986, †16 pp.225-247)

Boer, Catherine, *The Maitland Riot, Presbyterian Church Union 1865: An Analysis of Religious Conflict* (Sociology IV Honours, U of Newcastle,1981)

Boer, Catherine, *An Early Clergyman of the Hunter - William McIntyre 1806-1870* (RAHSJ, October 1986, pp.130-148).

Breward, Ian, *Christianity Must Be Interpreted* (Trinity Occasional Papers, UCA Brisbane, April 1985, pp.24-34)

Bridges, B.J.,*The Presbyterian Churches in New South Wales 1823-1865 with Particular Reference to their Scottish Relations* (PhD,U of St Andrews,1985

Bridges, B.J., *The Presbyterian Contribution to Education in New South Wales to 1866* (PhD, U of Newcastle 1985).

Bridges, B.J., *Rev John McGarvie: A Scottish Moderate in the Presbyterian Church in New South Wales 1826-1853* (MTh, U of Sydney 1987).

Bridges, B.J., *Ministers, Licentiates and Catechists of the Presbyterian Churches in New South Wales 1823-1865* (A typescript of about 180 pages providing data in great detail with sources. R.S.Ward is arranging a limited edition for publication in 1989).

Bridges, B.J., *Review of 'Days of Wrath' by D.W.A.Baker* (CH, September 1986, pp.271-280).

Bridges, B.J., *The Reverend John McGarvie* (CH, September 1986, pp.231-244, and following issue pp.1-17. [Written before above thesis completed.])

Campbell, Keith R., *Presbyterian Conflicts in New South Wales 1837-1865* (JRH, June 1962, pp.233-247).

Chambers, Don, *Calvinists and Capitalists in Colonial Victoria* (Melbourne Historical Journal, 4, 1964, pp.9-16).

Chambers, Don, *A History of Ormond College 1881-1945* (MA, U of Melbourne, 1966).

Clements, Helen., *The Presbyterian Struggle 1970-1977* (PhD, U of New South Wales, 1983).

Dougan, A.A., *The Kirk and Social Problems of the 1830s in New South Wales* (RAHSJ, March 1961, pp.457-475).

Emilsen, Susan, *Samuel Angus and the Presbyterian Church in the State of New South Wales* (PhD, U of Sydney 1985).

Grocott, Allan M., *Rev William Purves' Journey to New England 1844* (CH, September 1979, pp.101-113).

Grose, Kelvin, *The Status of the Church of Scotland in the Colonies in the 1820s* (RAHSJ, October 1988, pp.112-113).

Hansen, D.E., *The Long Road to Union: Negotiations and Developments 1919-1939* (CH, September 1979, pp.81-99).

Hansen, D.E., *The Origin and Early Years of the New South Wales Council of Churches* (JRH, June 1981, pp.452-471).[Covers period 1925-39.]

Jack, R. Ian, *Andrew Brown Laird of Cooerwull* (RAHSJ, December 1987, pp.173-186).

Lucy, R.J.M., *Presbyterian Politics: a study of politics within the Presbyterian Church of Australia in the twentieth century on the issue of union with the Methodist and Congregational Churches* (PhD, U of New South Wales, 1976).

Lyon, Mark, *Aspects of Sectarianism in New South Wales circa 1865-1880* (PhD, A.N.U., 1972).

Parker, David, *Fundamentalism and Conservative Protestantism in Australia 1920-1980* (PhD, U of Queensland, 1982).

Parker, David, *The Bible Union: A Case Study in Australian Fundamentalism* (JRH, June 1986, pp.71-99).

Phillips, Walter, *The Churches and the Sunday Question in the 1880s* (JRH, June 1970, pp.41ff.).

Phillips, Walter, *The Defence of Christian Belief in Australia 1875-1914 - The Response to Evolution and Higher Criticism* (JRH, Dec. 1977, pp.402-423).

Piggin, Stuart, *Towards a Bicentennial History of Australian Evangelicalism* (JRH, June 1988, pp.20-37).

Prentis, Malcolm, *Colonial Ecumenism: Aspects of Presbyterian Reunion in New South Wales* (CH, March 1980, pp.219-239).

Prentis, Malcolm, *The Defection of Scots from their Kirk in New South Wales: the significance of 1838* (*The Push from the Bush*, September 1980, pp.51-57).

Prentis, Malcolm, *Scottish Religious Influences in Colonial Australia 1788-1900* (*Scottish Church History Society Records*, XX,I (1981) pp.79-90).

Prentis, Malcolm, *Changes in Presbyterian Worship in Colonial Australia, 1860-1900* (CH, March 1981, pp.46-57).

Prentis, Malcolm, *The Presbyterian Ministry in Australia 1822-1900: Recruitment and Composition* (JRH, June 1984, pp.46-65).

Prentis M & Bridges, B.J., *A Biographical Register of Presbyterian Ministers in New South Wales 1823-1865* (CH, March 1984, pp.185-208). NB: This should be treated as work in progress.

Seaton, Gladys, *Divers people and far sundered lands: John and Elizabeth Tait, and the Scottish and Gaelic Free Churches* (*Investigator*, Geelong Historical Society, December 1972, pp.95-107; March 1973, pp.8-15; and June 1983, pp.56-63).

Udy, J.S., *Australian Negotiations Towards Union: An Historical Survey 1901-1977* (CH, September 1978, pp.1-32).

Udy, J.S., *Ecumenical Initiatives in Shaping the Ministry in New South Wales* (CH, September 1985, pp.95-121).

Uidam, C., *Why the Church Union Movement Failed in Australia 1901-1925* (JRH, Vol 13, †4 (1985) pp.393-410).

Walker, R.B., *Presbyterian Church and People in the Colony of New South Wales in the Late Nineteenth Century* (JRH, June 1969, pp. 49-65).

Weeks, Phillipa, *John Dunmore Lang and the Colonist 1835-40* (ANU Historical Journal, 13 ,1977, pp.41-54).

(D) Other material

Entries for prominent Australians pre 1939 appear in the *Australian Dictionary of Biography* (1966-   ). The footnotes to the text indicate sources in manuscript and printed form. Space precludes a full listing here. However, limiting oneself to recent publications, the following literature is among the most useful for gaining insight into things Presbyterian.

Baker, D.W.A., *Days of Wrath - A Life of John Dunmore Lang* (Melb. 1985).

Brown, Callum, *The Social History of Religion in Scotland Since 1730* (London 1987).

Cheyne, A.C., *The Transforming of the Kirk* (Edinburgh 1983).

Clifford, N. Keith, *The Resistance to Church Union in Canada 1904-1939* (Vancouver 1985).

Collins, G.N.M., *The Heritage of our Fathers* (Edinburgh 1974)

Kuyper, Abraham, *Lectures on Calvinism* (1898, reprinted Grand Rapids 1961 and since).

Lyall, Francis, *Of Presbyters and Kings - Church and State in the Law of Scotland* (Aberdeen 1980)

Macleod, John, *Scottish Theology in relation to Church History since the Reformation* (Edinburgh, 3rd edition 1974).

Prentis, Malcolm D., *The Scots in Australia - A study of New South Wales, Victoria and Queensland 1788-1900* (Sydney 1983).

Reid, W.Stanford, *Trumpeter of God - A Biography of John Knox* (New York 1974, reprinted Grand Rapids 1982).

Ward, Rowland S., *Learning the Christian Faith* (The Shorter Catechism modernised with notes) 3rd edition, Melbourne, 1987.

Williamson, G.I., *The Westminster Confession of Faith for Study Classes* (Philadelphia 1964 and reprinted since).

Note for Researchers

At the time of union in 1977, the theory was that the Uniting Church would hold Methodist and Congregational records, while the (Continuing) Presbyterian Church would retain Presbyterian records. In practice the division was not quite so clear cut, and some Presbyterian records have been lodged with the Uniting Church. Those seeking information re baptisms, marriages etc. should enquire first of the local congregation and then make enquiry, if necessary, through state offices of the church. Many South Australian and Tasmanian records are in the State Government Archives. Western Australian Presbyterian records were destroyed in a fire some years ago.

ORDAINED MINISTERS OF THE PCEA/FPCV/FPCSA IN AUSTRALIA
FROM DIVISION RE UNION (May 1864 in Victoria, May 1865 in South Australia and September 1865 in New South Wales) TO THE PRESENT
NB: Gaelic preachers indicated as such but Gaelic usage rare after 1890.

1. McINTYRE, William (1806-1870)   Gaelic NSW

Born March 6, 1806 at Kilmonivaig, near Fort William, the 5th son of Duncan McIntyre, sheep farmer, and his wife Catherine (nee Kennedy). Educated at parish school and U of Glasgow (MA 1829). Taught with his brother Allan in McIntyre's School, Laurieston. After divinity studies in Glasgow was licensed by the Presbytery of Dunoon, but continued teaching and preaching. Lang was impressed by him and invited him to Australia where he had several cousins engaged in pastoral pursuits (Peter McIntyre and his brothers John and Donald). McIntyre acted as chaplain on the Midlothian, and arrived at Sydney on December 12, 1837. He delivered the first Gaelic sermon in Australia on December 17, 1837, and joined Lang's Synod of NSW on January 31, 1838. Assistant to Lang at Scots' Church, Sydney 1838 to 1840 and also taught in the Australian College, and assisted in editing The Colonist. Regularly visited the Hunter to conduct Gaelic services. Active in achieving the formation of the Synod of Australia in 1840. Settled at West Maitland early in 1841; in 1844 he married his cousin Mary (1786-1872), Peter's sister and heir; but no issue. Led in formation of PCEA in 1846 Commenced the High School at Maitland (see p.117) and acted as Principal for a time. Transferred to St George's, Sydney and inducted there on February 20, 1862 and remained until his death on July 12, 1870, serving without stipend. He wrote much in defence of Biblical Principles and the position of the PCEA. Editor: The Voice in the Wilderness (1846-52 fortnightly) and The Testimony (1865-70 monthly). Chief published works: Exposition of the Sermon on the Mount (Edinburgh 1854); The Token of the Covenant, Sydney 1861, much enlarged 1869; The Christian Sabbath, Sydney 1866; Faith, Sydney 1869; and many pamphlets. A man of stature.

2. McINTYRE, Allan (1798-1870)   Gaelic NSW

Born July 15, 1798 at Kilmonivaig, near Fort William, the 2nd son of Duncan and Catherine McIntyre. Educated at U of Glasgow and New College, Edinburgh 1843-45. Conducted school at Laurieston from 1832/33 with his brother William. Joined Free Church at Disruption, was licensed by the Presbytery of Dunoon and ordained and inducted to Paisley Free Gaelic Church in 1846. When William was visiting Scotland in 1854, Allan resolved to go to Australia and was duly appointed by the Free Church Colonial Committee in June and arrived in Sydney per Berhampore on November 6, 1854 with Rev James McCulloch, a nephew by marriage. Arrived on the Manning on December 18, 1854 and held first service the next day. He was formally inducted on January 7, 1854 and remained until his death on May 28, 1870 except for a period from the end of 1862 to August 1865 when he was at Grafton (see p.130). Married Jemima Pilcher late in 1862 and had issue. In the late 1850s there was quite a spiritual movement on the Manning under Allan's sin-exposing preaching. His outlook was rather severe. He was consistent throughout the union controversy, and he was a much appreciated pastor of his people.

3. McCULLOCH, James (1823-1873)   NSW

Born at Muthil, Perthshire in 1823, the youngest son of John McCulloch, a godly elder in the parish. Educated at the U of Glasgow and at New College 1843-47 and licensed by the Presbytery of Auchterarder. He served as a home missionary at Kilmacolm and at Rothesay. His was not a strong constitution and this contributed to him offering for service in Australia along with Allan McIntyre. His wife (nee McKinnon) was a niece of William and Allan McIntyre, and they came out with Allan arriving on November 6, 1854. He was appointed to the Upper Hunter based at Singleton, and was inducted there on September 6, 1855. He became minister on the Lower Hunter at Ahalton (see p.120) near Raymond Terrace in 1861, making the latter place his main centre about 1865, and giving service to East Maitland as well. He did not have Gaelic but was highly acceptable to the Highlanders and was of a pleasant nature and well regarded. He died on May 20, 1873 after a period of ill health and was buried at Raymond Terrace.

4. McSKIMMING, John Locke (1826-1886)   NSW

Born about 1826 at Paisley the 2nd son of William McSkimming, a games teacher. Educated at the U of Glasgow and at New College, Edinburgh (1850/55). He was licensed by the Free Church and appointed by the Colonial Committee. He arrived near the close of 1859, was appointed to supply Chalmers' Church, Redfern and was inducted in 1860. He had a major drinking problem, the congregation declined markedly and he was suspended for 6 months and resignation of the charge recommended. This took place February 3, 1864. In September 1864 he was assigned to the Presbytery of Maitland and on May 23, 1866 was inducted to that section of Singleton which remained with the PCEA. He married Elizabeth Urquhart in June 1867, resigned charge August 21, 1867, and was deposed on November 6, 1867 upon confession of antenuptial fornication. Sought readmission to Synod November 1870, and the application was referred to the Presbytery but not accepted. He taught at Kempsy Public School (c.1873-84) and at Collector, and died at Sydney on June 11, 1886. Had issue.

5. GREIG, Colin Rogers (1826-1913)   NSW

Born about 1826 near Dundee, and educated at the U of St Andrews and at New College, Edinburgh 1847-51. He arrived in Sydney late in 1860 (see p.101), and served Twofold Bay, where he was ordained in 1861, until transferred to Bombala in May 1864. St Andrew's Church was opened on February 6, 1870. Greig resigned this charge and joined the PCNSW in 1872 (some matter of stipend arrears seems to have been involved). He served Dubbo (1872-75), Hill End (1876-81), and Walcha (1881-86) and was then without charge. He applied to the PCEA to be readmitted, but the Synod resolved on February 15, 1890 in the negative. Greig died October 19, 1913.

6. PAUL, Arthur (1826-1910)   V

Born on May 1, 1826 at Greenock, eldest son of Colin Paul, an artificer. Educated at the U of Glasgow and at New College, Edinburgh 1847-51. Ordained by the Free Church in 1853 with a view to working in Sydney where he arrived in the latter part of the year and was received by the PCEA on November 2, 1853. He was appointed to labour in Sydney with a view to establishing a new congregation but was not successful in this. On November 23, 1854 he became a member of the Melbourne Presbytery of the FPCV, and was appointed to a relatively new cause at Richmond (Bridge Road) using the Presbyterian Schoolhouse opened earlier that year as the place of worship. Paul gave a fair measure of supply to St Kilda, where services were commenced in May 1855, and on October 2, 1855 he was inducted to this charge and remained until his death on August 13, 1910. He was a man of great logical capacity, but he was not a popular preacher or an active visitor and he did not hold a large congregation. He wrote many pamphlets but his major literary work was as editor of **The Presbyter** 1878-81, 1884-86, and the large volume **Latter Day Light on the Apocalypse** (London 1898, 2nd edition 1902) The union controversies contributed to a contraction of his sympathies in the last 20 years of his life, and he maintained a rather isolated position. He married in Victoria a Miss Janet Moffat by whom he had 12 children. William Paul, the second eldest, was a very prominent barrister.

7. McINTYRE, Alexander (1807-1878)   Gaelic NSW/V

Born about 1807 at Rannachan, Strontian, son of Donald McIntyre, merchant. He studied for the ministry but his 'moderate' Presbytery so delayed that he went north and was licensed by the Presbytery of Locharron on August 17, 1836, having fulfilled the 6 month's residence requirement. Dr John Macleod regarded him as 'one of the most fervid evangelists and most alarming preachers raised in his day.' He would not accept a call but devoted his life to itinerant evangelism among Gaelic-speaking communities. He was active in the parish of Strontian at the time of the Disruption and was associated with the early days of 'the floating church' on Loch Sunart, launched in July 1846 as a consequence of the proprietor's refusal to grant a site for a church. On October 16, 1846, McIntyre was appointed by the Colonial Committee to Prince Edward Island. He was ordained by the Presbytery of Pictou on September 30, 1847. Returned to Scotland in 1850 and laboured in the bounds of the Presbytery of Abertaff. Declined a call from Knapdale in 1852 and offered for Australia. Appointed to Ahalton in April 1852, he arrived in Melbourne in March 1853. After a time with a brother in Geelong, reached Sydney in June and received by the PCEA on November 2, 1853 and appointed to Ahalton where he laboured about four years with great success, having extra burdens when William McIntyre (apparently no relation) was in Scotland 1854-55. Went to Victoria early in 1858 and joined FPCV and had oversight of Geelong from February 10, 1858 until his death on June 9, 1878, except that he undertook frequent preaching tours, commonly spending the winter at Maclean to which place many of his Ahalton hearers had moved. He was at Ascot (near Ballarat) 1861-62 and at Grafton 1865-66, while he also played a significant part in gathering the Hamilton/Branxholme cause in the late 1860s. McIntyre did not marry and lived with his brother in Geelong. He was somewhat distant and reserved to strangers and a trifle eccentric. He blew the trumpet of the law hard sometimes but he preached splendid gospel sermons too. Gaelic was the language in which he excelled although he had few desiring that tongue in his closing years at Geelong. He died intestate leaving something over 6,000 pounds, and was buried in Geelong. He had a remarkable influence on the Gaels in Australia, and many found rich spiritual blessing through his ministry.

8. MacPHERSON, Peter (1826-1886)   V/NSW

Born NSW July 2, 1826, son of a pastoralist, educated at the Australian College, U of Edinburgh (MA) & New College. Returned to Victoria and was licensed by the FPCV in February 1858. After period supplying in several centres, he was appointed to Meredith/Lethbridge early in 1862 and ordained and inducted on June 18, 1862. In 1866 he married Miss Elizabeth Armstrong of Mortlake by whom he had 4 sons and a daughter. He left at the end of May 1874 and moved to Raymond Terrace/East Maitland PCEA and was inducted there on June 9, 1874. In 1875 he lost his wife and daughter due to typhoid and his own health deteriorated towards the end of 1876. From May 1877 he was on sick leave for most of the time until he resigned the charge on September 4, 1878. He removed to Sydney. In November 1879 he accepted position as Professor of Sacred Languages to the Synod of EA, but clashed with Rev George Sutherland and contributed to a painful church dispute. Quite fearless and uncompromising but somewhat too minute in pressing his position, he was a man of conspicuous ability. As well as many pamphlets on church questions, he contributed several articles on aboriginal culture and religion to the journal of the Royal Society of NSW (1881,84,85,86). He edited The Standard (1859-61) and contributed to The Testimony (1865-70) and The Free Churchman (1884-86). In January 1886 he married Isabella, 2nd daughter of William Buyers. He died at Sydney on July 30, 1886. A brother was twice Chief Secretary of Victoria and a sister was married to Rev Allan McVean. He presented a valuable collection of papers on Presbyterianism to the State Library of Victoria.

9. BENNY, James (1824-1910)   SA

Born about 1824 of Stirlingshire stock, it appears Benny came to South Australia with his brother John about 1839 and ran a sheep station near Clare returning to Scotland about 1842. I cannot confirm this but it is certain that James witnessed the 'Disruption' in May 1843 and carried with him the inspiring memories of that event. It appears James and John arrived per the 'Symmetry' on February 21, 1844 and that the parents, James and Margaret, arrived with two younger sons (William and Thomas) in November 1845. James, John and William had legal training and the latter two formed the legal firm of Benny Brothers, but James trained for the ministry under Rev John Gardner of Chalmers Church, Adelaide where he was an elder and session clerk. James was licensed on July 3, 1854 and ordained and inducted to Morphett Vale, which he had been supplying since December 1853. Opened John Knox Church on April 13, 1856, a church in Ryans Road, Aldinga on December 14, 1856, and another in Yankalilla on May 30, 1858. On January 5, 1858, the Presbytery purported to depose Benny for contumacy arising out of a discipline case in the Morphett Vale Session. The Presbytery was in the wrong and its action had little practical effect, except to drive Benny out. He continued the FPCSA after the union of 1865, operated a Presbytery 1869-81, and exercised a fruitful ministry over a wide area from his centre at Morphett Vale. Formally retired on September 8, 1904 and died on May 3, 1910. Benny was an excellently organised man, an attractive preacher and a first rate visitor. He trained three men for the ministry and exercised a valued evangelical ministry. He was moderately pre-millennial in the McCheyne tradition. He edited The Free Presbyterian (1875-81).

10. BENNY, George (1829-1881)   SA

Born in 1829, George was a younger brother of James who came to South Australia in 1852. He had some medical training and was a good scholar. He completed training for the ministry under his brother's oversight, and was ordained and inducted by James to the charge of Aldinga on January 17, 1867. He demitted on May 3, 1870 and became Master of John Knox School at Morphett Vale. When the school closed in 1878 he became the master of Oatlands School on Yorke Peninsula where he died in May 1881. A son (Benjamin 1869-1935) became a lawyer and Senator for South Australia.

11. DONALD, William Scott (1812-1890)   NSW

Born 1812 near Montrose, trained for the ministry and was licensed by the Presbytery of Brechin prior to the Disruption. He joined the Free Church and was ordained and inducted to Fraserburgh in 1843. He was granted leave to come to NSW to wind up the affairs of his deceased brother near Dubbo, and arrived in January 1863. Resigned Fraserburgh in 1864 and joined PCEA supplying in several areas, particularly Newtown but declined calls to unionist congregations. In mid 1868 he formally joined the continuing PCEA and acted as missionary in the Clarence Town district. He died on June 9, 1890, and was buried at East Maitland.

12. McINNES, Duncan (1827-1908)   Gaelic NSW

Born at Blaich, Ardgour c. 1827, McInnes arrived in Sydney in 1849 with his mother and sisters and settled on the Hunter at Bolwarra. Remained out of the union and supplied at East Maitland while completing studies for the ministry supervised by Rev William McIntyre. He was licensed in November 1867 and ordained and inducted at East Maitland to the Maclean charge on July 30, 1868 where he remained until his death on August 12, 1908. He was a man of reverence and piety who kept an even keel during the church dispute of the 1880s, and was highly regarded. His first wife, by whom he had 8 or 9 children, died in 1869 and most of the children died when relatively young. In 1872 he married Caroline, daughter of Peter Stewart of Sydney.

13. SINCLAIR, John (1851-1932)   SA/V

Born in Glasgow February 15, 1851, the family being connected with Hope Street Free Church. Hugh, his father, was a shoemaker. They attended Morphett Vale FPC and in 1862 John commenced studies under James Benny with a view to the ministry. He was ordained and inducted at Yankalilla November 5, 1868, translated to Kingston SE in June 1872 (inducted November 8, 1872), and to Geelong FPCV May 3, 1881 where he continued in active ministry until his death on August 18, 1932. He married Elizabeth Hensley in 1878 by whom he had 8 children. Mrs Sinclair died in 1942. Sinclair was an excellent minister, hardworking and methodical like his mentor. He was gentle, kindly and gracious, while his sermons were long and solid. He carried a major load in Victoria in the lean years. He was the editor of The Free Church Quarterly (1889-1913), the FPCV paper, and then of the FPCA magazines, The Australian Free Presbyterian (1913-1924) and The Free Church Monthly (1924-28). A memorial volume was issued in1939.

14. McLEOD, John (1844- ?)   Gaelic NSW

Born in Scotland in 1844, McLeod was an adherent of the Free Church and afterwards a member of the PCV under whose auspices he became a student for the ministry. Moved to NSW c.1868, was licensed by the PCEA after further studies on November 6, 1868. During most of 1869 he supplied on the Hastings, and he was ordained minister at large on November 12, 1869. Early in 1870 he was admitted minister of Grafton following a call bearing 108 signatures. He built up the work and the Fry Street church was erected. His resignation was accepted in July 1872. He joined the PCNSW, proceeded to Canada later that year, and took a medical degree in Montreal, but became minister of Tiree FCS in 1878. After two years he again went to Canada.

15. McINTYRE, Duncan Kennedy (1817-1899)   Gaelic NSW

Born on April 16, 1817, the youngest of the 12 children of Duncan and Catherine McIntyre and the brother of Allan and William. He came to NSW in 1854, and at the time of union in 1864/65 resided at Inverell where there were family interests (see p.95). He trained for the ministry with a view to filling the place left by Allan's death. About the middle of 1872 he commenced his ministry on the Manning although the date of ordination that year has not been located. On April 3, 1878, his resignation of the charge due to poor health was accepted, but he remained in the district for a further year before retiring to Sydney. Here he interested himself in extension work, particularly at Newtown. He was faithful, zealous and given to hospitality and liberality without ostentation. However, not a great deal is known about him. A bachelor he died at Sydney on December 17, 1899.

16. SUTHERLAND, George (1830-1893)   NSW

Born 1830 at New Glasgow, Nova Scotia, graduated from the Presbyterian College, Halifax, was ordained at Montreal in 1854 and was inducted minister of Charlottetown, Prince Edward Island, on August 27, 1856. He resigned this charge on November 21, 1866 with a view to visiting Australia. Arriving in New Zealand in July 1867, preached at First Church, Dunedin, and was duly called and inducted as colleague to Dr Thomas Burns; became sole minister upon the latter's death in 1871. As a result of a visit to NSW, Sutherland received a call from St George's and was inducted on November 4, 1872. He collapsed and died on July 27, 1893, having just come home from pastoral duties. Sutherland was a man of great intellectual vigor and scholarly culture, and was always active by tongue and pen in the advancement of the cause of Christ. His was a catholic vision. He was not always the easiest man to deal with, and there had been some friction with his deacons in Dunedin, but he was an outstanding man, well suited for a city pulpit. While at Charlottetown he was instrumental in establishing De Louis College, by whom he was honoured by a doctorate in 1890. His literary output was considerable. As well as editing a weekly religious paper from 1872-84 ('The Witness'), he wrote: **Urgent Appeals to the Unsaved** (Canada 1867, 261pp; 2nd edition Dunedin 1869; **Baptism** (Dunedin 1868, 204pp); **The Lord's Supper** (Dunedin 1869, 200pp); **The Magdalen Islands** (copy not sighted); **Christian Psychology** (Sydney 1874, 480pp); and **The True Church** (Sydney 1877, 208pp).

17. MACKAY, Isaac (1839-1900)   Gaelic NSW

Born Annandale, Scotland, November 1839. He completed divinity studies at New College, Edinburgh and was ordained in the Presbytery of Nova Scotia about 1863. In 1869 he became minister of Warwick PCQ. He was Moderator of the PCQ Assembly in May 1873 when he sought admission into the PCEA. He was received on August 13,1873 and was inducted to the Grafton charge on June 24, 1874. Here he remained, despite the difficulties of the Synod dispute which much reduced the congregation, until his death on March 3, 1900. Mackay was a cultured gentleman, well read on religious subjects and of an even temper. He was keenly interested in Foreign Missions, and the Bible Society, and was Clerk of Synod 1885-1900. He married in 1881 and a son, Iven, was knighted in 1941.

18. BUTTROSE, William Robert (1852-1913)   SA/V

Born February 2, 1852 on voyage from Scotland, the son of William and Frances Buttrose. His father was a policeman. The son studied for the ministry under James Benny, and also did some teaching in Adelaide. Ordained and inducted to the newly organised Robe congregation on September 17, 1875. The population declining, he demitted August 5, 1878. He served Nareen FPCV from December 19, 1878 to May 1888, then supplied elsewhere in Victoria until December 1890 when he returned to South Australia. He was admitted minister of the new congregation of Adelaide on October 27, 1892, and also gave a monthly service to Yankalilla, 80kms distant. Not a man of robust health, he was a man of consistency and fidelity. He married Frances, daughter of Rev James Benny, and there were 3 sons. He died of cancer of the throat on March 17, 1913. Friends in NSW and Victoria contributed about 200 pounds as a token of love and appreciation for his ministry.

19. LIVINGSTONE, Hugh (1844-1922)
NSW/V

Born about 1844 he was a catechist on the Hastings & Wilson rivers in 1871, completed his studies under George Sutherland, and was ordained in St George's Church for a new work at Parkes on November 3, 1875 in response to a call bearing 43 names. The goldfield declining, he was appointed to the Richmond River and arrived there in June 1876 residing at Casino then Lismore. Work progressed; he was inducted June 20, 1878, exercised an influential ministry and was a vigorous correspondent in the local press. He left for Victoria in May 1886, and was inducted to the Wimmera FPCV on July 28, 1886. He ministered over a wide area giving special attention to catechetical work and to psalmody. He resigned on March 6, 1902 and served the PCV and also the PCT, being inducted at Stanley August 25, 1908. He retired on March 3, 1914. He was wont to worship at St Kilda FPCV towards the close of his life, and died in Melbourne on September 25, 1922 leaving a widow and four children.

20. McDONALD, William (1848-1930)
V/NSW

Born Dunvegan, Skye in June1848; came to Victoria in 1852 with his parents and 4 older brothers. Educated in Geelong, he attended the RP Church when there was no service in the Free Church of which he became a member. After a period as a teacher, in 1874 he became a student for the ministry under Rev George Sutherland of Sydney, and was a catechist at Brushgrove for much of this period. He was licensed by the Presbytery of Sydney on March 6, 1876. After a short period of supply, he was called by the Hamilton/Branxholme charge and ordained and inducted there on March 28, 1877. Here he exercised an energetic and appreciated ministry until he was translated to the charge of St George's (inducted December 13, 1901) which was then at a low ebb. He did excellent work in rallying the church and furthering unity. He visited Scotland in 1920. For several years before his death on December 13, 1930, McDonald was unable to preach but still gave diligent attention to the meetings and activities of the church. He married Christina McLean of Branxholme by whom he had 2 daughters (Jean and Susan) and a son (Gordon). He was the editor of **The Free Presbyterian Magazine** 1905-1912, published quarterly.

21. DAVIS, John (1854-1897)
NSW

Born about 1854 in Northern Island and came to NSW when very young. He became a student about 1874, probably through the influence of Rev George Sutherland under whom he trained. He was licensed by the Presbytery of Sydney on March 6, 1876 and appointed to Bombala. Due to the efforts of the union party, the use of the church was denied (though it was PCEA property) and services were held in the Court House with acceptance. On June 6, 1877, he was ordained as missionary on the Hastings and Macleay rivers, the work prospered and he was inducted on February 3, 1879. He took a keen interest in the youth of the church, while his policy in Synod was clear-sighted and moderate. His health failing his resignation of the charge was accepted on February 17, 1891. He removed to Sydney where he was connected with the extension work in Newtown. In the early part of 1894 he resumed his ministry on the Hastings and Wilson rivers, but his valued labours were cut short when he was killed by a falling tree branch at the back of the manse on November 25, 1897. He left a wife (nee McDonald of the Macleay) and six children who returned to Sydney and were active in the church. In 1987 the last of the children, Iain, who had attained prominence in public life, conveyed a total of $260,000 to the church for various objects as the Davis Memorial Gifts.

22. MACPHERSON, John Shiret (1844-1921)
NSW/SA

Born about 1844 at Montrose, Scotland, and came to Sydney to engage in business. His educational background is not known but he was a man of considerable ability. He became a student for the ministry in 1877 and assisted at Raymond Terrace/East Maitland from May 1877, was licensed in May 1878 and ordained and inducted to this charge as successor to Peter MacPherson on October 22, 1878. Excessively rigid in the Synod dispute of the 1880s, he lost support as the 20th century arrived. He left for South Australia in April 1904, following a call bearing 63 names from Morphett Vale

FPC. Here he continued, not without difficulties, until his death on June 22, 1921. He was a man of kindly disposition and pleasant personality in everyday things, but his intense religious zeal was not always fully informed or wisely directed.

23. NICOL, John Arnot (c1850- ?) NSW/V

Born 1850 or later, little is known of him. He became a student in May 1874, and was a catechist in various centres, visting on the Richmond at the end of 1875. He was licensed Nov 1976, supplied Aberdeen, was ordained July 2,1878 and inducted to the Aberdeen charge on October 23,1878. Following a call signed by 207 persons, he was translated to the Wimmera FPCV and was inducted at North Rupanyup on January 12, 1881. He was caught up in the Synod dispute, but appears to have been weak morally, and also refused to comply with the direction to establish a session. He was deposed on January 3, 1884.

24. STEWART, Samuel Pentleton (1856-1936) NSW

Born November 29, 1856 at Bolong on the Shoalhaven River, one of ten children of James Stewart. About 1862 the family moved to Port Macquarie where Samuel was educated. Later the family resided at Upper Rolland's Plains. In 1875 he was recognised as first teacher of the Macksville School, but he resigned this post later that year to train for the ministry. Most of his training was supervised by Rev George Sutherland, and he proved a diligent and capable student, and was proficient in Hebrew, Latin and Greek. He served as a catechist (home missionary) at Camden and Picton during most of 1877, and on the Manning River during much of 1878. He was licensed by the Presbytery of Sydney on July 2, 1878, and was duly ordained and inducted to the Manning charge at Tinonee on February 5, 1879. Here he laboured with acceptance until even after his resignation took effect on March 27, 1929. Stewart was a tall man (over 6 feet) as well as a fearless horseman. For a number of years his charge included the Barrington district as well as the Hastings. Possessed of a well furnished mind and a retentive memory, Stewart had a remarkable facility in the use of the English language and never lacked an audience. He was staunch upholder of Protestantism and possessed of kindly sympathy in his personal relations. He married Annie MacKinnon of Picton in 1888. She died in 1895 and he married Mary Plummer of Taree in 1898. There were 7 children in all. Stewart's sight gave way in his old age, but he continued preaching, obtained a successor in 1929, and died at Taree on May 17, 1936.

25. GRANT, William (1838-1919) NSW

Born about 1838 at Strathspey, Scotland and went to Canada about 1842. He trained for the ministry at McGill College, Toronto, and was ordained and inducted to Vankleek, Ontario in 1869. Rev George Sutherland's brother in law, Rev William Ross of Lochiel in Canada, was a friend, and through him he came to Australia and was settled at Brushgrove about August 1879. In the aftermath of the Synod dispute he resigned (January 14, 1885) and was overseas for a year or so. Upon his return in 1886 he laboured for a time in his old charge but on May 3, 1888, was inducted to the Upper Hunter based at Aberdeen. Here he remained until the ill-health of his wife forced his retirement to Sydney in July 1908. His wife died in 1909, but Grant continued assisting as he could. It is thought he could preach in Gaelic although express evidence has not been located. Grant was a modest and capable man who did good work. He died in Sydney on February 11, 1919.

26. BUNTINE, Hugh Symington (c1860-1925) NSW

Formerly connected with the PCV, Buntine was received as a student by the PCEA on November 5, 1880. He supplied at Aberdeen 1881-82 but a call by the congregation did not proceed due to the Synod dispute. His studies were completed under Rev Peter MacPherson, and he was ordained February 6, 1883 and appointed to the Namoi. He was inducted to this charge at Boggabri on August 30, 1884. Early in 1887 he joined the PCNSW with his congregation, resigned the charge within the year and served at Narrandera 1889-91, Broken Hill 891-94, Port Macquarie 1894-1901, St Marys & Rupertswood 1901-05, Armidale 1901-1925; died July 9, 1925.

27. MARSHALL, James (1856-1930)   NSW

Born 1856 of Northern Ireland Presbyterian stock, he became a regular student on February 10, 1885, but had acted as catechist at Wellington for a year or so previous. [William H Marshall (a cousin born on the Macleay in 1861) became a student about 1886 and spent some two years to March 1891 at Wellington when he went to the Nambucca River; he and the congregation at Macksville were received by the PCNSW on July 12, 1900, and WHM was ordained on that date, served various places and retired in 1931.] James Marshall was appointed to supply Casino from March 1885, was licensed in June and ordained and inducted November 2, 1885. He demitted the charge on July 4, 1889 and joined the PCNSW serving Cooma (1891-94), Pymble/Hornsby (1896-1907), Canterbury/Rosedale/Campsie 1907-09) and Bowral (1919-20); died 1930.

28. WILSON, William Nathaniel (1856-1922)   NSW

Born about 1856 in Sydney, he became a student about 1879, and during his studies he supplied different centres, particularly Barrington and the Upper Hunter. He was licensed by the Presbytery of Maitland on December 24, 1884, and ordained and inducted to the Upper Hunter on February 4, 1886 with Rouchel and Westbrook his chief centres. In 1904 he took the oversight of the Lower Hunter based at East Maitland and formally joined the original Synod (see p.248) on February 3, 1906, becoming Synod Clerk. An excellent pastor, good with young people, a man of integrity and amiable disposition. He died at East Maitland on May 28, 1922 leaving a widow Helen (nee Greer), who died at Grafton in 1937, and six daughters.

29. FINLAYSON, John (1847-1890)   Gaelic NSW

Born April 15, 1848 at Portree. At first a teacher, he trained for the ministry at the Free Church College, Glasgow; licensed Presbytery of Skye June 1880; ordained & inducted Coigach in December of that year. He demitted this charge and accepted an invitation to Brushgrove on medical advice, arriving January 1887. As a consequence of the difficulties in the church he became a member of the Maclean session and acted as ordained missionary at Brushgrove. He was a faithful and exemplary minister. He died of a ruptured blood vessel on October 10, 1890. His widow (nee Nicholson) and infant son returned to Scotland. Mrs Finlayson died at Raasay in 1921.

30. GREIG, George Brown   NSW

Ordained April 3,1884 To Knox Church, Paisley, Ontario, Greig was admitted a minister of the PCEA on February 8, 1887. He supplied briefly at Wellington and for a longer period at Newtown, but considered his sphere of usefulness was limited and had thoughts of returning to Canada where he had had a large congregation. About September 1888 he gave supply to the PCNSW at Waverley, resigned from the PCEA, joined the PCNSW and was inducted at Waverley on May 31, 1889. However he demitted after one year and returned to North America.

31. MacKENZIE, Farquhar   Gaelic NSW

A licentiate of the FCS previously in charge of the mission church at Kyleakin, Inverness-shire, MacKenzie was invited to NSW on the recommendation of Rev John Finlayson. He arrived in December 1887, and was ordained by the Presbytery of Maitland in connection with the 'Reconstituted Synod' (see p. 248). He laboured on the Barrington, Manning and Hastings rivers, his facility in Gaelic being appreciated. He was not so good in English, while some thought him somewhat inactive. Concluding his engagement with the Reconstituted Synod he applied to the original Synod. On February 3, 1894, the Synod declined his application chiefly on the grounds that no suitable sphere of labour was available, and MacKenzie returned to Scotland

32. ARCHIBALD, William (? -1941)   NSW

Adequate information has not been located, but it appears Archibald became a student in 1881, and subsequently supplied in several less established centres including Wellington and Nambucca. He was ordained 1887 or 1888, and served Casino for about two years to 1891. He visited Scotland and on his return in mid 1893 a call issued from Casino but was not accepted. He supplied at Barrington and later at Newtown. He resigned as a minister of the PCEA April 10, 1911, but attended St George's as able. It appears that his wife was related to Rev John Edwards, liberal minister of PCNSW at Rose Bay, which may have affected things. He died in 1941 leaving his Rose Bay home to the FCS for missions, probably anticipating organic union of the PCEA with the FCS. This bequest (some 29,000 pounds sterling) became available in 1978 following the death of Archibald's daughter.

33. STEWART, James Johnstone (1852-1896)   V

Born 1852 at Blairgowrie, Scotland, son of Provost. Gained MA with distinction U of Edinburgh, and studied medicine but his health failed near the end of the course. Studied at New College, Edinburgh in the time of Professor George Smeaton (died 1889), and licensed by the Presbytery of Meigle. Assistant at Logie 2½ years and to Dr William Balfour of Holyrood 1 year. He was editor of **The Signal**, a magazine of the constitutionalists in the FCS. Medical advice favoured him coming to Victoria and he arrived in April 1891. He supplied in several centres and on May 25, 1892 was ordained and inducted to Glendonald/Durham Lead to which Meredith was also added. He remained four years until his health failed. His resignation of the charge was effective May 25, 1896. He died at Blairgowrie November 18, 1896. He married a Miss Stewart in 1893, but had no children. Stewart was a staunch upholder of the principles of the church. He was no mere traditionalist, was in touch with the thought of his time and wanted to see the truth applied. His literary work in Victoria includes: **The Scientific Possibility of Miracles** (Geelong, June 1891, 16pp., also in FCQ), **An Appeal for the Improvement of Psalmody** (Geelong, April 1893, 16pp), in which he advocated improved metrical versions of the psalms, and **The Disruption Conflict and its Present Commemorators** (Geelong 1893, 26 pages), being an expanded version of his address as Presbytery Moderator (also in FCQ 1893) and an excellent analysis. A man of principle, understanding and vision.

34. SCOTT, Walter (1854-1916)   V/NSW

Born October 8, 1854 at Edinburgh, son of Arthur W. Scott, an army officer of strict religious principles. His formative years were spent in Perth where he attended Free St Leonard's. In 1874 he joined a small Anti-Burgher Church in Edinburgh and renewed the 17th century covenants. Engaged in the legal profession, and also studied Arts at the U of Edinburgh 1883-87. He came to Australia for his health's sake through the generosity of Sir William Mackinnon, and arrived in Queensland in 1889 per 'Jumna'. In 1890, when in NSW, Scott wrote to W.J.Reid , a prominent pastoralist and elder of the Geelong FPC, with a introduction from Rev William Balfour of Holyrood Free Church, a mutual friend whom Reid had visited some years before. On January 8, 1891, Scott was received as a student of the FPCV, was licensed February 3, 1892, and ordained as missionary to the 'Back Country' in the far north-west of NSW on August 25, 1892, based on Yancannia station, a 1700 square mile property in which Reid had a half share. Scott's coming corresponded with severe drought and the mission was abandoned after a year, and Scott supplied in Victoria. (Reid sold out of Yancannia in July 1895). Scott received calls from Hamilton (assistant) and Brushgrove. The latter, which bore 65 signatures, was accepted and he commenced work there on July 21, 1895 and was inducted on September 23, 1895. He married a daughter of Hugh MacDonald of Dunfield in 1897, visited Scotland in 1900 as representing the 'Reconstituted Synod' at the meeting of the FPCS that year, and concluded his Brushgrove ministry in the latter part of 1908, and sailed for Scotland in 1909. He was received by the FPCS on January 2, 1911 after that church had passed its 'Declaration anent Reformation Attainments' (re covenanting principles). In April 1912 he proceeded to Canada as FPCS deputy, was called by Chesley, Ontario, inducted in Glasgow, Scotland to this charge on October 4, 1912 and commenced his ministry at Chesley on November 5, 1912. There he died on January 18, 1916. His widow returned to Grafton and died in 1959. Scott was a man of principle, steeped in the covenanting history of Scotland, but of a narrowly severe outlook in his NSW and Canadian ministry.

35. LEWIS, James Payn (1879- ?) V

Born July 8, 1879 at Buchan Station, Hunter River. Served under the Home Missions Committee of the PCNSW and when at Kyogle in December 1906 cast in his lot with the PCEA. Rev William Hamilton was instrumental in his taking up work at Hamilton in 1907 and he was duly ordained and inducted July 26, 1907, although he had not undergone a full course of training. In May 1910, he intimated his intention of entering politics at the close of 1911, which led the congregation to seek his resignation. Lewis left in July, his resignation being accepted by the Presbytery on August 18, 1910. Lewis went to Melbourne and supplied at Auburn PCV. He applied to the GAA of 1912 for recognition as a minister (application dated December 7, 1910). Further studies were required. Subsequent career uncertain.

36. RAMSAY, John David (1880-1933) V

Born c.1880 near Wingham, son of John Ramsay of the Macleay. Received as a student in 1903, completed his studies in difficult financial circumstances, was licensed 1908 and at the end of that year served in Victoria at Branxholme within the Hamilton charge. He was ordained and inducted to Hamilton/Branxholme on May 10, 1911 but concluded his ministry in March 1913, following the death of his first wife, a niece of Rev S.P.Stewart. He went to Scotland and served the FCS until his death on June 7, 1933 (Dalmally 1914-18; Rothesay 1918-33). An above average minister, well read and with a retentive memory.

37. RAMSAY, Herbert William (1876-1945) NSW

Born September 18, 1876 at Dingo Creek, Manning River, the eldest son of John Ramsay of the Macleay. Accepted as a student in 1909 and studies prescribed. In August 1911 he was appointed to supply Grafton/Brushgrove while continuing his studies. He was licensed September 16, 1913 and ordained and inducted to the charge on February 5, 1915 where he remained until his death on February 18, 1945. His first wife died in 1914 leaving 5 children. In 1916 he married Miss Flora McQueen who died in 1977. Ramsay was a well read man, an able pastor, ready with the pen, and an efficient Clerk of Synod (1922-45) and Assembly (1923-39).

38. McCLEAN, Thomas Morrin (1880-1960) V/NSW

Born about 1880 in Northern Ireland, studied under Dr Petticrew at Magee College and at the FCS College, Edinburgh. Licensed by the FCS he came to give assistance for a year or two. Arrived in Melbourne October 24, 1913. Served Hamilton/Branxholme from November 14, 1913, declined a call but did excellent work until farewelled on October 23, 1916 upon his acceptance of a call from Maclean PCEA where he was ordained and inducted on November 10, 1916. A practical and vigorous preacher, the congregation saw marked growth under his ministry. He resigned with effect from January 8, 1936, and returned with his bride to the UK. He died at Portrush, NI in May 1960. His widow (nee McPherson) returned to Australia and died at Maclean in 1985.

39. GRAHAM, Isaac Lester (1888-1964) V

Born on the Hastings River January 2, 1888 and received as a student in 1909. He gained his MA from the U of Edinburgh (part Sydney) and completed divinity at the Free Church College. Licensed by the Free Presbytery of Edinburgh he returned to Australia in January 1917, and was ordained and inducted to the charge of Hamilton/Branxholme on January 3, 1918. He obtained a colleague for 1951-53, resigned the charge with effect April 16, 1954, but continued to supply 3 or 4 services each Lord's Day until his death on July 10, 1964. Graham was a Christian gentleman. Perhaps he could make too much out of little points but he was of generous disposition and prayerful spirit. He was diligent, active in church courts, having a concern for the needs of aboriginals in the district, and for missionary work. He left a widow and 3 children.

40. ROBINSON, James Campbell (1884-1952)   V

Born on the Manning River in 1884 of Northern Ireland stock, he was converted at age 21 and received as a student in 1909. He proceeded to Scotland in 1911, completed studies at the U of Edinburgh and Free Church College, and was licensed in Scotland, returning to Australia in November 1918. He supplied the Hastings in 1919, St George's for a time in 1920, visited UK and returned via USA . Ordained and inducted to East St Kilda August 18, 1921. Did excellent work in literature distribution. Tendered resignation February 29, 1952 but given 12 months leave of absence. He died of a heart condition October 15, 1952. Robinson had married Miss Flora McSwan of the Clarence in October 1951, and she currently (1989) resides in Grafton. Robinson was a devotional preacher, much attached to the church. He edited the children's paper 1923-29, the general magazine 7/1928-1/1929 and 1933-40. His main literary work included **An Infant's Catechism of the Early Life of Christ** (1924), **Melbourne's First Settled Minister** (1928, 26pp), **The Rev Alexander McIntyre, Evangelist** (1929, 60pp), **The Free Presbyterian Church of Australia** (1947 , 446pp) and the collection of sermons entitled **The Glorious Gospel** (1953).

41. RAMSAY, Malcolm Campbell (1890-1973)   NSW

Born 1890, the third son of John Ramsay of the Macleay. Received as a student in 1912; BA (1913-15) and MA (1916) U of Sydney and divinity at the Free Church College (1917-1920); licensed in Edinburgh and returned to NSW September 1920. Ramsay desired to go to Russia as a missionary but home needs too pressing. He was ordained and inducted to the Hastings September 8, 1921, translated to the Manning June 2, 1937 and resigned this charge on retirement April 1, 1965. 'M.C.', as he was affectionately known, continued to serve the church as able until his death in Sydney on April 18, 1973. He overcame an early stutter to be an acceptable preacher. He had a good mind, a lucid pen and a pastor's heart. He took a great interest in young people. Tenacious defender of the Reformed faith and the principles of the church. His major published items were **The Cross as a Symbol** (1962, 29pp), **Purity of Worship** (1968) and **Psalms Only: Objections Answered** (1971, 56pp). A daughter, Dr Helen Ramsay, was a medical missionary of the church in Central India.

42. MacLEOD, Neil (1905-   )   Gaelic NSW

Born Lewis, Scotland, May 29, 1905; MA at U of Edinburgh and divinity at the Free Church College. Two College Professors who had visited Australia (D. Maclean and J. Macleod) urged him to assist on the Manning. MacLeod was ordained in Hope Street Free Church, Glasgow on August 27, 1929 with a view to work in Australia, Rev John D. Ramsay († 36 above) being one of the preachers on that occasion. MacLeod arrived in October and was inducted to the Manning on December 17, 1930. He gave attention to work among the young in particular. He was translated to St George's on March 19, 1936, and was the impetus behind the 'Free Kirk Youth Fellowship.' Gained BD at U of Sydney 1942. A chaplaincy was not available to the FPCA but the PCA offered to take MacLeod and he accepted on the understanding he reported to his own church. Taking 6 months leave of absence, he was called up June 1943, resigned the pastoral charge later that year, was Moderator of Synod & Assembly in 1944. Mentioned in despatches. Resigned April 1946 and joined PCA. Subsequently served St Andrew's, Perth, WA (1946-52), Hamilton, Victoria (1952-60) and Hurstville, Sydney (1960-74). He was Moderator of the PCNSW Assembly 1973-74 and of the continuing GAA 1974. DD from Central School of Religion, London, 1978; Member of the Order of Australia. Has made a notable contribution to Australian Presbyterian life.

43. MACDONALD, Malcolm Murdo (c1904-1970)   Gaelic NSW

Ordained 1927 by the FCS. Minister of Shiskine, Arran but invited to Australia by St George's.'He arrived in May 1931, and inducted to St G's March 24, 1932. He was a careful sermon craftsman and the congregation grew. He was overseas for some 6 months from late March 1934, and resigned the charge in April 1935 to return to Scotland, where he served the FCS, and married an Australian girl. To Australia 1948 where he served the PCNSW at Murrumburrah/Harden, then inducted to Murwillumbah (1951),

Wentworthville (1961) and Manilla (1967). He remained Reformed in his theology and directed at least one Australian to the Free Church College for study (Ian McKenzie, from 1964 FCS missionary in India). Macdonald died about 1970.

44. WEBSTER, James Alexander (1895-1987) NSW/V

Born Scotland July 1895, served on the western front in WWI and migrated to Australia in 1920. Married Leila Paine of CHatsworth in 1925. Received as a student in 1929 he began studies in Sydney that year, and in October 1930 commenced a 2 year course in the Free Church College, Edinburgh. He returned to Australia and commenced work on the Hunter in June 1932 while completing a further year of study. He was ordained and inducted to the Hunter/Barrington on October 31, 1933. He did excellent work in this vast charge. A devotional preacher he was particularly noted for his pastoral visiting. He was translated to Geelong on June 29, 1946 and from there to Maclean (inducted July 27, 1949). He resigned with effect December 3, 1969 as a consequence of ill health. In retirement he and his like-minded wife lived at Mowll Village, Castle Hill, Sydney and still found opportunity for service. His death occurred on June 30, 1987, and his wife died the following day. Five of the 7 children reached adulthood, and the 3 sons have all served as elders.

45. HARMAN, Joseph Albert (1899-1976) NSW

Born May 18, 1899, one of the 9 children of Joseph Harman of Long Flat on the Hastings. Active as a young Christian in forming Sabbath schools at Ellenborough and Kindee, in 1921 he was received as a student for the ministry of the FPCA. His studies were dogged by long periods of poor health. He completed the course in divinity at the Free Church College 1929-32. He did important work in reviving the old Richmond/ Brunswick cause and was ordained on May 17, 1934 the better to facilitate his labours there. He was inducted to the Hastings on February 8, 1938 following a call bearing 74 signatures. In this charge he continued through joys and sorrows until he retired on May 3, 1967. Harman had wanted to go to Peru as a missionary but the needs of the home church were more pressing. He rejoiced to see one blessed by his ministry go as a missionary teacher to Peru in 1965 (Hugh Varnes). He was a busy, practical, missionary-minded pastor. He was Clerk of Synod (1941-66) and of the Assembly for many years, and was Convener of the Missions Committee 1945-71. There were three children.

46. TROTTER, Dudley G.C. (1909-   ) NSW

Born 1909 and brought up in the Huntingdon district in the Hastings charge. Received as a student by Assembly April 15, 1930; to Scotland 1932; completed MA, U of Edinburgh 1935, and Free Church College course. Licensed in Scotland and returned to NSW June 1937. He was ordained and inducted to Maclean on March 10, 1938 following a call bearing 212 signatures. He married Miss Christina Anderson in 1939. A man of ability he did good service but made an issue of the psalms/paraphrases question and resolved to resign effective September 7, 1948. He took up farming at Huntingdon.

47. ALLEN, Arthur (1902-1958) V/NSW

Born Sydney November 23, 1902 of godly parents long active in the church, his father Robert (died 1915) having served as a catechist/home missionary for many years. Converted in 1929, received as a student in 1933, he proceeded to Scotland that year. He completed one year of the Arts course, gained the Dip Anthro with distinction and completed the divinity course at the Free Church College. He proved an able student, and was licensed in Edinburgh on April 27, 1937 and returned to Australia. He married Catherine Anderson, who was from the Clarence, in 1937, and was ordained and inducted to Geelong June 18, 1938 where he remained until the close of 1943. He was inducted to St George's, Sydney on March 1, 1944 and continued in this charge until his death on September 23, 1958. Allen was a thorough Calvinist who corresponded world-wide. He helped inaugurate the **Calvinistic Society of Victoria**, and the **Reformed Theological Review** (of which he was an original editor, 1942). He planned and pressed for such a body as the Reformed Ecumenical Synod, and gave much assistance to Dutch migrants in the early 1950s. He was editor of the church magazine 1944-58, and played an important part in bringing about the 1953 union. His deep convictions were expressed with force and originality. His widow died in Sydney 1985. A selection of his work was published as **Writings and Addresses** (Sydney 1964, 70pp).

48. ANDREWS, James Campbell (1909-   )   Sth Africa/NSW

Born August 26, 1909 at Wauchope. Received as a student April 15, 1930. Matriculated Sydney 1931, and to Scotland with Dudley Trotter. MA U of Edinburgh 1937; MB, ChB (Edin) 1940; completed Free Church College course 1937, and licensed April 27, 1937. To Australia   April 1941, married Ruby Elvery of Alstonville, medical experience including a year at Lismore Base Hospital, joined AIF and with Army Medical Corps from mid 1943 but apart from 6 months in Borneo at the end of the war served in Australia. Ordained at Wauchope on October 9, 1946 with a view to missionary service in South Africa. Sailed at the end of 1947 and arrived in January 1948. Appointed to Pirie district of the FCS Mission 1948-64; inducted to Manning PCEA June 11, 1965, and resigned February 1970 to return to the South African field. Seconded to Mt Coke Methodist Hospital, Kingwilliamstown March 1970 to March 1975. Retired to Wauchope. A man of many gifts, Dr Andrews made a remarkable contribution to the South African church as medical missionary, preacher and church builder. The first foreign missionary sent out by the PCEA his catholicity of vision and humble Christian character has commended the Gospel to many. He and his wife have four children.

49. McINTOSH, Alvan Donald (1911-1983)   NSW/V

Born December 26, 1911, son of John and Sarah McIntosh of Chatsworth Island, NSW. Received as a student in 1933, he proceeded to Scotland in 1934 for studies at Skerry College, the U of Edinburgh and the Free Church College. He was licensed by the Free Presbytery of Edinburgh and in October 1943 was ordained and served the Aberdeen FCS congregation (Dee Street) for some 2 years. He married Anne Rattray of Edinburgh in 1943 by whom he had 3 sons. He returned to Australia in March 1945, gave supply to Geelong, but was called and inducted to Grafton July 17, 1946, translated to Hamilton May 3, 1951 as colleague and successor, but was inducted to Geelong on July 31, 1953 and to Grafton a second time August 14, 1957, and then to St George's January 19, 1961. His wife died in 1961 and in 1966 he married Miss Eva Kearns of Grafton. McIntosh retired on July 18, 1981 and died in Sydney on April 19, 1983. McIntosh was noted as a preacher. Particularly in his earlier years there was an evangelistic note of frshness and power seen, for example, in the conversion of a number on the Hastings in 1947.   His love for Christ, concern for souls, generous hospitality and kindliness never changed even if he held some rather conservative views on matters of church life.

50. RAMSAY, Stewart Neil (1917-   )   NSW

Born Grafton January 26, 1917, the son of Rev H.W.Ramsay. Received as student in 1936 and proceeded to matriculation. Married Beatrice Faulks of Tamworth in 1940. In AIF 1940-44 (Middle East & New Guinea). Studied 3 years at U of Sydney and 3 years at Geelong under Rev H.K.Mack (retired) and Rev A. Barkley, RP ministers. Gave some supply to Geelong 1949-50; licensed by the Central Presbytery on December 14, 1950. From mid 1951 he supplied at Grafton and was ordained and inducted there on February 24, 1953. He was translated to the Hunter/Barrington (inducted November 11, 1954)   and completed 30 years service, retiring on November 12, 1984. This was a widespread charge   but was served conscientiously. Mr Ramsay edited the church magazine from 1958-66 and was Clerk of Synod 1966-82. He and his wife retired to Bonny Hills.

51. BEATON, Angus Ramsay (1930-   )   Peru/T/NSW

Born Gloucester, NSW 1930, son of John Beaton; received as student 1949; gained Matriculation and did most of an Arts course at U of Sydney, and completed divinity at the Free Church College 1954-57. Licensed and ordained by the Presbytery of Inverness for the Peruvian Mission and returned to Australia July 1957. Supplied St Kilda (6 mths) and Richmond/Brunswick (2½ years) and sailed with his family for Peru in September

1960. He served briefly at Lima but then took up work at Cajamarca where he worked with energy and devotion returning to Australia late in 1968 due to the educational needs of his family. In August 1969 began supply of Penguin, Tas (now Ulverstone), inducted December 5, 1969 translated to Maclean February 1, 1974 and resigned this charge on August 17, 1981 to accept a call to Springwood PCNSW which he served until settled at Noorat PCV 1989.

52. LEE, Edwin Roughton (1922-   )   V/NSW

Born Leicester UK 1922. He was a Chief Petty Officer in Naval Air Arm and was converted through a RAF chaplain, and had contact with Rev J.M.MacLeod, FCS minister at Greenock, 1942. Studied for the ministry after the war; MA U of Edinburgh 1953-56, divinity at Free Church College 1956-59, and licensed by the Presbytery of Edinburgh. Invited to supply St Kilda he and his wife and 3 children arrived in July 1959. He was ordained and inducted to St Kilda on October 21, 1959 but demitted April 17, 1966 to return to Scotland. The congregation experienced a considerable growth during his ministry. Inducted to Dundee FCS June 1, 1966. This was a small congregation and it was necessary for him to teach part-time in the last 2 years. He demitted 11/1970; inducted to Manning PCEA December 11, 1970. Has served this parish well in pulpit, visitation and radio ministry. Editor church magazine 1979-81.

53. HARMAN, Allan Macdonald (1936-   )   V

Born Lismore, NSW 1936 son of Rev J.A.Harman. Received as a student in 1953. BA (Sydney), Free Church College course and BD (Edin) 1960 and licensed in Edinburgh. Married 1961. MTh (Westminster, Pa) 1961. Ordained and inducted to Geelong PCEA March 21, 1962; on leave of absence 8/64 to 5/66, and gained ThD (Westminster) [Paul's Use of the Psalms]. Resigned Geelong effective June 15, 1966, and inducted to Hebrew & OT Professorship at the Free Church College, September 13, 1966. MLitt (Edin). Prof of OT at Reformed Theological College Geelong 1974-77. Appointed Visiting Professor with Life Tenure at Presbyterian Theological Hall, Melbourne, with effect from January 1, 1978. Resigned from the PCEA ministry effective July 10, 1981; joined PCV and inducted as Professor December 19, 1981, thereafter becoming Principal also. Editor church magazine 1975-79. Ed. R.S.Miller, **Thomas Dove & the Australian Aboriginals** 1985; jointly with A.M.Renwick, **The Story of the Church**, 1985.

54. CAMPBELL, Alexander Donald (1931-   )   NSW

Born Mullumbimby NSW, son of A.A.Campbell, an elder in the PCEA. Spent some years on the family farm, became student in 1956, proceeded to Scotland in 1960, divinity at the Free Church College and licensed May 1963. Married Mary Matheson in Scotland 1963 and returned to Australia in September. He was ordained and inducted to Grafton on January 16, 1964. He resigned this charge effective July 26. 1971 to return to Scotland for family reasons. Editor church magazine 1966-70. Minister of Wick FCS to 1977; visited Australia 1977/78; has not held charge since.

55. TURNBULL, Eric Stanley (1928-   )   T/V

Born Perth, Tasmania in April 1928. After some 10 years preaching in connection with the Baptist Union he resigned from the Baptist Home Mission Dept on February 21, 1960, the issue being Calvinistic doctrine, and continued as a Baptist Reformed Church at Penguin with those who adhered. Coming to a full Presbyterian position, he was ordained by a special presbytery of PCEA ministers September 28, 1961, and the congregation became part of what is now called the Evangelical Presbyterian Church when instituted the following day. On June 13, 1964 the resignation of Turnbull and the congregation was submitted to the EPC Presbytery but not accepted. However, after discussions with the PCEA, the EPC released minister and congregation and Turnbull was added to the roll of PCEA ministers with effect from September 14, 1965. A change of ministry was indicated, and after some months leave of absence preaching on the mainland, Turnbull was inducted to Hamilton on October 25, 1967, and was translated to St Kilda on June 29, 1973. A strongly doctrinal preacher, though with less than adequate training, he provided spiritual help to many but went off on a tangent and would not heed advice of other Reformed brethren - something of which he had accused the EPC in 1964 with some justice. Suspended on libel August 31, 1979 by Southern Presbytery for his teaching concerning the King James Version. Libel proved by special Synod, October 13, 1979. Refusing to desist or else resign, he was declared no longer a PCEA minister on November 2, 1979. The larger portion of the congregation adhered to him, and they purchased a small place of worship in Chadstone in 1988.

56. TRIPOVICH, Alan Leslie (1929-   )   NSW

Born Melbourne in July 1929, he was raised in the Roman Catholic Church and became a carpenter and joiner. Converted in 1958 he was a student at the WEC Training College in Tasmania in 1960 when the College was divided over the Reformed Faith. Returned to Melbourne, received as a student 1961, obtained Leaving Certificate 1962, and studied under Messrs Lee and A.M.Harman from 1963. Licensed on November 15, 1966, supplied in various centres, and was ordained and inducted to the Hastings on February 23, 1968.

57. MURRAY, Raymond William (1941-   )   V/NSW

Born Nabiac NSW 1941, raised at Bunyah within the Manning charge. Received as student 1961; BA (Newcastle) 1961-64 and Free Church College 1964-67. Licensed in Scotland. Married Roberta MacPherson in Scotland. At Westminster Theological Seminary, Pa., 1967/68 [ThM granted 1978: The Idea of History in the thought of R.G.Collingwood]. Ordained and inducted to St Kilda December 11, 1968, translated to Brisbane July 21, 1972. On leave of absence in Scotland 1975/76 and on LSL in Scotland 11/80, he resigned the Brisbane charge and was inducted to Glenurquhart FCS on March 24, 1981. Returning to Australia in November 1983, he commenced supply of the Grafton congregation to which he was inducted on March 29, 1984. Since 1987 he has been Special Religious Education teacher in the high schools of Grafton, while continuing to serve the Grafton congregation. Editor of the church magazine 6/70-5/72 and 7/87-4/88.

58. MacLEOD, Kenneth (1933-   )   Gaelic NSW

Born Lewis, 1933. After 12 years in the merchant navy, he studied at U of Aberdeen and completed the Free Church of Scotland College course in 1968. He arrived in Australia October of that year to take up work at Lismore. He was ordained and inducted to the charge covering the Richmond Brunswick, on April 24, 1969, and did excellent work as the first settled minister this century. He returned to Scotland in September 1973, decided to remain and accordingly his resignation of the charge was accepted December 13, 1973. Inducted to Tain FCS February 24, 1974, demitted April 30, 1982 and returned to Australia and was inducted to Maclean PCEA June 18, 1982.

59. NIBBS, David Roy (1933-1988)   V/NSW/T

Born Smithton, Tasmania , April 15, 1933, one of 4 sons of Gordon Nibbs, a Baptist pastor. Active in street preaching and evangelism from 1950. Student for Baptist ministry and studied at Baptist College in Melbourne, and gave supply in Tasmania during vacations. Gained L.Th; ordained November 21, 1962 to Georgetown Baptist Ch Church, Tas. His Reformed convictions growing he resigned in mid 1964; worked in draper's shop until May 1965 when called to Dingley Union Church, Vic., where he spent 3 happy years. Applied to the Victorian Presbytery for admission to the PCEA, March 1967. From July 1968, while completing requisite studies and probation, Nibbs supplied St Kilda (5 mths), then Geelong. Admitted minister of the PCEA May 6, 1969; supplied Brisbane (3 mths) then Geelong to which he was inducted on February 11, 1970. Translated to Grafton May 19, 1972, and thence Ulverstone (inducted February 11, 1982). He died suddenly while reading the Scriptures, October 5, 1988, leaving a widow and 3 sons). A warm-hearted and genial pastor of prayerful and devotional spirit.

60. HEENAN, John Dennis (1913-   )   NSW

Born Hawkes Bay, NZ 1913. An elder in the Bucklands Beach Reformed Church, he trained for the ministry at the RTC, Geelong, and was ordained in 1958 serving as minister of evangelism in the Reformed Churches of Australia at Blacktown, NSW, and organising the 'Back to God Hour' radio ministry. Influenced by developments in Tasmania, he resigned early 1964, and adopted the principles of worship held by the PCEA, and went to Scotland. Minister of Perth FCS to 1970, thence Maclean PCEA (inducted February 24, 1970) but resigned May 11, 1973 to return to Scotland for family reasons. Subsequently minister of Kiltarlity/Kirkhill and retired 1978.

61. BRADBEER, Graham Morrison (1945-   )   NSW

Born Glasgow, Scotland 1945, the family came to Melbourne. He became a member at St Kilda in May 1964. Received as a student 1965. BSc (U of Strathclyde) 1965-68, Free Church College 1969-72, and licensed June 28, 1972. Returning to Australia he was ordained as assistant minister at Maclean with responsibility for the new work at Armidale on September 15, 1972. He did this work with considerable success but resigned effective January 25, 1980, and was settled as minister of Warburton PCV February 4, 1980. He closed his ministry at Warburton in December 1983 to become Chaplain at Scotch College, Melbourne.

62. WEBER, Graeme Lindsay (1946-   )   T/V

Born Kemsey, NSW, 1946. Father an office-bearer on the Manning. Received as a student 1965; studied U of Newcastle 1965-68 and Free Church College 1969-72. Licensed in Australia, married in 1972. Early in 1973 he commenced residential supply at Winnaleah, NE Tasmania and was ordained but not inducted on June 29, 1973. He accepted a call to Hamilton and was inducted February 8, 1974. His ministry was valued but he resigned July 28, 1978 in order to accept a call to Murwillumbah PCNSW, where he was inducted on October 20, 1978. In 1983 he was translated to St George's, Geelong PCV.

63. WARD, Rowland Skipsey (1945-   )   T/V

Born December 28, 1945 at Melbourne. Member PCV to 1968 then PCEA St Kilda. BA (U of Sth Africa, correspondence) 1969-73. After about 10 years in general insurance received as student 1971. Married Anna Hilliard 1972. Free Church College course 1972-75. Licensed Melbourne October 17, 1975 and supplied Ulverstone to which charge ordained and inducted March 16, 1976. BTh (Hons) 1976/81 (Unisa). Worked part and then full time 1978/81 due to parlous Synod finances. Concluded ministry there August 25, 1981 and supplied St Kilda in the aftermath of the Turnbull ministry, and inducted June 2, 1984, the Melbourne work being subsequently reorganised. Editor of church magazine 6/81 to 6/86 and author of a number of publications.

64. NICHOLDS, Donald Eric (1926-   )   NSW

Born Melbourne 1926; in merchant navy during WWII. Subsequently held a variety of posts in accounting, sales etc. Member St Kilda PCEA 1963. Commenced study at RTC Geelong as a private student, received as a student 1973, graduated BD in 1975, and licensed April 6, 1975. After a period supplying Brisbane and then Lismore, he was ordained and inducted to the latter charge on October 29, 1976, and resigned same September 17, 1982, and proceeded to Melbourne to work on an unpaid basis with Christian Witness to Israel. After a year he discontinued this and resigned from the PCEA effective December 31, 1984, to accept an appointment with the PCQ parish of the Gold Coast. In 1986 distressing circumstances came to light which led to the termination of his ministry.

65. CROMARTY, John Macintosh (1940-   )   V

Born at Raymond Terrace in 1940, the 2nd son of John J. Cromarty, dairy farmer. Trained as teacher and taught 1961-72, principally in Hunter Valley primary schools, concluding as Vice Principal of Maitland Primary. Elder on Hunter 1963 and married Elizabeth King that year. Received as a student 1972, entered on course at RTC, Geelong in February 1973 and also supplied the Geelong congregation. Having been withdrawn from the RTC 10/75, he completed the prescribed studies and was licensed September 17, 1976, and ordained and inducted to Geelong on December 3, 1976, following a call bearing 18 signatures. Mr Cromarty has had the joy of seeing a marked numerical growth in the congregation.

66. GADSBY, William Peter (1948-   )   Q/NSW

Born Shropshire, England 1948 and migrated to Melbourne at the end of 1961. Member at St Kilda 1969. Employed by Country Roads Board 1967-74; BSc (Melb) 1970. Commenced studies at RTC Geelong 2/74 at which time he was received as a student. Graduated BD with distinction; licensed December 9, 1976. After a short period assisting in Lismore, he was ordained and inducted as second minister of Brisbane August 18, 1977. Seconded to supply Armidale February 1980, and inducted to this charge on October 30, 1981. Appointed Clerk of Synod 1982. Author of **Essentials of Christian Living** (1985, 60pp). Editor: **The Presbyterian Banner** since May 1988. He married Lindy Humphries of Melbourne in 1973.

67. DOLE, Brian Leslie (1939-   )   NSW

Born Sydney January 1939. Worked in the Computer field. Member of St George's, received as student 1972. Passed HSC and to Scotland, Free Church College 1974-77. Returning to Australia, he was licensed by Central Presbytery and commenced services in the Sydney western suburbs at Werrington on October 9, 1977. To this charge he was ordained and inducted August 11, 1978 but resigned effective August 9, 1981 when he was found in the wrong in a procedural matter. He continued a small congregation on independent lines. His position had some similarities to that of E.S.Turnbull.

68. GRAHAM, John Stewart (1939-   )   NSW

Born Lewis, December 24, 1939. He worked as a motor mechanic, MA U of Aberdeen 1972-75; received as a student 1975; Free Church College course 1975-78 and ordained by the Presbytery of Lewis October 17, 1978. He supplied various centres and arrived in Sydney in September 1979 to be missioner of Christian Witness to Israel in that city, a work he still continues. Married in 1964 and has 2 children.

69. TAMATA, Sauyawa Ravarava [Sam] (1941-   )   Fiji

Born Fiji 1941, served in British Army. Free Church of Scotland 4 year course 1977-81, thence to Australia with a view to work in Fiji. Licensed at Wingham by the Southern Presbytery May 10, 1981, ordained by the Northern Presbytery August 22, 1981. He supplied at Brisbane and left with his family for Fiji in January 1983 and remained 2 years (see p.433). To Scotland 1985, and inducted to Assynt FCS September 3, 1986.

70. VARNES, Hugh Crawford (1937-   )   NSW

Born Toowoomba Q, son of a Baptist minister. Teacher Wauchope 1957-61; completed MBI Diploma, Melbourne 1962-63, and taught at Carey BGS 1964. Missionary teacher in Peru 1965-74 (see p.432). Received as student and commenced RTC course 1975 and PCEA tutors 1976,77, and supplied at Winnaleah 2/1976-8/1978. Released from student -ship 12/1977. To Scotland as private student, and received by Central Presbytery October 19, 1978. Completed Free Church College course 1981. Licensed in Australia and ordained and inducted to Sydney Western Districts March 5, 1982.

71. BLOOMFIELD, Peter John (1947-   )   Q

Born Kilcoy, Q 1947. Trained as High School teacher, BEc (ANU), Dip Ed. and taught in NSW for 8 years. Moved to Geelong 1978. Received as student March 10, 1978, graduated BD with distinction from RTC (1978-81). Licensed November 15, 1981, he supplied Brisbane from May 1982 and was ordained and inducted there October 29, 1982. Married with two daughters.

72. CORNFORD, Paul (1952-   )   NSW

Born Maryborough Q, qualified as teacher (BSc. Dip Ed) and undertook course at RTC as private student, and graduated with distinction November 1981. Received as student July 10, 1981. Supplied at Grafton (6 mths) and Lismore where ordained and inducted July 6, 1984 but resigned March 29, 1985. Joined PCA and currently serves PCQ.

73. McCALLUM, John Alexander (1942-   ) NSW

Born Fort William 1942. After 3 years in the merchant navy he studied at U of Aberdeen (MA) and at the Free Church College. Ordained and inducted to Govanhill FCS Sept. 22, 1978. He demitted April 13, 1985 and was inducted to St George's June 28, 1985.

74. MACKAY, William Morton (1934-   )

Born Dundee, Scotland. MA (Hons) U of St Andrews 1952-56, Dip Ed. 1957 and completed course at Free Church of Scotland College 1959. Ordained October 10, 1961, a few days before proceeding to Peru. Teacher at Colegio San Andres 1961-65, Headmaster 1966-78. Returned to Scotland and teaching 1978-85. Principal of PLC Melbourne 1986. Married with three children.

75. CROMARTY, James Alexander (1937-   ) NSW

Born Raymond Terrace1937, older brother of JMC, trained as Primary teacher (BA, MLitt, Newcastle and New England). Taught to close of 1983, finishing as Principal of Chatham Primary School. Accepted as Home Missionary 1984 and completed studies under PCEA tutors. Supplied Manning and Hunter in 1984, Hunter alone from November 1984. Licensed November 11, 1985 and ordained and inducted to Hunter April 11, 1986.

76. PATEMAN, John (1930-   ) V

Born Tutbury, Staffordshire 1930. Trained at the Free Church of Scotland College and ordained and inducted to East Kilbride FCS September 3, 1973. Translated to Hamilton PCEA April 25, 1986.

77. LEGGOTT, Trevor Ian (1949-   ) V

Born Sydney March 22, 1949. In electrical trade holding management position 1971-74. Moved to Wingham 1974, joined PCEA from Uniting Church 1985. He was encouraged to apply for status as a Home Missionary. Received, Dip Min Tahlee Bible College 1985-87, and property manager at Tahlee 1988. Licensed by Southern Presbytery January 27, 1989. Ordained and inducted as assistant to the minister at Melbourne on March 11, 1989 with special responsibility for the new work in the City of Berwick.

557

ORDAINED PRESBYTERIAN MINISTERS SERVING IN AUSTRALIA TO 1865

The following list of 306 ministers comprises all ministers known to the writer who served to the time of union in Queensland (November 1863), South Australia (May 1865) and New South Wales (September 1865), and to the end of 1865 in respect of Tasmania and Victoria, together with D.Meiklejohn (†9 p.153) and D.McKenzie (†29 p.155). The lists in the body of the text are found on pages 110-115, 150-157, 159, 161 & 162. I do not purport to include licentiates or catechists, nor ordained ministers who came to Australia to 1865 but did not serve as inducted ministers or the equivalent.

The sources for such a listing so far as New South Wales is concerned include a provisional 'Biographical Register' in **Church Heritage**, 1984, pages 185-208. This work was prepared by Dr Malcolm Prentis and utilised some material collected by Dr Barry Bridges. However, various corrections need to made to it in the light of mistakes noted and new information. This listing includes corrections known to the present writer who has compared notes with Dr Bridges and Dr Prentis to a certain extent. The definitive work for New South Wales will be Dr Bridges' Register currently being prepared for publication (see Bibliography). Dr Prentis is assembling data on all Presbyterian ministers to 1900, and this may be published in a few years. Note the caveat for Victoria on p 155. A few corrections have been made to Scrimgeour's listing for South Australia.

In this alphabetical listing, the bracketed numbers refer to the page where the man is listed, and the unbracketed numbers to other references to him in this book. An * indicates the other references are included in the main index, while † indicates that a more detailed entry occurs in the Biographical Register of 'Free Church' ministers which follows.

Abernethy, J McL (155) 279
Adam, George (156)
Adam, James (156)
Allan, James (110)*
Anderson, John, MA (Tas) (159)
Anderson, John (SA) (161)
Atchison, C. (110)*
Bain, William (113) 126,221
Baird, James (159,151)
Ballantyne, D.H. (153)
Ballantyne, John (154)
Battersby, M R (157)
Begg, Andrew (155)
Bell, Thomas (114,162)
Black, Alex (114)
Blair, David (114) 254n
Blair, Hugh (150)
Boddie, A C (113) 101
Boyd, J S (156)   Brown P. (157)
Cairns, Adam (151)*
Caldwell, R A (157)
Cameron, James (112) 93,97,210,239
Campbell, Lauchlin (159) 223
Chapman, David (153)
Clark, John (152)
Clow, James (150) 137
Colquhoun, M (110) 41,47
Cooper, John (154) 144
Coutts, James (111) 88,103,125,178
Crawford, Archibald (157)
Dalrymple, J R (153)

Adam, Alex (151)
Adam, James, MA (111) 97
Adam, Matthew (111)41,55,93
Anderson, George (110)*
Anderson, John (Vic) (155)
Anderson, Robert (155)
Bagley, John (157)
Baird, C.J. (157)
Baker, William (111)
Ballantyne,James (154)149, 189
Barnet, John (151)
Beg, Wazir, MD (156,115)296
Bell, James (159)
Benny, James (161)*†
Blain, Robert (110)*
Blair, Edward (155)
Boag, Robt (111,114,115)119
Boyd, David (150)
Brownlee, J (157)
Caldwell, James (155)
Cameron, Arch (112)95
Campbell, A J (155)253
Carter, J T (111,114)*
Chaucer, W (114) 125,126
Cleland, John (110)*
Collins, James (114) 134
Comrie, W (110) 53
Corrie, Samuel (150)
Craig, Thomas (150,111)
Cullen, W (157)
Darling, Hugh (154,156)

INDEX TO DOCUMENTS INCORPORATED IN THE TEXT

INDEX TO MAPS AND TABLES INCORPORATED IN THE TEXT

INDEX TO MAIN REFERENCES TO AUTHORS & SOURCE PERSONS

References have been given to the **Port Phillip Christian Herald** and to the **Voice in the Wilderness** since in most cases the writers were respectively James Forbes and William McIntyre.

PRINCIPAL REFERENCES TO PRESBYTERIAN PARISHES BEFORE 1900
FOR PCEA PARISHES SEE ALSO DETAILED ENTRIES IN PART NINE

GENERAL INDEX (ABBREVIATED)

566